PRINCIPLES OF MACROECONOMICS

Second Edition

W • W • NORTON & COMPANY • INC • NEW YORK

EDWIN MANSFIELD

UNIVERSITY OF PENNSYLVANIA

PRINCIPLES OF MACROECONOMICS

SECOND EDITION

To Ted,
the macro part of the household

Published simultaneously in Canada by George J. McLeod Limited,

Toronto. Printed in the United States of America.

ISBN 0 393 09120 1

1 2 3 4 5 6 7 8 9 0

Permission from the following sources to reprint photographs is hereby gratefully acknowledged: Mansell Collection (pp. 22, 394); New York Port Authority (p. 92); The Department of the Treasury (p. 128); Edward C. Topple, New York Stock Exchange Photographer (p. 139); British Airways (p. 166); United Press International (pp. 237, 364, 526); Board of Governors of the Federal Reserve System (pp. 338, 341); New York *Times* (p. 357); Dow Chemical U.S.A. (p. 425); Time-LIFE Picture Agency (p. 430); Swiss Bank Corporation (p. 505).

(Picture Research by Liesel Bennett)

CONTENTS

PART THREE NATIONAL OUTPUT, INCOME, AND EMPLOYMENT

PREFACE

This volume, drawn from the second edition of my text, *Economics: Principles, Problems, Decisions,* once again is a self-contained introduction to macroeconomics. Many instructors used the previous edition in conjunction with its companion volume, *Principles of Microeconomics,* in a full-year principles course, others assigned it separately in one-semester courses. That choice remains, for this second edition covers the same ground as its predecessor.

Several aims converged in the planning and preparation of this new edition. Foremost was the need to examine the pressures exerted on economic theory by shock waves of inflation, high unemployment, and a relentless demand on the world's supply of natural resources. The turbulence that beset the domestic and international economies over the past few years has forced economists to rethink some of their favorite constructs, to modify others. A time of ferment, however, has its uses, and I have sought to give maximum exposure in this revision to the fresh thinking stimulated under stress. A second aim has been once again to take theory beyond the classroom and demonstrate how economics can be, and has been, utilized by decision makers in both the private and public sectors. With record numbers of students enrolling in the introductory course, an economics text that concentrates exclusively on principles will fail to tap the surge of new interest in the field. While economics has its share of elegant theories, I continue to believe that their elegance is enhanced, not diminished, by application to real problems of the economy.

No matter how carefully conceived and developed, a textbook requires the seasoning that only course use can give it. This volume is no exception. And so a third major concern in this edition was to respond to the reports, comments, and suggestions generously provided by teachers and students from many of the campuses where the first edition was used. I have worked hard to iron out wrinkles without singeing the fabric in the process. No page or paragraph has escaped reconsideration. While the structure and proportion of the text may not have been significantly altered, much of the content has. It almost goes without saying that extensive updating was necessary throughout in the text, tables, and diagrams. But this new edition also gave me an opportunity to clarify points and to improve over-all readability. Such changes are not cosmetic. Though sometimes they involve only a sentence or two, often they have led to the rewriting of entire sections. In the paragraphs that follow, I provide a brief guided tour of the areas that have undergone the most substantial reworking.

First, the material on the determination of national income, fiscal policy, money, monetary policy, and the debate between the monetarists and Keynesians has been extensively rewritten, extended, and deepened. Consumption, saving, and investment now are taken up in an entirely separate chapter. The original exposition has been bolstered by the leakage-injections approach to the determination of national output, an expanded and simplified treatment of the multiplier, and new sections on the paradox of thrift and the permanent-income hypothesis. In Chapter 11, the material on fiscal policy now includes the balanced-budget multiplier, an analysis of the case where taxes are independent of NNP, a treatment of recessionary and inflationary gaps, and more discussion of the effects of how a deficit or surplus is financed, while in Chapter 12 a closer look is given to the accuracy of forecasting models. In Part Four, considerably more space is devoted to the demand for money, the effects of the money supply on NNP, and the discussion of monetary policy. The sections on the Keynesian-monetarist debate have been refined and extended in a variety of ways, stagflation is accorded far more attention, and the Phillips curve comes under extended and critical scrutiny.

Second, *IS* and *LM* curves, though accorded a much fuller exposition, now form an appendix to Chapter 16. For those instructors who want to include this topic, the material is just as accessible as it was in the first edition. For those who do not, its current position makes it less obtrusive and it can be skipped without loss of continuity.

Third, the introductory chapters have been altered so that the student encounters many key analytical concepts in economics, and the nature of fundamental economic problems, more quickly. Chapter 1 now has major sections on resources, scarcity, choice, and opportunity costs (together with several case studies), as well as a discussion of the functions of any economic system and the major principles of economic organization. Chapter 2 now has some new material on the Industrial Revolution and a basic treatment of graphs. Chapter 3 takes up the law of increasing cost, Chapter 4 deals at greater length with price ceilings and floors, Chapter 5 has a better analysis of the effects of external economies and diseconomies, and Chapter 6 explores in greater depth tax incidence, the public debt, and alternative ways of financing government expenditures.

Fourth, formerly given brief mention, our nation's energy problems now occupy nearly half of Chapter 19. Included are substantial discussions about the Organization of Petroleum Exporting Countries, the relationship between energy and economic growth, the ways that our energy choices can affect the environment, and the shortage of natural gas. Close examination is given to policy measures that might be adopted, such as a tax on fuel, and on new energy technologies, such as oil from shale, coal gasification, and solar energy.

Fifth, recent developments on the international stage have demonstrated that the United States economy cannot be examined *in vacuo.* Much of the new content in Part Six is a direct outgrowth of these events. The treatments of the terms of trade and of nontariff barriers have been made less cryptic. New sections have been added on our experience with floating exchange rates, on the interpretation of the balance of payments under a regime of floating exchange rates, on the Trade Act of 1974 and on the Tokyo Round, and on the likelihood that OPEC will become a model for other less developed countries.

Sixth, many more one-page inserts have been added to provide in-depth commentaries on timely and important issues and topics. Among the new topics taken up are New York's fiscal crisis, income-tax loopholes, the stock market, international comparisons of inflation and unemployment, indexation, and the alleged capital crisis. These inserts add spice to the discussion, as well as insight into important topics.

Seventh, the questions at the end of each chapter have been increased in number with greater emphasis given to problem solving. These questions should be useful both for review and examination purposes as well as bases for classroom discussion.

In addition to changes in the text itself, major improvements have been made in the ancillaries: *The Study Guide for Principles of Macroeconomics,* second edition, now contains a listing of new Behavioral Objectives for each chapter, a far greater percentage of problems that require the student to work with quantitative matter in applying concepts to practical situations, a number of Discussion Questions drawn from economic issues in the news, and some Extension Questions aimed at developing skill in economic reasoning. *Principles of Macroeconomics: Readings, Issues, and Cases,* second edition, provides a substantial set of supplementary articles, carefully correlated with the text for instructors who want to introduce their students to the writings of major contemporary economists.

Finally, it is a pleasure to acknowledge the debts that I owe to the many teachers at various colleges and universities who have commented in detail on various parts of the manuscript. The first edition has benefited greatly from the advice I received from the following distinguished economists, none of whom is responsible, of course, for the outcome: Bela Balassa, Johns Hopkins; Robert Baldwin, University of Wisconsin (Madison); William Branson, Princeton; Martin Bronfenbrenner, Duke; Richard Cooper, Yale; Robert Dorfman, Harvard; James Duesenberry, Harvard; David Fand, Wayne State; Robert Gordon, Northwestern; Herschel Grossman, Brown; Albert Hirschman, Harvard; Ronald Jones, Rochester; John Kareken, Minnesota; Ann Krueger, Minnesota; Simon Kuznets, Harvard; Raymond Lubitz, Columbia and the Federal Reserve; Sherman Maisel, University of California (Berkeley); Thomas Mayer, University of California (Davis); Arthur Okun, Brookings Institution; and David Schulze, Florida.

Among the teachers who contributed comments and suggestions for changes in the first edition are: Wallace Atherton, California State University at Long Beach; James Duesenberry, Harvard; Richard Easterlin, University of Pennsylvania; Judith Fernandez, University of California (Berkeley); David Gay, University of Arkansas; Howard A. Gilbert, South Dakota State University; Judy Herman, Queens College; Alan Heston, University of Pennsylvania; Ronald Jones, University of Rochester; Leonard Martin, Cleveland State University; Thomas Mayer, University of California (Davis); William McEachern, University of Connecticut; Steven Morrison, University of California (Berkeley); E. Dwight Phaup, Union College; Charles Ratliff, Davidson College; Anthony Romeo, University of Connecticut; Warren St. James, Nassau County Community College; Stephen Sacks, University of Connecticut; Allen Sanderson, William and Mary; Richard Sutch, University of California (Berkeley); Frank Tansey, City University of New York; Thomas Tidrick, Clayton Junior College; Simon Whitney, Iona

College; William Whitney, University of Pennsylvania; and Harold Williams, Kent State University.

I would like to thank Elisabeth Allison of Harvard University for contributing the inserts that appear (over her initials) in various chapters, and Donald S. Lamm and Mary Shuford of W. W. Norton for their efficient handling of the editorial and publishing end of the work. As always, my wife, Lucile, has contributed an enormous amount to the completion of this book.

Philadelphia, 1977 E.M.

PART ONE

Introduction to Economics

1 Economic Problems, Policies, and Decisions

A French sage had a point when he said, "I finally know what distinguishes man from the other beasts: economic worries." Rich people, poor people, beggars, and kings: all have economic worries, though not of equal degree. And so do all the nations of the world. This is the nature of the human condition—and the basic reason why economics enters into a vast array of everyday activities, and plays an important role in the solution of national problems. Perhaps the best way to get an idea of what economics is all about is to look at some of the problems it can help solve. In these opening pages you will encounter six fairly typical economic problems. Although this is only a small sample, it is designed to give you a reasonable first impression of how the study of economics bears directly on the real world.

Economic Problems: A Sampler

Unemployment and Inflation

The history of the American economy is for the most part a story of growth. Our output—the amount of goods and services we produce annually—has grown rapidly over the years, giving us a standard of living that could not have been imagined a century ago. For example, output per person in the United States was about $7,000 in 1975; in 1909 it was about $1,840. Nonetheless, the growth of output has not been steady or uninterrupted; instead, our output has tended to fluctuate—and so has unemployment. In periods when output has fallen, thousands, even millions, of people have been thrown out of work. In the Great Depression of the 1930s, for example, over 20 percent of the labor force was unemployed (see Figure 1.1). Unemployment on this scale results in enormous economic waste and social misery.

The first of our sample of economic problems is: *What determines the extent of unemployment in the American economy, and what can be done to reduce it?* This problem is complicated by a related phenomenon: the level of prices may rise when we reduce the level of unemployment. In other words, inflation may occur. Thus, the problem is not only to curb unemployment, but to do this without producing an inflation so ruinous to the nation's economic health that the cure proves more dangerous than the ailment. As Figure 1.2 shows, we have experienced considerable inflation since 1929; the dollar has lost about ¾ of its purchasing power during this period. Moreover, in the 1970s, our economy has been bedeviled by "stagflation"—that is, a combination of high unemployment and high inflation.

During the past 50 years, economists have learned a great deal about the factors that determine the extent of unemployment. Since, contrary to earlier opinion, our economy has no automatic regulator that keeps it moving quickly and dependably toward minimal unemployment with stable prices, the American people, as well as people in other lands, have given their government the responsibility of promoting conditions favoring a high level of employment without serious inflation. Economists have developed useful techniques to help the government do this job. In particular, they have shown how government can use its control over the money supply and interest rates, as well as its power to spend and tax, to pro-

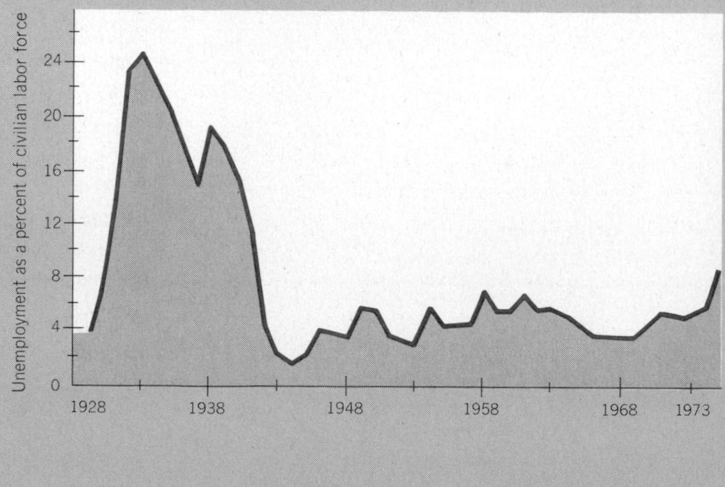

Figure 1.1
Unemployment Rates, United States, 1929–75
The unemployment rate has varied substantially from year to year. In the Great Depression, it reached a high of about 25 percent. In 1975, it rose to 8½ percent.

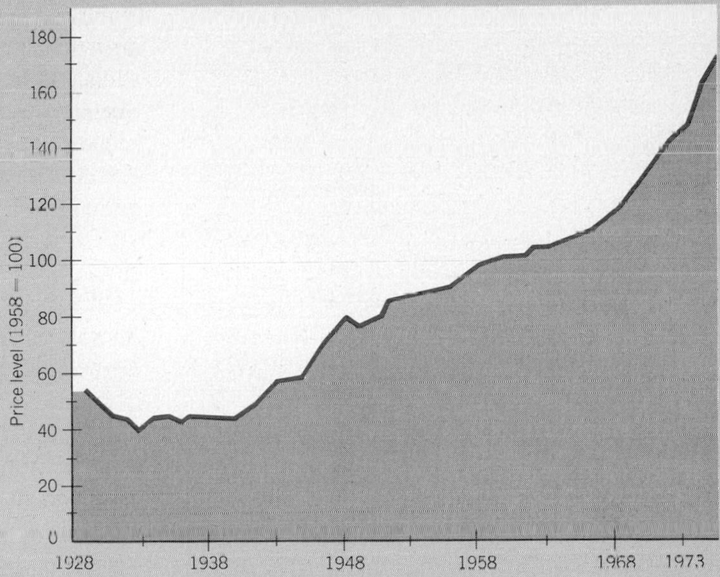

Figure 1.2
Changes in Price Level, United States, 1929–75
The price level has increased steadily since the 1930s, and is now about four times as high as it was in 1935.

mote high employment with reasonably stable prices. As a responsible citizen, you must be interested in this matter. To judge how well Congress and the president are doing their jobs, and to determine how you should vote, you must know what the government can do to reduce unemployment and how much it is doing. Also, to understand the fallacies in many apparently simple remedies for the complex economic problems in this area, you need to know some economics.

Government Regulation of Business

The 100 largest manufacturing firms control about ½ of all manufacturing assets in the United States (and their share of total assets seems to have increased since World War II). In certain industries, like automobiles, the four largest firms account for over 90 percent of the market (see Table 1.1). Nonetheless, although the large corporations obviously wield considerable power in their markets, the American economic system is built on the idea that firms should compete with one another. In particular, the producers of steel, automobiles, oil, toothpicks, and other goods are expected to set their prices independently and not to collude. Certain acts of Congress, often referred to as the antitrust laws, make it illegal for firms to get together and set the price of a product.

Our second example of an economic problem is: *Why is competition of this sort socially desirable?* More specifically, why should we be in favor of the antitrust laws? What reasons are there to believe that such laws will result in a more efficient economic system? (And what do we mean by "efficient"?) To a business executive, lawyer, government official, or judge, these questions are very important, since it is likely that at one time or another these people will be concerned with an antitrust case. But these issues also matter to every citizen, because they deal with the basic rules of the game for firms in our economy. Of course, one reason why Americans have traditionally favored competition over collusion, and relatively

Table 1.1
Market Share of Four Largest Firms, Selected Manufacturing Product Markets, United States, 1972.

Industry	Market share of four largest firms (percent)
Automobiles	93
Cigarettes	84
Soap	62
Tires	73
Aircraft	66
Metal cans	66
Blast furnaces and steel plants	45

Source: Statistical Abstract of the United States.

small firms over giant ones, is that they have mistrusted the concentration of economic power, and obviously, this mistrust was based on both political and economic considerations. But beyond this, you should know when competition generally benefits society, and when it does not.

One way that society has attempted to control the economic power of corporations that dominate an entire industry is through public regulation. Take the case of radio and TV. The Federal Communications Commission, a government agency, monitors the activities of broadcasting stations and networks to prevent misuse of the airwaves. Other regulatory commissions supervise the activities of the power companies, the airlines, the railroads, and other industries where it is felt that competition cannot be relied on to produce socially desirable results.

The regulatory commissions and the principles they use are currently a subject of tremendous controversy. Many observers feel that they tend to be lax, or, worse still, to be captured by the industries they are supposed to regulate. Since these regulated industries produce about 10 percent of national income, we all have a big stake in understanding how they operate and whether they are being regulated properly. This is another aspect of the same general problem of how industries should be organized.

The Elimination of Poverty

As pointed out by Philip Wicksteed, a prominent twentieth-century British economist, "A man can be neither a saint, nor a lover, nor a poet, unless he has comparatively recently had something to eat." Although relatively few people in the United States lack food desperately, about 25 million American people, about 12 percent of the population of the United States, live in what is officially designated as poverty. These people have frequently been called invisible in a nation where the average yearly income per person is about $7,000; but the poor are invisible only to those who shut their eyes, since they exist in ghettos in the wealthiest American cities like New York, Chicago, and Los Angeles, as well as near Main Street in thousands of small towns. They can also be found in areas where industry has come and gone, as in the former coal-mining towns of Pennsylvania and West Virginia, and in areas where decades of farming have depleted the soil.

Table 1.2 shows the distribution of income in the United States in 1974. Clearly, there are very substantial differences among families in income level. Indeed, the cats and dogs of the very rich eat better than some human beings. You as a citizen and a human being need to understand the social mechanisms underlying the distribution of income, both in the United States and in other countries, and how reasonable and just they are. Our third economic problem is: *Why does poverty exist in the world today, and what can be done to abolish it?* To help the poor effectively, we must understand

Table 1.2
Percentage Distribution of Families, by Income, United States, 1974.

Money income (dollars)	Percent of all families
Under 2,000	3
2,000– 3,999	6
4,000– 6,999	13
7,000– 9,999	14
10,000–14,999	24
15,000–24,999	28
25,000 and over	12
Total	100

Source: Statistical Abstract of the United States.

the causes of poverty. Does it make sense, for example, to pour billions of dollars into programs often denounced by politicians and even the recipients themselves as a "welfare mess"?

Since poverty is intimately bound up with our racial problems and the decay of our cities, the success or failure of measures designed to eradicate poverty may also help us determine whether we can achieve a society where equality of opportunity is more than a slogan and where people do not have to escape to the suburbs to enjoy green space and fresh air. Nor does the economist's concern with poverty stop at our shoreline. One of the biggest problems of the world today is the plight of the poor countries of Asia, Africa, and Latin America–the so-called less developed countries. The industrialized countries of the world, like the United States, Western Europe, Japan, and the Soviet Union, are really just rich little islands surrounded by seas of poverty. Over two billion people live in countries where income per person is less than $750 per year. These countries lack equipment, technology, and education; sometimes (but by no means always) they also suffer from overpopulation. Economists have devoted considerable attention to the problems of the less developed countries, and to developing techniques to assist them.

Pollution and Energy Problems

The poor seem always to be with us; and in our industrialized world, so too is pollution. For many years, people in the United States paid relatively little attention to the environment and what they were doing to it, but this attitude has changed markedly in the past decade. Now the public is really concerned about environmental pollution.

You may have seen the considerable air pollution in Los Angeles, New York, or many other cities. Chances are that a river near you is no longer fit for swimming or an abundant fish life, even if it is not as badly polluted as Cleveland's Cuyahoga, which was so full of wastes that it literally caught fire in 1969. In response to the pollution problem, the government and interested groups of private citizens are trying to control pollution, whether from auto exhausts, combustion of fossil fuels, solid-waste disposal, or the noise of sirens and jackhammers. But this is a difficult task, not unlike the job performed by Hercules in the Augean stables.

Besides pollution, another problem we face is concerned with energy. In early 1974, the major oil-exporting countries in the Middle East, Africa, and South America raised the price of crude oil very sharply, helping to increase inflation here and transferring tens of billions of dollars from the oil-consuming nations to the oil-exporting nations. The American people have become increasingly uneasy about their growing dependence on foreign oil. Some observers, rightly or wrongly, believe that we must reduce our current rate of energy consumption. Our energy and environmental problems are intertwined. Many suggested solutions to our energy problems would result in further environmental deterioration; many suggested solutions to our environmental problems would make our energy problems worse.

Our fourth example of an economic problem is: *What causes environmental pollution, and how can we reduce it to the proper levels? What is the nature of our energy problems, and how can they be resolved?* Economists have devoted substantial attention to questions like these in recent years. Of course, these questions entail technological considerations as well as purely economic ones. For example, in dealing with our energy problems, one must know something about the costs of producing electricity in nuclear plants and the possible hazards involved. But technological considerations are not the only ones. To a considerable extent, our environmental and energy problems are economic problems—and economics must play an important role in any attempted solution.

The Planned Economies and East-West Relations

Roughly ⅓ of the world's people live and work under a set of economic rules quite different from ours. The object of the game—achieving material prosperity and living the good life—may be broadly similar, but differences in how it is played account for a distinct cleavage between Communist and capitalist countries. Some of these differences can be spotted at once. For example, the steel mills of the Soviet Union are owned and operated by the government, whereas the steel mills of Gary, Indiana, or Pittsburgh belong to private corporations. Under the Communist system, the productive activities of a country are planned by a small group of bureaucrats in government ministries. In the capitalist world, industrial decision making is dispersed among many firms, each sizing up the demand for its products and choosing its own methods of production.

For many years, there has been intense economic, political, and ideological rivalry between the West and the Communist countries. During the 1970s, the United States, as part of its policy of *détente* with the Soviet Union, began to increase its trade with the Soviets. Particularly in fields of advanced technology such as electronics, the United States entered into a number of cooperative programs with the Soviet Union, the purpose being to share and exchange technological information. Many American firms and government agencies have taken part in this program, which has been an important aspect of East-West relations in the 1970s.

Our fifth example of an economic problem is: *How do the economic systems of the Communist countries work? Have they been performing as well as our economic system in recent years? What are the potential costs of greater technological and economic cooperation with the Soviets? What are the potential benefits?* Economics helps you to understand the differences between Communism and capitalism, and the relationships between them. Economists, here and in the Communist countries, have devoted considerable time and effort to studying each other's economic systems, in the process laying to rest many pernicious myths. This is all to the good, because sensible dealings with other nations must rest on fact, not myth. It will be a long time before the tensions between the Communist and capitalist blocs are eliminated, but a realistic understanding of the Communist systems is bound to promote the chances of harmonious international relations.

Organizational Efficiency

The problems discussed in previous sections are problems that concern our entire society. Obviously, they merit study by economists. But much of economics deals with narrower problems, such as the operations of the business firm.

Our sixth example of an economic problem is: *How should a firm decide what to produce, and how to produce it?* For example, consider the cost calculations that must be made by the management of Continental Air Lines to determine how many flights to run between Houston and Los Angeles. Or take the case of the International Business Machines Corporation (IBM), which must decide how to make, market, and price its next generation of electronic computers. These firms face very difficult problems, often involving millions of dollars. It is important, both to the firms themselves and to society at large, that they make the best decisions possible.

Economics is divided into two parts: macroeconomics and microeconomics. **Macroeconomics** deals with the behavior of economic aggregates like national output, the price level, and the level of unemployment, while **microeconomics** deals with the economic behavior of individual units like consumers, firms, and resource owners. This volume is concerned primarily with macroeconomics, but since one must know some microeconomics to understand macroeconomics, we include some microeconomics as well. However, the economic problem cited in this section is too purely microeconomic in nature to be taken up in detail here. For a more intensive discussion of this sort of problem, see the companion volume to this one, *Principles of Microeconomics.*

What Is Economics?

Resources, Scarcity, and Choice

Now that we have looked at a number of specific economic problems, we are in a position to set forth and probe the following basic definition: *economics is concerned with the way resources are allocated among alternative uses to satisfy human wants.* This definition will help get you oriented, but to understand it fully, you must know what resources are, why they are scarce and how choices are made as to their use and allocation.

To economists, a ***resource*** is a material or service used to produce goods or services that can be used to satisfy human wants. For present purposes, all that we want to emphasize about resources is that for the most part, they are scarce. No matter how rich any society may be, it has only a limited amount of resources. Even the United States, which is clearly among the richest of nations, has only a finite amount of resources. Not all resources are scarce: ***Free resources,*** such as air, are so abundant that they can be obtained without charge. But the number of free resources is actually quite limited. For instance, although the earth contains a huge amount of water, it is not a free resource to the typical urban or suburban homeowner, who must pay a local water authority for providing and maintaining his water supply. Despite the reassuring lyrics of the old ballad, "The Best Things In Life Are Free," a great many resources are not free at all.

Those resources that are scarce are called ***economic resources.*** The test of whether a resource is an economic resource or a free resource is price: economic resources command a nonzero price but free resources do not. Economists often classify economic resources into three categories: ***land, labor,*** and ***capital.***

Land. A shorthand expression for natural resources, land includes minerals, as well as plots of ground. Clearly, land is an important and valuable resource in both agriculture and industry. In addition, it is a major part of our environment, and it provides enjoyment above and beyond its contribution to agricultural and industrial output.

Labor. Human efforts, both physical and mental, are included in the category of labor. Thus, when you study for a final examination or make out an income tax return, this is as much labor as if you were to dig a ditch. The available supply of labor is, of course, an important resource in any society.

Capital. Buildings, equipment, inventories, and other nonhuman producible resources that contribute to the production, marketing, and distribution of goods and services all fall within the economist's definition of capital. Examples of capital are blast furnaces, oil refineries, machine tools, and warehouses. But not all types of capital are big or bulky. For example, a hand calculator, or a pencil for that matter, is a type of capital.

The amount of goods and services that can be obtained from the amount of resources at hand is dependent upon the existing technology. ***Technology*** is society's pool of knowledge concerning the industrial arts. It includes knowledge, needed in industry, of the principles of social and physical phenomena (such as the laws of motion and the properties of fluids); knowledge regarding the application of these principles to production (such as applying various aspects of genetic theory to the breeding of new plants); and knowledge regarding the day-to-day operation of productive processes (such as the rules of thumb of the skilled craftsman). Note that technology is different from the techniques in use, since not all that is known is likely to be applied. Also, technology is different from pure science, although the distinction is not very precise. Pure science is directed toward understanding, whereas technology is directed toward use.

Given the existing technology, the fact that resources are scarce means that only a limited amount of goods and services can be produced from them. In other words, the capacity to produce goods and services is limited—*far more limited than human wants.* ***Human wants*** are the goods, services, and circumstances people desire. Wants vary greatly among individuals, and, for a given individual, they vary greatly over time. Some people like to ride horseback, others like to read. Some want to carouse until 3:00 A.M.; others follow Ben Franklin's maxim of early to bed, early to rise. For present purposes, the important thing to note about human wants is that they seem to be insatiable in the aggregate (even though an individual's desire for a particular good in a particular period of time is not infinite). In part, this is because wants arise from cultural factors—advertising, social pressures, education, and emulation of other people—as well as the basic human drives for food, shelter, and clothing. In other words, people's wants tend to increase and multiply as they see ads for products that look attractive, and as they hear about and come into contact with affluent people. Although many people claim to prefer the simple life, it often turns out they mean a steak fixed simply in a simple $80,000 split-level house in the suburbs.

Since the amount of goods and services that can be produced is less than what is wanted, there arises the necessity for ***choice.*** Somehow or other, a choice must be made as to how the available resources will be used (or if they will be used at all). Somehow or other, a choice must be made as to how the output produced from these resources will be distributed among the population. Economics is concerned with how such choices are made. Economists have spent a great deal of time, energy, and talent (their own and other peoples') trying to determine how such choices *are* made in various circumstances, and how they *should* be made. Indeed, as we shall see in the next section, the basic questions that economics deals with are problems of choice of this sort. Note that these problems of choice go beyond the problems of particular individuals in choosing how to allocate their own resources; they are problems of social choice.

Central Questions in Economics

Economists are particularly concerned with four basic questions regarding the working of any economic system—ours or any other. These questions are: (1) What determines what is produced? (2) What determines how it is produced? (3) What determines how the society's output is distributed among the members? (4) What determines the rate at which the society's productive capacity will grow? These questions lie at the core of economics, because they are directed at the most fundamental characteristics of economic systems.

To illustrate the nature and basic importance of these questions, suppose that, because of war or natural catastrophe, your town is isolated from the adjoining territory. No longer is it possible for the town's inhabitants to leave, or for people or goods to enter. (Lest you regard this as fanciful, it is perhaps worthwhile to note that Leningrad was under siege in World War II for over two years.) In this situation, you and your fellow townspeople must somehow resolve each of these questions. You must decide what goods and services will be produced, how each will be produced, who will receive what, and how much provision there will be for increased output in the future.

In a situation of this sort, your very survival will depend on how effectively you answer these questions. If a decision is made to produce too much clothing and too little food, some of the townspeople may starve. If a decision is made to produce wheat from soil that is inappropriate for wheat, but excellent for potatoes, much the same result may occur. If a decision is made to allot practically all of the town's output to friends and political cronies of the mayor, those who oppose him may have a very rough time. And if a decision is made to eat, drink, and be merry today, and not to worry about tomorrow, life may be very meager in the days ahead.

Because we are considering a relatively small and isolated population, the importance of these questions may seem more obvious than in a huge country like the United States, which is constantly communicating, trading, and interacting with the rest of the world. But the truth is that these questions are every bit as important to the United States as to the isolated town. And, for this reason, it is important that we understand how these decisions are made, and whether they are being made effectively. Just as in the hypothetical case of the isolated town, your survival depends on these decisions—but in the United States the situation isn't hypothetical!

Three Basic Principles of Economic Organization

Based on their studies of how various societies have gone about answering these four basic questions, economists have found that the methods used fall into three categories—tradition, command, and the price system. Throughout all history, societies have relied on one of these three methods (or some mixture of them) to answer the basic economic questions. In view of the fact that human ingenuity seems to have been able to construct only these three methods, it is worthwhile describing each of them briefly.

Tradition. For much of recorded time, tradition was the basic principle of economic organization. A host of procedures, inherited from the far distant past and frequently hallowed by religion and enforced by law, guided the behavior of individuals and groups. For example, in ancient societies, sons frequently followed the occupations of their fathers. You were born into a particular station in life, and tradition dictated that you stayed in that station. In India, such a caste system remained in existence until quite recently. In many parts of the world, tradition continues to play a major role in determining how the economic system functions. Tradition is a particularly important determinant of economic behavior in many of the less developed countries.

Command. Throughout human history, various kinds of political authorities have imposed their will on society to determine how the basic economic questions would be answered. In ancient times, the Roman emperors decreed that the economic system would respond in particular ways to their desires. In modern times, the governments of China and the Soviet Union have brought about radical changes in the economic order. In the Soviet Union, for example, the government has pushed industrialization at a rapid pace, and has tried hard to catch up with the West. In every economy, the basic economic questions are answered to some extent by command, but in a democratic society the commands are in accord with, and in response to, majority opinion.

Price system. Of the three basic ways to organize an economy, the price system is in many respects the most difficult to understand; and for that reason we shall devote considerable attention to the price system in Chapter 4, below. At this point, it is sufficient to point out that, under the price system, consumers are free to buy what they please, firms are free to sell what they please, and resource owners are free to use them as they please. Under the price system, the four basic economic questions are answered through the working of free markets.

It is worth emphasizing that the United States relies on a combination of all three of these methods. Tradition unquestionably plays a role, although less than in many other societies. For example, some families, like the Adamses or Kennedys, have had a tradition of going into public service; and others, like the Pattons, have gone into the military. Command plays a major role too. For example, the government decides how much is spent on defense. (As we shall see in subsequent chapters, the government intervenes in our economic affairs in myriad ways, often to the applause of liberals and the consternation of conservatives.) And although it is not allowed to operate unfettered, the price system plays a central role in our economy. Thus, even though our economy relies more heavily on the price system than many other economies do, command and (to some extent) tradition are also important.

The Basic Problem of Choice

In a previous section, we illustrated the nature of the basic economic questions by taking up the case of a town that is isolated from the adjoining territory, because of a war or natural catastrophe. To show some essential elements of any problem of choice, let's return to this illustration. Suppose that you are a member of the town council that is organized to determine how the town's resources should be utilized. To keep things simple, suppose that only two goods—food and clothing—can be produced. (This is an innocuous assumption that allows us to strip the problem to its essentials.) You must somehow figure out how much of each good should be produced. How can you go about solving this problem?

Clearly, the first step toward a solution is to list the various resources contained within the town. Using the technology available to the townspeople, each of these resources can be used to produce either food or clothing. Some of these resources are much more effective at producing one good than the other. For example, a tailor probably is better able to produce clothing than to produce food. But nonetheless most resources can be adapted to produce either good. For example, the tailor can be put to work on a farm, even though he may not be very good at farming.

After listing the various available resources and having determined how effective each is at producing food or clothing, the next step is to see how much food the town could produce per year, if it produced nothing but food, and how much clothing it could produce per year, if it produced nothing but clothing. Also, you should determine, if various amounts of food are produced per year, the maximum amount of clothing that the town can produce per year. For example, if the town produces 100 tons of food per year, what is the maximum amount of clothing it can produce per year? If the town produces 200 tons of food per year, what is the maximum amount of clothing it can produce per year? And so on.

Having carried out this step, suppose that the results are as shown in Table 1.3. According to this table, the town can produce (at most) 200 tons of clothing per year if it produces nothing but clothing. It can produce (at most) 180 tons of clothing per year if it produces 100 tons of food per year. It can produce (at most) 150 tons of clothing per year, if it produces 200 tons of food per year. It can produce (at most) 100 tons of clothing per year, if it produces 300 tons of food per year. And it can produce (at most) 400 tons of food per year, if it produces no clothing at all. (These five possible combinations of food output and clothing output are labeled *A* to *E* in Table 1.3.)

Table 1.3
Combinations of Output of Food and Clothing That the Town Can Produce Per Year.

Possibility	Amount of food produced per year (tons)	Amount of clothing produced per year (tons)
A	0	200
B	100	180
C	200	150
D	300	100
E	400	0

The data in Table 1.3 put in bold relief the basic problem of choice facing you and the other members of the town council. Because the town's resources are limited, the town can only produce limited amounts of each good. There is no way, for example, that the town can produce 200 tons of clothing per year and 200 tons of food per year. This is beyond the capacity of the town's resources. If the town wants to produce 200 tons of clothing, it can produce no food—which is hardly a pleasant prospect. And if the town wants to produce 200 tons of food, it can produce 150 (not 200) tons of clothing per year. Table 1.3 shows what combinations of food and clothing outputs are attainable.

A very important fact illustrated by Table 1.3 is that, whenever the town increases its production of one good, it must cut back its production of the other good. For example, if the town increases its production of food from 100 to 200 tons per year, it must cut back its production of clothing from 180 to 150 tons per year. Thus, in a very real sense, *the cost to the town of increasing its food output from 100 to 200 tons per year is that it must reduce its clothing output from 180 to 150 tons per year.*

Economists refer to this cost as ***alternative cost***; it is one of the most fundamental concepts in economics. *The alternative cost of using resources in a certain way is the value of what these resources could have produced if they had been used in the best alternative way.* In this case, the alternative cost of the extra 100 tons of food per year is the 30 tons of clothing per year that must be given up.

Finally, based on the data in Table 1.3, you and the other members of the town council must determine which combination of food and clothing output is best. To come to a conclusion on this score, you must decide, explicitly or implicitly, the relative importance—that is, the relative value to the townspeople—of food and clothing. In other words, you must decide at what point an increase in the output of one good is no longer worth what it costs in terms of reduced output of the other good. For example, the town council may agree that it is worthwhile to increase food output from 100 to 200 tons per year, because the extra 100 tons of food is worth more to the town's welfare than the 30 tons of clothing that is given up. But the town council may feel that it is unwise to increase food output beyond this point (from 200 to 300 tons per year), because the extra 100 tons of food is not worth as much to the town's welfare as the 50 tons of clothing that is given up by doing so.

On Parks and Schooling: Applications of Alternative Costs

As an example of the application of the concept of alternative costs to contemporary social issues, consider a case where a bill is presented to Congress to set aside certain wilderness areas as national parks. At first glance, it may appear that such a step entails no cost to society, since the land is not being utilized and the resources required to designate the areas as national parks are trivial. But using the concept of alternative cost, it is clear that this step may have very substantial costs to society. For instance, if these lands are made part of the national park system, the minerals, timber, and other natural resources contained within the areas cannot be extracted nor can the lands be used as sites for factories or processing plants. As pointed out in the previous section, the alternative cost of using resources in one way is the value of what these resources could have produced had they been used in the best alternative way. Suppose that if these lands are not turned into national parks, their most valuable alternative use is for development of copper mines which would produce benefits amounting to $25 million per year to the society. Then the actual cost to society of using these lands and parks is $25 million per year, since this is the amount that society is giving up when it uses them in this way (rather than selecting the most valuable alternative). Thus, whether these lands should be used as parks depends on whether the society believes that it is worth $25 million or more to do so.

Besides being applicable to social issues, the concept of alternative cost has direct relevance to the decision-making process of private citizens. For example, consider the case of a student who must decide whether or not a college education is worth its cost. In making this decision, the student should recognize that the true cost of going to college is considerably in excess of the out-of-pocket expenses because one can obtain wages by working rather than attending classes and studying. In other words, the time spent in school has alternative costs, since it could be devoted to a job rather than to education. For the sake of concreteness, let's assume that the student could earn $5,000 during each school year if he or she works rather than goes to college. Also, let's assume that the student goes to a college where the annual tuition and fees equal $2,500, and additional expenses amount to $2,000. Under these rather arbitrary assumptions (which may be quite different from your own situation), Table 1.4 shows that the total annual cost—including the alternative cost of the student's time—of a college education amounts to $9,500. This, of course, is much higher than the annual out-of-pocket cost which is $4,500. Whether or not the cost is worthwhile depends on how much the student's subsequent earnings will be raised by a college diploma—and how much enjoyment he or she will get from the experience at college and the knowledge obtained there.

Table 1.4
Annual Cost (dollars) to the Student of a College Education: A Hypothetical Case

Out-of-pocket costs:	
Tuition and fees	2,500
Books, travel, and other expenses	2,000
Alternative cost of student's time	5,000
Total	9,500

Note: These figures vary greatly from college to college and from individual to individual. Also, the "other expenses" cited in the second line include living expenses in excess of those which would have been incurred whether or not the student went to college.

In recent years, economists have carried out a number of important studies concerned with actual policy making in fields such as conservation of natural resources and education, often utilizing the concept of alternative costs in the process. This may come as a surprise to many who assume that economics deals only with subjects that are closely related to the market place.

Some Important Characteristics of Economic Problems

As stressed in previous sections, economic problems generally involve choice. Several common threads often characterize these problems of choice.

Forecasting. To choose among a number of feasible solutions to an economic problem, it frequently is necessary to forecast what will occur if each solution is adopted. This emphasis on the future necessarily entails some uncertainty. For example, in a period of substantial unemployment, the government can reduce the extent of unemployment in a variety of ways: it can reduce taxes, increase its expenditures, or increase the amount of money in circulation, among other methods. Which measure is best depends on the magnitude and nature of the effects of each one, which must be forecasted. Unfortunately, economic forecasting is by no means an exact science, but there is no way to avoid making such forecasts. One way or another, a choice will be made, and any choice involves a forecast, explicit or implicit. Each year, thousands of studies are carried out by economists in an effort to improve their ability to forecast various phenomena. Judging by the available evidence, these efforts have been paying off, and economic forecasting has become increasingly reliable. However, it would be foolish to claim that forecasts of this sort are anything other than rough guides to the future.

Role of Government. Many economic problems involve choices concerning the role of government in economic affairs. Consider the problem of stemming inflation. Should the government impose wage and price controls, or should the government leave prices and wages to private bargaining and markets? Or, how much government intervention to reduce pollution should be accepted? Should the Environmental Protection Agency be given the power to impose regulations of various kinds on the extent to which any firm or individual can pollute the environment, or should we allow firms and individuals to make these decisions themselves?

Turn to a different area: the antitrust laws, which are designed to stimulate and preserve competition and to discourage monopoly. In the Von's Grocery case of 1965, the Supreme Court disallowed a merger between two supermarkets that together had less than 8 percent of the Los Angeles market. Is this carrying government intervention too far? Or consider the regulation of natural gas prices by the Federal Power Commission. When it instructed the Commission to regulate these prices, the Supreme Court said that the producers of natural gas had appreciable power over the market; but there are thousands of natural gas producers, and many observers believe that the industry is highly competitive. Is governmental regulation of this sort justified?

Interdependence. Many economic problems cannot be considered in isolation, because attempts to solve one problem may worsen another problem. For example, measures designed to reduce the rate of inflation may increase unemployment, unless the government is very careful. Similarly, stepping up the rate of increase of national output may also increase environmental pollution, and attempts to reduce pollution may worsen the poverty problem, because the antipollution programs may hurt the poor more than the rich. Needless to say, an attempt to solve a particular problem does not always aggravate another problem. However, since it *may* make another problem worse, we must determine its side effects before we act.

Economics in Action

The Role of Economics in Public Policy

The problems we have touched on in this chapter are only a sample of the ways economics affects your life as a citizen, administrator, worker, investor, or consumer. But even this small sample makes it clear that some economic problems are problems facing our entire society. For example, avoiding excessive unemployment is not a task that can be assigned to a particular individual, family, or firm. It requires the concerted effort of our entire society. In other words, it is a problem of public policy—a problem that is considered and debated in the political arena. As citizens, we are all entitled to take part in making public policy—and we are all affected by the policies adopted.

Economics, and economists, play an extremely important role in the formulation of public policy. Skim through the articles in a daily newspaper. Chances are that you will find a report of an economist testifying before Congress, perhaps on the costs and benefits of a program to reduce unemployment among black teenagers in the Bedford-Stuyvesant area of New York City, or on the steps that can be taken to make American goods more competitive with those produced by Japan or West Germany. Still another economist may crop up on the sports page, arguing that professional athletes should be allowed to sell their talents to any team, not merely the team that has acquired the right to negotiate with them through a players' draft.

Economics and economists play a key role at the highest levels of our government. The president, whether Democrat or Republican, relies heavily on his economic advisers in making the decisions that help to shape the future of the country. Like his predecessors in the White House, President Carter works closely and continually with his economic advisers, some of whom were involved in his successful campaign for the presidency in 1976. In addition, economics plays a very important role in the decisions made by individual government agencies. For example, the Energy Research and Development Administration (ERDA) is charged with the responsibility of devising a program of research and development to help us overcome our energy problems. To carry out this responsibility, ERDA must take careful account of economic factors, and use economic techniques to allocate its multi-billion-dollar budget efficiently.

In the Congress, too, economics plays a major role. Economists are frequent witnesses before congressional committees, staff members for the committees, and advisers to individual congressmen and senators. Many congressional committees focus largely on economic matters. For example, some, including the powerful Ways and Means Committee of the House of Representatives, deal with taxes. In recent years, tax reform has been a hot subject, as the public has clamored for the reduction of various loopholes in the tax laws. (These loopholes frequently favor the rich at the expense of the poor.) The Congress also decides how much the government will spend each year on various programs. There is frequently considerable politicking over the size and distribution of government expenditures. For example, in 1976, many congressmen fought hard against President Ford's attempt to keep a tight lid on government spending, and there was considerable debate over the adequacy of the amounts allotted for antipoverty, health, and educational programs.

Finally, perhaps the most dramatic evidence of the importance of economics in the formulation of public policy is provided during presidential elections, when each candidate—with his or her own cadre of economic advisers supplying ideas and reports—stakes out a position on the major economic issues of the day. This position can be of crucial importance in determining victory or defeat, and you, the citizen, must know some economics to understand whether a candidate is talking sense or nonsense (or merely evading an issue). For example, if a candidate promises to increase government expenditures, lower taxes, and reduce the federal deficit, you can be pretty certain that he is talking through his hat. This may not be obvious to you now, but it should be later on.

The Role of Economics in Private Decision Making

Not all economic problems affect all, or even a major part, of our society: some affect a particular individual, household, or firm, and are largely a matter of private decision making. Because these problems tend to be narrow and localized, they are sometimes viewed as less important or interesting than those involving public policy. But this is not the case. If individuals, households, and firms do a reasonably good job of solving their own problems, many social problems are solved automatically. Moreover, most of us spend most of our lives wrestling with these narrower questions. Thus we all have an interest in learning how to cope better with them.

Economics and economists play an extremely important role in private decision making. Their role in the decision-making process in business firms is particularly great, since many of the nation's business executives have studied economics in college or in postgraduate programs, and many of the nation's larger corporations hire professional economists to forecast their sales, reduce their costs, increase their efficiency, negotiate with labor and government, and carry out a host of other tasks. Judging from the fancy salaries business economists are paid, the firms seem to think they can deliver the goods; and in fact the available evidence seems to indicate that they do provide important guidance to firms in many areas of their operations.

As an illustration, consider the Magnavox Company, a major manufacturer of television sets. In 1971, Magnavox's president, Robert Platt, decided to move slowly in converting Magnavox's TV sets from electron tubes to all solid-state sets, because he did not believe that the solid-state sets would catch on quickly with the public, and because he wanted to wait until an improved picture tube was available in 1973 before making the transition. This was a mistake. Consumers rushed to buy the solid-state sets, and Magnavox's sales fell to $226 million in 1972, down 36 percent from their peak in 1968. Economics is concerned with decisions of this sort, and although it cannot insure success or prevent mistakes, it can shed important light on the way such decisions should be made.

Finally, economics and economists influence the decision making of households as well as firms. Few households—other, perhaps, than the Rockefellers and the Gettys—can afford to hire their own professional economist, but this does not mean that many households do not receive and use a considerable amount of economic advice. On the contrary, most households take magazines and newspapers that contain a great deal of economic information. The *Wall Street Journal* is packed with it; so are the financial pages of the *New York Times* and other leading newspapers. Even a general news magazine like *Time* now has a board of economic advisers—and puts an economist on its cover from time to time. (*Newsweek*, its competitor, features columns by economists.) Based on information provided in such publications, households can make more informed decisions on their investments and expenditures. Through this channel, among others, economics can play a major role in their decision making.

Summary

Economics helps you to understand the nature and organization of our society (and other societies), the arguments underlying many of the great public issues of the day, and the operation and behavior of business firms and other economic decision-making units. It is no exaggeration to say that everyone must know something about economics to function responsibly and effectively as a citizen, administrator, worker, or consumer.

According to one standard definition, economics is concerned with the way resources are allocated among alternative uses to satisfy human wants. A resource is a material or service used to produce goods or services. Not all resources are scarce. Free resources, such as air, are so abundant that they can be obtained without charge. Those resources that are scarce are called economic resources. The test of whether a resource is an economic resource or a free resource is price: economic resources command a nonzero price but free resources do not. Economists often classify economic resources into three categories: land, labor, and capital.

Since economic resources are scarce, only a limited amount of goods and services can be produced from them, and there arises the necessity for choice. For example, if an isolated town has a certain amount of resources, it must choose how much of each good it will produce from these resources. If it increases the amount produced of one good, it must reduce the amount produced of another good. The alternative cost of using resources to increase the production of the one good is the reduction in the output of the other good. To illustrate the use of the concept of alternative cost, which is one of the most important in economics, we discussed the cases of public parks and a college education.

Economists are particularly concerned with four basic questions regarding the working of any economic system, ours or any other. These questions are: (1) What determines what is produced? (2) What determines how it is produced? (3) What determines how the society's output is distributed among the members? (4) What determines the rate at which the society's productive capacity will grow? To answer these questions societies have relied on one of three methods (or some mixture of them): tradition, command, and the price system. The American economy relies more heavily on the price system than many other economies do, but command and (to some extent) tradition are important too.

CONCEPTS FOR REVIEW

Economics	Government regulation	Interdependence	Capital
Unemployment	Poverty	Resources	Technology
Inflation	Pollution	Labor	Macroeconomics
Forecasting	Economic resources	Free resources	Microeconomics
Choice	Planned economy	Land	

QUESTIONS FOR DISCUSSION AND REVIEW

1. Alfred Marshall, the great British economist, defined economics as follows: "Economics is a study of men as they live and move and think in the ordinary business of life. But it concerns itself chiefly with those motives which affect, most powerfully and most steadily, man's conduct *in the business part of his life*. . . . [The] steadiest motive to ordinary business work is the desire for the pay which is the material reward of work."[1] Does this definition encompass all of the examples of economic analysis and problems contained in this chapter? Do you agree with this definition? If not, how would you modify it?

2. Herbert Spencer, the English philosopher, wrote that "the poverty of the incapable, the distresses that come upon the imprudent, the starvation of the idle, and those shoulderings aside of the weak by the strong, which leave so many 'in shallows and in miseries,' are the decrees of a large, far-seeing benevolence." Interpret and explain this view. Do you agree with it? Why or why not?

3. "Resources are scarce and once a decision is made to use them for one purpose, they are no longer available for another. One opportunity cost of reading [an] . . . article, for example, is not simultaneously being able to read [another article]."[2] Explain, and relate to the question of how much society should spend on defense.

4. "The analytical approach to choice is the hallmark of the [economics] profession. It is the essence of the discipline to focus on, and especially to quantify, the dimensions of choice—the costs, the benefits, and the alternative ways to achieve a given result."[3] Give three specific situations where data concerning the annual costs of operating a car would throw important light on a problem of choice faced by a household or firm.

5. Suppose that it costs a college student $1,000 per year more for room and board than if he or she works (and lives at home). If this assumption is correct, why is this amount, rather than the full cost of room and board, the proper amount to use in Table 1.4?

6. "Modern economics can and has successfully prescribed the means of preventing large-scale unemployment without bringing on major inflation."[4] Explain what this statement means, and suggest ways to test whether it is true.

[1] A. Marshall, *Principles of Economics*, London: Macmillan, 1920.
[2] D. Eastburn, "Economic Man in Conflict with His Economic Self," *New York Times Magazine*, July 26, 1970.
[3] A. Okun, *The Political Economy of Prosperity*, New York: Norton, 1970.
[4] C. Schultze, "Is Economics Obsolete? No, Underemployed," *Saturday Review*, January 22, 1972.

7. In this chapter, we described four basic questions that any economic system must answer. Which of these questions is involved in each of the following specific problems: (a) Should the United States use natural gas to produce ammonia? (b) Should taxes on the poor be lower? (c) Should American consumers save more? (d) Should more of our nation's industry be used to produce food?

8. Consider "a Melanesian native group, the Aztec empire, a Greek city state, an English medieval manor, modern America, or modern Russia. Each of these economic systems represents a configuration of institutions almost totally unlike that of any of the others, yet each has a practicable means by which the fundamental tasks of the economic order have been accomplished."[5] What are these fundamental tasks? In which of these cases do you think that tradition played the biggest role? In which of these cases do you think that command played the biggest role? In which of these cases do you think that the price system played the biggest role?

9. "Unemployment can be cured by public employment. In other words, the government can give a job to anyone who wants it." Do you agree? What problems do you see in this approach to the problem?

10. "Inflation is of little consequence. If prices go up, wages must go up commensurately, so who cares if prices go up?" Comment in detail, and explain why you agree or disagree.

[5] H. Bowen, *Toward Social Economy*, New York: Holt, Rinehart, and Winston, 1948.

2 Economic Analysis: Models and Measurement

As a formal field of study, economics is a Johnny-come-lately. Copernicus paved the way for modern astronomy 400 years ago, and Newton started his revolution in physics in the seventeenth century. By contrast, modern economics is generally said to have begun in 1776, the same year as the American Revolution, with the publication of Adam Smith's *The Wealth of Nations*, and to have developed into a science only a century or so ago. But despite its relative youth, economics has influenced generations of statesmen, philosophers, and ordinary citizens, and has played a significant role in shaping our society today. To understand the great ideas that underlie important parts of our civilization and to appreciate great segments of our intellectual heritage, you must understand some economics.

Apart from its value as an intellectual discipline, economics provides keys that help to interpret the broad sweep of the world's history. Economic forces have strongly influenced the course of human events. It would be a gross oversimplification to argue that taxes levied by the British on the American colonies were the sole cause of the American Revolution; yet the movement for independence cannot be understood without some knowledge of the economic ties of the colonies to the mother country. Few historians would call the triumph of Nazism in the 1930s solely a consequence of raging inflation; yet Hitler used the economic plight of Germany as a lever in his rise to power.

In 1960, John F. Kennedy's pledge "to get the economy moving ahead" scored effectively at the political box office. In 1976, Jimmy Carter's promise to reduce unemployment helped him defeat Gerald Ford for the presidency. It is safe to say that many elections have turned on economic issues, that many wars have resulted from economic causes, and that many revolutions have occurred because of economic discontent. Of course, economics is only one key to history; political, social, religious, and cultural factors are extremely important too. But to understand much about history—either the history of ideas or the history of events—you need to know something about economics.

The Industrial Revolution and Adam Smith

The Industrial Revolution

To illustrate the importance of economics in understanding the history of events, let's consider one of the most fundamental and remarkable developments in human history, the so-called Industrial Revolution. Until the middle of the eighteenth century, industry, as distinct from agriculture or commerce, played a small role in the economies of Europe or America. But during the late eighteenth and early nineteenth centuries, a host of important technological innovations, such as James Watt's steam engine and Richard Arkwright's spinning jenny, made possible a very rapid growth in the output of industrial goods (like textiles and pig iron). And accompanying this growth of industrial output was the advent of the factory—a social and economic institution that is taken for granted today, but which was largely unknown prior to the Industrial Revolution.

Economics is important in understanding the effects of the Industrial Revolution and the conditions that made it possible. The Industrial Revolution was characterized by major improvements in technology and by large increases in the amount of capital resources available to society. (Recall from the previous chapter that capital resources include buildings, equipment, and other nonhuman producible resources.) Both the improvements in technology and the additional capital made it possible for England (where the Industrial Revolution first took hold) to increase its total output. Why? Because improved technology made possible greater output from a given amount of resources, and because more capital constituted an increase in resources. Due to the increased output, the standard of living in England, as measured by per capita income, grew at an unprecedented rate. As the Industrial Revolution spread, this rise in living standards occurred too on the European continent and in the United States; it remained one of the lasting effects of industrialization.

However, this long-term increase in the standard of living took many years to be achieved. In the short run, the Industrial Revolution was marked by considerable human suffering (but perhaps not much more so than in previous years). Although a small segment of European society led rich lives in city drawing rooms or on country estates, the great bulk of the population at that time lived in abject poverty. To take one small example, in some coal mines, both men and women worked, often half-naked, for long hours; children worked in the mines too—and some seldom saw daylight for months. In the factory towns, as in the mines, the hours were long, and children often spent their early years at work. Shifts of 10 to 12 hours a day were not uncommon, and wages were very low.

As stressed above, the Industrial Revolution was characterized by considerable increases in capital. How did England (and other countries) bring about this increase in capital? By saving. In other words, the English people had to set aside some of their resources, and to say in effect, "These resources will not be used to satisfy the current needs of our population for food, clothing, and other forms of consumption. Instead, they will be used to produce capital—factories, machines, equipment, railroads, and canals—which will increase our future productive capacity." Much more will be said about this saving process in subsequent chapters. For now, the essential point is that this saving process was one of the necessary conditions that made possible the Industrial Revolution.

Adam Smith, Father of Modern Economics

To illustrate the importance of economics in understanding the history of ideas, let's consider Adam Smith (1723-90), the man who is often called the father of modern economics. Smith lived during the Industrial Revolution, and was one of the first scholars to understand many of the central mechanisms of a free, or unplanned, economy. Much of his life was spent as professor of moral philosophy at the University of Glasgow in Scotland. In 1759, he published *The Theory of Moral Sentiments,* which established him as one of Britain's foremost philosophers, but this was not the book for which he is famous today. His masterpiece, published in 1776 (while the American colonists were brewing rebellion), was *The Wealth of Nations,*[1] a long, encyclopedic book 12 years in the writing. It was not an instant success, but the laurels it eventually won undoubtedly compensated for its early neglect. It is unquestionably one of the most influential books ever written.

Much of *The Wealth of Nations* seems trite today, because it has been absorbed so thoroughly into modern thought, but it was not trite when it was written. On the contrary, Smith's ideas were revolutionary. *He was among the first to describe how the price system works and how a free, competitive economy can function—without central planning or government interference—to allocate resources efficiently. He recognized the virtues of the "invisible hand" that leads the private interests of firms and individuals toward socially desirable ends, and he was properly suspicious of firms that are sheltered from competition, since he recognized the potentially undesirable effects on resource allocation.*

In addition, Smith—with the dire poverty of his times staring him in the face—was interested in the forces that determined the evolution of the economy—that is, the forces determining the rate of growth of average income per person. Although Smith did not approve of avarice, he felt that saving was good because it enabled society to invest in machinery and other forms of capital. Accumulating more and more capital would, according to Smith, allow output to grow. In addition, he emphasized the importance of increased specialization and division of labor in bringing about economic progress. Moreover, he recognized that the rate of population increase was an important determinant of a country's economic development.

All in all, Smith's views were relatively optimistic, in keeping with the intellectual climate of his time—the era of Voltaire, Diderot, Franklin, and Jefferson, the age of the Enlight-

[1] Adam Smith, *The Wealth of Nations,* New York: Modern Library, 1937.

ADAM SMITH

on the "Invisible Hand" and Specialization

It is only for the sake of profit that any man employs [his] capital in the support of industry, and he will always, therefore, endeavor to employ it in the support of that industry of which the produce is likely to be of greatest value, or to exchange for the greatest quantity either of money or of other goods. But the annual revenue of every society is always precisely equal to the exchangeable value of the whole annual produce of its industry, or rather is precisely the same thing with that exchangeable value. As every individual, therefore, endeavors as much as he can both to employ his capital in the support of domestic industry, and so to direct that industry that its produce may be of the greatest value, every individual necessarily labors to render the annual revenue of the society as great as he can: He generally, indeed, neither intends to promote the public interest, nor knows how much he is promoting it. . . . He intends only his own security; and by directing that industry in such a manner as its produce may be of the greatest value, he intends only his own gain, and *he is in this, as in many other cases, led by an invisible hand to promote an end which was no part of his intention.* Nor is it always the worse for the society that it was no part of it. *By pursuing his own interest he frequently promotes that of the society more effectually than when he really intends to promote it.* I have never known much good done by those who affected to trade for the public good. It is an affectation, indeed, not very common among merchants, and very few words need be employed in dissuading them from it. . . .

It is the maxim of every prudent master of a family, never to attempt to make at home what it will cost him more to make than to buy. The tailor does not attempt to make his own shoes, but buys them of the shoemaker. The shoemaker does not attempt to make his own clothes, but employs a tailor. The farmer attempts to make neither the one nor the other, but employs those different artificers. All of them find it for their interest to employ their whole industry in a way in which they have some advantage over their neighbors, and to purchase with a part of its produce, or with the price of a part of it, whatever else they have occasion for.

Adam Smith, *The Wealth of Nations,* London: George Routledge, 1900, p. 345. Originally published in 1776. (Italics added.)

enment, when men believed so strongly in rationality. Leave markets alone, said Smith, and beware of firms with too much economic power and government meddling. If this is done, there is no reason why considerable economic progress cannot be achieved.

Economics: A Social Science

In the previous chapter, we tried to indicate the practical importance of economics. But economics is much more than a bag of techniques for solving practical problems. *Like any other natural or social science, it is concerned with explaining and predicting observed phenomena, whether or not these explanations and predictions have any immediate practical application.* One only need look at some of the books economists write for each other—books bristling with complicated mathematical formulas and highly theoretical arguments—to realize that not all economics is a search for immediate answers to the world's ailments. Instead, many fields of economics pursue abstract truth, immediately useful or not.

Thus much economic research is directed at questions like these: What determines the level of national output? (Why did the total amount of goods and services produced in the United States plummet by about 30 percent between 1929 and 1933?) What determines the price of various commodities? (Why are lamb chops more expensive than hot dogs?) What determines the over-all price level? (Why is the average level of prices so much higher now than it was 40 years ago?) What determines how much a worker makes? (Why are brain surgeons paid more than pipefitters?) What determines the rate of increase of per capita output? (Why has Japan's per capita output increased so much more rapidly than other industrialized countries' in recent years?) What determines how a consumer allocates his or her income among various commodities? (How will an increase in the price of honeydew melons influence the quantity you buy?) What determines the goods a country exports and those it imports? (Why do we export electronic computers and import transistor radios?) What determines the value of foreign money? (Why was a British pound worth about $1.60 in October 1976?)

As these questions and their parenthetical accompaniments stand, they are not in the form of practical problems. Yet a knowledge of the answers to these questions is obviously of interest and of value. In this respect, many branches of economics recall mathematics. Pure mathematics is not concerned with day-to-day affairs, but various branches of mathematics are very valuable in solving practical problems, and some knowledge of mathematics is indispensable for understanding the world around us and for professional and technical training. Or think of physics. Although many of its branches are rather far removed from practical application, a general knowledge of physics has proved necessary to solve many types of practical problems; and certain branches, like solid-state physics, have had enormous practical impact on technology and industry.

The crucial consideration is that *economics is a science*. Like other sciences, it formulates and tests basic propositions that can be used to predict and explain the phenomena we observe in the world around us. This does not mean it cannot be useful; but because it is a science—a social science—economics goes beyond problem-solving *to deal with the basic principles and mechanisms that make economic systems work as they do.*

Also, it is important to recognize that economics, although probably the most highly developed of the social sciences, is still far from being able to solve many of the pressing social issues we face. Nor will a knowledge of economics insure that your bank balance will soar. Economics can help solve important social problems, and it can help you come to better decisions, but it is no panacea. As you will see below, there are many economic questions that are unsettled and debated by the experts. Consequently, one should not expect too much. But even the most demanding student would probably admit that, to be valuable, a subject need not provide reliable answers to all interesting questions.

How Successful Are Economics and Economists?

Accuracy of Economic Propositions

Economics has come a long way since Adam Smith. Due to the efforts of such great figures as David Ricardo, Thomas Malthus, John Stuart Mill, Alfred Marshall, and John Maynard Keynes, as well as the work of countless other talented people, our understanding of the workings of the economic system has improved continually and significantly. But you may still have some doubts about how much of a science economics is, and whether it will give you valid, useful answers, or just ivory-tower concoctions with little or no applicability to the real world. These questions deserve an answer, although finding a concise one is not easy. One reason for the difficulty is that some aspects of economics are not as well understood as others, in part because less research has been done on them. Any discipline—physics, chemistry, or biology, for example—has such areas. Another reason is that all scientific predictions contain some error. Thus, the real question isn't whether economic predictions and propositions are accurate, but *how* accurate they are.

Even in this more meaningful form, the question is not easy to answer, however, since, as noted above, some economic predictions and propositions are much more accurate than others. For example, advances in economics and related disciplines in the postwar period have allowed economists to figure out more efficient ways for firms to run many aspects of their operations. Linear programming and related economic techniques have been applied to petroleum refineries, for example, to determine the minimum-cost blend of gasoline stocks and the most profitable outputs of regular and premium gasoline, enabling firms to increase their profits substantially. Short-range forecasting of changes in business conditions is another area where economics has proved very useful. Such forecasts are used by the government, as well as a host of firms, to guide major decisions involving billions of dollars.

On the other hand, economic knowledge in other areas is very limited. For example, economists are still uncertain about many effects of the government's monetary and fiscal policies. Most economists believe that both *monetary policy* (the government's policy concerning the money supply and interest rates) and *fiscal policy* (the government's policy concerning spending and taxes) play an important role in determining the size of national output, the extent of unemployment, and the rate of inflation. But an influential minority of the economics profession believes monetary policy to be far more important than fiscal policy, and the available evidence is too weak to show conclusively whether they are right or wrong. Our knowledge of the modern process of inflation is also limited. This the Nixon administration found out in the late 1960s when it tried to control the inflation occurring then. The standard remedies it applied did not work as many distinguished economists predicted they would.

However, even though economic knowledge in some areas is much more limited than we would like, you should recognize this important fact: *judging from all available evidence, a knowledge of economics will enable you to solve economic problems better than you would without it. Even though economic predictions and propositions are not always very precise, they tend to work better than predictions and propositions not based on economics.* And this, if you think about it, is really the crucial consideration.

Signals of Progress

One important signal that economics had become a full-fledged science was the establishment in 1969 of a Nobel Prize in economics. The beginning of these awards was an indication that economics was the first of the social sciences to "arrive." The first Nobel Prizes went to Professors Ragnar Frisch of Norway and Jan Tinbergen of Holland. Paul Samuelson, Simon Kuznets, Kenneth Arrow, Wassily Leontief, Tjalling Koopmans, and Milton Friedman were the first Americans to receive these prizes. All these scholars have contributed greatly to economics, but each in a quite different way: Samuelson, Arrow, and Koopmans have been responsible primarily for theoretical advances, while Kuznets has done basic empirical work, and Frisch, Tinbergen, Leontief, and Friedman have pioneered in the blending of theoretical and statistical techniques. Like any science, economics requires advances of many types—theoretical, empirical, statistical—to develop and flourish.

Another clear signal that economics has become a useful science is the very high salaries economists pull down in industry and government. Years ago, the taunt may have been, "If you're so smart, why aren't you rich?" Today the reply could be, "Those economists who are interested in making money seem to be doing very well indeed!" Of course, this does not mean that most economists in universities are making loads of money. Like other academic scientists, they are willing to earn less than they could in industry or government in order to enjoy the freedom to do research and teach. But if an economist wants to make lots of money, he certain has the opportunity.

The Methodology of Economics

Model Building in Economics

By now, you may think it worthwhile to devote a little time to economics, but you still don't know anything about how economists approach their subject or the methods they use. In the rest of this chapter, we will provide a general description of the methodology of economics. Like other types of scientific analysis, economics is based on the formulation of ***models***. *A model is a theory. It is composed of a number of assumptions from which conclusions—or predictions—are deduced.* If an astronomer wants to formulate a model of the solar system, he might represent each planet by a point in space and assume that each would change position in accord with certain mathematical equations. Based on this model, he might predict when an eclipse would occur, or estimate the probability of a planetary collision. The economist proceeds along similar lines when he sets forth a model of economic behavior.

There are several important aspects of models. First, *to be useful, a model must in general simplify and abstract from the real situation.* The assumptions made by a model need not be exact replicas of reality. If they were, the model would be too complicated to use. The basic reason for using a model is that the real world is so complex that masses of detail often obscure underlying patterns. The economist faces the familiar problem of seeing the forest, as distinct from just the trees. Other scientists must do the same; physicists work with simplified models of atoms, just as economists work with simplified models of markets. However, this does not mean that *all* models are good or useful. A model may be so oversimplified and distorted that it is utterly useless. The trick is to construct a model so that irrelevant and unimportant considerations and variables are neglected, but the major factors—those that seriously affect the phenomena the model is designed to predict—are included.

Second, *the purpose of a model is to make predictions about the real world, and in many respects the most important test of a model is how well it predicts.* In this sense, a model that predicts the price of copper within plus or minus $.01 a pound is better than a model that predicts it within plus or minus $.02 a pound. Of course, this does not mean that a model is useless if it cannot predict very accurately. We do not always need a very accurate prediction. For example, a road map is a model that can be used to make predictions about the route a driver should take to get to a particular destination. Sometimes, a very crude map is good enough to get you where you want to go, but such a map would not, for instance, serve the hiker who needs to know the characteristics of the terrain through which he plans to walk. How detailed a map you need depends on where you are going and how you want to get there.

Third, *if one wants to predict the outcome of a particular event, he will be forced to use the model that predicts best, even if this model does not predict very well.* The choice is not between a model and no model; it is between one model and another. After all, if one must make a forecast, he will use the most accurate device available—and any such device is a model of some sort. Consequently, when economists make simplifying assumptions and derive conclusions that are only approximately true, it is somewhat beside the point to complain that the assumptions are simpler than reality or that the predictions are not always accurate. This may be true, but if the predictions based on the economists' model are better than those obtained on the basis of other models, their model must, and will, be used until something better comes along. Thus, if a model can predict the price of copper to within plus or minus $.01 per pound, and no other model can do better, this model will be used even if those interested in the predictions bewail the model's limitations and wish it could be improved.

Economic Measurement

To utilize and test economic models, economists need facts of many kinds. As Lord William Beveridge said almost 40 years ago, "There can be no science of society until the facts about society are available. . . . It matters little how wrong we are with our existing theories, if we are honest and careful with our observations." As economics has become more of a science, more and more economists have spent more and more time digging out the facts and seeing what their implications are. Each economic model yields predictions, and to determine whether these predictions are accurate enough to be worth anything, economists must continually collect data to see how accurate the predictions are. For example, if a model predicts that the price of copper should be $.03 a pound higher in 1978 than in 1977, it is important to determine what price change really occurred, and how close the model's predictions were to reality.

At the outset, note that, to a very large extent, economics is not an experimental, or laboratory, science. In other words, economists, unlike physicists, chemists, or biologists, cannot generally carry out experiments under carefully controlled conditions. Consequently, they usually cannot study the effects of varying one factor, while holding constant other factors that may influence the outcome. Such controlled experiments are common in the natural sciences and in technology. For example, a controlled experiment might be performed in agriculture to learn the effect of various amounts of fertilizer on the amount of wheat produced on an acre of land. A sample of plots of ground might be planted with wheat, the amount of fertilizer varying from plot to plot. Then the yield obtained from each plot might be related to the amount of fertilizer used on that plot.

Since controlled experimentation of this sort is often, but not always, impossible in economics, economists must rely on data generated by the economic system. For example, to test a model of consumer behavior, an economist may set out to estimate the effect of a household's income on the amount of money it spends per year on clothing. To make such an estimate, the economist cannot perform an experiment in which he varies the income of a household and sees the effect on its clothing expenditures. Instead, he must gather data concerning the incomes and clothing expenditures of a large number of households, and study the relationship between them. The relationship he finds may, for example, resemble that shown in Figure 2.1: The line *AA′* represents an average relationship between household income and household clothing expenditure. If this relationship is in accord with the model, he will accept this model (at least tentatively); if not, he will reject it, and search for a better model.

Graphs and Relationships

Economists find it useful to present data and relationships between variables in graphs, such as Figure 2.1. Several things should be noted concerning graphs. First, a graph has a horizontal axis and a vertical axis, each of which has a scale of numerical values. For example, in Figure 2.1, the horizontal axis shows a household's annual income, and the vertical axis shows the annual amount spent by the household on clothing. The intersection of the two axes is called the origin, and is the point where both the variable measured along the horizontal axis and the variable measured along the vertical axis are zero. In Figure 2.1, the origin is at the lower lefthand corner of the figure, labeled *0*.

Second, to show the relationship between two variables, one can plot the value of one variable against the value of the other variable. Thus, in Figure 2.1, each family is represented by a dot. For example, the dot for the Buchanan family is in the position shown in Figure 2.1, because its income was \$5,000 and its clothing expenditure was \$400. Clearly, the relationship, *AA′* does not fit all the families exactly, since all the points do not fall on the line. *AA′* does, however, give the average clothing

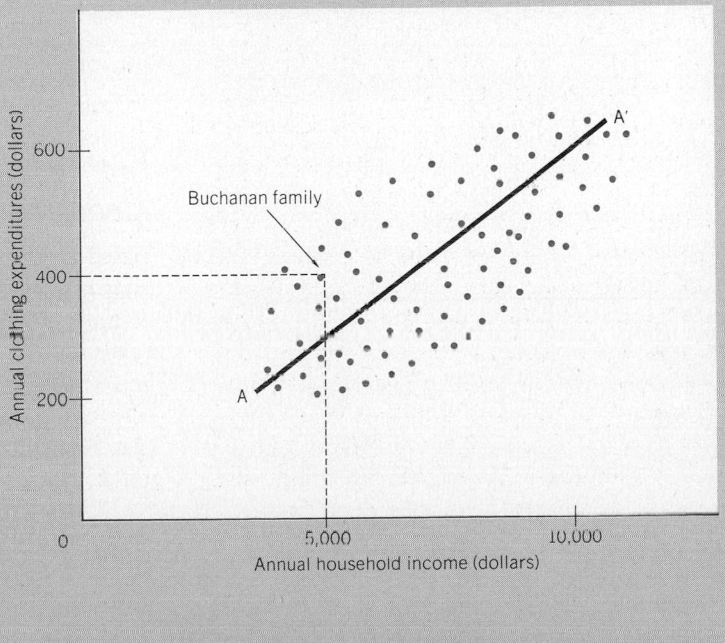

Figure 2.1
Relationship between Annual Clothing Expenditures and Annual Household Income
The line *AA′* represents an average relationship. Each family is represented by a dot. Clearly, *AA′* does not fit all families exactly, since all the points do not fall on the line. *AA′* does, however, give average clothing expenditure for each income level.

Figure 2.2
Relationship between Quantity Demanded and Price of Tennis Balls (as shown in Table 2.1).

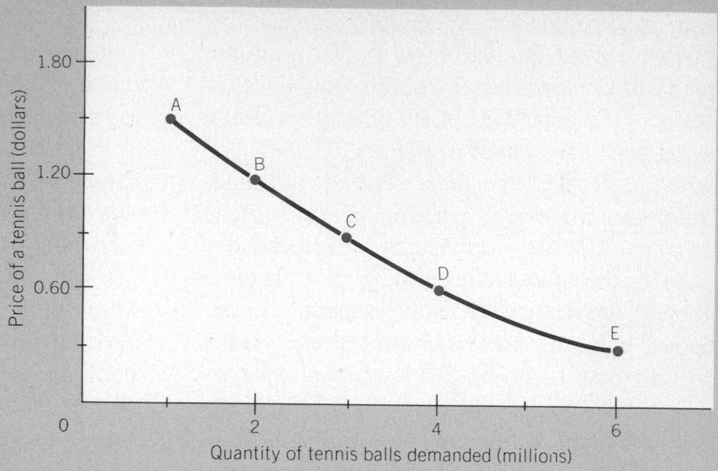

expenditure for each level of income: it is an average relationship.

Third, the relationship between two variables is *direct* if, as in Figure 2.1, the line of average relationship is upward sloping. In other words, if the variable measured along the vertical axis tends to increase (decrease) in response to increases (decreases) in the variable measured along the horizontal axis, the relationship is direct. On the other hand, if the line of average relationship is downward sloping, as in Figure 2.2, the relationship is *inverse.* In other words, if the variable measured along the vertical axis tends to decrease (increase) in response to increases (decreases) in the variable measured along the horizontal axis, the relationship is inverse.

Table 2.1
Quantity of Tennis Balls Demanded in a Particular Market at Various Prices

Price of a tennis ball (dollars)	Quantity of tennis balls demanded (millions)
1.50	1
1.20	2
0.90	3
0.60	4
0.30	6

To illustrate how one can graph a relationship between two variables, consider Table 2.1, which shows the amount of tennis balls demanded in a particular market at various prices. Putting price on the vertical axis and quantity demanded on the horizontal axis, one can plot each combination of price and quantity in this table as a point on a graph; and that is precisely what has been done in Figure 2.2 (points *A* to *E*). Note that, in contrast to the line in Figure 2.1, the line in Figure 2.2 goes through all of the points.

Statistical Tests and Quantitative Models

Based on the study of relationships like those shown in Figures 2.1 and 2.2, economists determine how well various models fit reality. In other words, they perform statistical tests to see whether a particular model is satisfactory. Two types of error can be made: they can reject a satisfactory model, or they can accept an unsatisfactory one. Which of these errors is more important will depend, of course, on the costs involved. For example, if the cost of accepting an unsatisfactory model is low, while the cost of rejecting a satisfactory model is high, then one should worry more about the latter type of error than the former. Using standard statistical methods, economists formulate their tests so that the probability that they will commit each type of error is roughly commensurate with the costs. Generally, it is impossible to eliminate completely the probability of error; the expense of doing so would be prohibitive.

Measurements like those in Figures 2.1 and 2.2 enable economists to ***quantify*** their models: in other words, they enable them to construct models that predict *how much* effect one variable has on another. For example, economists could be content with a model that predicts that higher household income results in higher household clothing expenditures; but this model would not be interesting or useful, since you don't need an economist to tell you that. A more valuable model is one that is quantitative, that predicts *how much* clothing expenditure will increase if household income increases by a certain amount.

A model of this sort might predict that clothing expenditures tend to increase by $60 when income increases by $1,000. Judging by Figure 2.1, such a model would be reasonably accurate, at least for households with incomes between $5,000 and $10,000 per year. Such quantitative models, tested against data like those in Figure 2.1, can be extremely valuable to firms that sell clothing and related products, to government agencies concerned with consumer expenditures, and to economists and other social scientists interested in consumer behavior.[2]

[2] It is worth noting that, although it is useful to see how well a model would have fit the historical facts, this is no substitute for seeing how well it will predict the future. As a distinguished mentor of mine once observed, "It's a darned poor person who can't predict the past."

Examples of Economic Models

The Pricing of Urban Transportation: A Case Study

For a first glimpse of the practical importance of economic models, consider the situation faced by the Boston and Maine Railroad in the early 1960s. The Boston and Maine wanted to discontinue its unprofitable railroad passenger commuter service into Boston. According to the railroad, the revenues it obtained from its commuter operations did not and could not meet the costs of providing the service. However, the Mass Transportation Commission of Massachusetts was not at all sure that such service had to be unprofitable for the Boston and Maine. The commission thought that lowering the price of commuter tickets might increase the service's profitability. This issue was of considerable importance both to the railroad and to Boston commuters.

To understand the Commission's view, we need the concept of a demand curve. Assuming that the incomes and tastes of the Boston commuting public, as well as the cost of commuting by alternative means of transportation, remain constant, it is extremely likely that the number of commuter tickets sold by the Boston and Maine will be inversely related to the price it charges for a ticket. In other words, holding constant these other factors, the lower the price, the greater the quantity of tickets sold. *This relationship between price and quantity of tickets sold can be represented graphically by a* ***demand curve,*** *which shows the number of tickets that will be sold at each price.*

The Commission suspected that the demand curve might be shaped like BB' in Figure 2.3, in which case the quantity of tickets sold would increase very substantially in response to a price cut. If BB' is the demand curve, and if

Figure 2.3
Demand Curve for Commuter Tickets, the Commission's View and the Skeptics' View
The commission suspected the demand curve might be *BB′*; the skeptics thought it might be *AA′*.

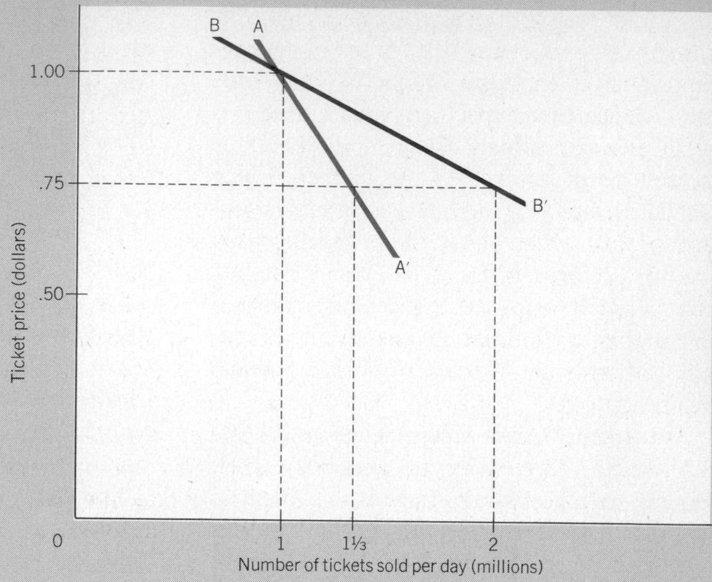

the price of a ticket is reduced from $1 to $.75, the quantity of tickets sold per day increases from 1 million to 2 million, with the result that the railroad's total revenue from suburban passenger service increases from $1 million per day (if the ticket price is $1) to $1.5 million per day (if the ticket price is $.75).[3] Since the extra $500,000 per day in revenue is greater than the extra cost of carrying the extra million passengers per day, such a price reduction would increase the railroad's profits. Indeed, according to the Commission, it might increase the Boston and Maine's profits enough to push its suburban passenger service into the black.

On the other hand, skeptics had a different model of the situation. According to their model, the demand curve was shaped like *AA′* in Figure 2.3, in which case the quantity of tickets sold does not increase very much in response to price cuts. If the price of a ticket is reduced from $1 to $.75, the quantity of tickets sold per day increases only from 1 million to 1⅓ million, with the result that the total revenues of the railroad remain constant at $1 million per day. Since it will cost the railroad more to transport 1⅓ million people than 1 million people per day, it follows that the railroad will make less money by reducing the price of a ticket. Thus, according to the skeptics, a price cut of this sort would not make the Boston and Maine's suburban passenger service profitable. On the contrary, it would make it more unprofitable.

Which model was correct? The Commission's or the skeptics'? As in any science, a question of this sort must be answered by an appeal to facts. Measurements must be made, and data gathered to shed light on the shape of this demand curve. Once such data are in hand, statistical tests can be carried out to see which model is closer to reality. The Commission asked the Boston and Maine to experiment with a reduction in ticket prices to see its effect on the quantity of tickets sold. This experiment, made in 1963, indicated that the skep-

[3] The total revenue equals 1 million tickets times $1 when the price is $1, and 2 million tickets times $.75 when the price is $.75. Thus it is $1 million in the former case and $1.5 million in the latter. Of course, the demand curves in Figure 2.3 (and the other numbers in this example) are hypothetical, but they illustrate the essential point.

ties' model was more nearly correct than the Commission's, and the railroad continued with its petition to terminate commuter passenger service when the experiment ended. However, public subsidies eventually were instituted to keep the service from terminating.

The models used in the Boston and Maine case were very simple, relative to most others employed by economists. All economic models are not this straightforward. Moreover, in this brief sketch we cannot do justice to all the subtleties and nuances involved in interpreting and testing these models: there are lots of problems and pitfalls. Yet, even so, this case study is a useful introduction to the construction and use of economic models.

The Battle against Unemployment: Another Case Study

Turning to more complicated economic models, let's look at some techniques used by government economists to combat unemployment. In early 1975, when the national unemployment rate exceeded 8 percent and was the highest in over 30 years, President Ford and the Congress both expressed grave concern. Fortunately, decades of research by economists all over the world had produced models that indicated the factors influencing the unemployment rate—among them, the level of taxes, government expenditures, and the money supply. These models indicated a number of ways by which the government could reduce the unemployment rate. One was to increase government expenditure, another was to reduce taxes. Having made their own evaluations of the advantages and disadvantages of each approach, the Congress and the Ford administration decided on a tax cut. A $23 billion tax cut was passed in March 1975. During late 1975 and early 1976, unemployment fell, and the tax cut was given considerable credit for it.

This was by no means the first time that models of this sort had been used. For example, when the Kennedy administration took office in 1961, it was confronted with a relatively high unemployment rate. (About 7 percent of the labor force was unemployed in mid-1961.) Based on these same kinds of economic models, Walter W. Heller, chairman of President Kennedy's Council of Economic Advisers, and other administration officials argued strongly for a tax cut, which was passed in 1964. According to available studies, this measure seemed to work: unemployment fell, as the models predicted it would. Of course, the models used by Heller and his colleagues may have been wrong; perhaps unemployment fell for reasons other than the tax cut. One cannot rule out this possibility, but it seems unlikely.[4]

Values and Decisions

Positive Economics versus Normative Economics

Economists make an important distinction between positive economics and normative economics. ***Positive economics*** *contains descriptive statements, propositions, and predictions about the world.* For instance, an economic model may predict that the price of copper will increase by $.01 a pound if income per person in the United States rises by 10 percent; this is positive economics. Positive economics tells us only what will happen under certain circumstances. It says nothing about whether the results are good or bad—or about what we should do. ***Normative economics,*** *on the other hand, makes statements about what ought to be, or about what a person, organization, or nation ought to do.* For instance, a model might say

[4] However, it should be noted that some prominent economists—the monetarists—feel that the models used by Heller and his colleagues were wrong, at least in part. To understand this issue, you need to know more about fiscal and monetary policy, discussed in Chapters 11 and 15.

that Chile should nationalize its copper industry and use the profits to reduce poverty; this is normative economics.

Clearly, positive economics and normative economics must be treated differently. Positive economics is science in the ordinary sense of the word. Propositions in positive economics can be tested by an appeal to the facts. Needless to say, in a nonexperimental science like economics, it is sometimes difficult to get the facts you need to test particular propositions. For example, if income per person in the United States does not rise by 10 percent, it may be difficult to tell what the effect of such an increase would be on the price of copper. Moreover, even if per capita income does increase by this amount, it may be difficult to separate the effect of the increase in income per person on the price of copper from the effect of other factors. But nonetheless, we can, in principle, test propositions in positive economics by an appeal to the facts.

In normative economics, however, this is not the case. *In normative economics, the results you get depend on your values or preferences.* For example, if you believe that reducing unemployment is more important than maintaining the purchasing power of the dollar, you will get one answer to certain questions; whereas if you believe that maintaining the purchasing power of the dollar is more important than reducing unemployment, you are likely to get a different answer to the same questions. This is not at all strange. After all, if people desire different things (which is another way of saying that they have different values), they may well make different decisions and advocate different policies. It would be strange if they did not.

The Role of Values

People sometimes make fun of economists because they disagree, and their differences are sometimes held up as evidence that economics is really not a science at all. In truth, of course, they prove nothing of the kind. *Because economists—like physicists, mathematicians, lawyers, and plumbers—differ in their preferences and values, they come to different conclusions when they enter the realm of normative economics.* Thus liberal economists often differ from conservative economists in their conclusions on public policy, and the disagreements can be over means as well as ends. *However, there is very substantial agreement on most of the propositions of positive economics.* Of course, this does not mean that everything is settled, but the areas of disagreement are generally relatively narrow. And this, it should be noted, is the important thing, since the pure science of economics is positive economics.

This book will spend a lot of time on the principles of positive economics—the principles and propositions concerning the workings of the economic system about which practically all economists tend to agree. Also, normative economics will be treated as well, since we must discuss questions of policy—and all policy discussions involve individual preferences, not solely hard facts. In these discussions, we shall try to indicate how the conclusions depend on one's values. Then you can let your own values be your guide. The purpose of this book is not to convert you to a particular set of values. It is to teach you how to obtain better solutions to economic problems, whatever set of values you may have.

Methodological Hazards in Economics

There are lots of impediments to straight thinking in economics that are not present in other disciplines like chemistry or biology. Some of the most important impediments are the following:

Bias. People have preconceptions about economic matters that they don't have about chemical or biological matters. Few people have a long-standing bias against two hydrogen atoms combining with an oxygen atom to form water, but some people grow up with the idea that profits are a bad thing or that unions are a social evil. These biases get in the way of objective analysis, because people tend to believe what they want to believe. If you want to learn any economics, you must respect facts, unpleasant though they may be at times.

Loaded words. Another hazard in economics is the use of loaded, emotional words. Unless you school yourself to look carefully at what words mean—and don't mean—you can be gulled by misleading terminology. For example, Marxists often refer to the exploitation of labor by capitalists, which sounds bad, since no one can be in favor of exploitation. But you must remember that labels can be misleading. What the Marxists call exploitation, most Western economists do not regard as exploitation at all.

Jargon. Social scientists are often and justly accused of using unfamiliar words, or jargon, to describe common phenomena. Economists do not escape this charge. You would probably not refer to your checking account in a bank as a demand deposit: economists do. What is more, economists define some terms in a different way from the man on the street. You will find out that rent to the economist is not an amount paid each month for an apartment, but a payment for a resource that is fixed in supply. Of course, economists have a right to define terms as they please, but you can be confused if you assume that seemingly familiar terms mean what you think they mean.

Post hoc ergo propter hoc. Still another pitfall is to assume that, because one event follows another, the former event is caused by the latter. The Romans had a phrase for this kind of reasoning: *post hoc ergo propter hoc* ("after this, therefore because of this"). This fallacy occurs all the time. Consider the people who attributed a spell of bad weather that occurred after the first moon landing to the astronauts' trip to the moon. The bad weather followed the lunar trip—therefore it must have been caused by it. Needless to say, this sort of reasoning is treacherous indeed, since many events occur on the heels of other events without being caused by them. To jump to the conclusion that an event following another event is caused by the earlier event is clearly to court disaster.

Fallacy of composition. Some people assume that what is true of part of a system must be true for the whole system. This can be quite wrong. For example, it may be true that a farmer will gain from producing a larger crop. But it may not be true that farmers as a whole will gain if all produce a larger crop. Or consider another case: a business firm will go bankrupt by continuing to spend more than it takes in, but it does not follow that an entire nation will go bankrupt if its government spends more than it takes in. The fallacy of composition—that what is true of the part must be true of the whole—lies in wait for the unwary student of economics, and for the experienced economist too. Grievous errors can be avoided by keeping clear of this fallacy's clutches.

Myopic specialization. Since economic factors are closely intertwined with social, psychological, and political factors, there is no well defined border between economics and the other social sciences—sociology, anthropology, psychology, and political science. To understand many problems in society, one must consider the sociological and political, as well as economic angles. For example, noneconomic factors are important in explaining why some countries are richer than others. Even in solving narrower problems, such as why consumers buy a particular product, psychological as well as economic factors must be considered. Thus, the economist must continually keep abreast of the advances made in other fields, since they can help him solve his own problems. Conversely, political scientists, psychologists, and other social scientists can often use economic techniques in their work. A myopic refusal to cross disciplinary boundaries can result in poor or misleading results.

Summary

Economics—and economists—have played a significant role in shaping the present nature of society. A knowledge of economics is necessary to understand the history of human events, and the masterpieces of economics produced in the past are important segments of our intellectual heritage. The methodology used by economists is much the same as that used in any other kind of scientific analysis. The basic procedure is the formulation and testing of models. A model must in general simplify and abstract from the real world. Its purpose is to make predictions concerning phenomena in the real world, and in many respects the most important test of a model is how well it predicts these phenomena. One illustration of the construction and use of an economic model was the discussion concerning the Boston and Maine's decision to discontinue suburban passenger service. Another example of the use of economic models was the decision made by the Congress and the Ford administration to pass a tax cut in 1975 to reduce unemployment.

To test and quantify their models, economists gather data and utilize various statistical techniques. Economists often distinguish between positive economics and normative economics. Positive economics contains descriptive statements, propositions, and predictions about the world; whereas normative economics contains statements about what ought to be, or about what a person, organization, or nation ought to do. In normative economics, the results you get depend on your basic values and preferences; in positive economics, the results are testable, at least in principle, by an appeal to the facts.

Although economics plays an important role in helping to solve basic social and private problems, you should not jump to the conclusion that economics is wholly a bag of techniques designed to solve practical problems; this is far from the case. Economics—like any natural or social science—is concerned with explaining and predicting observed phenomena, whether or not these explanations or predictions have any immediate application to practical problems. Also, it is important to recognize that, although economics can help solve social and private problems, it is no panacea. Nor is economics able to answer every important question about the workings of the economic system. As we shall see, our understanding of some questions is far from adequate. Nonetheless, a knowledge of economics is very useful and important in understanding the world around us.

CONCEPTS FOR REVIEW

Model
Measurement
Demand curve
Positive economics
Normative economics
Fallacy of composition

QUESTIONS FOR DISCUSSION AND REVIEW

1. In Adam Smith's words, "I have never known much good done by those who affected to trade for the public good." Did he mean that public officials do little good? Or didn't he include them among those who "trade"? Some American corporations claim to support many activities, such as the arts, because they are "for the public good." Does this contradict Smith's statement? How valid do you regard his statement to be?

2. Companies that invest a relatively large amount in research and development frequently tend to have relatively high rates of growth of sales. Does this mean that large expenditures on research and development *cause* high rates of growth of sales? Can you think of other explanations for the observed correlation? (Hint: Firms that spend a great deal on research and development may tend to have relatively progressive managements.)

3. Suppose that the quantity of corn demanded annually by American consumers at each price of corn is as follows:

Price (dollars per bushel)	Quantity of corn (millions of bushels)
1	2.0
2	1.0
3	0.5
4	0.4

How much will farmers receive for their corn crop if it is 2 million bushels? If it is 1 million bushels? If you owned all of the farms producing corn, would you produce 2 million bushels? Why or why not?

4. Plot the relationship between price and quantity demanded in Question 3 in a graph. Is the relationship direct or inverse? Based on your graph, estimate how much corn is likely to be demanded if the price is (a) \$1.50, (b) \$2.50, and (c) \$3.50.

5. Suppose that you wanted to construct a model to explain and predict the breakfast food that your neighbor will choose tomorrow. What factors would you include? How well do you think you could predict?

6. Suppose that you were given the job of estimating the demand curve for commuter tickets in metropolitan Boston. How would you proceed? What sorts of difficulties would you anticipate?

7. "If one firm cuts its price, it will make more money, so if all firms cut their price, they will make more money." Do you agree? If so, prove that it is true. If not, cite the kind of methodological error that is committed.

8. "Models are useless because they cannot include all of the variables that influence the phenomenon we want to predict." Comment.

9. On the basis of positive economics alone, which of the following statements can be determined to be true or false: (a) The tax cut of 1975 reduced unemployment in the United States by 1 percent. (b) The tax cut was timed improperly. (c) The tax cut was a less equitable way of reducing unemployment than a program whereby the unemployed were hired by the government to perform important social functions.

10. "For its unwillingness to indulge in sociopolitical 'guesswork,' out of fear of transgressing the limits of proper scientific procedure, economics is placed in a position in which its findings *must* be partial and imcomplete and very possibly erroneous."[5] Comment.

[5] R. Heilbroner, "On the Limited 'Relevance' of Economics," *The Public Interest,* 1970.

PART TWO

The Private Sector and the Public Sector: an Overview

3 The American Economy: Our Mixed Capitalist System

The economy of the United States is beset by many problems. As pointed out in Chapter 1, the mid-seventies have been a period of excessive unemployment and excessive inflation. Also, we are confronted by serious environmental, energy, and poverty problems, among others. Yet, despite these problems, the American economy is clearly among the most prosperous in the world. The typical American family has plenty of food, clothing, housing, appliances, and luxuries of many kinds, and the typical American worker is well educated and well trained. The tremendous strength and vitality of the American economy should be recognized, as well as its shortcomings. Nothing is gained by overlooking either the successes or the faults of our system.

As a first step toward understanding why we are so well off in some respects and so lacking in others, we need to understand how our economy works. Of course, this is a big task. Indeed, you could say that this whole book is devoted to discussing this subject. So we will not try to present a detailed picture of the operation of the American economy at this point. All we shall do now is give a preliminary sketch, a basic blueprint of some of the highlights. The details will be provided later, as they are needed.

The American Economy: Some Salient Facts

To begin with, let's take up a few elementary facts about the American economy. First, it is huge. The United States contains over 210 million people, about 95 million of whom are in the labor force. Table 3.1 shows how large our population is, relative to other major nations. In addition, the American economy contains over 12 million business firms, and thousands of local and state governments, as well as the enormous federal government with its many departments and agencies. By practically any standard, ours is one of the biggest economic shows on earth.

Second, the American economy is very rich and productive. In 1975, our income per capita was about $7,000 per year. In other words, if you take the total amount of income that Americans made that year and divide by the number of Americans in existence (including all ages), the result equals about $7,000. Table 3.2 shows some rough estimates of income per capita in selected countries in 1976; the results put the United States at the top of the list. Moreover, the United States produces an enormous amount of such basic products as steel, petroleum, chemicals, electric power, automobiles, electronic computers, and a myriad of other goods. For example, we lead the world in steel production, electric energy production, and computer production, three basic indices of industrial might.

Table 3.1
Population, 1974, Selected Countries

Country	Population (millions of people)
China	800
India	586
Soviet Union	251
United States	211
Japan	110
Germany	62
United Kingdom	56
Italy	56

Source: United Nations.

Table 3.2
Income Per Capita, 1976, Selected Countries

Country	Income per capita (dollars)
United States	7,700
Canada	7,500
Sweden	7,100
France	6,400
Germany	6,200
Japan	4,900
United Kingdom	4,800
Italy	4,000
Soviet Union	3,700
Egypt	700
India	500
China	400

These estimates are rough, because of problems in converting other currencies into dollars, and for other reasons. Nonetheless, they should provide reasonable indications of relative orders of magnitude.

Third, our economy is based heavily on freedom of choice. Consumers can buy what they like, and reject what they do not like; workers can take jobs when and where they please, and quit if they please; firms can produce whatever products they want to produce, and use whatever techniques they want to use. Of course, this freedom is not unlimited. For example, there are laws to prevent people and firms from engaging in antisocial dealings. Moreover, this freedom is not all it might be. For example, it is sometimes difficult for a firm to enter a market, or for a person to get a particular type of job. Yet relative to other countries, our economy is very free.

Fourth, the American economy is rich in economic resources. As you will recall from Chapter 1, economic resources are the land, labor, and capital used to produce the goods and services that people want. The United States is blessed with a big, industrious, well-educated labor force, as well as a large amount of plant and equipment. Also, the United States has a great deal of fertile soil and natural resources. Even in the case of energy resources, where fear has been expressed that we shall become increasingly dependent on foreign sources of supply, the United States is by no means poor. We lead the world in coal reserves, and have a considerable amount of oil.

Finally, the American economy is noted for its sophisticated and advanced technology. In contrast to pure science (where, until World War II, the United States was not a leader), the United States has long been a leader in many areas of technology. This technological lead seems to have narrowed somewhat in recent decades, but it still exists. According to data collected by the National Science Board and the Organization for Economic Cooperation and Development, the United States has been responsible for a very large share of the major new processes and products introduced since World War II.

The Tasks of an Economic System

Although many of the statistics concerning the American economy are impressive, we cannot evaluate how well an economic system (or any system) is working unless we know what it is meant to do. Basically, as we saw in Chapter 1, there are four things that any economic system—*ours or any other*—must do. First, *it must determine the level and composition of society's output.* That is, it must answer questions like. To what extent should society's resources be used to produce new destroyers and missiles? To what extent should they be used to produce sewage plants to reduce water pollution? To what extent should they be used to produce swimming pools for the rich? To what extent should they be used to produce low-cost housing for the poor? Pause for a moment to think about how important—and how vast—this function is. Most people simply take for granted that somehow it is decided what we as a society are going to produce, and far too few people really think about the social mechanisms that determine the answers to such questions.

Second, *an economic system must determine how each good and service is to be produced.* Given existing technology, a society's resources can be used in various ways. Should the skilled labor in Birmingham, Alabama, be used to produce cotton or steel? Should a particular machine tool be used to produce aircraft or automobiles? The way questions of this sort are answered will determine the way each good and service is produced. In other words, it will determine which resources are used to produce which goods and services. If this function is performed badly, society's resources are put to the wrong uses, resulting in less output than if this function is performed well.

Third, *an economic system must determine*

how the goods and services that are produced are to be distributed among the members of society. In other words, how much of each type of good and service should each person receive? Should there be a considerable amount of income inequality, the rich receiving much more than the poor? Or should incomes be relatively equal? Take your own case: somehow or other, the economic system determines how much income you will receive. In our economic system, your income depends on your skills, the property you own, how hard you work, and prevailing prices, as we shall see in succeeding chapters. But in other economic systems, your income might depend on quite different factors. This function of the economic system has generated, and will continue to generate, heated controversy. Some people favor a relatively egalitarian society where the amount received by one family varies little from that received by another family of the same size. Other people favor a less egalitarian society where the amount a family or person receives varies a great deal. Few people favor a thoroughly egalitarian society, if for no other reason than that some differences in income are required to stimulate workers to do certain types of work.

Fourth, *an economic system must determine the rate of growth of per capita income.* An adequate growth rate has come to be regarded as an important economic goal, particularly in the less developed countries of Africa, Asia, and Latin America. There is very strong pressure in these countries for changes in technology, the adoption of superior techniques, increases in the stock of capital resources, and better and more extensive education and training of the labor force. These are viewed as some of the major ways to promote the growth of per capita income. In the industrialized nations, the goal of economic growth has become somewhat more controversial. Some observers claim that we have become rich enough, while others point out that since so many of the world's people, here and abroad, are poor, it seems hard to believe that extra output would not be useful.

The Economic System: A Simple Introductory Model

The Product Transformation Curve and the Determination of What Is Produced

In the previous chapter, we said that economists use models to throw light on economic problems. At this point, let's try our hand at constructing a simple model to illuminate the basic functions any economic system, ours included, must perform. To keep things simple, suppose that society produces only two goods, food and tractors. This, of course, is unrealistic, but, as we stressed in the previous chapter, a model does not have to be realistic to be useful. Here, by assuming that there are only two goods, we eliminate a lot of unnecessary complexity and lay bare the essentials. In addition, we suppose that society has at its disposal a certain amount of resources, and that this amount is fixed for the duration of the period in question. This assumption is quite realistic. So long as the period is relatively short, the amount of a society's resources is relatively fixed (except, of course, under unusual circumstances, such as if a country annexes additional land). Finally, we suppose as well that society's technology is fixed. So long as the period is relatively short, this assumption too is realistic.

Under these circumstances, it is possible to figure out the various amounts of food and tractors that society can produce. Specifically, we can proceed as in Chapter 1, where we determined the amounts of food and clothing that an isolated town could produce. Let's begin with how many tractors society can produce if all resources are devoted to tractor production:

Table 3.3
Alternative Combinations of Outputs of Food and Tractors That Can Be Produced

Possibility	Food (millions of tons)	Tractors (millions)
A	0	15
B	2	14
C	4	12
D	6	10
E	8	7
F	10	4
G	12	0

According to Table 3.3, the answer is 15 million tractors. Next, let's consider the opposite extreme, where society devotes all its resources to food production: According to Table 3.3, it can produce 12 million tons of food in this case. Next, let's consider cases where both products are being produced: Such cases are represented by possibilities *B* to *F* in the table. As emphasized in Chapter 1, the more of one good that is produced, the less of the other good can be produced. Why? Because to produce more of one good, resources must be taken away from the production of the other good, lessening the amount of the other good produced.

Figure 3.1 shows how we can use a graph (based on the principles in Chapter 2) to show the various production possibilities society can attain. It is merely a different way of presenting the data in Table 3.3; the output of food is plotted on the horizontal axis and the output of tractors on the vertical axis. The curve in Figure 3.1, which shows the various combinations of output of food and tractors that society can produce, is called a ***product transformation curve.*** Economists are fond of inelegant labels of this sort. Like Eliza Doolittle, heroine of *My Fair Lady* (and *Pygmalion,* in her earlier incarnation), economics is sometimes guilty of "cold-blooded murder of the English tongue." But so are other sciences. You just have to roll with the punches—and learn what these strange-sounding terms mean.

The product transformation curve is a useful indicator of the economic tasks facing any society. It shows the various production possibilities open to society. For example, in Figure

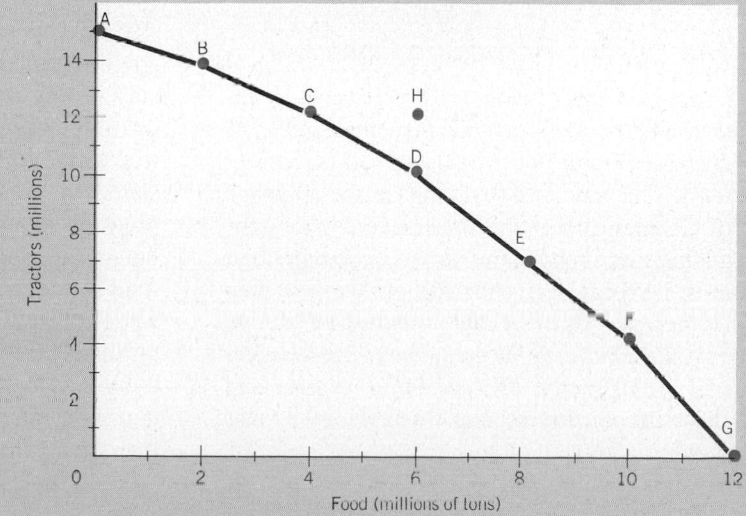

Figure 3.1
Product Transformation Curve
This curve shows the various combinations of tractors and food that can be produced efficiently with given resources and technology. Point *H* is unattainable.

3.1, society can choose to produce 4 million tons of food and 12 million tractors (point *C*), or 6 million tons of food and 10 million tractors (point *D*), but it cannot choose to produce 6 million tons of food and 12 million tractors (point *H*). Point *H* is inaccessible with this society's resources and technology: Perhaps it will become accessible if the society's resources increase or if its technology improves, but for the present, point *H* is out of reach.

Since society must wind up somewhere on the product transformation curve, it is clear that *the first function of any economic system—to determine the level and composition of society's output—is really a problem of determining at what point along the product transformation curve society should be.* Should society choose point *A, B, C, D, E, F,* or *G?* In making this choice, one thing is obvious from the product transformation curve: *you cannot get more of one good without giving up some of the other good.* In other words, you cannot escape the problem of choice. So long as resources are limited and technology is less than magic, you must reckon with the fact (emphasized in Chapter 1) that more of one thing means less of another. The old saw that you don't "get something for nothing" is hackneyed, but true, so long as resources are fully and efficiently utilized.

The Law of Increasing Cost

In the previous section, we stressed that an increased output of one good (say, food) means a decreased output of the other good (say, tractors). This amounts to saying (in the language of Chapter 1) that the alternative cost of producing more food is the output of tractors that must be forgone. In this section, we go a step further: we point out that, *as more and more of a good is produced, the production of yet another unit of this good is likely to entail a larger and larger alternative cost* and we explain why this is true.

This so-called law of increasing cost can be demonstrated in Figure 3.1. What is the cost of increasing food output from 0 to 2 million tons? It is 1 million tractors (since this is the amount that tractor output must be reduced if this increase in food output takes place). What is the cost of increasing food output from 2 to 4 million tons? It is 2 million tractors. What is the cost of increasing food output from 4 to 6 million tons? It is 2 million tractors. What is the cost of increasing food output from 6 to 8 million tons? It is 3 million tractors. Similarly, the cost of increasing food output from 8 to 10 million tons is 3 million tractors, and the cost of increasing food output from 10 to 12 million tons is 4 million tractors.

The important point here is that, as more and more food is produced, the cost of increasing food output by 2 million tons increases. To see this, note that the *first* 2 million tons of food cost 1 million tractors, the *second* 2 million tons of food cost 2 million tractors, the *third* 2 million tons of food cost 2 million tractors, the *fourth* 2 million tons of food cost 3 million tractors, the *fifth* 2 million tons of food cost 3 million tractors, and the *sixth* 2 million tons of food cost 4 million tractors. Clearly, the more food that is already being produced, the greater the cost of producing an additional 2 million tons.

Why is this the case? Basically, it is because resources are not as effective in producing one good as in producing the other. When society only produces a small amount of food, it can use in food production those resources that are well suited to producing food and not so well suited to producing tractors. But as society produces more and more food, it tends to run out of such resources, and must absorb into food production those resources that are less suited to producing food and better suited to producing tractors. To increase food output by 2 million tons with the latter type of resources, a greater reduction must occur in tractor output than when the 2-million-ton increase in food output occurred with the resources that were well suited to food production (and not so well suited to producing tractors). Thus the cost of producing an additional 2 million tons of food tends to increase as more food is already being produced.

This law of increasing cost explains why a product transformation curve has the shape shown in Figure 3.1. That is, it explains why the product transformation curve has the "bowed-out" shape (rather than the "bowed-in" shape) indicated in Figure 3.2. Because the cost of increasing food output by a certain amount increases as more of it is already produced, the product transformation curve tends to fall more steeply as one moves from left to right along the horizontal axis—which explains why the product transformation curve has the "bowed-out" shape.

The Product Transformation Curve and the Determination of How Goods Are Produced

Let's turn now to the second basic function of any economic system: to determine how each good and service should be produced. In Table 3.3, we assumed implicitly that society's resources would be fully utilized and that the available technology would be applied in a way that would get the most out of the available resources. In other words, we assumed that the firms making food and tractors were as efficient as possible and that there was no unemployment of resources. But if there is widespread unemployment of people and machines, will society still be able to choose a point on the product transformation curve? Clearly, the answer is no. Since society is not using all of its resources, it will not be able to produce as much as if it used them all. Thus, *if there is less than full employment of resources, society will have to settle for points inside the product transformation curve.* For example, the best society may be able to do under these circumstances is to attain point K in Figure 3.3. Clearly, K is a less desirable point than C or D—but that is the price of unemployment.

Suppose, on the other hand, that there is full employment of resources but that firms are inefficient. Perhaps they promote relatives of the boss, regardless of their ability; perhaps the managers are lazy or not much interested in efficiency; or perhaps the workers like to take long coffee breaks and are unwilling to work hard. Whatever the reason, will society still be able to choose a point on the product transformation curve? Again, the answer is no. Since society is not getting as much as it could out of its resources, it will not be able to produce as

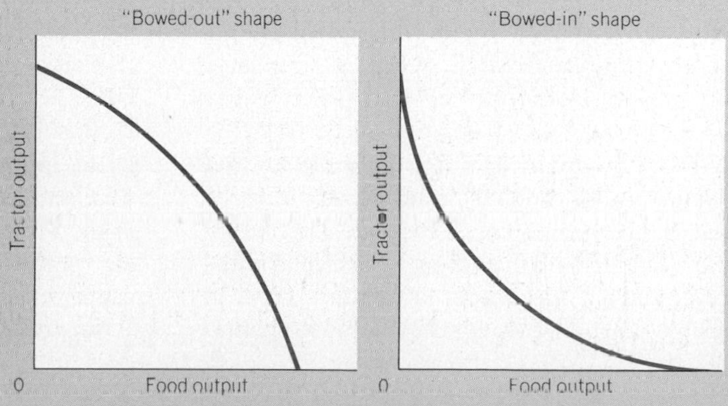

Figure 3.2
Shape of the Product Transformation Curve.
So long as the law of increasing cost holds true, the product transformation curve will have the shape on the left ("bowed-out"), *not* the shape on the right ("bowed-in").

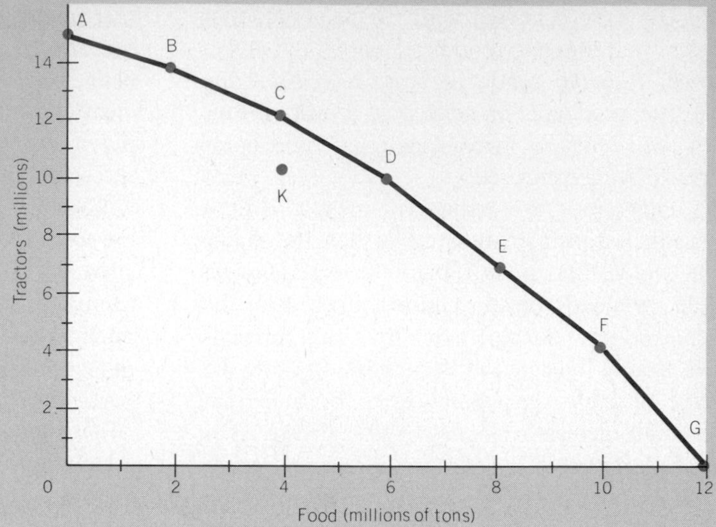

Figure 3.3
Product Transformation Curve
This curve, like Figure 3.1, shows the various combinations of tractors and food that can be produced efficiently with given resources and technology. Point *K* is less desirable than points *C* or *D*, because less output is produced at this point. But because of unemployment or inefficiency, society may wind up at point *K*.

much as it would if its resources were used efficiently. Thus, *if resources are used inefficiently, society will have to settle for points inside the product transformation curve.* Perhaps in these circumstances, too, the best society can do may be point *K* in Figure 3.3. This less desirable position is the price of inefficiency.

At this point, it should be obvious that our model at least partially answers the question of how each good and service should be produced. The answer is to *produce each good and service in such a way that you wind up on the product transformation curve, not on a point inside it.* Of course, this is easier said than done, but at least our model indicates a couple of villains to watch out for: unemployment of resources and inefficiency. When these villains are present, we can be sure that society is not on the product transformation curve. Also, the old saw is wrong and it is possible to "get something for nothing" when society is inside the product transformation curve. That is, society can increase the output of one good without reducing the output of another good in such a situation. Society need not give up anything—in the way of production of other goods—to increase the production of this good under these circumstances.

This simple model helps illuminate the sequence of events in various countries at the beginning of World War II. In certain countries, like the Soviet Union, the war effort meant a substantial decrease in the standard of living on the home front. Resources had to be diverted from the production of civilian goods to the production of military goods, and the war struck a severe blow at the living standards of the civilian population. In other countries, like the United States, it was possible to increase the production of military goods without making such a dent in the living standards of the civilian population. This happened because the United States at the beginning of World War II was still struggling to emerge from the Great Depression, and several million people were still unemployed. The same was not true in the Soviet Union. Thus, we could increase the production of both guns and butter, whereas they could not.

Suppose that we divide all goods into two

classes: war goods and civilian goods. Then, as shown in Figure 3.4, *we were inside our product transformation curve at the beginning of the war, while the Russians were not.* Consequently, for the reasons discussed above, we could increase our production of war goods without reducing our production of civilian goods, while the Russians could not. (Note that in Figure 3.4, the two goods are war goods and civilian goods, not food and tractors).

The Product Transformation Curve, Income Distribution, and Growth

Let's return now to the case where our economy produces food and tractors. The third basic function of any economic system is to distribute the goods and services that are produced among the members of society. Each point on the product transformation curve in Figure 3.3 represents society's total pie, but to deal with the third function, we must know how the pie is divided up among society's members. Since the product transformation curve does not tell us this, it cannot shed light on this third function.

Fortunately, the product transformation curve is of more use in analyzing the fourth basic function of any economic system: to determine the society's rate of growth of per capita income. Suppose that the society in Figure 3.3 invests a considerable amount of its resources in developing improved processes and products. For example, it might establish agricultural experiment stations to improve farming techniques and industrial research laboratories to improve tractor designs. As shown in Figure 3.5, the product transformation curve will be pushed outward. This will be the result of improved technology, enabling more food and/or more tractors to be produced from the same amount of resources. Thus one way for an economy to increase its output—and its per capita income—may be to invest in research and development.

Another way is by devoting more of its resources to the production of capital goods rather than consumers' goods. ***Capital goods*** consist of plant and equipment that are used to make other goods; ***consumers' goods*** are items that consumers purchase like clothing, food, and drink. Since capital goods are themselves resources, a society that chooses to produce lots of capital goods and few consumers'

Figure 3.4
Effect of Increased Production of War Goods at the Beginning of World War II
Because the United States was at a point inside its product transformation curve, we could increase our production of war goods without reducing production of civilian goods. Because the Russians were on their product transformation curve, they could increase their output of war goods only by reducing output of civilian goods.

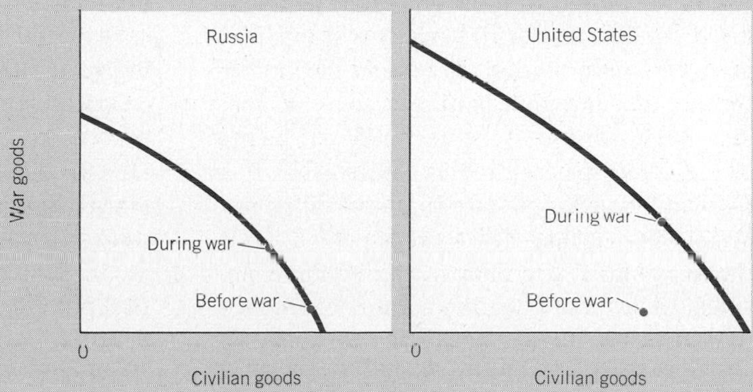

Figure 3.5
Effect of Improvement in Technology on Product Transformation Curve
An improvement in technology results in an outward shift of the product transformation curve.

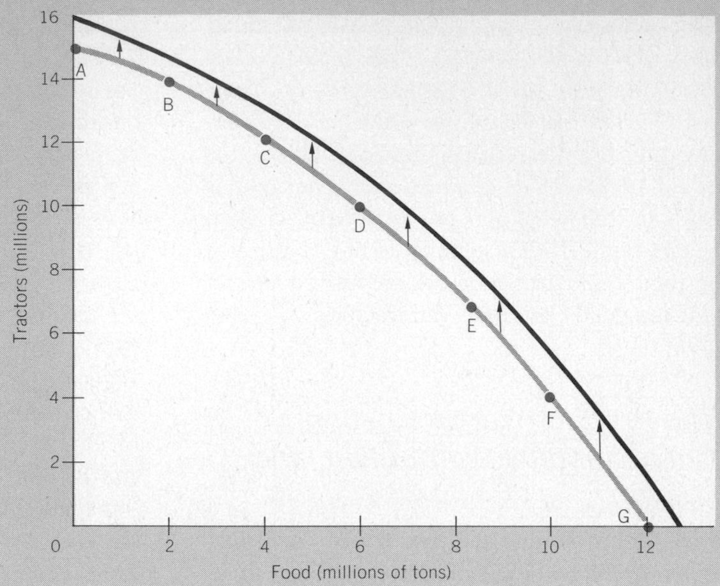

goods will push out its product transformation curve much farther than a society that chooses to produce lots of consumers' goods and few capital goods.

To illustrate this point, consider our simple society that produces food and tractors. The more tractors (and the less food) this society produces, the more tractors it will have in the next period; and the more tractors it has in the next period, the more of both goods—food and tractors—it will be able to produce then. Thus the more tractors (and the less food) this society produces, the farther out it will push its product transformation curve—and the greater the increase in output (and per capita income) that it will achieve in the next period. For example, if this society chooses point *F* (shown in Figures 3.5, 3.3, or 3.1), the effect will be entirely different than if it chooses point *C*. If it chooses point *F*, it produces 4 million tractors, which we assume to be the number of tractors worn out each year. Thus, if it chooses point *F*, it adds nothing to its stock of tractors: it merely replaces those that wear out. Since it has no more tractors in the next period than in the current period, the product transformation curve does not shift out at all if point *F* is chosen. On the other hand, if point *C* is chosen, the society produces 12 million tractors, which means that it has 8 million additional tractors at the beginning of the next period. Thus, as shown in Figure 3.6, the product transformation curve is pushed outward. By producing more capital goods (and less consumers' goods) our society has increased its production possibilities and its per capita income.

Essentially, this is the saving process described in Chapter 2 in connection with the Industrial Revolution. As pointed out there, England (and the other countries where the Industrial Revolution occurred) set aside some of its resources during the late eighteenth and early nineteenth centuries, and used them to produce capital goods, not consumption goods. In this way, the productive capacity of the nation was increased. But this was not the only reason for such an increase in productive capacity at that time. In addition, there were a

Figure 3.6
Effect of Increase in Capital Goods on Product Transformation Curve
An increase in the amount of capital goods results in an outward shift of the product transformation curve. The choice of point *C* means the production of more capital goods than the choice of point *F*.

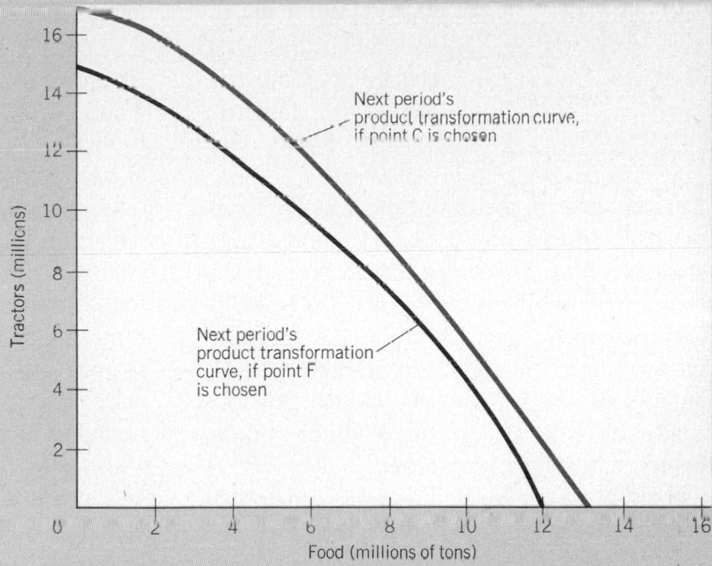

host of important technological advances, such as the steam engine and the spinning jenny, which also pushed the product transformation curve outward. Thus both the process of capital formation (illustrated in Figure 3.6) and the process of technological change (illustrated in Figure 3.5) were at work.

Capitalism: An Economic System

What Is Capitalism?

The particular kind of economic system the United States has adopted to carry out the four basic economic functions is ***capitalism.*** Capitalism is one of those terms that is frequently used but seldom defined, and even less frequently understood. Its operation is complex, but its principal characteristics can be lumped into four major categories.

Private ownership of capital. Under capitalism you or I can buy the tools of production. We can own factories, equipment, inventories, and other forms of capital. In a capitalistic system, somebody owns each piece of capital—and receives the income from it. Each piece of equipment has some sort of legal instrument indicating to whom it belongs. (If it belongs to a corporation, its owners basically are the stockholders who own the corporation.) Moreover, each piece of capital has a money market value. This system is in marked contrast to a Communist or socialist state where the government owns the capital. In these states, the government decides how much and what kinds of capital goods will be produced; it owns the capital goods; and it receives and distributes the income they produce. In the Soviet Union or China, no one can buy or put up a new steel plant: it simply isn't allowed.

The United States is basically a capitalistic system, but there are certain areas where the government, not individuals, owns capital, and where individual property rights are limited in various ways by the government. The government owns much of the tooling used in the defense industries; it owns dams and the Tennessee Valley Authority; and it owns research laboratories in such diverse fields as atomic energy, space exploration, and health. Further, the government determines how much of a man's assets can go to his heirs when he dies. (The rest goes to the government in the form of estate and inheritance taxes.) Also, the government can make a person sell his property to allow a road or other public project to be built. There are many such limitations on property rights. Ours is basically a capitalistic system, but it must be recognized that the government's role is important. More will be said on this score in subsequent sections.

Freedom of choice and enterprise. Another important characteristic of capitalism is freedom of choice and freedom of enterprise. ***Freedom of choice*** means that consumers are free to buy what they please and reject what they please; that laborers are free to work where, when, and if they please; and that investors are free to invest in whatever property they please. By ***freedom of enterprise,*** we mean that firms are free to enter whatever markets they please, obtain resources in whatever ways they can, and organize their affairs as best they can. Needless to say, this does not mean that firms can run roughshod over consumers and workers. Even the strongest champions of capitalism are quick to admit that the government must set "rules of the game" to prevent firms from engaging in sharp or unfair practices. But granting such limitations, the name of the game under capitalism is economic freedom.

Freedom to do what? Under capitalism, individuals and firms are free to pursue their own self-interest. Put in today's idiom, each individual or firm can do his, her, or its own thing. However, it is important to note that this freedom is circumscribed by one's financial resources. Consumers in a capitalistic system can buy practically anything they like—if they have the money to pay for it. Similarly, workers can work wherever or whenever they please—if they don't mind the wages. And a firm can run its business as it likes—if it remains solvent. Thus an important regulator of economic activity under capitalism is the pattern of income and prices that emerges in the market place.

Competition. Still another important characteristic of capitalism is ***competition.*** Firms compete with one another for sales. Under perfect competition, there are a large number of firms producing each product; indeed, there are so many that no firm controls the product's price. Because of this competition, firms are forced to jump to the tune of the consumer. If a firm doesn't produce what consumers want—at a price at least as low as other firms are charging—it will lose sales to other firms. Eventually, unless it mends its ways, such a firm will go out of business. Of course, in real-life American markets, the number of producers is not always so large that no firm has any control over price. (Much more will be said on this score below.) But in the purest form of capitalism, such imperfections do not exist. Also, lest you think that competition under capitalism is confined to producers, it must be remembered that owners of resources also compete. They are expected to offer their resources—including labor—to the buyer who gives them the best deal, and buyers of resources and products are supposed to compete openly and freely.

Reliance upon markets. Finally, another very important characteristic of capitalism is its reliance upon markets. *Under pure capitalism, the market—the free market—plays a central role.* Firms and individuals buy and sell products and resources in competitive markets. Some firms and individuals make money and prosper; others lose money and fail. Each firm or individual is allowed freedom to pursue his interests in the market place, while the government guards against shady and dishonest dealings. Such is the nature of the economic system under pure capitalism.

How Does Capitalism Perform the Four Basic Economic Tasks?

The ***price system*** lies at the heart of any capitalist economy. In a purely capitalist economy, it is used to carry out the four basic economic functions discussed above. The price system is a way to organize an economy. Under such a system, every commodity and every service, including labor, has a price. Everyone receives money for what he sells, including labor, and uses this money to buy the goods and services he wants. If more is wanted of a certain good, the price of this good tends to rise; if less is wanted, the price of the good tends to fall. Producers base their production decisions on the prices of commodities and inputs. Thus increases in a commodity's price generally tend to increase the amount of it produced, and decreases generally tend to decrease the amount produced. In this way, firms' output decisions are brought into balance with consumers' desires.

The very important question of how the price system performs the basic economic functions we discussed above will be answered in some detail in the next chapter. All we can do here is provide a preliminary sketch of the way the price system carries out each of these four tasks. First, consider the determination of what the society will produce. In a substantially capitalistic economy, such as ours, consumers choose the amount of each good that they want, and producers act in accord with these decisions. The importance consumers attach to a good is indicated by the price they are willing to pay for it. Of course, the principle of ***consumer sovereignty***—producers dancing to the tune of consumers' tastes—should not be viewed as always and completely true, since producers do attempt to manipulate the tastes of consumers through advertising and other devices, but it is certainly a reasonable first approximation.

In its second fundamental task, the price system helps determine how each good and service will be produced by indicating the desires of workers and the relative value of various types of materials and equipment as well as the desires of consumers. For example, if plumbers are scarce relative to the demand for them, their price in the labor market—their wage—will be bid up, and they will tend to be used only in the places where they are productive enough so that their employers can afford to pay them the higher wages. The forces that push firms toward actually carrying out the proper decisions are profits and losses. Profits are the carrot and losses are the stick used to eliminate the less efficient and less alert firms and to increase the more efficient and the more alert.

How does the price system accomplish its third task, of determining how much in the way of goods and services each member of the society is to receive? In general, an individual's income depends largely on the quantities of resources of various kinds that he owns and the prices he gets for them. For example, if a man both works and rents out farm land he owns, his income is the number of hours he works per year times his hourly wage rate plus the number of acres of land he owns times the annual rental per acre. Thus the distribution of income depends on the way resource ownership—including talent, intelligence, training, work habits, and, yes, even character—is distributed among the population. Also, to be candid, it depends on just plain luck.

Finally, how does the price system determine the nation's rate of growth of per capita income? A nation's rate of growth of per capita income depends on the rate of growth of its resources and the rate of increase of the efficiency with which they are used. In our economy, the rate at which labor and capital resources are increased is motivated, at least in part, through the price system. Higher wages for more skilled work are an incentive for an individual to undergo further education and training. Capital accumulation occurs in response to the expectation of profit. Increases in efficiency, due in considerable measure to the advance of technology, are also stimulated by the price system.

Our Mixed Capitalist System

The Role of Government

Since the days of Adam Smith, economists have been fascinated by the features of a purely capitalistic economic system—an economy that relies entirely on the price system. Smith, and many generations of economists since, have gone to great pains to explain that in such an economic system, *the price system, although it is not controlled by any person or small group, results in economic order, not chaos.* The basic economic tasks any economy must perform can, as we have said, be carried out in such an economic system by the price system. It is an effective means of coordinating economic activity through decentralized decision making based on information disseminated through prices and related data.

But does this mean that the American economy is purely capitalistic? As we have noted repeatedly in previous sections, the answer is no. A purely capitalistic system is a useful model of reality, not a description of our economy as it exists now or in the past. It is useful because a purely capitalistic economy is, for some purposes, a reasonably close fit to our own. However, this does not mean that such a model is useful for all purposes. Many American markets are not entirely competitive and never will be; they are dominated by a few producers or buyers who can influence price and thus distort the workings of the price system. Moreover, *the American economy is a mixed capitalistic economy, an economy where both government and private decisions are important.* The role of the government in American economic activity is very large indeed. Although it is essential to understand the workings of a purely capitalistic system, any model that omits the government entirely cannot purport to be adequate for the analysis of many major present-day economic issues.

To create a more balanced picture of the workings of the American economy, we must recognize that, although the price system plays an extremely important role, it is not permitted to solve all of the basic economic problems of our society. Consumer sovereignty does not extend—and cannot realistically be extended—to all areas of society. For example, certain public services cannot be left to private enterprise. The provision of fire protection, the operation of schools, and the development of weapons systems are examples of areas where we rely on political decision making, not the price system alone. Moreover, with regard to the consumption of commodities like drugs, society imposes limits on the decisions of individuals.

In addition, certain consequences of the price system are, by general agreement, unacceptable. Reliance on the price system alone does not assure a just or equitable or optimal distribution of income. It is possible, for example, that one person will literally have money to burn while another person will live in degrading poverty. Consequently, the government modifies the distribution of income by imposing taxes that take more from the rich than the poor, and by welfare programs that try to keep the poor from reaching the point where they lack decent food, adequate clothing, or shelter. Besides providing public services and maintaining certain minimum income standards, the government also carries out a variety of regulatory functions. Industries do not police the actions of their constituent firms, so it falls to the government to establish laws that impose limits on the economic behavior of firms. For example, these laws say that firms must not misrepresent their products, that child labor must not be employed, and that firms must not collude and form monopolies to interfere with the proper functioning of the price system. In this way, the government tries, with varying effectiveness, to establish the "rules of the game"—the limits within which the economic behavior of firms (and consumers) should lie.

Capital, Specialization, and Money: Other Characteristics of the American Economy

Finally, we must point out three additional characteristics of the American economy: the use of a great deal of capital per worker, specialization, and the use of money. These characteristics are common to all modern, industrialized nations, not just the United States, and they are so obvious that you may take them for granted. But they are too important to be ignored.

First, consider the enormous amount of capital American labor has to work with. Think of the oil refineries in New Jersey and Philadelphia, the blast furnaces and open hearths in Pittsburgh and Cleveland, the railroad yards of Chicago and Wichita, the aircraft plants in California and Georgia, the skyscrapers of New York, and the host of additional types of capital that we have and use in this country. To understand this idea fully, stop and think about what we mean by capital. As noted in Chapter 1, to the economist capital is not the same as money. A man with a hot-dog stand who has $100 in his pocket may say that he has $100 in capital. But his definition is different from that of the economist, who would include in the man's capital the value of his stand; the value of his equipment, the value of his inventories of hot dogs, buns, and mustard; and the value of other nonlabor resources (other than land) that he uses.

Defining capital as economists do, it is evident that American workers have an enormous amount of capital to work with. And it is evident as well that this enormous amount of capital, together with an advanced technology, and a well-trained labor force, is responsible for the tremendous amount of goods and services the American economy produces. All this capital contributes to increased production because it is often more efficient to adopt ***roundabout methods of production.*** For example, it is often more efficient to build a blast furnace and open hearth to produce steel rather than to try to produce steel directly. On the other hand, harking back to our discussion of Figure 3.6, it is also true that the production of capital goods means that less consumers' goods can be produced in the current period. In other words, although a greater amount of capital means greater production, consumers must be willing—or forced—to forgo current consumption of goods and services to produce this capital.

Next, consider the tremendous amount of specialization in the American economy. You may decide to specialize in tax law (and a particular branch of tax law at that), a classmate may specialize in brain surgery, another may specialize in repairing hi-fi sets, and another in monitoring certain types of equipment in an oil refinery. In contrast to more primitive economies, where people specialize much less, the American economy is characterized by an intricate web of specialization. What does it accomplish? As stressed by Adam Smith over two centuries ago, it results in much greater output than if people attempted to be Jacks-of-all-trades. Because of this specialization, people can concentrate on the tasks they do best. For example, Bobby Fischer, the world champion chess player, can concentrate on chess and leave the hi-fi repairs to people who understand more about woofers and tweeters. However, it should be recognized that this specialization also results in great interdependence. Because each of us performs such specialized tasks, each of us depends on others for most of the things he needs. For example, unless you are much better at farming than I am, you would lose a lot of weight—and not because you wanted to—if farmers decided that they no longer wanted to provide us city folks with the fruits (and vegetables) of their labor.

Finally, the use of money is another important characteristic of all economies, including the American economy. Unquestionably you take the use of money as much for granted as you do the fact that the moon revolves about the earth. But money is a social invention. There is no evidence that Adam and Eve were created with the idea of money. They, or their descendants, had to think it up themselves, and this took time, as evidenced by the fact that extremely primitive cultures resorted to barter, which meant that to get a particular commodity, you had to swap a commodity that you owned for it. Since the exchange of commodities and services by barter was very difficult, the use of money has made trade and exchange much, much easier and facilitated the specialization of labor.

Summary

The product transformation curve, which shows the various production possibilities a society can attain, is useful in indicating the nature of the economic tasks any society faces. The task of determining the level and composition of society's output is really a problem of determining at what point along the product transformation curve society should be. Society, in performing this task, has to recognize that it cannot get more of one good without giving up some of another good, if resources are fully and efficiently used. However, if they are not fully and efficiently used, society will have to settle for points inside the product transformation curve—and it will be possible to obtain more of one good without giving up some of another good.

Clearly, the task of determining how each good and service should be produced is, to a considerable extent, a problem of keeping society on its product transformation curve, rather than at points inside the curve. The product transformation curve does not tell us anything about the distribution of income, but it does indicate various ways that a society can promote growth in per capita income. By doing research and development, or by producing capital goods (rather than consumers'goods), society may push its product transformation curve outward, thus increasing per capita income.

The American economy is one of the richest in the world. Based on freedom of enterprise, the American economy is rich in resources—land, labor, and capital—and American technology is among the most advanced in the world. Ours is a capitalistic economy, an economic system in which there is private ownership of capital, freedom of choice, freedom of enterprise, competition, and reliance upon markets. Many countries do not have a capitalistic economy, and even ours is not a purely capitalistic system. Under pure capitalism, the price system is used to perform the four basic economic tasks. Although it is not controlled by any person or small group, the price system results in order, not chaos.

A purely capitalistic system is a useful model of reality, not a description of our economy as it exists now or in the past. The American economy is a mixed capitalistic economy, in which both government and private decisions are important. For example, certain public services, like fire protection and schools, cannot be left to private enterprise. In addition, society has said that certain consequences of the price system—like the existence of abject poverty—are unacceptable. For this reason and others, the government carries out a long and impressive array of additional functions, many of which are discussed in subsequent chapters.

CONCEPTS FOR REVIEW

Product transformation curve
Capital goods
Consumers' goods
Capitalism
Capital
Consumer sovereignty
Money

QUESTIONS FOR DISCUSSION AND REVIEW

1. In a famous passage from *The Wealth of Nations,* Adam Smith said that "the great increase of the quantity of work, which, in consequence of the division of labor, the same number of people are capable of performing, is owing to three different circumstances; first, to the increase of dexterity in every particular workman; secondly, to the saving of the time which is commonly lost in passing from one species of work to another; and lastly, to the invention of a great number of machines which facilitate and abridge labor, and enable one man to do the work of many." Taking medicine, law, engineering, or some other profession, describe in detail how specialization tends to increase productivity. Then indicate whether more and more specialization is a good thing. (Beyond some point, is more specialization counterproductive?)

2. "[How] does New York City each day obtain about the quantity of milk that it demands? Of the thousands of people engaged in supplying New York with milk, almost none knows how much the city consumes or how much is being produced.[1]"

3. "The English obtain about twice as many bushels of wheat per acre as do the Americans, but we obtain about twice as many bushels per man.[2]" Why do you think this is true? Does it indicate that the price system is not working properly in the United States, England, or both?

4. According to Karl Marx, "the division of labor seizes upon not only the economic but every other sphere of society and everywhere lays the foundation of that all-engrossing system of specializing and sorting men, that development in a man of one single faculty at the expense of all other faculties, which caused A. Ferguson, the master of Adam Smith, to exclaim: 'We make a nation of helots, and have no free citizens.' " Comment.

5. "Libertarians fail to realize that the price system is, and ought to be, a method of coercion. . . . The very term 'rationing by the purse" illustrates the point. Economists defend such forms of rationing, but they have to do so primarily in terms of its efficiency and its fairness."[3] Comment.

6. "The great advantage of the [price system] . . . is that it permits wide diversity. It is, in political terms, a system of proportional representation. Each man can vote, as it were, for the color of tie he wants and get it; he does not have to see what color the majority wants and then, if he is in the minority, submit."[4] Comment.

[1] S. Slichter, *Modern Economic Society,* New York: Holt, 1928.
[2] *Ibid.*
[3] P. Samuelson, "The Economic Role of Private Activity," *A Dialogue on the Proper Economic Role of the State,* Chicago: University of Chicago Press, 1963.
[4] M. Friedman, *Capitalism and Freedom,* Chicago: University of Chicago Press, 1962, p. 15.

7. Suppose that a society's product transformation curve is as follows:

	Output (per year)	
Possibility	Food (millions of tons)	Tractors (millions)
A	0	30
B	4	28
C	8	24
D	12	20
E	16	14
F	20	8
G	24	0

(a) Is it possible for the society to produce 30 million tons of food per year? (b) Can it produce 30 million tractors per year? (c) Suppose this society produces 20 million tons of food and 6 million tractors per year. Is it operating on the product transformation curve? If not, what factors might account for this?

8. Plot the product transformation curve in Question 7 in a graph. At what point along the horizontal axis does the curve cut the axis? At what point along the vertical axis does the curve cut the axis?

9. Suppose that, because of important technological improvements, the society in Question 7 can double its production of tractors at each level of food production. If so, is this society on its new product transformation curve if it produces 20 million tons of food and 16 million tractors? Plot the new product transformation curve. At what point along the horizontal axis does the new curve cut the axis? At what point along the vertical axis does it cut the axis?

10. Given its present resources, a university like Harvard or Yale can choose to accept and graduate more graduate students and less undergraduates, or less graduate students and more undergraduates. Show how the concept of the product transformation curve can be used to represent the choices open to such a university.

4 The Price System: Consumers, Firms, and Markets

Capitalist economies use the price system to perform the four basic tasks any economic system must carry out. Of course, as we pointed out in the previous chapter, the American economy is a mixed capitalist system, not a pure one. But this does not mean that the price system is unimportant. On the contrary, the price system plays a vital role in the American economy, and to obtain even a minimal grasp of the workings of our economic system, one must understand how the price system operates. This chapter takes up the nature and functions of the price system, as well as some applications of our theoretical results to real-life problems. For example, we show how the price system determines the quantity produced of a commodity like wheat, and how the pricing policies of the Broadway theater hurt show business in a variety of ways. These applications should help illustrate the basic theory and indicate its usefulness.

Consumers

We begin by describing and discussing consumers and firms, the basic building blocks that make up the private, or nongovernmental, sector of the economy. What is a consumer? Sometimes—for example, when a person buys a beer on a warm day—the consumer is an individual. In other cases—for example, when a family buys a new car—the consumer may be an entire household. Consumers purchase the goods and services that are the ultimate end-products of the economic system. When a man buys tickets to a ball game, he is a consumer; when he buys himself a Coke at the game, he is a consumer; and when he buys his wife a book on baseball for their twentieth wedding anniversary, he is also a consumer.

Consumers—whether individuals or households—are an extremely varied lot. To get some idea of the variation, let's look at two families, the Rockefellers and the Ríoses. First, consider the Rockefeller family. *Fortune* magazine has credited seven Rockefellers with a minimum combined wealth of $1 billion, and a maximum of $1.9 billion. These descendants of John D. Rockefeller, who amassed an enormous fortune in the oil business (and founded Standard Oil), live in regal style. The grandsons of John D.—including former Governor and Vice-President Nelson Rockefeller and David Rockefeller, chairman of the Chase Manhattan Bank—each have a large house on the Rockefeller estate of over 4,000 acres at Pocantico Hills, New York. The estate has scores of buildings, including a $1 million recreation facility that contains bowling alleys, a tennis court, a swimming pool, and a squash court. Further, the Rockefeller brothers have New York City homes, and plantations in Venezuela, Hawaii, and elsewhere. Certainly, the Rockefellers consume on a mammoth scale. And they can afford it. Since they are estimated to be worth at least $1 billion, even if they put their money in a savings account at 5 percent interest, they would have more than $50 million per year coming in. Clearly, the Rockefellers have kept the wolf at a remarkable distance from the door!

In contrast, let's look at the Ríoses, a Puerto Rican family living in La Esmeralda, a slum section of San Juan. There are three branches of the Ríos family. One is headed by a man who works as a messenger and makes about $1,700 a year, another by a woman who works as a barmaid and makes about $1,500 a year, and another by a woman who makes about $500 a year. The Ríoses consume relatively little. They live in crowded quarters with inadequate sanitary facilities, none of them has a refrigerator, and on the average, the members of this family have spent about four years in school. Excluding clothing, the total value of the possessions of these households is $436, $149, and $120; and the total value of each household's clothing is $496, $70, and $53.[1] Clearly, the Ríos family, which is quite typical of the families in La Esmeralda, is an example of abject poverty. To compare the level of consumption of the Rockefellers with that of the Ríoses is to compare an ocean liner with a frail canoe: yet both are consumers.

Firms

There are over 12 million firms in the United States. About $^9/_{10}$ of the goods and services produced in this country are produced by firms. (The rest are provided by government and not-for-profit institutions like universities and hospitals.) A firm is an organization that produces a good or service for sale. In contrast to not-for-profit organizations, firms attempt to make a profit. It doesn't take great analytical power to see that an economy like ours is centered around the activities of firms.

Like consumers, firms are extremely varied in size, age, power, and purpose. Consider two examples, Peter Amacher's drugstore on Chi-

[1] Oscar Lewis, *La Vida,* New York: Random House, 1966.

cago's South Side and the General Motors Corporation. The Amacher drugstore, started in 1922 by Mr. Amacher's father-in-law, is known in the retail drug trade as an independent, because it has no affiliation with a chain-store organization. Mr. Amacher and two other pharmacists keep the store open for business 13 hours a day, except on Sundays. The store sells about $150,000 worth of merchandise per year. Prescriptions account for about 25 percent of total sales, and cosmetics and greeting cards are the other principal sales items. Amacher's drugstore is an example of the small-business segment of the American business community.

In contrast, General Motors is one of the giants of American industry. It is the largest manufacturer of automobiles in the United States, with sales in 1975 of over $35 billion. Besides cars, it makes trucks, locomotives, aircraft engines, household applicances, and other products. Its total assets amounted to about $22 billion in 1975; and its total employment was about 700,000. General Motors, which was formed by merger, was set up as a holding company in 1908 by William C. Durant, owner of the Buick Motor Car Company. Durant acquired about 50 auto companies and parts manufacturers and put them all together as General Motors. Its present share of the market is greater than it was in 1908, when it produced about 25 percent of all cars in this country. In 1974, for example, it produced abut 50 percent of all domestically produced cars.[2]

Markets

Consumers and firms come together in a market. The concept of a market is not quite as straightforward as it may seem, since most markets are not well defined geographically or physically. For example, the New York Stock Exchange is an atypical market because it is located principally in a particular building. For present purposes, *a **market** can be defined as a group of firms and individuals that are in touch with each other in order to buy or sell some good.* Of course, not every person in a market has to be in contact with every other person in the market. A person or firm is part of a market even if it is in contact with only a subset of the other persons or firms in the market.

Markets vary enormously in their size and procedures. For some toothpastes, most people who have their own teeth (and are interested in keeping them) are members of the same market; while for other goods like Picasso paintings, only a few dealers, collectors, and museums in certain parts of the world may be members of the market. And for still other goods, like lemonade sold by neighborhood children for a nickel a glass at a sidewalk stand, only people who walk by the stand—and are brave enough to drink the stuff—are members of the market. Basically, however, all markets consist primarily of buyers and sellers, although third parties like brokers and agents may be present as well.

Markets also vary in the extent to which they are dominated by a few large buyers or sellers. For example, in the United States, there was for many years only one producer of aluminum. Clearly this firm, the Aluminum Corporation of America, had great power in the market for aluminum. In contrast, the number of buyers and sellers in some other markets is so large that no single buyer or seller has any power over the price of the product. This is true in various agricultural markets, for example. When a market for a product contains so many buyers and sellers that none of them can influence the price, economists call the market ***perfectly competitive.*** In these introductory chapters, we make the simplifying assumptions that markets are perfectly competitive. We will relax that assumption later.

[2] L. Weiss, *Economics and American Industry,* New York: Wiley, 1961, p. 329; and General Motors' 1975 annual report.

Demand and Supply

The Demand Side of a Market

There are two sides of every market, just as there are of every argument. A market has a demand side and a supply side. *The **demand** side can be represented by a market demand curve, which shows the amount of the commodity buyers demand at various prices.* Consider Figure 4.1, which shows the demand curve for wheat in the American market during the middle 1970s.[3] The figure shows that about 1,850 million bushels of wheat will be demanded annually if the farm price is $3 per bushel, about 1,650 million bushels will be demanded annually if the farm price is $4 per bushel, and about 1,500 million bushels will be demanded annually if the farm price is $5 per bushel. The total demand for wheat is of several types: to produce bread and other food products for domestic use, as well as for feed use, for export purposes, and for industrial uses. The demand curve in Figure 4.1 shows the total demand—including all these components—at each price. Any demand curve pertains to a particular period of time, and its shape and position depend on the length of this period.

Take a good look at the demand curve for wheat in Figure 4.1. This simple, innocent-looking curve influences a great many people's lives. After all, wheat is the principal grain used for direct human consumption in the United States. To states like Kansas, North Dakota, Oklahoma, Montana, Washington, Nebraska, Texas, Illinois, Indiana, and Ohio, wheat is a mighty important cash crop. Note that the demand curve for wheat slopes downward to the right. In other words, the quantity of wheat demanded increases as the price falls. This is true of the demand curve for most commodities: they almost always slope downward to the right. This makes sense; one would expect increases in a good's price to result in a smaller quantity demanded.

[3] I am indebted to officials of the U.S. Department of Agriculture for providing me with this information. Of course, these estimates are only rough approximations, but they are good enough for present purposes.

What determines the position of the demand curve for a commodity? Why isn't the demand curve for wheat higher or lower, and what factors will cause it to shift? Although the position of the demand curve for a commodity depends on many and varied factors, those discussed below are generally of primary importance.

Consumer tastes. If consumers show an increasing preference for a product, the demand curve will shift to the right; that is, at each price, consumers will desire to buy more than previously. On the other hand, if consumers show a decreasing preference for a product, the demand curve will shift to the left, since, at each price, consumers will desire to buy less than previously. Take wheat. If consumers become convinced that foods containing wheat prolong life and promote happiness, the demand curve may shift, as shown in Figure 4.2; and the greater the shift in preferences, the larger the shift in the demand curve.

Income level of consumers. For some types of products, the demand curve shifts to the right if per capita income increases; whereas for other types of commodities, the demand curve shifts to the left if per capita income rises. Economists can explain why some goods fall into one category and other goods fall into the other, but, at present, this need not concern us. All that is important here is that changes in per capita income affect the demand curve, the size and direction of this effect varying from product to product. For example, in the case of wheat, a 10 percent increase in per capita income would probably have a relatively small effect on the demand curve, as shown in Figure 4.3.

Number of consumers in the market. Compare Austria's demand for wheat with America's. Austria is a small country with a population of about 7 million; the United States is a huge country with a population of about 211 million. Clearly, at a given price of wheat, the quantity

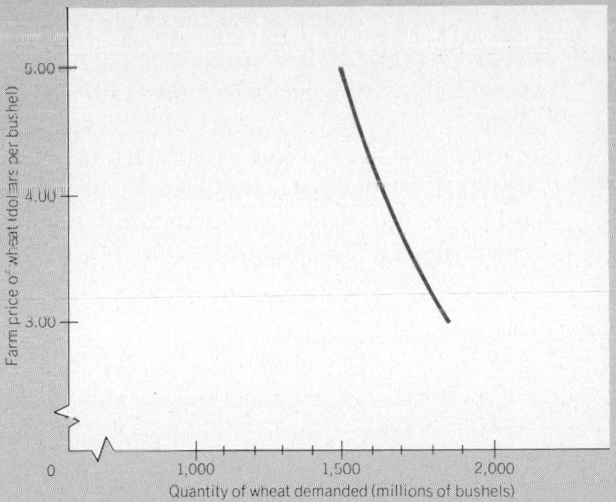

Figure 4.1
Market Demand Curve for Wheat, Middle 1970s
The curve shows the amount of wheat buyers would demand at various prices. At $3.00 per bushel, over 20 percent more wheat can be sold than at $5.00 per bushel.

Figure 4.2
Effect of Increased Preference for Wheat on Market Demand Curve
An increased preference for wheat would shift the demand curve to the right.

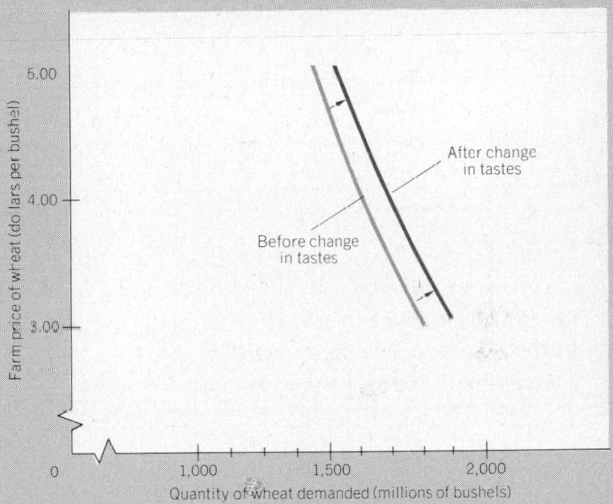

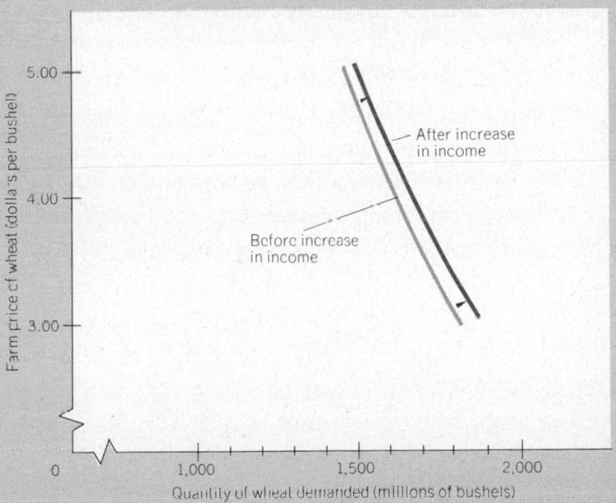

Figure 4.3
Effect of Increase in Income on Market Demand Curve for Wheat
An increase in income would shift the demand curve for wheat to the right, but only slightly.

Figure 4.4
Market Demand Curve for Wheat, Austria and the United States
Since the United States has far more consumers than Austria, the demand curve in the United States is far to the right of Austria's.

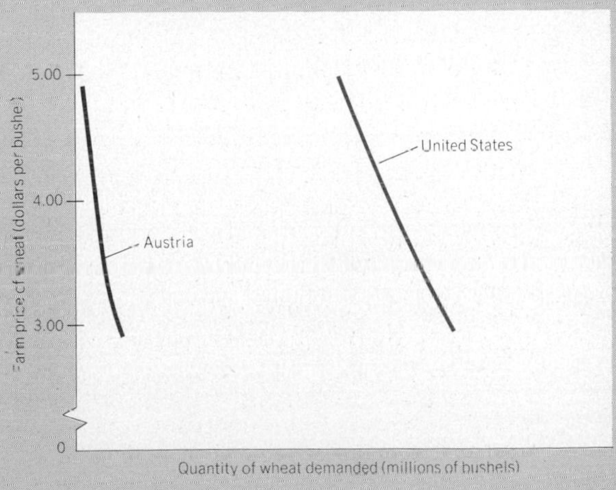

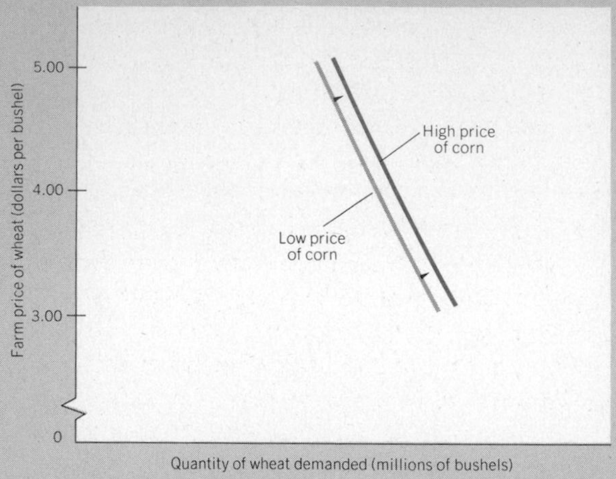

Figure 4.5
Effect of Price of Corn on Market Demand Curve for Wheat
Price increases for corn will shift the demand curve for wheat to the right.

Figure 4.6
Market Supply Curve for Wheat, Middle 1970s
The curve shows the amount of wheat sellers would supply at various prices. At $5.00 per bushel, over ⅓ more wheat would be supplied than at $3.00 per bushel.

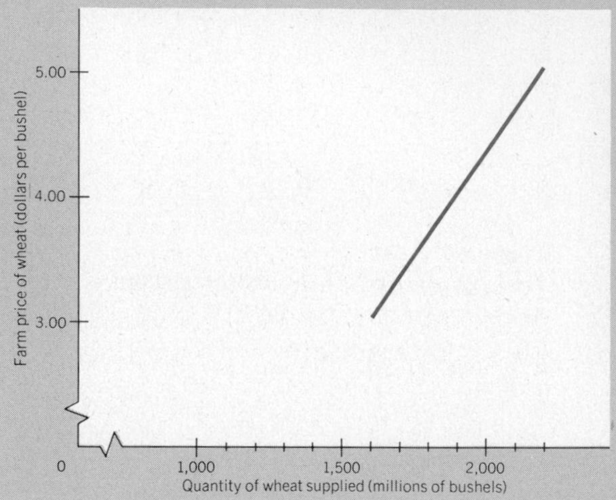

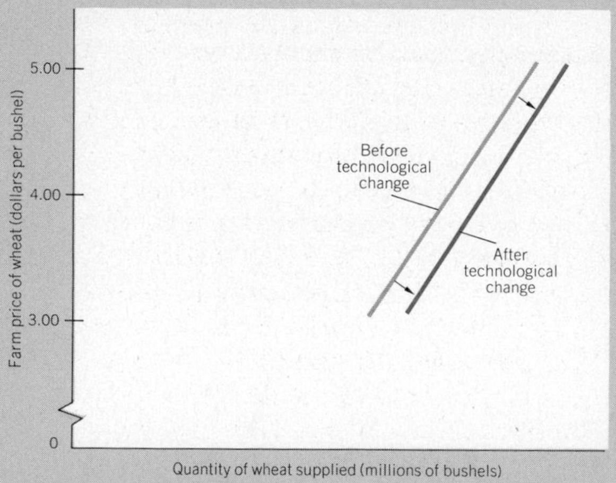

Figure 4.7
Effect of Technological Change on Market Supply Curve for Wheat
Improvements in technology often shift the supply curve to the right.

Figure 4.8
Effect of Increase in Farm Wage Rates on Market Supply Curve for Wheat
An increase in the wage rate might shift the supply curve to the left.

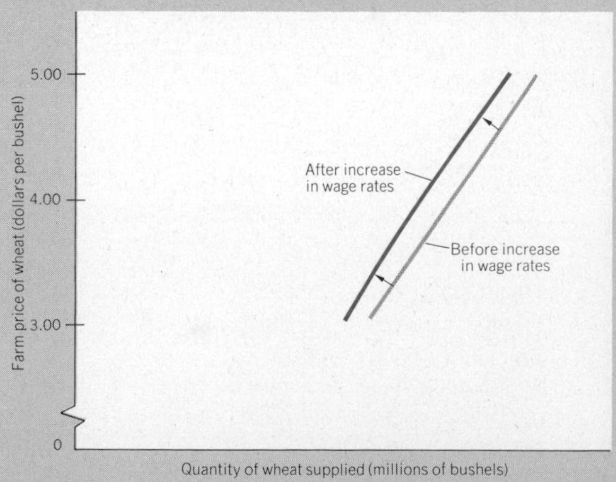

demanded by American consumers will greatly exceed the quantity demanded by Austrian consumers, as shown in Figure 4.4. Even if consumer tastes, income, and other factors were held constant, this would still be true simply because the United States has so many more consumers in the relevant market.[4]

Level of other prices. Since wheat can be substituted to some extent for corn as livestock feed, the quantity of wheat demanded depends on the price of corn as well as on the price of wheat. If the price of corn is high, more wheat will be demanded since it will be profitable to substitute wheat for corn. If the price of corn is low, less wheat will be demanded since it will be profitable to substitute corn for wheat. Thus, as shown in Figure 4.5, increases in the price of corn will shift the demand curve for wheat to the right, and decreases in the price of corn will shift it to the left.

The Supply Side of a Market

So much for our first look at demand. What about the other side of the market: supply? *The* ***supply*** *side of a market can be represented by a market supply curve that shows the amount of the commodity sellers will supply at various prices.* Let's continue with the case of wheat. Figure 4.6 shows the supply curve for wheat in the United States in the middle 1970s, based on estimates made informally by government experts.[5] According to the figure, about 1,600 million bushels of wheat would be supplied if the farm price were $3 per bushel, about 1,900 million bushels if the farm price were $4 per bushel, and about 2,200 million bushels if the farm price were $5 per bushel.

Look carefully at the supply curve shown in Figure 4.6. Although it looks innocuous enough, it summarizes the potential behavior of thousands of American wheat farmers—and their behavior plays an important role in determining the prosperity of many states and communities. Note that the supply curve for wheat slopes upward to the right. In other words, the quantity of wheat supplied increases as the price increases. This seems plausible, since increases in price give a greater incentive for farms to produce wheat and offer it for sale. Empirical studies indicate that the supply curves for a great many commodities share this characteristic of sloping upward to the right.

What determines the position of the supply curve for a commodity? As you might expect, it depends on a host of factors. But the following stand out.

Technology. Recall that technology was defined in Chapter 1 as society's pool of knowledge concerning the industrial arts. As technology progresses, it becomes possible to produce commodities more cheaply, so that firms often are willing to supply a given amount at a lower price than formerly. Thus technological change often causes the supply curve to shift to the right. For example, this certainly has occurred in the case of wheat, as shown in Figure 4.7. There have been many important technological changes in wheat production, ranging from advances in tractors to the development of improved varieties, like semidwarf wheats.

Input prices. The supply curve for a commodity is affected by the prices of the resources (labor, capital, and land) used to produce it. Decreases in the price of these inputs make it possible to produce commodities more cheaply, so that firms may be willing to supply a given amount at a lower price than they formerly would. Thus decreases in the price of inputs may cause the supply curve to shift to the right. On the other hand, increases in the price of inputs may cause it to shift to the left. For example, if the wage rates of farm labor increase, the supply curve for wheat may shift to the left, as shown in Figure 4.8.

[4] Note that no figures are given along the horizontal axis in Figure 4.4. This is because we do not have reasonably precise estimates of the demand curve in Austria. Nonetheless, the hypothetical demand curves in Figure 4.4 are close enough to the mark for present purposes.

[5] Officials of the U.S. Department of Agriculture provided me with these estimates. Although rough approximations, they are good enough for present purposes.

The Determination of Price

Equilibrium Price

The two sides of a market, demand and supply, interact to determine the price of a commodity. Recall from the previous chapter that prices in a capitalistic system are important determinants of what is produced, how it is produced, who receives it, and how rapidly per capita income grows. It behooves us, therefore, to look carefully at how prices themselves are determined in a capitalist system. As a first step toward describing this process, we must define the equilibrium price of a product. At various points in this book, you will encounter the concept of an equilibrium, which is very important in economics, as in many other scientific fields.

Put briefly, *an **equilibrium** is a situation where there is no tendency for change;* in other words, it is a situation that can persist. Thus, *an **equilibrium price** is a price that can be maintained.* Any price that it is not an equilibrium price cannot be maintained for long, since there are basic forces at work to stimulate a change in price. The best way to understand what we mean by an equilibrium price is to take a particular case, such as the wheat market. Let's put both the demand curve for wheat (in Figure 4.1) and the supply curve for wheat (in Figure 4.6) together in the same diagram. The result, shown in Figure 4.9, will help us determine the equilibrium price of wheat.

We begin by seeing what would happen if various prices were established in the market. For example, if the price were $4 per bushel, the demand curve indicates that 1,650 million bushels of wheat would be demanded, while the supply curve indicates that 1,900 million bushels would be supplied. Thus, if the price were $4 a bushel, there would be a mismatch between the quantity supplied and the quantity demanded per year, since the rate at which wheat is supplied would be greater than the rate at which it is demanded. Specifically, as shown in Figure 4.9, there would be an *excess supply* of 250 million bushels. Under these circumstances, some of the wheat supplied by farmers could not be sold, and as inventories of wheat built up, suppliers would tend to cut

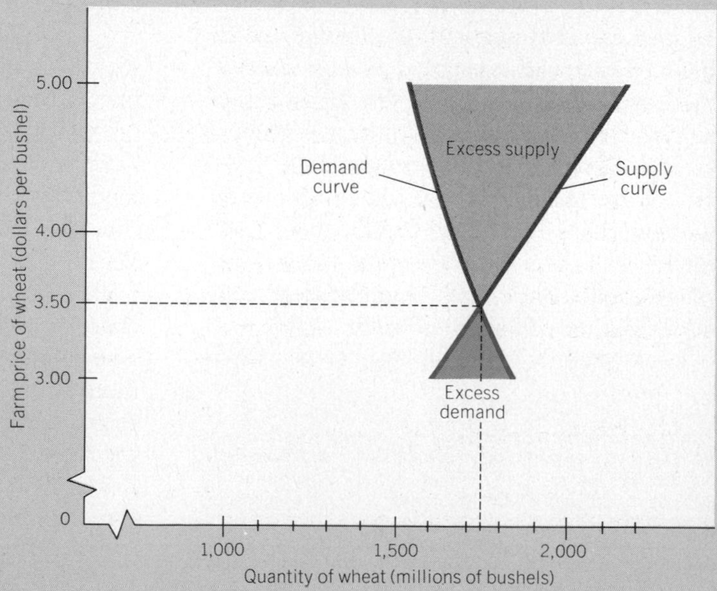

Figure 4.9
Determination of the Equilibrium Price of Wheat, Middle 1970s
The equilibrium price is $3.50 per bushel, and the equilibrium quantity is 1,750 million bushels. At a price of $4.00 per bushel, there would be an excess supply of 250 million bushels. At a price of $3.00 per bushel, there would be an excess demand of 250 million bushels.

their prices in order to get rid of unwanted inventories. Thus a price of $4 per bushel would not be maintained for long—and for this reason, $4 per bushel is not an equilibrium price.

If the price were $3 per bushel, on the other hand, the demand curve indicates that 1,850 million bushels would be demanded, while the supply curve indicates that 1,600 million bushels would be supplied. Again we find a mismatch between the quantity supplied and the quantity demanded per year, since the rate at which wheat is supplied would be less than the rate at which it is demanded. Specifically, as shown in Figure 4.9, there would be an *excess demand* of 250 million bushels. Under these circumstances, some of the consumers who want wheat at this price would have to be turned away empty-handed. There would be a shortage. And given this shortage, suppliers would find it profitable to increase the price, and competition among buyers would bid the price up. Thus, a price of $3 per bushel could not be maintained for long—so $3 per bushel is not an equilibrium price.

Under these circumstances, the equilibrium price must be the price where the quantity demanded equals the quantity supplied. Obviously, this is the only price at which there is no mismatch between the quantity demanded and the quantity supplied; and consequently the only price that can be maintained for long. In Figure 4.9, the price at which the quantity supplied equals the quantity demanded is $3.50 per bushel, the price where the demand curve intersects the supply curve. Thus $3.50 per bushel is the equilibrium price of wheat under the circumstances visualized in Figure 4.9, and 1,750 million bushels is the equilibrium quantity.

Actual Price versus Equilibrium Price

The price that counts in the real world, however, is the actual price, not the equilibrium price, and it is the actual price that we set out to explain. In general, economists simply assume that the actual price will approximate the equilibrium price, which seems reasonable enough, since the basic forces at work tend to push the actual price toward the equilibrium price. Thus, if conditions remain fairly stable for a time, the actual price should move toward the equilibrium price.

To see that this is the case, consider the market for wheat, as described by Figure 4.9. What if the price somehow is set at $4 per bushel? As we saw in the previous section, there is downward pressure on the price of wheat under these conditions. Suppose the price, responding to this pressure, falls to $3.75. Comparing the quantity demanded with the quantity supplied at $3.75, we find that there is still downward pressure on price, since the quantity supplied exceeds the quantity demanded at $3.75. The price, responding to this pressure, may fall to $3.60, but comparing the quantity demanded with the quantity supplied at this price, we find that there is still a downward pressure on price, since the quantity supplied exceeds the quantity demanded at $3.60.

So long as the actual price exceeds the equilibrium price, there will be a downward pressure on price. Similarly, so long as the actual price is less than the equilibrium price, there will be an upward pressure on price. Thus there is always a tendency for the actual price to move toward the equilibrium price. But it should not be assumed that this movement is always rapid. Sometimes it takes a long time for the actual price to get close to the equilibrium price. Sometimes the actual price never gets to the equilibrium price because by the time it gets close, the equilibrium price changes. All that safely can be said is that the actual price will move toward the equilibrium price. But of course this information is of great value, both theoretically and practically. For many purposes, all that is needed is a correct prediction of the direction in which the price will move.

Changes in the Demand and Supply Curves

Heraclitus, the ancient Greek philosopher, said you cannot step in the same stream twice: everything changes, sooner or later. One need not be a disciple of Heraclitus to recognize that demand curves and supply curves shift. Indeed, we have already seen that demand curves shift in response to changes in tastes, income, population, and prices of other products, and that supply curves shift in response to changes in technology and input prices. Any supply-and-demand diagram like Figure 4.9 is essentially a snapshot of the situation during a particular period of time. The results in Figure 4.9 are limited to a particular period because the demand and supply curves in the figure, like any demand and supply curves, pertain only to a certain period.

Changes in the demand curve. What happens to the equilibrium price of a product when its demand curve changes? This is an important question because it sheds a good deal of light on how the price system works. Suppose that consumer tastes shift in favor of foods containing wheat, causing the demand curve for wheat to shift to the right. This state of affairs is shown in Figure 4.10, where the demand curve shifts from DD' to D_1D_1'. It is not hard to see the effect on the equilibrium price of wheat. When DD' is the demand curve, the equilibrium price is OP. But when the demand curve shifts to D_1D_1', a shortage of $(OQ_2 - OQ)$ develops at this price: that is, the quantity demanded exceeds the quantity supplied at this price by $(OQ_2 - OQ)$. Consequently, suppliers raise their prices. After some testing of market reactions and trial-and-error adjustments, the price will tend to settle at OP_1, the new equilibrium price, and quantity will tend to settle at OQ_1. On the other hand, suppose that consumer demand for wheat products falls off, perhaps because of a great drop in the price of corn products. The demand for wheat now shifts to the left. Specifically, as shown in Figure 4.11, it shifts from DD' to D_2D_2'. What will be the effect on the equilibrium price of wheat? Clearly, the new equilibrium price will be OP_2, where the new demand curve intersects the supply curve.

In general, *a shift to the right in the demand curve results in an increase in the equilibrium price, and a shift to the left in the demand curve results in a decrease in the equilibrium price.* This is the lesson of Figures 4.10 and 4.11. Of course, this conclusion depends on the assumption that the supply curve slopes upward to the right, but, as we noted in a previous section, this assumption is generally true.

At this point, since all of this is theory, you may be wondering how well this theory works in practice. In 1972 and 1973, there was a vivid demonstration of the accuracy of this model in various agricultural markets, including wheat. Because of poor harvests abroad and greatly increased foreign demand for American wheat, the demand curve for wheat shifted markedly to the right. What happened to the price of wheat? In accord with our model, the price increased spectacularly, from about \$1.35 a bushel in the early summer of 1972 to over \$4 a year later. Anyone who witnessed this phenomenon could not help but be impressed by the usefulness of this model.

Changes in the supply curve. Suppose that because of technological advances in wheat production, wheat farmers are willing and able to supply more wheat at a given price than they used to. Specifically, suppose that the supply curve shifts from SS' to S_1S_1' in Figure 4.12. What will be the effect on the equilibrium price? Clearly, it will fall from OP (where the SS' supply curve intersects the demand curve) to OP_3 (where the S_1S_1' supply curve intersects the demand curve). On the other hand,

Figure 4.10
Effect on the Equilibrium Price of a Shift to the Right of the Market Demand Curve
A shift to the right from DD' to D_1D_1' results in an increase in the equilibrium price from OP to OP_1 and an increase in the equilibrium quantity from OQ to OQ_1.

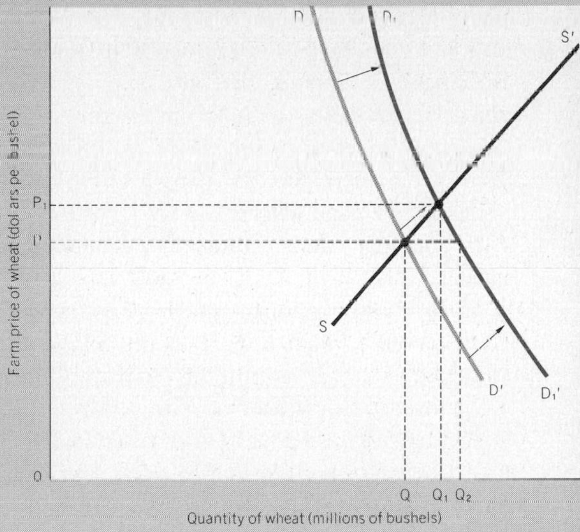

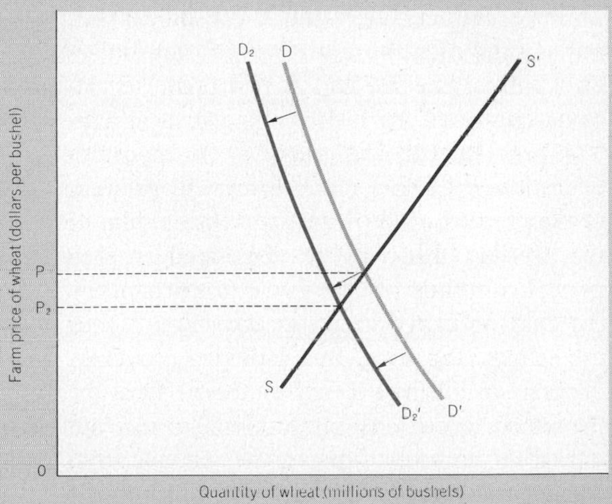

Figure 4.11
Effect on the Equilibrium Price of a Shift to the Left of the Market Demand Curve
A shift to the left from DD' to D_2D_2' results in a decrease in the equilibrium price from OP to OP_2 and a decrease in the equilibrium quantity.

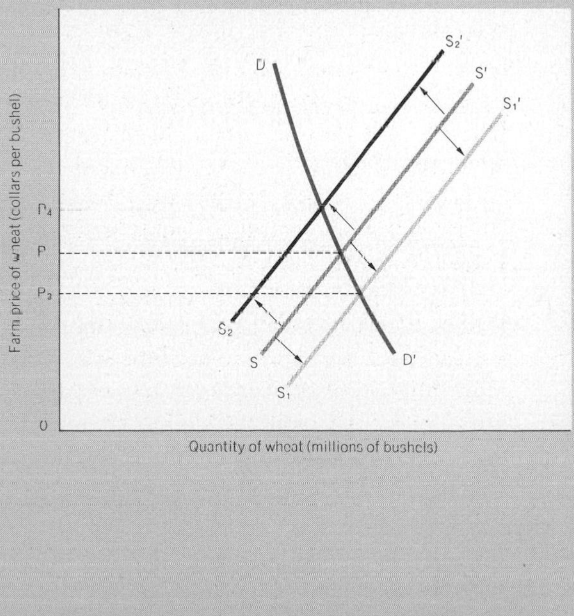

Figure 4.12
Effects on the Equilibrium Price of Shifts in the Market Supply Curve
A shift to the right from SS' to S_1S_1' results in a decrease in the equilibrium price from OP to OP_3. A shift to the left from SS' to S_2S_2' increases the equilibrium price from OP to OP_4.

suppose that the weather is poor, with the result that the supply curve shifts to the left. Specifically, suppose that the supply curve shifts from *SS'* to S_2S_2' in Figure 4.12. Clearly, the equilibrium price will increase from *OP* (where the *SS'* supply curve intersects the demand curve) to OP_4 (where the S_2S_2' supply curve intersects the demand curve).

In 1976, American consumers of coffee were shown vividly what a shift to the left in the supply curve of a commodity will do. There were three major reasons for this shift in the supply curve for coffee: (1) A frost in Brazil killed over 500 million coffee trees, and damaged many more. (2) A civil war in Angola, a major supplier of coffee, cut back its crop. (3) An earthquake in Guatemala disrupted the flow of coffee. The result was just what our theory would predict: a big jump in coffee prices. For example, Brazilian coffee, upon arrival in New York, sold for $1.25 per lb. in May 1976, compared with 69 cents per lb. a year before.

In general, *a shift to the right in the supply curve results in a decrease in the equilibrium price, and a shift to the left in the supply curve results in an increase in the equilibrium price.* Of course, this conclusion depends on the assumption that the demand curve slopes downward to the right, but, as we noted in a previous section, this assumption is generally true.

How the Price System Functions

The Price System and the Determination of What Is Produced

Having described how prices are determined in free markets, we can now describe somewhat more fully how the price system goes about performing the four basic tasks that face any economic system. (In the previous chapter, we sketched out the functions of the price system, but in a very cursory manner.) Let's begin by considering the determination of what society will produce: How does the price system carry out this task? As pointed out in the previous chapter, consumers indicate what goods and services they want in the market place, and producers try to meet these wants. More specifically, the demand curve for a product shows how much of that product consumers want at various prices. If consumers don't want much of it at a certain price, its demand curve will indicate that fact by being positioned close to the vertical axis at that price. In other words, the demand curve will show that, at this price for the product, the amount consumers will buy is small. On the other hand, if consumers want lots of the product at this price, its demand curve will be far from the vertical axis.

A product's demand curve is an important determinant of how much firms will produce of the product, since it indicates the amount of the product that will be demanded at each price. From the point of view of the producers, the demand curve indicates the amount they can sell at each price. In a capitalist economy, firms are in business to make money. Thus the manufacturers of any product will turn it out only if the amount of money they receive from consumers exceeds the cost of putting the product on the market. Acting in accord with the profit motive, firms are led to produce what the consumers desire. For example, we saw in the previous section that if consumers' tastes shift in favor of foods containing wheat, the demand curve for wheat will shift to the right, which will result in an increase in the price of wheat. This increase will stimulate farmers to produce more wheat. For example, when the demand curve shifts from *DD'* to D_1D_1' in Figure 4.10, the equilibrium quantity produced increases from *OQ* to OQ_1. Given the shift in the demand curve, it is profitable for firms to step up their production. Acting in their own self-interest, they are led to make production decisions geared to the wants of the consumers.

Thus the price system uses the self-interest of the producers to get them to produce what consumers want. Consumers register what they want in the market place by their purchasing decisions—shown by their demand curves. Producers can make more money by responding to consumer wants than by ignoring them. Consequently, they are led to produce what consumers want—and are willing to pay enough for to cover the producers' costs. Note that costs as well as demand determine what will be produced, and that producers are not forced by anyone to do anything. They can produce air conditioners for Eskimos if they like—and if they are prepared to absorb the losses. The price system uses prices to communicate the relevant signals to producers, and metes out the penalties and rewards in the form of losses or profits.

The Price System and the Determination of How Goods Are Produced

Next, consider how society determines how each good and service is produced. How does the price system carry out this task? As pointed out in the previous chapter, the price of each resource gives producers an indication of how scarce this resource is, and how valuable in other uses. Clearly, firms should produce goods and services at minimum cost. Suppose that there are two ways of producing tables: Technique *A* and Technique *B*. Technique *A* requires 4 man-hours of labor and $10 worth of wood per table, whereas Technique *B* requires 5 man-hours of labor and $8 worth of wood. If the price of a man-hour of labor is $4, Technique *A* should be used since a table costs $26 with this technique, as opposed to $28 with Technique *B*.[6] In other words, Technique *A* uses fewer resources per table.

The price system nudges producers to opt for Technique *A* rather than Technique *B* through profits and losses. If each table commands a price of $35, then by using Technique *A*, producers make a profit of $35 − $26 = $9 per table. If they use Technique *B*, they make a profit of $35 − $28 = $7 per table. Thus producers, if they maximize profit, will be led to adopt Technique *A*. Their desire for profit leads them to adopt the techniques that will enable society to get the most out of its resources. No one commands firms to use particular techniques. Washington officials do not order steel plants to substitute the basic oxygen process for open hearths, or petroleum refineries to substitute catalytic cracking for thermal cracking. It is all done through the impersonal market place.

You should not, however, get the idea that the price system operates with kid gloves. Suppose all firms producing tables used Technique *B* until this past year, when Technique *A* was developed: in other words, Technique *A* is based on a new technology. Given this technological change, the supply curve for tables will shift to the right, as we saw in a previous section, and the price of a table will fall. Suppose it drops to $27. If some firm insists on sticking with Technique *B*, it will lose money at the rate of $1 a table; and as these losses mount, the firm's owners will become increasingly uncomfortable. The firm will either switch to Technique *A* or go bankrupt. The price system leans awfully hard on producers who try to ignore its signals.

The Price System and the Determination of Who Gets What

Let's turn now to how society's output will be distributed among the people: How does the price system carry out this task? How much a

[6] To obtain these figures, note that the cost with Technique *A* is 4 man-hours times $4 plus $10, or $26, while the cost with Technique *B* is 5 man-hours times $4 plus $8, or $28.

person receives in goods and services depends on his money income, which in turn is determined under the price system by the amount of various resources that he owns and by the price of each resource. Thus, under the price system, each person's income is determined in the market place: he comes to the market place with certain resources to sell, and his income depends on how much he can get for them.

The question of who gets what is solved at two levels by the price system. Consider an individual product—for example, the tables discussed in the previous section. For the individual product, the question of who gets what is solved by the equality of quantity demanded and quantity supplied. If the price of these tables is at its equilibrium level, the quantity demanded will equal the quantity supplied. Consumers who are willing and able to pay the equilibrium price (or more) get the tables, while those who are unwilling or unable to pay it do not get them. It is just as simple—and as impersonal—as that. It doesn't matter whether you are a nice guy or a scoundrel, or whether you are a connoisseur of tables or someone who doesn't know good workmanship from poor: all that matters is whether you are able and willing to pay the equilibrium price.

Next, consider the question of who gets what at a somewhat more fundamental level. After all, whether a consumer is able and willing to pay the equilibrium price for a good depends on his money income. Thus the Rockefellers can pay the equilibrium price for an astonishing variety of things, whereas the Ríos family can scrape up the equilibrium price for very little. As we have already seen, a consumer's money income depends on the amount of resources of various kinds that he owns and the price that he can get for them. Some people have lots of resources: they are endowed with skill and intelligence and industry, or they have lots of capital or land. Other people have little in the way of resources. Moreover, some people have resources that command a high price, while others have resources that are of little monetary value. The result is that, under the price system, some consumers, like the Rockefellers, get a lot more of society's output than other consumers, like the Ríos family.

The Price System and Economic Growth

Let's turn now to the task of determining a society's rate of growth of per capita income. How does the price system do this? As pointed out in the previous chapter, a nation's rate of increase of per capita income depends on the rate of growth of its resources and the rate of increase of the efficiency with which they are used. First, consider the rate of growth of society's resources. The price system controls the amount of new capital goods produced much as it controls the amount of consumer goods produced. Similarly, the price system influences the amount society invests in educating, training, and upgrading its labor resources. To a considerable extent, the amount invested in such resource-augmenting activities is determined by the profitability of such investments, which is determined in turn by the pattern of prices.

Next, consider the rate of increase of the efficiency with which a society's resources are used. Clearly, this factor depends heavily on the rate of technological change. If technology is advancing at a rapid rate, it should be possible to get more and more out of a society's resources. But if technology is advancing rather slowly, it is likely to be difficult to get much more out of them. The price system affects the rate of technological change in a variety of ways: it influences the profitability of investing in research and development, the profitability of introducing new processes and products into commercial practice, and the profitability of accepting technological change—as well as the losses involved in spurning it.

The price system establishes strong incentives for firms to introduce new technology. Any firm that can find a cheaper way to produce an existing product, or a way to produce a better product, will have a profitable jump on its competitors. Until its competitors can do the same thing, this firm can reap higher profits than it otherwise could. Of course, these higher profits will eventually be competed away, as other firms begin to imitate this firm's innovation. But lots of money can be made in the period during which this firm has a lead over its competitors. These profits are an important incentive for the introduction of new technology.

Two Case Studies

The Price System in Action behind Enemy Lines

Just as general discussions of tennis will take a neophyte only so far, after which he or she must watch and participate in a few matches, so a general discussion of the price system will take a student only so far. Then he should look at real-life examples of the price system at work. Our first illustration of the price system in operation is a prisoner-of-war camp in World War II. This case is not chosen because of its inherent importance, but because of its simplicity. Just as certain elementary forms of life illustrate important biological principles in a simple way, so the economic organization of a prisoner-of-war camp is an elementary form of economic system that illustrates certain important economic principles simply and well.

The prisoner-of-war camp was so elementary because no goods were produced there. All commodities were provided by the country running the camp, by the Red Cross, and by other outside donors. Each prisoner received an equal amount of food and supplies—canned milk, jam, butter, cookies, cigarettes, and so on. In addition, private parcels of clothing, cigarettes, and other supplies were received, with different prisoners, of course, receiving different quantities. Because no goods were produced in the prisoner-of-war camp, the first two tasks of an economic system (What will be produced? How will it be produced?) were not relevant; neither was the fourth task (What provision is to be made for growth?)

All that did matter in this elementary economic system was the third task: to determine who would consume the various available goods. At first blush, the answer may seem obvious: each prisoner would consume the goods he received from the detaining country, the Red Cross, and private packages. But this assumes that prisoners would not trade goods back and forth ("I'll swap you a cigarette for some milk"), which is clearly unrealistic. After all, some prisoners smoked cigarettes, others did not; some liked jam and didn't like canned beef, others liked canned beef and didn't like jam. Thus there was bound to be exchange of this sort, and the real question is in what way and on what terms such exchange took place.

How did the prisoners go about exchanging goods? According to one observer, the process developed as follows:

> Starting with simple direct barter, such as a nonsmoker giving a smoker friend his cigarette issue in exchange for a chocolate ration, more complex exchanges soon became an accepted custom. . . . Within a week or two, as the volume of trade grew, rough scales of exchange values came into existence. [Some prisoners], who had at first exchanged tinned beef for practically any other foodstuff, began to insist on jam and margarine. It was realized that a tin of jam was worth one-half pound of margarine plus something else, that a cigarette issue was worth several chocolate issues, and a tin of diced carrots was worth practically nothing. . . . By the end of the month, there was a lively trade in all com-

> modities and their relative values were well known, and expressed not in terms of one another—one didn't quote [jam] in terms of sugar—but in terms of cigarettes. The cigarette became the standard of value.[7]

Thus the prisoners used the price system to solve the problem of allocating the available supply of goods among consumers. A market developed for each good. This market had, of course, both a demand and a supply side. Each good had its price—but this price was quoted in cigarettes, not dollars and cents. These markets were not started in a self-conscious, deliberate way. No one said, "Let's adopt the price system to allocate available supplies," or "Let's vote on whether or not to adopt the price system." Instead, the system just evolved . . . and it worked.

To see how the supply of a particular good—jam, say—was allocated, look at Figure 4.13, which shows the market supply curve for jam, SS'. In the short run, this supply was fixed, so SS' is a vertical line. Figure 4.13 also provides the market demand curve for jam, DD', which shows the amount of jam the prisoners wanted to consume at various prices of jam—expressed in terms of cigarettes. For example, DD' shows that the prisoners wanted OQ_1 tins of jam when a tin of jam cost OP_1 cigarettes, and OQ_2 tins of jam when a tin of jam cost OP_2 cigarettes. For the quantity demanded to equal the available supply, the price of a tin of jam had to be OP cigarettes: one tin of jam had to exchange for OP cigarettes. At this price, the available supply of jam was rationed, without resort to fights among prisoners or intervention by the prison authorities. Those prisoners who could and would pay the price had the jam—and there were just enough such consumers to exhaust the available supply. Moreover, this held true for each of the other goods (including cigarettes) as well.

[7] R. A. Radford, "The Economic Organization of a P.O.W. Camp," reprinted in E. Mansfield, *Economics: Readings, Issues, and Cases,* 2d ed., New York: Norton, 1977.

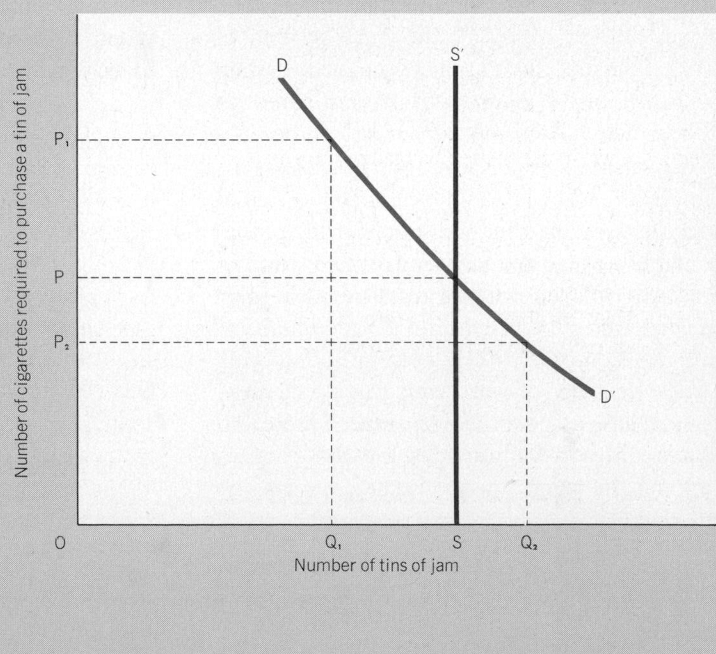

Figure 4.13
Determinants of Equilibrium Price of a Tin of Jam (in terms of cigarettes) in a P.O.W. Camp
The market supply for jam is fixed at *OS* tins. The market demand curve is *DD′*. Thus the equilibrium price of a tin of jam is *OP* cigarettes. If the price were OP_1, OQ_1 tins would be demanded; if the price were OP_2, OQ_2 tins would be demanded.

The Price System in Action on the Great White Way

It is a long way from a prisoner-of-war camp to the Broadway theater, but economics, like any good tool of analysis, applies to a very wide variety of problems. In this section, we discuss the theater's pricing problems—and the role of the price system in helping to solve these problems. Prices for tickets to Broadway shows are established at levels that are much the same whether the show is a success or a flop. For example, an orchestra ticket to *Kelly* (which managed to hold out for one performance before closing) cost about as much as an orchestra ticket to such hits as *Fiddler on the Roof* or *A Chorus Line*. And once a play opens, the price of a ticket remains much the same whether the play is greeted with universal praise or with discontented critics and customers.

Because of these pricing methods, the Broadway theater has been beset for many years by serious problems. Here they are described by two veteran observers of the Broadway stage:

> For centuries the sale of theater tickets has brought on corruption and confusion. When there are more buyers than sellers, a black market results. The so-called "retail" price, the price printed on the ticket, becomes meaningless. Speculation doubles, triples, or quadruples the "real" as opposed to the "legal" asking price. A smash hit on Broadway means "ice"—the difference between the real and legal prices—a well-hidden but substantial cash flow that is divided among shadowy middlemen. Ticket scandals break out in New York as regularly as the flu. The scenario is familiar. A play opens and becomes a superhit. Tickets become difficult, then impossible, to obtain. There are letters to the newspapers. . . . Shocking corruption is discovered. Someone . . . is convicted of overcharging and accepting illegal gratuities. Someone may even go to jail. The black market, valiantly scotched, *never stops for a single moment.*[8]

[8] S. Little and A. Cantor, *The Playmakers,* New York: Norton, 1970, p. 220.

Besides enriching crooked box-office men and managers, as well as other shadowy elements of society, the black market for theater tickets has the additional undesirable effect of excluding the authors, composers, directors, and stars of the play from participation in the premium revenue. Almost all of these people receive a percentage of the play's revenues; and if the revenues at the box office are less than the customers pay for their seats (because of "ice"), these people receive less than they would if no black market existed. The amount of "ice" can be substantial. For example, Rodgers and Hammerstein estimated that, at one performance of their play, *South Pacific,* the public probably paid about $25,000 for tickets with a face value of $7,000, the amount turned in at the box office.

To focus on the problem here, let's look at the market for tickets to a particular performance of *My Fair Lady* (one of Broadway's all-time big hits) when it was at the height of its popularity. Since the supply of tickets to a given performance is fixed, the market supply curve, *SS′* in Figure 4.14, is a vertical line at the quantity of tickets corresponding to the capacity of the theater. The price set officially on the price of a ticket was $8. But because the show was enormously popular, the market demand curve was *DD′* in Figure 4.14, and the equilibrium price for a ticket was $50.[9]

Figure 4.14 makes the nature of the problem apparent: at the official price of $8, the quantity of tickets demanded is much greater than the quantity supplied. Supply and demand don't match. Obviously, there is an incentive for people to buy the tickets from the box office at $8 and sell them at the higher prices customers are willing to pay. There is also an incentive for box-office men to sell them surreptitiously at higher prices and turn in only $8. The price system cannot play the role it did in the prisoner-of-war camp for jam and

[9] This figure is an estimate based on an article in *Variety.*

Figure 4.14
Equilibrium Price for Tickets to *My Fair Lady*
The market supply for tickets is fixed at *OS* per performance. If the demand curve is *DD'*, the equilibrium price of a ticket is \$50. (If the demand curve is D_1D_1', the equilibrium price is \$7.) If the demand curve is *DD'* and the price of a ticket is \$8, the quantity of tickets demanded will far exceed the quantity supplied.

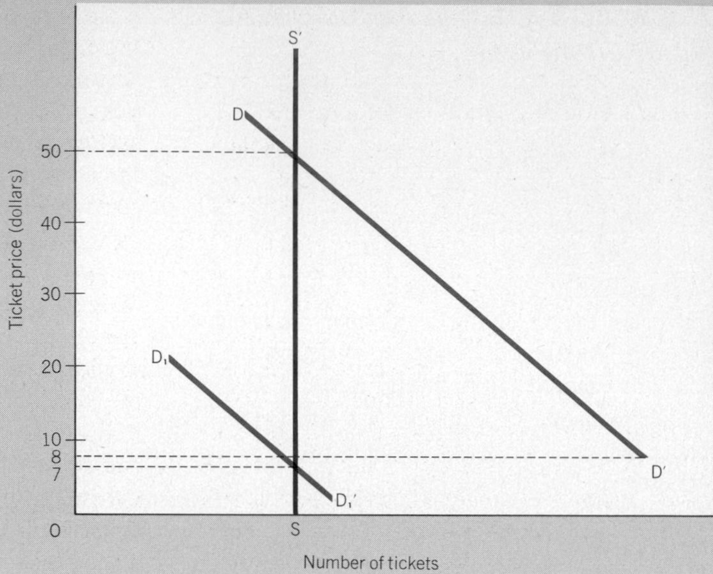

other goods. It cannot act as an effective rationing device because, to do so, the price of tickets would have to increase to its equilibrium level, \$50.

Many theater experts believe that the solution to Broadway's pricing problems lies in allowing the price system to work more effectively by permitting ticket prices to vary depending on a show's popularity. For example, the official ticket price would be allowed to rise to \$50 for *My Fair Lady.* On the other hand, if *My Fair Lady* had been much less popular and its market demand curve had been D_1D_1' in Figure 4.14, its official ticket price would have been allowed to fall to \$7. In this way, the black market for tickets would be eliminated, since the equilibrium price–which equates supply and demand–would be the official price. "Ice" would also be eliminated, since there would be no difference between the official and the actual price paid, and the people responsible for the show would receive its full receipts, not share them with crooked box-office men and illegal operators.[10]

Price Ceilings and Price Supports

During national emergencies, the government sometimes puts a lid on prices, not allowing them to reach their equilibrium levels. For example, during World War II, the government did not allow the prices of various foodstuffs to rise to their equilibrium levels, because it felt that this would have been inequitable (and highly unpopular). Under such circumstances, the quantity demanded of a product exceeds the quantity supplied. In other words, the situation is like that in Figure 4.14, where the quantity demanded of tickets for *My Fair*

[10] In the mid-1970s, a step was taken toward somewhat greater price flexibility for Broadway shows. A booth was established in Times Square where tickets to some shows were on sale at (approximately) half of the official ticket price. In this way, a show was enabled to cut its price, if it was unable to fill the theater at the official ticket price. Apparently, this innovation has worked quite well, both for the producers of the shows and the theater-going public.

Lady exceeds the quantity supplied at a price of $8. There is a shortage.

Since the price system is not allowed to perform its rationing function, some formal system of rationing or allocating the available supply of the product may be required. Thus, in World War II, families were issued ration coupons which determined how much they could buy of various commodities. And in late 1973, when supplies of gasoline seemed to be cut by the curtailment of Arab exports of oil to the United States, there was serious talk that gasoline and oil might be rationed in a similar way. Such rationing schemes may be justified in emergencies (of reasonably short duration), but they can result eventually in serious distortions, since prices are not allowed to do the job normally expected of them.

To illustrate the sorts of problems that can arise when price ceilings are imposed, consider the rent ceilings that exist on some apartments in New York City. Originally imposed to prevent dwelling costs from soaring during World War II, these ceilings have been defended on the ground that they help the poor, at least in the short run. Although this may be so, they have also resulted in a shortage of housing in New York City. Because they have pushed the price of housing below the equilibrium price, less housing has been supplied than has been demanded. The depressed price of housing has discouraged investors from building new housing, and has made it unprofitable for some owners of existing housing to maintain their buildings. Thus, although it would be socially desirable to channel more resources into New York housing, the rent ceilings have prevented this from occurring.

Government authorities may also impose price floors—or price supports, as they often are called. These floors are generally defended on the ground that they enable the producers of the good in question to make a better living. For example, the federal government imposed price supports on a wide range of agricultural commodities until 1973, the purpose being to increase farm incomes. Just as in the case in Figure 4.14 where the demand curve is D_1D_1' and where a price floor of $8 exists, the result is that the quantity supplied exceeds the quantity demanded at the support price. Thus there is a surplus of the commodity—and, in the case of agricultural commodities, the government had to buy up and store these surpluses. As in the case of a price ceiling, the result is that the price system is not allowed to do the job expected of it.

Whether price ceilings or floors are socially desirable depends on whether the loss in social efficiency resulting from them is exceeded by the gain in equity they achieve. As indicated above, their purpose is to help or protect particular parts of the population which would be treated inequitably by the unfettered price system. Since one person's views of what is equitable differ from another person's, this is an area of considerable controversy. More will be said about both price ceilings and floors in subsequent chapters, particularly Chapters 5 and 16.

The Circular Flows of Money and Products

So far we have been concerned largely with the workings of a single market—the market for wheat or tables or jam or tickets to *My Fair Lady*. But how do all of the various markets fit together? This is a very important question. Perhaps the best way to begin answering it is to distinguish between product markets and resource markets. As their names indicate, ***product markets*** *are markets where products are bought and sold; and* ***resource markets*** *are markets where resources are bought and sold.* Let's first consider product markets. As shown in Figure 4.15, firms provide products to consumers in product markets, and receive money in return. The money the firms receive is their receipts; to consumers, on the other hand, it represents their expenditures.

Next, let's consider resource markets. Figure 4.15 shows that consumers provide resources—including labor—to firms in resource markets, and they receive money in return. The money the consumers receive is their income; to firms, on the other hand, it represents their costs. Note that the flow of resources and products in Figure 4.15 is counterclockwise: that is, *consumers provide resources to firms which in turn provide goods and services to consumers.* On the other hand, the flow of money in Figure 4.15 is clockwise: that is, *firms pay money for resources to consumers who in turn use the money to buy goods and services from the firms.* Both flows—that of resources and products, and that of money—go on simultaneously and repeatedly.

So long as consumers spend all their income, the flow of money income from firms to consumers is exactly equal to the flow of expenditure from consumers to firms. Thus these circular flows, like Ole Man River, just keep rolling along. As a first approximation, this is a perfectly good model. But as we pointed out in Chapter 1, capitalist economies have experienced periods of widespread unemployment and severe inflation that this model cannot explain. Also, note that our simple economy in Figure 4.15 has no government sector. In the following chapter, we shall bring the government into the picture. Under pure capitalism, the government would play a limited role in the economic system, but in the mixed capitalistic system we have in the United States, the government plays an important role indeed.

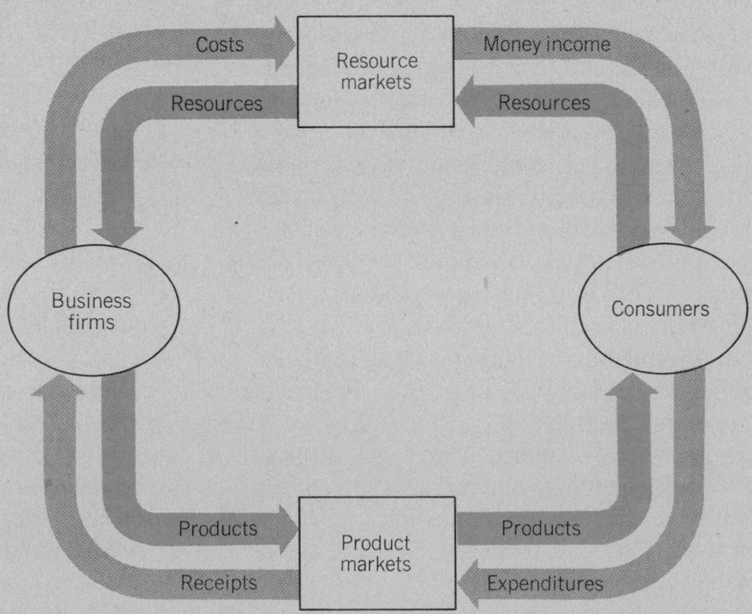

Figure 4.15
The Circular Flows of Money and Products
In product markets, consumers exchange money for products and firms exchange products for money. In resource markets, consumers exchange resources for money and firms exchange money for resources.

Summary

Consumers and firms are the basic units comprising the private sector of the economy. Consumers, whether individuals or households, purchase the goods and services that are the ultimate end-products of the economic system. Consumers are obviously an extremely varied lot, as a brief comparison of the Rockefeller and Ríos families indicates. A firm is a unit that produces a good or service for sale. About $^9/_{10}$ of the goods and services produced in the United States are produced by firms, which number in the millions. Like consumers, they are extremely varied in size, age, power, and purpose, as illustrated by a comparison of Amacher's drugstore and General Motors. A market is a group of firms and individuals that are in touch with each other in order to buy or sell some commodity or service. When a market for a homogeneous product contains so many buyers and sellers that none of them can influence the price, economists call it a perfectly competitive market.

There are two sides of every market: the demand side and the supply side. The demand side can be represented by the market demand curve, which almost always slopes downward to the right and whose location depends on consumer tastes, the number and income of consumers, and the prices of other commodities. The supply side of the market can be represented by the market supply curve, which generally slopes upward to the right and whose location depends on technology and resource prices. The equilibrium price and equilibrium quantity of the commodity are given by the intersection of the market demand and supply curves. If conditions remain reasonably stable for a time, the actual price and quantity should move close to the equilibrium price and quantity. Changes in the position and shape of the demand curve—in response to changes in consumer tastes, income, population, and prices of other commodities—result in changes in the equilibrium price and equilibrium output of a product. Similarly, changes in the position and shape of the supply curve in response to changes in technology and resource prices, among other things—also result in changes in the equilibrium price and equilibrium output of a product.

To determine what goods and services society will produce, the price system sets up incentives for firms to produce what consumers want. To the extent that they produce what consumers want and are willing to pay for, firms reap profits; to the extent that they don't, they experience losses. Similarly, the price system sets up strong incentives for firms to produce these goods at minimum cost. These incentives take the form of profits for firms that minimize costs and losses for firms that operate with relatively high costs. To determine who gets what, the price system results in each person's receiving an income that depends on the quantity of resources he owns and the prices that they command. The price system also establishes incentives for activities that result in increases in a society's per capita income. The very simple case of a prisoner-of-war camp and the more complicated case of the Broadway theater provide real illustrations of the price system in action.

There are circular flows of money and products in a capitalist economy. In product markets, firms provide products to consumers and receive money in return. In resource markets, consumers provide resources to firms, and receive money in return. The flow of resources and products is as follows: consumers provide resources to firms which in turn provide goods and services to consumers. The flow of money is as follows: firms pay money for resources to consumers who in turn use the money to buy goods and services from firms. Both flows go on simultaneously and repeatedly.

CONCEPTS FOR REVIEW

Consumer	Supply	Equilibrium price
Firm	Perfect competition	Product market
Market	Market demand curve	Resource market
Demand	Market supply curve	Actual price

QUESTIONS FOR DISCUSSION AND REVIEW

1. Assume that the market for electric toasters is competitive, and that the quantity supplied per year depends as follows on the price of a toaster:

Price of a toaster (dollars)	Number of toasters supplied (millions)
6	4.0
8	5.0
10	5.5
12	6.0
14	6.3

Plot the supply curve for toasters. Is this a direct or inverse relationship? Are supply curves generally direct or inverse relationships?

2. Suppose that the quantity of toasters demanded per year depends as follows on the price of a toaster:

Price of toaster (dollars)	Number of toasters demanded (millions)
6	7.0
8	6.5
10	6.2
12	6.0
14	5.8

Plot the demand curve for toasters. If the price is $8, will there be an excess demand of toasters? If the price is $14, will there be an excess demand? What is the equilibrium price of a toaster? What is the equilibrium quantity? (Use the data in Question 1.)

3. Suppose that the government imposes a price ceiling on toasters. In particular, suppose that it decrees that a toaster cannot sell for more than $8. Will the quantity supplied equal the quantity demanded? What sorts of devices may come into being to allocate the available supply of toasters to consumers? What problems will the government encounter in keeping the price at $8? What social purposes, if any, might such a price ceiling serve? (Use the data in Questions 1 and 2.)

4. Suppose that the government imposes a price floor on toasters. In particular, suppose that it decrees that a toaster cannot sell for less than $14. Will the quantity supplied equal the quantity demanded? How will the resulting supply of toasters be taken off the market? What problems will the government encounter in keeping the price at $14? What social purposes, if any, might such a price floor serve? (Use the data above.)

5. Will each of the following tend to shift the demand curve for toasters to the right, to the left, or not at all? (a) Consumer incomes rise by 20 percent. (b) The price of bread falls by 10 percent. (c) The price of electricity increases by 5 percent. (d) Medical reports indicate that toast prevents heart attacks. (e) The cost of producing a toaster increases by 10 percent.

6. Will each of the following tend to shift the supply curve for toasters to the right, to the left, or not at all? (a) The wage of workers producing toasters increases by 5 percent. (b) The price of the metal used to make toasters falls by 10 percent. (c) The price of bread falls by 10 percent. (d) Consumer incomes rise by 20 percent. (e) New technology makes toaster production much more efficient.

7. If both the demand and supply curve for a product shift to the right, can one predict whether the product's equilibrium price will increase or decrease? Can one predict whether its equilibrium quantity will increase or decrease?

8. According to W. Allen Wallis, "Not only do prices convey information on how an individual should act, but they provide at the same time a powerful inducement for him to do so." Do you agree? If you do, explain why it is true. If you don't, explain where it is wrong.

9. Suppose that you were appointed head of a blue-ribbon commission to recommend changes in pricing practices for the entertainment industry. Would you recommend a free market for tickets for Broadway shows? For tickets to the San Francisco Opera? For the Dallas Cowboys games? In each case, why or why not?

10. Suppose that the American public becomes convinced that beets are more desirable, and string beans are less so. Describe the shifts that will occur in the demand and supply curves in the relevant markets, and the mechanisms that will signal and trigger a redeployment of resources.

11. (Advanced) If the demand curve for butter is $Q_D = 20 - 4P$ (where Q_D is the quantity demanded and P is the price of butter) and the supply curve for butter is $Q_S = 2P$ (where Q_S is the quantity supplied), what is the equilibrium price? What is the equilibrium quantity? (Both Q_D and Q_S are measured in millions of pounds, and price is measured in dollars per pound.)

5

The Economic Role of the Government

To state that the United States is a mixed capitalist system, in which both government decisions and the price system play important roles, is hardly to provoke a controversy. But going a step beyond, as we shall in this chapter, takes us into areas where viewpoints often diverge. The proper functions of government and the desirable size and nature of government expenditures and taxes are not matters on which all agree. Indeed, the question of how big government should be, and what its proper functions are, is hotly debated by conservatives and liberals throughout the land. Of course, this is only a preliminary airing of many of these issues. As the base of economic analysis is broadened in subsequent chapters, much more will be said on these matters, and you will be in a far better position to judge them for yourself.

In the latter part of this chapter, we describe

the nature and causes of our farm problem, and indicate the extent to which government programs seem to have solved this problem. This is an interesting application of the supply and demand theory presented in the previous chapter, as well as an example of the economic role of the government. Whether you are from the city or the country, you should be interested in the nature and success of our farm programs—if for no other reason than that you and your tax-paying and food-consuming friends and relatives pay for them.

Limitations of the Price System

Despite its many advantages, the price system suffers from serious limitations. Because these limitations are both prominent and well known, no one believes that the price system, left to its own devices, can be trusted to solve our society's basic economic problems. Indeed, some economists argue that the price system's limitations are so great that it should be scrapped. In fact, however, we have not scrapped it. Instead, we have charged the government with the responsibility for correcting many of its shortcomings. Thus, to a considerable extent, the goverment's role in the economy has developed in response to the limitations of the price system, which are described below.

Distribution of income. There is *no* reason to believe that the distribution of income generated by the price system is *fair* or, in some sense, *best.* Some rich families receive much more income in a day than the Ríos family does in a year. Most people feel that the distribution of income generated by the price system should be altered to suit humanitarian needs; in particular, that help should be given to the poor. Both liberals and conservatives tend to agree on this score, although there are arguments over the extent to which the poor should be helped and the conditions under which they should be eligible for help. But the general principle that the government should step in to redistribute income in favor of the poor is generally accepted in the United States today.[1]

Public goods. Some goods and services *cannot be provided through the price system because there is no way to exclude a citizen from consuming the good whether he pays for it or not.* For example, there is no way to prevent a citizen from benefiting from national expenditures on defense, whether he pays money toward defense or not. Consequently, the price system cannot be used to provide such goods; no one will pay for them since they will receive them whether they pay or not. Further, some goods, like the quality of the environment and national defense (and others cited below), *can be enjoyed by one person without depriving others of the same enjoyment.* Such goods are called ***public goods.*** The government provides many public goods. Such goods are consumed collectively or jointly, and it is inefficient to try to price them in a market. They tend to be indivisible; thus, they frequently cannot be split into pieces and be bought and sold in a market.

External economies and diseconomies. In cases where *the production or consumption of a good by one firm or consumer has adverse or beneficial uncompensated effects on other firms or consumers, the price system will not operate effectively.* An ***external economy*** is said to occur when consumption or production by one person or firm results in uncompensated benefits to another person or firm. A good example of an external economy exists where fundamental research carried out by one firm is used by another firm. (To cite one such case, there were external economies from the Bell Telephone Laboratories' invention of the transistor.)

[1] Also, because the wealthy have more "dollar votes" than the poor, the sorts of goods and services that society produces will reflect this fact. Thus luxuries for the rich may be produced in larger amounts and necessities for the poor may be produced in smaller amounts than some critics regard as sensible and equitable. This is another frequently encountered criticism of the price system.

Where external economies exist, it is generally agreed that the price system will produce too little of the good in question and that the government should supplement the amount produced by private enterprise. This is the basic rationale for much of the government's huge investment in basic science. An ***external diseconomy*** is said to occur when consumption or production by one person or firm results in uncompensated costs to another person or firm. A good example of an external diseconomy occurs when a firm dumps pollutants into a stream and makes the water unfit for use by firms and people downstream. Where activities result in external diseconomies, it is generally agreed that the price system will tolerate too much of the activity and that the government should curb it. For example, as we shall see in Chapter 19, the government, in keeping with this doctrine, has involved itself increasingly in environmental protection and the reduction of air and water pollution.[2]

What Functions Should the Government Perform?

There are wide differences of opinion on the proper role of government in economic affairs. Although it is generally agreed that the government should redistribute income in favor of the poor, provide public goods, and offset the effects of external economies and diseconomies, there is considerable disagreement over how far the government should go in these areas, and what additional areas the government should be responsible for. Some people feel that "Big Government" is already a problem; that government is doing too much. Others believe that the public sector of the economy is being undernourished and that government should be allowed to do more. This is a fundamental question, and one that involves a great deal more than economics.

Conservative view. On the one hand, conservatives, such as the University of Chicago's recent Nobel laureate, Milton Friedman, believe that the government's role should be limited severely. They feel that economic and political freedom is likely to be undermined by excessive reliance on the state. Moreover, they tend to be skeptical about the government's ability to solve the social and economic problems at hand. They feel that the prevailing faith in the government's power to make a substantial dent in these problems is unreasonable, and they call for more and better information concerning the sorts of tasks government can reasonably be expected to do—and do well. They point to the slowness of the government bureaucracy, the difficulty in controlling huge government organizations, the inefficiencies political considerations can breed, and the difficulties in telling whether government programs are successful or not. On the basis of these considerations, they argue that the government's role should be carefully circumscribed.

The flavor of the conservative position on this question, as well as a generous helping of sarcasm and wit, is evident in the remarks of George Stigler, another distinguished economist at the University of Chicago:

> I consider myself courageous, or at least obtuse, in arguing for a reduction in governmental controls over economic life. You are surely desirous of improving this world, and it assuredly needs an immense amount of improvement. No method of displaying one's public-spiritedness is more popular than to notice a problem and pass a law. It combines ease, the warmth of benevolence, and a suitable disrespect for a less enlightened era. What I propose is, for most people, much less attractive: close study of the comparative performance of public and private economy, and the dispassionate appraisal of special reme-

[2] The effects of external economies and diseconomies can also be taken care of by legal arrangements that assign liabilities for damages and compensate for benefits. However, such arrangements often are impractical or too costly to be used.

dies that is involved in compassion for the community at large.[3]

Liberal view. To such remarks, liberals respond with very telling salvos of their own. Just as conservatives tend to be skeptical of the government's ability to solve important social and economic problems, so liberals tend to be skeptical about the price system's ability to solve these problems. They point to the important limitations of the price system, discussed above, and they assert that the government can do a great deal to overcome these limitations, by regulating private activity, and by subsidizing and providing goods and services that the private sector produces too little of.

According to some distinguished liberals, like Harvard's John Kenneth Galbraith, the public sector of the economy has been starved of needed resources, while the private sector has catered to relatively unimportant wants. In his best-selling book, *The Affluent Society*, Galbraith argued that consumers are led by advertising and other promotional efforts to purchase more and more goods of marginal significance to them. On the other hand, in his opinion, the nation is suffering because too little is spent on government services like education, transportation, and urban renewal.[4] In the next chapter, we shall discuss this proposition in more detail.

Liberals tend to be less concerned than conservatives about the effects of greater governmental intervention in the economy on personal freedom. They point out that the price system also involves coercion, since the fact that the price system awards the available goods and services to those who can pay their equilibrium price can be viewed as a form of coercion. Moreover, some people are awarded only a pittance by the price system: in a real sense, they are coerced into discomfort and malnutrition.[5]

A Legal, Social, and Competitive Framework

Although there is considerable disagreement over the proper role of the government, both conservatives and liberals agree that it must do certain things. The first of these is to establish the "rules of the game"—that is, a legal, social, and competitive framework enabling the price system to function as it should. Specifically, the government must see to it that contracts are enforced, that private ownership is protected, and that fraud is prevented. Clearly, these matters must be tended to if the price system is to work properly. Also, the government must maintain order (through the establishment of police and other forces), establish a monetary system (so that money can be used to facilitate trade and exchange), and provide standards for the weight and quality of products.

As an example of this sort of government intervention, consider the Pure Food and Drug Act. This act, originally passed in 1906 and subsequently amended in various ways, protects the consumer against improper and fraudulent activities on the part of producers of foods and drugs. It prohibits the merchandising of impure or falsely labeled food or drugs, and it forces producers to specify the quantity and quality of the contents on labels. These requirements strengthen the price system. Without them, the typical consumer would be unable to tell whether food or drugs are pure or properly labeled. Unless the con-

[3] G. Stigler, "The Government of the Economy," *A Dialogue on the Proper Economic Role of the State*, University of Chicago, Graduate School of Business, Selected Paper no. 7, reprinted in E. Mansfield, *Economics: Readings, Issues, and Cases*, 2d ed., New York: Norton, 1977. Also, see M. Friedman, *Capitalism and Freedom*, Chicago: University of Chicago Press, 1962.

[4] J. K. Galbraith, *The Affluent Society*, Boston: Houghton Mifflin, 1958.

[5] See P. Samuelson, "The Economic Role of Private Activity," *A Dialogue on the Proper Economic Role of the State*, University of Chicago, Graduate School of Business, Selected Paper no. 7, reprinted in E. Mansfield, *Economics: Readings, Issues, and Cases.*

sumer can be sure that he is getting what he is paying for, the basic logic underlying the price system breaks down. Similar regulation and legislation have been instituted in fields other than food and drugs–and for similar reasons.

Besides establishing a legal and social framework that will enable the price system to do its job, the government must also see to it that markets remain reasonably competitive. Only if they are will prices reflect consumer desires properly. If, on the other hand, markets are dominated by a few sellers (or a few buyers), prices may be "rigged" by these sellers (or buyers) to promote their own interests. For example, if a single firm is the sole producer of aluminum, it is a safe bet that this firm will establish a higher price than if there were many aluminum producers competing among themselves. The unfortunate thing about prices determined in noncompetitive markets–rigged prices, if you will–is that they give incorrect signals concerning what consumers want and how scarce resources and commodities are. Producers, responding to these incorrect signals, do not produce the right things in the right quantities. Consumers respond to these incorrect signals by not supplying the right resources in the right amounts, and by not consuming the proper amounts of the goods that are produced. Thus the price system is not permitted to solve the four basic economic problems properly in the absence of reasonable competition.

To try to encourage and preserve competition, the Congress has enacted a series of antitrust laws, such as the Sherman Antitrust Act and the Clayton Act, and it has established the Federal Trade Commission. The antitrust laws make it illegal for firms to collude or to attempt to monopolize the sale of a product. Both conservative and liberal economists, with some notable exceptions, tend to favor the intent and operation of the antitrust laws. In addition, the government tries to control the activities of firms in markets where competition cannot be expected to prevail (as in the telephone industry, where efficient operations would be destroyed if more than a very few firms got in the act). In industries of this sort, the government often establishes commissions to regulate prices and standards of service. Such regulatory commissions are common in the communications, transportation, electric, and gas industries.

Redistribution of Income

We have already noted at several points the general agreement that the government should redistribute income in favor of the poor. In other words, it is usually felt that help should be given to people who are ill, handicapped, old and infirm, disabled, and unable for other reasons to provide for themselves. To some extent, the nation has decided that income–or at least a certain minimum income–should be divorced from productive services. Of course, this doesn't mean that people who are too lazy to work should be given a handout. It does mean that people who cannot provide for themselves should be helped. To implement this principle, various payments are made by the government to needy people–including the aged, the handicapped, the unemployed, pensioners, and veterans.

These welfare payments are to some extent a "depression baby," for they grew substantially during the Great Depression of the 1930s, when relief payments became a necessity. But they also represent a feeling shared by a large segment of the population that human beings should be assured that, however the Wheel of Fortune spins and whatever number comes up, they will not starve and their children will not be deprived of a healthy environment and basic schooling. Of course, someone has to pay for this. Welfare payments allow the poor to take more from the nation's output than they produce. In general, the more affluent members of society contribute some of their claims on output to pay for these programs, their contributions being in the form of taxes. By using its expenditures to help certain groups and by taxing other groups to pay for these programs, the government accomplishes each year, without revolt and without bayonets, a substantial redistribution of income. This is a crucial aspect of the government's role in our economy.

It should not be assumed, however, that all government programs transfer income from the rich to the poor. On the contrary, some programs, intentionally or unintentionally, soak the poor to give to the rich. Some government programs fatten the purses of rich farmers, some tax loopholes allow the affluent to dodge taxes through the creation of trusts and other legal devices, and some important taxes—such as sales taxes—hit the poor harder than the rich. Nonetheless, the best available evidence indicates that, when all its activities are taken into account, the government does take from the rich to give to the poor. In other words, taking account of both its expenditures and the taxes it levies, the government redistributes income in favor of the poor. Whether it goes as far as it should in this direction is a more nettlesome question, the answer to which will depend on your own ethical values.

Economic Stabilization

It is also generally agreed that the government should see to it that the economy maintains reasonably full employment with reasonably stable prices. Capitalist economies have tended to alternate between booms and depressions in the past. The Great Depression of the 1930s hit the American economy—and the world economy—a particularly devastating blow, putting millions of people out of work and in desperate shape. When World War II ended, the American people vowed that they would not let a depression of this sort occur again. The Congress passed the Employment Act of 1946, which stated that it was the responsibility of the federal government to maintain full employment in the United States. In particular, the federal government was not supposed to tolerate unemployment of the sort that materialized during severe depressions in the past.

Of course, it is one thing to charge the federal government with the responsibility for maintaining full employment and quite another thing to tell the federal government how to achieve this goal. Without a good deal of economic knowledge, this law would have been as empty as Atlantic City in December—since it is useless to tell the federal government to do something no one knows how to do. Fortunately, advances in economic knowledge during the 1930s made it much more likely that the federal government could carry out the responsibility of maintaining full employment. The man who contributed much of this new economic knowledge was John Maynard Keynes, one of the great figures of modern economics, whom we will discuss in some detail in Chapter 9.

Besides maintaining full employment, the government must also maintain a reasonably stable price level. No economy can function well if prices are gyrating wildly. Through its control of the money supply and its decisions regarding expenditures and taxation, the government has considerable impact on the price level, as well as on the level of employment.

Public Goods

As we have indicated, the government provides many public goods. Let's consider the nature of public goods in more detail. One hallmark of a public good is that it can be consumed by one person without diminishing the amount that other people consume of it. Public goods tend to be relatively indivisible: they often come in such large units that they cannot be broken into pieces that can be bought or sold in ordinary markets. Also, once such goods are produced, there often is no way to bar certain citizens from consuming them. Whether or not a citizen contributes toward their cost, he benefits from them. As pointed out in a previous section, this means that the price system cannot be used to handle the production and distribution of such goods.

An obvious example of a public good is a lighthouse. There might be general agreement that the cost of building a particular lighthouse would be more than justified by the benefits (saving of lives, fewer shipwrecks, cheaper transportation). Nonetheless, no firm or person would build and operate such a lighthouse because they could not find any way to charge the ships using the lighthouse for the service. Nor would any single user gain enough from the lighthouse to warrant constructing and operating it. Moreover, voluntary contributions are very unlikely to support such a lighthouse because each user is likely to feel that his contribution will not affect whether or not it is built, and that he will be able to use the lighthouse whether or not he contributes. Consequently, the lighthouse will be established and operated only if the government intervenes.

National defense is another example. The benefits of expenditure on national defense extend to the entire nation. Extension of the benefits of national defense to an additional citizen does not mean that any other citizen gets less of these benefits. Also, there is no way of preventing a citizen from benefiting from them, whether he contributes to their cost or not. Thus there is no way to use the price system to provide for national defense. Since it is a public good, national defense must be provided by the government. Similarly with flood control, roads, police and fire protection, public parks, and a host of other such services. In each case, although the people who benefit may not contribute to the costs of these services voluntarily, they may feel better off when the government taxes them to make such services possible.

Other services, such as education and health, can be provided by private enterprise on a fee basis, but much of the population feels that the government should intervene to see to it that everyone, regardless of income level, receives a certain minimum amount of education and health care. Free public education has, of course, been an important and conspicuous part of American society, and in recent years the government has begun to play a more significant role in the health field. Both in health and education, an important argument for government intervention has been that the social benefits of these services exceed the private benefits. However, opponents of such intervention assert that it is paternalistic and that it results in less efficiency in education and health. This is an area of controversy.

Essentially, deciding how much to produce of a public good is a political decision. The citizens of the United States elect senators and congressmen who decide how much should be spent on national defense or education, and how it should be spent. These elected representatives are responsive to special-interest groups, as well as to the people as a whole. Many special-interest groups lobby hard for the production of certain public goods. For example, an alliance of military and industrial groups presses for increased defense expenditures, and other interested groups promote expenditures on highways, health, education, and other functions.

The tax system is used to pay for the production of public goods. In effect, the government says to each citizen, "Fork over a certain amount of money to pay for the expenses incurred by the government." The amount a particular citizen is assessed may depend on his income (as in the income tax), the value of all or specific types of his property (as in the property tax), the amount he spends on certain types of goods and services (as in the sales tax), or on still other criteria. Much more will be said about the tax system in a later section of this chapter and in the next chapter.

Externalities

It is generally agreed that the government should encourage the production of goods and services that entail external economies and discourage the production of those that entail external diseconomies. Take the pollution of air and water. When a firm or individual dumps wastes into the water or air, other firms or individuals often must pay all or part of the cost of putting the water or air back into a usable condition. Thus the disposal of these wastes entails external diseconomies. Unless the government prohibits certain kinds of pollution, or enforces air and water quality standards, or charges polluters in accord with the amount of waste they dump into the environment, there will be socially undesirable levels of pollution.

To see how such externalities affect the social desirability of the output of a competitive industry, consider Figure 5.1, where the industry's demand and supply curves are contained in the top panel. As shown there, the equilibrium output of the industry is OQ_0. If the industry results in no external economies or diseconomies, this is likely to be the socially optimal output. But what if the industry results in external diseconomies, such as the pollution described above? Then the industry's supply curve, SS', does not fully reflect the true social costs of producing the product. The supply curve that reflects these social costs is S_1S_1', which, as shown in the middle panel of Figure 5.1, lies to the left of SS'. The optimal output of the good is OQ_1, which is less than the competitive output, OQ_0.

What can the government do to correct the situation? There are a variety of ways that it can intervene to reduce the industry's output from OQ_0 to OQ_1. For example, it can impose

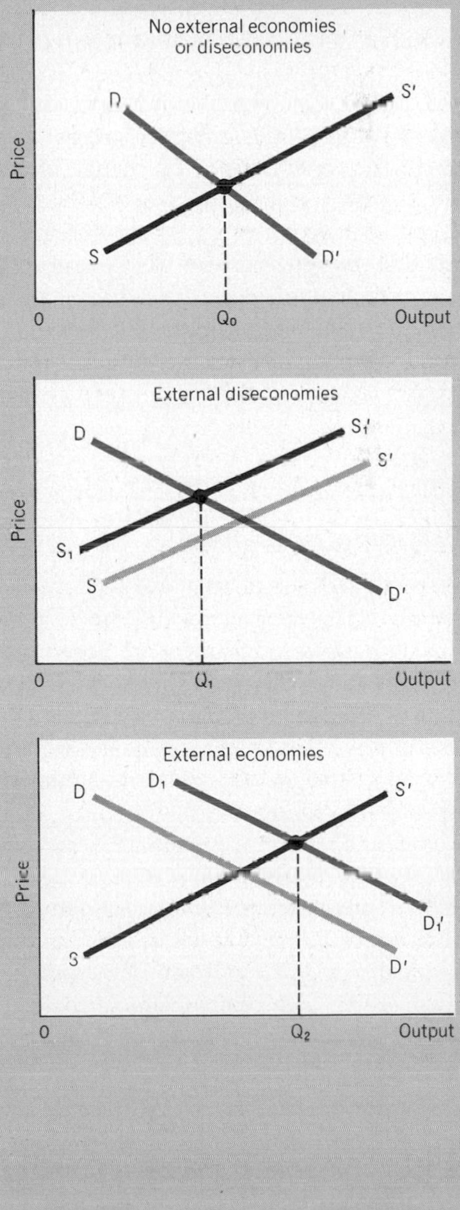

Figure 5.1
Effect of External Economies and Diseconomies on the Optimal Output of a Competitive Industry
The optimal output is OQ_0 if neither external economies nor diseconomies are present. If there are external diseconomies, S_1S_1' reflects the true social costs of producing the product, and OQ_1 is the optimal output. If there are external economies, D_1D_1' reflects the true social benefits of producing the product, and OQ_2 is the optimal output.

taxes on the industry, as we shall see in Chapter 6. If these taxes are of the right type and amount, they will result in the desired reduction of output.

What if the industry results in external economies? For example, what if the manufacture of one industrial product makes it cheaper to produce other products? Then the industry's demand curve, DD', underestimates the true social benefits of producing the product. The demand curve that reflects these social benefits correctly is D_1D_1', which, as shown in the bottom panel of Figure 5.1, lies to the right of DD'. The optimal output of the good is OQ_2, which is greater than the competitive output, OQ_0.

As in the case where the industry results in external diseconomies, the government can intervene in various ways to change the industry's output. But in this case, the object is to increase, not decrease, its output. To accomplish this, the government can, among other things, grant subsidies to the industry. If they are of the right type and amount, they can be used to increase the industry's output from OQ_0 to OQ_2.

Government Production and "Creeping Socialism"

As we pointed out in previous sections, it is generally accepted that, in the case of public goods and goods where there are very important externalities, the government should intervene to influence their production. But this does not mean that the government must actually produce the good in question. On the contrary, *the government does not produce most of the goods and services it provides.* For example, the federal government supports over ½ of the research and development carried out in the United States, but only about 30 percent of federally supported research and development is carried out in government laboratories. The rest is carried out by firms and universities working under government contracts.[6]

Some of the areas in which our government actually becomes involved in the production of goods and services are familiar. In the United States the post office, the airports, and many water, gas, and electric companies are publicly owned and operated. In these cases it would be inefficient to have many producers, and since competition is not feasible, the courts have held that such industries must be publicly owned or regulated. But there is no very clear line between them and other industries that have not been publicly owned. For example, many other countries have publicly owned telephone, telegraph, railroad, airline, and broadcasting industries. These industries are not under public ownership in the United States for historical and cultural reasons, as well as because the feeling exists that public ownership tends to result in too much bureaucracy and inefficiency.

For many years, this country has been suspicious of anything smacking of "creeping socialism." As we explained in Chapter 3, socialism means government ownership and operation of plants, farms, and mines. Clearly, *there has been little movement toward public ownership in the United States,* despite occasional cries to the contrary on the hustings and in the press. Perhaps the most important and controversial area where government ownership has been extended appreciably in the last 40 years has been in electric power. During the administration of Franklin D. Roosevelt, the Tennessee Valley Authority, Bonneville Dam, and Hoover Dam, among others, were established. But this was hardly a widespread thrust toward public ownership—and it took place several decades ago.

However, although there has been little

[6] Edwin Mansfield, "Federal Support of R and D Activities in the Private Sector," *Priorities and Efficiency in Federal Research and Development,* Joint Economic Committee of Congress, 1976.

movement toward government ownership and operation, *there has been a tendency in certain fields for the boundaries between the private sector and the public sector to become extremely blurred.* Particularly in the field of defense, it is difficult to know how to categorize some organizations. To what extent is a firm like Lockheed Aircraft Corporation really part of the private sector? Although it is privately owned, most of its output (92 percent in 1971) goes to a single customer—the government. Much of its supply of tools is provided by the government, and government officials play an important role in influencing its decisions, auditing its books, regulating its profits, and so forth. The same tendency toward blurred boundaries between the private and public sectors has occurred in atomic energy, space exploration, and other areas. To a certain extent, it appears that—in the words of Don Price, dean of Harvard's Kennedy School of Government—the government "has learned to socialize without assuming ownership."[7] This blurring of the boundaries between the private and public sectors is an important recent development, with repercussions on many aspects of our daily life.

Size and Nature of Government Activities

How Big Is the Government?

Up to this point, we have been concerned primarily with the reasons why the government must intervene in our economy—and the types of role it should play—but we have made little or no attempt to describe its role in quantita-

[7] Don Price, *The Scientific Estate,* Cambridge, Mass.: Belknap Press, 1965, p. 43.

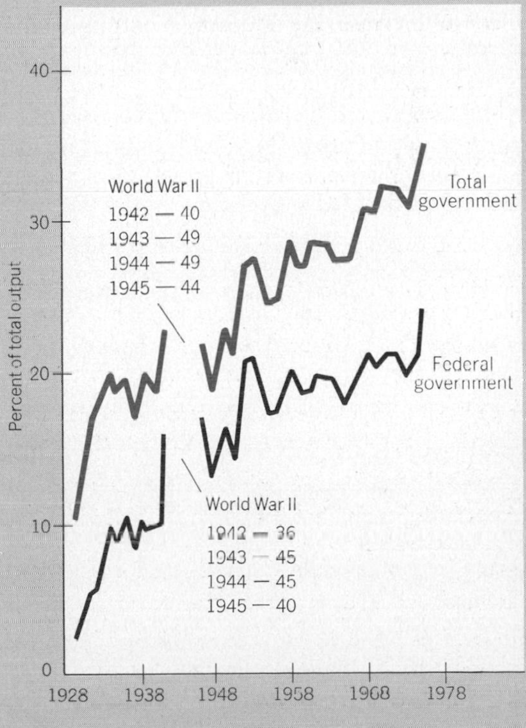

Figure 5.2
Government Spending as a Percent of Total Output, United States.
Government expenditures—federal, state, and local—totaled about $525 billion in 1975. These expenditures, which include transfer payments, have grown more rapidly than total output in this period.

tive terms. It is time now to turn to some of the relevant facts. One useful measure of the extent of the government's role in the American economy is the size of government expenditures, both in absolute terms and as a percent of our nation's total output.

The sum total of government expenditures—federal, state, and local—was about $525 billion in 1975. Since our nation's total output was about $1.5 trillion, this means that government expenditures were about ⅓ of our total output. The ratio of government expenditures to total output in the United States has not always been this large, as Figure 5.2 shows. In 1929, the ratio was about 10 percent, as contrasted with about 35 percent in 1975. (Of course, the ratio of government spending to total output is smaller now than during World War II, but in a wartime economy, one would expect this ratio to be abnormally high.)

There are many reasons why government expenditures have grown so much faster than total output. Three of these are particularly important. First, the United States did not maintain anything like the kind of military force in pre-World-War-II days that it does now. In earlier days, when weapons were relatively simple and cheap, and when we viewed our military and political responsibilities much more narrowly than we do now, our military budget was relatively small. The cost of being a superpower in the days of nuclear weaponry is high by any standards. Second, there has been a long-term increase in the demand for the services provided by government, like more and better schooling, more extensive highways, more complete police and fire protection, and so forth. As incomes rise, people want more of these services. Third, ***government transfer payments***—payments in return for no products or services—have grown substantially. For example, various types of welfare payments have increased markedly. Since transfer payments do not entail any reallocation of resources from private to public goods, but a transfer of income from one private citizen or group to another, Figure 5.2 is, in some respects, an overstatement of the role of the public sector.

Table 5.1
Taxes as Percentages of Total Output, 1970

Country	Percentage
Sweden	43
France	39
West Germany	35
United Kingdom	35
Canada	32
United States	32
Japan	21
India	15
Nigeria	9

When in Table 5.1 we compare the size of government spending in the United States (relative to total output) with that in other countries, we learn that the governments of Sweden, France, West Germany, and the United Kingdom spend more—as a percent of total output—than we do. In part, of course, this is because of the extensive welfare programs in Sweden and the United Kingdom. It is interesting, however, that, despite our huge military programs, we do not spend more (relative to total output) than these countries. It is also noteworthy that poor countries like Nigeria—ones with little industry and at a relatively early stage of economic development—spend the least on government services. This is understandable, since such countries must devote more of their output to the basic necessities of life. In many cases, as we saw in Chapter 1, they have a difficult time merely feeding their populations.

What the Federal, State, and Local Governments Spend Money On

There are three levels of government in the

United States federal, state, and local. The state governments spend the least, while the federal government spends the most. This was not always the case. Before World War I, the local governments spent more than the federal government. In those days, the federal government did not maintain the large military establishment it does now, nor did it engage in the many programs in health, education, welfare, and other areas that it currently does. Figure 5.2 shows that federal spending is now a much larger percentage of the total than it was 40 years ago. Table 5.2 shows how the federal government spends its money. *About ⅓ of the federal expenditures goes for defense and other items connected with international relations and national security. About ½ goes for welfare (and other income security) programs, health, and education. The rest goes to support farm, transportation, housing, and other such programs, as well as to run Congress, the courts, and the executive branch of the federal government.*

Table 5.2
Federal Expenditures, Fiscal 1977.

Purpose	Amount (billions of dollars)	Percent of total
National defense	101	26
International affairs and finance	7	2
Veterans' benefits	17	4
General science, space, and technology	4	1
Agriculture	2	[b]
Education, training, employment, and social services	17	4
Health	34	9
Natural resources, environment, and energy	14	4
Commerce and transportation	17	4
Community and regional development	6	1
Interest	41	11
General government	3	1
Income security	137	35
Law enforcement and justice	3	1
Revenue sharing	7	2
Allowances	2	1
Offsetting receipts	−19	−5
Total[a]	394	100

[a] Because of rounding errors, the figures may not sum to the totals.
[b] Less than ½ of 1 percent.
Source: The Budget in Brief, 1977. These are estimates made in 1976.

What about the local and state governments? On what do they spend their money? Table 5.3 shows that *the biggest expenditure of the state and local governments is on schools.* After the end of World War II, these expenditures increased greatly because of the baby boom—the increase in the number of school-age children. Traditionally, schools in the United States have been a responsibility of local governments—cities and towns. *State governments spend most of their money on highways; welfare,*

Table 5.3
Expenditures of State and Local Governments, United States, 1973

Type of expenditure	Amount (billions of dollars)	Percent of total
Education	93.0	41.7
Highways	21.6	9.7
Natural resources	3.4	1.5
Health and hospitals	14.9	6.7
Public welfare	31.4	14.1
Housing and urban renewal	3.3	1.5
Interest on debt	6.8	3.0
Other	48.3	21.8
Total	222.7	100.0

Source: Statistical Abstract of the United States.

Urban Fiscal Crisis: The Case of New York City

On June 16, 1975, *Time* magazine's cover read, "How New York Went Broke." It was hard for people (both New Yorkers and others) to believe, but New York City was in danger of defaulting on its obligations. It had to borrow huge sums of money to meet its expenses, pay its workers, and refinance its mammoth debt—and the banks were no longer willing to lend the city the money. How did New York get into this fix? First, it has taken responsibility for many services and programs not undertaken by most other major cities, and its pays relatively high wages (and fringe benefits) and has a large municipal work force. (In 1973, its per capita expenditures were about $1,400, as opposed to about $400 in Los Angeles, Philadelphia, and Detroit.) Second, as the poor have moved in and the rich have moved out, New York, like many large cities, has not been able to increase its taxes commensurately. Third, instead of bringing expenditures into better balance with revenues, the city resorted to various kinds of accounting sleight-of-hand to make it appear that its budget was closer to a balance than in fact it was. By 1975, the city had borrowed so much money that about 17 percent of its budget went for debt service—and the banks were unwilling to lend any more.

In response to the crisis, state and city officials established the Municipal Assistance Corporation (called "Big Mac") to convert some of the city's short-term debt into long-term bonds.* But despite a valiant effort on the part of "Big Mac," investors were unwilling to buy the required amount of such bonds. In September 1975, when it appeared that New York City would be unable to meet its financial obligations, the New York state legislature created an Emergency Financial Control Board to impose budgetary reform on the city. At the same time, the state helped the city meet its most pressing obligations. This put the state's financial position in considerable jeopardy and many observers claimed that, if New York City defaulted (that is, if it failed to pay its debts when due), it would not be long before New York State defaulted too.

Both city and state officials petitioned the federal government for help. They pointed out that, if the city or state defaulted, this would make it difficult, if not impossible, for many other local governments throughout the nation to borrow money. Both President Gerald Ford and Secretary of the Treasury William Simon replied that it was a local matter, and that it would be improper for the federal government to intervene. However, in October 1975, Simon softened his stand a bit, saying that if the state as well as the city were forced to default, "that would add a new dimension to the problem that would require close scrutiny."

Finally, in November 1975, a financial package was put together by Governor Hugh Carey of New York, some of the major banks which held the city's debt, the unions of municipal employees, the state legislature, and President Ford. Its major provisions were as follows: First, the pension funds of the municipal employees agreed to purchase $2.5 billion in city debt. Second, the banks agreed to refinance $1 billion of the city's maturing notes (which are short term debt). Third, there was a moratorium on the payment of $1.6 billion in maturing city notes. (Holders of these notes could exchange them for long-term bonds issued by "Big Mac," or they could hold them and receive 6 percent interest, but they could not get their principal for three years and perhaps longer.) Fourth, New York City taxes were increased by $200 million per year. Fifth, New York state agreed to advance the city $800 million. Sixth, President Ford asked the Congress to approve a loan of $2.3 billion to the city. This loan was to enable the city to get past seasonal problems in matching income with outgo, and was supposed to be repaid at the end of each year.

In November 1976, this financial package came apart when New York's highest court ruled that the moratorium on payment of $1.6 billion in notes was illegal. According to this court, it was an unconstitutional avoidance of the fact that the city owed the money and didn't pay it when due. How New York City will surmount its financial problems is by no means obvious, even to its highest officials. But, regardless of how it gets through its short-term problems, two things are clear. First, investors will never again look on municipal notes and bonds with the same confidence that they did in the past. Second, New York City will have to walk on a financial tightrope for some time to come.

The extent to which the city will continue to impose cutbacks on its services will depend, of course, on the behavior of the Carter administration. Many New Yorkers hope that President Carter and the Congress will help the city out of its fiscal predicament. Only time will tell how much aid of this sort will be forthcoming.

* Basically, a bond is an IOU issued either by a private or public entity. More will be said about bonds in Chapter 7.

old age, and unemployment benefits; and providing help to localities to cover the cost of education, as well as supporting education directly. In addition, the local and state governments support hospitals, redevelopment programs, and courts, police, and fire departments.

Table 5.4
Federal Receipts, by Tax, Fiscal 1977

Type of tax	Amount (billions of dollars)	Percent of total
Personal income tax	154	40
Corporation income tax	50	14
Employment taxes	113	32
Excise taxes	18	5
Estate and gift taxes	6	2
Other revenues	11	3
Total[a]	351	100

[a] Because of rounding errors, the figures may not sum to the totals.
Source: The Budget in Brief, 1977. These are estimates made in 1976.

Changes in View of Government Responsibilities

We have already seen that government expenditures in the United States have grown considerably, both in absolute amount and as a percentage of our total output. It must be recognized that this growth in government expenditure has been part of a general trend in the United States toward a different view of the government's role. Two hundred years ago, it was not uncommon for people to believe in the slogan "That government governs best which governs least." There was considerable suspicion of government interference and meddling, freedom was the watchword, and governments were viewed as potential tyrants. In the nineteenth century, the United States prospered mightily under this *laissez-faire* system, but gradually—and not without considerable protest—the nation began to interpret the role of the government more broadly.

Responding to the dangers of noncompetitive markets, states were given the power to regulate public utilities and railroads. The Interstate Commerce Commission was established in 1887 to regulate railroads operating across state lines; and the Sherman Antitrust Act was passed in 1890 to curb monopoly and promote competition. To help control recurring business fluctuations and financial panics, banking and finance were regulated. In 1913, the Federal Reserve System was established as a central bank controlling the member commercial banks. In 1933, the Federal Deposit Insurance Corporation was established to insure bank deposits. And in 1934, the Securities and Exchange Commission was established to watch over the financial markets. Responding to the "buyer-beware" attitudes of unscrupulous and careless sellers, the Pure Food and Drug Act was passed by Congress in 1906 to insure proper quality for drugs and food.

In addition, the government's role in the fields of labor and welfare expanded considerably. For example, in the 1930s, minimum wage laws were enacted, old-age pensions and unemployment insurance were established, and the government became an important force in collective bargaining and labor relations. Furthermore, the power of government has been used increasingly to insure that citizens will not fall below a certain economic level. Food-stamp programs and programs that provide aid to dependent children have been established. *In general, the broad trend in the United States in the past century has been for the government to be used to a greater and greater extent to achieve social objectives.*

Recall from your study of American history the programs of Theodore Roosevelt, Franklin D. Roosevelt, John F. Kennedy, and Lyndon

B. Johnson. Although they were quite different sorts of presidents faced with quite different sorts of situations, they all had one thing in common: they promoted a broader view of government responsibilities. Theodore Roosevelt's "Square Deal," Franklin D. Roosevelt's "New Deal," John F. Kennedy's "New Frontier," and Lyndon B. Johnson's "Great Society" all extended government responsibilities. Some of these extensions were highly controversial at the time. For example, the ill-feeling generated by FDR's "wild-eyed schemes" is legendary. Yet, when the Republicans took office subsequently, these schemes were not repudiated. This has been the typical pattern. Although the rate at which government involvement has grown has depended heavily on who was in power, neither political party has reversed the direction of change. As you would expect, conservatives view this trend with suspicion and alarm, while liberals view it with favor and satisfaction. Your own view will depend inevitably on your own political beliefs and preferences.

What the Federal, State, and Local Governments Receive in Taxes

To get the money to cover most of the expenditures discussed in previous sections, governments collect taxes from individuals and firms. As Table 5.4 shows, at the federal level the personal income tax is the biggest single money raiser. It brings in about ⅖ of the tax revenue collected by the federal government. The next most important taxes at the federal level are the Social Security, payroll, and employment taxes, and the corporation income tax. Other important taxes are excise taxes—levied on the sale of tobacco, liquor, imports, and certain other items—and death and gift taxes. (Even when the Grim Reaper shows up, the Tax Man is not far behind.)

At the local level, on the other hand, the most important form of taxation and source of revenue is the property tax (see Table 5.5). This is a tax levied primarily on real estate. Other important local taxes—although dwarfed

Table 5.5
State and Local Tax Revenues, by Source, 1973

Source	State: Revenues (billions of dollars)	State: Percent of total	Local: Revenues (billions of dollars)	Local: Percent of total
General sales tax	20	29	3	6
Property tax	1	2	44	83
Selective excise taxes	17	25	2	3
Personal income tax	16	23	2	5
Corporate income tax	5	8	—	—
Motor vehicle licenses	3	5	—	—
Estate and gift taxes	1	2	—	
Other taxes	4	6	2	3
Total[a]	68	100	53	100

[a] Because of rounding errors, the figures may not sum to the totals.
Source: Statistical Abstract of the United States.

in importance by the property tax—are local sales taxes and local income taxes. Many cities—for example, New York City—levy a sales tax, equal to a certain percent—4 percent in New York City—of the value of each retail sale. The tax is simply added on to the amount charged the customer. Also, many cities—for example, Philadelphia and Pittsburgh—levy an income (or wage) tax on their residents and even on people who work in the city but live outside it. At the state level, sales (and excise) taxes are the biggest money raisers, followed by income taxes and highway user taxes. Highway user taxes include taxes on gasoline and license fees for vehicles and drivers. Often they exceed the amount spent on roads, and the balance is used for a variety of nonhighway uses.

The Role of Government in American Agriculture

Thus far, we have been discussing the government's role in the American economy in rather general terms. Now we need to consider in some detail a particular example of the economic programs carried out by our government. The government's farm programs are a logical choice, because they illustrate the usefulness of the supply-and-demand analysis presented in the previous chapter. It is important to recognize at the outset that these farm programs are not being held up as a representative sample of what the government does. There are a host of other government economic programs—poverty programs, urban programs, defense programs, research programs, education programs, transportation programs, fiscal programs, monetary programs, and many more. Many of these programs will be discussed at some point in this book.

Agriculture is an enormously important sector of the American economy. Even though its size has been decreasing steadily—and this contraction has been going on for many decades—agriculture still employs about 4 million Americans. Its importance, moreover, cannot be measured entirely by its size. You need only think about how difficult it would be to get along without food to see the strategic role agriculture plays in our economic life. Also, when it comes to technological change, agriculture is one of the most progressive parts of the American economy. Output per man-hour has grown more rapidly there than in any other major sector of the American economy, in considerable part because of government-financed agricultural research programs. The efficiency of American agriculture is admired throughout the world.

Nonetheless, it is widely acknowledged that American agriculture has had serious problems. Perhaps the clearest indication of these problems is shown by a comparison of per capita income of American farmers with per capita income among the rest of the population. Until the past few years, it is clear that farm incomes have tended to be much lower than nonfarm incomes. For example, in 1970, per capita income on the farms was about 20 percent below that for the nonfarm population. Moreover, a large proportion of the rural population is poor. Thus the National Advisory Commission on Rural Poverty found that "rural poverty is so widespread, and so acute, as to be a national disgrace."[8] Of course, this does not mean that all farmers are poor: on the contrary, many do very well indeed. But a large percentage of the nation's farmers are poor by any standard.

This farm problem is nothing new. During the first two decades of the twentieth century, farmers enjoyed relatively high prices and relatively high incomes. But in 1920, the country experienced a sharp depression that jolted agri-

[8] National Advisory Committee on Rural Poverty, *The People Left Behind,* Washington, D.C., 1967, part of which is reprinted in E. Mansfield, *Economics: Readings, Issues, and Cases.*

culture as well as the rest of the economy. Whereas the Roaring Twenties saw a recovery and boom in the nonfarm sector of the economy, agriculture did not recover as completely, and the 1930s were dreadful years; the Great Depression resulted in a sickening decline in farm prices and farm incomes. World War II brought prosperity to agriculture, but in the postwar period, farm incomes continually have been well below nonfarm incomes. All in all, agriculture has been experiencing difficulties for several decades. In 1973, as we shall see, prosperity began to return to the farms. How long-lived it will be is anyone's guess.

Causes of the Farm Problem

In Chapter 1, we claimed that relatively simple economic models are of considerable use in understanding important public and private problems. To back up this claim, we will apply the simple models of market behavior presented in the previous chapter—the models involving market demand curves and market supply curves—to explain the basic causes of the problems that, until 1973, besieged agriculture. Let's start with the market demand curve for farm products. If you think about it for a moment, you will agree that this market demand curve must have two important characteristics. First, its shape must reflect the fact that food is a necessity and that the quantity demanded will not vary much with the price of food. Second, the market demand curve for food is unlikely to shift to the right very much as per capita income rises, because consumption of food per capita faces natural biological and other limitations.

Next, consider the market supply curve for farm products. Again, you should be aware of two important characteristics of this market supply curve. First, the quantity of farm products supplied tends to be relatively insensitive to price, because the farmers have only limited control over their output. (Weather, floods, insects, and other such factors are very important.) Second, because of the rapid technological change emphasized in the previous section, the market supply curve has been shifting markedly and rapidly to the right.

If you understand these simple characteristics of the market demand curve and market supply curve for farm products, it is no trick at all to understand why we had the sort of farm problem just described. Figure 5.3 shows the market demand and market supply curves for farm products at various points in time. As you would expect, the market demand curve for farm products shifts rather slowly to the right

Figure 5.3
Shifts over Time in Market Demand and Supply Curves for Farm Products
The market demand curve has shifted rather slowly to the right (from *DD'* to D_1D_1' to D_2D_2'), whereas the market supply curve has shifted rapidly to the right (from *SS'* to S_1S_1' to S_2S_2'), with the result that the equilibrium price has declined (from *OP* to OP_1 to OP_2).

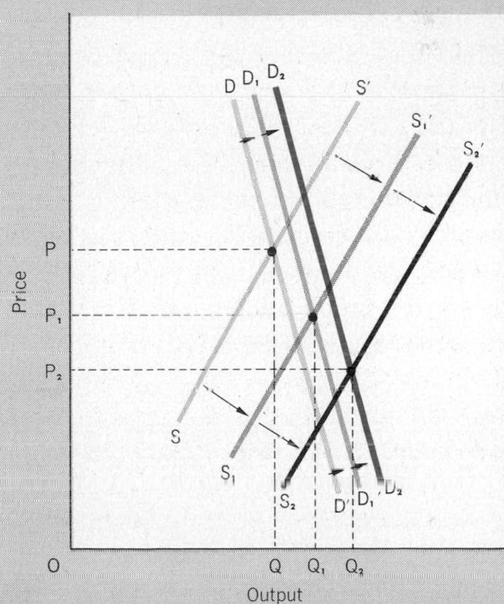

as incomes (and population) grow over time. Specifically, the market demand curve shifted from DD' in the first period to D_1D_1' in the second period to D_2D_2' in the third period. On the other hand, the market supply curve for farm products shifted rapidly to the right as technology improved over time. Specifically, it shifted from SS' in the first period to S_1S_1' in the second period to S_2S_2' in the third period.

What was the consequence of these shifts in the market demand and supply curves for food products? Clearly, *the equilibrium price of food products fell* (*relative to other products*). Specifically, the equilibrium price fell from OP to OP_1 to OP_2 in Figure 5.3. This price decrease was, of course, a large part of the farm problem. If we correct for changes in the general level of prices (which have tended to rise over time), there was, until 1973, a declining trend in farm prices. That is, agricultural prices generally fell, relative to other prices, in the last 60 years. Moreover, *given this fall in farm prices, farm incomes tended to fall, because, although lower prices were associated with greater amounts sold, the reduction in price was much greater than the increase in quantity sold,* as shown in Figure 5.3.[9]

Thus the simple model of market behavior described in the previous chapter makes it possible to explain the fact that, until recently, farm prices and farm incomes have tended to fall in the United States. Certainly there is nothing mysterious about these trends. Given the nature and characteristics of the market demand curve and market supply curve for farm products, our simple model shows that these trends are as much to be expected as parades on the Fourth of July.

However, one additional fact must be noted to understand the farm problem: *people and nonhuman resources have been relatively slow to move out of agriculture in response to these trends.* Recall from the previous chapter that the price system uses such trends—lower prices and lower incomes—to signal producers that they should use their resources elsewhere. Farmers have been loath to move out of agriculture (even though they often could make more money elsewhere)—and this was a primary cause of the farm problem that existed over most of the past 40 years. If more people and resources had left farming, agricultural prices and incomes would have risen, and ultimately farm incomes would have come closer to nonfarm incomes. (Poor education and color were, of course, significant barriers to migration.)

Nonetheless, even though farmers have been slow to move out of agriculture, they have left the farm in the long run. For example, in 1930 the farm population was about 30 million, or 25 percent of the total population; in 1950, it was about 23 million, or 15 percent of the total population; and in 1974, it was about 9 million, or 4 percent of the total population. Thus the price system has had its way. Resources have been moving out of agriculture in response to the signals and pressures of the price system. This movement of people and nonhuman resources unquestionably has contributed to greater efficiency and production for the nation as a whole. But during most of the past 40 years, we have continued to have a "surplus" of farmers—and this has been the root of the farm problem.

Government Aid to Agriculture

Traditionally, farmers have had a disproportionately large influence in Congress; and faced with declining economic fortunes, they appealed to the government for help. They extolled the virtues of rural life, emphasized that agriculture is a competitive industry, and claimed that it was unfair for their prices to fall relative to the prices they have had to pay. In

[9] The amount farmers receive is the amount they sell times the price. Thus, in Figure 5.3, the amount farmers receive in income is $OP \times OQ$ in the first period, $OP_1 \times OQ_1$ in the second period, and $OP_2 \times OQ_2$ in the third period. Clearly, since the price is decreasing much more rapidly than the quantity is increasing, farm incomes are falling.

addition, they pointed out that the movement of resources out of agriculture has entailed large human costs, since this movement, although beneficial to the nation as a whole, has been traumatic for the farm population. For reasons of this sort, they argued that the government should help farmers; and in particular, that the government should act to bolster farm prices and farm incomes.

Their voices were heard. In the Agricultural Adjustment Act of 1933, the Congress announced the concept of parity as the major objective of American farm policy. This concept acquired great importance—and must be clearly understood. Put in its simplest terms, the concept of ***parity*** says that a farmer should be able to exchange a given quantity of his output for as much in the way of nonfarm goods and services as he could at some time in the past. For example, if a farmer could take a bushel of wheat to market in 1912 and get enough money to buy a pair of gloves, today he should be able to get enough money for a bushel of wheat to buy a pair of gloves.

To see what the concept of parity implies for farm prices, suppose that the price of gloves triples. Obviously, if parity is to be maintained, the price of wheat must triple too. Thus the concept of parity implies that farm prices must increase at the same rate as the prices of the goods and services farmers buy. Of course, farmers buy lots of things besides gloves, so in actual practice the parity price of wheat or other farm products is determined by the changes over time in the average price of all the goods and services farmers buy.

Two major points should be noted about parity. First, to use this concept, one must agree on some base period, such as 1912 in the example above, during which the relationship of farm to nonfarm prices is regarded as equitable. Obviously, the higher farm prices were relative to nonfarm prices in the base period, the higher farm prices will be in subsequent periods if parity is maintained. It is interesting to note that 1910–14 was used for many years as the base period. Since this was a period of relatively high farm prices and of agricultural prosperity, the farm bloc must have wielded considerable political clout on this issue. Second, note that the concept of parity is an ethical, not a scientific proposition. It states what the relative economic position of a bushel of wheat ought to be—or more precisely, it states one particular view of what the relative economic position of a bushel of wheat should be. Based on purely scientific considerations, there is no way to prove (or disprove) this proposition, since it is based on one's values and political preferences. Using the terminology of Chapter 2, it is a proposition in normative, not positive economics.

Price Supports and Surplus Controls

During the four decades up to 1973, the concept of parity was the cornerstone of a system of government price supports. In many cases, the government did not support farm prices at the full 100 percent of parity. For example, Congress may have enacted a bill saying that the secretary of agriculture could establish a price of wheat, corn, cotton, or some other product that is between 65 and 90 percent of parity. But whatever the exact level of the price supports, the idea behind them was perfectly simple: it was to maintain farm prices above the level that would result in a free market.

Using the simple supply-and-demand model developed in the previous chapter, we can see more clearly the effects of these price supports. The situation is shown in Figure 5.4. A support price, OP', was set by the government. Since this support price was above the equilibrium price, OP, the public bought *less* of farm products (OQ_2 rather than OQ) and paid a *higher* price for them. Farmers gained from the price supports, since the amount they received for their crop under the price support was equal to $OP' \times OQ_1$, a greater amount than what they would have received in a free market, which was $OP \times OQ$.

Note, however, that since the support price exceeded the equilibrium price, the quantity supplied of the farm product, OQ_1, exceeded the quantity demanded, OQ_2. That is, *there was a surplus of the farm product in question,* which the government had to purchase, since no one else would. These surpluses were an embarrassment, both economically and politically. They showed that society's scarce resources were being utilized to produce products consumers simply did not want at existing prices. Moreover the cost of storing these surpluses was very large indeed: in some years, these storage costs alone hit the $1 billion mark.

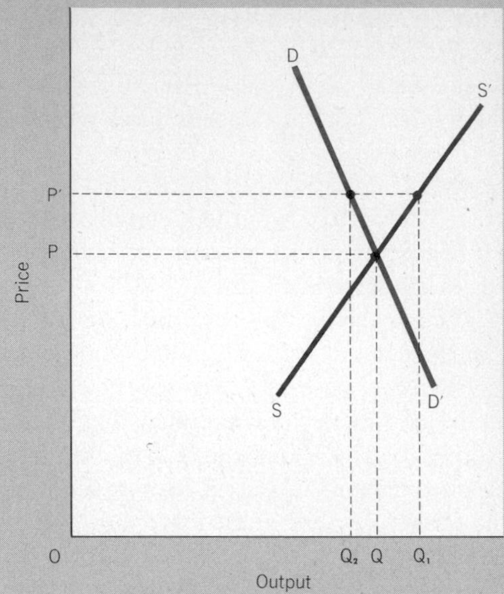

Figure 5.4
Effects of Farm Price Support Program
The support price, OP', is above the equilibrium price, OP, so the public buys OQ_2, farmers supply OQ_1 units of output, and the government buys the difference ($OQ_1 - OQ_2$).

To help reduce these surpluses, the government followed two basic strategies. First, it tried to restrict output of farm products. In particular, the government established an acreage allotment program, which said that farmers had to limit the number of acres they planted in order to get price supports on their crops. The Department of Agriculture estimated how much of each product would be demanded by buyers (other than the government) at the support price, and tried to cut back the total acreage planted with this crop to the point where the quantity supplied equaled the quantity demanded. These output restrictions did not eliminate the surpluses, because farmers managed to increase the yields from acreage they were allowed to plant, but undoubtedly they reduced the surpluses. With these restrictions, the situation was as shown in Figure 5.5, where OQ_3 was the total output that could be grown on the acreage that could be planted with the crop. Because of the imposition of this output control, the surplus—which the government had to purchase—was reduced from $(OQ_1 - OQ_2)$ to $(OQ_3 - OQ_2)$. Farmers continued to benefit from price supports because the amount they received for their crop—$OP' \times OQ_3$—was still greater than they would have received in a free market, because the amount demanded of farm products was not very sensitive to their price.

Second, the government tried to shift the demand curve for farm products to the right. An effort was made to find new uses for various farm products. Also, various antipoverty programs, such as the food-stamp program, used our farm surpluses to help the poor. In addition, the government tried to expand the export markets for American farm products. Western Europe and Japan increased their demand for food, and the Communist countries purchased our farm products to offset their own agricultural deficiencies. Moreover, the less developed countries were permitted by

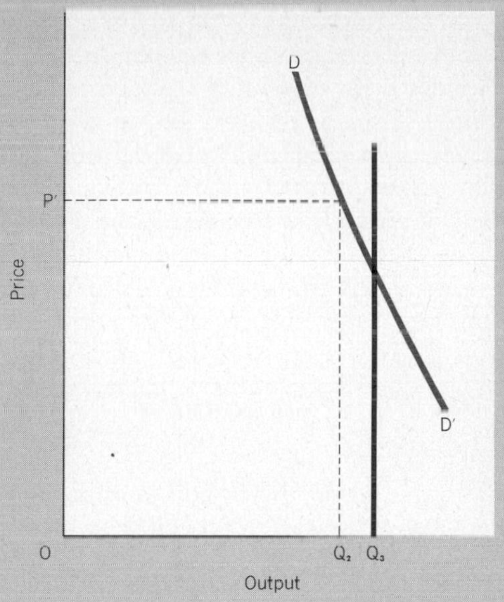

Figure 5.5
Effects of Price Supports and Output Restrictions
The government restricts output to OQ_3, with the result that it buys (OQ_3 — OQ_2) units of output.

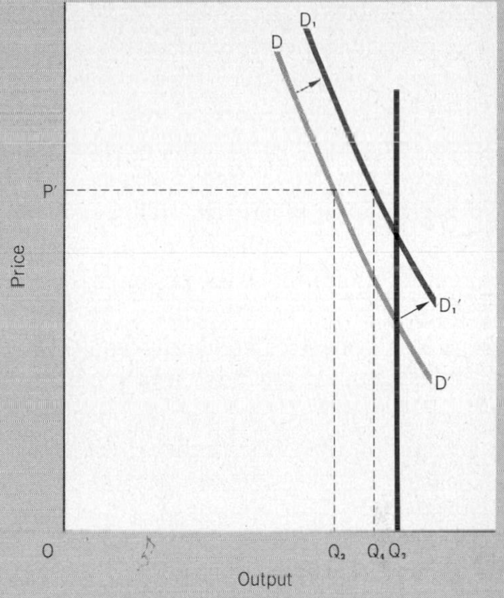

Figure 5.6
Effects of Price Supports, Output Restrictions, and a Shift to the Right in the Demand Curve for Farm Products
By shifting the demand curve from *DD′* to D_1D_1', the goverment reduces the surplus from (OQ_3 — OQ_2) to (OQ_3—OQ_4) units of output.

Public Law 480 to buy our farm products with their own currencies, rather than dollars. The result was a reduction in farm surpluses, as shown in Figure 5.6. Since the market demand curve for farm products shifted from *DD′* to D_1D_1', the surplus was reduced from ($OQ_3 - OQ_2$) to ($OQ_3 - OQ_4$). Because of these demand-augmenting and output-restricting measures, surpluses during the late 1960s and early 1970s were considerably smaller than they were during the late 1950s and early 1960s.

The 1973 Farm Bill and More Recent Developments

In 1973, farm prices increased markedly, due partly to very great increases in foreign demand for American agricultural products. This increase in foreign demand was due partly to poor harvests in the Soviet Union, Australia, Argentina, and elsewhere, as well as to devaluations of the dollar. (In 1972-73, the Soviet Union alone bought over $1 billion of grain—on terms that provoked considerable controversy in the United States.) As a result, farm incomes reached very high levels, farm surpluses disappeared, and for the first time in 30 years the government was trying to stimulate farm production rather than restrict it.

Taking advantage of this new climate, Congress passed a new farm bill which ended price supports. This bill, the Agriculture and Consumer Protection Act of 1973, aimed at reducing government involvement in agriculture and at a return to freer markets. Specifically, agricultural prices were allowed to fluctuate freely in accord with supply and demand. However, the government makes cash payments to farmers if prices fall below certain "target" levels established by the law. These target levels are above the prices that generally prevailed in the past, but they are below the high levels of prices prevailing in 1973.

A program of this kind was originally proposed in 1949 by Charles F. Brannan, who was secretary of agriculture under President Harry Truman. Farm organizations and their supporters in Congress succeeded in killing the proposal. One important reason why it was passed in 1973 was that farm prices were so high. This meant that a program of this sort would cost little or nothing, so long as prices remained above the target levels. However, it must be recognized that, if prices fall back to their pre-1973 levels, this program will be very expensive to the taxpayers.

Besides establishing these new forms of subsidies, the 1973 farm bill limited total subsidy payments to any individual farmer to $20,000 per year. This provision is meant to deal more effectively than did the prior law with the problem of very large subsidies being paid to wealthy farmers. Also, the 1973 law states that whether or not land is taken out of production is at the discretion of the secretary of agriculture. In 1974, Secretary Earl Butz said that none should be taken out of production, and encouraged farmers to produce as much as they wanted. Nonetheless, in 1974, American crop production as a whole suffered its biggest setback in almost 40 years, due primarily to bad weather. Coupled with continued strong foreign demand for farm products, as well as domestic demand, the result was another year of high farm prices.

By 1975, it appeared to many knowledgeable observers that the farm sector no longer was suffering from overcapacity, and that, in this respect at least, an equilibrium had been achieved. However, it is too soon to be at all sure that this is the case. Just as one swallow doesn't make a spring, so a few good years for the farmers may not mean a new era. Nonetheless, it certainly is true that in the mid-1970s, excess agricultural capacity declined, and crop reserves were drawn down. As we have seen, this was a noticeable change from earlier years.

The Wheat Program: A Case Study

To get a better idea of how government programs have worked in agriculture, we will narrow our focus to the case of wheat. In the previous chapter, we described how the price of wheat would be determined in a free market. But the market for wheat has been influenced by government programs for many decades. Let's begin our brief account of the wheat program with the situation after World War II. During the war, a rural political coalition succeeded in getting guarantees of 100 percent of parity price. After the war, there was some movement away from rigid price supports by important government officials, including President Eisenhower's secretary of agriculture, Ezra Taft Benson, who wanted the government to reduce its involvement in the farm economy, both because he felt that the government's programs were not succeeding and because he wanted to see a reversal of "the trend toward government invasion of farm freedoms." [10]

During Secretary Benson's eight years in office (1953–61), there was a chronic mismatch between the quantity supplied and quantity demanded of wheat. Because of rapid advances in agricultural technology, wheat farmers were able to maintain production in the face of seri-

[10] D. Hadwiger, *Federal Wheat Commodity Programs,* Ames: Iowa State University Press, 1970, Chapter 8.

ous droughts, production controls, and moderate reductions in wheat prices. The government was forced to buy up enormous surpluses of wheat. A big issue in the 1950s was whether price supports should remain at the high levels established during World War II. Rural interests, which included commercial wheat farmers, wanted price supports to stay high: specifically, they wanted them to be at least 90 percent of parity. Secretary Benson, on the other hand, wanted to institute flexible support levels so that they could be used to help reduce overproduction. He succeeded in reducing price support levels—as well as in alienating farmers, farm leaders, and many political liberals.

In 1960, with the election of John F. Kennedy as president, Orville Freeman became secretary of agriculture. In contrast to Benson, Secretary Freeman felt that the government should play a major role in American agriculture. Faced with the prospect of continuing large surpluses of wheat, he pushed for great reductions in acreage, which was held at little more than half its postwar high. Also, he urged the export of wheat to the less developed countries, both to help promote their economic growth and to stave off famine. Rather than attempt to maintain 90 percent of parity, Freeman adopted the more modest goal of maintaining 100 percent of parity prices *on the production used for domestic food* (less than half the total crop in the 1960s).

The Cotton-Wheat Act of 1964 established a voluntary wheat-marketing certificate program for 1964 and 1965, later extended with only limited changes to 1969. Under this program, farmers who complied with acreage allotments and agreed to participate in a land-diversion program received price supports, marketing certificates, and payments for land diversion, but farmers who did not comply did not receive benefits. During 1964 to 1969, the price of wheat ranged from about $1.15 to $1.74 per bushel. However, the total price to farmers was more than this, because participants in the wheat program also got direct marketing certificate payments amounting to $.65 per bushel in 1969. During the early 1970s, the wheat program remained conceptually the same, although some modifications were made.[11]

In August 1973, the wheat program, like other agricultural programs, changed drastically. Price supports were ended, and, as we know from the previous section, the government pledged to make cash payments to farmers if the price fell below a certain target level—$2.05 per bushel in 1975. The price of wheat exceeded $4 per bushel in 1973, and was well above the target level. In contrast to previous years, the secretary of agriculture imposed no restrictions on the acreage that wheat farmers could plant in 1974. Given the enormous increase in the demand for American wheat, the emphasis was on expanding, not curtailing production.

Evaluation of Government Farm Programs

It is obviously hard to evaluate the success of the government's farm programs. Farmers will certainly take a different view of price supports and other measures than their city cousins. Nonetheless, from the point of view of the nation as a whole, these farm programs have received considerable criticism. To understand these criticisms, we must hark back to our discussion earlier in this chapter of the proper functions of government, and ask what justification there is for the government's intervening in this way in agriculture. Perhaps the most convincing justification is that the government ought to help the rural poor. As we saw in previous sections, most people agree that the gov

[11] See G. Shepherd and G. Futrell, *Marketing Farm Products*, Ames: Iowa State University Press, 1969, p. 417; and W. Rasmussen and G. Baker, "Programs for Agriculture, 1933–1965," *Agriculture Economics Research*, July 1966.

ernment should redistribute income in this way.

Unfortunately, however, *our farm programs have done little for the farmers most in need of help,* because the amount of money a farmer has gotten from these programs has depended on how much he produced. Thus the big farmer has gotten the lion's share of the subsidies—and he, of course, needed help least. On the other hand, the small farmer, the farmer who is mired most deeply in poverty, has received little from these programs. Recognizing this fact, many observers have pointed out that, if these programs are really aimed at helping the rural poor, it would be more sensible to channel the money to them through direct subsidies, than to finance programs where much of the benefits go to prosperous commercial farmers.

It must also be recognized that *our farm programs have not dealt with the basic causes of the farm problem.* In the past at least, we have had too many people and resources in agriculture. This, as we stressed in previous sections, is why farmers' incomes have tended to be low. Yet the government's farm programs have been directed more toward supporting farm prices and incomes (and stabilizing a sector of the economy that historically has been unstable), rather than toward promoting the needed movement of people and resources out of agriculture. Indeed, some people would say that the government's farm programs have made it more difficult for the necessary adjustments to take place.

Given these defects, many proposals have been made to alter our farm programs. In the view of many observers, agriculture should return to something more closely approximating free markets, and the price system should be allowed to work more freely. The changes that occurred in 1973 are in that direction, but it is important to note that the government is still intervening heavily in agriculture. (Moreover, it should be emphasized that if farm prices recede from the high levels prevailing since 1973, the taxpayers may have to pay very heavy subsidies to farmers, according to the new law.) Although further movements toward a free market in agriculture may not be popular among many farm groups, there are signs that such changes may occur in the years ahead.

Finally, before closing this chapter, we must point out a fundamental moral of our farm programs: *the government, like the price system, can bungle the job of organizing a nation's economic activities.* We began this chapter by stressing the fact that the price system breaks down under some circumstances, and that the government must intervene. It is also worth stressing that the government sometimes intervenes when it shouldn't—and that even when it should intervene, it sometimes does so in a way that wastes resources. This, of course, doesn't mean that the government should play no part in the American economy. On the contrary, the government must—and does—play an enormously important role. What it does mean is that, just as the price system is no all-purpose cure-all, neither is the government.

Summary

The price system, despite its many virtues, suffers from serious limitations. There is no reason to believe that the distribution of income generated by the price system is equitable or optimal. Also, there is no way for the price system to handle public goods, and because of external economies or diseconomies, the price system may result in too little or too much of certain goods being produced. To a considerable extent, the government's role in the economy has developed in response to these limitations of the price system. There is considerable agreement that government should redistribute income in favor of the poor, provide public goods, and offset the effects of external economies and diseconomies. Also, it is generally felt that the government should establish a proper legal, social, and competitive framework for the price system, and that it should see to it that the economy maintains relatively full employment with reasonably stable prices. Beyond this, however, there are wide differences of opinion on the proper role of government in economic affairs. Conservatives tend to be suspicious of "big government" while liberals are inclined to believe that the government should do more.

In the past 50 years, government spending has increased considerably, both in absolute terms and as a percent of total output. (It is now about $\frac{1}{3}$ of our total output.) To a large extent, this increase has been due to our greater military responsibilities, as well as to the fact that, as their incomes have risen, our citizens have demanded more schools, highways, and other goods and services provided by government. The growth in government expenditures has also been part of a general trend in the United States whereby, more and more, the power of the government has been used to achieve social objectives. To get the money to cover most of these expenditures, governments collect taxes from individuals and firms. At the federal level, the most important form of taxation is the personal income tax.

One example of the role of government in the American economy is the farm program. American agriculture has been plagued by relatively low incomes. Until 1973, the demand for farm products grew slowly, while rapid technological change meant that the people and resources currently in agriculture could supply more and more farm products. Because people and resources did not move out of agriculture as rapidly as the price system dictated, farm incomes tended to be relatively low. In response to political pressures from the farm blocs, the government set in motion a series of programs to aid farmers. A cornerstone of these programs was the concept of parity, which said that the prices farmers receive should increase at the same rate as the prices of the goods and services farmers buy. The government instituted price supports to keep farm prices above their equilibrium level. But since the support prices exceeded the equilibrium prices, there was a surplus of the commodities that the government had to purchase and store. To help reduce these surpluses, the government tried to restrict the output of farm products and expand the demand for them.

These farm programs received considerable criticism. From the point of view of income redistribution, they suffered from the fact that they did little for the farmers most in need of help. As tools of resource allocation, they suffered because they dealt more with the symptoms of the farm problem than with its basic causes. In 1973, price supports were ended, but the government pledged to make cash payments to farmers if farm prices fall below certain target levels. The government's farm programs illustrate the fact that government intervention, like the price system, has plenty of limitations. Neither the price system nor government intervention is an all-purpose cure-all.

CONCEPTS FOR REVIEW

Public goods
External economy
External diseconomy
Transfer payments
Antitrust laws
Welfare payments
Price supports
Parity
Depression
Private sector
Public sector
Income tax
Sales tax
Property tax

QUESTIONS FOR DISCUSSION AND REVIEW

1. "The government that governs least governs best." What does this mean? Does it have any implications for economic policy? If so, what? Do you agree with this proposition? Is it testable? If so, how?

2. "I believe the government should do only that which private citizens cannot do for themselves, or which they cannot do so well for themselves." Interpret and comment. Indicate how one might determine in practice what the legitimate functions of government are, according to this proposition.

3. "The ideal public policy, from the viewpoint of the state, is one with identifiable beneficiaries, each of whom is helped appreciably, at the cost of many unidentifiable persons, none of whom is hurt much."[12] Interpret and comment. Indicate how this proposition might be used to help predict government behavior.

4. Suppose that the demand and supply curves for paper are as shown below.

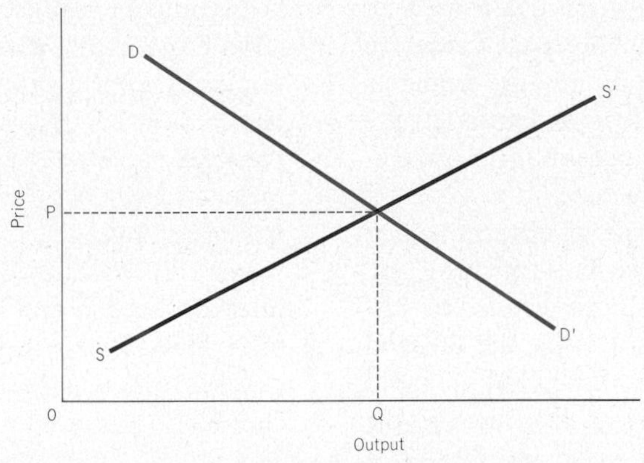

If paper production results in serious pollution of rivers and streams, is the socially optimal output of paper less than, greater than, or equal to *OQ*? Does the supply curve reflecting the true social costs of producing paper lie to the right of *SS'*, to the left of *SS'*, or at *SS'*? Why?

[12] G. Stigler, "The Government of the Economy," in E. Mansfield, *Economics: Readings, Issues, and Cases.*

5. Suppose that paper production results in some important uncompensated benefits to other industries. If there are major external economies of this sort (and if paper production no longer results in any pollution), is the socially optimal output of paper less than, greater than, or equal to *OQ* in Question 4? Does the demand curve reflecting the true social benefits from paper output lie to the right of *DD′*, to the left of *DD′*, or at *DD′*? Why?

6. "An uncrowded bridge is an example of a public good." Do you agree? Why or why not? Can this good—or more accurately, this service—be provided by private firms? Why or why not?

7. What are some of the major factors that have tended to reduce the rate at which people and resources have moved out of agriculture? Consider the cultural factors, relevant differences in birth rates, and institutions of land tenure and ownership.

8. Suppose that the demand curve for corn is as follows:

Price (dollars per bushel)	Quantity demanded per year (millions of bushels)
1	70
2	65
3	60
4	55
5	50
6	45

If the government supports the price of corn at $4 per bushel, and if it restricts output to 60 million bushels per year, how much corn will the government have to buy each year? If the government stopped supporting the price of corn, what would its price be?

9. "During the mid-1970s, the American agricultural problem turned from one of overcapacity to shortage." Explain whether you agree or disagree, and cite the evidence that leads you to whichever conclusion you reach. Be sure to define "overcapacity" and "shortage."

10. "The sharp increases in the price of wheat during the mid-1970s have been due primarily to shifts in the supply curve for wheat." Comment.

11. "I cannot get the amount of national defense I want and you, a different amount."[13] Explain. Is this true of all public goods?

12. Is delivery of the mail a public good? Why should the government provide this service? What are the arguments against its providing it?

[13] M. Friedman, *Capitalism and Freedom*.

6 Government Expenditures, Taxation, and the Public Debt

The government plays an extremely important role in the American economy. It is obvious that it influences our economic lives and fortunes in countless ways. At this point, we must look in detail at how decisions are made concerning the level and distribution of government expenditures. Also, we must discuss the principles of taxation. These topics are of central importance in understanding the public sector of our economy.

In addition, we must discuss some of the salient issues concerning the public sector, including the so-called military-industrial complex, tax reform, and revenue sharing. Further, we must describe in some detail the nature, size, and burden of the public debt, a subject that has been surrounded by as many myths as any in economics.

Government Expenditures

The Federal Budgetary Process

Determining how much the federal government should spend is a mammoth undertaking, involving literally thousands of people and hundreds of thousands of man-hours. Decisions on expenditures are part of the budgetary process. The ***budget*** is a statement of the government's anticipated expenditures and revenues. The federal budget is for a fiscal year, from October 1 to September 30. Let's consider the budget for the fiscal year beginning October 1, 1976. In the summer of 1975, the various agencies of the federal government began to prepare their program proposals. By the fall they had made detailed budget requests which the president, with his Office of Management and Budget, went over from October to December 1975. Since the agencies generally wanted more than the president wanted to spend, he usually cut down their requests.

In January 1976, the president submitted his budget to Congress, which then spent several months in intensive deliberation and negotiation. Congressional committees concerned with particular areas like defense or education recommended changes in the president's budget. The Congressional Budget Office, headed by Alice Rivlin (formerly an economist at the Brookings Institution), made various types of economic analyses to help congressmen evaluate alternative programs. By mid-May, the Congress passed a resolution setting tentative targets for over-all spending and revenues; this resolution was based on the joint recommendations by the House and Senate Budget Committees. The targets in the resolution had to be kept in mind by the various congressional committees dealing with specific spending or tax actions. If these actions added up to bigger totals than the resolution called for, the budget committees and the Congress had to decide how the discrepancies were to be reconciled: by changes in expenditures, taxes, or initial targets. Before late September 1976, the Congress adopted a second resolution, setting final ceilings for over-all expenditure and a floor on revenues.

This budgetary procedure is new. The Congressional Budget and Impoundment Control Act of 1974 established this series of steps that Congress must go through in considering the president's budget. Prior to the middle 1970s, the decision-making process in Congress was fragmented. Separate committees and subcommittees of the Appropriations Committees considered various parts of the president's recommended budget, and it was hard for Congress to establish any over-all policy for total government expenditure and taxes. Moreover, the Congressional Budget Office did not exist, and Congress lacked the staff required to analyze and examine the benefits and costs of various proposed programs. This new procedure attempted to bolster Congress's role in the budgetary process, and to force Congress to look at the over-all budgetary picture so that the total would be more than the sum of largely uncoordinated parts.

Benefit-Cost Analysis

How much should the government spend on various activities and services? Basically, the answer must be provided by the nation's political processes. For example, with regard to the provision of public goods

> voting by ballot must be resorted to in place of dollar voting. . . . Decision making by voting becomes a substitute for preference revelation through the market. The results will not please everybody, but they will approximate—more or less perfectly, depending on the efficiency of the voting process and the homogeneity of preferences the community's preferences.[1]

[1] Richard and Peggy Musgrave, *Public Finance in Theory and Practice,* New York: McGraw Hill, 1973, p. 8.

Under certain circumstances, particular types of economic analysis can prove helpful to the policy makers and citizens who must determine how much the government should spend on various programs. Let's begin by supposing that we can measure the benefits and costs of each such program. What is the optimal amount to spend on each one? The answer, clearly enough, is that *spending on the program should be pushed to the point where the extra benefit from an extra dollar spent is at least equal to the dollar of cost.* This would insure that the amount spent on each government program yields a benefit at least as great as the value of output forgone in the private sector. This would also make sure that one government program is not being expanded at the expense of other programs that would yield greater benefits if they were expanded instead.

The principle that extra benefit should be compared with extra cost is valuable—and, as we shall see in the next section, widely applicable—but it can solve only a small part of the problem of allocating resources in the public sector. Why? Because it is impossible to measure the benefits from defense or police protection or the courts in dollars and cents. Only in certain cases can benefits be quantified at all precisely. And it is not only a question of the amount of the benefits and costs; it is also a question of who benefits and who pays. Nonetheless, it is difficult to see how rational choices can be made without paying attention to costs and benefits—even if they are measured imprecisely, and are by no means the whole story.[2]

Preventing School Dropouts: A Case Study[3]

Despite the difficulties involved, in recent years more and more benefit-cost analyses have been carried out to help guide public policy. For example, consider the following study, by the University of Wisconsin's Burton Weisbrod, of a program to reduce the dropout rate in a high school in St. Louis. In this program, potential dropouts were given counseling and help in getting part-time jobs. It cost over $500 per student. The question, of course, was whether the program did enough good to be worth the cost. To help answer this question, the experience of the students in the program was compared with the experience of a control group of comparable students who were not included in the program. It turned out that, despite the help they received, 44 percent of the students in the program dropped out of school before graduation, while 52 percent of the students in the control group dropped out before graduation. Thus the program seemed to reduce the dropout rate by 8 percentage points.

How much was this benefit worth? Weisbrod pointed out that one principal gain was the increased income earned by students who complete high school. A high school graduate earns about $2,750 more than a dropout over a lifetime. Let us use this figure—$2,750—as a measure of the benefit of preventing a student from dropping out. Was the program worthwhile? Since the program reduced the probability of dropping out by 8 percentage points, the average benefit per student was .08 times $2,750, or $220. Since this was less than the cost per student, the program did not seem worthwhile. Of course, one can object that the measure of the benefit from preventing a student from dropping out is incomplete. It does not include the psychic and social benefits from putting people in a position to earn their own keep rather than to be prime candidates for public assistance, and even perhaps jail. Nonetheless, this study raised important questions and had significant effects.

---

[2] See Charles Schultze, *The Politics and Economics of Public Spending,* Washington, D.C.: Brookings Institution, 1968. Also, see Bernard Herber, *Modern Public Finance,* Homewood, Ill.: Irwin, 1971, pp. 389-91.

[3] This section is based on Burton Weisbrod, "Preventing High School Dropouts," in Robert Dorfman, ed., *Measuring Benefits of Government Investments,* Washington, D.C.: Brookings Institution, 1965. A brief discussion of this study is also provided in Otto Eckstein, *Public Finance,* Englewood Cliffs, N.J.: Prentice-Hall, 1967.

Benefit-cost analyses have proved useful in many areas of government. In particular, they have been used for many years in the Department of Defense. Decisions to develop one weapons system rather than another, or to procure a certain amount of a given weapon, have been based in part on such studies. Other areas where benefit-cost analyses have been used extensively are water projects (irrigation, flood control, hydroelectric, and other projects), transportation projects, and urban renewal, recreation, and health projects. For example, in water projects, benefit-cost analysis has frequently been used by the Corps of Engineers and others to determine whether it is worthwhile to spend additional money on flood control, and if so, how much extra expenditure is justified.

A highly simplified example of a benefit-cost analysis of the construction of a dam is shown in Table 6.1. The alternative policies are to build a low dam or a high dam. Table 6.1 shows the annual costs and benefits associated with each of these policies. Clearly, the high dam should be built because the extra cost involved ($150,000 more than for the low dam) is more than outweighed by the extra benefits received ($200,000 more than for the low dam). Note, however, that this is a very simple case. In general, data on costs and benefits are not laid out so straightforwardly. Instead, there are very wide bands of uncertainty about the relevant costs and benefits.

Table 6.1
Benefit-Cost Analysis for Constructing a Dam

Alternative policies	Annual cost (dollars)	Annual benefit (dollars)
Build a low dam	600,000	650,000
Build a high dam	750,000	850,000

Government Expenditures and the Problem of Social Balance

It is not easy to decide how large government expenditures should be. As we saw in Chapter 5, opinions differ widely on the proper role of government in economic affairs, and it is often impossible to measure the costs and benefits of government programs with dependable accuracy. Nonetheless, some economists—led by Harvard's John Kenneth Galbraith—believe that the public sector of the economy has been deprived of needed resources, whereas the private sector has catered to relatively unimportant wants. For example, in *The Affluent Society,* Galbraith argued that consumers are led by advertising and other promotional efforts to purchase more and more goods of marginal importance to them. On the other hand, in his opinion, the nation is suffering from too little spending on government services. Thus he writes,

> In the years following World War II, the papers of any major city . . . told daily of the shortages and shortcomings in the elementary municipal and metropolitan services. The schools were old and overcrowded. The police force was understrength and underpaid. The parks and playgrounds were insufficient. Streets and empty lots were filthy, and the sanitation staff was underequipped and in need of men. Access to the city by those who work there was uncertain and painful and becoming more so. Internal transportation was overcrowded, unhealthy, and dirty. So was the air. Parking on the streets had to be prohibited, and there was no space elsewhere. These deficiencies were not in new and novel services, but in old established ones.[4]

Many economists agree with Galbraith. Particularly among liberals, there is a widespread feeling that resources are being malallocated, too much going for deodorants, comic books,

[4] John Kenneth Galbraith, *The Affluent Society,* Boston: Houghton Mifflin, 1958, p. 252. Incidentally, Galbraith opposed the tax cut of 1964 because he felt that government spending should be increased instead.

and mouth wash, and too little going for schools and public services. But this feeling is not shared by all economists. Galbraith's critics point out that expenditures often benefit particular interest groups, which lobby hard for them in federal and state legislatures. The result is that spending programs may be carried beyond the optimal point. Further, they point out that Galbraith's assertion that private wants are becoming more and more trivial and synthetic is not scientifically verifiable and that, in any case, it ignores the large number of people living in very modest circumstances, indeed, even in dire poverty.

Economic theory alone cannot settle this basic question. It is obviously a matter of politics as well as economics. However, in trying to reach an opinion, bear in mind that both sides may be partly correct. For certain types of government services, you may agree with Galbraith and his followers that too little is being spent, but for other types of government services you may agree with his critics that too much is being spent. For example, you may feel that too little is being spent on pollution control and urban problems, but that too much is being spent on agricultural subsidies (many of which go to wealthy farmers) and subsidies to the merchant marine (which are meant to keep the American shipping industry competitive with other nations).

Finally, it is important to distinguish between decisions concerning the *scope* of government activities and decisions concerning the *efficiency* of government. Thus far in this section we have been discussing the proper scope of government. Assume that we can divide all goods into public goods and private goods, and that Figure 6.1 shows the society's product transformation curve. In other words, as you recall from Chapter 3, Figure 6.1 shows the maximum amount of public goods that can be produced, given each quantity produced of private goods. Then the question that we have been discussing is: At what point along the product transformation curve should society be? For example, should society choose point *A* (where more public goods and less private goods are produced) or point *B* (where less public goods and more private goods are produced)?

But there is another important question: How can we attain a point *on* the product transformation curve, rather than one (like point *C*) that is *inside* it? As we know from Chapter 3, inefficiency will result in society's being on a point inside the product transformation curve. Thus, to attain a point on the

Figure 6.1
Product Transformation Curve, Public versus Private Goods
At point *B*, society produces less public goods and more private goods than at point *A*. Thus, a movement from point *A* to point *B* reduces government expenditures by reducing the *scope* of government services. At point *C*, society is producing inefficiently, and a movement from point *C* to point *B* or point *A* can be attained by increasing the *efficiency* of government (and/or private) operations.

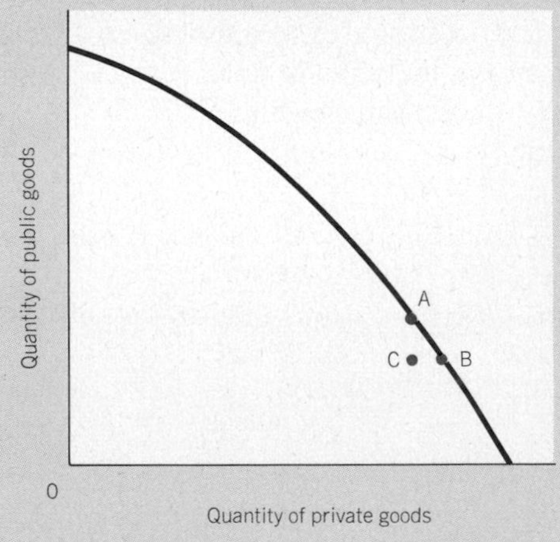

product transformation curve, government officials (and others) must do their best to eliminate inefficiency. By doing so, society can get more from the available resources. For example, it can attain points *A* or *B* rather than point *C*. Whether society wants to use its added efficiency to attain point *A* or point *B* is then a political question. However, regardless of how this question is decided, society is better off to eliminate inefficiency.

Two Case Studies: Defense and Coal Research

Military Spending and the Military-Industrial Complex

At this point, it is worthwhile to look briefly at two federal agencies, the Department of Defense and the Office of Coal Research (formerly in the Department of Interior, and now part of the Energy Research and Development Administration). Although these two agencies cannot be held up as typical, they do represent interesting case studies. On the one hand, the Department of Defense has repeatedly been charged with overspending. But since it is hard to tell what level of defense capability is optimal, it is equally difficult to tell whether defense spending is too much or too little. However, there can be no doubt about the enormous size of our defense expenditures. In 1970, American military expenditures were more than $80 billion, which means that they constituted over 40 percent of national output. (Moreover, this figure excludes defense-related spending by the Energy Research and Development Administration and National Aeronautics and Space Administration.) Some people claim that this exaggerates the cost of defense, because if defense expenditures were cut appreciably, our national output would fall. But this assumes that other forms of government spending would not be substituted for defense, or that fiscal and monetary policies could not keep the economy at a high employment level without defense spending—both very unrealistic assumptions.

However, some forms of defense and space spending, particularly on research and development, do provide important benefits to the civilian economy. The electronic computer, numerical control, integrated circuits, atomic energy, synthetic rubber, and many other significant inventions stemmed at least partly from military R and D. Moreover, there is undoubtedly considerable opportunity for such spillover from current military and space R and D. Nonetheless, there seems to be a widespread feeling that the spillover per dollar of military-space R and D is unlikely to be as great as in the past, because the capabilities that are being developed and the environment that is being probed are less intimately connected with civilian activities than formerly. For example, the devices needed to send a man to the moon may have relatively little applicability in the civilian economy because they "oversatisfy" civilian requirements and few people or firms are willing to pay for them.

There is considerable evidence that the weapons acquisition process has not been as efficient as it might have been. There have been spectacular overruns in development and production costs. For example, the cost of the Lockheed C5A transport plane increased from the $3.4 billion estimated in 1965 to $5.3 billion in 1968. To some extent, such cost increases reflect the fact that new weapons systems tend to push the state of the art, so that unexpected problems must be expected. But in addition, the firms that develop and produce these weapons systems often submit unrealistically low bids to get a contract, knowing that they are likely to get approval for cost increases later on. According to some observers, like Merton J. Peck of Yale University and F. M. Scherer of Northwestern University, these cost overruns have also been due to "inadequate attention to the efficient utilization of technical, production, and administrative manpower—areas in which major cost reductions are possible."[5]

In addition, some observers believe that the major defense contractors, in conjunction with the military services, apply undue political pressure in support of high defense budgets. For example, President Dwight D. Eisenhower, himself a distinguished military commander, warned of the dangers involved in this "military-industrial complex." In his last speech to the nation as president, he said, "In the councils of government, we must guard against the acquisition of unwarranted influence, whether sought or unsought, by the military-industrial complex. The potential for the disastrous rise of misplaced power exists and will persist." It seems unlikely that there is any real conspiracy, but military contractors, with their political allies, are undoubtedly a powerful lobby for defense spending.

In a world marked by international tensions, few people argue that our defense establishment should be dismantled. Many, indeed, argue that we should be careful to avoid a decline in our military strength relative to our potential adversaries. But this is no argument for inefficiency. Almost all agree that, given the size of the defense budget, sound economic controls must be exercised by Pentagon officials to prevent waste of resources on a mammoth scale.

The Office of Coal Research

Just as it is sometimes charged that certain agencies, like the Department of Defense, may have been spending too much, so it is sometimes charged that other agencies, like the Office of Coal Research, may have been spending too little. In recent years, there has been considerable discussion and alarm over the so-called energy crisis, a situation where a marked shortage seems to have arisen in clean domestic fuels. One way to avoid such a crisis is to develop new technologies to convert our relatively plentiful coal supplies into a clean gas or other forms of fuel that would be less polluting than coal. The Office of Coal Research was responsible for financing research of this kind, and in accord with President Nixon's energy message of June 4, 1971, it was charged with accelerating the coal gasification program to develop a process or processes to produce clean, high-quality gas from coal on a commercial scale by 1980.

The expenditures of the Office of Coal Research (OCR) increased very substantially during the early 1970s. Its budget was about $60 million in 1974, about $30 million in 1972, and about $15 million in 1970. Much of this money was spent for coal gasification work; about $30 million was spent in 1973 on this program, ⅔ being funded by OCR and about ⅓ by industry. The Office of Coal Research helped to finance several approaches to coal gasification, including the Institute of Gas Technology's HYGAS pilot plant, the Consolidation Coal Company's CO_2 Acceptor pilot plant, FMC Corporation's COED pilot plant, and others. Each of these pilot plants cost millions of dollars. Because it was felt that the social returns from the information gained from them would exceed the private returns to the companies operating them, the government subsidized this research and development.

Despite the increase in OCR's expenditures, many knowledgeable people felt that such work should be expanded even more rapidly. For example, in 1973 Senator Henry Jackson of Washington called for a 10-year R and D program on coal gasification costing $660 million (60 percent to be paid for by government, 40 percent by industry), and a 12-year R and D program on coal liquefaction costing $750 mil-

[5] M. J. Peck and F. M. Scherer, *The Weapons Acquisition Process*, Cambridge, Mass.: Harvard University Press, 1962, p. 594.

lion (75 percent to be paid for by government). Also, the Office of Science and Technology's Energy Advisory Panel called in 1972 for an expanded R and D program for coal liquefaction, as well as continued emphasis on coal gasification.

During the mid-1970s, the amount spent on coal research did increase dramatically—from the $60 million spent in 1974 to about $280 million in 1976. Besides the coal gasification program, the Energy Research and Development Administration (which now includes what formerly was the Office of Coal Research) is carrying out considerable research concerning coal liquefaction and direct combustion of coal. The United States has over 300 billion tons of coal reserves, more than any other country in the world. In view of this fact, and our recent energy problems, many observers feel that this increase in government support for coal research was justified and perhaps overdue.

Taxation and Government Revenues

The Federal Tax Legislative Process

It is one thing for the federal government to decide how much to spend and on what; it is another to raise the money to underwrite these programs. This section describes how the federal government decides how much to tax. Of course, this problem is not solved from scratch every year. Instead, the government takes the existing tax structure as given and changes it from time to time as seems desirable. Frequently the major initiative leading to a change in the tax laws comes from the president, who requests tax changes in his State of the Union message, his budget message, or a special tax message. Much of the spadework underlying his proposals will have been carried out by the Treasury Department, particularly the Treasury's Office of Tax Analysis, Office of the Tax Legislative Counsel, and Internal Revenue Service.

The proposal of a major tax change generally brings about considerable public debate. Representatives of labor, industry, agriculture, and other economic and social groups present their opinions. Newspaper articles, radio shows, and television commentators analyze the issues. By the time the Congress begins to look seriously at the proposal, the battle lines between those who favor the change and those who oppose it are generally pretty clearly drawn. The tax bill incorporating the change is first considered by the Ways and Means Committee of the House of Representatives, a very powerful committee composed of members drawn from both political parties. After public hearings, the committee goes into executive session and reviews each proposed change with its staff and with the Treasury staff. After careful study, the committee arrives at a bill it recommends—though this bill may or may not conform to what the president asked for. Then the bill is referred to the entire House of Representatives for approval. Only rarely is a major tax bill recommended by the committee turned down by the House.

Next, the bill is sent to the Senate. There it is referred to the Finance Committee, which is organized like the House Ways and Means Committee. The Finance Committee also holds hearings, discusses the bill at length, makes changes in it, and sends its version of the bill to the entire Senate, where there frequently is considerable debate. Ultimately, it is brought to a vote. If it does not pass, that ends the process. If it does pass (and if it differs from the House version of the bill, which is generally the case), then a conference committee must be formed to iron out the differences between the House and Senate versions. Finally, when this compromise is worked out, the result must be passed by both houses and sent to the president. The president rarely vetoes a tax bill, although it has occasionally been done.[6]

Principles of Taxation

According to the English political philosopher, Edmund Burke, "To tax and to please, no more than to love and to be wise, is not given to men." What constitutes a rational tax system? Are there any generally accepted principles to guide the nation in determining who should pay how much? The answer is that there are some principles most people accept, but they are so broad and general that they leave plenty of room for argument and compromise. Specifically, two general principles of taxation command widespread agreement.

Benefit principle. The first principle is that *people who receive more from a certain government service should pay more in taxes to support it.* Certainly few people would argue with this idea. However, it is frequently difficult, if not impossible, to apply. For example, there is no good way to measure the amount of the benefits received by a particular taxpayer from many public services, such as police protection.

Ability-to-pay principle. The second principle is that *people should be taxed so as to result in a socially desirable redistribution of income.* In practice, this has ordinarily meant that the wealthy have been asked to pay more than the poor. This idea, too, has generally commanded widespread assent—although this, of course, has not prevented the wealthy from trying to avoid its application to them.

It follows from these principles that if two people are in essentially the same circumstances (their income, purchases, utilization of public services are the same), then they should pay the same taxes. This is an important rule, innocuous though it may seem. It says that equals should be treated equally—*whether one is a Republican and the other is a Democrat, or whether one is a friend of the president and the other is his enemy, or whether one has purely salary income and the other has property income, they should be treated equally.* Certainly, this is a basic characteristic of an equitable tax system.

It is easy to relate most of the taxes in our tax structure to these principles. For example, the first principle—the benefit principle—is the basic rationale behind taxes on gasoline and license fees for vehicles and drivers. Those who use the roads are asked to pay for their construction and upkeep. Also, the property tax, levied primarily on real estate, is often supported on these grounds. It is argued that property owners receive important benefits—fire and police protection, for example—and that the extent of the benefits is related to the extent of their property.

The personal income tax is based squarely on the second principle—ability to pay. A person with a large income pays a higher proportion of income in personal income taxes than does a person with a smaller income. For example, in 1975, if a couple's income (after deductions but before exemptions) were $10,000, their federal income tax would be $1,430, whereas if their income were $50,000, their federal income tax would be $16,250. (However, the wealthy can avoid taxes in various perfectly legal ways, as we shall see in a later section.) Also, estate and inheritance taxes hit the rich much harder than the poor; but again, it is possible to take some of the sting out of them if you have a good lawyer.

The principles cited above are useful and important, but they do not take us very far toward establishing a rational tax structure. They are too vague and leave too many ques-

[6] For an excellent discussion of the federal tax legislative process, see J. Pechman, *Federal Tax Policy,* rev. ed., New York: Norton, 1970, part of which is reprinted in E. Mansfield, *Economics: Readings, Issues, and Cases,* 2d ed., New York: Norton, 1977.

tions unanswered. For example, if I use about the same amount of public services as you do, but my income is twice yours, how much more should I pay in taxes? Twice as much? Three times as much? Fifty percent more? These principles throw no real light on many of the detailed questions that must be answered by a real-life tax code.

The Personal and Corporate Income Taxes

The federal personal income tax brings in over $150 billion a year. Yet a great many people are perhaps unaware of just how much they are contributing because it is deducted from their wages each month or each week, so that they owe little extra when April 15 rolls around. (Indeed, they may even be due a refund.) This pay-as-you-go scheme reduces the pain, but, of course, it does not eliminate it: taxes are never painless.

Obviously, how much a family has to pay in personal income taxes depends on the family's income. The tax schedule (as of 1975) is as shown in Table 6.2. The second column shows how much a couple would have to pay if their income was the amount shown in the first column. For example, at an income of $5,000, their income tax would be $475; at an income of $20,000, their income tax would be $3,900. Clearly, the percentage of income owed in income tax increases as income increases, but this percentage does not increase indefinitely. The percentage of income going for personal income taxes never exceeds 70 percent, no matter how much money the couple makes. (And on income from wages and personal effort, it never exceeds 50 percent.)

It is instructive to look further at how the "tax bite" increases with income. In particular, let's ask ourselves what proportion of an *extra* dollar of income the couple will have to pay in personal income taxes. In other words, what is the ***marginal tax rate***—the tax on an extra dollar of income? The fourth column of Table 6.2 shows that the marginal tax rate is 17 percent if the couple's income is $5,000, 28 percent if their income is $20,000, 50 percent if their income is $50,000, and 70 percent if their income is $1 million. Thus, the greater the couple's income, the greater the proportion of

Table 6.2
Federal Personal Income Tax, Couple without Children, 1975[a]

Income (after deductions but before personal exemptions) (dollars)	Personal income tax (dollars)	Average tax rate (percent)	Marginal tax rate (percent)
Below 1,500	0	0	0
3,000	155	5.2	15
5,000	475	9.5	17
10,000	1,430	14.3	22
20,000	3,900	19.5	28
50,000	16,250	32.5	50
100,000	44,220	44.2	60
1,000,000	669,870	67.0	70

[a] If a family contained dependent children and its income was less than $8,000 per year, it could get a credit of up to $400, which might wipe out any income tax liability and result in a cash payment to the family.

an extra dollar that goes for personal income taxes.

Clearly, the personal income tax tends to reduce the inequality of after-tax income, since the rich are taxed more heavily than the poor. However, the personal income tax does not bear down as heavily on the rich as one might surmise from Table 6.2. This is because, as we shall see in a subsequent section, there are a variety of perfectly legal ways for people to avoid paying taxes on their incomes. Current tax laws are favorable to homeowners, who can deduct the payment of local real estate taxes and the interest on their mortgage from their income to get the adjusted level of income on which they pay income taxes. Also, money a person makes on the stock market or from some other situation where his assets go up in value, known as a ***capital gain,*** is subject to lower personal income tax rates than other income. Interest paid by state and local governments on their bonds is not taxable at all by the federal government. In addition, of course, there is some illegal tax evasion, such as underreporting of income, fake expenses, and imaginary dependents. But evasion is much less important than legal tax avoidance, despite Will Rogers's quip that the income tax has made more liars among the American public than golf.

The federal government imposes a tax on the incomes of corporations as well as of people. Corporations must pay 20 percent of their first $25,000 of annual profits, 22 percent of their second $25,000 of annual profits, and 48 percent of the rest as corporate income tax. For example, a corporation with annual profits of $150,000 would pay $58,500 in corporate income tax—$5,000 (20 percent of the first $25,000) plus $5,500 (22 percent of the next $25,000) plus $48,000 (48 percent of the remaining $100,000). The corporate income tax involves double taxation. The federal government taxes a corporation's earnings both through the corporate income tax (when the corporation earns the profits) and through the personal income tax (when the corporation's earnings are distributed to the stockholders as dividends).

It is generally agreed that the personal income tax is paid by the person whose income is taxed: he or she cannot shift this tax to someone else. But the incidence of the corporate income tax is not so clear. To some extent, corporations may pass along some of their income tax bill to customers in the form of higher prices or to workers in the form of lower wages. Some economists feel that a corporation shifts much of the tax burden in this way; others disagree. This is a controversial issue that has proved very difficult to resolve.

Fiscal Relations between Federal, State, and Local Government

It is important to recognize that there are several levels of government in the United States—federal, state, and local—and that each level of government spends and taxes. Thus all levels of government, not just the federal government, play a role in our economic affairs. Unfortunately, however, there has been limited coordination between the spending and tax decisions of the federal government and those of the state and local governments. From the point of view of promoting full employment without inflation, it would be desirable for the federal, state, and local governments to work in unison, or at least in the same direction, to fight excessive unemployment or inflation. But in fact they often have worked at cross-purposes.

In this country the state and local governments are traditionally entrusted with the responsibility for some of the services that have had to be expanded most rapidly—education, highways, municipal facilities, and so forth. Yet the kinds of taxes the state and local governments rely on—notably sales and property taxes—do not provide a yield that increases very rapidly with increases in income. Thus a basic question arises: How can the state and local governments get the money they need to expand their services at the desired rate? Presently, the state and local governments are caught in a fiscal bind. Their expenditures are being pushed up more rapidly than their revenues. On the other hand, because the personal income tax generates a great deal of additional money as income increases, the federal government is in the fortunate position of having its revenues increase at a relatively rapid rate.

Recognizing that it has access to greater sources of revenue, the federal government has been making more and more grants to states and—on a smaller scale—to local governments. These grants have been earmarked primarily for highways, welfare, and education, the major expenditure areas for state and local governments. One effect of these grants is to offset the considerable regional differences in income. Since some states—particularly those in the Deep South—are poor, less tax revenue is generated there than in richer states even if tax rates are the same. Thus, to equalize the extent and quality of public services, the federal government in effect takes from the richer states—like New York and California—and gives to the poorer states—like Mississippi and Alabama.

Revenue Sharing

In recent years, a great deal of attention has been given to ***revenue sharing***—large and unconditional grants by the federal government to the state and local governments. Initially suggested by Walter W. Heller of the University of Minnesota and Joseph Pechman of the Brookings Institution, this idea was accepted by the Nixon administration, and eventually by Congress. At first it was opposed on the ground that those who spend money should have the responsibility of raising it, since the divorce of expenditure from financing responsibilities might lead to wasteful expenditures. Initially, other objections were raised as well. But the fiscal plight of the state and local governments is serious and undesirable: there is a mismatch between their responsibilities and their resources. Recognizing that some device must be adopted to help the local and state governments, Congress passed the first revenue-sharing bill in 1972.

However, this bill did not establish revenue sharing as a permanent program. Instead, it was given a termination date of December 31, 1976, to be sure that it would be examined in the light of several years of experience to see how effective revenue sharing proved in practice. There are great difficulties in making such an examination (since the effects of revenue sharing are hard to measure), but the studies carried out to date seem to suggest that the program has been working out reasonably well. According to Richard Nathan of the Brookings Institution, the adoption of revenue sharing has helped to promote a desirable decentralization of government power. To improve the program, he feels that the formula for dividing the shared funds between state and local governments should be made more flexible. At present, local governments *in each state* receive $2 for every $1 received by the state government. In late 1976, Congress and the Ford administration extended the program (with little modification) to 1980.

The Property Tax and the Sales Tax

The ***property tax*** is the fiscal bulwark of our local governments. The way it works is simple enough. Most towns and cities estimate the amount they will spend in the next year or two, and then determine a property tax based on the assessed property values in the town or city. For example, if there is $500 million in assessed property values in the town and the town needs to raise $5 million, the tax rate will be 1 percent of assessed property value. In other words, each property owner will have to pay 1 percent of the assessed value of his property. There are well-known problems in the administration of the property tax. First, assessed values of property often depart significantly from actual market values; the former are typically much lower than the latter. And the ratio of assessed to actual value is often lower among higher-priced pieces of property; thus wealthier people tend to get off easier. Second, there is widespread evasion of taxes on ***personal property***—securities, bank accounts, and so on. Many people simply do not pay up. Third, the property tax is not very flexible: assessments and rates tend to change rather slowly.

The ***sales tax,*** of course, is a bulwark of state taxation. It provides a high yield with relatively low collection costs. As Table 6.3 indicates, most of the states have some form of general sales tax, the rate being usually between 3 and 5 percent. Retailers add to the price of goods sold to consumers an amount equal to 3 to 5 percent of the consumer's bill. This extra amount is submitted to the state as the general sales tax. Some states exempt food purchases from this tax, and a few exempt medical supplies. Where they exist, these exemptions help reduce the impact of the sales tax on the poor; but in general the sales tax imposes a greater burden relative to income on the poor than on the rich, for the simple reason that the rich save a larger percentage of their income. Practically all of a poor family's income may be subject to sales taxes; a great deal of a rich family's income may not be, because it is not spent on consumer goods, but is saved.

Who really pays the property tax or the sales tax? To what extent can these taxes be shifted to other people? The answer is not as straightforward as one might expect. For the property tax, the owner of unrented residential property swallows the tax, since there is no one else to shift it to. But the owner of rented property

Table 6.3
State Retail Sales Tax Rates, 1975

State	Percentage	State	Percentage	State	Percentage
Alabama	4	Louisiana	3	Oklahoma	2
Arizona	4	Maine	5	Pennsylvania	6
Arkansas	3	Maryland	4	Rhode Island	5
California	4¾	Massachusetts	3	South Carolina	4
Colorado	3	Michigan	4	South Dakota	4
Connecticut	7	Minnesota	4	Tennessee	3½
District of Columbia	5	Mississippi	5	Texas	4
Florida	4	Missouri	3	Utah	4
Georgia	3	Nebraska	2½	Vermont	3
Hawaii	4	Nevada	3	Virginia	3
Idaho	3	New Jersey	5	Washington	4½
Illinois	4	New Mexico	4	West Virginia	3
Indiana	4	New York	4	Wisconsin	4
Iowa	3	North Carolina	3	Wyoming	3
Kansas	3	North Dakota	4		
Kentucky	5	Ohio	4		

Source: Advisory Commission on Intergovernmental Relations.

Figure 6.2
Effect of a \$1.00 Tax on a Case of Beer.
The tax shifts the supply curve upward by \$1.00 (from SS' to $S_T S_T'$). Since the demand curve is unaffected, the equilibrium price of beer increases from \$6.00 to \$6.50 per case.

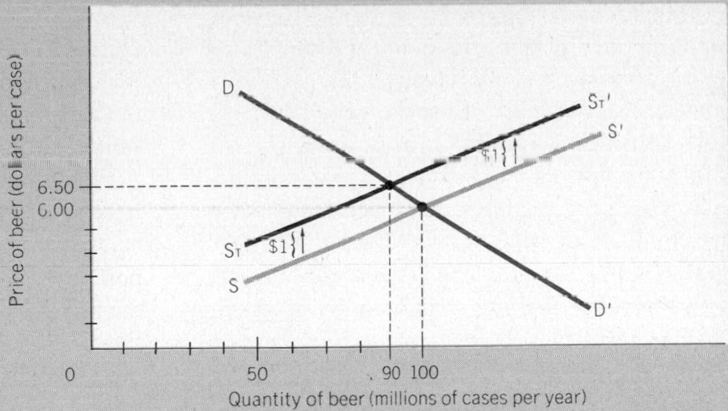

may attempt to pass along some of the tax to the tenant. In the case of a general sales tax, it is generally concluded that the consumer pays the tax. But if the tax is imposed on only a single commodity, the extent to which it can be shifted to the consumer depends on the demand and supply curves for the taxed commodity. The following section explains in some detail why this is the case.

Tax Incidence

Suppose that a sales or excise tax is imposed on a particular good, say beer. In Figure 6.2, we show the demand and supply curves, DD' and SS', for beer before the imposition of the tax. Obviously, the equilibrium price of a case of beer is \$6, and the equilibrium quantity is 100 million cases. If a tax of \$1 is imposed on each case produced, what is the effect on the price of each case? Or to see it from the beer guzzler's perspective, how much of the tax is passed on to the consumer in the form of a higher price?

Since the tax is collected from the sellers, the supply curve is shifted upward by the amount of the tax. In Figure 6.2, the posttax supply curve is $S_T S_T'$. For example, if the pretax price had to be \$5 a case to induce sellers to supply 80 million cases of beer, the posttax price would have to be \$1 higher—or \$6 a case—to induce the same supply. Similarly, if the pretax price had to be \$6 a case to induce sellers to supply 100 million cases of beer, the posttax price would have to be \$1 higher—or \$7 a case—to induce the same supply. The reason why the sellers require \$1 more per case to supply the pretax amount is that they must pay the tax of \$1 per case to the government. Thus, to wind up with the same amount as before (after paying the tax), they require the extra \$1 per case.

Figure 6.2 shows that, after the tax is imposed, the equilibrium price of beer is \$6.50, an increase of \$.50 over its pretax level. Consequently, in this case, ½ of the tax is passed on to consumers, who pay \$.50 per case more for beer. And ½ of the tax is swallowed by the sellers, who receive (after they pay the tax) \$.50 per case less for beer. But it is not always true that sellers pass half of the tax on to consumers and absorb the rest themselves. On the contrary, in some cases, consumers may bear almost all of the tax (and sellers may bear practically none of it), while in other cases consumers may bear almost none of the tax (and sellers may bear practically all of it). The result will depend on how sensitive the quantity demanded and the quantity supplied are to the price of the good.

In particular, holding the supply curve constant, *the less sensitive the quantity demanded is to the price of the good, the bigger the portion of the tax that is shifted to consumers.* To illustrate this, consider Figure 6.3, which shows the effect of a $1 per case tax on beer in two markets, one where the quantity demanded (D_1D_1') is much more sensitive to price than in the other case (D_2D_2'). As is evident, the price increase to consumers resulting from the tax is much greater in the latter case than in the former. And the amount of the tax that is absorbed by producers is much less in the latter case (where D_2D_2' prevails) than in the former (where D_1D_1' prevails).

It can also be shown that, holding the demand curve constant, *the less sensitive the quantity supplied is to the price of the good, the bigger the portion of the tax that is absorbed by producers.* To illustrate this, consider Figure 6.4, which shows the effect of a $1 per case tax on beer in two markets, one where the quantity supplied (S_1S_1') is much more sensitive to price than in the other case (S_2S_2'). As is evident, the price increase to consumers resulting from the tax is much greater in the former case than in the latter. And the amount of the tax that is absorbed by producers is much less in the former case (where S_1S_1' prevails) than in the latter case (where S_2S_2' prevails).

Finally, note that the tax reduces the equilibrium quantity of the good that is taxed—beer in this case. One reason why governments impose taxes on goods like cigarettes and liquor is that they are regarded (in some circles at least) as socially undesirable. Clearly, the more sensitive the quantity demanded and quantity supplied are to price, the larger the reduction in the equilibrium quantity. Thus, if the government imposes a tax of this sort to reduce the quantity consumed of the good, the effect will be greater if both the quantity demanded and the quantity supplied are relatively sensitive to price.

Tax Reform

Because the tax structure of the United States contains so many exemptions and loopholes, there is continual pressure for tax reform. Sen-

Figure 6.3
Effect on Tax Incidence of the Sensitivity of the Quantity Demanded to Price
Before the tax, the equilibrium price is OP_0, regardless of whether D_1D_1' or D_2D_2' is the demand curve. After the tax, the equilibrium price is OP_1, if the demand curve is D_1D_1', or OP_2 if the demand curve is D_2D_2'. Clearly, the increase in price to the consumer is greater if the quantity demanded is less sensitive to price (D_2D_2') than if it is more sensitive (D_1D_1').

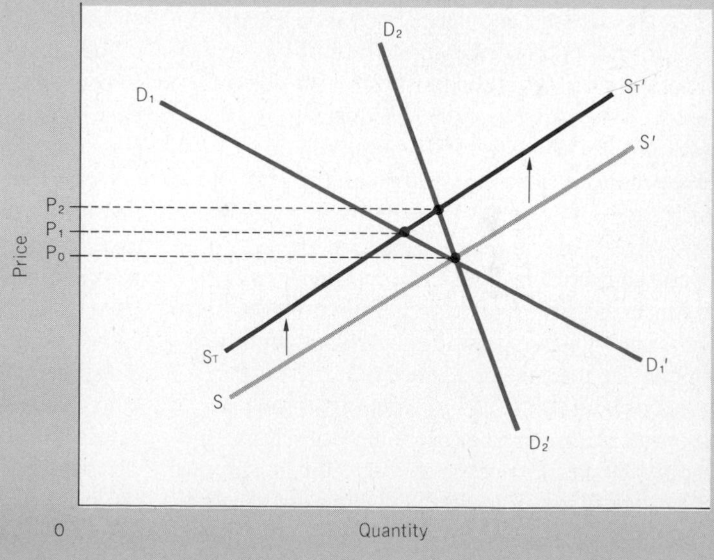

ator George McGovern, in his bid for the presidency in 1972, stressed the importance of tax reform, stating, "The tax code . . . is riddled with loopholes, special exemptions, and shelters. . . . Income which is earned on an assembly line or in an office should no longer be more heavily taxed than profits from oil or securities." President Carter, in his 1976 presidential campaign, also emphasized tax reform. In particular, there are questions about the equity of the relatively low tax rates on capital gains, the tax-free status of interest on state and local bonds, and other aspects of the tax code.

Because there are so many exemptions, exclusions, and deductions, a surprisingly small percentage of all income is subject to the federal personal income tax. In 1960, only about $\frac{3}{7}$ of personal income in the United States was subject to the income tax. This erosion of the tax base, lamented frequently by experts on public finance, means that tax rates must be higher than they would be if the tax base were broader. In other words, if a larger proportion of all income were subject to the personal income tax, a smaller tax could be imposed on each dollar of income subject to tax. Many tax experts feel strongly that the erosion of the tax base should be stopped, and that the tax base should be broadened appreciably. But it is difficult to take away the various exemptions and deductions that have been granted in the past.

When the time seems ripe for a change in tax rates to stabilize the economy, there is often a tendency to try to accomplish tax reform as well. For example, if a tax cut seems advisable to reduce excessive unemployment, there may be an attempt to combine tax reform with tax reduction. Although the attempt to kill two birds—economic stabilization and tax reform—with one stone seems laudable in theory, in practice it can spell trouble. For example, here is how Thomas Dernburg of American University and Duncan McDougall of the University of Kansas describe the attempts in the early 1960s to mix tax reduction and tax reform:

> During the debate of the early 1960s, the Treasury proposed that the tax bill contain a comprehensive package of reform. Aware that congress-

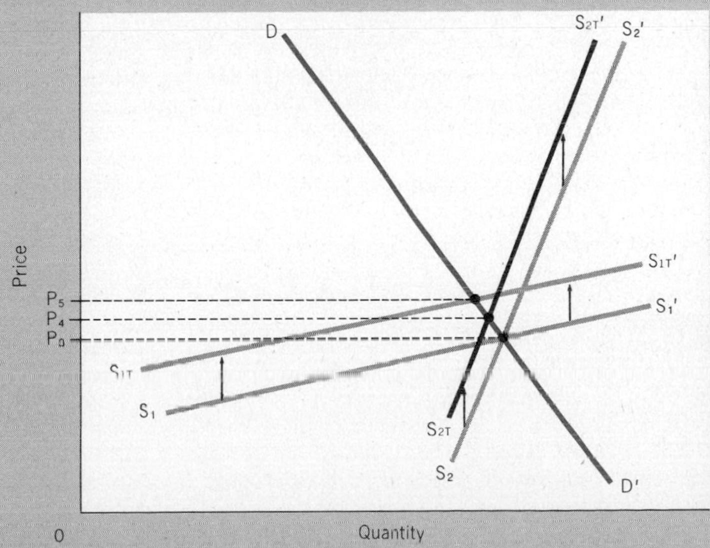

Figure 6.4
Effect on Tax Incidence of the Sensitivity of the Quantity Supplied to Price
Before the tax, the equilibrium price is OP_3, regardless of whether S_1S_1' or S_2S_2' is the pretax supply curve. After the tax, the equilibrium price is OP_4, if the (pretax) supply curve is S_2S_2', or OP_5 if the (pretax) supply curve is S_1S_1'. Clearly, the increase in price to the consumer is greater if the quantity supplied is more sensitive to price (S_1S_1') than if it is less sensitive (S_2S_2').

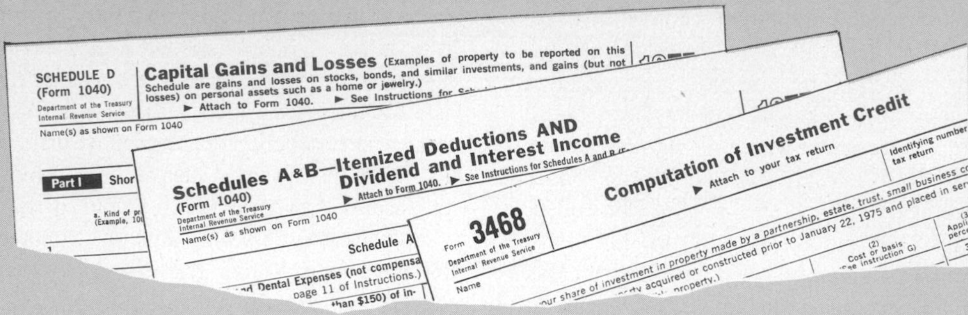

How People Reduce Their Income Tax without Cheating

Lawyers and accountants like to distinguish between tax *avoidance* and tax *evasion.* Tax avoidance occurs when a taxpayer takes legal steps to minimize his tax bill. Tax evasion occurs when a taxpayer misreports his income or takes other illegal steps to cut down on what he pays Uncle Sam. Tax avoidance is a particularly profitable pastime of the well-to-do. With the help of a good lawyer or accountant, one frequently can cut his or her income taxes considerably. To illustrate, consider the following three cases.

George Adams has savings of $50,000, which he has invested in stocks. The dividends from these stocks amount to $3,000 per year. Since his marginal income tax rate is 28 percent, he pays $840 per year in federal income tax on his dividend income. (Why? Because he must pay 28 cents in taxes on every extra dollar of income he receives. Thus 0.28 times $3,000, or $840, is the amount of tax he must pay on an extra $3,000 of income.) If he invests his $50,000 in state and local bonds instead, he can obtain $2,800 per year in interest. Since the interest from state and local bonds is exempt from federal income taxes, he can cut his income tax bill by $840—and, allowing for the fact that he receives $200 less in income per year, he will increase his after-tax income by $640.

William Smith has an 8-year-old daughter. Each year, he saves $1,000, which he invests in stocks in her name. The income from these stocks is not taxable, since his daughter can receive up to $750 per year in income without having to file any federal income tax return. Thus, by the time that she is 18 (and he has given her $10,000 in stocks), the annual income from these stocks will be $700, if the stocks yield 7 percent. And, assuming that his marginal federal income tax rate is 30 percent, he will avoid $210 per year (.30 times $700) in federal income taxes. Why? Because, if he had bought the stocks in his own name, he would have had to pay this much in taxes on this income. At age 18, his daughter can apply this money to her college bills, rather than have him provide it.

Now take the actual case of a wealthy socialite who took a job as an editor. Because of this job, she may be able to deduct many expenses that she would have incurred anyhow. For example, if she takes a trip to Europe, many of her expenses may be deductible, if she can argue (convincingly) that the trip is somehow related to the development of a book. A deduction is an item that is subtracted from one's income to obtain the net income figure on which the amount of income tax is figured. If you can deduct an expense that otherwise would not be deductible, this reduces your income tax by an amount equal to your marginal income tax rate times the expense. Thus, in the case of the socialite, if she spends $5,000 on a trip to Europe, and if her marginal tax rate is 60 percent, she will save $3,000 in income taxes (that is, $.60 \times \$5,000$) if she can convince the Internal Revenue Service that the trip pertained to her business interests.

Many economists feel that the tax system would be more equitable if the tax code were simplified and if many of these ways to avoid income taxes were eliminated. Clearly, some people are better able to take advantage of these loopholes than others. In particular, the wealthy frequently are in a better position to benefit from them than the poor. For this reason, among others, the personal income tax does not bear down as heavily on the rich as one might presume from the official tax rates.

men cannot be interested in reforms that penalize wealthy constituents and potential campaign contributors, the Treasury attempted to tack the reform package onto the tax reduction proposed by the President. The hope was that the tasty carrot of a tax reduction might be strong enough to drag along the refractory donkey of reform. Tax reform got nowhere in Congress. Realizing that the entire bill was in jeopardy, the Administration eventually gave up on reform, and the final bill represented rate reduction and not much else. Undoubtedly, the attempt to gain reform was one factor making for delay in obtaining passage of the tax bill.[7]

Government Debt

The National Debt: Size and Growth

No subject in economics has more confused the public than the national debt. When the federal government spends more than it receives in taxes, it borrows money to cover the difference. The national debt—composed of bonds, notes, and other government IOUs of various kinds—is the result of such borrowing. These IOUs are held by individuals, firms, banks, and public agencies. There is a large and very important market for government securities, which are relatively riskless and highly liquid. If you look at the *New York Times* or *Wall Street Journal*, for example, you can find each day the prices at which each of a large number of issues of these bonds, notes, and bills are quoted.

How large is the national debt? In 1975, as shown in Figure 6.5, it was almost $600 billion. This certainly seems to be a large amount, but it is important to relate the size of the national debt to the size of our national output. After all, a $600 billion debt means one thing if our annual output is $1 trillion, and another thing if our annual output is $100 billion. As a percent of output, the national debt is smaller now than in 1939, and no larger now than shortly after the Civil War. In 1975, the debt was about 40 percent of output; in 1939, it was about 50 percent of output; and in 1868, it was about 40 percent of output. The debt—expressed as a percentage of output—is shown in Figure 6.6. Surely the figures do not seem to provide any cause for alarm. The popular misconception that the national debt is growing at a dangerous rate seems hard to square with the facts.

It is obvious from Figure 6.5 that the size of our national debt is due largely to one thing: World War II. In 1939, the national debt was less than $50 billion; by 1945, it was close to $300 billion. This huge increase occurred to finance the war. Since 1945, the national debt has not grown fast. Indeed, as a percent of national output, it has decreased substantially since 1945. Consequently, as Richard and Peggy Musgrave point out, "The specter of an ever-rising debt to [output] ratio, which so agitated the public only a few decades ago, has become of more or less anthropological interest, a striking example of the demise of a once burning issue."[8]

Burdens and Advantages of the National Debt

Although a discussion of many aspects of the national debt must be postponed to later chapters, it is essential that we look more closely at why the public has been so agitated about the debt's size. One important reason has been that they have felt that the debt was a burden that was being thrust on future generations. To evaluate this idea it is important to recognize that a public debt is not like your debt or mine, which must be paid off at a certain time in the

[7] Thomas Dernburg and Duncan McDougall, *Macroeconomics*, New York: McGraw-Hill, 1972, p. 414.

[8] Richard and Peggy Musgrave, *Public Finance in Theory and Practice*, p. 587. Note too that much of the public debt is in the hands of government agencies, not held by the public. For example, in 1975 only about $350 billion was held by private investors.

Figure 6.5
Size of the National Debt, United States, 1929–75
The national debt, currently almost $600 billion, is due largely to World War II.

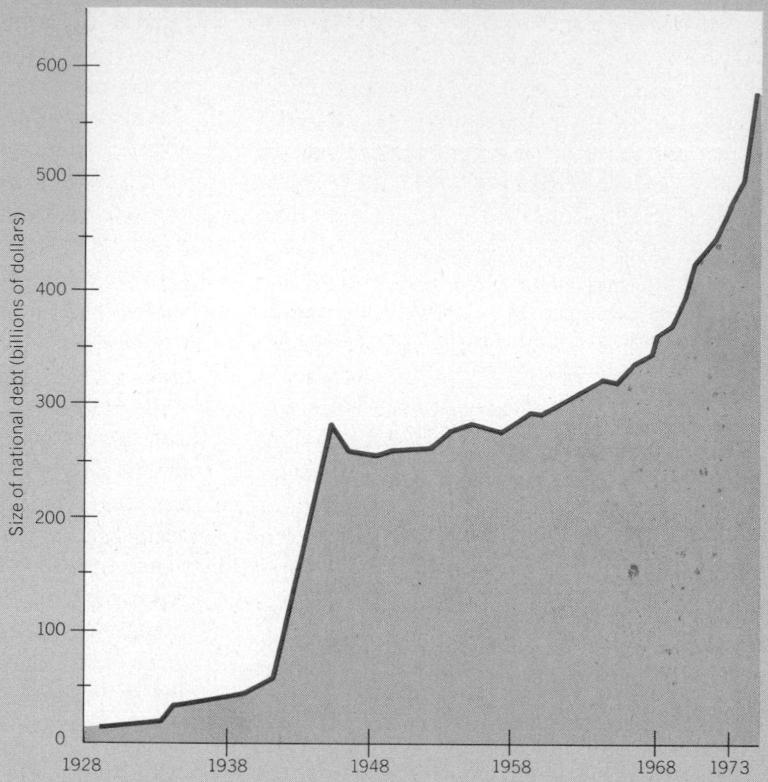

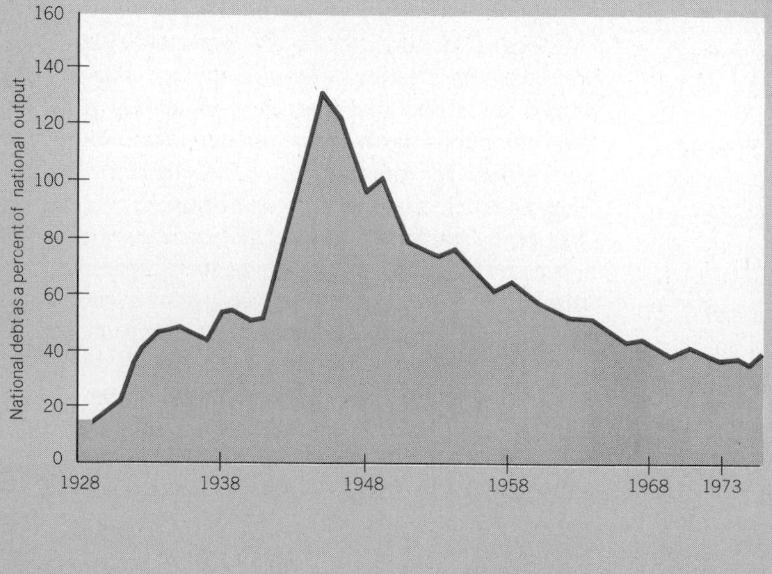

Figure 6.6
National Debt as a Percent of National Output, United States, 1929–75
As a percent of national output, the national debt has declined steadily since World War II.

future. In practice, new government debt is floated to pay off maturing public debt. There never comes a time when we must collectively reach into our pockets to pay off the debt. And even if we did pay it off, the same generation would collect as the one that paid.

Of course, this does not mean that the debt is of no economic consequence. On the contrary, to the extent that the debt is held by foreigners, we must send goods and services overseas to pay the interest on it. This means that less goods and services are available for our citizens. Thus, if we finance a particular government activity by borrowing from foreigners, the costs may be transferred to future generations, since they must pay the interest. But from the point of view of the world as a whole, the current generation sacrifices goods and services, since the lending country forgoes current goods and services. Also, it must be recognized that, if the debt is incurred to purchase capital goods, they may produce enough extra output to cover the interest payments.

Even if the debt is internally held, it may have some undesirable effects. Taxes must be collected from the public at large to pay interest to the holders of government bonds, notes, and other obligations. To the extent that the bondholders receiving the interest are wealthier than the public as a whole, there is some redistribution of income from the poor to the rich. To the extent that the taxes needed to obtain the money to pay interest on the debt reduce incentives, the result also may be a smaller national output.

Beyond this, the existence of all those government bonds, notes, and so forth in the portfolios of people and firms may make them feel richer, and this may make them spend more. Whether this is good or bad depends upon whether we are at less than full employment. If so, it is a good thing; if not, it is bad. In addition, the existence of a large, broadly marketed national debt enables the Federal Reserve System to buy and sell government securities to help stabilize the economy, as we shall see in Chapter 15. This is a good thing—or at least a convenience.

A final word should be added about the idea that the national debt imposes a burden on future generations. *The principal way in which one generation can impose such a burden on another is by using up some of the country's productive capacity or by failing to add a normal increment to this capacity.* This, of course, is quite different from incurring debt. For example, World War II would have imposed a burden on subsequent generations whether or not the national debt was increased. However it was financed, the war would have meant that our resources had to be used for tanks and war planes rather than for keeping up and expanding our productive capacity during 1941–45. And this imposed a burden, a real burden, on Americans living after 1945—as well, of course, as on those living during the war.

Alternative Ways of Financing Government Expenditures—and Their Effects

To complete the present discussion of public finance, it is important to recognize that there are three ways that the federal government can finance any expenditure. The first way is to *raise taxes* to cover the expenditure. The effect of this method of financing the expenditure is straightforward: purchasing power is transferred from the people paying the extra taxes to the government. Thus the costs are borne by the taxpayer. The second way is to *borrow the money* from willing lenders. In this case, too, the effect is straightforward: purchasing power is transferred from the lenders to the government. The current costs of the government programs are borne by the lenders, who receive interest subsequently in return.

The third way the federal government can finance any expenditure is to *create new money.* In other words, it can print extra currency (or

The Department of the Treasury and the National Debt

The average U.S. citizen has very little direct contact with the Department of the Treasury. If he works for the federal government, he receives a bimonthly check; if he is so fortunate as to have overpaid his income tax, he may receive a lovely green refund check. In fact, the processing of checks is (at least, to the nonrecipient economist) much less important than many other functions of the Treasury. Should the Congress or the president wish technical advice on the effect of a new tax measure, the Treasury Department will supply the analysis. In addition, it represents American interests in negotiations over international monetary arrangements with other countries; and, through the Internal Revenue Service and the Customs Service, it collects most federal taxes.*

But from an economist's point of view, one of the most interesting tasks the Treasury performs may be the management of the national debt. Imagine yourself with a debt of about $350 billion (held by private investors), with a few billion coming due each week. Obviously, much of the Treasury's time must be spent scratching for new Peters in order to pay old Pauls. This may not sound like an easy task; and, in fact, it isn't. Over the years the Treasury has developed a bewildering array of devices—refinancing Series E bonds, U.S. savings bonds, short-term bills, long-term bonds—for coaxing new lenders to release their cash, or persuading old lenders to defer collection. The most important of these instruments is U.S. Treasury bills, which in 1973 amounted to almost $103 billion. (Should you ever have a spare $10,000, the smallest denomination in which Treasury bills are sold, their current prices can be found in the financial pages of any major newspaper.)

Almost every month the undersecretary of the Treasury for monetary affairs must decide in what form the portion of the debt coming due should be refinanced. Are interest rates going up? If so, he might refinance by selling long-term bonds, locking up money at the present low rate. Will interest rates fall? If so, he might prefer the 90-day bill. Before an issue is floated, he gets a reading of market conditions from committees of the American Bankers Association and the Investment Bankers Association. But cost is not his only problem. He must also worry about the effect of Treasury operations on financial markets and must have developed future refunding policies. In any case, an elaborate financial network of banks, big insurance companies, pension funds, and investment houses is always waiting to respond to the Treasury's next offering.

E.A.

* Moreover, faithful television fans may realize that, through its Bureau of Customs, the Treasury is responsible for controlling the importation of narcotics.

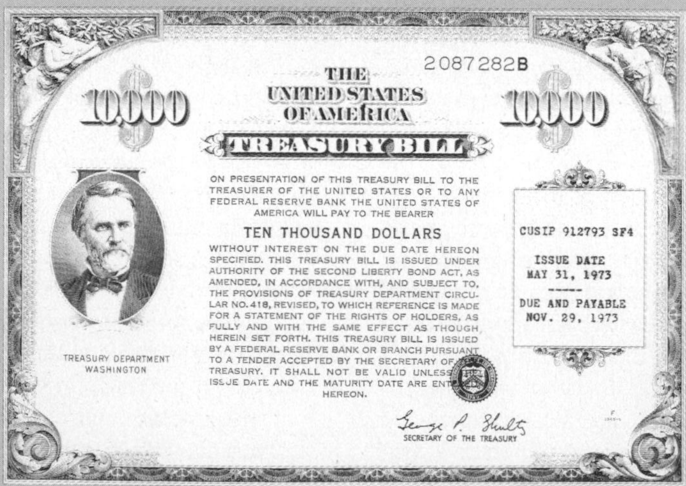
2087282B

10,000 THE UNITED STATES OF AMERICA 10,000

TREASURY BILL

ON PRESENTATION OF THIS TREASURY BILL TO THE TREASURER OF THE UNITED STATES OR TO ANY FEDERAL RESERVE BANK THE UNITED STATES OF AMERICA WILL PAY TO THE BEARER

TEN THOUSAND DOLLARS

WITHOUT INTEREST ON THE DUE DATE HEREON SPECIFIED. THIS TREASURY BILL IS ISSUED UNDER AUTHORITY OF THE SECOND LIBERTY BOND ACT, AS AMENDED, IN ACCORDANCE WITH, AND SUBJECT TO, THE PROVISIONS OF TREASURY DEPARTMENT CIRCULAR NO. 418, REVISED, TO WHICH REFERENCE IS MADE FOR A STATEMENT OF THE RIGHTS OF HOLDERS, AS FULLY AND WITH THE SAME EFFECT AS THOUGH HEREIN SET FORTH. THIS TREASURY BILL IS ISSUED BY A FEDERAL RESERVE BANK OR BRANCH PURSUANT TO A TENDER ACCEPTED BY THE SECRETARY OF TREASURY. IT SHALL NOT BE VALID UNLESS ISSUE DATE AND THE MATURITY DATE ARE ENT HEREON.

CUSIP 912793 SF4

ISSUE DATE
MAY 31, 1973

DUE AND PAYABLE
NOV. 29, 1973

TREASURY DEPARTMENT
WASHINGTON

SECRETARY OF THE TREASURY

create new money in other ways that will be described in Chapters 13 to 15). If the economy is already at full employment, this procedure is likely to cause inflation. The increase in the price level will mean that households and firms will have to buy less than would otherwise have been the case. At the same time, the government will use the new money to finance the expenditure (and obtain the resources it wants). Thus purchasing power is transferred from the consumers and firms whose incomes and receipts do not keep pace with inflation to the government. One disadvantage of this means of finance is that these consumers and firms are often the weakest and least able to bear this burden.

If the economy is not at full employment, the alternative costs of government programs may be much less than if the economy is at full employment. Recall from Chapter 1 that the alternative cost of using resources in a particular way is the value of the output that could have been obtained if these resources had been used in some other way. Clearly, if the resources used in a particular government program would have been unemployed if this program had not been started, society is giving up very little by using these resources in this program. Why? Because they would have been idle otherwise. On the other hand, if there is full employment, these resources would not have been idle, and the alternative costs of the program would be the value of what they could produce elsewhere.

Summary

The spending decisions of the federal government take place in the context of the budgetary process. The president submits his budget, which is a statement of anticipated expenditures and revenues, to Congress, which votes appropriations. Basically, the amount that the government spends on various activities and services must be decided through the nation's political processes. Voting by ballots must be substituted for dollar voting. In making such decisions, it is important to distinguish between changes in government expenditure that alter the scope of government and changes in government expenditures due to changes in efficiency.

Spending on each government program should be pushed to the point where the extra benefit from an extra dollar spent is at least equal to the dollar of cost. In some areas, benefit-cost analyses have proved useful in determining which of a variety of projects can accomplish a particular goal most economically, and whether any of them is worth carrying out. However, accurate measurement of the relevant benefits and costs is frequently difficult.

The Ways and Means Committee of the House of Representatives and the Senate Finance Committee play important roles in the federal tax legislative process. It is generally agreed that people who receive more in benefits from a certain government service should pay more in taxes to support it. It is also generally agreed that people should be taxed so that the result is a socially desirable redistribution of income, and that equals should be treated equally. But these general principles, although useful, cannot throw light on many of the detailed questions a real-life tax code must answer.

The personal and corporate income taxes are very important sources of federal revenue, the sales tax is an important source of state revenues, and the property tax is an important source of local revenues. In recent years, there has been continual pressure for tax reform, since the tax structure of the United States contains many exemptions and loopholes. Also, recognizing the mismatch between the responsibilities and resources of the state and local governments, the federal government has begun a program of revenue sharing.

When the government spends more than it receives in revenues, the difference is called a deficit. The national debt is the result of previous deficits, since the government borrows money to cover a deficit. It could simply print money for this purpose, but it has chosen to borrow a considerable proportion of what was needed. Despite much public worry about the size of the national debt, as a percentage of national output it has been declining over the past 25 years. There are important differences between government debt and private debt. Although the size of the debt is certainly of consequence, it is not true that it somehow transmits a serious burden to future generations or that it may lead to bankruptcy.

CONCEPTS FOR REVIEW

Benefit-cost analysis	Tax reform	Capital gains
Revenue sharing	Benefit principle	Tax incidence
Military-industrial complex	Personal income tax	Public debt
Marginal tax rate	Sales tax	Tax evasion
	Ability to pay	Tax avoidance

QUESTIONS FOR DISCUSSION AND REVIEW

1. "Cost-benefit analysis necessarily involves groping and the making of subjective judgments, not just briskly proceeding with dispassionate scientific measurements."[9] Suppose that such an analysis were made to determine which of a number of roads should be built. Indicate the kinds of subjective judgments that would have to be made.

2. Suppose that the government is trying to determine whether it should build a road from *A* to *B*, or whether it should build one that goes from *B* to *C* as well. The annual costs and benefits from the two alternative projects are as follows:

	Road from *A* to *B*	Road from *A* to *B* to *C*
Annual cost (millions of dollars)	10	15
Annual benefit (millions of dollars)	20	22

Which project, if any, should the government accept? Why?

3. Can you be sent to jail for tax avoidance? Why do people often prefer to receive capital gains rather than ordinary forms of income? If a person's marginal income tax rate is 25 percent and he receives $100 in tax-free income, how much does this equal in before-tax income?

[9] R. McKean, "The Nature of Cost-Benefit Analysis," in E. Mansfield, *Microeconomics: Selected Readings,* 2d ed. New York: Norton, 1975, p. 371.

4. Suppose that if it produces the indicated amount of private goods, the maximum amount of public goods that a society can produce is as follows:

Quantity of private goods	Quantity of public goods
0	12
1	11
5	6
8	1
10	0

If this society produces 5 units of private goods and 5 units of public goods, is it being as efficient as it could be? If not, can we tell whether the inefficiency occurs in the private or public sector? And if so, how?

5. "The national debt is of little or no economic consequence because we owe it to ourselves." Comment and evaluate.

6. Is it possible to test Galbraith's proposition that too little is being spent on government services? What sorts of tests would you propose? In 1973, President Nixon proposed a greatly expanded program of energy research and development. What sorts of information would you look at in order to decide whether the president's proposal should have been accepted or rejected?

7 Make a detailed set of recommendations concerning changes that should be made in the American tax system. With regard to every change that you propose, state your reasons for advocating the change.

8. Suppose that the supply curve for gin is as follows:

Price of gin (dollars per quart)	Quantity supplied (millions of quarts)
4	10
5	9
6	8
7	7
8	6
9	5

Plot the supply curve on graph paper. Suppose that the government imposes a tax of $2 per quart on gin, and that the tax is collected from the sellers. Plot the posttax supply curve on graph paper.

9. Under the circumstances described in Question 8, suppose that the quantity of gin demanded is 7 million quarts, regardless of the price (so long as it is between $4 and $9 per quart). What will be the equilibrium price of gin before the tax, and after it? How much of the tax is passed on to the consumer?

10. Under the circumstances described in Question 8, suppose that the demand curve for gin is a horizontal line at $6 per quart. If this is the case, what will be the equilibrium price of gin before the tax, and after it? How much of the tax is passed on to the consumer?

7

The Business Firm: Organization, Motivation, and Technology

It is hard to overstate the importance of business firms in the American economy. They produce the bulk of our goods and services, hire most of the nation's workers, and issue stocks and bonds that represent a large percentage of the nation's wealth. Judged by any yardstick—even less complimentary ones like the responsibility for environmental pollution—business firms are an extremely important part of the American economy. In this chapter, we discuss the various types of business firms, such as proprietorships and corporations. Then we describe the various types of securities—common stock, bonds, and so forth—issued by firms, and discuss the workings of the stock market. Next, we take up the motivation and structure of firms, as well as their technology. Finally, we provide some essential elements of accounting. This material is a necessary introduction to the workings of the business enterprise, absolutely essential to anyone who works for, manages, or invests in a firm.

Types and Functions of Firms

General Motors: A Case Study

In Chapter 4, when we first discussed the role of the business firm in the American economy, we cited two examples of American business firms: Peter Amacher's drugstore and the General Motors Corporation. Now that we are considering the operations of the business firm in more detail, let's look more closely at the General Motors Corporation. A description of its formation and vicissitudes should give you a better feel for what firms do and the sorts of problems they face.

General Motors was formed in 1908 by William C. Durant, an energetic and imaginative businessman who made over a million dollars in the carriage business before he was 40. After taking over the bankrupt Buick Motor Company in 1904, Durant built it into a very successful operation. Then, in 1908, he gained control of a number of small automobile companies (including Cadillac and Olds), several truck firms, and ten parts and accessory firms. The resulting amalgamation was General Motors.

In 1910, General Motors' sales fell below scheduled production, and Durant lacked the funds to pay his work force and suppliers. To get the money he needed, he went to a banking syndicate, which lent him $15 million–but required him to turn over the management of the company to them. By 1915, Durant had acquired another auto producer, Chevrolet, and had picked up formidable financial allies in the Du Ponts, the owners of the famous chemical firm. Using both these levers, Durant regained full control of General Motors in 1916; and between 1916 and 1920, he concentrated on expanding the productive capacity of the General Motors Corporation. A man of extraordinary vision, he recognized, as did few of his contemporaries, a great potential demand for moderately priced cars, and devoted his energy to putting General Motors in a position to satisfy this demand.

Although Durant was a man of great vision, he was not the sort of administrator who created a tidy organizational structure. The General Motors Corporation under Durant was a very large agglomeration of companies in a variety of product lines, with somewhat tangled lines of communication and diffuse control. When automobile sales did not come up to expectations in 1920, the firm suffered a reduction in profits. The ensuing crisis resulted in Durant's retirement as president of General Motors, and the adoption by the firm of a new organizational plan created by Alfred Sloan, a young M.I.T.-trained engineer, who soon became president. This plan divided General Motors into a number of divisions: the Buick division, the Chevrolet division, the accessory division, and so forth. Each division was given considerable freedom, but greater attention was devoted to central control and coordination than under Durant's more anarchic organization. Sloan's organizational plan, an important innovation in its day, has remained in effect with little change from 1920 to the present: Figure 7.1 shows the organization of General Motors today.

During the 1920s General Motors prospered: its sales rose from $600 million in 1920 to $1,500 million in 1929, and its profits rose from about $38 million in 1920 to about $248 million in 1929. The next decade was different: the 1930s were the years of the Great Depression, when sales and profits of most firms, including General Motors, were hard hit. But during the 1940s General Motors entered another period of prosperity and growth. Its sales rose from about $1.8 billion in 1940 to about $5.7 billion in 1949, and its profits rose from about $196 million in 1940 to about $656 million in 1949. The 1950s and 1960s saw the prosperity of General Motors continue. Of course there were short intervals when sales

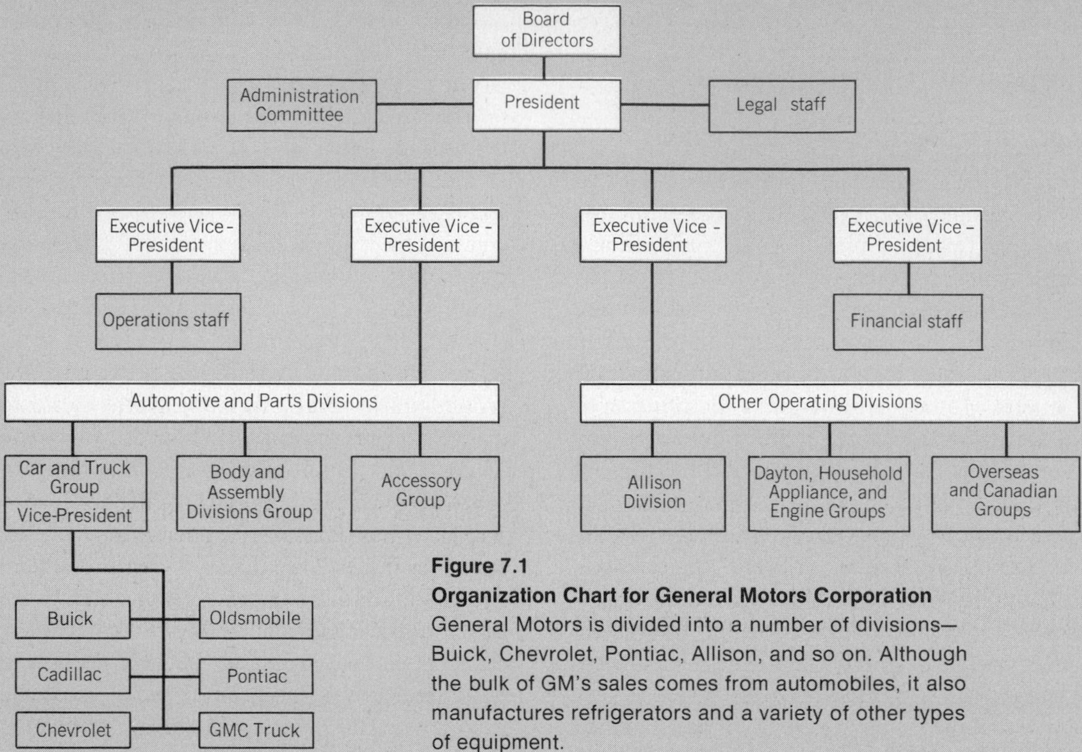

Figure 7.1
Organization Chart for General Motors Corporation
General Motors is divided into a number of divisions—Buick, Chevrolet, Pontiac, Allison, and so on. Although the bulk of GM's sales comes from automobiles, it also manufactures refrigerators and a variety of other types of equipment.

and profits fell, but the trend was upward—in part because of population growth and because higher incomes have meant bigger sales of automobiles. The firm has experienced no prolonged period of low profits or considerable excess capacity, as was the case in the 1930s. By 1975, General Motors had sales of over $35 billion. The somewhat jumbled organization William Durant assembled in 1908 had become one of the biggest industrial companies in the United States, a symbol of industrial might around the world.

Characteristics of American Firms: Some Salient Facts

General Motors is an economic colossus—a huge organization with almost 700,000 employees. Of course it is not typical of American business firms. If we broaden our focus to take in the entire population of business firms in the United States, the first thing we note is their tremendous number; according to government statistics, there are over twelve million. The vast majority of these firms, as one would expect, is very small. There are lots of grocery stores, gas stations, auto dealers, drugstores (like Mr. Amacher's), clothing shops, restaurants, and so on. You see hundreds of them as you walk along practically any downtown city street. But these small firms, although numerous, do not control the bulk of the nation's productive capacity. The several hundred largest firms have great economic power, measured by their sales, assets, employment, or other such indices. The small firms tend to be weak and short-lived. On the average, they tend to go out of business before they have been in existence seven years.

The next thing to note is that most of the nation's business firms are engaged in agriculture, services, and retail trade. Table 7.1 shows that almost ¾ of the firms in the United States are in these industries, an understandable figure since these industries tend to have lots and lots of small businesses. Although manufacturing firms constitute only about 3 percent of all American firms, they account for more than ⅓ of all business receipts. On the other hand, agriculture (including forestry and fisheries) includes about 30 percent of the nation's business firms, but accounts for only 3 percent of the total receipts. Clearly, this is because manufacturing firms tend to be much bigger, in terms of receipts, employment, and assets, than agricultural firms. Think, for example, of the steel plants in Pittsburgh or Cleveland, or of the aircraft plants in California or Georgia. They dwarf the typical farm—and they are only parts of a manufacturing firm.

Finally, note that most of the nation's business firms are proprietorships: indeed, almost ⅘ fall into this category, while about 13 percent are corporations, and about 8 percent are partnerships. You often hear the terms *proprietorship, partnership, corporation.* What do these terms mean?

Proprietorships

A proprietorship is a legal form of business organization—the most common form, as we saw in the previous section, and also the simplest. Specifically, a ***proprietorship*** is a firm owned by a single individual. A great many of the nation's small businesses are proprietorships. For example, the corner drugstore may well be one. If so, it has a single owner. He hires the people he needs to wait on customers, deliver orders, do the bookkeeping, and so forth. He borrows, if he can, whatever money he feels he needs. He reaps the profits, or incurs the losses. All his personal assets—his house, his furniture, his

Table 7.1
Number and Receipts of Business Firms, by Industry, United States, 1972

Industry	Number of firms (millions)	Receipts of firms (millions of dollars)
Agriculture, forestry, and fisheries	3.4	77
Mining	0.1	25
Construction	1.0	143
Manufacturing	0.4	855
Transportation, communication[a]	0.4	172
Wholesale trade	0.6	349
Retail trade	2.3	470
Financial	1.5	148
Services	3.2	146
Total	12.9	2,385

Source: Statistical Abstract of the United States.

[a] Includes electric and gas.

car—can be taken by creditors to meet the drugstore's bills: that is, he has unlimited liability for the debts of the business.

What Lincoln said about the common man applies as well to proprietorships: God must love them, or He wouldn't have created so many of them. If proprietorships didn't have advantages over other legal forms of business organization under many sorts of circumstances, there wouldn't be so many of them. What are these advantages? First, the owner of a proprietorship has complete control over the business. He doesn't have to negotiate with partners or other co-owners. He is the boss—and the only boss. Anyone who has been in a position of complete authority knows the joy it can bring: many proprietors treasure this feeling of independence. Second, a proprietorship is easy and inexpensive to establish: all you have to do is hang out your shingle and announce you are in business. This too is a great advantage.

But proprietorships have important disadvantages as well—and for this reason, they are seldom found in many important industries. One disadvantage is that it is difficult for a proprietor to put together enough financial resources to enter industries like automobiles or steel. No one in the world has enough money to establish, by himself, a firm of General Motors' present size. Another disadvantage is that the proprietor is liable for all of the debts of the firm. If his business fails, his personal assets can be taken by his creditors, and he can be completely wiped out.

Partnerships

A ***partnership*** is somewhat more complicated than a proprietorship. As its name implies, it is a form of business organization where two or more people agree to own and conduct a business. Each partner agrees to contribute some proportion of the capital and labor used by the business, and to receive some proportion of the profits or losses. There are a variety of types of partnerships. In some cases, one or more of the partners may be "silent partners," who put up some of the money, but have little or nothing to do with the operations of the firm. The partnership is a common form of business organization in some industries and professions, like the law. But as we saw in a previous section, partnerships are found less frequently than proprietorships or corporations in the United States.

A partnership has certain advantages. Like a proprietorship, it can be established without great expense or legal red tape. (However, if you ever go into partnership with someone, you would be well advised to have a good lawyer draw up a written agreement establishing such things as the salaries of each partner and how profits are to be shared.) In addition, a partnership can avoid some of the problems involved in a proprietorship. It can usually put together more financial resources and specialized know-how than a proprietorship—and this can be an important advantage.

But the partnership also has certain drawbacks. First, each partner is liable without limit for the bills of the firm. For example, even if one partner of a law firm has only a 30 percent share of the firm, he may be called upon to pay all the firm's debts if the other partners cannot do so. Second, there is some red tape in keeping a partnership in existence. Whenever a partner dies or withdraws, or whenever a new partner is admitted, a new partnership must be established. Third, like the proprietorship, the partnership is not a very effective way to obtain the large amounts of capital required for some modern industries. A modern automobile plant may cost $500 million, and not many partnerships could assemble that much capital. For these reasons, as well as others discussed in the next section, the corporation has become the dominant form of business organization.

Corporations

A far more complicated form of business organization than either the proprietorship or partnership, the ***corporation*** is a fictitious legal person, separate and distinct from its owners. A businessman forms a corporation by having his lawyer draw up the necessary papers stating (in general terms) what sorts of activities he and the other owners of the corporation intend to engage in. The owners of the corporation are the stockholders. ***Stock,*** pieces of paper signifying ownership of the corporation, is issued to the owners, generally in exchange for their cash. Ordinarily, each ***share*** of stock gives its owner one vote. The corporation's ***board of directors,*** which is responsible for setting over-all policy for the firm, is elected by the stockholders. Any of the firm's owners can, if he is dissatisfied with the company's policies or thinks he has better opportunities elsewhere, sell his stock to someone else, assuming, of course, that he can find a buyer.

The corporation has many advantages over the partnership or proprietorship. In particular, each of the corporation's owners has limited, not unlimited, liability. If I decide to become one of the owners of General Motors and if a share of General Motors common stock sells for $65 a share, I can buy ten shares of General Motors stock for $650. And I can be sure that, if General Motors falls on hard times, I cannot lose more than the $650 I paid for the stock. There is no way that I can be assessed beyond this. Moreover, the corporation, unlike the partnership or proprietorship, has unlimited life. If several stockholders want to withdraw from the firm, they simply sell their stock. The corporation goes on, although the identity of the owners changes. For these reasons, the corporation is clearly a better device for raising large sums of money than the partnership or proprietorship. This is an enormous advantage of the corporation, particularly in industries like automobiles and steel, which could not otherwise finance their operations.

Without question, the corporation is a very important social invention. It permits people to assemble the large quantities of capital required for efficient production in many industries. Without limited liability and the other advantages of the corporation, it is doubtful that the opportunities and benefits of large-scale production could have been reaped. However, this does not mean that the corporate form will work for all firms. In many cases, a firm requires only a modest amount of capital, and there is no reason to go to the extra trouble and expense of establishing a corporation. Moreover, one disadvantage of the corporation is ***double taxation of income,*** since, as you will recall from Chapter 6, corporations pay income taxes—and the tax rate is often about ½ of every extra dollar earned. Thus every dollar earned by a corporation and distributed to stockholders is taxed twice by the federal government—once when it is counted as income by the corporation, and once when the remainder is counted as income by the stockholders. This disadvantage of the corporation must be balanced against the advantage that the top tax rates for corporations are less than those that may apply to unincorporated businesses.

The Modern Corporation: Financing, Organization, and Power

Corporate Securities

The corporation raises money by issuing various kinds of securities; of these, three kinds—common stock, preferred stock, and bonds—are particularly significant. Each of these types of securities is important to the workings of the corporation and to people's investment decisions. ***Common stock*** is the ordinary certificate of ownership of the corporation. A holder of common stock is an owner of the firm. He shares in the firm's profits—if there are any profits. At frequent intervals, the board of directors of the firm may declare a dividend of so much per share for the common stockholders. For example, the common stockholders of General Motors received dividends of $2.40 per share in 1975. ***Dividends*** are thus the income the owners of common stock receive. (In addition, of course, common stockholders may make money by selling their stock for more than they paid for it; as noted in the previous chapter, such income is called ***capital gains.***) Common stock is generally regarded as more risky than preferred stock or bonds, for reasons that will be explained.

Preferred stock is a special kind of certificate of ownership that pays at most a stated dividend. For example, owners of one type of General Motors preferred stock receive $5 a share per year, as long as the firm makes enough to pay this dividend. To protect the owners of preferred stock, it is stipulated that no dividends can be paid on the common stock unless the dividends on the preferred stock are paid in full. Since the common stockholders cannot receive their dividends unless the preferred stock's dividends have been paid, common stock is obviously more risky than preferred stock. But by the same token, the amount preferred stockholders have to gain if the company prospers is less than the amount common stockholders have to gain, since however high its profits may be, the firm will pay only the stated dividend—for example, $5 per share per year in the case of General Motors—to the owners of preferred stock.

Bonds are quite different from both common and preferred stocks. ***Bonds*** are debts of the firm; in other words, they are IOUs issued by the firm. In contrast to stockholders, the bondholders are not owners of a firm: they are its creditors, and receive interest, not dividends. Specifically, a bond is a certificate bearing the firm's promise to pay the interest every six months until the bond matures, at which time the firm also promises to pay the bondholder the principal (the amount he lent the firm) as well. Often, bonds are sold in $1,000 denominations. For example, one type of bond issued by General Motors is a 3¼ percent bond, due in 1979. The owner of each such bond receives $32.50 per year in interest, and General Motors promises to pay him the principal of $1,000 when the bond falls due in 1979. A firm must pay the interest on the bonds and the principal when it is due, or it can be declared bankrupt. In other words, the bondholders are legally entitled to receive what is due them before the stockholders can get anything.

Thus, from the point of view of the investor, bonds are generally considered less risky than preferred stock, and preferred stocks are considered less risky than common stock. But we have ignored another fact: inflation. The tendency for the price level in the United States to increase over time has meant that bondholders have been paid off with dollars that were worth less than those they lent. For this reason, together with the fact that owners of common stocks reaped substantial capital gains during the 1960s and early 1970s, many investors in recent years have tended to favor common stocks. Indeed, during the 1960s, a "cult of equities" developed; these were the years when it appeared that stock prices were headed only one way—ever higher. It became very fashionable to buy common stock. But in the middle 1970s, the public's infatuation with common stocks seemed to fade, as stock prices fell. To understand why the value of stocks can gyrate so considerably, it is necessary to look briefly at the workings of the stock market.

The Stock Market

In general, large corporations do not sell stock directly to the investor. Instead, the investor

Buying and Selling Common Stocks

Over 30 million Americans own common stocks, which indicates that you don't have to be wealthy to be an investor. Suppose that you are interested in buying General Motors stock. To determine its current price, you need only look at the financial pages of any major newspaper. For example, on April 24, 1976, the *New York Times* showed the following information concerning General Motors common stock:

1976				Sales				
High	*Low*	*Stock*	*Div*	*100s*	*High*	*Low*	*Last*	*Net Change*
$72\frac{3}{4}$	$57\frac{3}{4}$	Gn Mot	2.40	1513	$70\frac{1}{2}$	$69\frac{3}{4}$	$69\frac{7}{8}$	$-\frac{5}{8}$

Reading from left to right, \$72.75 and \$57.75 are the highest and lowest prices of GM stock in 1976 (up to this date), Gn Mot is the symbol used for General Motors, and \$2.40 is the level of GM's dividends in the previous year. The last five figures show the number of shares sold (151,300), the highest price (\$70.50), the lowest price (\$69.75), and the final price (\$69.87$\frac{1}{2}$) of a share on the previous day, as well as the change in the price from the day before (down \$.62$\frac{1}{2}$ per share). Knowing what these symbols mean, you can tell at a glance what GM common stock sold for yesterday. (And any broker will be glad to give you current quotations.)

To determine whether GM common stock is a good buy, you would be well advised to look at GM's recent earnings record and to obtain as much information as you can concerning the firm's earnings prospects in the future. This is because, as a firm's earnings (per share of common stock) go up, the price of its stock tends to go up too. Some economists and business analysts have gone so far as to publish formulas by which one can determine, on the basis of forecasts of what a firm's earnings will be, how much the stock is worth. They believe that one should buy if the current price of the stock is below this measure of the stock's intrinsic value and sell if the price is above it.

In contrast, other economists believe that the movement of stock prices has more to do with psychology than with financial valuation of this sort. As John Maynard Keynes put it, "[Most persons] are concerned, not with what an investment is really worth to a man who buys it 'for keeps,' but with what the market will value it at, under the influence of mass psychology, three months or a year hence. . . . For it is not sensible to pay 25 for an investment of which you believe the prospective yields to justify a value of 30, if you also believe that the market will value it at 20 three months hence." As Princeton's Burton Malkiel observes, "This theory might . . . be called the 'greater-fool theory.' It's perfectly all right to pay three times what a stock is worth as long as later on you can find some innocent to pay five times what it's worth."*

There is no simple, foolproof way to determine whether GM common stock is a good buy. Certainly, the firm's earnings prospects are of basic importance, but it is difficult, even for the firm itself, to predict what its earnings will be. And psychological factors can outweigh earnings changes in any event. Since even the most astute traders on Wall Street frequently do no better than one could do by buying the Dow-Jones average, you would do well to approach the stock market with caution. More than one economic savant has lost his or her shirt.

* B. Malkiel, *A Random Walk Down Wall Street,* New York: Norton, 1973.

buys stock on the stock market. Two major stock exchanges in the United States are the New York Stock Exchange and the American Stock Exchange, both in New York City. On these and similar exchanges in other cities, the common stocks of thousands of corporations are bought and sold. The price of each common stock fluctuates from day to day, indeed from minute to minute. Basically, the factors responsible for these price fluctuations are the shifts in the demand curve and supply curve for each kind of common stock. For example, if a strike breaks out at a General Motors plant, this may cause the demand curve for General Motors stock to shift downward to the left, since the strike is liable to mean lower profits for General Motors. Because of this downward, or leftward, shift in the demand curve, the price of General Motors common stock will tend to fall, as in fact happened during a United Auto Workers strike in 1974.

Occasionally, the stock market gets a case of jitters over economic conditions, stock prices tumble, and old investors think back to the Great Crash of 1929. The 1920s witnessed a feverish interest in investing in the stock market. Along with raccoon coats, Stutz Bearcats, and the Charleston, common stocks were the rage. Both the professionals on Wall Street and the neophytes on Main Street bought common stocks and more common stocks. Naturally, as the demand curves for common stocks shifted upward to the right, their prices rose, thus whetting the appetites of investors for still more common stocks. This upward spiral continued until 1929, when the bubble burst. Suddenly the prices of common stocks fell precipitously—and continued to drop during the early 1930s. The most famous average of industrial stock prices, the Dow-Jones average, fell from 381 in 1929 to 41 in 1933. Many investors, large and small, were wiped out.

The Great Crash made investors wary of common stocks for many years. But by the 1960s confidence in them was fully restored, and there certainly was no tendency for investors to shy away from them. In the 1970s, although many small investors (and some large ones) lost their shirts, the stock market remained a major outlet for savings. Judging from historical experience, the public's taste for common stocks seems to be justified. Studies show that, during the course of a lifetime, the typical investor would have done better to invest in common stocks than in the best-quality bonds, because stock prices have tended to rise. This tended to apply in a great many cases, even for investors who lived through the Great Crash. And it has certainly been borne out during the past 40 years. Thus, although common stocks are riskier in some respects than bonds or preferred stocks, they seem to have performed better, on the average, at least in recent times.

During periods when the average of stock prices is going up, such as the 1920s and much of the 1950s and 1960s, it is relatively easy to be a financial wizard, whether by luck or calculation. A much more exacting test of your financial acumen is how well you can pick which stocks will outperform the averages. If you can predict that increases will occur in a certain firm's profits, and if other people don't predict the same thing, you may be able to pass this test. However, the sobering truth is that "playing the stock market" is much more an art than a science. The stock market is affected by psychological as well as economic considerations. Moreover, when you try to spot stocks that will increase in price, you are pitting your knowledge and experience against those of skilled professionals with big research staffs and with friends and acquaintances working for the companies in question. And even these professionals can do surprisingly poorly at times.

Do economists have a nose for good investments? John Maynard Keynes was an extremely successful speculator who made millions of dollars. Other economists have been far less successful. Certainly, a knowledge of basic economics is not sufficient to enable you to make money on the stock market, but insofar as the market reflects economic realities, a knowledge of basic economics should be helpful.

The Giant Corporation

Much of the trading on the stock market centers around the relatively small number of giant corporations that control a very substantial percentage of the total assets and employment in the American economy. And well it might, for the largest 100 manufacturing corporations control about ½ of this country's manufacturing assets. These firms have tremendous economic and political power. They include the giant automobile manufacturers (General Motors, Ford, and Chrysler), the big oil firms (Exxon, Gulf, Standard Oil of Indiana, Mobil, Standard Oil of California, Texaco, Atlantic-Richfield), the big steel firms (U.S. Steel, Bethlehem, Jones and Laughlin, Armco), the big computer and office machinery producers (IBM and Xerox), the leading tobacco firms (American Brands, R. J. Reynolds, Philip Morris), and many others.

The large corporation is generally organized into various operating divisions. We saw in Figure 7.1 how General Motors is divided along various product lines. An automotive division like Buick is part of the Car and Truck Group, the head of which reports to an executive vice-president, who reports in turn to the president of General Motors. Usually, the president is the chief operations officer in the firm, although sometimes the chairman of the board of directors fills this role. As for the board of directors, some members are chosen for their reputations and contacts, while others are chosen for their knowledge of the firm, the industry, or some profession or specialty. Usually, the board contains at least one representative of the financial community, and a university president or former government official is often included to show that the firm is responsive to broad social issues. Members of GM's board include Charles Townes, a professor at the University of California, John Connor, a former secretary of commerce; and Leon Sullivan, pastor of Zion Baptist Church of Philadelphia. The board of directors is concerned with over-all policy. Since it meets only a few times a year, it seldom becomes involved in day-to-day decisions; and it usually goes along with management's policies, so long as management retains the board's confidence.

An interesting and important feature of the large corporation is the fact that it is owned by many, many people, practically all of whom have little or no detailed information about the firm's operations. For example, the owners of the American Telephone and Telegraph Company, the giant public utility, number several million but most of them know relatively little about what is going on in the firm. Moreover, because of the wide diffusion of ownership, working control of a large corporation can often be maintained by a group with only ⅕ or less of all the voting stock. The result is a *separation of ownership from control.* In other words, the owners control the firm in only a limited and somewhat sporadic sense.

So long as a firm's management is not obviously incompetent or corrupt, it is difficult for insurgent stockholders to remove the management from office. Most stockholders do not go to the annual meetings to vote for members of the firm's board of directors. Instead, they receive *proxies,* which, if returned, permit the management to exercise their votes. Usually enough shareholders mail in their proxies to give management the votes it needs to elect a friendly board of directors. In recent years, the Securities and Exchange Commission, which oversees and regulates the financial markets, has attempted to make the giant corporations more democratic by enabling insurgent groups to gain access to mailing lists of stockholders and so forth. But there is still a noteworthy and widespread separation of ownership from control.

The New Industrial State

The large corporation is a subject of considerable debate among economists. Many feel that bigness can be a detriment to society, whereas others are more impressed by its virtues. One view of the large corporation that has received considerable attention in recent years can be found in John Kenneth Galbraith's *The New Industrial State.*[1] Galbraith is less concerned than most economists with the disadvantages of the large corporation; indeed, he feels that large corporations are required for much of society's business. According to Galbraith, the large corporation is free of most of the restraints imposed by the market place. It can, by a judicious mixture of advertising and other devices, influence the demand for its own products. Indeed, according to Galbraith, it can control its demand curve to a very considerable extent. In addition, the management of the large corporation is, in Galbraith's view, largely emancipated from the control of the stockholders, since there is a considerable separation of ownership from control. Moreover, the large corporation is free from the obligation to borrow in the capital markets, since it can reinvest its own earnings.

Under these circumstances, who runs the large corporation, and for what purpose? Galbraith's answer is that the large corporation is run by the ***"technostructure"***—the professional managers, engineers, and technicians who are the corporate bureaucracy—and the large corporation's overriding goal is its own survival and autonomy. Consequently, the large corporation tries to avoid risk, and emphasizes planning and stability. It is interested in corporate growth, even if this means some sacrifice of profits. Moreover, it is often interested in technological leadership. Galbraith does not view this situation as bad. Instead, he regards it as inevitable since, in his view, modern technology requires that huge amounts of money and huge organizations dominate the modern economy. Whether you like it or not, he says, this is the way it must be.

Although Galbraith's book has generated much useful and interesting discussion, it has not escaped criticism by the economics profession. For one thing, as Robert Solow of M.I.T. has pointed out, the large corporation does not dominate many parts of the American economy. Nor is it at all clear that modern technology requires very large firms in many industries. Nor is Galbraith's assumption that firms attempt to maximize their rate of growth of sales necessarily better than the more conventional assumption that firms maximize their profits. As we shall see, most economists seem to regard profit maximization as the more fruitful assumption.

Motivation and Technology of the Firm

Profit Maximization

What determines the behavior of the business firm? As a first approximation, *economists generally assume that firms attempt to maximize* ***profits,*** *which are defined as the difference between the firm's revenue and its costs.* In other words, economists generally assume, contrary to Galbraith, that firms try to make as much money as possible. This assumption certainly does not seem unreasonable: most businessmen appear to be interested in making money. Nonetheless, the assumption of profit maximization oversimplifies the situation. Although businessmen certainly want profits, they are interested in other things as well. For example, some firms claim that they want to promote

[1] John Kenneth Galbraith, *The New Industrial State,* Boston: Houghton Mifflin, 1967.

better cultural activities or better racial relations in their community. At a less lofty level, other firms say that their aim is to increase their share of the market. Whether or not one takes these self-proclaimed goals very seriously, it is clear that firms are not interested *only* in making money—often for the same reason that Dr. Johnson gave for not becoming a philosopher: "because cheerfulness keeps breaking in."[2]

In a large corporation, there are some fairly obvious reasons why firms may not maximize profits. Various groups within such firms develop their own party lines, and intrafirm politics is an important part of the process determining firm behavior. Whereas in a small firm it may be fairly accurate to regard the goals of the firm as being the goals of the proprietor, in the large corporation the decision on the goals of the firm is a matter of politics, with various groups within the organization struggling for power. In addition, because of the separation of ownership from control, top management usually has a great deal of freedom as long as it seems to be performing reasonably well. Under these circumstances, the behavior of the firm may be dictated in part by the interests of the management group, resulting in higher salaries, more perquisites, and a bigger staff for their own benefit than would otherwise be the case.

Also, in a world of risk and uncertainty, it is difficult to know exactly what profit maximization means, since the firm cannot be sure that a certain level of profit will result from a certain action. Instead, the best the firm can do is to estimate that a certain probability distribution of profit levels will result from a certain action. Under these circumstances, the firm may choose less risky actions, even though they have a lower expectation of profit than other actions. In a world where ruin is ruinous, this may be perfectly rational policy.

Nonetheless, profit maximization remains the standard assumption in economics. As we agreed in our discussion of model building in Chapter 2, to be useful models need not be exact replicas of reality. Economic models based on profit maximization have been very useful indeed. For one thing, they help to show how the price system functions. For another, in the real world, they suggest how a firm should operate if it wants to make as much money as possible. Even if a firm does not want to maximize profit, these theories can be utilized. For example, they can show how much the firm is losing by taking certain courses of action. In recent years, the theory of the profit-maximizing firm has been studied more and more for the sake of determining profit-maximizing rules of business behavior.

Technology and Inputs

The decisions a firm should make in order to maximize its profits are determined by the current state of technology. Technology, it will be recalled from Chapter 1, is the sum total of society's knowledge concerning the industrial arts. Just as the consumer is limited by his income, the firm is limited by the current state of technology. If the current state of technology is such that we do not know how to produce more than 40 bushels of corn per year from an acre of land and 2 man-years of labor, then this is as much as the firm can produce from this combination of land and labor. In making its decisions, the firm must take this into account.

In constructing his model of the profit-maximizing firm, the economist must somehow represent the state of technology and include it in his model. As a first step toward this end, we must define an ***input.*** Perhaps the simplest definition of an input is that it is anything the

[2] This quote is taken from R. Solow, "The New Industrial State, or Son of Affluence," *The Public Interest,* Fall 1967. Since footnotes are so often used to cite dreary material, it seems worthwhile to use them occasionally to cite humor as well.

firm uses in its production process. For example, some of the inputs of a farm producing corn might be seed, land, labor, water, fertilizer, various types of machinery, as well as the time of the people managing the farm. In analyzing production processes, we suppose that all inputs can be classified into two categories: fixed and variable inputs.

A ***fixed input*** is one whose quantity cannot change during the period of time under consideration. This period will vary: it may be six months in one case, six years in another case. Among the most important inputs often included as fixed are the firm's plant and equipment—that is, its factory and office buildings, its machinery, its tooling, and its transportation facilities. A ***variable input*** is one whose quantity can be changed during the relevant period. For example, it is generally possible to increase or decrease the number of workers engaged in a particular activity (although this is not always the case, since they may have long-term contracts). Similarly, it frequently is possible to alter the amount of raw material that is used.

The Short Run and the Long Run

Whether an input is considered variable or fixed depends on the length of the period under consideration. The longer the period, the more inputs are variable, not fixed. Although the length of the period varies from case to case, economists have found it very useful to focus special attention on two time periods: the short run and the long run. The ***short run*** is defined as the period of time in which some of the firm's inputs are fixed. More specifically, since the firm's plant and equipment are among the most difficult inputs to change quickly, *the short run is generally understood to mean the length of time during which the firm's plant and equipment are fixed.* On the other hand, *the **long run** is that period of time in which all inputs are variable.* In the long run, the firm can make a complete adjustment to any change in its environment.

To illustrate the distinction between the short run and the long run, let's return to the General Motors Corporation. Any period of time during which GM's plant and equipment cannot be altered freely is the short run. For example, a period of one year is certainly a case of the short run, because in a year GM could not vary the quantity of its plant and equipment. It takes longer than a year to construct an automotive plant, or to alter an existing plant to produce a new kind of automobile. For example, the tooling phase of the model changeover cycle currently takes about 2 years. On the other hand, any period of time during which GM can vary the quantity of all inputs is the long run: for example, a period of 50 years is certainly a case of the long run. Whether a shorter period of time—10 years, say—is a long-run situation depends on the problem at hand. If all the relevant inputs can be varied, it is a long-run situation; if not, it is a short-run situation.

The Production Function

Having defined an input and distinguished between the short and long runs, we can now describe how economists represent the state of technology. The basic concept economists use for this purpose is the production function. For any commodity, *the **production function** is the relationship between the quantities of various inputs used per period of time and the maximum quantity of the commodity that can be produced per period of time.* More specifically, the production function is a table, a graph, or an equation showing the maximum output rate that can be achieved from any specified set of usage rates of inputs. The production function summarizes the characteristics of existing technology at a given point in time. It shows the technological constraints the firm must reckon with.

To see more clearly what we mean by a production function, consider the Milwaukee Machine Company, a hypothetical machine shop that produces a simple metal part. Suppose that we are dealing with the short run. The firm's basic plant and equipment are fixed, and the only variable input is the amount of labor used by the machine shop. Suppose that the firm collects data showing the relationship between the quantity of its output and the quantity of labor it uses. This relationship, shown in Table 7.2, is the firm's production function. It shows that, when 1 worker is employed, 100 parts are produced per month; when 2 workers are employed, 210 parts are produced per month; and so on.

Table 7.2
Production Function, Milwaukee Machine Company

Quantity of labor used per month (number of men employed)	Output per month (number of parts)
0	0
1	100
2	210
3	315
4	415
5	500

To illustrate what a production function looks like in a real case, let's consider a crude oil pipeline that transports petroleum from oilfields and storage areas over hundreds of miles to major urban and industrial centers. We begin by noting that the output of such a pipeline is the amount of oil carried per day, and that the two principal inputs are the diameter of the pipeline and the horsepower applied to the oil carried. Both inputs are important. Clearly, the bigger the diameter of the pipe, the more oil the pipeline can carry, holding constant the horsepower applied. And the greater the horsepower applied, the more oil the pipeline can carry, holding constant the diameter of the pipeline.

The production function shows the maximum output rate that can be derived from each combination of input rates. Thus, in this case, the production function shows the maximum amount of oil carried per day as a function of the pipeline's diameter and the amount of horsepower applied. On the basis of engineering estimates, one can derive the production function for crude oil pipelines. For example, Leslie Cookenboo of the Exxon Corporation derived such a production function, assuming that the pipeline carries Mid-Continent crude, has ¼-inch pipe throughout the lines, has lines 1,000 miles in length with a 5 percent terrain variation, and no net gravity flow in the line.[3] Some of his results are shown in Table 7.3. For example, the production function shows that if the diameter of the pipeline is 22 inches and the horsepower is 40,000, the pipeline can carry 215,000 barrels per day. Certainly, any firm operating a pipeline or considering the construction of one is vitally interested in such information. The production function plays a strategic role in the decision making of any firm.

Elements of Accounting

The Firm's Balance Sheet

In a previous section, we stated that economists generally assume that firms attempt to maximize profits. Viewed as a first approximation, this assumption does not seem too hard to swallow, but exactly what do we mean by profit? This is an important question, of inter-

[3] L. Cookenboo, *Crude Oil Pipe Lines and Competition in the Oil Industry*, Cambridge: Harvard University Press, 1955.

Table 7.3
Production Function, Crude Oil Pipeline[a]

Line diameter (inches)	Horsepower (thousands)				
	20	30	40	50	60
	Output rate (thousands of barrels per day)				
14	70	90	95	100	104
18	115	140	155	165	170
22	160	190	215	235	250
26	220	255	290	320	340

Source: Leslie Cookenboo, *Crude Oil Pipe Lines and Competition in the Oil Industry,* Cambridge: Harvard University Press, 1955.
[a]The output rates given in this table are only approximate, since they were read from Cookenboo's graph on p. 16.

est to businessmen and investors as well as to economists. The accounting profession provides the basic figures that are reported in the newspapers and in a firm's annual reports to its stockholders. If General Motors reports that it made $1.5 billion last year, this figure is provided by GM's accountants. How do the accountants obtain this figure? What are its limitations?

Basically, accounting concepts are built around two very important statements: the balance sheet and the profit and loss statement. *A firm's* ***balance sheet*** *shows the nature of its assets, tangible and intangible, at a certain point in time.* For example, let us return to the Milwaukee Machine Company. Its balance sheet might be as shown in Table 7.4. The lefthand side of the balance sheet shows the assets of the firm as of December 31, 1976. ***Current assets*** are assets that will be converted into

Table 7.4
Balance Sheet, Milwaukee Machine Company, as of December 31, 1976

Assets (dollars)		Liabilities and net worth (dollars)	
Current assets:		Current liabilities:	
Cash	20,000	Accounts payable	20,000
Inventory	120,000	Notes payable	40,000
Fixed assets:		Long-term liabilities:	
Equipment	160,000	Bonds	160,000
Buildings	180,000		
		Net worth:	
		Preferred stock	100,000
		Common stock	100,000
		Retained earnings	60,000
Total	480,000	Total	480,000

cash relatively quickly (generally within a year), whereas ***fixed assets*** generally will not be liquidated quickly. The firm has $20,000 in cash, $120,000 in inventory, $160,000 in equipment, and $180,000 in buildings. At first glance, these figures may seem more accurate than they are likely to be. It is very difficult to know how to value various assets. For example, should they be valued at what the firm paid for them, or at what it would cost to replace them? More will be said about these problems in the next section.

The righthand side of the firm's balance sheet shows the claims by creditors on the firm's assets and the value of the firm's ownership. For example, in Table 7.4, the Milwaukee Machine Company has total liabilities—or debts—of $220,000. There is $60,000 in ***current liabilities,*** which come due in less than a year; and $160,000 in ***long-term liabilities,*** which come due in a year or more. Specifically, there is $20,000 in ***accounts payable,*** which are bills owed for goods and services that the firm bought; $40,000 in ***notes payable,*** short-term notes owed to banks, finance companies, or other creditors; and $160,000 in ***bonds payable,*** or bonds outstanding.

The difference between the value of a firm's assets and the value of its liabilities is its ***net worth,*** which is the value of the firm's owners' claims against the firm's assets. In other words, the value of the firm to its owners is the total value of its assets less the value of the debts owed by the firm. Since

total value of assets − total liabilities = net worth,

it follows that

total value of assets = total liabilities + net worth.

That is, *the sum of the items on the lefthand side of the balance sheet must equal the sum of the items on the righthand side.* This, of course, must be true because of the way we define net worth. In the case of the Milwaukee Machine Company, the firm's net worth—the difference between its assets and its liabilities—is $260,000. Specifically, there is $100,000 worth of preferred stock and $100,000 worth of common stock; there is also $60,000 in retained earnings, which we shall explain below.

The Firm's Profit and Loss Statement

*A firm's **profit and loss statement** shows its sales during a particular period, its costs incurred in connection with these sales, and its profits during this period.* Table 7.5 shows the Milwaukee Machine Company's profit and loss statement during the period January 1, 1977 to December 31, 1977. Sales during this period were $240,000. The cost of manufacturing the items made during this period was $110,000—$30,000 for materials, $40,000 for labor, $34,000 for depreciation (discussed below), and $6,000 for miscellaneous operating expenses.

However, because the firm has reduced its inventory from $120,000 to $110,000 during the period, the cost of manufacturing the items *made* during the period does not equal the cost of manufacturing the items *sold* during the period. To find the *cost of goods sold*—which is the amount that logically should be deducted from sales to get the profits made from the sale of these goods—we must add the decrease in the value of inventory to the total manufacturing cost. (Why? Because the firm sold more items than it produced during this period. Thus the cost of the items it sold equals the cost of the items it produced during this period plus the cost of the items it sold from its inventory. Since the cost of the items it sold from its inventory equals the decrease in the value of its inventory, the cost of the items it sold equals the cost of the items it produced during this period plus the decrease in inventory.) Putting

Table 7.5
Profit and Loss Statement, Milwaukee Machine Company, January 1, 1977, to December 31, 1977 (dollars)

Net Sales		240,000
Manufacturing cost of goods sold		120,000
Materials	30,000	
Labor	40,000	
Depreciation	34,000	
Miscellaneous operating cost	6,000	
Total	110,000	
Plus beginning inventory	120,000	
Less closing inventory	−110,000	
Adjusted total	120,000	
Selling and administrative costs		20,000
Fixed interest charges and state and local taxes		10,000
Net earnings before income taxes		90,000
Corporation income taxes		40,000
Net earnings after taxes		50,000
Dividends on preferred stock		4,000
Net profits of common stockholders		46,000
Dividends paid on common stock		20,000
Addition to retained earnings		26,000

it another way, we must add the beginning inventory and subtract the closing inventory, as shown in Table 7.5. The resulting figure for cost of goods sold is $120,000.

But manufacturing costs are not the only costs the firm incurs. To estimate the firm's profits, we must also deduct from sales its selling and administrative expenses, its interest charges, and its state and local taxes, as well as its federal income taxes. Table 7.5 shows that the Milwaukee Machine Company's after-tax earnings during 1977 were $50,000. This is the amount left for the owners of the business. The profit and loss statement also shows what the owners do with what is left. For example, Table 7.5 shows that the Milwaukee Machine Company used $4,000 to pay dividends to holders of preferred stock. When this was done, the holders of common stock were free to distribute some of the profits to themselves. According to Table 7.5, they distributed $20,000 to themselves in dividends on the common stock, and plowed the rest—$26,000—back into the business as retained earnings.

Before leaving the profit and loss statement, we should explain one element of manufacturing cost—***depreciation.*** While the other elements of manufacturing cost are self-explanatory, this one is not. The idea behind depreciation is that the buildings and equipment will not last forever; eventually they will have to replaced. Clearly, it would be foolish to charge the entire cost of replacing them to the year when they are replaced. Instead, a better picture of the firm's true profitability will be drawn if the cost of replacing them is spread gradually over the life of buildings and equipment, thus recognizing that each year's output has a hand in wearing them out. One frequently used technique is so-called ***straight-line depreciation,*** which spreads the cost of buildings and equipment (less their scrap value) evenly over their life. Thus, if the Milwaukee Machine Company buys a piece of equipment for $20,000 and if it is expected to last ten years (its scrap value being zero), it would charge depreciation of $2,000 per year for this machine (for ten years after its purchase). The $34,000 charge for depreciation in Table 7.5 is the sum of such charges. Clearly, this is only a rough way to estimate the true depreciation charges, but it is good enough for many purposes.

Relationship between the Balance Sheet and Profit and Loss Statement

The balance sheet and profit and loss statement are closely related. To see the relationship, let's compare the Milwaukee Machine Company's balance sheet at the end of the period covered by the profit and loss statement in Table 7.5 with the balance sheet at the beginning of this period. The balance sheet at the beginning of the period was shown in Table 7.4. The balance sheet at the end of the period is now given in Table 7.6. At first glance, it may not be obvious how the two balance sheets and the profit and loss statement are related; but after a little reflection, it should be clear that the firm's net worth as shown by the end-of-period balance sheet must equal the firm's net worth as shown by the beginning-of-period balance sheet plus the addition to retained earnings shown in the profit and loss statement.

The reason for this lies in the definition of ***addition to retained earnings.*** This is the amount the common stockholders plow back into the firm; in other words, the amount they add to the net worth of the firm. Since this is so, the increase (or decrease, if addition to retained earnings is negative) in the net worth of the firm must equal the addition to retained earnings (assuming, of course, that the net worth of the firm is not changed by altering the amount of stock outstanding).[4] Thus, for example, in the case of the Milwaukee Machine Company, the firm's net worth had to increase by $26,000 during 1977; and since it was $260,000 at the beginning of 1977, it must

[4] This statement also makes some other assumptions. For a more complete treatment, see any college accounting textbook.

Table 7.6
Balance Sheet, Milwaukee Machine Company, as of December 31, 1977

Assets (dollars)		Liabilities and net worth (dollars)	
Current assets:		Current liabilities:	
Cash	36,000	Accounts payable	10,000
Inventory	110,000	Notes payable	40,000
Fixed assets		Long-term liabilities	
Equipment	170,000	Bonds	160,000
Buildings	180,000		
		Net worth:	
		Preferred stock	100,000
		Common stock	100,000
		Retained earnings	86,000
Total	496,000	Total	496,000

have been $286,000 at the end of 1977. Where on the balance sheet does this $26,000 show up? What part of net worth increased by $26,000? The answer is that ***retained earnings,*** which shows the total amount that the stockholders have plowed back into the firm in the past, went up by $26,000.

Economic versus Accounting Profits

The previous sections described the nature of profit, as defined by accountants. This is the concept on which practically all published figures in business reports are based. But economists define profits somewhat differently. In particular, the economist does not assume that the firm attempts to maximize the current, short-run profits measured by the accountant. Instead he assumes that the firm will attempt to maximize the sum of profits over a long period of time.[5] Also, when the economist speaks of profits, he means profit after taking account of the capital and labor provided by the owners. Thus, suppose that the owners of the Milwaukee Machine Company, who receive profits but no salary or wages, put in long hours for which they could receive $30,000 in 1977 if they worked for someone else. Also suppose that if they invested their capital somewhere other than in this firm, they could obtain a return of $22,000 on it in 1977. Under these circumstances, economists would say that the firm's after-tax profits in 1977 were $50,000 − $30,000 − $22,000, or − $2,000, rather than the $50,000 shown in Table 7.5. In other words, the economist's concept of profit includes only what the owners make above and beyond what their labor and capital employed in the business could have earned elsewhere. In this case, that amount is negative.

[5] The profits earned at various points in time should be *discounted* before being added together, but, for simplicity's sake, we neglect this point here.

To a considerable extent, the differences between the concepts used by the accountant and the economist reflect the difference in their functions. The accountant is concerned with controlling the firm's day-to-day operations, detecting fraud or embezzlement, satisfying tax and other laws, and producing records for various interested groups. On the other hand, the economist is concerned primarily with decision making and rational choice among prospective alternatives. Although the figures published on profits almost always conform to the accountant's, not the economist's, concept, the economist's concept is the more relevant one for many kinds of decisions. (And this, of course, is recognized by sophisticated accountants.) For example, suppose the owners of the Milwaukee Machine Company are trying to decide whether they should continue in business. If they are interested in making as much money as possible, the answer depends on the firm's profits as measured by the economist, not the accountant. If the firm's economic profits are greater than zero, the firm should continue in existence; otherwise, it should not. Thus the Milwaukee Machine Company should not stay in existence if 1977 is a good indicator of its future profitability.

The Financial Statements of General Motors: A Case Study

To conclude this chapter, let's return once again to General Motors, and examine its financial statements—its balance sheet and profit and loss statement. These are a bit more detailed than the hypothetical statements of the Milwaukee Machine Company, but they are constructed on the same principles. Each year, General Motors issues an annual report to its stockholders, which includes these financial statements. Table 7.7 reproduces GM's balance sheet as of December 31, 1974; and Table 7.8 reproduces GM's profit and loss statement

Table 7.7
Balance Sheet, General Motors Corporation, as of December 31, 1974

Assets (millions of dollars)		Liabilities and net worth (millions of dollars)	
Current assets:		Current liabilities:	
Cash	401	Accounts payable	3,600
Government securities	938	Taxes owed	2,499
Accounts receivable	3,001	Other	3
Inventories	6,405		
		Long-term liabilities	
Fixed Assets:		Bonds	122
		Other	1713
Investments	1,552		
Real estate, plant, and equipment	6,215	Net worth:	
Other	1,956	Preferred stock	284
		Common stock	479
		Retained earnings[a]	11,769
Total	20,468	Total	20,468

Source: Moody's.
[a] Includes capital surplus.

Table 7.8
Profit and Loss Statement, General Motors Corporation, January 1, 1974, to December 31, 1974 (millions of dollars)

Net sales (and other income)		31,861
Manufacturing cost of goods sold		28,624
Materials, labor, and miscellaneous operating costs	28,147	
Depreciation	1,705	
Total	29,852	
Plus beginning inventory	5,177	
Less closing inventory	−6,405	
Adjusted total	28,624	
Selling and administrative costs (and interest charges)		1,560
Net earnings before U.S. and foreign taxes		1,677
U.S. and foreign taxes		727
Net earnings after taxes		950
Dividends on preferred stock		13
Net profits of common stockholders		937
Dividends paid on common stock		970
Addition to retained earnings		−30

Source: Moody's.

for 1974. Take a close look at these tables, and see if you understand what each item means. For example, Table 7.7 says that GM had $3,001 million in accounts receivable at the end of 1974. What are accounts receivable? (Bills its customers owe General Motors.) It also says that GM had $284 million in preferred stock at the end of 1974. What is preferred stock? (If you don't recall, turn back to the section on "Corporate Securities.") According to Table 7.8, GM incurred depreciation costs of $1,705 million in 1974. What is depreciation? (Turn back to "The Firm's Profit and Loss Statement" if you need to.) Also, GM's addition to retained earnings was negative in 1974. What does this mean? (See the section on "Relationship between Balance Sheet and Profit and Loss Statement.")

Financial analysts spend an enormous amount of time poring over the financial statements of various companies to estimate whether their stock is a good or bad investment. Banks look at a firm's financial statements when they decide whether or not to grant the firm a loan. The financial pages of the major newspapers, as well as magazines specializing in financial and business news, are sprinkled liberally with summaries of these financial statements. You would do well to make sure you understand the basic definitions and principles of accounting presented in previous sections. In dealing with practical problems, this information will serve you well.

Summary

There are three principal types of business firms: proprietorships, partnerships, and corporations. The corporation has many advantages over the other two—limited liability, unlimited life, and greater ability to raise large sums of money. The corporation raises money by issuing various kinds of securities, of which three kinds—common stock, preferred stock, and bonds—are particularly important. A relatively small number of giant corporations control a very substantial proportion of the total assets and employment in the American economy. In the large corporation, ownership and control tend to be separated. So long as a firm's management is not obviously incompetent or corrupt, it is difficult for insurgent stockholders to remove the management from office.

As a first approximation, economists generally assume that firms attempt to maximize profits. In large part, this is because it is a close enough approximation to reality for many of the most important purposes of economics. Also, economists are interested in the theory of the profit-maximizing firm because it provides rules of behavior for firms that do want to maximize profits. In constructing his model of the profit-maximizing firm, the economist must somehow represent the state of technology and include it in his model. He classifies inputs used by the firm into two categories: fixed and variable. He also differentiates between the short run and the long run. Then, to summarize the characteristics of existing technology at a given point in time, he uses the concept of the production function, which shows the maximum output rate of a given commodity that can be achieved from any specified set of usage rates of inputs.

Accounting concepts are built around two very important statements: the balance sheet and the profit and loss statement. The balance sheet shows the nature of the firm's assets and liabilities at a given point in time. The difference between its assets and its liabilities is its net worth, which is the value of the firm's owners' claims against its assets. A firm's profit and loss statement shows its sales during a particular period, its costs incurred in connection with these sales, and its profits during the period. The balance sheet and the profit and loss statement are closely related. Economists define profits somewhat differently than accountants do. In particular, the economist excludes from profit the value of the capital and labor provided by the owners, and he is interested in longer periods than those to which accounting statements apply. Although the profit figures that are published almost always conform to the accountant's concept, the economist's concept is the more relevant one for many kinds of decisions.

CONCEPTS FOR REVIEW

Proprietorship	Preferred stock	Production function
Partnership	Bond	Balance Sheet
Corporation	Profit	Current Assets
Liability	Input	Fixed Assets
Board of directors	Fixed input	Profit and loss statement
Common stock	Variable input	Depreciation

QUESTIONS FOR DISCUSSION AND REVIEW

1. Which of the following are inputs in the steel industry? (a) coke, (b) iron ore, (c) labor, (d) bread, (e) capital, (f) water, (g) oxygen, (h) yeast.

2. "Modern technology, says Galbraith, makes planning essential, and the giant corporation is its chosen instrument. This planning, in turn, requires the corporation to eliminate risk and uncertainty, to create for itself an environment of stability and security, and to free itself from all outside interference with its planning function."[6] Comment.

3. "The long run in one industry or situation may be shorter than the short run in another industry or situation." Explain and evaluate. If you agree, give several specific examples.

4. Assume that a partnership wanted to enter the automobile industry. What problems would such a legal form of organization impose upon the potential entrants? Are there any partnerships that produce automobiles? Why?

5. The great English economist, John Maynard Keynes, said that investing in stocks was like "entering a newspaper beauty-judging contest in which you have to select the six prettiest faces out of 100 photographs. The prize goes to the person whose selections most nearly conform to those of the group as a whole."[7] Explain and evaluate.

[6] W. Adams, "Another View of the New Industrial State," in E. Mansfield, *Economics: Readings, Issues, and Cases*, 2d ed., New York: Norton, 1977.

[7] B. Malkiel, *A Random Walk Down Wall Street.*

6. Suppose that a firm's balance sheet is as follows:

Assets (dollars)		Liabilities and net worth (dollars)	
Current assets		Current liabilities	
Cash	200,000	Accounts payable	100,000
Inventory	300,000	Notes payable	_______
Fixed Assets		Long-term liabilities	
Equipment	_______	Bonds	400,000
Buildings	800,000		
		Net Worth	400,000
Total	2,000,000	Total	_______

Fill in the three blanks. What is the total amount that the firm owes? How much have the owners contributed? What is the difference between current assets and fixed assets?

7. Suppose that a firm's accounting profits for 1976 are $20,000. The firm is a proprietorship, and the owner worked 500 hours managing the business during 1976, for which he received no compensation other than the profits. If he could have gotten $10 an hour working for someone else, how much were his economic profits during 1976? Suppose that he also contributed $50,000 in capital to the firm, and that he could have obtained 6 percent interest on this capital if he had invested it elsewhere. In this case, how much were his economic profits?

8. Do you think that General Motors maximizes profits? What do you think William C. Durant would have replied if you had asked him this question? For economic models to be useful, must firms maximize profits?

9. Suppose that a friend offered to sell you some stock in a small company. How would the firm's balance sheet and profit and loss statement be useful in evaluating how much the stock is worth?

10. Based on the data in Table 7.3, if line diameter is held constant and horsepower is increased, does an extra 1,000 horsepower seem to increase the output of a pipeline by the same amount, regardless of how many horsepower are already applied? Why or why not?

PART THREE

National Output, Income, and Employment

8 Unemployment, Inflation, and National Output

Three of the most important indicators of the health of any nation's economy are its unemployment rate, its rate of inflation, and the size of its national output. Every government, including our own, watches these indicators with great interest. Moreover, most societies today are committed to policies designed to influence each of them, in particular to keeping unemployment and inflation to a reasonable minimum, and to promoting the growth of national output. These social goals certainly seem sensible, since high rates of unemployment can cause enormous social waste and private hardship. Also, most societies seem to believe that the benefits of greater national output outweigh the costs, and that serious inflation should not be tolerated.

In this chapter, we begin to study unemployment, inflation, and national output. Our first objective is to discuss the nature of unemployment and inflation, and how the rate of inflation is related to the rate of unemployment.

Then we turn to a detailed examination of how national output is measured, our purpose being to describe such concepts as gross national product and its components: consumption, investment, government spending, and net exports. Finally, we discuss how the gap between actual and potential output is related to the level of unemployment.

Unemployment

Types of Unemployment

Almost a century ago, Pope Leo XIII said, "Among the purposes of a society should be to arrange for a continuous supply of work at all times and seasons."[1] The word *unemployment* is one of the most frightening in the English language–and for good reason. Unemployed people become demoralized, suffer loss of prestige and status, and their families tend to break apart. Sometimes they are pushed toward crime and drugs; often they feel terrible despair. Their children are innocent victims too. Indeed, perhaps the most devastating effects of unemployment are on children, whose education, health, and security may be ruined. After a few minutes' thought, most people would agree that in this or any other country every citizen who is able and willing to work should be able to get a job.

Of course we are not saying that all unemployment, whatever its cause or nature, should be eliminated. According to the U.S. government, *any person 16 years old or more who does not have a job and is looking for one is* ***unemployed.*** Since this definition is necessarily quite broad, it is important that we distinguish among several quite different kinds of unemployment.

Frictional unemployment. This sort of unemployment is related to the entrance of new workers into the labor market and the movement of workers from one position to another. For example, Tom Smith may quit his job after the boss calls him a fathead. It may take him a month to find another job, perhaps because he is unaware of job opportunities or perhaps because the boss was right. During this month, he is numbered among the unemployed. It would not make much sense to try to eliminate all such temporary unemployment. On the contrary, a free labor market could not function without a certain amount of frictional unemployment.

Structural unemployment. Unemployment of this kind exists when jobs are available for qualified workers, but the unemployed do not have the necessary qualifications. This sort of unemployment results from a mismatch between job requirements and the skills of the unemployed, as in the case of a 58-year-old cotton picker thrown out of work by the introduction of mechanical cotton pickers who lacks the skills needed to get a job in another field. To some extent, structural unemployment can be reduced by monetary and fiscal policies of the sort described in the following chapters. But in many cases, the principal way to attack it is by retraining workers whose skills are no longer in demand for jobs in other occupations, industries, or areas.

Cyclical unemployment. This type of unemployment occurs when, because of an insufficiency of aggregate demand, there are more workers than jobs. Cyclical unemployment is associated with business fluctuations, or the so-called business cycle. Industrialized capitalistic economies have been subject to fluctuations, with booms often succeeding busts and vice versa. Before World War II the American economy periodically went through serious depressions, during which unemployment was very high. The Great Depression of the 1930s was particularly long and severe, and when World War II ended, the American people resolved that the gigantic social costs of the enormous unemployment of the 1930s must

[1] Pope Leo XIII, *Encyclical Letter on the Conditions of Labor,* May 15, 1891.

not be repeated in the postwar period. To avoid this, Congress passed the Employment Act of 1946, which says,

> It is the continuing policy and responsibility of the Federal Government to use all practicable means . . . [to create and maintain] conditions under which there will be afforded useful employment opportunities, including self-employment, for those able, willing, and seeking to work and to promote maximum employment, production, and purchasing power.

The Employment Act of 1946 was an extremely important piece of legislation, for it committed the federal government to combat cyclical unemployment.

How Much Unemployment Is There?

To get some idea of the extent of unemployment, we can consult Figure 8.1, which shows the percent of the labor force unemployed during each year from 1929 to 1975. Note the wide fluctuations in the unemployment rate, and the very high unemployment rates during the 1930s. Fortunately, unemployment since World War II has never approached the tragically high levels of the Great Depression of the 1930s. In 1949 and 1950, and again in 1954, the unemployment rate pushed up toward 6 percent, but in general it remained at about 4 percent or less until 1958, when it increased to almost 7 percent. Between 1958 and 1964, it averaged about 6 percent, and then declined steadily until it fell below 4 percent in 1966–69. In 1970–74, it bounced back up to 5 or 6 percent, and then rose to 8½ percent in 1975, after which it receded. Although many of these variations in the unemployment rate may seem small, they are by no means unimportant. Any administration, Democratic or Republican, watches these figures closely, and tries to avoid significant increases in unemployment.

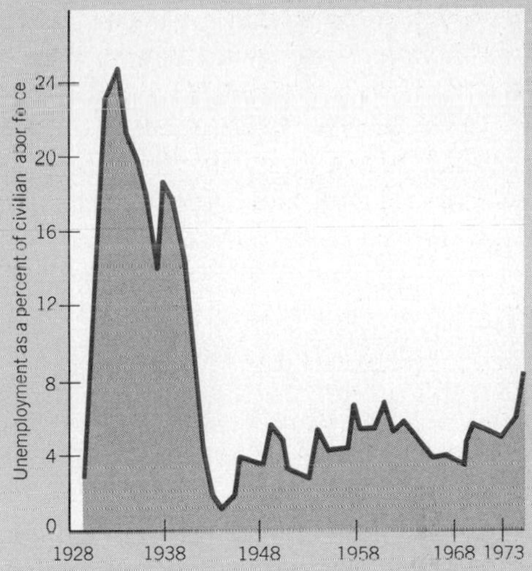

Figure 8.1
Unemployment Rates, United States, 1929–75
The unemployment rate has varied substantially. Fortunately, since World War II it has not approached the very high levels of the Great Depression of the 1930s. But the recent recession of 1974–75 showed that the nation is not immune to severe bouts of unemployment.

The importance of unemployment statistics makes it worthwhile to see how they are collected. The federal government periodically conducts a scientific survey of the American people, asking a carefully selected sample of the population whether they have a job, and, if not, whether they are looking for one. According to most expert opinion, the resulting figures are quite reliable within certain limits. One of these is that they do not indicate the extent to which people are ***underemployed.*** Some people work only part-time, or at jobs well below their level of education or skill, but the government figures count them as fully employed. Also, some people have given up looking for a job and are no longer listed among the unemployed, even though they would be glad to get work if any was offered. To count as unemployed in the government figures, one must be actively seeking employment.

In addition, aggregate figures on unemployment cover up very substantial differences among groups within a society. Unemployment rates among blacks and other minorities are much higher than among whites. Also, unemployment rates among teenagers and women tend to be disproportionately high. For example, in 1975, although the unemployment rate for all workers was 8.5 percent, it was 19.9 percent among people 16 to 19 years of age and 13.9 percent among nonwhites. Consequently, since unemployment tends to be concentrated in particular segments of the population, overall unemployment rates can be somewhat misleading.

Finally, some critics of the official unemployment statistics would use a definition of unemployment that focuses attention on "serious" cases of joblessness. They would exclude unemployed people with a working spouse, unemployed teenagers living with a parent with a job, and unemployed people who have been out of work less than a month. Also, they would have the government try harder to find out whether those who say they are unemployed are making a serious effort to find work. Officials of the Bureau of Labor Statistics reply that such a change in definition would convert the statistics into a measure of hardship rather than of unemployment.

Unemployment: A Case Study

Since general descriptions of the plight of the unemployed often have relatively little impact, a real-life case study may give you a better feel for what unemployment is like. Consider Joseph Torrio, a New Haven factory worker who was laid off after 18 years on the job. He describes in his own words how he spent several mornings:

> Up at seven, cup of coffee, and off to Sargent's. Like to be there when the gang comes to work, the lucky devils. Employment manager not in. Waited in his outer office. . . . Three others waiting, two reporting for compensation. Other one laid off two weeks ago and said he called at office every day. He inquired what I was doing and when I said "looking for work" he laughed. "You never work here? No? What chance you think you got when 400 like me who belong here out?" Employment manager showed up at 9:30. I had waited two hours. My time has no value. A pleasant fellow; told me in a kind but snappy way business was very bad. What about the future, would he take my name? Said he referred only to the present. Nothing more for me to say, so left. Two more had drifted into office. Suppose they got the same story. Must be a lot of men in New Haven that have heard it by now.
>
> [On May 21], interview with sales manager of the Real Silk Hosiery Mills. Had seen their ads for salesmen in the paper. Sales manager approached me with his hand sticking out, the first one who had offered to shake hands with me. I told him my name and inquired about the position. He took me into his private office, well furnished, and asked me if I had had any selling experience. I told him that I hadn't any but I thought I could do the work. . . . Asked me to report at 9 A.M. the next morning for further instructions. . . . [On May 22], I kept my appointment with the sales manager. Spent the morning learning about different kinds of stockings. Made another appointment for the afternoon which I did not keep because he wanted me to bring along $6 as security on a bag and some stock. I did not have the $6.[2]

No single case study can give you an adequate picture of the impact on people of being without a job. There are a wide variety of responses to unemployment. Some people weather it pretty well, others sink into despair; some people have substantial savings they can

[2] E. W. Bakke, *The Unemployed Worker,* Hamden, Conn.: Archon, 1969, pp. 168, 169, 174, and 175.

draw on, others are hard pressed; some people manage to shield their families from the blow, others allow their misfortunes to spread to the rest of the family. But despite these variations, being without work deals a heavy blow to a person's feeling of worth. It hits hard at a person's self-image, indicating that he or she is not needed, cannot support a family, is not really a full and valuable member of society. It can strike a cruel blow at men and women alike, since many women are vitally interested in achievement outside the home, sometimes because they are the family breadwinners. The impact of widespread and persistent unemployment is most clearly visible at present among the blacks and other racial minorities, where unemployment rates are much higher than among the white population. Unquestionably, the prevalence of unemployment among blacks greatly influences how the blacks view themselves, as well as the way they interact with the rest of the community.

Inflation

Nature and Effects of Inflation

It is hard to find anyone these days who does not know the meaning of inflation firsthand. Try to think of commodities you regularly purchase that cost less now than they did several years ago. Chances are that you can come up with precious few. ***Inflation** is a general upward movement of prices.* In other words, inflation means that goods and services that currently cost $10 may soon be priced at $11 or even $12, and wages and other input prices increase as well. It is essential to distinguish between the movements of individual prices and the movement of the entire price level. As we saw in Chapter 4, the price of an individual commodity can move up or down with shifts in the commodity's demand or supply curve. If the price of a particular good—corn, say—goes up, this need not be inflation, since the prices of other goods may be going down at the same time, so that the over-all price level—the general average level of prices—remains much the same. Inflation occurs only if most prices for goods and services in the society move upward—that is, if the average level of prices increases.

Inflation may seem no more than a petty annoyance: after all, most people care about relative, not absolute, prices. For example, if wages (the price of labor) increase at the same rate as prices, a family may be no better or worse off under inflation than under a constant price level. But this view ignores the people—civil service employees, teachers, and many others—who cannot increase their wages to compensate for price increases because they work under long-term contracts, among other reasons. These people and people living on pensions and other fixed incomes take a considerable beating from inflation.

Also, inflation hurts lenders and benefits borrowers, since it results in the depreciation of money. A dollar is worth what it will buy, and what it will buy is determined by the price level. If the price level increases, a dollar is worth less than it was before. Consequently, if you lend Bill Jones $100 in 1977 and he pays you $100 in 1987—when a dollar will buy much less than in 1977—you are losing on the deal. In terms of what the money will buy, he is paying you less than what he borrowed. Of course, if you anticipate considerable inflation, you may be able to recoup by charging him a high enough interest rate to offset the depreciation of the dollar, but it is not so easy to forecast the rate of inflation and protect yourself.

Unlike unemployment, inflation (at least in small doses) does not seem to reduce national output: in the short run, output may increase. The principal effect of inflation is on the distribution of income and wealth. Many inflations are not anticipated; and even if they are, we have just noted that many people are not knowledgeable enough to protect themselves.[3] The poor worker who has put aside some money for his old age, only to find that it will buy a fraction of what he hoped, has been victimized by inflation. Why should he bear this loss? As Arthur Okun, a former chairman of the Council of Economic Advisers, has put it, " 'sharpies' . . . make sophisticated choices and often reap gains on inflation which do not seem to reflect any real contribution to economic growth. On the other hand, the unsophisticated saver who is merely preparing for the proverbial rainy day becomes a sucker."[4]

Citizens and policy makers generally agree that inflation, like unemployment, should be minimized. For example, when President Ford convened a national Summit Conference of business people, labor leaders, and others in the fall of 1974, almost all agreed that inflation was "Public Enemy Number One," or close to it. However, such sentiment has not prevented the United States from suffering from considerable inflation. As shown in Figure 8.2, the price level has tended to increase considerably in the United States during the past 40 years. Substantial inflation followed World War II; the price level increased by about 33 percent between 1945 and 1948. Bursts of inflation recurred during the Korean War and then during the Vietnam War. And in the 1960s and 1970s, despite the government's efforts, inflation has continued. (Indeed, during 1974, prices rose by about 12 percent.) Our government's policy is to avoid both excessive unemployment and excessive inflation, but this goal, like many desirable social objectives, is by no means easy to achieve. Indeed, under certain circumstances, it may be impossible to have both stable prices and high employment, as we shall see in the next section.

[3] Economists often distinguish between anticipated and unanticipated inflation because if inflation is anticipated, people may be able to compensate for it by charging higher interest rates and by similar devices.

[4] Arthur Okun, "The Costs of Inflation," in his *The Battle against Unemployment*, rev. ed., New York, Norton, 1972.

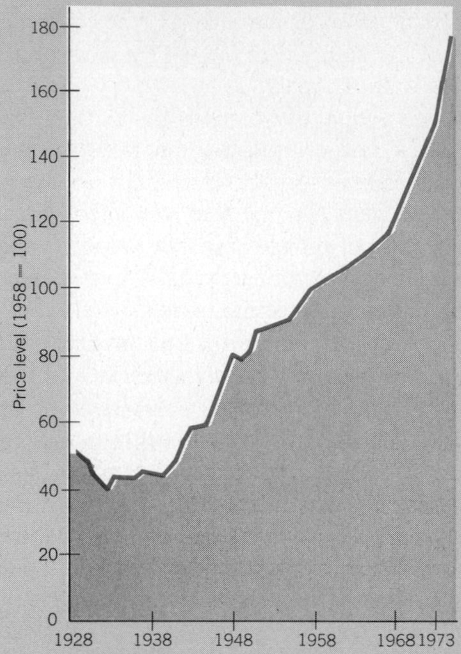

Figure 8.2
The Price Level, United States, 1929–75
The price level has increased considerably in the United States during the past 40 years. In recent years, inflation has been a stubborn problem.

The Relationship between Inflation and Unemployment

According to many economists, in the short run the unemployment rate is inversely related to the rate of inflation: that is, the lower the unemployment rate, the higher the rate of inflation. This relationship is by no means fixed and immutable, and the factors underlying its shape and position are still matters of debate. But, as a first approximation, we assume that this relationship is like that shown in Figure

8.3. In Chapter 16, we shall discuss in detail the reasons why many economists believe this relationship exists (and some recent controversies over its existence). At this point, it is sufficient to point out that both the unemployment rate and the inflation rate are determined by the total level of spending on the goods and services produced by the economy. Consumers, firms, and governments all spend money on the goods and services the nation produces. The level of output in our economy depends on how much money they spend. If their expenditures are very low, this means that the economy will operate in Range *A* in Figure 8.4, where national output is far below its maximum. Because the low level of expenditure means a low level of demand for the nation's goods and services, firms cannot sell enough goods and services to make it profitable to hire many of the workers who want to work. Thus employment is low, and the unemployment rate is high. As for the inflation rate, it is low, since there are plenty of excess capacity and unemployed resources. It is no time to raise prices.

Under these circumstances, suppose that an increase occurs in the total level of spending. National output and employment will rise, and the unemployment rate will fall, but there will be little or no increase in the price level since output can be increased without bidding up the prices of labor and other inputs. When the level of expenditure increases to the point where output and employment are in Range *B*, the unemployment rate will be substantially lower than in Range *A*, but the price level will begin to rise. Why? Because bottlenecks occur in some parts of the economy, and labor pushes harder for wage increases (and firms are more willing to agree to such increases). Finally, if the level of spending increases to the point where output and employment are in Range *C*, there will be no further decreases in the unemployment rate, since national output, which has reached its maximum, can grow no longer. In this range, the rate of inflation is very high, since total spending far exceeds the value of national output at initial prices. There are "too many dollars chasing too few goods."

As indicated in Figure 8.4, the inflation rate is likely to increase as output and employment

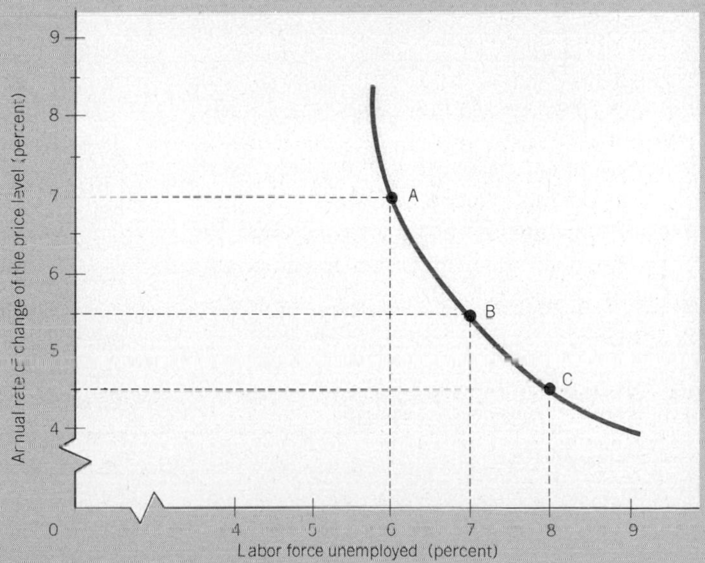

Figure 8.3
Relationship between Unemployment Rate and Rate of Inflation
According to many economists, there is an inverse short-run relationship between the unemployment rate and the rate of inflation. If the relationship is as shown here, a 6 percent unemployment rate means a 7 percent rate of inflation, a 7 percent unemployment rate means a 5.5 percent rate of inflation, and an 8 percent unemployment rate means a 4.5 percent rate of inflation.

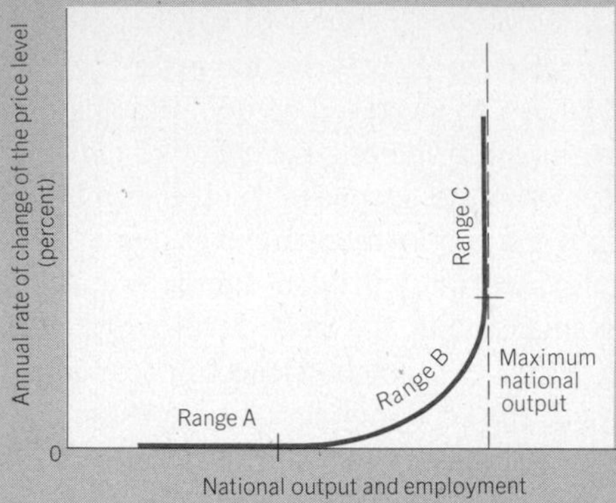

Figure 8.4
Output, Employment, and the Rate of Inflation
Chapter 3 pointed out that any economy can only produce so much, given its resources and the existing technology. The maximum output level, if all the economy's resources are fully and efficiently employed, is shown by the broken vertical line. In Range *A*, where national output is far below this maximum, the rate of inflation is very low but the unemployment rate is very high. In Range *B*, the unemployment rate is substantially less than in Range *A*, but the price level begins to rise. In Range *C*, national output is at its maximum, and increases in total spending result only in inflation.

increase—which means that it is likely to increase as unemployment decreases. Thus there may be the inverse relationship between the unemployment rate and the inflation rate shown in Figure 8.3.

Shifts in the Inflation-Unemployment Relationship

The curve in Figure 8.3 is a fascinating tool. At first glance it may seem that the government can simply aim at any point along the curve. For example, it might choose point *A* (where the unemployment rate is 6 percent and the inflation rate is 7 percent) or point *C* (where the unemployment rate is 8 percent and the inflation rate is $4\frac{1}{2}$ percent). To reach point *A* or point *C*, monetary and fiscal policies can be used, as we shall see in subsequent chapters.

If the curve remains fixed, this choice among points on the curve is a real one—and a relevant one. Some administrations are more inclined than others to tolerate more unemployment in order to stem inflation. Some are more willing than others to tolerate inflation in order to reduce unemployment. The target you choose depends, of course, on your evaluation of the relative social costs associated with unemployment and inflation. The more importance you give to the costs of unemployment, and the less importance to the costs of inflation, the farther *up* the curve you will want to be. (For example, you will prefer point *A* to point *B*.) The more importance you attach to the costs of inflation, and the less to the costs of unemployment, the farther *down* on the curve you will want to be. (For example, you will prefer point *C* to point *B*.)

But fortunately or unfortunately, government policy making is not as simple as this. Perhaps the most important reason is that the curve in Figure 8.3 shifts. For example, it shifted upward during the early 1970s, as shown in Figure 8.5, for reasons that will be discussed in Chapter 16. Because of this shift the American economy was confronted simultaneously with excessive unemployment and excessive inflation—an uncomfortable combination known as "stagflation."

To repeat, *although there may be an inverse relationship in the short run between inflation and unemployment, this relationship may shift, with the result that one cannot be sure that increased unemployment will mean an eventual decline in inflation, or that increased inflation will mean an eventual decline in unemployment.* For example, if the relationship shifts in the

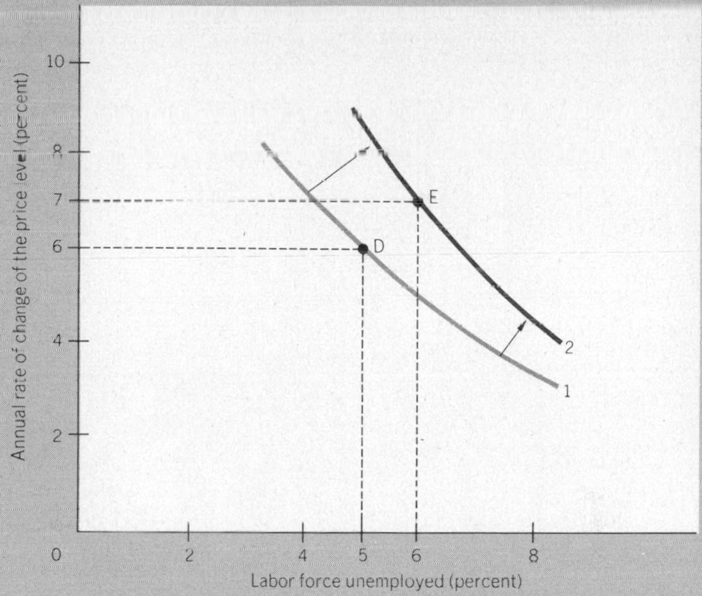

Figure 8.5
Shift in Relationship Between Unemployment Rate and Rate of Inflation
If the relationship between the unemployment rate and the inflation rate shifts from position 1 to position 2, the economy may move from point *D* to point *E*, in which case increased inflation is associated with increased unemployment.

way shown in Figure 8.5, the inflation rate may increase from 6 to 7 percent, even though the unemployment rate increases from 5 to 6 percent. To see why, note that an unemployment rate of 5 percent means an inflation rate of 6 percent when the relationship is in its original position—position 1 in Figure 8.5. But after the relationship shifts to position 2, an unemployment rate of 6 percent means an inflation rate of 7 percent. Thus the economy can move from point *D* to point *E* in Figure 8.5, in which case increased inflation is associated with increased unemployment. The fact that shifts of this sort can occur in this relationship means that it is less useful than might appear at first glance in guiding public policy.

Gross National Product

Estimates of Gross National Product: Uses and History

Unemployment and inflation statistics help us gauge how well an economy is performing. In addition, there is another major measuring rod that reflects the nation's over-all economic condition: the gross national product. Put in the simplest terms, *the* ***gross national product****—or* ***GNP,*** *as it is often called—is a measure of the total amount of goods and services produced by our economy during a particular period of time.* This measure is important both for its own sake, and because it helps us to understand both inflation and unemployment. The federal government and the business community watch the GNP figures avidly. Government officials, from the president down, are interested because these figures indicate how prosperous we are, and because they are useful in forecasting the future health of the economy. Politicians are well aware that the political party in power generally gets clobbered when GNP falls substantially. Business executives are also extremely interested in the GNP figures because the sales of their firms are related to the level of GNP, and so the figures are useful in forecasting the future health of their businesses. All in all, it is no exaggeration to say that the gross national product is one of the most closely watched numbers in existence.

Unemployment and Inflation: An International Overview

Economic problems, like smugglers, have no respect for international boundaries. In the mid-1970s, unemployment and inflation afflicted most of the industrialized world. As shown in the accompanying table, the unemployment rate in the fall of 1975 was about 8 percent in the United States and Canada, about 4 percent in France, Germany, Italy, and Britain, and about 2 percent in Japan. Compared with previous experience since World War II, these unemployment rates were very high. For example, in 1969, West Germany's unemployment rate was only 0.9 percent, as compared with 4.5 percent in late 1975.

A comparison of the U.S. unemployment rate with that in other countries shows that our unemployment rate (and Canada's) tends to be higher than the others, both in 1975 and 1969. To some extent, this is due to the fact that unemployment is defined differently in one country than in another. For example, in some countries, to be counted as unemployed, you must register with government unemployment exchanges. Another reason for the international differences in unemployment rates is that institutional and cultural arrangements differ from country to country. Thus, in Japan, many large firms commit themselves to a policy of lifetime employment for workers. This is one reason for Japan's relatively low unemployment rates. Still another reason for the international differences in unemployment rates is differences among countries in their fiscal and monetary policies (discussed in Chapters 11 and 15).

Lest you jump to the conclusion that present-day unemployment means starvation, note that there are substantial unemployment benefits in all of these countries. The percentage of workers covered by such plans in each country is: United States, 95; Canada, 99; Britain, 80; West Germany, 93; France, 61; Italy, 51; and Japan, 45. In the case of some U.S. auto workers who were laid off in 1974, unemployment benefits were almost equal to what they made when they were working. But this is the exception, not the rule. In general, although jobless benefits are an important cushion, they are far from big enough to prevent the unemployed from taking a substantial cut in income.*

* In the United States, unemployment insurance typically replaces only ⅓ to ½ of an unemployed worker's previous before-tax wages. But it replaces a great deal more of his or her *after-tax* income, because jobless benefits are exempt from taxes. Thus, according to Martin Feldstein of Harvard University, unemployment insurance increases unemployment, since it encourages (or at least enables) the jobless to remain unemployed longer than they otherwise would. Many economists agree with Feldstein, but there is considerable argument over the extent of this effect. Stephen Marston of the Brookings Institution estimates that unemployment insurance increases the unemployment rate by about 0.25 percentage points, while Feldstein estimates the increase at about 1.25 percentage points.

Unemployment Rate and Inflation Rate in the United States and Six Other Major Countries

Country	Unemployment rate[a] 1975	Unemployment rate[a] 1969	Inflation rate[b] 1975	Inflation rate[b] 1974
United States	8.4	3.5	7.1	12.2
Canada	7.2	4.7	10.0	12.5
France	4.0	1.7	10.1	21.5
Germany	4.5	0.9	6.0	5.9
Italy	3.4	3.4	10.2	25.0
Japan	1.7	1.1	19.8	21.5
Great Britain	4.7	2.4	28.7	19.2

[a] The number of people unemployed as a percentage of the labor force. 1975 figures pertain to the third quarter.
[b] Annual percentage rate of increase of consumer prices. 1975 figures pertain to the first three quarters of the year.

As for the rate of inflation, the accompanying table shows that the price level increased at a rapid rate during 1974 and 1975 in all of these countries. The U.S. performance actually seemed somewhat better than in the other countries. While Great Britain, Canada, France, and Italy experienced increases in consumer prices of 10 percent per year or more during the first three quarters of 1975, we managed to keep the rate of inflation down to an average of 7 percent per year during that period. But a 7 percent annual rate of inflation is hardly anything to brag about. Many economists, and citizens as well, would be glad to return to the days when the price level seldom rose at more than a few percentage points per year—and unemployment rarely exceeded 4 or 5 percent.

In view of their importance, it is noteworthy that estimates of the gross national product are of comparatively recent vintage. The Department of Commerce first made such estimates in 1932, after experiments at various universities and at the National Bureau of Economic Research. A leading pioneer in this field was Nobel laureate Simon Kuznets, then at the University of Pennsylvania. The concepts that Kuznets and others developed are often called the ***national income accounts,*** and the Bureau of Economic Analysis of the U.S. Department of Commerce compiles these figures on a continuing basis. Just as the accounts of a firm are used to describe and analyze its financial health, so the national income accounts are used to describe and analyze the economic health of the nation as a whole.

Measuring Gross National Product

The American economy produces millions of types of goods and services. How can we add together everything from lemon meringue pie to helicopters, from books to houses? The only feasible answer is to use money as a common denominator and to make the price of a good or service—the amount the buyer is willing to pay—the measure of value. In other words, we add up the value in money terms of the total output of goods and services in the economy during a certain period, normally a year, and the result is the gross national product during that period.

At the outset, we must note several important points about the gross national product. First, it does not include the value of *all* goods and services produced: it includes only the value of *final* goods and services produced. ***Final goods and services*** are goods and services destined for the ultimate user. For example, flour purchased for family consumption is a final good, but flour to be used in manufacturing bread is an ***intermediate good,*** not a final good. Clearly, we would be double counting if we counted both the bread and the flour used to make the bread as output. Thus the output of intermediate goods—goods that are not destined for the ultimate user, but are used as inputs in producing final goods and services—must not be included in gross national product. For example, steel used in the production of automobiles and cotton used in the production of blue jeans must not be included. To avoid double counting, we include only the value of final goods and services in gross national product.

Second, some final goods and services that must be included in gross national product are not bought and sold in the market place, so they are valued at what they cost. For example, consider the services performed by government—police protection, fire protection, the use of the courts, defense, and so forth. Such services are not bought and sold in any market (despite the old saw about the New Jersey judge who was "the best that money could buy"). Yet they are an important part of our economy's final output. Economists and statisticians have decided to value them at what they cost the taxpayers. This is by no means ideal, but it is the best practical solution advanced to date.

Third, it is necessary for practical reasons to omit certain types of final output from gross national product. In particular, some nonmarketed goods and services, such as the services performed by housewives, are excluded from the gross national product. This is not because economists fail to appreciate these services, but because it would be extremely difficult to get reasonably reliable estimates of the money value of a housewife's services. At first glance, this may seem to be a very important weakness in our measure of total output, but so long as the value of these services does not change much (in relation to total output), the variation in gross national product will provide a reasonably accurate picture of the variation in total output—and, for many purposes, this is all that is required.

Fourth, purely financial transactions are excluded from the gross national product. Such financial transactions include government transfer payments, private transfer payments, and the sale and purchase of securities. ***Government transfer payments*** are payments made by the government to individuals who do not contribute to production in exchange for them. Payments to welfare recipients are a good example of government transfer payments. Since these payments are not for production, it would be incorrect to include them in GNP. ***Private transfer payments*** are gifts or other transfers of wealth from one person or private organization to another. Again these are not payments for production, so there is no reason to include them in GNP. The sale and purchase of securities are not payments for production, as you will recall from our discussion in Chapter 7, so they too are excluded from GNP.

Finally, the sale of secondhand goods is also excluded from the gross national product. The reason for this is clear. When a good is produced, its value is included in GNP. If its value is also included when it is sold on the secondhand market, it will be counted twice, thus leading to an overstatement of the true GNP. For example, suppose that you buy a new bicycle and resell it a year later. The value of the new bicycle is included in GNP when the bicycle is produced. But the resale value of the bicycle is not included in GNP; to do so would be double counting.

Gross National Product: Adjusting for Price Changes

In discussing inflation, we stressed that the general price level has changed over time. Since gross national product values all goods and services at their current prices, it is bound to be affected by changes in the price level as well as by changes in total output. If all prices doubled tomorrow, this would produce a doubling of gross national product. Clearly, if gross national product is to be a reliable measure of changes in total output, we must correct it somehow to eliminate the effects of such changes in the price level.

To make such a correction, economists choose some ***base year*** and express the value of all goods and services in terms of their prices during the base year. For example, if 1970 is taken as the base year and if the price of beef was $1 per pound in 1970, beef is valued at $1 per pound in all other years. Thus, if 200 million pounds of beef were produced in 1975, this total output is valued at $200 million even though the price of beef in 1975 was actually higher than $1 per pound. In this way, distortions caused by changes in the price level are eliminated.

It is customary to express gross national product either in current dollars or in constant dollars. Figures expressed in ***current dollars*** are actual dollar amounts, whereas those expressed in ***constant dollars*** are corrected in this way for changes in the price level. Expressed in current dollars, gross national product is affected by changes in the price level. Expressed in constant dollars, gross national product is not affected by the price level because the prices of all goods are maintained at their base-year level. GNP, after being corrected for changes in the price level, is called ***real GNP.*** Inflation has caused GNP expressed in current dollars to increase more rapidly than GNP in constant dollars (Figure 8.6).

It is often useful to have some measure of how much prices have changed over a certain period of time. One way to obtain such a measure is to divide the value of a set of goods and services expressed in current dollars by the value of the same set of goods and services expressed in constant (or base-year) dollars. For example, suppose that a set of goods and services costs $100 when valued at 1977 prices, but $70 when valued at 1970 prices. Apparently, prices have risen an average of 43

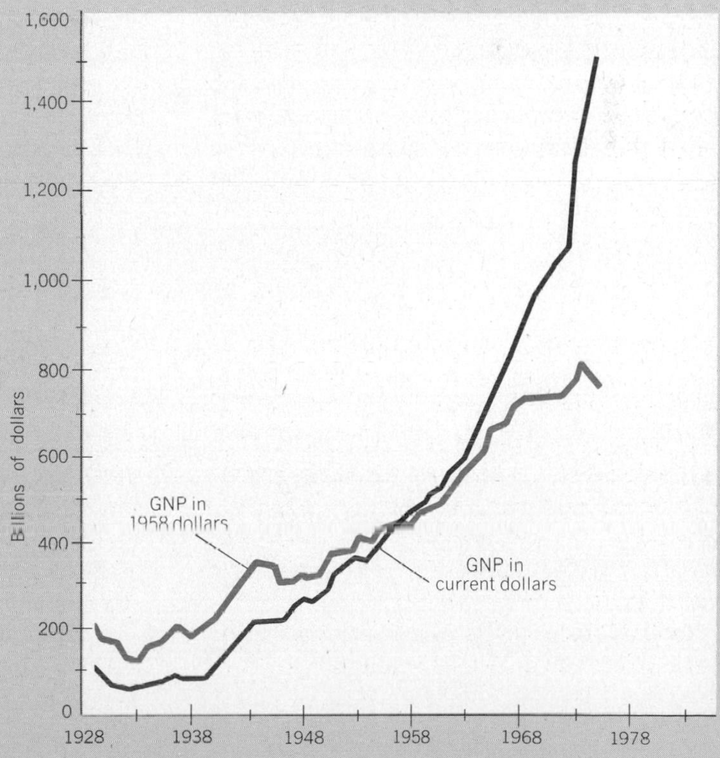

Figure 8.6
Gross National Product, Expressed in Current Dollars and in 1958 Dollars, United States, 1929–75
Because of inflation, GNP expressed in current dollars has increased more rapidly in recent years than GNP in constant (1958) dollars. This has been particularly true in the mid-1970s, reflecting the price surge then.

percent for this set of goods between 1970 and 1977. How do we get 43 percent? The ratio of the cost in 1977 prices to the cost in 1970 prices is 100 ÷ 70 = 1.43; thus prices must have risen on the average by 43 percent for this set of goods.

The ratio of the value of a set of goods and services in current dollars to the value of the same set of goods and services in constant (base-year) dollars is a ***price index.*** Thus 1.43 is a price index in the example above. An important function of a price index is to convert values expressed in current dollars into values expressed in constant dollars. This conversion, known as ***deflating,*** can be achieved simply by dividing values expressed in current dollars by the price index. For example, in the illustration above, values expressed in 1977 dollars can be converted into constant (i.e., 1970) dollars by dividing by 1.43. This procedure is an important one, with applications in many fields other than the measurement of gross national product. For example, firms use it to compare their output in various years. To correct for price changes, they deflate their sales by a price index for their products.

To illustrate how a price index can be used to solve such problems, suppose that we want to measure how much the output of bread rose ***in real terms***—that is, in constant dollars—between 1973 and 1977. We know that the value of output of bread in current dollars during each year was as shown in the first column of Table 8.1, and that the price of bread during each year was as shown in the second column. To determine the value of output of bread in 1973 dollars, we form a price index with 1973 as base year, as shown in the third column. Then dividing the figures in the first column by this price index, we get the value of output of bread during each year in 1973 dollars, shown in the fourth column. Thus the fourth column shows how much the output of bread has grown in real terms. For example, the real output of bread has risen by 19 percent—(1,900 − 1,600) ÷ 1,600—between 1973 and 1977.

Intermediate Goods, Value-Added, and Net National Product

We have pointed out that gross national product includes the value of only the final goods and services produced. Obviously, however, the output of final goods and services is not due solely to the efforts of the producers of the final goods and services. The total value of an automobile when it leaves the plant, for example, represents the work of many industries besides the automobile manufacturers. The steel, tires, glass, and many other components of the

Table 8.1
Use of Price Index to Convert from Current to Constant Dollars

Year	(1) Output of bread in current dollars	(2) Price of bread (dollars)	(3) Price index (price ÷ 1973 price)	(4) Output of bread in 1973 dollars[a]
1973	1,600 million	0.50	1.00	1,600 million
1974	1,768 million	0.52	1.04	1,700 million
1975	1,980 million	0.55	1.10	1,800 million
1976	2,090 million	0.55	1.10	1,900 million
1977	2,204 million	0.58	1.16	1,900 million

[a]This column was derived by dividing column 1 by column 3.

Table 8.2
Value-added by Various Industries, United States, 1975

Industry	Value-added (billions of dollars)
Agriculture, forestry, and fisheries	55
Mining	38
Construction	67
Manufacturing	346
Transportation	57
Communication	38
Electricity, gas, and sanitation	37
Wholesale and retail trade	272
Finance, insurance, and real estate	209
Other services	182
Government[a]	201
Rest of the world	11
Gross national product	1,516[b]

[a] Equals wages and salaries of government workers.
[b] Because of rounding errors, figures do not sum to total.
Source: Survey of Current Business, July 1976.

automobile were not produced by the automobile manufacturers. In reality, the automobile manufacturers only added a certain amount of value to the value of the intermediate goods—steel, tires, glass, and so forth—they purchased. This point is basic to an understanding of how the gross national product is calculated.

To measure the contribution of a firm or industry to the final output, we use the concept of value-added. ***Value-added*** means just what it says: *the amount of value added by a firm or industry to the total worth of the product.* It is a measure in money terms of the extent of production taking place in a particular firm or industry. Suppose that $160 million of bread was produced in the United States in 1976. To produce it, farmers harvested $50 million of wheat, which was used as an intermediate product by flour mills, which turned out $80 million of flour. This flour was used as an intermediate product by the bakers who produced the $160 million of bread. What is the value-added at each stage of the process? For simplicity, assume that the farmers did not have to purchase any materials from other firms in order to produce the wheat. Then the value added by the wheat farmers is $50 million, the value-added by the flour mills is $30 million ($80 million − $50 million); and the value-added by the bakers is $80 million ($160 million − $80 million). Of course, the total of the value-added at all stages of the process ($50 million + $30 million + $80 million) must equal the value of the output of final product ($160 million), because each stage's value-added is its contribution to this value.

Table 8.2 shows the value-added by various industrial groups in the United States in 1975. Since the total of the value-added by all industries must equal the value of all final goods and services, which, of course, is gross national product, it follows that $1,516 billion—the total of the figures in Table 8.2—must have been equal to gross national product in 1975. It is interesting to note that most of the value-added in the American economy in 1975 was not contributed by manufacturing, mining, construction, transportation, communication, or electricity or gas. Instead, most of it came from services—wholesale and retail trade, finance, insurance, real estate, government services, and other services. This is a sign of a basic change taking place in the American economy, which is turning more and more toward producing services, rather than goods.

Gross national product has one drawback as a measure that must now be faced: it does not take into account the fact that plant and equipment wear out with use, and that a certain amount of each year's national output must be devoted to replacing the capital goods worn out in producing the year's output. Economists have therefore developed another important measure, net national product (or NNP), that recognizes what every accountant knows—the relevance of depreciation. (Recall the discussion in Chapter 7.) Specifically, ***net national product*** *equals gross national product minus depreciation.* To obtain net national product, government statisticians estimate the amount of depreciation—the amount of the nation's plant, equipment, and structures that are worn out during the period—and deduct it from gross national product. Net national product is a more accurate measure of the economy's output than gross national product because it takes depreciation into account, but estimates of net national product contain whatever errors are made in estimating depreciation (which is not easy to measure). As we shall see in succeeding chapters, data on gross national product are more often used, even if net national product may be a somewhat better measure. Actually, since GNP and NNP move together quite closely, which one you use doesn't matter much for most practical purposes.

The Limitations of Gross National Product and Net National Product

It is essential that the limitations of both gross national product and net national product be understood. Although they are very useful, these figures are by no means ideal measures of economic well-being. At least five limitations of these measures must always be borne in mind:

Population. GNP and NNP are not very meaningful unless one knows the size of the population of the country in question. For example, the fact that a particular nation's GNP equals $50 billion means one thing if the nation has 10 million inhabitants, and quite another thing if it has 500 million inhabitants. To correct for the size of the population, GNP per capita—GNP divided by the population—is often used as a rough measure of output per person in a particular country.

Leisure. GNP and NNP do not take account of one of mankind's most prized activities, leisure. During the past century, the average work week in the United States has decreased substantially. It has gone from almost 70 hours in 1850 to about 40 hours today. As people have become more affluent, they have chosen to substitute leisure for increased production. Yet this increase in leisure time, which surely contributes to our well-being, does not show up in GNP or NNP. Neither does the personal satisfaction (or displeasure and alienation) people get from their jobs.

Quality changes. GNP and NNP do not take adequate account of changes in the quality of goods. An improvement in a product is not reflected accurately in GNP and NNP unless its price reflects the improvement. For example, if a new type of drug is put on the market at the same price as an old drug, and if the output and cost of the new drug are the same as the old drug, GNP will not increase, even though the new drug is twice as effective as the old one. Because GNP and NNP do not reflect such increases in product quality, it is sometimes argued that the commonly used price indices overestimate the amount of inflation, since, although prices may have gone up, quality may have gone up too.

Value and distribution. GNP and NNP say nothing about the social desirability of the composition and distribution of the nation's output. Each good and service produced is valued at its price. If the price of a Bible is $5 and the price of a pornographic novel is $5, both are valued at $5, whatever you or I may think about their respective worth. Moreover, GNP and NNP measure only the total quantity of goods and services produced. They tell us nothing about how this output is distributed among the people. If a nation's GNP is $500 billion, this is its GNP whether 90 percent of the output is consumed by a relatively few rich families or whether the output is distributed relatively equally among the citizens.

Social costs. GNP and NNP do not reflect some of the social costs arising from the production of goods and services. In particular, they do not reflect the environmental damage resulting from the operation of our nation's factories, offices, and farms. It is common knowledge that the atmosphere and water supplies are being polluted in various ways by firms, consumers, and governments. Yet these costs are not deducted from GNP or NNP, even through the failure to do so results in an overestimate of our true economic welfare.

Economists are beginning to correct the GNP figures to eliminate some of these problems. For example, William Nordhaus and James Tobin at Yale University have tried to correct the GNP figures to take proper account of the value of leisure, the value of housewives' services, and the environmental costs of production, among other things.[5] They have found that, when these corrections were made, the increase in economic well-being since World War II has been much less than is indicated by the growth of uncorrected GNP per capita. Unquestionably, more work along this line is needed, and will be done. However, it is also worth noting that many of these adjustments and corrections are necessarily quite rough, since there is no accurate way to measure the relevant values and costs.

[5] W. Nordhaus and J. Tobin, "Is Growth Obsolete?" *Fiftieth Anniversary Colloquium,* New York: National Bureau of Economic Research, 1972.

Measures of National Income

Gross National Income Equals GNP

We have been dealing with the measurement of national product, or output. Now we must recognize *the identity between gross national product and gross national income.* ***Gross national income*** is the total annual flow of income paid out (or owed) as wages, rent, interest, and profits, plus two other items: indirect business taxes and depreciation. (*Indirect business taxes* are sales taxes, excise taxes, and other such taxes that firms view as part of their costs.) In other words, gross national income exactly equals the total claims on output—the sum total of the wages of the workers who participated in the productive efforts, the interest paid to the investors who lent money to the firms that produced the output, the profits of the owners of the firms who produced the output, and the rents paid the owners of land used to produce the output, as well as indirect business taxes and depreciation. If you think back to the circular flows of money and products described in Chapter 4, you can see (at least vaguely) why gross national income must equal gross national product.

To provide you with a real proof that this equality must hold, let's start with a single firm, the General Electric Corporation, a huge producer of electrical equipment, appliances, and other products. By the simple rules of accounting discussed in Chapter 7,

$$\text{profit} = \text{sales} - \text{costs}. \qquad (8.1)$$

Thus it follows that

$$\text{sales} = \text{costs} + \text{profit}. \qquad (8.2)$$

Table 8.3
Sales, Costs, and Profit, General Electric Company, 1974

Sales (millions of dollars)		Costs and profit (millions of dollars)	
Sales:	13,599	Employee compensation	5,223
		Interest and rent	180
		Depreciation	376
		Indirect business taxes	123
		Intermediate products bought from other firms	6,696
		Total costs	12,598
		Profits	1,001
Total	13,599	Total	13,599

Source: Moody's.

Suppose we put the value of General Electric's output (i.e., its sales) on the lefthand side of Table 8.3 and its costs and profits on the righthand side. Clearly, by Equation (8.2), the total of the righthand side must equal the total of the lefthand side.

Now, suppose that we deduct one element of costs, "Intermediate products bought from other firms," from both sides of Table 8.3, and present the results in Table 8.4. Since the lefthand total equals the righthand total in Table 8.3, the same must hold in Table 8.4. The total of the lefthand side of Table 8.4 equals value-added, since General Electric's value-added equals its sales minus its expenditures on intermediate goods bought from other firms. The total of the righthand side of Table 8.4 equals the total claims against General Electric's output, which is the total of income paid out (or owed) by the firm—wages, interest, rent, profits—plus indirect business taxes and depreciation. And, as pointed out above, the total of the lefthand side must equal the total of the righthand side of Table 8.4.

Next, imagine constructing a table like Table 8.4 for each employer in the economy, putting sales less intermediate products bought from other firms on the left and costs plus profits less intermediate products bought from other firms on the right. For every employer,

Table 8.4
Value-added and Claims against Output, General Electric Company, 1974

Value-added (millions of dollars)			Claims against output	
	Sales:	13,599	Employee compensation	5,223
			Interest and rent	180
Subtract:	Intermediate products bought from other firms:	6,696	Profits	1,001
			Depreciation	376
			Indirect business taxes	123
	Value-added	6,903	Total	6,903

Source: Moody's.

the total of the left side must equal the total of the right side. Thus, if we add up the total of the lefthand sides for all employers in the economy, the result must equal the total of the righthand sides for all the employers in the economy. But what is the total of the left hand sides for all employers in the economy? It is the sum of value-added for all employers, which, as we saw in a previous section, equals gross national product. And the total of the righthand sides for all employers in the economy is the total of all income paid out (or owed) in the economy—wages, interest, rent, profits—plus indirect business taxes and depreciation. Consequently, gross national product must equal the total of all income paid out (or owed) in the economy plus indirect business taxes and depreciation.

Table 8.5 shows the total amounts of various types of income paid out (or owed) in the American economy during 1975. It also shows depreciation and indirect business taxes. You can see for yourself that the total of these items equals gross national product. Besides helping to prove the point stated at the beginning of this section, this table is an interesting description of the relative importance of various types of income. For example, it shows the great importance of wages and salaries in the total income stream in the United States. In 1975, roughly 60 percent of gross national income was paid out in wages and salaries.

Table 8.5
Gross National Income, United States, 1975

Type of claim on output	Amount of claim (billions of dollars)
Employee compensation	929
Rental income	22
Net interest	75
Income of proprietors and professionals	90
Corporate profits	92
Indirect business taxes	139
Depreciation	161
Statistical discrepancy[a]	8
Gross national income	1,516

[a] This also includes some minor items that need not be of concern here. See the source.
Source: Survey of Current Business, July 1976.

National Income, Personal Income, and Disposable Income

There is more to gross national income than the total amount of income paid out (or owed) by employers (including government). As noted in the previous section, it also includes indirect business taxes and depreciation. We are sometimes interested only in the total amount of income paid out (or owed) by employers, an amount called ***national income.*** Clearly, it is easy to derive national income if you know gross national income. All you have to do is subtract indirect business taxes and depreciation from gross national income. Or putting it another way, all you have to do is subtract indirect business taxes from net national product, since gross national income minus depreciation equals net national product.[6] Table 8.6 shows the result for 1975.

For some purposes, we also need to know how much the people of a nation receive in income. This is ***personal income,*** and it differs from national income in two ways. First, some people who have a claim on income do not actually receive it. For example, although all a firm's profits belong to the owners, not all of its profits are paid out to them. As we saw in

[6] Two other small items must also be taken into account. As shown in Table 8.6, we must subtract *business transfer payments*—pensions and other payments made by firms that are transfer payments—and add *subsidies less surpluses of government enterprises,* which corrects for the fact that some government agencies pay out more to income recipients than they produce in value-added. In addition, of course, there is a statistical discrepancy that must be recognized. It is purely a statistical matter. (Also, there are some miscellaneous items totaling only $4 billion that need not be specified in detail here.)

Table 8.6
Gross National Product, Net National Product, National Income, Personal Income, and Disposable Income, United States, 1975

Measure	Amount (billions of dollars)
Gross national product	1,516
Subtract: Depreciation	161
Net national product	1,355
Subtract: Indirect business taxes	139
Business transfers	6
Statistical discrepancy	4
Add: Subsidies less surpluses of government enterprises	2
National income	1,208
Subtract: Corporate profits	92
Contributions for social insurance	110
Add: Government transfers to persons	169
Dividends	32
Interest paid by government	33
Business transfers	6
Other items	4
Personal income	1,250
Subtract: Personal taxes	169
Disposable personal income	1,081

Source: Survey of Current Business, July 1976.

Chapter 7, part of the profits are plowed back into the business, and part go to the government for corporate income taxes. Also, wage earners do not actually receive the amounts they and their employers pay currently for Social Security. Second, some people receive income that is not obtained in exchange for services rendered. You will recall from an earlier section that government transfer payments are made to welfare recipients, people receiving unemployment compensation or Social Security, and so forth. Also, there are business transfer payments—pensions and other payments made by firms that are not in exchange for current productive services.

If you know national income, it is easy to derive personal income. You begin by subtracting profits from national income and adding dividends to the result. This will correct for the fact that profits not distributed as dividends do not actually enter people's hands. Then you must deduct contributions for social insurance, and add government and business transfer payments. (Note that interest paid by governments on their debt is regarded as a transfer payment, on the grounds that it is not a payment for current goods and services.) These calculations are shown in detail in Table 8.6.

Finally, it is also useful for many purposes to know how much the people of a nation receive in income and get to keep after personal income taxes. This is ***disposable income.*** If you know what personal income is, you can easily obtain disposable income by deducting personal income taxes from personal income, as shown in Table 8.6. Disposable income plays a very important role in subsequent chapters because it has a major influence on how much consumers spend. According to Table 8.6, disposable income equaled about 71 percent of gross national product (gross national income) in 1975.

Measures of National Expenditure

Consumption, Investment, Government Expenditure, and Net Exports

Up to this point, we have been concerned with national output and national income. Now we take up ***national expenditure.*** At the outset, note that if we include business spending for increased inventories as a form of expenditure, *the total amount spent on final goods and services must equal the total value of final goods and services produced.* In other words, *gross national expenditure must equal gross national product,* because all goods produced must either be bought by someone or added to the producer's inventories. In either case, the value of the goods is included in gross national expenditure.

The total amount spent on final goods and services is generally broken down into four parts, described below.

Consumption. This is the amount spent by households on durable goods, nondurable goods, and services. For example, consumption includes your expenditures on meals and clothing, and your family's expenditures on a car or on an electric washer and dryer. Table 8.7 shows that in 1975 consumption accounted for about 64 percent of the total amount spent on final goods and services in the United States. Expenditure on consumer durable goods is clearly much less than on consumer nondurable goods or services.

Table 8.7
Expenditure on Final Goods and Services, United States, 1975[a]

Type of Expenditure		Amount (billions of dollars)
Personal consumption		973
Durable goods	132	
Nondurable goods	409	
Services	432	
Gross private domestic investment		184
Expenditures on plant and equipment	147	
Residential structures	51	
Increase in inventories	−15	
Net exports		20
Exports	148	
Imports	128	
Government expenditures		339
Federal	124	
State and local	215	
Gross national product		1,516

[a] Because of rounding errors, figures sometimes do not sum to total.
Source: Survey of Current Business, July 1976.

Investment. This is the amount spent by firms for new plant and equipment, new housing, and increases in inventories, as well as the amount spent by households for new housing. (One reason why houses are treated as investment goods is that they can be rented out.) Table 8.7 shows that in 1975 investment accounted for about 12 percent of the total amount spent on final goods and services in the United States. This is ***gross investment,*** the gross amount of money spent on new plant, equipment, buildings, and extra inventory, not the net amount. Why? Because during the period in question, some plant, equipment, and so forth wore out: there was depreciation. Thus, to determine ***net investment*** we must deduct depreciation from gross investment. Net investment measures the change (net of depreciation) in the quantity of the nation's capital goods. If net investment is positive, the nation's productive capacity, as gauged by its capital stock, is growing. If net investment is negative, the nation's productive capacity, as gauged by its capital stock, is declining.

Government purchases of goods and services. This includes the expenditures of the federal, state, and local governments for the multitude of functions they perform: defense, education, police protection, and so forth. It does not include transfer payments, since they are not payments for current production. Table 8.7 shows that government spending in 1975 accounted for about 22 percent of the total amount spent on final goods and services in the United States. State and local expenditures are bigger than federal expenditures. As you recall

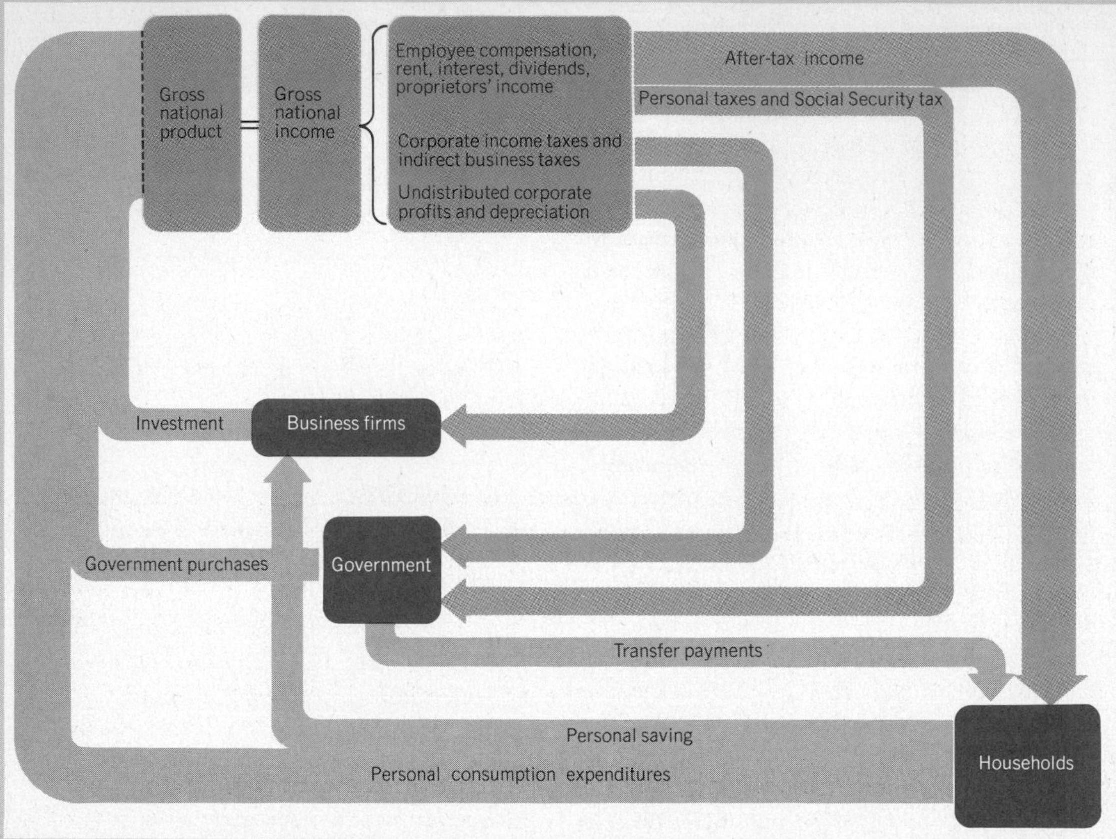

Figure 8.7
Flows of Output, Income, and Expenditures in the National Economy
This diagram shows that (1) gross national income equals GNP; (2) part of gross national income goes to households, part goes to firms, and part goes to government; and (3) households, firms, and government spend these receipts on GNP.

from Chapter 5, many of the expenditures of the federal government are connected with national defense, while at the state and local levels the biggest expenditure is for education.

Net exports of goods and services. This equals the amount spent by foreigners on our goods and services less the amount we spent on other nations' goods and services. Obviously, this factor must be included since some of our national output is destined for foreign markets, and since we import some of the goods and services we consume. There is no reason why this component of spending cannot be negative, since imports can exceed exports. The quantity of net exports tends to be quite small. Table 8.6 shows that net exports in 1975 were equal to about 1 percent of the total amount spent on final goods and services in the United States. Because net exports are so small, we shall generally ignore them until Chapters 20 and 21, when we shall focus attention exclusively on international trade and finance.

Finally, to see how these flows of expenditures are related to the flows of output and income, look carefully at Figure 8.7, which shows diagrammatically the relationships among them. Beginning at the top lefthand side of the figure, we see that gross national income equals GNP. Then moving to the right, we see that part of the gross national income goes to firms, part goes to the government, and the rest goes to households. These receipts are then used by households, firms, and the government to buy the gross national product, as shown on the lefthand side of the figure. (For simplicity, this figure assumes that net exports are zero and that the government has a balanced budget.)

The National Economy: Three Basic Facts

The measures of national output, national income, and national expenditure discussed above are some of the basic figures economists look at when trying to analyze the state of the economy. Using these measures, it is easy to demonstrate the following three facts, each of which will be needed in succeeding chapters. First, *disposable income, although it goes up and down with gross national product, does not fluctuate as much as gross national product.* This is shown in Figure 8.8. As we shall soon see, disposable income has a smoother path because our tax system and our social insurance programs, as well as other mechanisms, tend to dampen the effect of changes in gross national product on disposable income. When total output declines, the amount of after-tax income people receive does not go down so much; and when total output increases, the amount of after-tax income they receive does not go up so much. This, of course, cushions the effect of changes in GNP on people's expenditures.

Second, *consumption expenditure seems to depend closely on—and vary directly with—disposable income.* This observation, shown in Figure 8.9, is neither strange nor surprising. On the contrary, it would be odd if the amounts households spend on goods and services were *not* closely related to their after-tax income, for consumers can do only two things with their after-tax income: spend it or save it.

Third, *investment varies much more than the*

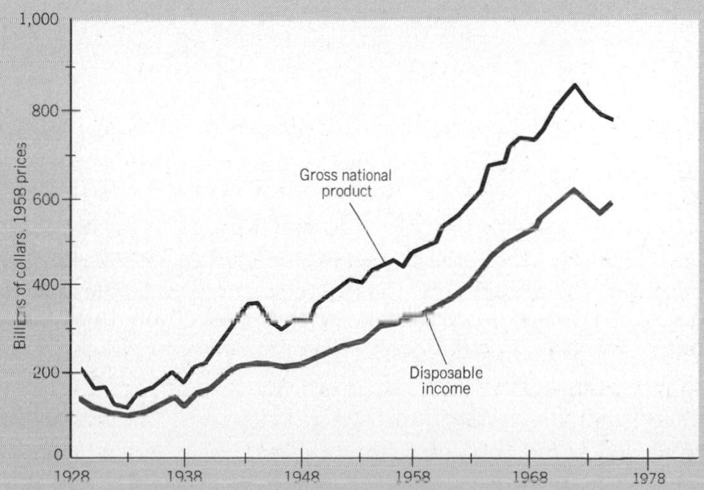

Figure 8.8
Relationship between Disposable Income and Gross National Product, United States, 1929–75
Disposable income, although it goes up and down with gross national product, does not fluctuate as much as GNP. To see this, note that the disposable income curve is smoother than the GNP curve.

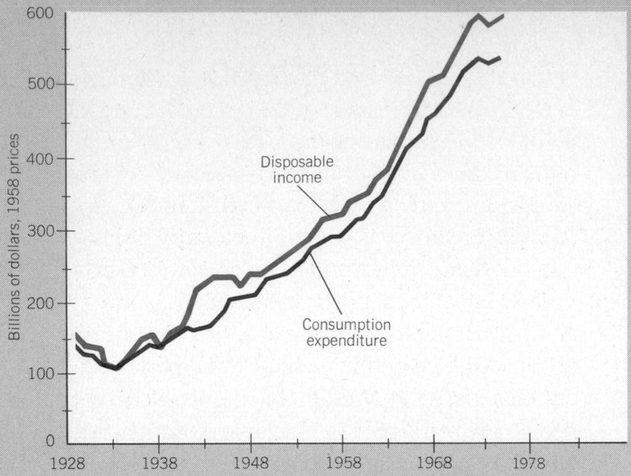

Figure 8.9
Relationship between Consumption and Disposable Income, United States, 1929–75
Consumption expenditure seems to depend closely on, and vary directly with, disposable income.

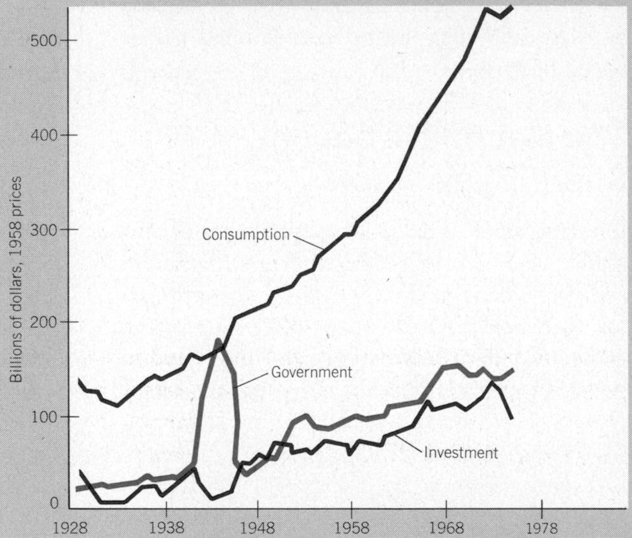

Figure 8.10
Consumption Expenditure, Gross Private Domestic Investment, and Government Expenditures, United States, 1929–75
Investment varies more than the other components of total spending. Also, because of wars, government spending moves up and down rather erratically.

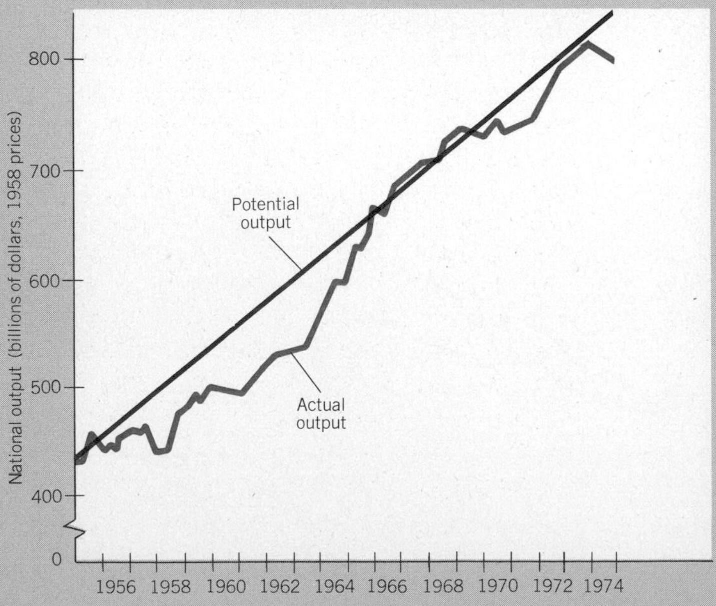

Figure 8.11
Actual and Potential Output, United States, 1955–74
The gap measures what it costs society each year, in output forgone, to tolerate an unemployment rate above 4 percent.

other components of total spending. Figure 8.10 shows that investment goes up and down, while consumption moves along with only slight bumps and dips, and government expenditures do not move up and down very much except when war breaks out.[7] (Note the bulges in government spending during World War II, the Korean War, and the Vietnam War.) The volatility of investment is an important factor in explaining the changes in national output over time. Also, the wartime bulges in government spending have been major causes of changes in national output. We shall have considerably more to say on this score in the next few chapters.

The Gap between Actual and Potential Output

Gross national product is a measure of the value of final goods and services produced in a given period: in other words, GNP measures actual output. Besides being concerned about actual output, economists are also interested in potential output. Specifically, they are interested in estimating how high the gross national product could have been *if the unemployment rate had been quite low, say 4 percent* (which is a common definition of full employment). An economy's potential output is determined by the size of its labor force, the average number of hours a worker is on the job per year, and the average amount of goods and services a worker can produce per hour. The average amount of goods and services a worker can produce per hour depends in turn on the extent and quality of the capital he has to work with, the level of technology, and his skill and schooling.

More specifically, the ***potential GNP*** is estimated by multiplying 96 percent of the labor force times the normal hours of work per year times the average output per man-hour at the relevant time. In the past few years, there has been some criticism of this definition of potential GNP on the grounds that an unemployment rate of 5 percent is a more realistic measure of full employment than 4 percent because there now are more young people, women, and minority workers in the labor force. All of these groups find it relatively difficult to find jobs. Since this debate is unresolved, we shall stick with the conventional definition, but the apparent difficulties in this measure should be noted.

If potential GNP is defined in this way, the gap between actual and potential GNP depends on the difference between the actual unemployment rate and 4 percent. Specifically, the gap will grow larger and larger as the unemployment rate exceeds 4 percent by greater and greater amounts. Figure 8.11 shows the estimated size of the gap between actual and potential GNP from 1955 to 1974. (Note that both actual and potential GNP are expressed in 1958 prices.) This gap is an extremely important measure of what it costs society to tolerate an unemployment rate above 4 percent. Besides the psychic costs of unemployment described in a previous section, society produces less than it could, so that human wants are less effectively fulfilled than they could be.

For example, consider 1975, a recession year when unemployment was about 8½ percent. According to Walter W. Heller, a former chairman of the Council of Economic Advisers, the gap between potential and actual GNP in 1975 was equal to about 12 percent of potential GNP. Although this estimate is very rough, it is accurate enough to suggest the social waste that accompanies large-scale unemployment. Clearly we must learn to curb the forces responsible for such waste. The following chapters will discuss some of the basic fac-

[7] Net exports are excluded from Figure 8.10. They were almost always under $10 billion during this period.

tors that cause excessive unemployment and excessive inflation, as well as various measures that can be taken to combat them.

Summary

Unemployment inflicts enormous social costs. Recognizing this fact, the Congress passed the Employment Act of 1946, which commits the federal government to combat excessive unemployment. Inflation is a general upward movement of prices. Since inflation results in an arbitrary and often inequitable redistribution of income, government policy makers attempt to curb inflation. Unfortunately, there may be an inverse relationship in the short run between the unemployment rate and the rate of inflation, because it is easier for unions and unorganized labor to increase wages and for firms to increase prices when there is little unemployment. What you regard as the optimal combination of unemployment and inflation depends on your political preferences and values. However, the relationship between unemployment and inflation is by no means fixed. In the middle 1970s, this relationship shifted upward, with the result that increased unemployment coexisted with increased inflation, this mixture being called "stagflation."

Besides unemployment and inflation, another very important indicator of the health of any economy is its gross national product, which measures the total value of the final goods and services it produces in a particular period. Since gross national product is affected by the price level, it must be deflated by a price index to correct for price-level changes. Gross national product is the sum of value-added by all industries. Net national product is gross national product minus depreciation. It indicates the value of net output when account is taken of capital used up.

Gross national product equals gross national income. Gross national income equals the sum of the total claims against output, including indirect business taxes and depreciation. National income is the total amount of income paid out (or owed) by employers; personal income is the total amount people actually receive in income; and disposable income is the total amount they get to keep after taxes.

Gross national product also equals gross national expenditure. Gross national expenditure equals the total amount spent on final goods and services, including business spending for increased inventories. The total amount spent on final goods and services is generally broken down into four parts: consumption, investment, government purchases, and net exports.

Based on the official data, investment appears to vary much more over time than other types of expenditure. As we shall see, this volatility is an important clue to the causes of change in national output. Also, there have been large variations in government expenditures associated with wars; these too have caused major changes in national output.

Clearly, one of the major social costs of unemployment is the fact that less goods and services are produced than could be produced with full employment. Estimates have been made of how the gap between actual and potential output is related to the unemployment rate. According to a rough estimate made by Walter Heller, this cost totaled about 12 percent of potential GNP in 1975.

CONCEPTS FOR REVIEW

Frictional unemployment
Structural unemployment
Cyclical unemployment
Gross national product
Intermediate good
Value-added
Current dollars
Constant dollars
Price index
Net national product
Gross national income
Personal income
Transfer payments
Disposable income
Inflation
National income
Consumption
Investment
Net exports

QUESTIONS FOR DISCUSSION AND REVIEW

1. "Unemployed workers make about as much as when they were employed because of unemployment insurance, so the nation need not worry about the unemployed." Specify at least two fundamental errors in this statement.

2. "The Employment Act of 1946 should be amended to include the goal of stabilizing the purchasing power of the dollar as well as the goal of maintaining high-level employment."[8] Comment and evaluate.

3. Suppose that if the unemployment rate in a particular nation is 5 percent, the inflation rate is 6 percent per year. In the short run, the inflation rate goes down by 1 percent if the unemployment rate goes up by 1 percent (so long as the unemployment rate is between 4 and 8 percent). Plot the relationship between inflation and unemployment in this nation on a graph, and discuss the policy choices open to its government in the short run. Can this relationship shift? If so, what effect will this have on the government's policy choices?

4. "Inflation is a necessary cost of economic progress." Comment and evaluate.

5. The following table shows the value of GNP in the nation of Puritania. The figures shown are in millions of 1960 dollars and current dollars. Fill in the blanks.

Year	GNP in millions of 1960 dollars	GNP in millions of current dollars	Price index $\left[\frac{\text{current price level}}{\text{1960 price level}}\right]$
1960	1,000	—	1.00
1965	—	1,440	1.20
1970	1,300	—	1.40
1975	1,500	—	1.60
1976	—	2,720	1.70

[8] J. Backman, "The Case against Creeping Inflation," *New York Times Magazine,* May 3, 1959.

6. Given the following data (in millions of dollars) concerning the Puritanian economy in 1974, compute its gross national product and net national product.

Gross private domestic investment	400
Personal consumption expenditure	1,000
Exports	300
Imports	100
Government expenditures	300
Increase in inventories	50
Depreciation	100

7. An economic historian, after careful research, makes the following estimates (in millions of dollars) concerning the Puritanian economy in 1910.

Disposable personal income	400
Business transfer payments	0
Statistical discrepancy	0
Subsidies less surpluses of government agencies	0
Net national product	600
National income	550
Personal income	460

How much were personal income taxes and indirect business taxes in Puritania in 1910?

8. Which of the following items are included in Puritania's gross national income? (a) The income of a lawyer, (b) interest received on government bonds, (c) the value of a housewife's services, (d) the allowance received by a ten-year-old, (e) donations to the Puritanian branch of the Salvation Army, (f) interest on corporate bonds, (g) dividends, (h) Social Security payments made by the Puritanian government, (i) the value of a 20-year-old house that is sold to a new owner, (j) the value of ten shares of U.S. Steel stock sold by one Puritanian citizen to another.

9. According to the September 1932 issue of *Fortune* magazine, "About 1,000,000 out of [New York City's] 3,200,000 working population are unemployed." What effect did this have on the city's population? During the past 30 years, has this experience been repeated? About how many New Yorkers are presently unemployed?

10. Suppose that you were given the job of estimating the gross national product of Monaco. How would you proceed?

9 Consumption, Saving, and Investment

In early 1975, the American economy was in the midst of a severe recession. Gross national product was well below its potential level, and unemployment in May 1975 reached 9 percent, the highest in decades. Early 1973, on the other hand, was a time of economic boom. GNP was moving ahead rapidly, and the unemployment rate was receding to less than 5 percent. Why the pronounced difference between these two periods? To answer this question, as well as to understand the causes of severe unemployment and inflation, and what can be done to avoid these problems, we must understand how the level of a nation's output is determined.

In this chapter, we take up some important elements of the modern theory of output and employment. To begin with, we describe the classical and Marxian views of unemployment, and Keynes's objections to these views. Then we discuss the determinants of consumption expenditure and investment. In the following chapter, we show how these elements are combined to form a model of the determination of national output—a model that lies at the heart of modern economics.

Theories of Unemployment

The Classical View of Unemployment

Until the 1930s, most economists were convinced that the price system, left to its own devices, would hold unemployment to a reasonable minimum. Thus most of the great names of economics in the nineteenth and early twentieth centuries—including John Stuart Mill, Alfred Marshall, and A. C. Pigou[1]—felt that there was no need for government intervention to promote a high level of employment. To be sure, they recognized that unemployment was sometimes large, but they regarded these lapses from high employment as temporary aberrations that the price system would cure automatically. We begin by taking an initial, brief look at why the classical economists felt this was true. (More will be said concerning their theories below and in later chapters.)

The classical economists recognized the fact, cited in the previous chapter, that the level of total spending determines the unemployment rate. They believed that total spending was unlikely to be too small to purchase the full-employment level of output, because of ***Say's Law*** (named after the nineteenth-century French economist, J. B. Say). According to this law, the production of a certain amount of goods and services results in the generation of an amount of income precisely sufficient to buy that output. (Recall the circular flow discussed in Chapters 4 and 8). In other words, *supply creates its own demand, since the total amount paid out by the producers of the goods and services to resource owners must equal the value of the goods and services. Thus, if this amount is spent, it must be sufficient to purchase all of the goods and services that are produced.*

But what if resource owners do not spend all of their income, but save some of it instead? How then will the necessary spending arise to take all of the output off the market? The answer the classical economists offered is that each dollar saved will be invested. Therefore, investment (made largely by business firms) will restore to the spending stream what resource owners take out through the saving process. Recall that the economist's definition of investment is different from the one often used in common parlance. To the economist, investment means expenditure on plant, equipment, and other productive assets. The classical economists believed that the amount invested would automatically equal the amount saved because the interest rate—the price paid for the use of money—would fluctuate in such a way as to maintain equality between them. In other words, there is a market for loanable funds, and the interest rate will vary so that the quantity of funds supplied equals the quantity demanded. Thus, since funds are demanded to be used—that is, invested—the amount saved will be invested.

Further, the classical economists said that the amount of goods and services businessmen can sell depends upon the prices businessmen charge, as well as on total spending. For example, $1 million in spending will take 200 cars off the market if the price is $5,000 per car, and 400 cars off the market if the price is $2,500 per car. Recognizing this, the classical economists argued that firms would cut prices to sell

[1] The ideas of John Stuart Mill (1806–73) and his arguments in support of individual freedom are particularly famous. He was one of the great philosophers of the nineteenth century. He was also a great economist; his *Principles of Political Economy* (1848) is his best-known work. He advocated many social reforms, including shorter working hours and tax reform.

Alfred Marshall (1842–1924) played an important role in the construction of the theories of supply and demand, the use of partial equilibrium techniques, and other major developments in economics. His *Principles of Economics* (1890), which had eight editions, was a leading economics text for many years.

A. C. Pigou (1877–1959) a student of Marshall, was professor of economics at Cambridge University from 1908 to 1943. His *Economics of Welfare* (1932) was a pathbreaking work that dealt in an important way with various aspects of welfare economics.

their output. Competition among firms would prod them to reduce their prices in this way, with the result that the high-employment level of output would be taken off the market.

Looking at this process more closely, it is obvious that the prices of resources must also be reduced under such circumstances. Otherwise firms would incur losses because they would be getting less for their product, but paying no less for resources. The classical economists believed that it was realistic to expect the prices of resources to decline in such a situation. Indeed they were quite willing to assume that the wage rate—the price of labor—would be flexible in this way. They expected this flexibility because of competition among laborers. Through the processes of competition, they felt that wage rates would be bid down to the level where everyone who really wanted to work could get a job.

The Views of Karl Marx

Quite a different view of unemployment was held by Karl Marx (1818–83), the intellectual father of communism. A man of unquestioned genius, he became an object of quasi-religious devotion to a large part of the world and a hated (and sometimes feared) revolutionary figure to another large part of the world. Because Marx the revolutionary has had such an enormous effect on modern history, it is difficult to discuss Marx the economist. But he was a very profound and influential economist. A meticulous German scholar who spent much of his life in poverty-ridden circumstances in Britain, he wrote a huge, four-volume work on economics, *Das Kapital.*[2] Eighteen years in the making, it remains one of the most influential books ever written.

To understand Marx, we need to know something about the times in which he lived. The period was characterized by revolutionary pressures against the ruling classes. In most of the countries of Europe, there was little democracy, as we know it. The masses participated little, if at all, in the world of political affairs, and very fully in the world of drudgery. For example, at one factory in Manchester, England, in 1862, people worked an average of about 80 hours per week. For these incredibly long hours of toil, the workers generally received small wages. They often could do little more than feed and clothe themselves. Given the circumstances of the times, it is little wonder that revolutionary pressures were manifest.

Marx, viewing the economic system of his day, believed that capitalism was doomed to collapse. He believed that the workers were exploited by the capitalists—the owners of factories, mines, and other types of capital. And he believed that the capitalists, by introducing new labor-saving technology, would throw more and more workers into unemployment. This army of unemployed workers, by competing for jobs, would keep wages at a subsistence level. As machinery was substituted for labor, Marx felt that profits would fall. Unemployment would become more severe. Big firms would absorb small ones. Eventually the capitalistic system was bound to collapse.

To get the flavor of his reasoning and emotions, consider the following passage from *Das Kapital,* a famous passage describing his vision of the death knell of the capitalist system:

> Along with the constantly diminishing number of the magnates of capital, who usurp and monopolize all advantages of this process of transformation, grows the mass of misery, oppression, slavery, degradation, exploitation; but with this too grows the revolt of the working-class, a class always increasing in numbers, and disciplined, united, organized by the very mechanism of the process of capitalist production itself . . . Centralization of the means of production and socialization of labor at last reach a point where they become incompatible with their capitalist integument. This integument bursts asunder. The knell of capitalist private property sounds. The expropriators are expropriated.[3]

[2] Karl Marx, *Das Kapital,* New York: Modern Library, 1906.

[3] Karl Marx, *Das Kapital,* pp. 836–37.

According to Marx, the inevitable successor to capitalism would be socialism, an economic system with no private property. Instead, property would be owned by society as a whole. Socialism, constituting a "dictatorship of the proletariat," would be only a transitional step to the promised land of communism. Marx did not spell out the characteristics of communism in detail. He was sure that it would be a classless society where everyone worked and no one owned capital, and he was sure that the state would "wither away," but he did not attempt to go much beyond this in his blueprint for communism. Even without examining Marx's doctrines, and their limitations, in greater detail, one can see that, although the classical view (discussed in the previous section) was the dominant one in the nineteenth century, it did not go unchallenged in its own time.

John Maynard Keynes and the Great Depression

The man who was responsible for much of the modern theory of the determination of national product was John Maynard Keynes (1883-1946). Son of a British economist who was justly famous in his own right, Keynes was enormously successful in a variety of fields. He published a brilliant book on the theory of probability while still a relatively young man. Working for a half-hour in bed each morning, he made millions of dollars as a stock market speculator. He was a distinguished patron of the arts and a member of the Bloomsbury set, a group of London intellectuals who were the intellectual pace-setters for British society. He was a faculty member at Cambridge University, and a key figure at the British Treasury. In short, he was an extraordinarily gifted and accomplished man.

Keynes lived and worked almost a century after Marx. His world was quite different from Marx's world; and Keynes himself—polished, successful, a member of the elite—was quite different from the poverty-stricken, revolutionary Marx. But the two great economists were linked in at least one important respect: both were preoccupied with unemployment and the future of the capitalistic system. As we saw in the previous section, Marx predicted that unemployment would get worse and worse, until at last the capitalist system would collapse. In the 1930s, when Keynes was at the height of his influence, the Great Depression seemed to many people to be proving Marx right.

In 1936, while the world was still in the throes of this economic disaster, Keynes published his masterpiece, *The General Theory of Employment, Interest, and Money.*[4] His purpose in this book was to explain how the capitalist economic system could get stalled in the sort of depressed state of equilibrium that existed in the 1930s. He also tried to indicate how governments might help to solve the problem. Contrary to the classical economists, Keynes concluded that no automatic mechanism in a capitalistic society would generate a high level of employment—or, at least, would generate it quickly enough to be relied on in practice. Instead, the equilibrium level of national output might for a long time be below the level required to achieve high employment. His reasons for believing that this could be the case are discussed in detail in this and subsequent chapters.

To push the economy toward a higher level of employment, Keynes advocated the conscious, forceful use of the government's power to spend and tax. As we shall see in Chapter 11, many years passed before these powers became accepted tools of national economic policy, but it was Keynes who provided much of the intellectual stimulus. And in so doing, he helped falsify the predictions of Marx. Keynes and his

[4] John Maynard Keynes, *The General Theory of Employment, Interest, and Money,* New York: Harcourt, Brace, 1936.

many followers showed how severe unemployment could be tamed, and how a capitalistic economy could be managed to avoid the sorts of debacles Marx predicted. It is no exaggeration to say that Keynes made a major contribution to saving the capitalist system.

Flaws in the Classical View

There were at least two basic flaws in the classical model, as Keynes and his followers pointed out. First, *there is no assurance that desired saving will equal desired investment at a level insuring high employment.* The people and firms who save are often not the same as the people and firms who invest, and they often have quite different motivations. In particular, a considerable amount of saving is done by families who want to put something aside for a rainy day or for a car or appliance. On the other hand, a considerable amount of investment is done by firms that are interested in increasing their profits by expanding their plants or by installing new equipment. Desired saving may not equal desired investment at a level insuring high employment. Instead, they may be equal at a level corresponding to considerable unemployment (or to considerable inflation). Thus a purely capitalist economic system, in the absence of appropriate government policies, has no dependable rudder to keep it clear of the shoals of serious unemployment or of serious inflation.

Second, *Keynes and his followers pointed out the unreality of the classical economists' assumption that prices and wages are flexible.* Contrary to the classical economists' argument, the modern economy contains many departures from perfect competition that are barriers to downward flexibility of prices and wages. In particular, many important industries are dominated by a few producers who try hard to avoid cutting price. Even in the face of a considerable drop in demand, such industries have sometimes maintained extraordinarily stable prices. Moreover, the labor unions fight tooth and nail to avoid wage cuts. In view of these facts of life, the classical assumption of wage and price flexibility seems unrealistic indeed. And it seems unlikely that price and wage reductions can be depended on to maintain full employment.

The Great Depression of the 1930s struck a severe blow against the classical view. When it continued for years, and millions and millions of people continued to be unemployed, it became increasingly difficult to accept the idea that unemployment was only a temporary aberration that the market economy would cure automatically in a reasonable length of time. Nonetheless, the diehard followers of the classical economists did not change their tune. They claimed that the economy would get back to high employment if the labor unions would allow more wage flexibility, if the big corporations would allow more price flexibility, and if President Franklin D. Roosevelt and his New Dealers would quit interfering with free markets.

Finally, when Keynes's *General Theory* appeared in 1936, it seemed to offer a more satisfactory model, even though, at first, only a minority of the economics profession was converted to the Keynesian view. Within 10 or 15 years of its publication, most economists were convinced that Keynes's theory was essentially sound; and his ideas now are generally accepted, although they have been refined and extended by his followers. Whether Republican or Democrat, any modern economist relies heavily on Keynesian ideas and concepts. But, of course, not all economists share Keynes's views on proper public policy. Moreover, as we shall see in subsequent chapters, under certain circumstances, more complicated models are likely to outperform the simple Keynesian model presented in this and the following chapters.

The Consumption Function: A Major Element of the Modern Theory

Keynes's *General Theory of Employment, Interest, and Money* is impenetrable for the general reader. Even among professional economists, it is not noted for its lucidity or liveliness. But the basic ideas that Keynes presented—and that subsequent economists have refined, extended, and reworked—are really quite simple. In the remainder of this chapter, we shall describe several of the most important elements of the modern theory of the determination of national output. The first such element to be discussed is the ***consumption function,*** *which is the relationship between consumption spending and disposable income.* Keynes emphasized that *consumption expenditures—whether those of a single household or the total consumption expenditures in the entire economy—are influenced heavily by income.* For individual households, Figure 9.1 shows that families with higher incomes spend more on consumption than families with lower incomes. Of course, individual families vary a good deal in their behavior; some spend more than others even if their incomes are the same. But, on the average, a family's consumption expenditure is tied very closely to its income.

What is true for individual families also holds for the entire economy: total consumption expenditures are closely related to disposable income. This fact, noted in the previous chapter, is shown in detail in Figure 9.2, a "scatter diagram" that plots total consumption expenditure in each year (from 1929 to 1974) against disposable income in the same year (from 1929 to 1974). The points fall very near the straight line drawn in Figure 9.2, but not right on it. For most practical purposes, however, we can regard the line drawn in Figure 9.2 as representing the relationship between total consumption expenditures and disposable income. In other words, we can regard this line as the consumption function.

The consumption function, the importance of which was stressed by John Maynard

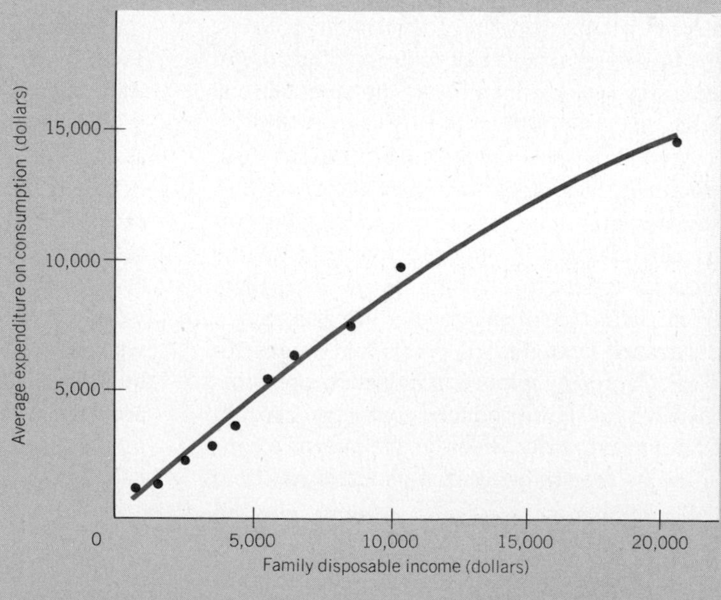

Figure 9.1
Relation between Family Expenditures on Consumption and Family Disposable Income, United States
Families with higher incomes spend more on consumption than families with lower incomes.

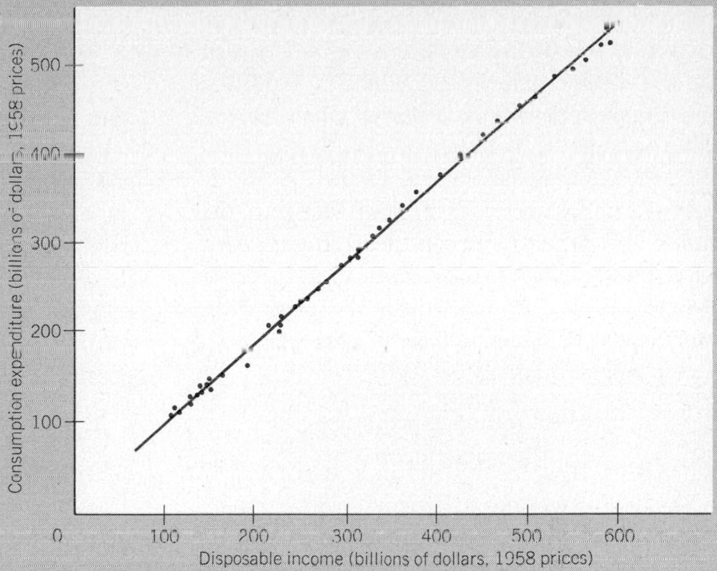

Figure 9.2
Relationship between Consumption Expenditure and Disposable Income, United States, 1929–74
There is a very close relationship between consumption expenditure and disposable income in the United States. In this figure a dot is given for each year. The dot's horizontal distance from the origin measures the disposable income that year, and its vertical position from the origin measures the consumption expenditure that year. As you can see, the dots generally are very close to the line.

Keynes, is at the heart of the modern theory of the determination of national output. It is a working tool that is used widely and often by economists to analyze and forecast the behavior of the economy. There have been many statistical studies of the consumption function. Some of these studies have been based on cross-section data—comparisons of the amount spent on consumption by families at various income levels. (Figure 9.1 is based on cross-section data.) Others have been based on time-series data—comparisons of the total amount spent on consumption in the economy with total income over various periods of time. (Figure 9.2 is based on time-series data.)

The Marginal Propensity to Consume

Suppose that we know what the consumption function for a given society looks like at a particular point in time. For example, suppose that it is given by the figures for disposable income and consumption expenditure in the first two columns of Table 9.1. Based on our knowledge of the consumption function, we can determine the *extra* amount families will spend on consumption if they receive an *extra* dollar of disposable income. *This amount—the fraction of an extra dollar of income that is spent on consumption—is called the* ***marginal propensity to consume.*** For reasons discussed in subsequent sections of this chapter, the marginal propensity to consume, shown in column 4 of Table 9.1, plays a major role in the modern theory of national output determination.

To make sure that you understand exactly what the marginal propensity to consume is, consult Table 9.1. What is the marginal propensity to consume when disposable income is between $1,000 billion and $1,050 billion? The second column shows that, when income rises from $1,000 billion to $1,050 billion, consumption rises from $950 billion to $980 billion. Consequently, the fraction of the extra $50 billion of income that is consumed is $30 billion ÷ $50 billion, or 0.60. Thus, the marginal propensity to consume is 0.60.[5] Based on

[5] Students with some knowledge of mathematics will recognize that this is an approximation since $50 billion is a substantial change in income, whereas the marginal propensity to consume pertains to a small change in income. But this is an innocuous simplification. Similar simplifications are made below.

similar calculations, the marginal propensity to consume when disposable income is between $1,050 billion and $1,100 billion is 0.60; the marginal propensity to consume when disposable income is between $1,100 billion and $1,150 billion is 0.60; and so forth.

It is important to distinguish between the marginal propensity to consume and the ***average propensity to consume.*** The average propensity to consume equals the proportion of disposable income that is consumed. In other words, it equals

$$\frac{\text{consumption expenditure}}{\text{disposable income}}$$

Clearly, this will not in general equal the marginal propensity to consume, which is

$$\frac{\text{change in consumption expenditure}}{\text{change in disposable income}}$$

The point is that the marginal propensity to consume is the proportion of *extra* income consumed, and this proportion generally is quite different from the proportion of *total* income consumed. For example, in Table 9.1, the average propensity to consume when disposable income is $1,100 billion is 0.92; but the marginal propensity to consume when disposable income is between $1,050 billion and $1,100 billion is 0.60.

The marginal propensity to consume can be interpreted geometrically as the slope of the consumption function. The slope of any line is, of course, the ratio of the vertical change to the

Table 9.1
The Consumption Function

Disposable income (billions of dollars)	Consumption expenditure (billions of dollars)	Average propensity to consume	Marginal propensity to consume	Saving (billions of dollars)	Marginal propensity to save
1,000	950	.95		50	
			$\frac{30}{50} = .60$		$\frac{20}{50} = .40$
1,050	980	.93		70	
			$\frac{30}{50} = .60$		$\frac{20}{50} = .40$
1,100	1,010	.92		90	
			$\frac{30}{50} = .60$		$\frac{20}{50} = .40$
1,150	1,040	.90		110	
			$\frac{30}{50} = .60$		$\frac{20}{50} = .40$
1,200	1,070	.89		130	
			$\frac{30}{50} = .60$		$\frac{20}{50} = .40$
1,250	1,100	.88		150	
			$\frac{30}{50} = .60$		$\frac{20}{50} = .40$
1,300	1,130	.87		170	

horizontal change when a small movement occurs along the line. As shown in Figure 9.3, the vertical change is the change in consumption expenditure, and the horizontal change is the change in disposable income. Thus the ratio of the vertical change to the horizontal change must equal the marginal propensity to consume.

In general, the marginal propensity to consume can differ, depending on the level of disposable income. For example, the marginal propensity to consume may be higher at lower levels than at higher levels of disposable income. Only if the consumption function is a straight line, as in Figure 9.2 and Table 9.1, will the marginal propensity to consume be the same at all levels of income. For simplicity, we assume in much of the subsequent analysis that the consumption function is a straight line, but this assumption can easily be relaxed without affecting the essential aspects of our conclusions.

The Saving Function and the Marginal Propensity to Save

If people don't devote their disposable income to consumption expenditure, what else can they do with it? Of course, they can save it. When families refrain from spending their income on consumption goods and services—that is, when they forgo present consumption to provide for larger consumption in the future—they save. Thus we can derive from the consumption function the total amount people will save at each level of disposable income. All we have to do is subtract the total consumption expenditure at each level of disposable income from disposable income. The difference is the total amount of saving at each level of disposable income. This difference is shown in the next to last column of Table 9.1. We can plot the total amount of saving against disposable income, as in Figure 9.4. The resulting rela-

Figure 9.3
The Marginal Propensity to Consume, Interpreted Geometrically as the Slope of the Consumption Function
The slope of the consumption function between points *A* and *B* equals the vertical change (which is the change in consumption expenditure) divided by the horizontal change (which is the change in disposable income). Since the marginal propensity to consume equals the change in consumption expenditure divided by the change in disposable income, it follows that the slope equals the marginal propensity to consume.

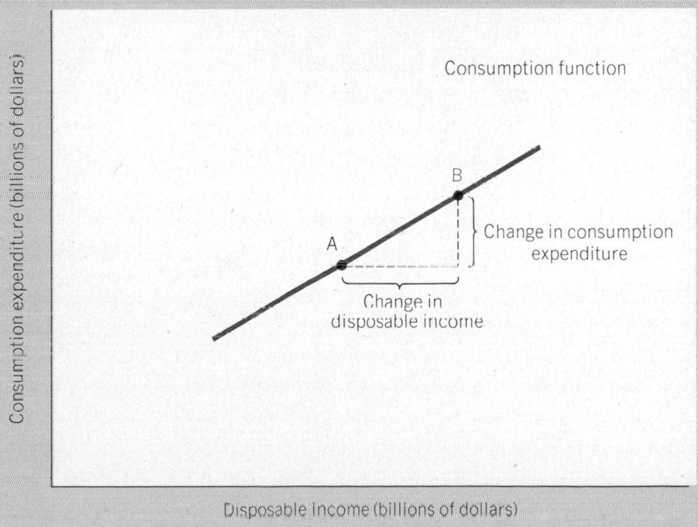

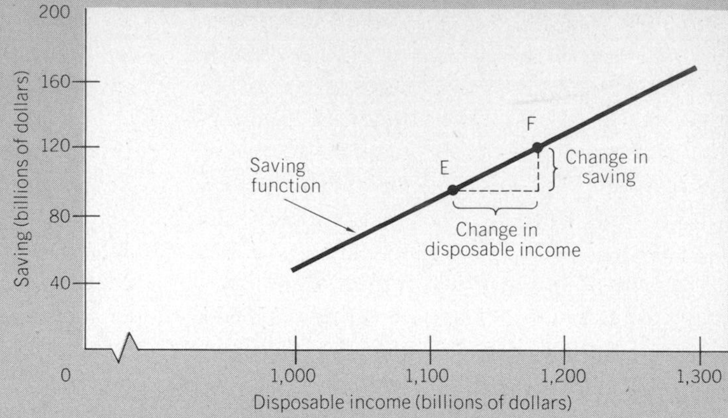

Figure 9.4
The Saving Function
The saving function describes the total amount of saving at each level of disposable income. The slope of the saving function equals the change in saving divided by the change in disposable income. Thus, the slope of the saving function equals the marginal propensity to save.

tionship between total saving and disposable income is called the ***saving function.*** Like the consumption function, it plays a major role in the modern theory of national output determination.

If we know the saving function, we can calculate the marginal propensity to save at any level of disposable income. The ***marginal propensity to save*** *is the proportion of an extra dollar of disposable income that is saved.* To see how to calculate it, consult Table 9.1 again. The fifth column shows that, when income rises from $1,000 billion to $1,050 billion, saving rises from $50 billion to $70 billion. Consequently, the fraction of the extra $50 billion of income that is saved is $20 billion ÷ $50 billion, or 0.40. Thus the marginal propensity to save is 0.40. Similar calculations show that the marginal propensity to save when disposable income is between $1,050 billion and $1,100 billion is 0.40; the marginal propensity to save when disposable income is between $1,100 billion and $1,150 billion is 0.40; and so forth.

Note that, *at any particular level of disposable income, the marginal propensity to save plus the marginal propensity to consume must equal one.* By definition, the marginal propensity to save equals the proportion of an extra dollar of disposable income that is saved, and the marginal propensity to consume equals the proportion of an extra dollar of income that is consumed. The sum of these two proportions must equal one, for, as stated above, the only things that people can do with an extra dollar of disposable income are consume it or save it. Table 9.1 shows this fact quite clearly.

Finally, it is worth noting that the marginal propensity to save equals the slope of the saving function—just as the marginal propensity to consume equals the slope of the consumption function. As pointed out above, the slope of a line equals the vertical distance between any two points on the line divided by the horizontal distance between them. Since (as shown in Figure 9.4) the vertical distance is the change in saving and the horizontal distance is the change in disposable income, the slope of the saving function must equal the marginal propensity to save.

Determinants of Consumption and Saving: Nonincome Factors

In previous sections, we have been concerned solely with the effect of changes in disposable income on total consumption expenditure and saving. It is important to recognize that many other factors besides disposable income also have an effect on total consumption expenditure and saving. Holding disposable income constant, total consumption expenditure is likely to vary with the amount of wealth in the hands of the public, the ease and cheapness with which consumers can borrow money, the expectations of the public, the amount of durable goods on hand, the income distribution, and the size of the population. In this section, we discuss the effects of these nonincome factors on consumption and saving.

Amount of wealth. Holding disposable income constant, it is clear that total consumption expenditure will be higher if the public has a large amount of wealth—stocks, bonds, savings accounts, and so on—than if it has a small amount. Why? Because people are more willing to spend out of current income when they have large assets to tide them over if their incomes fall. Thus, if the Merriwether family has $100,000 in stocks and bonds, it is more likely to spend a large percentage of its income than if it has little or nothing in wealth.

Ease and cheapness of borrowing. Holding disposable income constant, it is clear that total consumption expenditure will be higher if the public can borrow money easily and cheaply. This is particularly important for expenditures on consumer durables like automobiles and appliances. If required down payments are increased, and interest rates go up, some potential buyers will be persuaded (or forced) to postpone purchases of such items. For example, the Merriwethers may want a new car, and they may be quite willing to borrow the money to pay for it at 10 percent per year. But if the interest rate is raised to 15 percent per year, they may decide to stick with their old car until it is run into the ground.

Expectations. Holding disposable income constant, total consumption expenditure may be higher if the public feels that price increases are in the wind or that goods will become harder to get. Why? Because the public may want to stock up on goods before their prices rise and while they are still available. (In recent years, the expectation of price rises with regard to such items as autos and sugar seems to have had such an effect.) On the other hand, the expectation of price increases may have the opposite effect if the public is alarmed by the inflation, and wants to build up its savings to cushion it against hard times ahead. Recent experience, according to the Council of Economic Advisers, seems to indicate that consumers react to heightened inflationary expectations of this sort by cutting back their consumption expenditures.

Amount of durable goods on hand. Holding disposable income constant, total consumption expenditure may be higher if the public has few durable goods on hand. For example, during World War II, very few automobiles were produced for ordinary civilian purposes. When such goods became available once again immediately after the war, there was an increase in the proportion of disposable income spent on durable goods, particularly since the public came out of the war with considerable savings and liquid assets. More will be said about this in the next chapter.

Distribution of income. Holding disposable income constant, total consumption expenditure would be expected to increase as a nation's income becomes more nearly equally distributed. Why? Because one would expect that the marginal propensity to consume would be higher (and the marginal propensity to save would be lower) among poor families than among rich ones. Thus, if a dollar of income is transferred from a rich family to a poor one, the poor family would be expected to save a smaller proportion of this extra dollar than the rich family from whom it was taken. Consequently, total consumption expenditure would be expected to increase as a result of transfers of income of this sort.

Size of population. Holding disposable income constant, total consumption expenditure would be expected to increase as a nation's population increases. As there are more and more mouths to feed, bodies to clothe, and families to house, one would expect that more would be spent on consumption goods, and less would be saved.

Shifts in the Consumption and Saving Functions

Suppose that a change occurs in one of the factors discussed in the previous section. For example, suppose that there is a marked increase in the amount of wealth in the hands of the public. What effect will this have on the consumption function? Obviously, it will shift the consumption function upward, as from position 1 to position 2 in panel A of Figure 9.5. Or suppose that it becomes more difficult and expensive for consumers to borrow money. What effect will this have on the consumption function? Obviously, it will shift the consumption function downward, as from position 1 to position 3 in panel A of Figure 9.5.

It is important to distinguish between a *shift* in the consumption function and a *movement along* a given consumption function. A shift in the consumption function means that the public wants to spend a different amount on consumption goods out of a given amount of disposable income than in the past. Thus, if the consumption function shifts to position 2 in panel A of Figure 9.5, this means that the public wants to spend more on consumption goods out of a given amount of disposable income than when the consumption function was at position 1. And if the consumption function shifts to position 3 in panel A of Figure 9.5, this means that the public wants to spend less on consumption goods out of a given amount of disposable income than when the consumption function was at position 1.

In contrast, a movement along a given consumption function is a change in total consumption expenditure induced by a change in disposable income, with no change in the relationship between total consumption expenditure and disposable income. For example, the movement from point A to point B is a movement along a consumption function (in position 1). Similarly, the movement from point C to point D is a movement along a consumption function (in position 2). As we shall see in the next chapter, this distinction between a shift in the consumption function and a movement along a consumption function is important in many aspects of the theory of output and employment.

Note too that an *upward* shift in the consumption function must be accompanied by a *downward* shift in the saving function. If the public wants to spend *more* on consumption goods out of a given amount of disposable income, it must want to save *less* out of that amount of disposable income. (Why? Because consumption expenditure plus saving equals disposable income). Thus, if the consumption function shifts upward from position 1 to position 2 in panel A of Figure 9.5, the saving function must shift downward from position 4 to position 5 in panel B of Figure 9.5.

Also, a *downward* shift in the consumption function must be accompanied by an *upward* shift in the saving function. If the public wants to spend *less* on consumption goods out of a given amount of disposable income, it must want to save *more* out of that amount of disposable income. (Why? Because consumption expenditure plus saving equals disposable income.) Thus, if the consumption function shifts downward from position 1 to position 3 in panel A of Figure 9.5, the saving function must shift upward from position 4 to position 6 in panel B of Figure 9.5.

The Permanent-Income and Life-Cycle Hypotheses

The consumption function, as described in

Figure 9.5
Shifts in Consumption and Saving Functions
If the consumption function moves from position 1 to position 2 (or position 3), this is a *shift* in the consumption function. A movement from *A* to *B* (or from *C* to *D*) is a *movement along* a given consumption function.

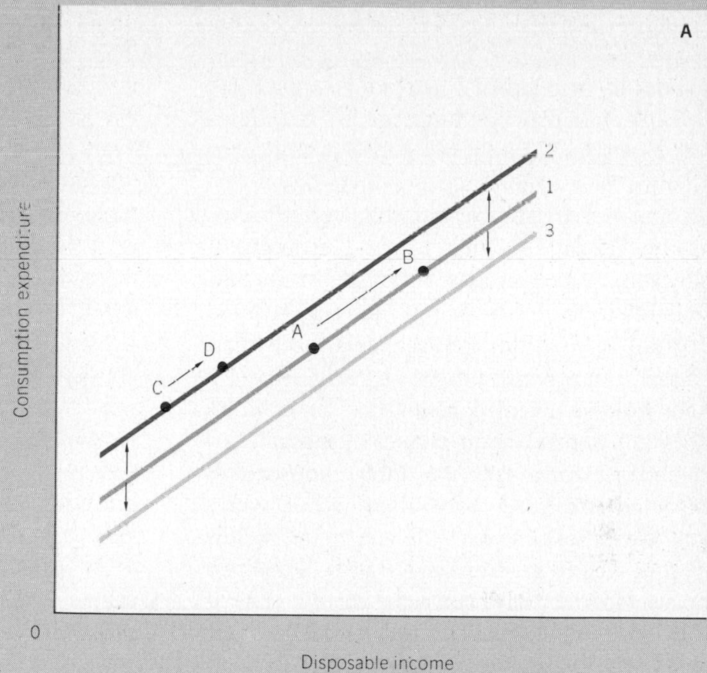

An *upward* shift in the consumption function (as from position 1 to position 2 in panel A) is accompanied by a *downward* shift in the saving function (from position 4 to position 5 in panel B). A *downward* shift in the consumption function (as from position 1 to position 3 in panel A) is accompanied by an *upward* shift in the saving function (from position 4 to position 6 in panel B).

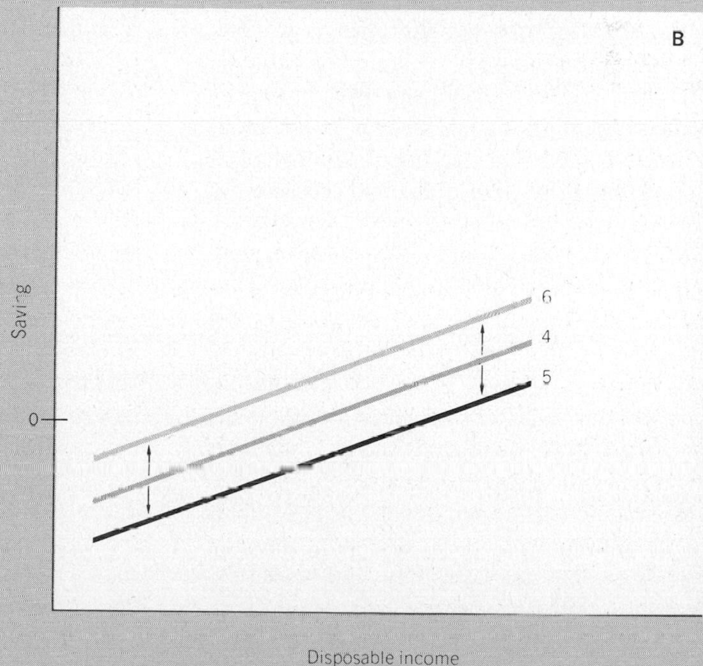

previous sections, is a relationship between *current* consumption expenditure and *current* disposable income. In Figures 9.1 and 9.2, for example, it is presumed that current consumption expenditure in a given period, whether for a family or a nation, depends upon disposable income in that same period. Some economists, led by Milton Friedman of the University of Chicago, Franco Modigliani of the Massachusetts Institute of Technology, and Albert Ando of the University of Pennsylvania, have challenged this presumption. In their view, a household's current consumption expenditure does not depend upon current disposable income; instead, it depends on the household's expected stream of disposable income over a long period of time (as well as the household's wealth, which we discussed above). Thus two households that have the same current disposable income may spend quite different amounts on consumption goods, if their expected income streams over the long term are quite different.

To illustrate what these economists mean, consider two hypothetical families: the Smiths and the Does. Although both Mr. Smith and Mr. Doe will earn $12,000 this year, their long-run income prospects are quite different. Mr. Smith is a businessman who ordinarily makes $50,000 per year, but whose income is much lower this year because of a foolish decision by one of his employees that caused a sizable one-time loss to Smith's firm. Based on all available evidence, Smith's annual income will return to about $50,000 in the future. Mr. Doe, on the other hand, has been unemployed for many years, and there is no prospect that he will return to work. His $12,000 income this year was due to his having won a lottery. What Friedman, Modigliani, and Ando are saying is that one would expect each family to spend an amount on consumption goods this year that is commensurate with its long-term income, not just its income this year. Thus one would expect the Smiths to spend a lot more on consumption goods than the Does, even though their current incomes are the same.

Although Friedman's theory (often called the permanent-income hypothesis) differs in many respects from the Modigliani-Ando theory (often called the life-cycle hypothesis), the differences need not concern us here. What is important for present purposes is that both of these theories predict that a transitory change in income may not have much impact on a household's consumption expenditure, if the household's long-run income prospects remain relatively unaffected. In contrast, the basic Keynesian consumption function assumes that consumption expenditure is dependent on current disposable income. To keep the analysis as simple as possible, we shall use the basic Keynesian consumption function in subsequent chapters; but the fact that it is a simplification should be recognized.

Determinants of Investment

In the previous chapter, we stressed that investment consists largely of the amount firms spend on new buildings and factories, new equipment, and increases in inventory. Investment plays a central role in the modern theory of output and employment. To understand this theory, it is essential that you understand the factors determining the level of net investment (which is gross investment less depreciation). Basically, there are two broad determinants of the level of net investment—the expected rate of return from capital, and the interest rate.

The ***expected rate of return from capital*** is the perceived rate of return that businessmen believe they can obtain if they put up new buildings or factories, add new equipment, or increase their inventories. Each of these forms of investment requires the expenditure of money. The rate of return measures the profitability of such an expenditure; it shows the annual profits to be obtained per dollar invested. Thus a rate of return of 10 percent means that, for every dollar invested, an annual profit of 10 cents is obtained. Clearly, the higher the expected rate of return from a particular investment, the more profitable the investment is expected to be.

The ***interest rate*** is the cost of borrowing money. More specifically, it is the annual amount that a borrower must pay for the use of a dollar for a year. Thus, if the interest rate is 8 percent, a borrower must pay 8 cents per year for the use of a dollar. And if the interest rate is 12 percent, a borrower must pay 12 cents per year for the use of a dollar. Anyone with a savings account knows what it is to earn interest; anyone who has borrowed money from a bank knows what it is to pay interest.

To determine whether to invest in a particular project (a new building, piece of equipment, or other form of investment), a firm must compare the expected rate of return from the project with the interest rate. If the expected rate of return is less than the interest rate, the firm will lose money if it borrows money to carry out the project. For example, if the firm invests in a project with a 10 percent rate of return and borrows the money to finance the project at 12 percent interest, it will receive profits of 10 cents per dollar invested and pay out interest of 12 cents per dollar invested. So it will lose 2 cents (12 cents minus 10 cents) per dollar invested.

Even if the firm does not borrow money to finance the project, it will be unlikely to invest in a project where the expected rate of return is less than the interest rate. Why? Because, if the firm can lend money to others at the prevailing interest rate, it can obtain a greater return from its money by doing this than by investing in the project. Thus, if the interest rate is 12 percent and an investment project has an expected rate of return of 10 percent, a firm will do better, if it has a certain amount of money, to lend it out at 12 percent than to earn 10 percent from the investment project.

Since firms are likely to invest only in projects where the expected rate of return exceeds the interest rate, it is obvious that *the level of investment depends on the total volume of investment projects where the expected rate of return exceeds the interest rate.* For example, if the interest rate is 10 percent, the level of investment depends on the total volume of investment projects where the expected rate of return exceeds 10 percent. The more such projects there are, the higher will be the level of (gross and net) investment. The fewer such projects there are, the lower will be the level of (gross and net) investment. In the next two sections, we discuss a number of factors that influence how many such projects there are.

Technological Change and the Existing Stock of Capital

The rate of technological change can have an important influence on the volume of investment projects where the rate of return exceeds the interest rate. New technology frequently opens up profitable investment opportunities. For example, DuPont, after successfully developing nylon in 1938, found it profitable to invest millions of dollars in new plant and equipment to produce this new synthetic fiber. In other words, the invention of nylon resulted in an additional number of investment projects where the rate of return was high enough to induce firms to invest. Another case of this sort was the continuous wide strip mill, one of the most important developments in steel technology in this century. After the invention of the continuous wide strip mill by Armco in the 1920s, American steel producers invested huge sums in new rolling mills to replace the old hand mills.

In general, *a more rapid rate of technological change is likely to result in a greater number of investment projects where the rate of return exceeds the interest rate. Thus a more rapid rate of technological change is likely to increase the level of investment.*

Another factor that influences the volume of investment projects where the rate of return exceeds the interest rate is the existing stock of capital. As a firm's sales go up, its need for plant, equipment, and inventories clearly goes up as well. Beyond some point, increases in sales result in pressure on the capacity of existing plant and equipment, so that the firm finds it profitable to invest in additional plant and equipment. Clearly, the crucial relationship is between a firm's sales and its stock of capital goods—that is, its stock of plant, equipment, and inventories. If its sales are well below the amount it can produce with its stock of capital goods, there is little pressure on the firm to invest in additional capital goods. But if its sales are at the upper limit of what can be produced with its capital goods, the firm is likely to view the purchase of additional capital goods as yielding a high rate of return.

In general, *the smaller the existing stock of capital goods—relative to present and prospective sales levels—the greater the number of investment projects where the expected rate of return exceeds the interest rate.* Conversely, *the bigger the existing stock of capital goods—relative to present and prospective sales levels—the smaller the number of investment projects where the expected rate of return exceeds the interest rate.*

Business Expectations and the Interest Rate

Still another factor that influences the number of investment projects where the expected rate of return exceeds the interest rate is the state of business expectations. Sometimes businessmen are optimistic; sometimes they are pessimistic. If they believe that their sales are about to drop dramatically, they will be unlikely to invest much in additional capital goods. On the other hand, if they believe that their sales are about to increase greatly, they may be led to invest heavily in capital goods. Firms must make investment decisions on the basis of forecasts. There is no way any firm can tell exactly what the future will bring, and the investment decisions it makes will be influenced by how optimistic or pessimistic its forecasts are. This in turn will depend on existing business conditions, as well as on many other factors. Sometimes government actions and political developments have an important impact on business expectations. Sometimes unexpected changes in the fortune of one industry have a major effect on expectations in other industries.

In general, *the more optimistic business expectations are, the larger the number of investment projects where the expected rate of return exceeds the interest rate. Conversely, the more pessimistic business expectations are, the smaller the number of investment projects where the expected rate of return exceeds the interest rate.*

Finally, the number of investment projects where the expected rate of return exceeds the interest rate clearly depends on the level of the interest rate. The higher the interest rate, the smaller the number of projects that have expected rates of return exceeding the interest rate. The lower the interest rate, the larger the number of projects that have expected rates of return exceeding the interest rate. To illustrate this fact, suppose that a firm is considering the six investment projects shown in Table 9.2. If the interest rate is 6 percent, all of them have expected rates of return exceeding the interest

Table 9.2
Expected Rates of Return from Investment Projects Considered by a Firm

Project	Expected rate of return (percent)
A	12
B	14
C	8
D	11
E	7
F	10

rate. If the interest rate is 10 percent, only three of them (projects *A*, *B*, and *D*) have expected rates of return exceeding the interest rate. And if the interest rate is 15 percent, none of them has an expected rate of return exceeding the interest rate.

In general, *increases in the interest rate tend to reduce investment, while decreases in the interest rate tend to increase investment.*

Why Is Investment So Volatile?

In the previous chapter, we pointed out the important fact that investment tends to be relatively unstable. That is, it varies from year to year by greater percentages than does consumption expenditure. Based on our discussion in the last few sections, it is easy to see why this is the case. First, technological innovation occurs irregularly—that is, in fits and starts—not at a constant rate. Thus investment (which, as we have seen, is dependent on the rate of technological change) also tends to occur irregularly. For example, investment booms seem to have occurred in response to major innovations like the railroad and the automobile.

Second, because capital goods tend to be quite durable, firms frequently can postpone investment decisions. For example, they can postpone the replacement of a piece of equipment by repairing it and extending its life. Or they can postpone the construction of a new building by tolerating crowded conditions in their existing buildings. Since many investment decisions are postponable, the exact time when projects are accepted may depend on the state of business expectations and the level of firms' profits, both of which are highly variable. Also, since the optimism or pessimism of business expectations tends to be contagious, firms often tend to invest at the same time.

Third, there are great differences from one year to the next in the extent to which existing productive capacity is being utilized. In some years, sales are so great that firms are working their plants at full capacity. In other years, sales are so slack that firms have plenty of excess capacity. In periods when the existing stock of capital goods is more than sufficient to meet current sales, the level of investment will tend to be lower than in periods when the existing stock of capital goods is only barely sufficient to meet current sales. Because of the year-to-year variation in the extent to which sales levels press against productive capacity, there is considerable variation in the level of investment.

Summary

Until the 1930s, most economists were convinced that the price system, left to its own devices, would insure the maintenance of full employment. They thought it unlikely that total spending would be too small to purchase the full-employment level of output, and argued that prices would be cut if any problem of this sort developed. A notable exception was Karl Marx, who felt that the capitalistic system would suffer from worse and worse unemployment, leading to its eventual collapse. John Maynard Keynes, in the 1930s, developed a theory to explain how the capitalist economic system remained mired in the Great Depression, with its tragically high levels of unemployment. Contrary to the classical economists, Keynes concluded that there was no automatic mechanism in a capitalistic system to generate and maintain full employment—or, at least, to generate it quickly enough to be relied on in practice. Keynes's ideas form the core of the modern theory of output and employment.

The consumption function—the relation between consumption expenditures and disposable income—is at the heart of this theory. There have been many studies of the consumption function, some based on cross-section data, some based on time-series data. From the consumption function, one can determine the marginal propensity to consume, which is the proportion of an extra dollar of income that is spent on consumption, as well as the saving function (the relationship between total saving and disposable income) and the marginal propensity to save (the proportion of an extra dollar of income that is saved).

Holding disposable income constant, total consumption expenditure is likely to depend on the amount of wealth in the hands of the public, the ease and cheapness with which consumers can borrow money, the expectations of the public, the amount of durable goods on hand, the income distribution, and the size of the population. Changes in these factors are likely to cause shifts in the consumption function. Also, it is widely accepted that current consumption expenditure does not depend solely on disposable income in the current period. Instead, as stressed by the permanent-income and life-cycle hypotheses, it depends on the expected stream of disposable income over a long period of time.

The level of investment is determined by the expected rate of return from capital and the interest rate. The expected rate of return from capital is the perceived rate of return that businessmen believe they can obtain if they put up new buildings, add new equipment, or increase their inventories. The interest rate is the cost of borrowing money. The level of investment is directly related to the expected rate of return from capital, and inversely related to the interest rate. The expected rate of return from capital is itself dependent upon the rate of technological change, the size of the existing stock of capital goods (relative to present and prospective sales levels), and the optimism or pessimism of businessmen's expectations.

CONCEPTS FOR REVIEW

Say's law
Consumption function
Saving function
Marginal propensity to consume
Marginal propensity to save
Average propensity to consume
Average propensity to save
Wealth
Permanent-income hypothesis
Interest rate
Expectations
Expected rate of return

QUESTIONS FOR DISCUSSION AND REVIEW

1. "If the government will leave things alone, competition in the product and input markets will cure a recession." Comment and evaluate.

2. Describe Say's Law in as much detail as you can. Explain the arguments given by the classical economists, and the counterarguments given by Keynes and his followers. Indicate what sorts of tests economists could conduct to determine which of these models is closer to the truth.

3. Suppose that only three families inhabit a nation and that each family spends 90 percent of its income on consumption goods. For the nation as a whole, what is the marginal propensity to save? How much difference is there between the marginal propensity to consume and the average propensity to consume? To what extent does the nation's marginal propensity to consume depend on the distribution of income? Is this realistic?

4. Assume that the consumption function is as follows:

Disposable income (billions of dollars)	Consumption expenditure (billions of dollars)
900	750
1,000	800
1,100	850
1,200	900
1,300	950
1,400	1,000

(a) How much will be saved if disposable income is $1,000 billion? (b) What is the average propensity to consume if disposable income is $1,000 billion? (c) What is the marginal propensity to consume if disposable income is between $1,000 billion and $1,100 billion? (d) What is the marginal propensity to save if disposable income is between $1,000 billion and $1,100 billion?

5. Suppose that the relationship between consumption expenditure and disposable income in the United States were as follows:

Consumption (billions of dollars)	Disposable income (billions of dollars)
750	700
830	800
910	900
970	1,000
1,030	1,100
1,100	1,200

Draw the consumption function on a graph. On another graph, draw the saving function. Is the marginal propensity to consume constant, or does it vary with the level of disposable income? Does the average propensity to consume rise or fall as disposable income arises?

6. "Unless firms make profits, they cannot invest in plant and equipment. Profits set an upper limit on how much they can invest." Comment and evaluate.

7. What effect would each of the following have on the position of the consumption function? That is, would each raise it, lower it, or have no effect on it? (a) An increase in interest rates; (b) expectations of greater inflation; (c) a catastrophe that wiped out half the nation's assets; (d) a marked increase in liquid assets held by people; (e) a rumor that major shortages of goods are about to occur.

8. What effect would each of the following have on the amount of investment? That is, would each increase it, decrease it, or have no effect on it? (a) Expectations of greater likelihood of impending recession by firms; (b) a decrease in interest rates; (c) increased rate of invention of important new synthetic materials; (d) a marked reduction in the percent of existing plant that is utilized; (e) an increase in the perceived profitability of building up inventories.

10 The Determination of National Output

National output varies substantially from year to year, as we have seen in previous chapters. One of the most important tasks of economic theory is to explain why these changes occur. Having explored the determinants of consumption and investment in the previous chapter, we now bring them together in the most basic Keynesian model to show how national output is determined. National output is defined as net national product in this chapter, since it is the best measure of how much the economy is producing when depreciation is taken into account. But since net national product and gross national product differ by relatively little, and since they move up and down together, this theory will also enable us to explain movements in gross national product, and to help forecast them.

In this chapter, we shall make three major simplifying assumptions. First, we assume that there are no government expenditures and that the economy is closed (no exports or imports).

Thus *total spending on final output—that is, on net national product—in this simple case equals consumption expenditure plus net investment.* (Why? Because the other two components of total spending—government expenditures and net exports—are zero.)

Second, we assume that there are no taxes, no transfer payments, and no undistributed corporate profits. Thus *NNP equals disposable income in this simple case,* because the items in Table 8.6 that are taken from, or added to, NNP to get disposable income total zero. Later chapters relax this and the first assumption.

Third, in most of this chapter, we shall assume that the total amount of desired investment is *independent* of the level of net national product. This, of course, is only a rough simplification, since, as we noted in the previous chapter, the amount firms invest will be affected by the level of output in the economy. But this simplification is very convenient and not too unrealistic. Moreover, as we shall show at the end of this chapter, it is relatively easy to extend the model to eliminate this assumption.

The Equilibrium Level of Net National Product

As stressed in Chapter 4, an equilibrium is a situation where there is no tendency for change; in other words, it is a situation that can persist. In Chapter 4, we studied the equilibrium value of a product's price. Here we are interested in the equilibrium value of net national product. In Chapter 4, we saw that price is at its equilibrium value when the quantity demanded equals the quantity supplied. Here we shall see that NNP is at its equilibrium value when the flow of income (generated by this value of NNP) results in a level of spending that is just sufficient (not too high, not too low) to take this level of output off the market.

To understand this equilibrium condition, it is essential to keep three points in mind. First, *the production of goods and services results in a flow of income to the workers, resource owners, and managers that help to produce them.* Each level of NNP results in a certain flow of income. More specifically, under the assumptions made here, NNP equals disposable income. Thus whatever the level of NNP may be, we can be sure that the level of disposable income will be equivalent to it.

Second, *the level of spending on final goods and services is dependent on the level of disposable income.* As we saw in the previous chapter, consumption expenditure depends on the level of disposable income. (For the moment, we assume that investment is independent of the level of output in the economy.) Thus, if we know the level of disposable income, we can predict what level of spending will be forthcoming.

Third, *the level of production is dependent mainly on the level of spending.* If producers find that they are selling goods faster than they are producing them, their inventories will decline. If they find that they are selling goods slower than they are producing them, their inventories will rise. *If NNP is at its equilibrium value, the desired level of spending must be just equal to NNP.* Why? Because otherwise there will be an undesired increase or decrease in producers' inventories—a situation which cannot persist. Much more will be said on this score in the sections that follow.

Aggregate Supply and Demand

Let's look in more detail at the process whereby national output (that is, NNP) determines the level of income, which in turn determines the level of spending. Suppose that the first column of Table 10.1 shows the various possible output levels—that is, the various possible values of NNP—that the economy might produce this year. This column is an ***aggregate supply*** schedule for the economy as a whole. It shows the various output levels that

Table 10.1
Determination of Equilibrium Level of Net National Product (billions of dollars)

(1) Net national product (= disposable income)	(2) Desired consumption expenditure	(3) Desired saving	(4) Desired investment	(5) Total desired spending (2) + (4)	(6) Tendency of national output
1,000	950	50	90	1,040	Upward
1,050	980	70	90	1,070	Upward
1,100	1,010	90	90	1,100	No change
1,150	1,040	110	90	1,130	Downward
1,200	1,070	130	90	1,160	Downward
1,250	1,100	150	90	1,190	Downward

might be produced, *if producers expect that there will be enough spending to take this much output off the market.*

Since NNP equals disposable income (under our current assumptions), the first column of Table 10.1 also shows the level of disposable income corresponding to each possible level of NNP. From this, it should be possible to determine the level of spending corresponding to each level of NNP. Specifically, suppose that the consumption function is as shown in Table 9.1 on page 192. In this case, desired consumption expenditure at each level of NNP will be as shown in column 2 of Table 10.1. And suppose that firms want to invest $90 billion (net of depreciation) regardless of the level of NNP. Under these circumstances, total desired spending at each level of NNP will be as shown in column 5 of Table 10.1. (Since total desired spending equals desired consumption expenditure plus desired investment, column 5 equals column 2 plus column 4.)

Column 5 of Table 10.1 is an ***aggregate demand*** schedule for the economy as a whole. It shows the level of total desired spending at each level of national output (and income). *If NNP is at its equilibrium value, aggregate demand must equal aggregate supply.* In other words, *if NNP is at its equilibrium value, desired spending must equal NNP.* The easiest way to show this is to show that, if desired spending is not equal to NNP, NNP is *not* at its equilibrium value. The following discussion provides such a proof. First we show that, if desired spending is greater than NNP, NNP is not at its equilibrium level. Then we show that, if desired spending is less than NNP, NNP is not at its equilibrium level.

If desired spending is *greater* than NNP, what will happen? Since the total amount that will be spent on final goods and services exceeds the total amount of final goods and services produced (the latter being, by definition, NNP), firms' inventories will be reduced. Consequently, firms will increase their output rate to avoid continued depletion of their inventories and to bring their output into balance with the rate of aggregate demand. Since an increase in the output rate means an increase in NNP, it follows that NNP will tend to increase if desired spending is greater than NNP. NNP therefore is not at its equilibrium level.

On the other hand, what will happen if desired spending is *less* than NNP? Since the total amount that will be spent on final goods and services falls short of the total amount of final goods and services produced (the latter being, by definition, NNP), firms' inventories will increase. As inventories pile up unexpectedly, firms will cut back their output to bring it into better balance with aggregate demand. Since a reduction in output means a reduction in NNP, it follows that NNP will tend to fall if desired spending is less than NNP. Once again, NNP is not at its equilibrium level.

Thus, if NNP tends to increase when desired spending is greater than NNP, and if NNP tends to decrease when desired spending is less than NNP, clearly NNP will be at its equilibrium level only if desired spending is equal to NNP.

The Process Leading toward Equilibrium: A Tabular Analysis

To get a better idea of why NNP tends to the level where desired spending on NNP equals NNP, consider three possible values of NNP—\$1,050 billion, \$1,100 billion, and \$1,150 billion—and see what would happen in our simple economy (in Table 10.1) if these values of NNP prevailed. First, what would happen if firms were to produce \$1,050 billion of final goods and services? Given our assumptions, disposable income would also equal \$1,050 billion (since disposable income equals NNP), so that consumers would spend \$980 billion on consumption goods and services. (This follows from the nature of the consumption function: see column 2 of Table 10.1). Since firms want to invest \$90 billion, total desired spending would be \$1,070 billion (\$980 billion + \$90 billion, as shown in column 5). But the total amount spent on final goods and services under these circumstances would exceed the total value of final goods and services produced by \$20 billion (\$1,070 billion − \$1,050 billion), so that firms' inventories would be drawn down by \$20 billion. Clearly, this situation could not persist very long. As firms become aware that their inventories are becoming depleted, they would step up their production rates, so that the value of output of final goods and services—NNP—would increase.

Second, what would happen if firms were to produce \$1,150 billion of final goods and services? Given our asumptions, disposable income would also equal \$1,150 billion (since disposable income equals NNP), with the result that consumers would spend \$1,040 billion on consumption goods and services. (Again, this follows from the consumption function: see column 2 of Table 10.1). Since firms want to invest \$90 billion, total spending would be \$1,130 billion (\$1,040 billion + \$90 billion, as shown in column 5). But the total amount spent on final goods and services under these circumstances would fall short of the total value of final goods and services produced by \$20 billion (\$1,150 billion − \$1,130 billion), so that firms' inventories would increase by \$20 billion. Clearly, this situation, like the previous one, could not continue very long. When firms see that their inventories are increasing, they reduce their production rates, causing the value of output of final goods and services—NNP—to decrease.

Finally, consider what would happen if firms were to produce \$1,100 billion of final goods and services? Disposable income would also equal \$1,100 billion (since disposable income equals NNP), so that consumers would spend \$1,010 billion on consumption goods and services. (Once again, this follows from the consumption function: see column 2 of Table 10.1.) Since firms want to invest \$90 billion, total spending would be \$1,100 billion (\$1,010 billion + \$90 billion, as shown in column 5). Thus the total amount spent on final goods and services under these circumstances would exactly equal the total value of final goods and services produced. Consequently, there would be no reason for firms to alter their production rates. Thus this would be an equilibrium situation—a set of circumstances where there is no tendency for NNP to change—and the equilibrium level of NNP in this situation would be \$1,100 billion.

These three cases illustrate the process that pushes NNP toward its equilibrium value. So long as NNP is below its equilibrium value, the situation is like that described in our first case. So long as NNP is above its equilibrium value, the situation is like that described in our second case. Whether NNP is below or above its equilibrium value, there is a tendency for production rates to be altered so that NNP moves toward its equilibrium value. Eventually, NNP will reach its equilibrium value, and the situation will be like that described in our third case. The important aspect of the third case—the equilibrium situation—is that, for it to occur, desired spending must equal NNP.

A Graphical Analysis

For the sake of absolute clarity, we can represent the same argument in a diagrammatic, rather than tabular, analysis. Let's show again that the equilibrium level of NNP is at the point where desired spending equals NNP, but now using a graph. Since disposable income equals net national product in this simple case, we can plot consumption expenditure (on the vertical axis) versus net national product (on the horizontal axis), as shown in Figure 10.1. This is the consumption function. Also, we can plot the sum of consumption expenditure and investment expenditure against NNP, as shown in Figure 10.1. This relationship, shown by the $C + I$ line, indicates the level of total desired spending on final goods and services for various amounts of NNP. Finally, we can plot a 45-degree line, as shown in Figure 10.1. This line contains all points where the amount on the horizontal axis equals the amount on the vertical axis. Thus, since NNP is on the horizontal axis and desired spending is on the vertical axis, it contains all points where total desired spending equals net national product.

The equilibrium level of net national product will be at the point where total desired spending equals NNP. Consequently, the *equilibrium level of NNP will be at the point on the horizontal axis where the $C + I$ line intersects the 45-degree line—$1,100 billion in Figure 10.1.* Under the conditions assumed here, no other level of NNP can be maintained for any considerable period of time. Let's begin by

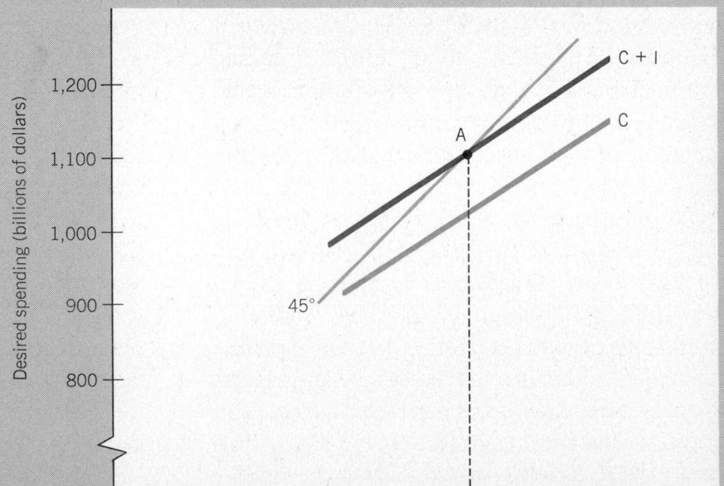

Figure 10.1
Determination of Equilibrium Value of Net National Product
The consumption function is *C*, and the sum of consumption and investment expenditure is $C + I$. The equilibrium value of NNP is at the point where the $C + I$ line intersects the 45-degree line, here $1,100 billion. The $C + I$ line shows aggregate demand and the 45-degree line shows aggregate supply.

proving that the point where the $C + I$ line intersects the 45-degree line is indeed the point where desired spending equals NNP. This is easy, since a 45-degree line is, by construction, a line that includes all points where the amount on the horizontal axis equals the amount on the vertical axis. In this case, as noted above, desired spending is on the vertical axis and NNP is on the horizontal axis. Thus at point A, the point where the $C + I$ line intersects the 45-degree line, desired spending must equal NNP, because such a point is on the 45-degree line.

Next, let's see why the equilibrium level of NNP must be at $1,100 billion, the point on the horizontal axis where the $C + I$ line intersects the 45-degree line. If NNP exceeds $1,100 billion the $C + I$ line lies below the 45-degree line. Since the $C + I$ line shows how much people desire to spend with a particular level of disposable income, this shows that total desired spending is less than NNP. Consequently, some production will not be sold, inventories will build up, production will be cut back, and NNP will decrease. If NNP is less than $1,100 billion, the $C + I$ line lies above the 45-degree line, which shows that total desired spending is greater than NNP. Consequently, inventories will decrease, production will be stepped up, and NNP will increase. Thus, since NNP tends to fall when it exceeds $1,100 billion, and to rise when it falls short of $1,100 billion, its equilibrium value must be $1,100 billion.

Leakages and Injections: Another Approach

In studying any topic, it helps to look at it from more than one angle. Another approach to the determination of national output is the so-called leakage-injection approach. The basic idea underlying this approach is that, under our assumptions, the production of a particular level of output (that is, NNP) results in a level of disposable income that is equivalent to this level of NNP. But, as we know from our previous discussions, not all of this disposable income is spent by households; some of it is saved. This saving is a ***leakage*** from the spending stream, because it withdraws spending from the flow of income and expenditure. Such a leakage tends to reduce the equilibrium value of NNP because, unless it is offset, it results in total spending being too small to take the entire output (that is, NNP) off the market.

But firms do not sell their whole output to consumers. As we know from previous chapters, some of NNP (including items like blast furnaces and oil refineries) is sold to firms, this spending being called investment. Investment is an ***injection*** into the spending stream, because it adds spending to the flow of income and expenditure. That is, it is a supplement to consumption expenditure. Such an injection tends to increase the equilibrium value of NNP because it offsets the leakage of saving. If desired investment is less than desired saving, it is only a partial offset of this leakage. If desired investment is greater than desired saving, it more than offsets this leakage.

The equilibrium value of NNP is the one where the leakages equal the injections. Why? Because desired spending will equal NNP only if the desired amount of income not spent on output (leakages) equals the desired spending on output that is a supplement to consumer expenditure (injections). If leakages are greater than injections, NNP is above its equilibrium value, since desired spending will be too small to take the existing NNP off the market. If leakages are less than injections, NNP is below its equilibrium value, since desired spending will be more than sufficient to take the existing NNP off the market.

To illustrate the use of the leakage-injection approach, consider Table 10.2, which is based on the same data as Table 10.1. Column 3 shows desired saving at each level of NNP.

Saving is, as we have seen, a leakage. Thus the total leakages at each level of NNP are given in column 3. Column 4 shows desired investment at each level on NNP. Investment is, as we have seen, an injection. Thus the total injections at each level of NNP are given in column 4.

If NNP is *less* than $1,100 billion, Table 10.2 indicates that the total leakages are less than the total injections. The desired amount withdrawn from the expenditure stream via saving is less than the desired amount added via investment. Thus total desired spending is greater than NNP, and, as we saw in previous sections, this will result in an increase in NNP. For example, suppose that NNP equals $1,050 billion. At this level of NNP, desired saving is $70 billion, whereas desired investment is $90 billion. Consumers want to withdraw $70 billion from the expenditure stream via saving, while firms want to add $90 billion to it via investment. Consequently, total desired spending exceeds NNP by $90 billion minus $70 billion, or $20 billion. Since firms' inventories are drawn down by $20 billion, there is a tendency for NNP to increase, as we saw in a previous section.

If NNP is *greater* than $1,100 billion, Table 10.2 indicates that the total leakages are more than the total injections. The desired amount withdrawn from the expenditure stream via saving is more than the desired amount added via investment. Thus total desired spending is less than NNP, and, as we saw in previous sections, this will result in a decrease in NNP. For example, suppose that NNP equals $1,150 billion. At this level of NNP, desired saving is $110 billion, whereas desired investment is $90 billion. Consumers want to withdraw $110 billion from the expenditure stream via saving, while firms want to add $90 billion to it via investment. Consequently, total desired spending falls short of NNP by $110 billion minus $90 billion, or $20 billion. Since firms' inventories increase by $20 billion, there is a tendency for NNP to fall, as we saw in a previous section.

Only when NNP *equals* $1,100 billion will there be no tendency for NNP to rise or fall. As shown in Table 10.2, this is the value of NNP where the total leakages equal the total injections. (Specifically, both desired saving and desired investment equal $90 billion at this level of NNP). Thus, as pointed out above, the equilibrium value of NNP is the one where the total leakages equal the total injections.

Note that the equilibrium value of NNP, as determined by the leakage-injection approach, is the same as the one determined by the approach used in the previous section. Using either approach, we get the same answer—an

Table 10.2
The Leakage-Injection Approach to the Determination of Net National Product (billions of dollars)

(1) Net national product (= disposable income)	(2) Desired consumption expenditure	(3) Leakages (desired saving)	(4) Injections (desired investment)	(5) Tendency of national output
1,000	950	50	90	Upward
1,050	980	70	90	Upward
1,100	1,010	90	90	No change
1,150	1,040	110	90	Downward
1,200	1,070	130	90	Downward
1,250	1,100	150	90	Downward

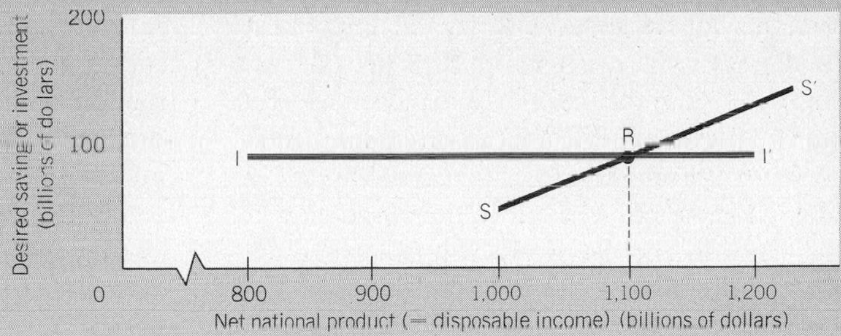

Figure 10.2
Determination of Equilibrium Value of Net National Product
The saving function is *SS'* and the investment function is *II'*. The equilibrium value of NNP is at the point where *SS'* intersects *II'*, which here is $1,100 billion. At this point, the total leakages equal the total injections, since the saving function represents the leakages and the investment function represents the injections.

equilibrium NNP of $1,100 billion. This will always be true. To see why, recall that according to the approach used in the previous section, NNP is at its equilibrium value when total desired spending on output equals NNP. It is easy to show that this condition will be met if and only if the total leakages (desired saving) equal the total injections (desired investment). Since

total desired spending = desired consumption expenditure + desired investment,

and

NNP = desired consumption expenditure + desired saving,

it follows that total desired spending will equal NNP if and only if desired saving equals desired investment. Thus, if we use one approach, we will get the same answer as if we use the other approach.

Leakages and Injections: A Graphical View

Graphs can be used to determine the equilibrium value of NNP when the leakage-injection approach is used. To do so, all that we have to do is plot the saving function and the investment function on the same graph. (The ***investment function*** is the relationship between NNP and desired investment.) The equilibrium value of NNP is the value of NNP at which these two functions intersect. Why? Because at the value of NNP at which they intersect, the total leakages (represented by the saving function) equal the total injections (represented by the investment function).

Based on the data in Table 10.2, the saving function (*SS'*) and investment function (*II'*) are as shown in Figure 10.2. Thus the equilibrium value of NNP must be $1,100 billion, since this is the point where the two functions intersect. For the reasons given in the previous section, the equilibrium value of NNP, as determined by a graph of this sort, must be the same as the one determined by Figure 10.1. And in accord with this fact, both Figures 10.1 and 10.2 yield the same answer—namely, that the equilibrium value of NNP is $1,100 billion.

Usefulness of the Leakage-Injection Approach

Why bother to look at the determination of NNP in terms of the leakage-injection approach? After all, as we have stated repeatedly, we can get the same answer by comparing total desired spending on final goods and services with NNP. One important reason for looking at the determination of NNP in terms of desired saving (leakage) and desired investment (injection) is that it helps to lay bare the reasons why equilibrium NNP may be different from the level of NNP that would result in reasonably full employment at reasonably stable prices. As we pointed out in our discussion of the flaws in the classical view of unemployment, these reasons revolve about the fact that desired saving and desired investment are carried out by different parts of society and for different reasons. Households do much of the saving. They abstain from consuming now in order to provide for retirement, college educations for their children, emergencies, and other ways of consuming later. Firms, on the other hand, do most of the investing. They build plants and equipment and expand their inventories in response to profit opportunities. Because of this cleavage between the savers and the investors, *there is no assurance that desired saving will equal desired investment at a level of NNP that results in reasonably full employment at reasonably stable prices.*[1]

Saving and Investment: Desired and Actual

In the previous sections, we stressed that desired saving need not equal desired investment. This is an important fact, which must be understood. At the same time, however, it must be recognized that, whether or not desired saving equals desired investment, *actual saving must always equal actual investment.* In other words, although the amount people *set out to save* during a particular year may not equal the amount firms *set out to invest,* the *actual amount saved* will always equal the *actual amount invested.* This must be true because, as pointed out in the previous chapter, NNP has to equal consumption plus net investment;[2] and it also has to equal consumption plus saving. Subtracting consumption from each of these expressions for NNP, saving must equal investment.

To see why, consider the case (in Table 10.1) where NNP is $1,050 billion. In this case, desired saving is $70 billion but desired investment is $90 billion. How does it turn out that actual saving equals actual investment? As pointed out in a previous section, there is an unintended ***disinvestment*** (i.e., negative investment) of −$20 billion in inventories if NNP is $1,050 billion. (Recall from Chapter 8 that a build-up of inventories is a form of investment, so a $1 billion increase in inventories equals $1 billion of investment.) Thus the actual investment is $90 billion (in intended investment) minus $20 billion (in unintended disinvestment), or $70 billion. Actual saving equals desired saving, or $70 billion. Thus actual saving equals actual investment.

As a further illustration, consider the case where NNP is $1,150 billion. In this case, desired saving is $110 billion but desired investment is $90 billion. How does it turn out that actual saving equals actual investment? As pointed out in a previous section, there is an unintended investment in inventories of $20 billion (because total spending falls short of NNP by this amount). Thus actual investment turns out to equal the desired investment of $90 billion plus the unintended investment of $20 billion, or $110 billion in all. Since actual saving also equals $110 billion, actual saving equals actual investment.[3]

In general, actual saving always must equal

[1] Note that, under the simplifying assumptions made in this chapter, there is only one leakage (saving) and one injection (investment). In subsequent chapters, we shall be concerned with models where other leakages (taxes and imports) and injections (government expenditures and exports) are involved.

[2] Recall from Chapter 8 that net national product equals consumption plus government expenditures plus net exports plus net investment. Since government expenditures and net exports are assumed to be zero, it follows that net national product equals consumption plus net investment.

[3] Note that we assume here that actual saving will equal desired saving and that unintended changes in inventories will make actual investment conform to actual and desired saving. There are other ways for adjustments to take place. The important thing is that, one way or another, actual saving will equal actual investment.

actual investment, even though desired saving does not always equal desired investment.

Effects of Change in Desired Investment

The Multiplier: A Geometric Formulation

In Chapter 8, we pointed out that investment is a particularly volatile form of expenditure. It is subject to large variations from year to year. For example, in 1975, business fixed investment was 12 percent (in real terms) below its 1974 level. Looking at the highly simplified model we have constructed, what is the effect of a change in the amount of desired investment? Specifically, if firms increase their desired investment by $1 billion, what effect will this increase have on the equilibrium value of net national product? This is a very important question, the answer to which sheds considerable light on the reasons for changes in national output. We devote the next several sections to answering this question.

Let's begin by noting once again that, if NNP is at its equilibrium level, desired saving must equal desired investment. Then let's apply the sort of graphical analysis that we used in Figure 10.2 to determine the effect of an increase in desired investment on equilibrium NNP. If the saving function in our simplified economy is SS' in Figure 10.3 and desired investment is shown by the horizontal line I_1I_1', what will be the effect of a $1 billion increase in desired investment on equilibrium NNP? Before the increase in desired investment, equilibrium NNP was equal to Y_0. The increase of $1 billion in desired investment will shift the investment function up by $1 billion, to the new position (I_2I_2') shown in Figure 10.3. This shift in the investment function will increase the equilibrium level of NNP, but by how much?

The resulting increase in equilibrium NNP, ΔY, can be derived by the following geometrical reasoning. First, the slope of SS' times the change in equilibrium NNP must equal the increase in desired investment, $1 billion. This follows from the definition of the slope of a line: The slope of SS' equals the vertical distance between any two points on SS' divided by the horizontal difference between them. The vertical distance between points A and B in Figure 10.3 is the increase in desired investment (ΔI), and the horizontal distance between points A and B is the change in equilibrium NNP (ΔY). Consequently, the change in equilibrium NNP must equal the increase in desired investment divided by the slope of SS'.

Figure 10.3
The Multiplier
If investment increases by ΔI, the equilibrium value of NNP increases by ΔY. Clearly $\frac{\Delta I}{\Delta Y}$ equals the slope of the saving function between A and B. Since this slope equals the marginal propensity to save (MPS), $\frac{\Delta I}{\Delta Y} = \text{MPS}$. Thus, $\Delta Y = \frac{\Delta I}{\text{MPS}}$ and if $\Delta I = 1$, $\Delta Y = \frac{1}{\text{MPS}}$.

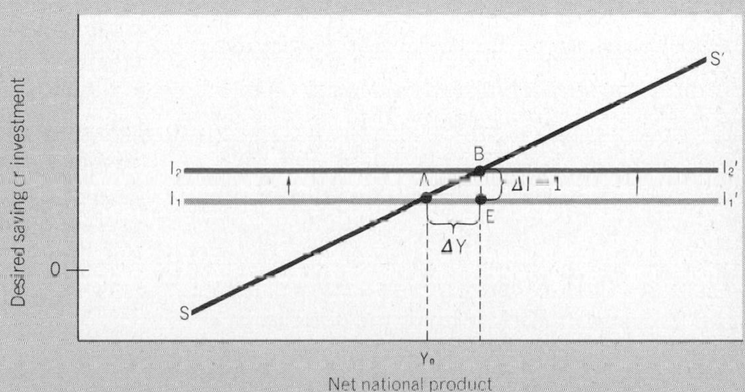

Since the slope of SS' is the marginal propensity to save—as pointed out in the previous chapter—it follows that *the change in equilibrium NNP equals the increase in desired investment divided by the marginal propensity to save. Thus a $1 billion increase in desired investment will result in an increase in equilibrium NNP of* $\left(\frac{1}{MPS}\right)$ *billions of dollars, where MPS is the marginal propensity to save.*

This is a very important conclusion. To understand more clearly what it means, let's consider a couple of numerical examples. For example, if the marginal propensity to save is ⅓, a $1 billion increase in desired investment will increase equilibrium NNP by 1 ÷ ⅓ billion dollars; that is, by $3 billion. Or take a somewhat more complicated case. If the consumption function is as shown in the first two columns of Table 10.1, what is the effect of an increase in desired investment from $90 billion to $91 billion? The first step in answering this question is to determine the marginal propensity to consume—which is 0.60 in Table 10.1. Then it is a simple matter to determine the marginal propensity to save—which must be 1 − 0.60 or 0.40. Finally, since the marginal propensity to save is 0.40, it follows from the previous paragraph that a $1 billion increase in desired investment must result in an increase in equilibrium NNP of $\frac{1}{0.40}$ billion dollars. That is, equilibrium NNP will increase by $2½ billion.

Since a dollar of extra desired investment results in $\left(\frac{1}{\text{MPS}}\right)$ dollars of extra NNP, $\left(\frac{1}{\text{MPS}}\right)$ is called the ***multiplier.*** If you want to estimate the effect of a given increase in desired investment on NNP, all you have to do is multiply the increase in desired investment by $\left(\frac{1}{\text{MPS}}\right)$: the result will be the resulting increase in NNP. Moreover, it is easy to show that the same multiplier holds for decreases in desired investment as well as for increases. That is, a dollar less of desired investment results in $\left(\frac{1}{\text{MPS}}\right)$ dollars less of NNP. Consequently, if you want to estimate the effect of a given change in desired investment (positive or negative) on NNP, all you have to do is multiply the change in desired investment by $\left(\frac{1}{\text{MPS}}\right)$.

It is important to note that, since MPS is less than one, the *multiplier must be greater than one.* In other words, an increase in desired investment of $1 will result in an increase in NNP of more than $1. This means, of course, that NNP is relatively sensitive to changes in desired investment. Moreover, since the multiplier is the reciprocal of the marginal propensity to save, the smaller the marginal propensity to save, the higher the multiplier—and the more sensitive is NNP to changes in desired investment. As we shall see, this result has important implications for public policy. For example, because our system of taxes and transfer payments tends to increase the marginal propensity to save out of NNP, the destabilizing effect of a sharp change in investment expenditures is reduced.

The Multiplier: An Algebraic Interpretation[4]

Equations speak more clearly to some than words, and so for those with a taste for (elementary) algebra, we will show how the results of the previous section can be derived algebraically. If you have trouble with equations, or if you feel that you already understand the material, go on to the next section. We begin by recalling that the equilibrium value of NNP is attained at the point where NNP equals total desired spending on output. This condition can be expressed in the following equation:

$$\text{NNP} = C + I, \tag{10.1}$$

[4] This section is optional and can be omitted without loss of continuity.

Figure 10.4
Consumption Function
The consumption function is derived from the data in Table 10.1. The marginal propensity to consume is 0.6, so the slope is 0.6.

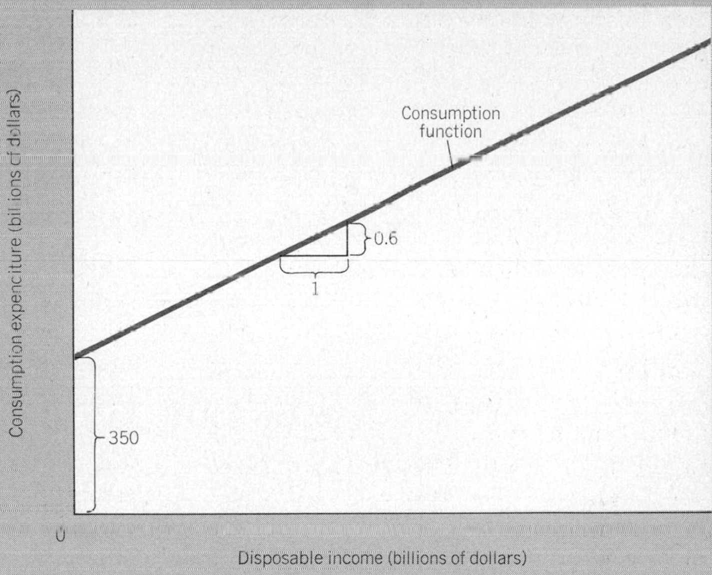

which says that NNP must equal desired expenditure on consumption goods (C) plus desired investment (I). Since desired consumption expenditures plus desired investment equals total desired spending, it follows that this equation states that NNP must equal total desired spending.

Next, let's introduce a friend from this and the previous chapter, the consumption function. The consumption function in the first two columns of Table 10.1 can be represented by the following equation:

$$C = 350 + 0.6D \qquad (10.2)$$

which says that desired consumption equals \$350 billion plus 0.6 times disposable income (D). Figure 10.4 shows the consumption function. As you can see, \$350 billion is the intercept on the vertical axis, while 0.6 is the slope of the consumption function. Since as we noted in the previous chapter—the slope of the consumption function equals the marginal propensity to consume, 0.6 equals the marginal propensity to consume.

The next step is to substitute the righthand side of equation (10.2) for C in Equation (10.1). The result is:

$$\text{NNP} = 350 + 0.6D + I. \qquad (10.3)$$

But recall that disposable income is equal to NNP in our simplified economy. Consequently, we can substitute NNP for D in this equation, to get

$$\text{NNP} = 350 + 0.6\text{NNP} + I. \qquad (10.4)$$

And going a step further, we can subtract 0.6 times NNP from both sides of Equation (10.4), which gives

$$\text{NNP} - 0.6\text{NNP} = 350 + I, \qquad (10.5)$$

or, collecting terms,

$$0.4\text{NNP} = 350 + I. \qquad (10.6)$$

Finally, dividing both sides by 0.4, we have

$$\text{NNP} = \frac{350}{0.4} + \frac{I}{0.4}. \qquad (10.7)$$

Now we can see what happens to NNP if there is a \$1 billion increase in I. In other words, suppose that I is increased from some amount, $X billion, to $(X + 1) billion. How much will this increase NNP? From Equation (10.7), it is clear that NNP will equal

$$\frac{350}{0.4} + \frac{X}{0.4}$$

if desired investment equals $X billion. It is also clear from Equation (10.7) that NNP will equal

$$\frac{350}{0.4} + \frac{(X + 1)}{0.4}$$

if desired investment is equal to $ (X + 1) billion. Consequently the increase in NNP due to the $1 billion increase in desired investment is equal to

$$\left[\frac{350}{0.4} + \frac{(X + 1)}{0.4}\right] - \left[\frac{350}{0.4} + \frac{X}{0.4}\right]$$

$$= \frac{X + 1}{0.4} - \frac{X}{0.4} = \frac{X}{0.4} + \frac{1}{0.4} - \frac{X}{0.4} = \frac{1}{0.4}$$

That is, a $1 billion increase in desired investment will result in an increase of $\frac{1}{0.4}$ billion dollars in NNP. Recalling that 0.6 is the marginal propensity to consume—and that the sum of the marginal propensity to consume and the marginal propensity to save equals one—it follows that *a $1 billion increase in desired investment will result in an increase of* $\left(\frac{1}{MPS}\right)$ *billions of dollars in NNP, where MPS is the marginal propensity to save—0.4 in this case.*

This is precisely the same conclusion we arrived at in the previous section. Thus we have derived the value of the multiplier by an algebraic route rather than the geometric route used before.

The Multiplier and the Spending Process

Now that we have shown in two ways that the multiplier equals $\frac{1}{\text{MPS}}$, we can leave the realm of graphs and equations and examine the operation of the multiplier in the real world. Specifically, what process in the real world insures that a $1 billion change in desired investment results in a change of $\left(\frac{1}{\text{MPS}}\right)$ billions of dollars in equilibrium NNP? It is worthwhile spelling this out in some detail.

If there is a $1 billion increase in desired investment, the effects can be divided into a number of stages. In the first stage, firms spend an additional $1 billion on plant and equipment. This extra $1 billion is received by workers and suppliers as extra income, which results in a second stage of extra spending on final goods and services. How much of their extra $1 billion in income will the workers and suppliers spend? If the marginal propensity to consume is 0.6, they will spend 0.6 times $1 billion, or $.6 billion. This extra expenditure of $.6 billion is received by firms and disbursed to workers, suppliers, and owners as extra income bringing about a third stage of extra spending on final goods and services. How much of this extra income of $.6 billion will be spent? Since the marginal propensity to consume is 0.6, they will spend 60 percent of this $.6 billion, or $.36 billion. This extra expenditure of $.36 billion is received by firms and disbursed to workers, suppliers, and owners as extra income, which results in a fourth stage of spending, then a fifth stage, a sixth stage, and so on.

Table 10.3 shows the total increase in expenditure on final goods and services arising from the original $1 billion increase in desired investment. The total increase in expenditures is the increase in the first stage, plus the increase in the second stage, plus the increase in the third stage, and so on. Since there is an endless chain of stages, we cannot list all the increases. But because the successive increases in spending get smaller and smaller, we can determine their sum, which in this case is $2.5

Table 10.3
The Multiplier Process

Stage	Amount of extra spending (billions of dollars)
1	1.00
2	.60
3	.36
4	.22
5	.13
6	.08
7	.05
8	.03
9 and beyond	.03
Total	2.50

billion. Thus the $1 billion increase in desired investment results—after all stages of the spending and respending process have worked themselves out—in a $2.5 billion increase in total expenditures on final goods and services. In other words, it results in a $2.5 billion increase in NNP.

It is important to note that this spending and respending process results in the same multiplier as indicated in previous sections. This happens because, if 0.6 is the marginal propensity to consume, a $1 billion increase in desired investment will result in increased total spending of $(1 + .6 + .6^2 + .6^3 + \ldots)$ billions of dollars. This is evident from Table 10.3, which shows that the increased spending in the first stage is $1 billion, the increased spending in the second stage is $.6 billion, the increased spending in the third stage is $\$.6^2$ billion, and so on. But it can be shown that $(1 + .6 + .6^2 + .6^3 + \ldots) = \dfrac{1}{1 - .6}$ (See footnote 5.)[5] Consequently, since $(1 - .6)$ is equal to the marginal propensity to save, a $1 billion increase in desired investment results in an increase of $\left(\dfrac{1}{\text{MPS}}\right)$ billions of dollars in NNP. Thus, however we look at it, the answer remains the same: the multiplier equals $\left(\dfrac{1}{\text{MPS}}\right)$.

Application of the Multiplier: A Case Study[6]

Now that we have discussed the modern theory of the determination of NNP in the abstract, it is time to look at a specific application of this theory. Consider a famous incident that occurred at the end of World War II. Economists, using the best models then available, had been able to forecast the pace of the economy reasonably well during the war. When the war was coming to an end, they were charged with forecasting the level of national product in 1946, the year immediately after the war. This was an important task, since the government was worried that the economy might suffer severe postwar unemployment. The Great Depression of the 1930s was a recent—and still bitter—memory.

A group of economists in Washington was given the responsibility for this forecast. They made it in terms of gross national product, not net national product, but they used essentially the same theory as that discussed in previous sections. To forecast gross national product in

---

[5] To see this, let's divide 1 by $(1 - m)$, where m is less than 1. Using the time-honored rules of long division, we find that

$$
\begin{array}{r|l}
 & 1 + m + m^2 + m^3 + \ldots \\
\hline
1 - m & 1 \\
 & \underline{1 - m} \\
 & m \\
 & \underline{m - m^2} \\
 & m^2 \\
 & \underline{m^2 - m^3} \\
 & m^3 \\
 & \underline{m^3 - m^4} \\
 & m^4
\end{array}
$$

Thus letting $m = 0.6$, it follows that 1 divided by $(1 - .6)$ equals $1 + .6 + .6^2 + .6^3 + \ldots$

[6] This account is based on Michael Sapir, "Review of Economic Forecasts for the Transition Period," *Conference on Research in Income and Wealth*, vol. 11, Princeton: National Bureau of Economic Research, 1949; and Lawrence Klein, "A Post-Mortem on Transition Predictions of National Product," *Journal of Political Economy*, August 1946.

Figure 10.5
Shift in the Consumption Function
If the consumption function shifts from C_1C_1' to C_2C_2' this means that, at each level of disposable income, consumers desire to spend \$1 billion more on consumption goods and services. Such a shift results in an increase of $\left(\frac{1}{MPS}\right)$ billion of dollars in equilibrium NNP, as shown in Figure 10.6.

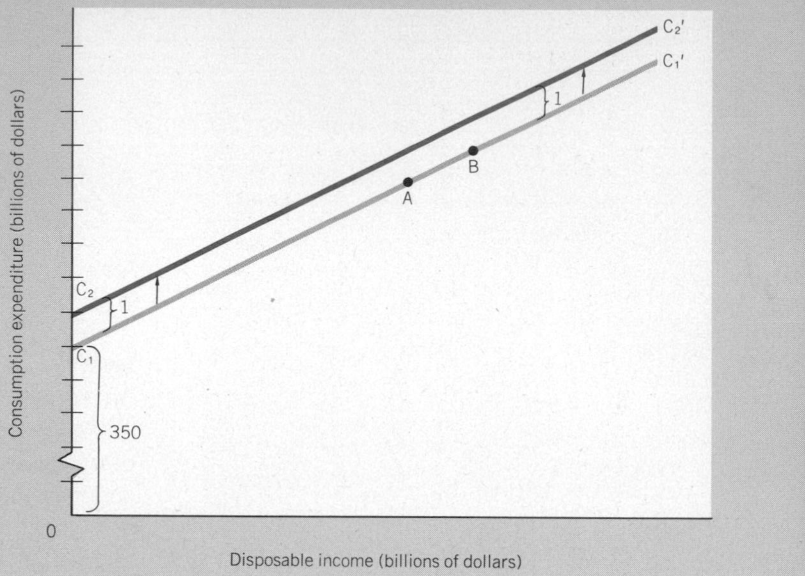

1946, these Washington economists began by using prewar data to estimate the consumption function. Then they estimated the amount of investment that would take place in 1946. Finally, to forecast gross national product in 1946, they performed the sort of calculations shown in Equation (10.7). In other words, they computed the multiplier $\left(\frac{1}{MPS}\right)$ and multiplied it by their estimate of investment for 1946. Then they added an amount analogous to the first term on the righthand side of Equation (10.7); and since their model—unlike ours—included government spending and taxes, other calculations, which will be discussed in Chapter 11, had to be made as well. The result was a forecast of a gross national product in 1946 of about \$170 billion. This forecast received considerable attention and publicity inside and outside the government.

Before discussing the accuracy of this forecast, an important empirical question must be considered: in real-world studies like this, what is the estimated value of the multiplier? Judging from our findings in the previous sections, we would guess a figure of at least $2\frac{1}{2}$, since the marginal propensity to consume should be at least 0.6. But these results are based on the assumption of no taxation. For reasons discussed in Chapter 11, the multiplier will be lower if there is taxation. Including the effects of taxation (and other factors like imports) most estimates of the multiplier seem to center around a value of 2. But these estimates can vary considerably, depending, of course, on the shape of the consumption function and other factors.

Effects of Shifts in the Consumption Function

Before discussing the accuracy of this forecast for 1946, we must look at the effects of shifts in the consumption function. So far, we have been concerned only with the effects of changes in desired investment on NNP. We have shown—repeatedly and in various ways—that changes in desired investment have an amplified effect on NNP, with the extent of the

Figure 10.6
Effect of a Downward Shift of the Saving Function
A $1 billion upward shift in the consumption function results in a $1 billion downward shift in the saving function. Thus, if the consumption function shifts from C_1C_1' to C_2C_2' in Figure 10.5, the saving function shifts downward from S_1S_1' to S_2S_2', as shown here. The point where the saving function intersects the investment function shifts from A to E, and the equilibrium value of NNP increases by ΔY, which is the same amount that it increases when desired investment increases by $1 billion. (See Figure 10.3.)

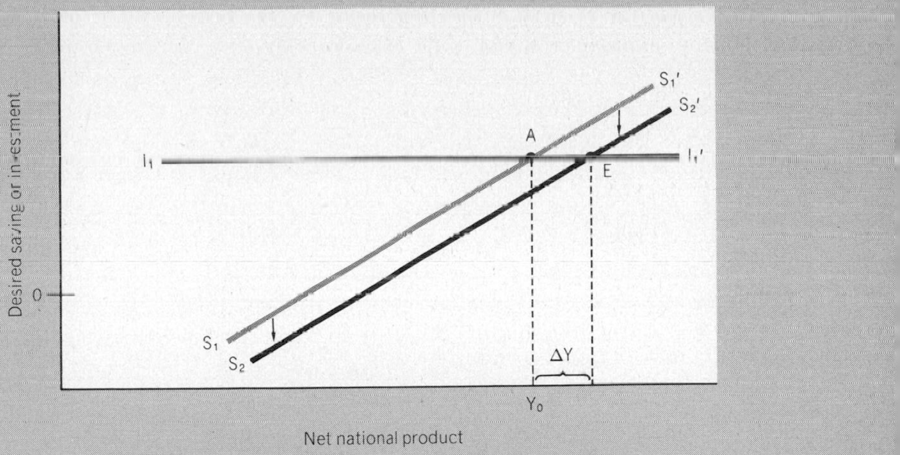

amplification measured by the multiplier. But it is important to note at this point that a shift in the consumption function will also have such an amplified effect on NNP. For example, in Figure 10.5, if the consumption function shifts from C_1C_1' to C_2C_2', this means that at each level of disposable income, consumers desire to spend $1 billion more on consumption goods and services than they did before. It is easy to show that *this $1 billion upward shift in the consumption function will have precisely the same effect on equilibrium NNP as a $1 billion increase in desired investment.*

To see that this is the case, recall from Chapter 9 that an upward shift in the consumption function results in a downward shift in the saving function. Specifically, a $1 billion upward shift in the consumption function means that the saving function shifts downward by $1 billion (because, if consumers desire to spend $1 billion *more* out of each level of disposable income than before, they must desire to save $1 billion *less* out of each level of disposable income than before). As shown in Figure 10.6, a $1 billion downward shift in the saving function results in an increase in the equilibrium value of NNP. And this increase is the same as when desired investment increases by $1 billion, the situation we observed in Figure 10.3. In either case, the increase equals $\left(\frac{1}{\text{MPS}}\right)$ billions of dollars.[7]

[7] For those of more mathematical bent, it may be worthwhile to use some simple algebra to prove that this is the case. Let's recall that in Equation (10.7), we showed that the equilibrium value of NNP equals

$$\frac{350}{0.4} + \frac{I}{0.4},$$

where 350 is the intercept on the vertical axis of the consumption function, 0.4 is the marginal propensity to save, and I is desired investment. A $1 billion shift upward in the consumption function causes the intercept to increase from its former amount, $350 billion, to $351 billion. What is the effect of this increase in the intercept on the equilibrium value of NNP? If the intercept is $350 billion, the equilibrium value of NNP will equal

$$\frac{350}{0.4} \times \frac{I}{0.4}.$$

If the intercept is $351 billion, the equilibrium value of NNP will equal

$$\frac{351}{0.4} + \frac{I}{0.4}.$$

Consequently, the increase in NNP from the $1 billion upward

Moreover, *a \$1 billion downward shift in the consumption function will have precisely the same effect on equilibrium NNP as a \$1 billion decrease in desired investment.* Thus both upward and downward shifts in the consumption function—from changes in tastes, assets, prices, population, and other factors—will have a magnified effect on NNP. In other words, NNP is sensitive to shifts in the consumption function in the same way that it is sensitive to changes in desired investment. This is an important point. Finally, to prevent misunderstanding, recall from Chapter 9 that a *shift* in the consumption function is quite different from a *movement along* a given consumption function. (An example of the latter would be the movement from point *A* to point *B* in Figure 10.5.) We are concerned here with shifts in the consumption function, not movements along a given consumption function.

The Accuracy of the Postwar Forecasts

We can now pick up the GNP forecasts for 1946 where we left off several paragraphs back. The government forecasters' estimate of a GNP of about \$170 billion caused a severe chill in many parts of the government, as well as among businessmen and consumers. A GNP of only about \$170 billion would have meant a great deal of unemployment in 1946. Indeed, according to some predictions, about eight million people would have been unemployed in the first quarter of 1946.

---

shift in the consumption function is

$$\left[\frac{351}{0.4} + \frac{I}{0.4}\right] - \left[\frac{350}{0.4} + \frac{I}{0.4}\right] = \frac{351}{0.4} - \frac{350}{0.4} = \frac{1}{0.4}$$

That is, a \$1 billion upward shift in the consumption function results in an increase of $\frac{1}{0.4}$ billions of dollars in NNP. Recalling that 0.4 = MPS, it follows that *a \$1 billion upward shift in the consumption function will result in an increase of* $\left(\frac{1}{MPS}\right)$ *billions of dollars in NNP.*

Unfortunately for the forecasters—but fortunately for the nation—the GNP in 1946 turned out to be not \$170 billion, but about \$190 billion. And unemployment was only about ⅓ of the forecasted amount. These are very large errors in practically anyone's book—so big that they continue to embarrass the economics profession 30 years later. Of course, our knowledge of the economy has expanded considerably over the past 30 years, and an error of this magnitude is much less likely now. Moreover, even at the end of World War II, some economists forecasted GNP in 1946 pretty well. Not everyone, by any means, agreed with the forecast of \$170 billion. But it is worth bearing this notable mistake in mind when considering economic forecasts of this sort. Economics is not as exact a science as physics or chemistry—and mischief can result if one assumes otherwise.

What went wrong in the Washington economists' forecast? To a considerable extent, the answer lies in the topic of the previous section: a shift in the consumption function. When World War II ended, households had a great deal of liquid assets on hand. They had saved money during the war. There had been rationing of many kinds of goods, and other goods—like automobiles or refrigerators—could not be obtained at all. When the war ended and these goods flowed back on the market, consumers spent more of their income on consumption goods than in the previous years. In other words, there was a pronounced upward shift of the consumption function.

To see why this shift in the consumption function caused the forecasters to underestimate GNP in 1946, recall from the previous section that an upward shift of \$1 billion in the consumption function will result in an increase of $\left(\frac{1}{MPS}\right)$ billions of dollars in national product. Bearing this in mind, suppose the forecasters assumed that the consumption function remained fixed, when in fact there was a \$8 billion shift upward. Then if the multiplier— $\frac{1}{\text{MPS}}$ —was $2\frac{1}{2}$, national product would turn out to be \$20 billion higher than the forecasters expected. (Since $\frac{1}{\text{MPS}}$ is assumed to be $2\frac{1}{2}$, national product will increase \$2.5 billion for every \$1 billion shift in the consumption function, so an \$8 billion shift in the consumption function will result in a \$20 billion increase in national product.) Of course, these figures—a multiplier of $2\frac{1}{2}$ and an \$8 billion shift in the consumption function—are only illustrative, not precise estimates of the actual situation. For one thing, as noted above, the multiplier is wrong because it assumes no taxation. But they indicate the sort of thing that occurred, and they show dramatically the effects of a shift in the consumption function.

The Paradox of Thrift

Now that we understand more fully the effects on NNP of a shift in the consumption function, we can appreciate the so-called paradox of thrift. Despite all of the praise heaped upon it by moral philosophers, thrift (as spendthrifts have long suspected) can be a dangerous thing. If society as a whole desires to save more, the result may well be a decrease in national output and no increase in saving. To see why this is so, consider Figure 10.7, which shows a situation where the saving function shifts upward from S_1S_1' to S_3S_3'. Since the investment function remains constant at II', the equilibrium level of NNP falls from Y_1 to Y_3. And despite the public's attempt to save more, saving remains fixed at \$80 billion, the amount that it equaled before the public's attempt to increase it.

Of course, the fact that an upward shift in the saving function is likely to cause a decrease in the equilibrium value of NNP is really no news. As we pointed out in the previous chapter, an upward shift in the saving function is accompanied by a downward shift in the consumption function. (Recall Figure 9.5.) And as we saw in an earlier section of this chapter, a downward shift in the consumption function will result in a decrease in the equilibrium value of NNP.

The important point here is that, *although thrift may be a private virtue, it can be a problem from the viewpoint of society as a whole.* Suppose, for example, that a recession occurs, with the result that NNP falls and unemployment rises. Under such circumstances, the public may well be inclined to cut back on its

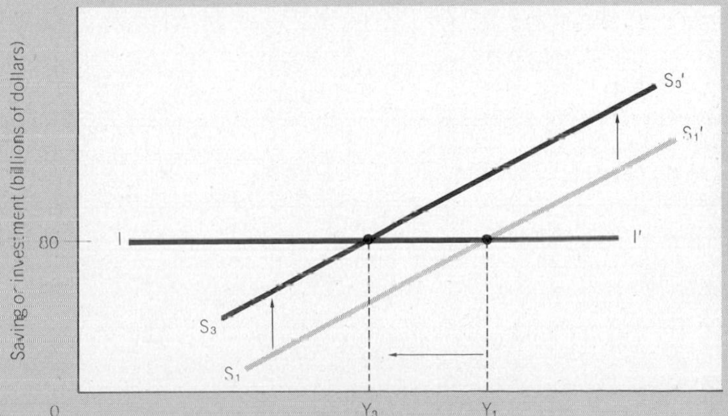

Figure 10.7
The Paradox of Thrift
If the saving function shifts upward from S_1S_1' to S_3S_3', the equilibrium value of NNP falls from Y_1 to Y_3—and, despite its attempt to save more, the public still saves \$80 billion, just as it did before. All that results is a reduction in NNP.

spending. That is, faced with economic storm signals, the public may try to save more. But what will be the unintended result? As indicated in Figure 10.7, the equilibrium value of NNP will be reduced, thus aggravating the recession. And to add insult to injury, the public may not be able to accomplish its goal of increasing saving. Thus all that will be achieved is an undesirable reduction in national ouput (and employment).

Induced Investment

Before concluding this chapter, one final point is worth noting. In previous sections, we have assumed that desired net investment is a certain amount, regardless of the level of NNP. This assumption has been reflected in the fact that the investment function—for example, in Figures 10.2 and 10.3—is horizontal. Although this assumption may be a useful first approximation, it neglects the fact that firms are much more likely to invest in plant and equipment when NNP is high than when it is low. After all, NNP measures output; and the greater the output of the economy, the greater the pressure on the capacity of existing plant and equipment—and the greater the pressure to expand this capacity by investing in additional plant and equipment.

It is relatively simple to extend the theory to take account of the fact that, to some extent, increases in NNP may increase desired investment. Rather than portraying the investment function as a horizontal line, we need only assume that it is positively sloped, as in Figure 10.8. Then, as before, the equilibrium level of NNP is at the point where the saving function intersects the investment function—that is, at point *A*, the point where desired saving equals desired investment. Much more will be said about *induced investment*—investment stimulated by increases in NNP—in Chapter 12.

Summary

The equilibrium level of net national product will be at the point where desired spending equals NNP. If desired spending exceeds NNP, NNP will tend to increase. If desired spending falls short of NNP, NNP will tend to fall.

Another way to describe this equilibrium condition is to say that NNP is at its equilibrium level if desired saving equals desired investment. This is the so-called leakage-injection approach. Because of the cleavage between

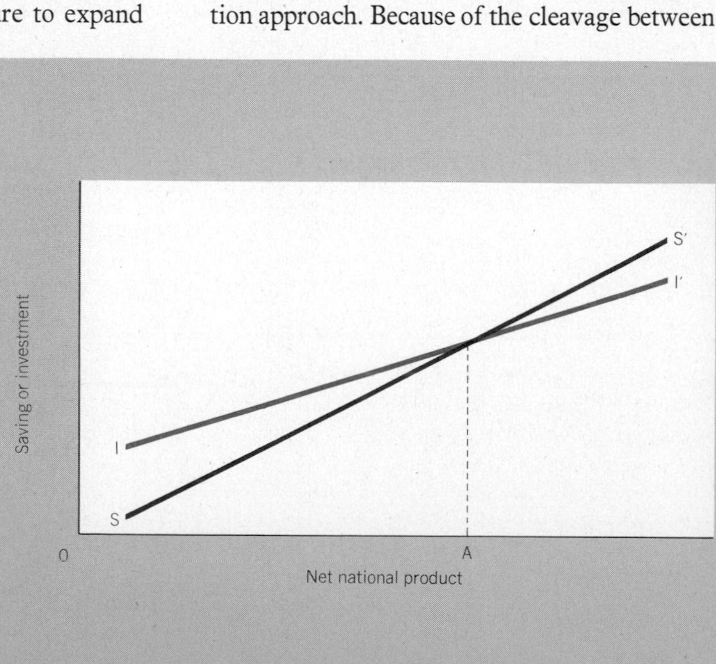

Figure 10.8
Determination of Equilibrium Value of Net National Product, with Induced Investment
If the level of investment depends on NNP, the investment function, *II′*, is positively sloped, and the equilibrium level of NNP is at the point where *II′* intersects *SS′*, the saving function.

savers and investors, there is no assurance that desired saving will equal desired investment at a level of NNP that results in reasonably full employment at stable prices. But actual saving and actual investment always must turn out to be equal.

A $1 billion change in desired investment will result in a change in equilibrium NNP of $\left(\frac{1}{\text{MPS}}\right)$ billions of dollars, where MPS is the marginal propensity to save. In other words, the multiplier is $\frac{1}{\text{MPS}}$. The multiplier can be interpreted in terms of—and derived from—the successive stages of the spending process. An example of the use of the multiplier was the formulation at the end of World War II of GNP forecasts for 1946.

A shift in the consumption function will also have an amplified effect on NNP, a $1 billion shift in the consumption function resulting in a change of $\left(\frac{1}{\text{MPS}}\right)$ billions of dollars in NNP. To a considerable extent, the large error in government forecasts of GNP in 1946 was due to an unanticipated shift in the consumption function. Responding to large accumulated wartime savings and pent-up wartime demands, consumers spent more of their income on consumption goods than in previous years.

Although thrift may be a private virtue, it can be a problem from the viewpoint of society as a whole. If society as a whole desires to save more, the result may well be a decrease in national output—and no increase in saving. This is the so-called paradox of thrift.

CONCEPTS FOR REVIEW

Aggregate demand
Aggregate supply
Leakage-injection approach
Desired investment
Desired saving
Multiplier
Induced investment
Shifts in the consumption function
45-degree line
Paradox of thrift

QUESTIONS FOR DISCUSSION AND REVIEW

1. Suppose that the consumption function in a particular economy is given by the following table:

Disposable income (billions of dollars)	Consumption expenditure (billions of dollars)
400	300
500	360
600	410
700	440
800	470

If firms want to invest $140 billion, what is the equilibrium value of NNP? Can we be sure that this is the full-employment value of NNP? Why or why not? (The full-employment value of NNP is defined as the value of NNP that can be produced if the unemployment rate is about 4 percent.)

2. Using the data in Question 1, plot the consumption function and the $C + I$ line on a graph, and derive the equilibrium value of NNP graphically. Is the consumption function a straight line? Does the answer to this question affect the validity of the analysis in any way?

3. Using the data in Question 1, plot the saving function and the investment function, and show how they can be used to determine the equilibrium value of NNP. Does desired saving equal desired investment if NNP equals $800 billion? If NNP were $800 billion, show how actual saving would turn out to equal actual investment.

4. Suppose that desired investment increases by $1 billion in Question 1. Using a graph like that derived in Question 2, show what effect this will have on the equilibrium value of NNP. Next, use a graph like that derived in Question 3 to do the same thing. Do you get the same answer? Why?

5. Suppose that consumers want to spend $50 billion more at each level of disposable income than indicated in Question 1. Using a graph like that derived in Question 2, show what effect this will have on the equilibrium value of NNP. Next, use a graph like that derived in Question 3 to do the same thing. Do you get the same answer? Why?

6. Suppose that the consumption function in a certain economy is $C = 100 + 0.8D$, where C is consumption expenditure and D is disposable income. If desired investment equals 10, what is the equilibrium value of NNP? What is the value of the multiplier? Is this a realistic figure for the United States?

7. In Question 6, suppose that desired investment falls from 10 to 6. What effect will this have on the equilibrium value of NNP? By how much, and in what direction, would the consumption function have to shift to offset this effect?

8. "The investment function is a horizontal line, so there must be a great deal of induced investment." Comment and evaluate.

9. (Advanced) In a certain economy, the average propensity to consume is always equal to the marginal propensity to consume. If the equilibrium level of NNP equals $300 billion and if desired investment equals $100 billion, what is the equation for the consumption function in this economy?

11

Fiscal Policy and National Output

In the period since World War II, the idea that the government's power to spend and tax should be used to stabilize the economy—that is, to reduce unemployment and fight inflation—has gained acceptance throughout the world. In many countries, including the United States, this acceptance was delayed by a fear of government deficits and of increases in the public debt, but with the passage of time these fears have receded or been put in proper perspective. However, time has also revealed that fiscal policy is no panacea. Witness the severe inflationary pressures and the high unemployment rates that have plagued the American economy in the mid-1970s. Both the power and the limitations of fiscal policy must be recognized.

This chapter presents a first look at fiscal policy, in the context of the simplest Keynesian model. In effect, we assume here that the money supply is fixed, and that the interest rate is not affected by changes in total desired spending (or that, if it is affected, it has little effect on total desired spending). In Chapter 16 (and its Appendix), a more sophisticated analysis of fiscal policy is presented, with money and financial assets included in the model.

Government Expenditure and Net National Product

In the previous chapter, we showed how the equilibrium level of net national product was determined in a simplified economy without government spending or taxation. We must now extend this theory to include both government spending and taxation. As we shall see, the results form the basis for much of our nation's past and present economic policy. In this section, we incorporate government spending into the theory of the determination of net national product. In so doing, we assume that government spending will not affect the consumption function or the level of desired investment. In other words, we assume that government spending does not reduce or increase private desires to spend out of each level of income. (Government includes here federal, state, and local.)

Suppose that the government purchases $50 billion worth of goods and services and that it will purchase this amount whatever the level of NNP. (Note that only government purchases, not transfer payments, are included here.) Clearly, adding this public expenditure to the private expenditures on consumption and investment results in a higher total level of desired spending. In an economy with government spending (but no net exports), total desired spending on output equals desired consumption expenditure plus desired investment expenditure plus desired government expenditure. Thus, since an increase in government expenditure (like increases in consumption or investment expenditure) results in an increase in total desired spending, and since the equilibrium value of net national product is at the point where total desired spending equals NNP, it follows that an increase in government expenditure, as well as the induced increase in private spending, brings about an increase in the equilibrium value of NNP.

To see the effects of government expenditure on the equilibrium value of NNP, we can use a simple graph similar to those introduced in the previous chapter. We begin by plotting the consumption function, which shows desired consumption expenditure at each level of

Figure 11.1
Determination of Net National Product, Including Government Expenditure
The consumption function is C, the sum of consumption and investment expenditures is $C + I$, and the sum of consumption, investment, and government expenditures is $C + I + G$. The equilibrium value of NNP is at the point where the $C + I + G$ line intersects the 45-degree line, which here is $1,225 billion. The $C + I + G$ line shows aggregate demand, and the 45-degree line shows aggregate supply.

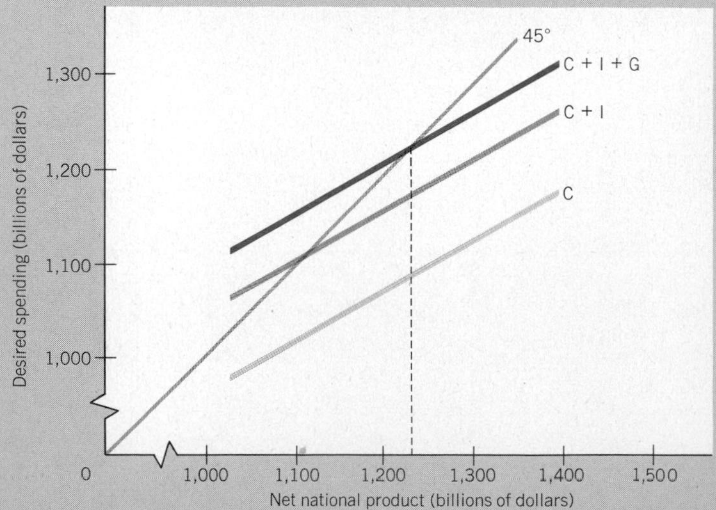

NNP (since NNP equals disposable income under our assumptions): the result is line C in Figure 11.1. Then, as in the previous chapter, we can plot the sum of desired consumption expenditure and investment expenditure at each level of NNP: the result is line $C + I$. Next, we plot the sum of desired consumption expenditure, investment expenditure, and government expenditure at each level of NNP, to get line $C + I + G$. Since the $C + I + G$ line shows total desired spending, and since, as we stressed in the previous chapter, the equilibrium value of NNP is at the point where total desired spending equals NNP, it follows that the equilibrium value of NNP is at the point where the $C + I + G$ line intersects the 45-degree line. This is at an output of $1,225 billion.

What happens to the equilibrium level of NNP if government expenditure increases? Figure 11.2 shows the results of a $5 billion increase in government spending. Obviously, the increased government expenditure (G_1) will raise the $C + I + G$ line by $5 billion, as the figure shows. Since the $C + I + G_1$ line must intersect the 45-degree line at a higher level of NNP, increases in government expenditure result in increases in the equilibrium level of NNP. In Figure 11.2, the $5 billion increase in government expenditure raises the equilibrium value of NNP from $1,225 billion to $1,237.5.

Figure 11.2 also shows what happens when government spending goes down by $5 billion (to G_2). The new $C + I + G_2$ line is $5 billion lower than the old $C + I + G$ line. Since the new $C + I + G_2$ line intersects the 45-degree line at a lower level of NNP, decreases in government expenditure result in decreases in the equilibrium level of NNP. In Figure 11.2, the $5 billion decrease in government expenditure reduces the equilibrium value of NNP from $1,225 billion to $1,212.5 billion.

How sensitive is the equilibrium level of NNP to changes in government spending? In the previous chapter, we found that a $1 billion change in desired investment—or a $1 billion shift in the consumption function—results in a change in equilibrium NNP of $\left(\frac{1}{MPS}\right)$ bil-

Figure 11.2
Effects on Equilibrium Net National Product of a $5 Billion Increase and Decrease in Government Expenditure
A $5 billion increase raises the equilibrium value of NNP from $1,225 billion to $1,237.5 billion. A $5 billion decrease reduces the equilibrium value of NNP from $1,225 billion to $1,212.5 billion.

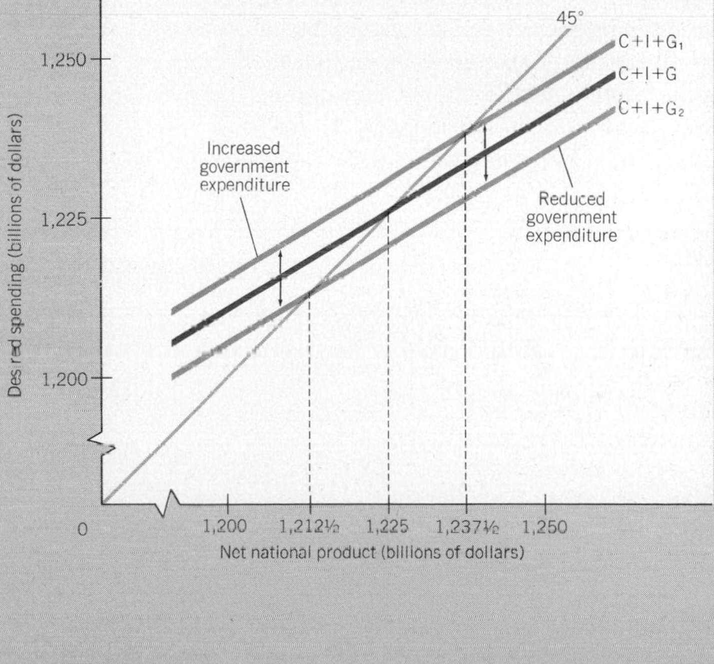

lions of dollars, where MPS is the marginal propensity to save. The effect of a $1 billion change in government expenditure is exactly the same. In other words, *it will result in a change in equilibrium NNP of* $\left(\frac{1}{MPS}\right)$ *billion dollars.* Thus *a change in government expenditure has the same multiplier effect on NNP as a change in investment or a shift in the consumption function.* For example, if the marginal propensity to consume is 0.6, an extra $1 billion in government expenditure will increase equilibrium NNP by $2.5 billion.

The mathematically inclined reader may be interested in proving that a $1 billion change in government expenditure will result in a change in equilibrium NNP of $\left(\frac{1}{\text{MPS}}\right)$ billions of dollars.* To prove this proposition, recall that the equilibrium value of NNP is at the point where desired spending—$C + I + G$—equals NNP. Thus,

$$NNP = C + I + G. \tag{11.1}$$

Assuming that the consumption function is as given in Table 9.1 (and Table 10.1), it follows that

$$C = 350 + 0.6\ NNP$$

where 0.6 is the marginal propensity to consume. (Note that NNP equals disposable income. This is because there are no taxes, no transfer payments, and no undistributed corporate profits. Taxes are brought into the picture in the next section.) Substituting the righthand side of equation (11.2) for C in Equation (11.1), we have

$$NNP = 350 + 0.6\ NNP + I + G \tag{11.3}$$

Thus

$$(1 - 0.6)\ NNP = 350 + I + G \tag{11.4}$$

$$NNP = \frac{350}{0.4} + \frac{I}{0.4} + \frac{G}{0.4}$$

What happens to NNP when G increases from $X billion to $(X + 1) billion? How much will this increase the equilibrium value of NNP? From Equation (11.4), it is clear that equilibrium NNP will be

$$\frac{350}{0.4} + \frac{I}{0.4} + \frac{X}{0.4}$$

if government expenditure equals $X billion. And it is equally clear from Equation (11.4) that NNP will equal

$$\frac{350}{0.4} + \frac{I}{0.4} + \frac{(X+1)}{0.4}$$

if government expenditure is $(X + 1) billion. Consequently the increase in NNP due to the $1 billion increase in government spending is

$$\left[\frac{350}{0.4} + \frac{I}{0.4} + \frac{(X+1)}{0.4}\right] - \left[\frac{350}{0.4} + \frac{I}{0.4} + \frac{X}{0.4}\right],$$

which equals

$$\frac{X+1}{0.4} - \frac{X}{0.4} = \frac{1}{0.4}.$$

That is, a $1 billion increase in government expenditure will result in an increase of $\frac{1}{0.4}$ billion dollars of NNP—which is equal to $\left(\frac{1}{\text{MPS}}\right)$ billions of dollars of NNP, since $0.4 = \text{MPS}$. This is what we set out to prove.

* The material in this box can be skipped without loss of continuity.

Taxation and Net National Product

The previous section added government expenditures to our theory, but it did not include taxes. Here we assume taxes to be net of transfer payments. For simplicity, it is assumed that all tax revenues stem from personal taxes. How do tax collections influence the equilibrium value of net national product? For example, if consumers pay 16⅔ percent of their income to the government in taxes, what effect does this have on NNP? Clearly, the imposition of this tax means that, for each level of NNP, people have less disposable income than they would with no taxes. In particular, disposable income now equals 83⅓ percent of NNP, whereas without taxes it equaled NNP. Thus the relationship between consumption expenditure and NNP is altered by the imposition of the tax. Before the tax was levied, the relationship was given by line C_0 in Figure 11.3; after the imposition of the tax, it is given by line C_1.

The relationship between consumption expenditure and national output changes in this way because consumption expenditure is determined by the level of disposable income. For instance, in the case in Figure 11.3, consumption expenditure equals $350 billion plus 60 percent of disposable income. Thus, since the tax reduces the amount of disposable income at each level of NNP, it also reduces the amount of consumption expenditure at each level of NNP. In other words, since people have less after-tax income to spend at each level of NNP, they spend less on consumption goods and services at each level of NNP. This seems eminently reasonable. It is illustrated in Figure 11.3, where, at each level of NNP, consumption expenditure after the tax (given by line C_1) is less than before the tax (given by line C_0).

Because the imposition of the tax influences the relationship between consumption expenditure and NNP, it also influences the equilib-

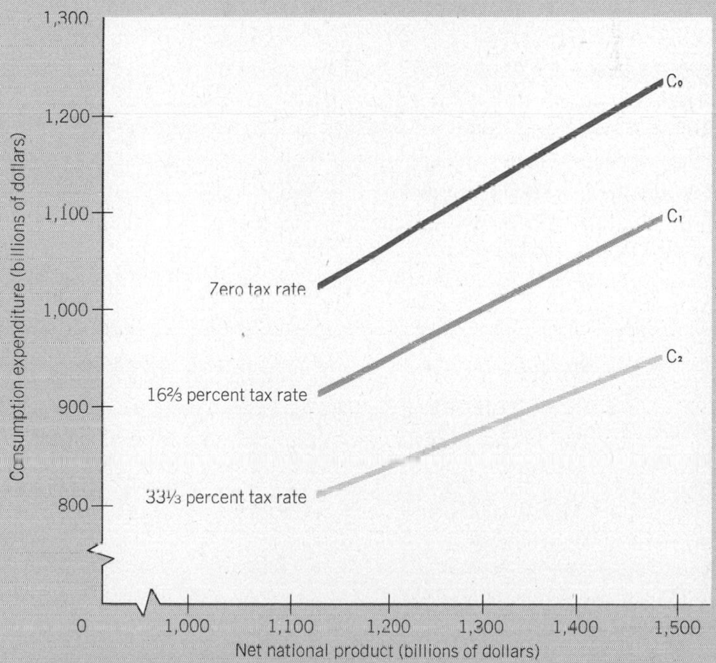

Figure 11.3
Relationship between Consumption Expenditure and Net National Product, Given Three Tax Rates
If taxes are zero, C_0 is the relationship between consumption expenditure and NNP. If consumers pay 16⅔ percent of their income in taxes, C_1 is the relationship; and if consumers pay 33⅓ percent of their income in taxes, C_2 is the relationship. Clearly, the higher the tax rate, the less consumers spend on consumption from a given NNP.

rium value of NNP. As we have stressed repeatedly, the equilibrium value of NNP is at the point where desired spending on output equals NNP. Lines C_0 and C_1 in Figure 11.3 show desired consumption expenditure at each level of NNP, before and after the tax. Adding desired investment and government expenditure to each of these lines, we get the total desired spending before and after the tax. The results are shown in Figure 11.4, under the assumption that the sum of desired investment and government spending equals $140 billion. The $C_0 + I + G$ line shows desired spending before the tax, while the $C_1 + I + G$ line shows desired spending after the tax.

Note that the equilibrium level of NNP is lower after the imposition of the tax than before. Specifically, as shown in Figure 11.4, it is $980 billion after the imposition of the tax and $1,225 billion before. The tax reduced the equilibrium level of NNP because it lowered the $C + I + G$ line from $C_0 + I + G$ to $C_1 + I + G$. It did this because, as pointed out above, it reduced the amount people wanted to spend on consumption goods at each level of NNP. People still wanted to spend the same amount *from each (after-tax) income level,* but because of the tax, their spending decisions had to be based on a *reduced (after-tax) income,* so that they spent less on consumption goods and services at each level of NNP.

Going a step further, *the higher the tax rate, the lower the equilibrium value of NNP; and the lower the tax rate, the higher the equilibrium value of NNP.* This is a very important proposition, as we shall see in subsequent sections. To demonstrate it, let's see what will happen to the equilibrium value of NNP when the tax rate is increased from 16⅔ percent of NNP to 33⅓ percent of NNP. If the tax rate is 33⅓ percent, total desired spending at each level of NNP will be given by line $C_2 + I + G$ in Figure 11.5. Since the equilibrium value of NNP will be at the point where the $C_2 + I + G$ line

Figure 11.4
Determination of Equilibrium Value of Net National Product, with Zero and 16⅔ Percent Tax Rates
The tax rate influences the relationship between consumption expenditure and NNP. (C_0 is this relationship with a zero tax rate, while C_1 is the relationship with a 16⅔ percent tax rate. See Figure 11.3.) The $C_0 + I + G$ line shows total desired spending at each level of NNP if the tax rate is zero, and the $C_1 + I + G$ line shows total desired spending at each level of NNP if the tax rate is 16⅔ percent. Consequently, the equilibrium value of NNP is $1,225 billion if the tax rate is zero, and $980 billion if it is 16⅔ percent.

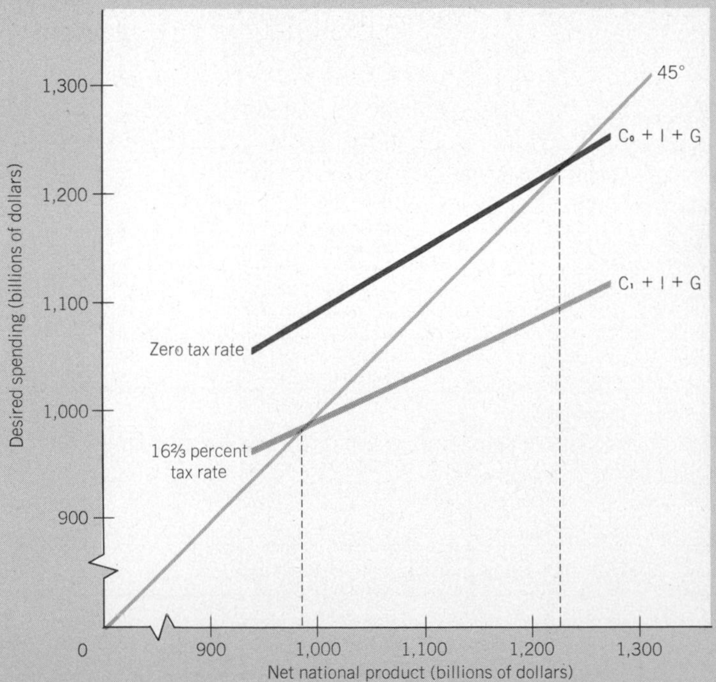

Figure 11.5
Determination of Equilibrium Value of Net National Product, with $16\frac{2}{3}$ Percent and $33\frac{1}{3}$ Percent Tax Rates
The $C_1 + I + G$ line shows total desired spending at each level of NNP if the tax rate is $16\frac{2}{3}$ percent, and the $C_2 + I + G$ line shows total desired spending at each level of NNP if the tax rate is $33\frac{1}{3}$ percent. Consequently, the equilibrium value of NNP is \$980 billion if the tax rate is $16\frac{2}{3}$ percent and \$$816\frac{2}{3}$ billion if it is $33\frac{1}{3}$ percent.

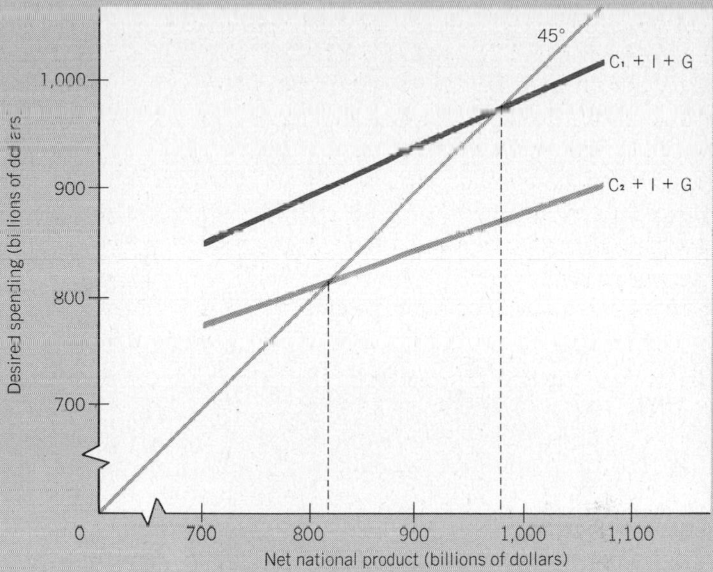

intersects the 45-degree line, the equilibrium value of NNP will be \$$816\frac{2}{3}$ billion, rather than \$980 billion (which was the equilibrium value when the tax rate was $16\frac{2}{3}$ percent). Thus the increase in the tax rate will reduce the equilibrium value of NNP. By reducing the amount people want to spend on consumption at each level of NNP, it will lower the $C + I + G$ line from $C_1 + I + G$ to $C_2 + I + G$.

On the other hand, suppose that the tax rate is lowered from $16\frac{2}{3}$ percent of NNP to a lesser amount. What will happen to the equilibrium value of NNP? If the tax rate is less than $16\frac{2}{3}$ percent, the desired spending on output at each level of NNP will be given by a $C + I + G$ line that lies between $C_0 + I + G$ and $C_1 + I + G$ line in Figure 11.4. Since the equilibrium value of NNP will be at the point where this line intersects the 45-degree line, the equilibrium value of NNP will be greater than \$980 billion. Thus the decrease in the tax rate will increase the equilibrium value of NNP. By increasing the amount people want to spend on consumption at each level of NNP, it will raise the $C + I + G$ line from $C_1 + I + G$ to a higher level.[1]

---

[1] Note that the slope of the relationship between consumption and NNP increases as the tax rate decreases. This means that the "marginal propensity to consume out of NNP" increases as the tax rate decreases. Consequently, the multiplier—the amount by which NNP changes if desired investment changes (or the consumption function shifts, or government expenditures change)—increases as the tax rate goes down, and conversely decreases as the tax rate goes up. In other words, as the tax rate increases, NNP becomes less sensitive to changes in investment, government spending, and the consumption function.

To see this, the mathematically inclined reader is encouraged to work through the following proof. Suppose that the consumption function is a straight line:

$$C = \alpha + \beta(1 - T)Y,$$

where Y = NNP, T equals the tax rate, i.e., the proportion of NNP consumers pay in taxes, α is the intercept of the consumption function, and β is the marginal propensity to consume. By definition,

$$Y = C + I + G.$$

Thus substituting for C,

$$Y = \alpha + \beta(1 - T)Y + I + G,$$

which means that

$$[1 - \beta(1 - T)]Y = \alpha + I + G,$$

or

$$Y = \frac{\alpha}{1 - \beta(1 - T)} + \frac{I}{1 - \beta(1 - T)} + \frac{G}{1 - \beta(1 - T)}.$$

Thus a \$1 billion increase in α, I, or G results in an increase of $\left[\frac{1}{1 - \beta(1 - T)}\right]$ billions of dollars in NNP. In other words, the multiplier is $\left[\frac{1}{1 - \beta(1 - T)}\right]$. But $\left[\frac{1}{1 - \beta(1 - T)}\right]$ gets bigger as T gets smaller; and conversely, $\left[\frac{1}{1 - \beta(1 - T)}\right]$ gets smaller as T gets bigger. This completes the proof.

Table 11.1
Determination of Equilibrium Level of Net National Product (billions of dollars)

(1) Net national product	(2) Taxes	(3) Disposable income (1)−(2)	(4) Desired consumption expenditure	(5) Desired saving (3)−(4)	(6) Desired invest-ment	(7) Government expenditure	(8) Total desired spending (4)+(6)+(7)	(9) Tendency of national output
1,000	50	950	920	30	90	50	1,060	Upward
1,050	50	1,000	950	50	90	50	1,090	Upward
1,100	50	1,050	980	70	90	50	1,120	Upward
1,150	50	1,100	1,010	90	90	50	1,150	No change
1,200	50	1,150	1,040	110	90	50	1,180	Downward
1,250	50	1,200	1,070	130	90	50	1,210	Downward
1,300	50	1,250	1,100	150	90	50	1,240	Downward

A Tabular Illustration

To illustrate how one can determine the equilibrium level of NNP when both government expenditure and taxation are included in our model, consider the numerical example shown in Table 11.1. The numbers in this table are the same as in Table 10.1, except that we now assume that the government spends $50 billion per year on goods and services and that it receives $50 billions in taxes per year. (For simplicity, we assume in this table that the amounts of both government expenditure and taxes are independent of the level of NNP. This is in contrast to the previous section where we assumed that taxes were proportional to NNP.) Column 1 of the table shows various possible levels of NNP. To obtain the level of disposable income corresponding to each level of NNP, we must subtract taxes (in column 2) from NNP, the result being shown in column 3.

Since the consumption function is assumed to be the same as in Table 10.1 (and Table 9.1), the desired consumption expenditure at each level of disposable income is as shown in column 4. Note that disposable income no longer equals NNP, as it did in Table 10.1, because taxes have entered the picture; this means that the relationship between desired consumption expenditure and NNP is also different. But since the consumption function is unchanged, the relationship between desired consumption expenditure and disposable income is the same as in Table 10.1.

Columns 5 to 8 of the table seem self-evident. Since desired saving equals disposable income less desired consumption expenditure, column 5 equals column 3 minus column 4. Column 6 shows desired investment, which is $90 billion. Column 7 shows government expenditure, which is $50 billion. And column 8 shows total desired spending on output at each level of NNP. Since total desired spending equals desired consumption expenditure plus desired investment expenditure plus desired government expenditure, column 8 equals column 4 plus column 6 plus column 7.

As emphasized in previous discussions (in this and the previous chapter), *national output will be at its equilibrium value only if total desired spending is equal (no more, no less) to NNP.* Thus, based on the data in Table 11.1, it is clear that the equilibrium value of NNP is $1,150 billion. Why? Because a comparison of columns 1 and 8 in Table 11.1 shows that this is the only value of NNP at which total desired spending (column 8) equals NNP (column 1).

If NNP is *less* than $1,150 billion, there will be a tendency for it to increase. Total spending will exceed the value of output produced, the result being that firms' inventories will be depleted. Firms will respond by raising their production rates, thus increasing NNP. If NNP is *greater* than $1,150 billion, there will be a tendency for it to decline. Total spending will fall short of the value of output produced, the result being that firms' inventories will mount. Firms will respond by lowering their production rates, thus decreasing NNP.

Finally, the leakage-injection approach described in the previous chapter is an alternative way of determining the equilibrium level of NNP. To use this approach, two points must be understood. First, *taxes are a leakage because they withdraw spending from the flow of income and expenditure.* After all, money that goes for taxes cannot be spent on output. Second, *government expenditure is an injection since it adds spending to the flow of income and expenditure.* It is a supplement to consumption expenditure and investment.

Since taxes are a leakage, the total leakages in Table 11.1 are desired saving plus taxes, or column 5 plus column 2. And since government expenditure is an injection, the total injections in Table 11.1 are desired investment plus government expenditure, or column 6 plus column 7. According to our discussion in the previous chapter, *the equilibrium value of NNP must be the value of NNP at which total leakages equal total injections*—in other words, the value of NNP at which desired saving plus taxes (column 5 plus column 2) equals desired investment plus government expenditure (column 6 plus column 7). Table 11.1 shows that this value of NNP is $1,150 billion. Of course, the answer obtained by the leakage-injection approach coincides, as it must, with that obtained by comparing the value of total desired spending (column 8) with the value of NNP (column 1).

The Balanced-Budget Multiplier

According to our previous conclusions, increases in government expenditures tend to increase NNP, while increases in tax receipts tend to reduce NNP. What will be the result when *both* government expenditures and tax receipts are increased *by the same amount?* Clearly, the increase in government expenditures will push NNP up, while the tax increase will push NNP down. But which force will prevail? According to an economic proposition called the balanced-budget multiplier, the result will be an *increase* in equilibrium NNP—and under the assumptions made in Table 11.1, this increase equals the increase in both government expenditures and taxes. (Although it is not very difficult to prove that this is the case, the proof involves some mathematics, and so will be omitted here.)

On the other hand, suppose that both government expenditures and tax receipts are *decreased* by the same amount. What will be the effect on NNP? Clearly, the decrease in government expenditures will push NNP down, while the tax cut will push NNP up. But which force will prevail? According to the balanced-budget multiplier, the result will be a *decrease* in equilibrium NNP—and under the assumptions made in Table 11.1, this decrease equals the decrease in both government expenditures and taxes.

To illustrate the application of this proposition, consider a proposal made by President Ford in 1975 to cut both taxes and government expenditures by $28 billion. Assuming that both the expenditure and tax cuts went into effect at the same time, this would have reduced NNP, as we have just seen. (However, if the tax cut occurred before the expenditure cut, as some observers claimed it would, the proposal might not have had this effect at all. Recall that the balanced-budget multiplier is concerned with a *simultaneous* change in government receipts and tax revenues.)

Recessionary and Inflationary Gaps

In this and the previous chapter, we have shown how the equilibrium level of net national product is determined. But it is of central importance to recognize that *this equilibrium level of NNP may not correspond to full employment.* As pointed out in Chapter 9, a basic theme of modern economics is that there is no automatic tendency for NNP to equal its full-employment level. For example, in Table 11.1, there is no assurance that $1,150 billion is the level of NNP corresponding to full employment. It may be below the full-employment level, in which case the unemployment rate will exceed 4 or 5 percent (the figures generally used to define full employment). Or it may be above the full-employment level, in which case there will be considerable inflation.

For simplicity, suppose that, so long as total spending does not exceed the value (at initial prices) of the full-employment level of output, the price level remains constant. (As pointed out in Chapter 8, this really is not true, but it is a useful simplification in the present context.) Then if the equilibrium NNP is *below* the full-employment level, the ***recessionary gap*** *is the increase in desired spending required to push the equilibrium NNP up to the full-employment level.* For example, if the full-employment level of NNP is Q_1 in Figure 11.6, the recessionary gap is $40 billion. Why? Because this is the amount by which desired spending must be increased if NNP is to rise from its current equilibrium level, Q_0, to Q_1. In other words, as shown in Figure 11.6, this is the amount by which the $C + I + G$ line must be raised in order to increase the equilibrium level of NNP from Q_0 to Q_1. *To prevent excessive unemployment, such a recessionary gap should be eliminated.*

Figure 11.6
Recessionary Gap
The equilibrium level of NNP, Q_0, is too low to result in full employment. The level of NNP corresponding to full employment is Q_1. To raise the equilibrium level of NNP from Q_0 to Q_1, desired spending must be increased by $40 billion. In other words, the $C + I + G$ line must be raised by $40 billion. This amount—the *vertical* distance between the 45-degree line and the $C + I + G$ line *at the full-employment level of NNP*—is called the *recessionary gap.*

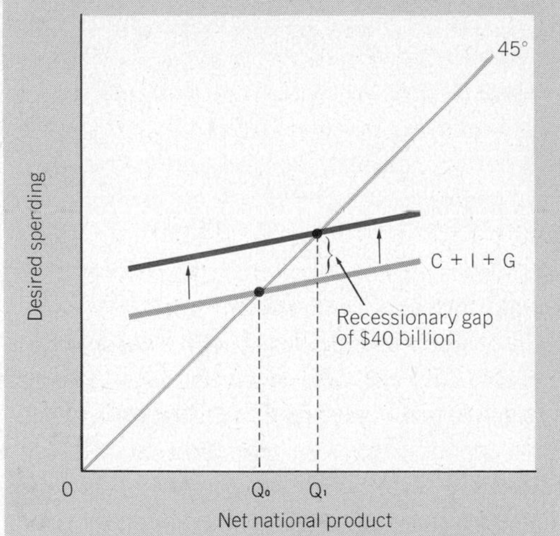

On the other hand, if the equilibrium NNP is *above* the full-employment level, the ***inflationary gap*** *is the reduction in desired spending required to push the equilibrium NNP down to the full-employment level.* For example, if the full-employment level of NNP is Q_2 in Figure 11.7, the inflationary gap is $40 billion. Why? Because this is the amount by which desired spending must be reduced if NNP is to fall from its current equilibrium level, Q_3, to Q_2.

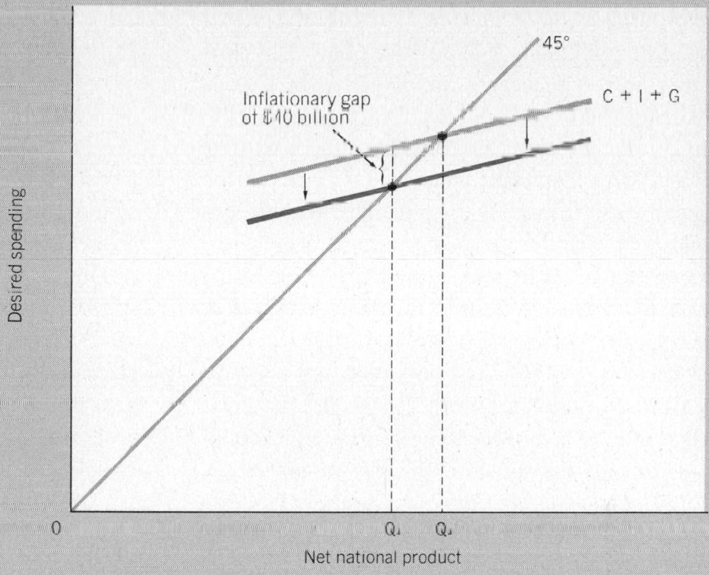

Figure 11.7
Inflationary Gap
For simplicity, assume that Q_2, the full-employment level of NNP, is the *maximum* value of *real* NNP (*in initial prices*) that can be achieved, thus any increase of *money* NNP above Q_2 is due entirely to inflation. To reduce the equilibrium NNP from Q_3 (its current level) to Q_2, desired spending must be reduced by $40 billion. In other words, the $C + I + G$ line must be lowered by $40 billion. This amount—the *vertical* distance between the 45-degree line and the $C + I + G$ line *at the full-employment level of NNP*—is called the *inflationary gap*.

In other words, as shown in Figure 11.7, this is the amount by which the $C + I + G$ line must fall in order to reduce the equilibrium level of NNP from Q_3 to Q_2. Assuming that Q_2 is the maximum value of real NNP (in initial prices) that can be achieved, any increase of money NNP above Q_2 is due entirely to inflation. Thus, *to curb inflationary pressures, such an inflationary gap should be eliminated.*

The Nature and Objectives of Fiscal Policy

Our discussions in previous sections make it easy to understand the basic ideas underlying modern fiscal policy. For example, suppose that the economy is suffering from an undesirably high unemployment rate. What should the government do? Since there is a recessionary gap, the economy needs increased spending. In other words, as shown in Figure 11.6, the economy needs an upward shift of the $C + I + G$ line, which by increasing NNP will increase employment as well. There are three ways that the government can try to bring this about. First, it can reduce taxes, which, as shown in a previous section, will shift the relation between consumption expenditure and NNP—and consequently the $C + I + G$ line—upward. Second, it can increase government expenditures, which will also shift the $C + I + G$ line upward. Third, the government can encourage firms to invest more, perhaps by enacting tax credits to make investment more profitable for them; an increase in desired investment will shift the $C + I + G$ line upward too.

On the other hand, perhaps we are suffering from an undesirably high rate of inflation. What should the government do? Since there is an inflationary gap, the economy needs reduced spending. In other words, what is required is a downward shift of the $C + I + G$ line, as shown in Figure 11.7. The government has three ways to try to bring this about. First, it can increase taxes; this, as shown in a previous section, will shift the relation between consumption expenditure and NNP—and consequently the $C + I + G$ line—downward. Second, it can cut government expenditures, which will also shift the $C + I + G$ curve downward. Third, it can change the tax laws and do other things to discourage firms from investing in plant and equipment or inventories; a decrease in desired investment will shift the $C + I + G$ line downward too.

Certainly, these ideas do not seem very hard to understand. Put bluntly, all we are saying is that, *if there is too much unemployment, the government should promote, directly or indirectly, additional public and/or private spending, which will result in additional output and jobs.* On the other hand, *if there is too much inflation, the government should reduce, directly or indirectly, spending (public and/or private); this will curb the inflationary pressure on prices.* Surely these propositions seem reasonable enough. And they are useful—although by themselves they cannot deal as effectively as one would like with times like the mid-1970s, when excessive unemployment and inflation have occurred together. We shall discuss such situations in detail in Chapter 16.

Perhaps the most surprising thing about these ideas is that they have been understood and accepted only very recently. Until the appearance of John Maynard Keynes's work in the 1930s, the economics profession really did not understand the effects of fiscal policy at all well. And once Keynes showed his fellow economists the way, it took over 20 years to convince congressmen, presidents, and other officials that these ideas were valid. Moreover, the educational process is still going on. Perhaps the most important reason why it has been so difficult to get across such simple ideas is that, until recently, the conventional wisdom passed down from father to son was that the government is no different from any other large enterprise: businesses must balance income against outgo, so should the government. In other words, it should spend no more than what it collects in taxes. This proposition is at odds with the ideas presented above. If those ideas are accepted, it may be necessary for the government to run a deficit or a surplus, depending on the economic situation. A ***deficit*** occurs when the government spends more than it collects in taxes; a ***surplus*** occurs when it spends less. It has taken a long time to convince people that full employment and stable prices—not a balanced budget—should be our goals. Some people still believe that the road to economic destruction is lined with unbalanced budgets.

Makers of Fiscal Policy

When you go to a ball game, you generally get a program telling you who on each team is playing each position. To understand the formulation and implementation of fiscal policy in the United States we need the same kind of information. Who are the people who establish our fiscal policy? Who decides that in view of the current and prospective economic situation, tax rates or government expenditures should be changed? This is not a simple question because lots of individuals and groups play an important role. In the Congress, the House and Senate Budget Committees—as well as the Congressional Budget Office—have been charged with important responsibilities in this area. Also, the Appropriations Committees, the House Ways and Means Committee, and the Senate Finance Committee have considerable influence. In addition, another congressional committee is of importance—the Joint Economic Committee of Congress. Established by the Employment Act of 1946, this committee goes over the annual Economic Report of the President on the state of the economy, and, through its hearings, provides a major forum for review of economic issues.

The Council of Economic Advisers

Before World War II, there was relatively little place in the government for economists. The Treasury had a small number, the antitrust division of the Justice Department a handful, but there was no place for economists who aspired to give advice on broad policy matters. The Employment Act of 1946 changed that situation by creating a council to "gather timely and authoritative information . . . to develop and recommend to the President national economic policies . . . and to make and furnish studies . . . as the President may request."

But as demonstrated by the first chairman, Edwin Nourse, the act was really a hunting license for a chairman to peddle his good counsel. Nourse, who believed that the Council's role was to "interpret literal facts . . . without becoming involved in any way in the advocacy of particular measures," found that such services were rarely required by the president. It is hard to find any trace of the Nourse era on the economic policies of the late forties.

THE FIRST COUNCIL OF ECONOMIC ADVISERS, EDWIN NOURSE, CHAIRMAN, AT LEFT.

Nourse's successor, Leon Keyserling, hunted so avidly that Congress almost suspended his license. Keyserling was temperamentally and politically inclined to activism. His advocacy of expansionist policies to a conservative Congress and a president concerned primarily with containing the Korean War inflation led to a bill reducing the CEA's budget by 25 percent. The Council was saved by the persuasiveness of a new chairman, Arthur F. Burns, and the support of a few senators. But the limits of independent advocacy had been established.

The Eisenhower years were quiet years for the Council. Even the election of John F. Kennedy, who was eager to increase the U.S. rate of economic growth, did not insure the Council's future. Kennedy was inclined to fiscal conservatism and less interested in domestic than in foreign affairs. It was Walter Heller, the new chairman under Kennedy, who made the CEA an integral part of the New Frontier. The tax cut of 1964, which Heller sold to a president committed to balanced budgets, is a tribute to his success in making a body without formal powers or legislative prerogatives an integral part of the policy making process. The new-found status of the Council was acknowledged in Washington by the establishment of a Quadriad, made up of representatives of the Council, the Bureau of the Budget, the Treasury, and the Federal Reserve, which met periodically to discuss economic affairs.

The Council's influence has risen and ebbed in recent years with both the state of the economy and with other pressures on the president. In 1966, as the Vietnam War intensified, the Council urged a tax increase; Lyndon Johnson, more attuned to the political realities, did not take action on the proposal until 1967. The Council's position in the Nixon administration further exemplified this process. Led by Paul McCracken and Herbert Stein, the Council championed restraint in fiscal and monetary policies early in Nixon's first term. But faced with mounting inflationary pressures, the Council members reluctantly joined other administration economists in setting up wage and price controls. In the Ford administration, the CEA played an important role, although the secretary of the Treasury, William Simon, often was the administration's leading economic spokesman. During 1974 and 1975, the Council had to help the president combat both double-digit inflation and the most severe recession since the thirties. In the Carter administration, the CEA has continued to play a major role in policy formation. E.A.

In the executive branch of government, the most important person in the establishment of fiscal policy is, of course, the president. Although he must operate in the context of the tax and expenditure laws passed by Congress, he and his advisers are the country's principal analysts of the need for fiscal expansion or restraint and its leading spokesmen for legislative changes to meet these needs. Needless to say, he doesn't pore over the latest economic data and make the decisions all by himself. The Office of Management and Budget, which is part of the Executive Office of the President, is a very powerful adviser to the president on expenditure policy, as is the Treasury Department on tax policy. In addition, there is the ***Council of Economic Advisers,*** which is part of the Executive Office of the President. Established by the Employment Act of 1946, its job is to help the president carry out the objectives of that act.

During the past 30 years, the Council of Economic Advisers, headed by a series of distinguished economists who left academic and other posts to contribute to public policy, has become a very important actor on the national economic policy stage. Its position has been well described by Stanford's G. L. Bach:

> Fundamentally, it is responsible for overseeing the state of the economy, for continually checking on the appropriateness of government policies for stable economic growth, and for working intimately with the President and other parts of the executive branch in developing overall legislative policy in the economic field. Some Council chairmen have worked closely with Congressional committees; others have remained more in the background as Presidential advisers. But for macroeconomic policy, the Council is now perhaps the President's most important single advisory group. It is *his* council and more specifically *his* part of the government than are the regular executive branch departments.[2]

[2] G. L. Bach, *Making Monetary and Fiscal Policy,* Washington, D.C.: Brookings Institution, 1971, pp. 30–31.

Automatic Stabilizers

Now that we have met some of the major players, we must point out that they get help from some ***automatic stabilizers***—some structural features of our economy that tend to stabilize national output. Although these economic stabilizers cannot do all that is required to keep the economy on an even keel, they help a lot. As soon as the economy turns down and unemployment mounts, they give the economy a helpful shot in the arm. As soon as the economy gets overheated and inflation crops up, they tend to restrain it.

Tax revenues. Changes in tax revenues are an important automatic stabilizer. One of the major points emphasized in Chapter 5 was that our federal system relies heavily on the income tax. The amount of income tax collected by the federal government goes up with increases in NNP and goes down with decreases in NNP. Moreover, because the income tax is progressive, the average tax rate goes up with increases in NNP, and goes down with decreases in NNP. This, of course, is just what we want to occur. When output falls off and unemployment mounts, tax collections fall off too, so disposable income falls less than NNP. This means less of a fall in consumption, which tends to brake the fall in NNP. When output rises too fast and the economy begins to suffer from serious inflation, tax collections rise too—which tends to brake the increase in NNP. Of course, corporation income taxes, as well as personal income taxes, play a significant role here.

Unemployment compensation and welfare payments. Unemployment compensation is paid to workers who are laid off, according to a system that has evolved over the past 40 years. When an unemployed worker goes back to work, he stops receiving unemployment compensation. Thus, when NNP falls off and unemployment mounts, the tax collections to finance unemployment compensation go down (because of lower employment), while the amount paid out to unemployed workers goes up. On the other hand, when NNP rises too fast and the economy begins to suffer from serious inflation, the tax collections to finance unemployment compensation go up, while the amount paid out goes down because there is much less unemployment. Again, this is just what we want to see happen. Spending is bolstered when unemployment is high and curbed when there are serious inflationary pressures. Various welfare programs have the same kind of automatic stabilizing effect on the economy.

Corporate dividends, family saving, and farm programs. Since corporations tend to maintain their dividends when their sales fall off, and moderate the increase in their dividends when their sales soar, their dividend policy tends to stabilize the economy. This is very important. Also, to the extent that consumers tend to be slow to raise or lower their spending in response to increases or decreases in their income, this too tends to stabilize the economy. Finally, there are the agricultural support programs, described in Chapter 5. The government has buttressed farm prices and incomes when business was bad and unemployment was high. When output was high and inflation occurred, the government distributed the commodities in its warehouses and received dollars. In both cases, these programs acted as stabilizers.

Having painted such a glowing picture of the economy's automatic stabilizers, we are in danger of suggesting that they can stabilize the economy all by themselves. It would be nice if this were true, but it isn't. All the automatic stabilizers do is *cut down* on variations in unemployment and inflation, not *eliminate* them. Discretionary tax and spending programs are needed to supplement the effects of these automatic stabilizers. Some economists wish strongly that it were possible to set well-defined rules for government action, rather than leave things to the discretion of policy makers. Indeed, Milton Friedman, among others, forcefully argues for greater reliance on such rules, but most economists feel that it is impossible to formulate a set of rules flexible and comprehensive enough to let us do away with the discretionary powers of policy makers. Instead their concern is with sharpening the tools available to government economic decision makers.

The Tools of Discretionary Fiscal Policy

Suppose that the Council of Economic Advisers, on the basis of information concerning recent economic developments, believes that national output may decline soon, causing serious unemployment, and that other agencies, like the Treasury and the Federal Reserve System, agree. What specific measures can the Council recommend that the government take under such circumstances?

First, *the government can vary its expenditure for public works and other programs.* If increased unemployment seems to be in the wind, it can step up outlays on roads, urban reconstruction, and other public programs. Of course, these programs must be well thought out and socially productive. There is no sense in pushing through wasteful and foolish public works programs merely to make jobs. Or if, as in 1969, the economy is plagued by inflation, it can (as President Nixon ordered) stop new federal construction programs temporarily.

Second, *the government can vary welfare payments and other types of transfer payments.* For example, a hike in Social Security benefits may provide a very healthy shot in the arm for an economy with too much unemployment. An increase in veterans' benefits or in aid to dependent children may do the same thing. The federal government has sometimes helped the states to extend the length of time that the unemployed can receive unemployment compensation; this too will have the desired effect. On the other hand, if there is full employment and inflation is a dangerous problem, it may be worthwhile to cut back on certain kinds of transfer payments. For example, if it is agreed that some veterans' benefits should be reduced, this reduction might be timed to occur during a period when inflationary pressures are evident.

Third, *the government can vary tax rates.* For example, if there is considerable unemployment, the government may cut tax rates, as it did in 1975. Or if inflation is the problem, the government may increase taxes, as it did in 1968 when, after considerable political maneuvering and buckpassing, the Congress was finally persuaded to put through a 10 percent tax surcharge to try to moderate the inflation caused by the Vietnam War. However, temporary tax changes may have less effect than permanent ones, since, as pointed out in Chapter 9, consumption expenditure may be influenced less by transitory changes in income than by permanent changes.

Of course there are advantages and disadvantages in each of these tools of fiscal policy. One of the big disadvantages of public works and similar spending programs is that they take so long to get started. Plans must be made, land must be acquired, and preliminary construction studies must be carried out. By the time the expenditures are finally made and have the desired effect, the dangers of excessive unemployment may have given way to dangers of inflation, so that the spending, coming too late, does more harm than good. To some extent, this problem may be ameliorated by having a backlog of productive projects ready to go at all times. In this way, at least a portion of the lag can be eliminated.

In recent years, there has been a widespread feeling that government expenditures should be set on the basis of their long-run desirability and productivity and not on the basis of short-term stabilization considerations. The optimal level of government expenditure is at the point where the value of the extra benefits to be derived from an extra dollar of government expenditure is at least equal to the dollar of cost. This optimal level is unlikely to change much in the short run, and it would be wasteful to spend more—or less—than this amount for stabilization purposes when tax changes could be used instead. Thus many economists believe that tax cuts or tax increases should be the primary fiscal weapons to fight unemployment or inflation.

However, one of the big problems with tax changes is that it is difficult to get Congress to take speedy action. There is often considerable debate over a tax bill, and sometimes it becomes a political football. Another difficulty with tax changes is that it generally is much easier to reduce taxes than it is to get them back up again. To politicians, lower taxes are attractive because they are popular, and higher taxes are dangerous because they may hurt a politician's chances of re-election. In discussing fiscal policy (or most other aspects of government operations, for that matter), to ignore politics is to risk losing touch with reality.

Two Hits and a Miss: Recent Applications of Economic Analysis

The Tax Cut of 1964

With some knowledge of the players and the plays they can call, we can look now at three examples of fiscal policy in action. When the Kennedy administration took office in 1961, it was confronted with a relatively high unemployment rate—about 7 percent in mid-1961. By 1962, although unemployment was somewhat lower (about 6 percent), the president's advisers, led by Walter W. Heller, chairman of the Council of Economic Advisers, pushed for a tax cut to reduce unemployment further. The president, after considerable discussion of the effects of such a tax cut, announced in June 1962 that he would propose such a measure to the Congress; and in January 1963, the bill was finally sent to Congress.

The proposed tax bill was a victory for modern ideas on fiscal policy. Even though it would mean a deliberately large deficit, the president had been convinced to cut taxes to push the economy closer to full employment. But the Congress was not so easily convinced. Many congressmen labeled the proposal irresponsible and reckless. Others wanted to couple tax reform with tax reduction. It was not until 1964, after President Kennedy's death, that the tax bill was enacted. It took a year from the time the bill was sent to Congress for it to be passed, and during this interval, there was a continuous debate in the executive branch and the Congress. The secretary of the Treasury, Douglas Dillon, the chairman of the Federal Reserve Board, William M. Martin, and numerous congressmen—all powerful and all initially cool to the proposal—were eventually won over. The result was a tax reduction of about $10 billion per year.

The effects of the tax cut are by no means easy to measure, but in line with the theory presented in earlier sections, consumption expenditure did increase sharply during 1964. Moreover, the additional consumption undoubtedly induced additional investment. According to some estimates, the tax cut resulted in an increase in GNP of about $24 billion in 1965 and more in subsequent years.[3] The unemployment rate, which had been about 5½ to 6 percent during 1962 and 1963, fell to 5 percent during 1964 and to 4.7 percent in the spring of 1965. It is fair to say that most economists were extremely pleased with themselves in 1965. Fiscal policy based on their theories seemed to work very well indeed! Unfortunately, however, this pleasure did not last very long, there being another, and sadder, tale to tell.

The Tax Surcharge of 1968

In late July 1965, President Lyndon Johnson announced that the United States would send 50,000 more men to Vietnam. From fiscal 1965 to fiscal 1966, defense expenditures rose from $50 billion to $62 billion—a large increase in government expenditure, and one that took place at a time of relatively full employment. On the basis of the theory presented earlier in this chapter, such an increase in government expenditure would be expected to cause inflationary pressures. The Council of Economic Advisers recognized this danger, and recommended in late 1965 that the president urge Congress to increase taxes. Johnson was reluctant. The inflationary pressures mounted during 1966, and little was done by fiscal policy makers to quell them.

Even in 1967, the Congress was unwilling to raise taxes. The case for fiscal restraint was, it felt, not clear enough. As for the president, he said, "It is not a popular thing for a President to do . . . to ask for a penny out of a dollar to pay for a war that is not popular either."[4] Finally, in mid-1968, a 10 percent surcharge on income taxes, together with some restraint in government spending, was enacted. This increase in taxes was obviously the right medicine, but it was at least two years too late, and its effects were delayed and insufficient.

The Tax Cut of 1975

In late 1974, the unemployment rate began to mount. Whereas it was 5.5 percent in August, it reached 7.2 percent in December. Although economists were rather slow to recognize that the economy was slumping into a severe recession, by early 1975 it was clear that some stimulus was needed. Inflation, which President

[3] Arthur Okun, "Measuring the Impact of the 1964 Tax Reduction," in Walter W. Heller, *Perspectives on Economic Growth,* New York: Random House, 1968, p. 33.

[4] Arthur Okun, *The Political Economy of Prosperity,* New York: Norton, 1970, p. 88.

Ford had labeled "Public Enemy Number One" in the fall of 1974, continued to be a problem, but most policy makers felt that unemployment rates were reaching intolerable levels. By March 1975, the unemployment rate was 8.7 percent, the highest level in over 30 years, and something clearly had to be done to lower it.

In early 1975, President Ford proposed a $16 billion tax cut. As his Council of Economic Advisers stated, its purpose was "to halt the decline in production and employment so that growth of output can resume and unemployment can be reduced."[5] In March 1975, Congress passed a $23 billion tax cut, which provided rebates (of $100 to $200) on 1974 personal income taxes as well as reductions in 1975 income taxes. Both personal and corporate income taxes were cut. Personal tax liabilities were reduced through a $30 credit for each taxpayer and each dependent, as well as through increased standard deductions and low-income allowances. Corporate tax liabilities were reduced through a liberalization of the investment tax credit, as well as changes in tax rates.

The evidence seems to indicate that the tax cut was the right kind of medicine. In accord with our theories, national output did, in fact, increase in the latter half of 1975, and unemployment eased somewhat. By the end of 1975, the recovery was well under way—due in part, according to most economists, to the tax cut.

Based on the histories of all three of these tax changes (1964, 1968, and 1975), it is clear that, although we know a great deal more than we used to about how fiscal policy should be employed to avoid inflation or considerable unemployment, there is no guarantee that it will be used in this way. In the early 1960s and in 1974-75, policy makers seemed to make reasonably correct choices; in 1965-68, they did not. Without question, mistakes will continue to be made: all that we can do is try to learn from past mistakes.

[5] Council of Economic Advisers, *1975 Annual Report,* Washington, D.C.: Government Printing Office, 1975.

Deficit and Surplus Financing

Now that you have studied the basic elements of fiscal policy, let's see how well you would fare with some of the problems that confront our nation's top policy makers. Suppose that, through some inexplicable malfunctioning of the democratic process, you are elected president of the United States. Your Council of Economic Advisers reports to you that, on the basis of various forecasts, national output is likely to drop next year, and unemployment is likely to be much higher. Naturally, you are concerned; and having absorbed the ideas presented in this chapter, you ask your advisers—the Council of Economic Advisers, the Treasury, and the Office of Management and Budget—what sort of fiscal policy should be adopted to head off this undesirable turn of events. On the basis of their advice, you suggest to Congress that taxes should be cut and government expenditures should be increased.

When they receive your message, a number of key congressmen point out that if the government cuts taxes and raises expenditures it will operate in the red. In other words, government revenue will fall short of government spending—there will be a deficit. They warn that such fiscal behavior is irresponsible, since it violates the fundamental tenet of public finance that the budget should be balanced: income should cover outgo. For further clarification on this point, you call in your advisers, who deny that the budget should be balanced each year. They point out that if a deficit is run in a particular year, the government can borrow the difference; and they claim that the national debt is in no sense dangerously large in the United States at present. Whose advice would you follow—that of your economic advisers or that of the congressmen?

Or suppose your advisers tell you that inflation is a growing problem and that you should cut back government spending and raise taxes. Since this advice seems eminently sensible, based on the principles set forth in this chapter, you propose this course of action to Congress. Some prominent newspapers point out that by raising taxes and cutting expenditures, the government will take in more than it spends. In other words, there will be a surplus. They say that there is no reason for the government to take more money from the people than it needs to pay for the services it performs, and argue that taxes should not be increased because the government can cover its expenditures without such an increase. Whose advice would you follow—that of your economic advisers or that of the newspapers?

You would be wise to go along with your economic advisers in both cases. Why? Because there is nothing particularly desirable about a balanced budget. Although it may well be prudent for individuals and families not to spend more than they earn, this does not carry over to the federal government. When we need to stimulate the economy and raise national output, it is perfectly legitimate and desirable for the federal government to run a deficit, provided it gets its full money's worth for what is spent. All that happens is that the government borrows the difference, and—as we pointed out in Chapter 6—there is no indication that the national debt is dangerously large. Thus, in the first case, you should not have been worried by the fact that a deficit would result. And in the second case, while it is true that the government could support its expenditures with lower taxes, this would defeat your purpose. What you want to do is to cut total spending, public and private, and raising taxes will cut private spending.

Deficit Spending in the 1930s: A Case Study

Some people—fewer than there used to be, but still some—are dead set against deficit spending by the government. Many, when pressed to explain their opposition, retort that it was tried by Franklin D. Roosevelt during the Great Depression of the 1930s and that it failed to eliminate the high levels of unemployment that prevailed then. This is both bad history and bad economics. The federal government did spend more than it took in during the Roosevelt administration, but the deficit was far too small to have much effect. GNP fell from about $100 billion in 1929 to less than $60 billion in 1933. Federal deficits in the 1930s were only a few billion dollars per year at most, and in many years these deficits were offset by surpluses run by the state and local governments. The situation somewhat resembled that described by the columnist Heywood Broun, when he wrote, "I have known people to stop and buy an apple on the corner and then walk away as if they had solved the whole unemployment problem."[6]

In a careful study of the effects of fiscal policy in the 1930s, Professor E. Cary Brown of M.I.T. concluded that fiscal policy "seems to have been an unsuccessful recovery device in the thirties—not because it did not work, but because it was not tried."[7] For those who know something of the political history of the period, this is not surprising. Few government officials of that day understood the power and effects of fiscal policy. The federal government did run a deficit, but largely in spite of itself. In that era, the golden rule of fiscal responsibility was a balanced budget, and deficits were regarded as unfortunate aberrations. If you contrast this attitude with the attitude of the federal government toward the tax cuts of 1964 and 1975, you will see how far the nation has come in its understanding of fiscal policy.

[6] Heywood Broun, *It Seems to Me,* 1933. Of course, this does not mean that the Roosevelt administration did not attempt to reduce unemployment. What we are saying is that the history of the period is not a very good test of the effectiveness of deficit spending.

[7] E. Cary Brown, "Fiscal Policy in the Thirties: A Reappraisal," *American Economic Review,* December 1956, pp. 865-66.

Alternative Budget Policies

At least three policies concerning the government budget are worthy of detailed examination. The first policy says that *the government's budget should be balanced each and every year.* This is the philosophy that generally prevailed, here and abroad, until the advent of Keynesian economics in the 1930s. Superficially, it seems eminently reasonable. After all, won't a family or firm go bankrupt if it continues to spend more than it takes in? Why should the government be any different? However, the truth is that the government has economic capabilities, powers, and responsibilities that are entirely different from those of any family or firm, and it is misleading—sometimes even pernicious—to assume that what is sensible for a family or firm is also sensible for the government.

If this policy of balancing the budget is accepted, the government cannot use fiscal policy as a tool to stabilize the economy. Indeed, if the government attempts to balance its budget each year, it is likely to make unemployment or inflation worse rather than better. For example, suppose that severe unemployment occurs because of a drop in national output. Since incomes drop, tax receipts drop as well. Thus, if the government attempts to balance its budget, it must cut its spending and/or increase tax rates, both of which will tend to lower, not raise, national output. On the other hand, suppose that inflation occurs because spending increases too rapidly. Since incomes increase, tax receipts increase too. Thus, for the government to balance its budget, it must increase its spending and/or decrease tax rates, both of which will tend to raise, not lower, spending.[8]

A second budgetary philosophy says that *the government's budget should be balanced over the course of each "business cycle."* As we shall see in Chapter 12, the rate of growth of national output tends to behave cyclically. As shown in Figure 8.6, it tends to increase for a while, then drop, increase, then drop. Unemployment also tends to ebb and flow in a similar cyclical fashion. This is the so-called business cycle. According to this second budgetary policy, the government is not expected to balance its budget each year, but is expected to run a big enough surplus during periods of high employment to offset the deficit it runs during the ensuing period of excessive unemployment. This policy seems to give the government enough flexibility to run the deficits or surpluses needed to stabilize the economy, while at the same time allaying any public fear of a chronically unbalanced budget. It certainly seems to be a neat way to reconcile the government's use of fiscal policy to promote noninflationary full employment with the public's uneasiness over chronically unbalanced budgets.

Unfortunately, however, it does contain one fundamental flaw: there is no reason to believe that the size of the deficits required to eliminate excessive unemployment will equal the size of the surpluses required to moderate the subsequent inflation. For example, suppose that national output falls sharply, causing severe and prolonged unemployment; then regains its full-employment level only briefly; then falls again. In such a case, the deficits incurred to get the economy back to full employment are likely to exceed by far the surpluses run during the brief period of full employment. Thus there would be no way to stabilize the economy without running an unbalanced

[8] In sophisticated circles, there is some support for this philosophy of a balanced budget, based on the idea that it makes it easier for the Office of Management and Budget to keep expenditures within reasonable limits. Once this philosophy is abandoned completely, it is feared that the individual departments and agencies of the government can challenge OMB's estimate of how big a surplus or deficit is appropriate, and argue that more spending on their part would be a good thing. In other words, it makes it easier to control spending.

Another point that is frequently made is that the government, through inappropriate fiscal or monetary policies, is often responsible for problems of unemployment and inflation. To many economists, the practical problem seems to be how to prevent the government from creating disturbances, rather than how to use the government budget (and monetary policy) to offset disturbances arising from the private sector. Unfortunately, as we noted in connection with the inflation arising from the Vietnam War, there is sometimes a good deal of truth to this.

budget over the course of this business cycle. If this policy were adopted, and if the government attempted to balance the budget over the course of each business cycle, this would interfere with an effective fiscal policy designed to promote full employment with stable prices.

Finally, a third budgetary policy says that *the government's budget should be set so as to promote whatever attainable combination of unemployment and inflation seems socially optimal,* even if this means that the budget is unbalanced over considerable periods of time. This policy is sometimes called ***functional finance.***[9] Proponents of functional finance point out that, although this policy may mean a continual growth in the public debt, the problems caused by a moderate growth in the public debt are small when compared with the social costs of unemployment and inflation.

Certainly, the history of the past 40 years has been characterized by enormous changes in the nation's attitude toward the government budget. Forty years ago, the prevailing attitude was that the government's budget should be balanced. The emergence of the modern theory of the determination of national output and employment shook this attitude, at least to the point where it became respectable to advocate a balanced budget over the business cycle, rather than in each year. Then, as modern ideas regarding fiscal policy have become accepted by more and more people, the idea that the budget should be balanced over the business cycle has been largely abandoned, and the government budget is now viewed as a means to reduce undesirable unemployment and inflation.

The Full-Employment Budget

Some of the misconceptions about budget deficits and surpluses can be avoided by the use of the ***full-employment budget,*** which shows the difference between tax revenues and government expenditures that would result if we had full employment, which is generally defined as 4 percent unemployed. For example, in 1958, the Eisenhower administration ran a deficit of over $10 billion—a reasonably large deficit by historical standards. Basically, the reason for this deficit was that, with the unemployment rate at about 7 percent, there was a substantial gap between actual and potential output. Net national product fell from 1957 to 1958, and, as a result, incomes and federal tax collections fell, and the government ran a deficit. But this $10 billion deficit was entirely due to the high level of unemployment the country was experiencing.

Had we been at full employment, there would have been a surplus of about $5 billion in 1958. NNP, incomes, and federal tax receipts would all have been higher. Government spending and the tax rates in 1958 were not such as to produce a deficit if full employment had been attained. On the contrary, the full-employment budget shows that, if full employment had prevailed, tax receipts would have increased so that federal revenues would have exceeded expenditure by about $5 billion. It is important to distinguish between the full-employment budget and the actual budget. When, as in 1958, the actual budget shows a deficit but the full-employment budget does not, most economists feel that fiscal policy is not too expansionary, since at full employment the federal government would be running a surplus.

Recognizing these considerations, recent administrations have officially adopted the full-employment budget as their measure of the stabilization impact of the budget. As you can see in Figure 11.8, President Nixon ran a full-employment surplus during his first term in office to combat inflation. In 1972, there was a full-employment deficit, but in 1973, and to a greater extent 1974, there were full-employment surpluses. This is in contrast to the actual budget, which was in deficit for most

[9] See Abba Lerner, *Economics of Control*, New York: Macmillan, 1944.

Figure 11.8
Full-Employment and Actual Budget Deficits and Surpluses, 1956–75.
The full-employment budget shows the difference between tax revenues and government expenditures that would result if there was full employment, which is generally defined as 4 percent unemployed. The Nixon administration was the first to officially adopt the full-employment budget as a measure of the stabilization impact of the budget.

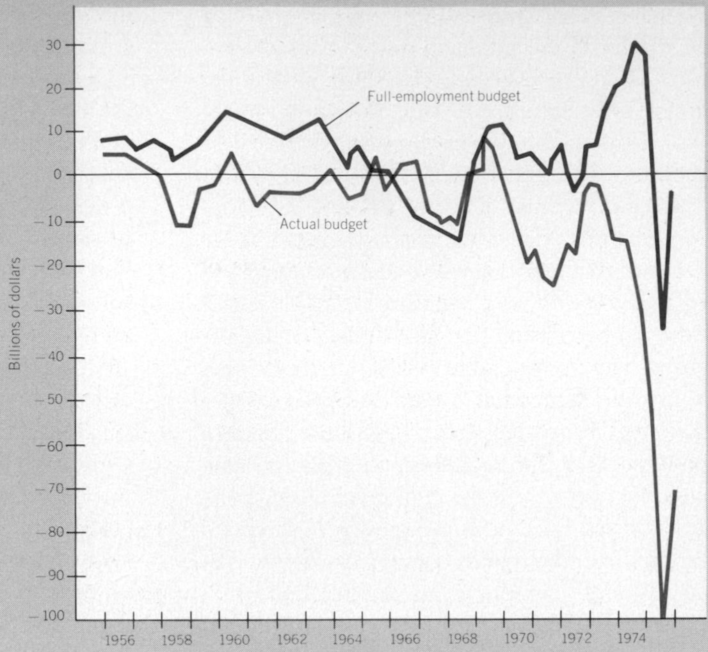

of these years. President Ford ran a substantial full-employment deficit in 1975 to promote recovery from the recession. As you can see in Figure 11.8, the full-employment budget can differ substantially from the actual budget. To understand whether fiscal policy is restrictive or stimulative, you must understand the difference.

Effects of How a Deficit Is Financed, or How a Surplus Is Used

Before leaving the topic of budget deficits and surpluses, it is important to note that the effect of a deficit may depend on how it is financed, as well as on its size. One way for the government to finance a deficit is *to borrow from consumers and business firms.* (Such borrowing results in increases in the national debt, discussed in Chapter 6.) When the government borrows from consumers and business firms, it takes funds from them that might otherwise be spent on consumption or investment goods. Thus, some of the expansionary effect of a budget deficit may be offset by reduced private spending, if a deficit is financed by borrowing from the public.

A second way for the government to finance a budget deficit is *to create new money.* For example, the government can simply print additional money to meet the deficit. (As will become clearer in Chapter 15, a similar result may be obtained if the government borrows from the central bank—the Federal Reserve in the United States.) When the government spends newly created money, it does not use funds that might otherwise be spent by the private sector. Consequently, *the expansionary effects of a deficit may be greater if it is financed by the creation of new money than if it is financed by borrowing from the public.*

Similarly, the effect of a surplus may depend on how it is used, as well as on its size. One way that the government can use a surplus is *to buy back some of its bonds from the public.* (Such purchases reduce the national debt.) When the government buys back some of its bonds, it provides the sellers of these bonds (consumers and firms) with additional spendable funds. Thus some of the anti-inflationary effects of a surplus may be offset by additional private spending. Another way that the government can use a surplus is to *impound the funds,* that is, keep the funds idle. Since this latter use of the surplus does not provide the private sector with additional spendable funds, there is no such offset to the surplus's anti-inflationary effect. Consequently, *the anti-inflationary effects of a surplus may be greater if the surplus is impounded than if it is used to reduce the national debt.*

Recent American Experience with Fiscal Policy

It should be evident by now that much more is known today about the impact of fiscal policy than at the time when the economy was staggered by the Great Depression. But this does not mean that economists have all the answers. Enough is known to keep the economy from careening off a bumpy road; avoiding the potholes is another matter.

The hard choices faced by economists in the top councils of government can be demonstrated by a close inspection of the recent attempts to give the economy a smoother ride. Let's begin with the situation in the late 1960s, when there was mounting inflation due partly to government spending on the Vietnam War. During 1969 and 1970, the administration restricted government expenditures and tried to run a surplus. As the administration's restrictive fiscal policies took hold, the nation's level of real output began to rise more slowly; and in 1970, gross national product in constant dollars fell below its 1969 level. Unemployment, which had been only 3.5 percent of the civilian labor force in 1969, rose to 4.9 percent in 1970 and to 5.9 percent in 1971.

During 1970 and 1971, many liberal economists accused the administration of being so absorbed with reducing inflation that it was creating serious unemployment. Yet despite the administration's efforts, the rate of inflation was not decreasing as fast as desired. Between 1969 and 1970, the index of consumer prices rose by about 6 percent. During the first half of 1971, it rose at an annual rate of about 4½ percent. Although this was an improvement, the inflationary process was proving difficult to quell.

In August 1971, the Nixon administration, reversing its previous attitudes, established controls on prices, wages, and rents. This was the first time that such controls had been adopted by an American government in peacetime. At the same time, the administration switched to a more expansionary fiscal policy in order to reduce the relatively high level of unemployment. Specifically, the president called for a tax reduction of about $7 or $8 billion. Included in his tax package was an investment tax credit, which encouraged investment by business firms, as well as a reduction in personal income taxes. This so-called New Economic Policy also was the subject of criticism, both from the left and the right. Some economists welcomed the shift to a more expansionary policy as long overdue; others viewed it as a mistake. Also, both the tax reduction and the controls were criticized on the grounds that they benefited business more than labor. But the unemployment rate did drop slightly, to 5½ percent in late 1972, and the rate of inflation declined to about 3 percent during the year.

After his re-election in November 1972, President Nixon indicated that he wanted to keep a tight lid on government spending, both to reduce inflation and to trim some programs that he regarded as secondary or of dubious value. In particular, he stressed the desirability of a $250 billion ceiling on federal spending. Critics of the president's economic policies claimed that his emphasis on restricting public expenditures was a mistake. In early 1973, the president phased out the wage and price controls he had imposed in 1971. Inflation, which never had been quelled, increased after the phaseout of the controls, and during early 1973 the economy was in the midst of a boom. In June 1973, the president imposed another price freeze, this time for 60 days. Then he instituted a program which attempted to limit price increases to an amount equal to cost increases. This program was largely ineffectual, and was phased out in 1974.

In early 1974, the price of foreign oil was increased very substantially by the OPEC countries. This price increase, as well as considerable increases in farm prices (recall Chapter 5), spearheaded a bewildering inflationary spurt. During 1974, consumer prices rose by about 12 percent! From the point of view of inflation, this was the worst year in decades. At the same time, the nation's real output fell, as the economy dropped into the most serious recession since World War II. The result was a marked increase in unemployment. By March 1975, the unemployment rate was 8.7 percent, as compared with 4.9 percent in December 1973.

Faced with a combination of excessive unemployment and excessive inflation, President Ford proposed a $16 billion tax cut, and, as we saw above, Congress passed a $23 billion tax cut in March 1975. Since federal expenditures increased considerably from 1974 to 1975, and federal receipts fell (because of the tax cut), there was a very large deficit in 1975—about $70 billion. But the full-employment deficit was only about $8 billion. As we have seen before, the economy began to revive in mid-1975, and unemployment fell from 8.7 percent in March 1975 to 7.5 percent in March 1976. However, "stagflation"—the combination of a high unemployment rate and a high rate of inflation—was by no means vanquished. On the contrary, both unemployment and inflation continued to be excessive in mid-1976.

Clearly, judging from our recent history, fiscal policy is no panacea. Policy makers are continually confronted with difficult choices, and the tools of fiscal policy, at least as they are currently understood and used, are not sufficient to solve or dispel many of the problems at hand. However, it is important to recognize that fiscal policy is not the only available means by which policy makers attempt to stabilize the economy. There is also monetary policy, which we shall discuss in detail in Chapter 15. Really, a sensible fiscal policy can be formulated only in conjunction with monetary policy, and although it is convenient to discuss them separately, in real life they must be coordinated. Also, lest you become overly pessimistic, you should note that, despite the problems that remain unsolved, our improved understanding of fiscal and monetary policy has enabled us to steer a better and more stable course than in the days before World War II. So far at least, bouts of severe unemployment and double-digit inflation have been moderated by government action.

Summary

The equilibrium level of net national product is the level where desired consumption plus desired investment plus desired government spending equals net national product. A $1 billion change in government expenditure will result in a change in equilibrium NNP of the same amount as a $1 billion change in desired investment or a $1 billion shift in the relation between consumption expenditures and NNP. In any of these cases, there is a multiplier effect. An increase in the tax rate shifts the relationship between consumption expenditure and NNP downward, thus reducing the equilibrium value of NNP. A decrease in the tax rate shifts the relationship upward, thus increasing the equilibrium value of NNP.

The equilibrium level of NNP may not be the level corresponding to full employment. A recessionary gap is the increase in desired spending required to push the equilibrium NNP up to the full-employment level. An inflationary gap is the decrease in desired spending required to push the equilibrium NNP down to its full-employment level (at initial prices).

Policy makers receive a lot of help in stabilizing the economy from our automatic stabilizers—automatic changes in tax revenues, unemployment compensation and welfare payments, corporate dividends, family saving, and farm aid. However, the automatic stabilizers can only cut down on variations in unemployment and inflation, not eliminate them. Discretionary programs are needed to supplement the effects of these automatic stabilizers. Such discretionary actions include changing government expenditure on public works and other programs, changing welfare payments and other such transfers, and changing tax rates. An important problem with some of these tools of fiscal policy is the lag in time before they can be brought into play.

At least three policies concerning the government budget have received considerable attention. First, the budget can be balanced each and every year. Second, the budget can be balanced over the course of the business cycle. Third, the budget can be set in a way that will promote full employment with stable prices whether or not this means that the budget is unbalanced over considerable periods of time. The history of the past 40 years has seen enormous changes in the public's attitude toward the government budget. Forty years ago, the prevailing doctrine was that the budget should be balanced each year; now the attitude seems to be that the budget should be used as a tool to reduce unemployment and inflation. Some of the popular misconceptions concerning budget deficits and budget surpluses can be avoided by the use of the full-employment budget, which shows the difference between tax revenue and government expenditure that would result if we had full employment.

CONCEPTS FOR REVIEW

$C + I + G$ line	Full-employment budget	Discretionary fiscal policy
Deficit	Functional finance	Balanced budget
Surplus	Automatic stabilizers	Recessionary gap
		Inflationary gap

QUESTIONS FOR DISCUSSION AND REVIEW

1. Suppose that the consumption function in a particular economy is given by the following table:

Disposable income (billions of dollars)	Consumption expenditure (billions of dollars)
400	350
500	425
600	500
700	575
800	650

Assuming that no taxes are imposed, what is the equilibrium value of NNP if government expenditures are $50 billion and desired investment is $50 billion?

2. Based on the data in Question 1, plot the $C + I + G$ line in a graph. Using a graph of this sort, estimate the effect on the equilibrium level of NNP of a \$10 billion increase in government spending.

3. Suppose that taxes are 20 percent of NNP. Using the data in Question 1, fill in the blanks below.

NNP (billions of dollars)	Consumption expenditure (billions of dollars)
—	350
—	425
—	500
—	575
—	650

4. Using the data in Question 3, what is the equilibrium value of NNP if government expenditures are \$50 billion and desired investment is \$50 billion? How does this result compare with that in Question 1? Explain the difference between these two results.

5. Using the data in Question 3, is the government's budget balanced at the equilibrium level of NNP if government expenditures are \$50 billion and desired investment is \$50 billion? If not, how big is the surplus or deficit?

6. Describe the balanced-budget multiplier. If both government expenditures and taxes rise by the same amount, what is the effect, according to the balanced-budget multiplier?

7. "An important advantage of public works as a tool of fiscal policy is that they can be started quickly. An important advantage of tax rate changes is that they almost never get embroiled in partisan politics." Comment and evaluate.

8. "The full-employment budget is just a lot of hocum to persuade the public that big deficits are smaller and less inflationary than they really are." Comment and evaluate.

9. According to Joseph Pechman, "Among taxes, the federal individual income tax is the leading [automatic] stabilizer." Explain why, and discuss the significance of this fact. He also says that "on the expenditure side, the major built-in stabilizer is unemployment compensation." Again, explain why, and discuss the significance of this fact.

10. According to Maurice Stans, "The federal government should have a balanced budget; its expenditures, especially in times like these, should not exceed its income." Do you agree? Why or why not?

12 Business Fluctuations and Economic Forecasting

The American economy has not grown at a constant rate: instead, output has expanded rapidly in some periods; little, if at all, in others; and actually contracted in still others. Our history indicates that national output, employment, and the price level tend to fluctuate. These fluctuations, often mild, sometimes violent, are frequently called business cycles. The average citizen, as well as the government official or the business executive, needs to know why these fluctuations occur and whether they can be avoided. This chapter summarizes some of the leading theories advanced to answer these questions.

We also take up a related question of great practical importance: can business fluctuations be forecasted? More and more, economic models are being used by government and industry to forecast changes in GNP and other economic variables. Economic forecasting has become a very important part of the economist's job. Although no reputable economist would claim that economic forecasting is very precise or reliable, the forecasts produced by relatively sophisticated models are watched closely by decision makers around the world. In the latter part of this chapter, we describe some of the more widely used forecasting techniques, and see how accurate they have proved in the past.

Business Fluctuations

To illustrate what we mean by "business fluctuations"—or the "business cycle"—let's look at how national output has grown in the United States since World War I. Figure 12.1 shows the behavior of real GNP (in constant dollars) in the United States since 1919. It is clear that output has grown considerably during this period; indeed, GNP is more than 5 times what it was 50 years ago. It is also clear that this growth has not been steady. On the contrary, although the long-term trend has been upward, there have been periods—like 1919-21, 1929-33, 1937-38, 1944-46, 1948-49, 1953-54, 1957-58, 1969-70, and 1973-75—when national output has declined.

Let's define the full-employment level of GNP as the total amount of goods and services that could have been produced if the unemployment rate had been 4 percent. Figure 12.1 shows that national output tends to rise and approach its full-employment level for a while, then falter and fall below this level, then rise to approach it once more, then fall below it again, and so on. For example, output remained close to the full-employment level in the prosperous mid-1920s, fell far below this level in the depressed 1930s, and rose again to this level once we entered World War II. This movement of national output is sometimes called the ***business cycle,*** but it must be recognized that these cycles are far from regular or consistent. On the contrary, they are very irregular.

Each cycle can be divided into four phases, as shown in Figure 12.2. The ***trough*** is the point where national output is lowest relative to its full-employment level. ***Expansion*** is the subsequent phase during which national output rises. The ***peak*** occurs when national output is highest relative to its full-employment level. Finally, ***recession*** is the subsequent phase during which national output falls.[1] Besides these four phases, two other

[1] More precisely, the peak and trough are generally defined in terms of deviations from the long-term trend of national output, rather than in terms of deviations from the full-employment level of national output. But the latter definition tends to be easier for beginners to grasp.

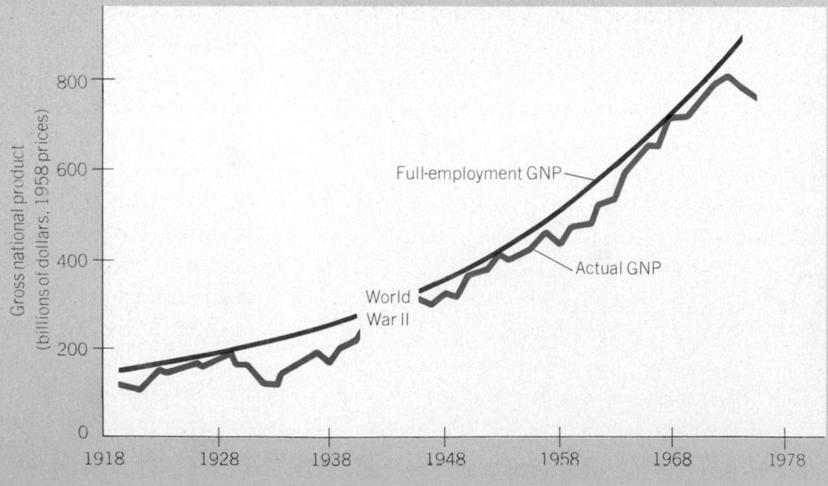

Figure 12.1
Gross National Product (in 1958 dollars), United States, 1918–74, Excluding World War II
Real GNP has not grown steadily. Instead, it has tended to approach its full-employment level, then to falter and fall below this level, then to rise once more, and so on. This movement of national output is sometimes called the business cycle.

Figure 12.2
Four Phases of Business Fluctuation
Each cycle can be divided into four phases: trough, expansion, peak, and recession.

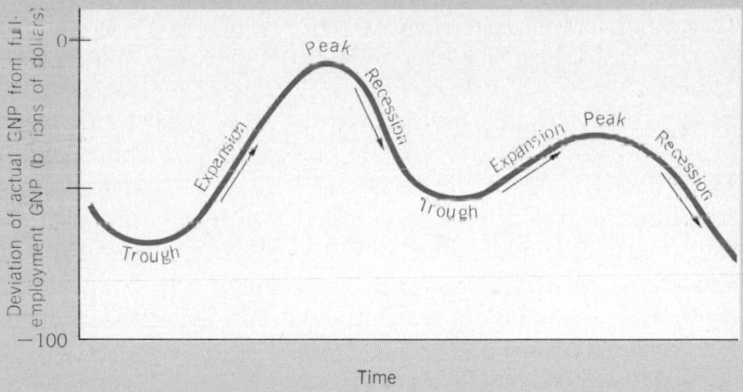

terms are frequently used to describe stages of the business cycle. A ***depression*** is a period when national output is well below its full-employment level; it is a severe recession. Depressions are, of course, periods of excessive unemployment. ***Prosperity*** is a period when national output is close to its full-employment level. Prosperity, if total spending is too high relative to potential output, can be a time of inflation. Of course, in some business cycles, the peak may not be a period of prosperity because output may be below its full-employment level, or the trough may not be a period of depression because output may not be far below its full-employment level.

Since World War II, peaks have occurred in 1948, 1953, 1957, 1960, 1969, and 1973, while troughs have occurred in 1949, 1954, 1958, 1961, 1970, and 1975. None of these recessions has been very long or very deep (although the 1974–75 recession was more severe than the others). We have done better since the war at avoiding and cushioning recessions, partly because of improvements in economic knowledge of the causes and cures of business cycles. Note that, although these cycles have certain things in common, they are highly individualistic. For certain classes of phenomena, it may be true that "if you've seen one, you've seen them all," but not for business cycles; they vary too much in length and nature. Moreover, the basic set of factors responsible for the recession and the expansion differs from cycle to cycle.[2] This means that any theory designed to explain them must be broad enough to accommodate their idiosyncracies.

It is also worth stressing that investment seems to be the component of total spending that varies most over the course of a business cycle. Investment goes down markedly during recessions and increases markedly during expansions; on the other hand, consumption generally moves along with only slight bumps and dips.[3] The volatility of investment, together with the reasons for this volatility, are important clues to the cause of many business cycles. We shall see that this variation in investment plus our old friend (of Chapter 10), the multiplier, can produce the sorts of business fluctuations that have occurred in the United States.

[2] For example, there is some evidence that every so often, a business boom, or peak, takes place at about the same time as a boom in building construction; thus such a peak is buoyed further by this favorable conjuncture—and every so often, a trough is lowered by it. These long swings in building (and other phenomena), lasting 15 to 25 years, are called Kuznets cycles after Harvard's Nobel laureate, Simon Kuznets, who has devoted considerable study to them. See Alvin Hansen, *Business Cycles and National Income*, New York: Norton, 1962.

[3] However, expenditure on consumer durables is more volatile than other consumption expenditure. Moreover, the consumption function can shift, as it did after World War II. (Recall the discussion of this shift in Chapter 10.)

Causes of Business Fluctuations

Government Spending and Expectations

Like investment, *government spending* too can sometimes cause business fluctuations. In Chapter 11, we described how government expenditures might be used to stabilize the economy. The unfortunate fact is that in the past the government's spending—particularly during and after wars—has sometimes been a major destabilizing force, resulting in business fluctuations. Recall from Chapter 8 the great bulge in government spending during World War II and the lesser bulges during the Korean and Vietnam Wars. These increases in spending produced strong inflationary pressures. The price level rose over 50 percent during 1940-46 (World War II), and major inflationary spurts also occurred during the wars in Korea and Vietnam.

Government spending has been a destabilizing force after, as well as during, wars. The recession in 1953-54 was caused primarily by the reduction in government expenditures when the Korean War came to a close. When hostilities terminated, government expenditures were reduced by more than $10 billion. Government spending sometimes has also had the same destabilizing effect in other than wartime or postwar situations. The recession in 1957-58 was aggravated by a drop in defense expenditures in late 1957. Faced with this drop, the defense contractors cut their inventories and expenditures for plant and equipment.

Another factor is the nature and behavior of *expectations.* For example, in the recession of 1974-75, businessmen's expectations became decidedly more pessimistic. Capital spending was cut by over $15 billion and inventory investment by over $17 billion. (Fortunately, the economy began to move upward in mid-1975.) Firms' expectations play a significant role in amplifying business fluctuations. Decisions made at any point in time depend on expectations concerning the future. For example, when a firm builds a new warehouse, it has certain expectations concerning the extent of its sales in the future, the price it will have to pay for labor and transportation, and so on. In forming their expectations, businessmen often tend to follow the leader. As more and more businessmen and analysts predict a rosy future, others tend to jump on the bandwagon. This means that, as the economy advances from a trough, optimistic expectations concerning sales and profits tend to spread, slowly at first, then more and more rapidly. These expectations generate investment, which in turn increases national output. Thus the rosy expectations are self-fulfilling, at least up to a point. (In this area, even if "wishing won't make it so," expecting may turn the trick!) The result is that the expansion is fueled by self-fulfilling and self-augmenting expectations.

Eventually, however, these expectations are not fulfilled, perhaps because full-employment ceilings cause national output to grow at a slower rate, perhaps because the government cuts back its spending (as in 1953-54), perhaps for some other reason. Now the process goes into reverse. Pessimistic expectations appear; and as national output begins to decline, these expectations spread more and more rapidly. These expectations also tend to be self-fulfilling. Businessmen, feeling that the outlook for sales and profits is unfavorable, cut back on their investing, which in turn reduces national output. Thus the recession is made more serious by the epidemic of gloom. In any theory of business fluctuations, it is necessary to recognize the importance of self-fulfilling expectations.

The Acceleration Principle

Investment in plant and equipment, as we know, varies considerably over the course of the business cycle. One of the most important reasons for this variation is illustrated by the following example. Suppose that the Johnson Shoe Corporation, a maker of women's shoes, requires 1 machine to make 50 pairs of shoes per year. Since each machine (and related plant and facilities) costs $2,000 and each pair of shoes costs $20, it takes $2 worth of plant and equipment to produce $1 worth of output per year. In 1968, we suppose that the quantity of the firm's plant and equipment was exactly in balance with its output. In other words, the firm had no excess capacity; sales were $10,000 and the actual stock of capital was $20,000. The firm's sales in subsequent years are shown in Table 12.1. For example, in 1969 its sales increased to $12,000; in 1970 they increased to $14,000; and so forth.

Table 12.1 also shows the amount the firm will have to invest each year in order to produce the amount it sells. Let's begin with 1969. To produce $12,000 worth of product, the firm must have $24,000 worth of capital. This means that it must increase its stock of capital from $20,000 the amount it has in 1968 to $24,000.[4] In other words, it must increase its stock of capital by $4,000, which means that its net investment in plant and equipment must equal $4,000. But this is not the same as its gross investment—the amount of plant and equipment the firm must buy—because the firm must also replace some plant and equipment that wears out. Suppose that $1,000 of plant and equipment wear out each year: then gross investment in 1969 must equal net investment ($4,000) plus $1,000, or $5,000.

Next, let's look at 1970. The firm's sales in that year are $14,000. To produce this much output, the firm must have $28,000 of capital, which means that it must increase its stock of capital by $4,000 from $24,000 to $28,000. In addition, there is $1,000 of replacement investment to replace plant and equipment that wear out in 1970. In all, the firm's gross investment must be $5,000. In 1971, the firm's sales are $15,000. To produce this output, this firm

[4] Note that the firm's stock of capital is an entirely different concept than its common stock or preferred stock. See Chapter 7.

Table 12.1
Relationship between Sales and Investment, Johnson Shoe Corporation

Year	Sales (thousands of dollars)	Needed stock of capital (thousands of dollars)	Actual stock of capital (thousands of dollars)	Replacement investment (thousands of dollars)	Net investment (thousands of dollars)	Gross investment (thousands of dollars)
1968	10	20	20	1	0	1
1969	12	24	24	1	4	5
1970	14	28	28	1	4	5
1971	15	30	30	1	2	3
1972	16	32	32	1	2	3
1973	16	32	32	1	0	1
1974	15	30	31	0	−1	0
1975	15	30	30	0	−1	0
1976	15	30	30	1	0	1
1977	17	34	34	1	4	5

must have $30,000 of capital, which means that it must increase its stock of capital by $2,000—from $28,000 to $30,000. In addition, there is $1,000 of replacement investment. In all, the firm's gross investment must be $3,000. Table 12.1 shows the results for subsequent years.

What conclusions can be drawn from Table 12.1? First, *changes in sales can result in magnified percentage changes in investment.* For example, between 1968 and 1969 sales went up by 20 percent, whereas gross investment went up by 400 percent. Between 1976 and 1977, sales went up by about 13 percent, whereas gross investment went up by 400 percent. The effect of a decrease in sales is even more spectacular because it tends to drive net investment to zero (or to negative values, as in 1974). Indeed, even gross investment may be driven to zero, as in 1974, if the firm wants to reduce the value of its plant and equipment. To accomplish this, the firm simply does not replace the plant and equipment that wear out.

Second, *the amount of gross investment depends on the rate of increase of sales.* In particular, for gross investment to remain constant year after year, the rate of increase of sales must also remain constant. You can see this in 1969 and 1970. In each of these years, since sales increased from the previous year by the same amount ($2,000), gross investment remained constant at $5,000 per year. It is very important to note that *gross investment will fall when sales begin to increase at a decreasing rate.* The fact that sales are increasing does not insure that gross investment will increase; on the contrary, if sales are increasing at a decreasing rate, gross investment will fall. This is a very important point.

This effect of changes in sales on gross investment is often called the ***acceleration principle,*** since changes in sales result in accelerated, or magnified, changes in investment, and since an increase in investment results from an increase in the growth rate (an ***acceleration***) of sales. The acceleration principle applies to kinds of investment other than plant and equipment. For example, it is easy to show that it applies to inventories and housing as well, since firms often try to maintain a certain amount of inventory for each dollar of sales—just as they often maintain a certain amount of plant and equipment for each dollar of sales.

The Interaction between the Acceleration Principle and the Multiplier

Economists—led by Nobel laureates Paul Samuelson and Sir John Hicks[5]—have shown that the acceleration principle combined with the multiplier may produce business cycles like those experienced in the real world. The basic idea is easy. Suppose that national output is increasing, and the economy is moving up toward full employment. Sales are increasing at an increasing rate. Because of the acceleration principle, the increases in sales result in a high level of investment. And via the multiplier, the high level of investment promotes further increases in national output. Thus the accelerator and multiplier tend to reinforce one another, resulting in a strong upward movement of national output. The economy is in an expansion. It is a good time to be president of the United States, president of a major corporation, or an average citizen.

Eventually, however, the economy nears full employment; and since we have only a certain amount of land, labor, and capital, it simply is impossible to increase national output at the rate experienced during the recovery. Sales, which cannot increase forever at the old rate, begin to increase more slowly. But as we saw in the previous section, the reduction in the rate of increase of sales is the kiss of death for in-

[5] Paul A. Samuelson, "The Interaction between the Multiplier Analysis and the Acceleration Principle," *Review of Economics and Statistics,* 1939; and John Hicks, *A Contribution to the Theory of the Trade Cycle,* Oxford: Oxford University Press, 1950. Also, see R. F. Harrod, *The Trade Cycle,* Oxford: Oxford University Press, 1936.

vestment. Even though sales continue to increase, the drop in the rate of increase means decreasing investment. And this reduction in investment sounds the death knell for the boom, since it reduces national output directly and via the multiplier. The reduction in national output means a reduction in sales, and the reduction in sales means a drastic reduction in investment, through the acceleration principle. The drastic reduction in investment means a further reduction in national output. The economy is in a recession. Everything is moving downward, with the notable exception of unemployment. People are getting increasingly nervous—including the president of the United States, the presidents of major corporations, and many average citizens.

Eventually, however, firms reduce their stock of capital to the point where it is in balance with their reduced sales. In other words, they go through the sort of process shown in Table 12.1 during 1974-75, when the Johnson Shoe Corporation reduced its stock of capital by refusing to replace worn-out plant and equipment. At the end of this process, the stock of capital is in balance with sales. To keep this balance, firms must now replace worn-out equipment, which means an increase in gross investment. Via the multiplier, this increase in investment results in an increase in national product, which means an increase in sales. Via the acceleration principle, this increase in sales results in an increase in investment, which in turn increases national product. The economy is once again in the midst of a recovery. It is again a good time to be president of the United States, president of a major corporation, or an average citizen. As moviegoers put it, this is where we came in.

This theory, although highly simplified, provides a great many insights into the nature of business fluctuations. One aspect of the theory in particular should be noted: business cycles are self-starting and self-terminating. Recession, trough, recovery, peak—each phase of the business cycle leads into the next. This theory shows that one need not look outside the economic system for causes of the upper and lower turning points—that is, the points where the economy begins to turn down after a recovery or begins to turn up after a recession. These turning points can occur for the reasons we have just indicated.

Inventory Cycles

Inventories also play an important role in business fluctuations. Indeed, the "minor" or "short" business cycle, lasting about two to four years, is sometimes called an ***inventory cycle*** because it is often due largely to variations in inventories. This cycle proceeds as follows. Businessmen, having let their inventories decline during a business slowdown, find that they are short of inventories. They increase their inventories, which means that they produce more than they sell. This investment in inventories has a stimulating effect on national output. So long as the rate of increase of their sales holds up, firms continue to increase their inventories at this rate.[6] Thus inventory investment continues to stimulate the economy. But when their sales begin to increase more slowly, firms begin to cut back on their inventory investment. This reduction in inventory investment has a depressing effect on national output. As their sales decrease, firms cut back again on their inventory investment, further damping national output. Then when inventories are cut to the bone, the process starts all over again.

As an illustration, consider the recession of 1974-75. During the fourth quarter of 1974, inventories were still increasing at an annual rate of about $10 billion. Then because of a drop in sales, businessmen found themselves

[6] As noted above, the acceleration effect discussed in previous sections applies to inventories as well as plant and equipment, since firms often try to maintain inventories equal to a certain percentage of sales. Thus the *rate of increase* of sales will affect the rate of investment in inventories as well as plant and equipment.

with excess inventories. They cut back their orders from suppliers, which in turn had to reduce output and employment. Inventories were reduced at an annual rate of about $20 billion during early 1975. This inventory liquidation played a major role in the recession. Production plummeted. Fortunately, the reduction in inventories all but ceased in the second half of 1975, and production and employment picked up.

Innovations and Random External Events

Let's turn now to a different sort of explanation of business fluctuations. Clearly, the acceleration principle is only one factor influencing gross investment. Since a firm will invest in any project where the returns exceed the costs involved, many investment projects are not triggered by changes in sales. For example, a new product may be invented, and large investments may be required to produce, distribute, and market it. Consider the automobile industry, currently one of America's largest industries. It took big investments by the pioneers in the auto business to get the automobile to the point where it was an important item in the average consumer's budget. Or consider nylon, which Du Pont spent several million dollars to develop. It took large investments before nylon was on its way.

Major innovations do not occur every day; neither do they occur at a constant rate. There are more in some years than in others, and sheer chance influences the number of innovations in a given year. Similarly, chance greatly influences the timing of many other types of events that bear on the level of output and investment. These include crop failures, hurricanes, and other such natural disasters, as well as man-made events, like strikes in major industries and financial panics, which also affect output and investment.

Let's suppose that these events—innovations and other occurrences that have a major effect on investment—occur more or less at random. Because so many factors influence the timing of each such event, we cannot predict how many will occur in a particular year. Instead, the number is subject to chance variation, like the number thrown in a dice game or the number of spades in a poker hand. In particular, suppose that the chance that one of these events occurs in one year is about the same as in another year.

If this is the case, economists—led by Norway's Nobel laureate, Ragnar Frisch[7]—have shown that business cycles are likely to result. The basic idea is simple enough. The economy, because of its internal structure, is like a pendulum or rocking chair. If it is subjected to random shocks—like pushing a rocking chair every now and then—it will move up and down. These random shocks are the bursts of investment that arise as a consequence of a great new invention or of the development of a new territory, or for some other such reason. These bursts play the role of the forces hitting the pendulum or the rocking chair. To a considerable extent, they may be due to noneconomic events or forces, but whatever their cause, they bang into the economy and shove it in one direction or another.

Of course, the occurrence of these shocks is not the whole story. Business fluctuations in this model do not occur only because of the random events that affect investment. In addition, the economy must respond to—and amplify—the effects of these stimuli. The economy must be like a rocking chair, not a sofa. (If you whack a sofa every now and then, you are likely to hurt your hand, but not to move the sofa much.) Frisch showed that the economy is likely to respond to, and amplify, these shocks. This model explains the fact, stressed in a previous section, that although cycles bear some

[7] Ragnar Frisch, "Propagation Problems and Impulse Problems in Dynamic Economics," *Economic Essays in Honor of Gustav Cassel,* London: Allen and Unwin, 1933.

family resemblance, no two are really alike. Thus the model has the advantage of not explaining more than it should. It does not imply that business fluctuations are more uniform and predictable than they are.

This theory provides valuable insight into the nature of business fluctuations. Like the theory of the interaction of the acceleration principle and the multiplier, it contains important elements of truth, although it obviously is highly simplified. Each of these theories focuses on factors that may be partly responsible for business fluctuations. They complement one another, in the sense that both processes—the interaction of the multiplier and the acceleration principle, and the random external stimuli to investment—may be at work. There is no need to choose between these theories: both help to explain business fluctuations, and both are far from the whole truth.

Monetary Factors

Finally, we must stress that *monetary factors are of great importance in causing business fluctuations.* By monetary factors we mean the rate at which the money supply grows, the rate of interest, and the availability of credit. The Federal Reserve System has major powers over these factors in the United States. As we shall see in Chapter 15, these factors figured significantly in slowing down the boom of the late 1960s and in reducing inflationary pressures during the 1970s. These factors are so important that we shall devote the next several chapters entirely to them. In economics as in other aspects of life, money counts.

Can Business Fluctuations Be Avoided?

Now that we have looked at some theories designed to explain business fluctuations, we are led to ask whether they (the fluctuations, not the theories) can be avoided in the future. To some extent, a discussion of this question is premature, since we have not yet taken up monetary policy. But there is no reason to postpone answering it in general terms, waiting for subsequent chapters to provide more detailed discussions of various aspects of the answer.

On the basis of our increased knowledge of the reasons for business fluctuations and the growing acceptance of modern monetary and fiscal policy, some people seem to think the business cycle has been licked. That is, they feel that we can now use monetary and fiscal policy to head off a recession or a boom, and in this way offset the processes and events that destabilize the economy. This is a rather optimistic view, although the evidence does indicate that we have been able to reduce the severity and frequency of major recessions in recent years. Our record in this regard has been distinctly better than in pre-World-War-II days, although the 1973-75 recession was rather severe.

Does this mean that a major depression—like that experienced in the 1930s—is impossible? The answer is no. Even though we now know how to prevent a depression, one could still occur through stupidity or some weird sequence of events. But the probability of such a depression is very, very small, given our automatic stabilizers and the fact that policy makers—and the electorate—know now that fiscal policy and monetary policy can be used to push the economy toward full employment.

It seems unlikely, however, that the small recessions—the "dips" and "pauses"—are a thing of the past. There will be ups and downs in spending on plant and equipment, there will be fluctuations in inventories, there will be military build-ups and cutbacks, and changes in government spending and in tax rates. All these things can be destabilizing, and existing economic knowledge is not sufficiently precise to allow policy makers to iron out the resulting small deviations of national output from its long-term upward trend. Although there has been a certain amount of optimistic talk about "fine-tuning" of the economy, the truth is that we lack the knowledge or the means to do it.

Finally, the prospect for inflation is not so bright. The recent record of the United States has not been particularly encouraging. We have just about learned that a balanced budget is not the touchstone of fiscal policy, but we have still to learn how to maintain reasonably full employment with reasonably stable prices. This is a very difficult problem, and an important one, which we shall discuss in much greater detail in Chapters 13, 15, and 16.

Can Business Fluctuations Be Forecasted?

How useful are modern economic theories in forecasting NNP? This is a perfectly reasonable question. After all, when you study physics or chemistry, you expect to come away with certain principles that will enable you to predict physical or chemical phenomena. To the extent that economics is a science, you have a right to expect the same thing, since an acid test of any science is how well it predicts.

This question is also of great practical importance. Government officials are enormously interested in what NNP is likely to be in the next year or so, since they must try to anticipate whether excessive unemployment or serious inflationary pressures are developing. Business executives are equally interested, since their firms' sales, profits, and needs for equipment depend on NNP. For these reasons, forecasting is one of the principal jobs of economists in government and industry.

The first thing that must be said is that, in forecasting as in most other areas, economics is not an exact science. If an economist tells you he can predict exactly what NNP will be next year, you can be pretty sure that he is talking through his hat. Of course, by luck, he may be able to predict correctly, but lucky guesses do not a science make. However, although economic forecasting is not perfectly accurate, economic forecasts are still useful. Since governments, firms, and private individuals must continually make decisions that hinge on what they expect will happen, there is no way that they can avoid making forecasts, explicit or implicit. Really the only question is how best to make them.

There is considerable evidence that, even though forecasts based on economic models are sometimes not very good, they are better—on the average—than those made by noneconomists. There is no substitute for economic analysis in accurate forecasting over the long haul. Of course, this really isn't very surprising. It would be strange if economists, whose profession it is to study and predict economic phenomena, were to do worse than those without this training—even if the others are tycoons or politicians. Further, it would be strange if government and industry were to hire platoons of economists at fancy prices—which they do—if they couldn't predict any better than anyone else.

In the realm of economic forecasting, what is a good batting average? According to M.I.T.'s Paul Samuelson,

> In economic forecasting of the direction of change, we ought to be able to do at least .500 just by tossing a coin. And taking advantage of the undoubted upward trend in all modern economies, we can bat .750 or better just by parrot-like repeating, "Up, Up." The difference between the men and the boys, then, comes between an .850 performance and an .800 performance. Put in other terms, the good forecaster, who must in November make a point-estimate of GNP for the calendar year ahead, will over a decade, have an average error of perhaps one percent, being in a range of $12 billion with reality being $6 billion on either side of the estimate. And a rather poor forecaster may, over

> the same period, average an error of 1½ percent. When we average the yearly results for a decade, it may be found that in the worst year the error was over 2 percent, compensated by rather small errors in many of the years not expected to represent turning points.[8]

Economists have no single method for forecasting NNP or GNP. They vary in their approaches just as physicians, for example, differ in theirs. But reputable economists tend to use one of a small number of forecasting techniques, each of which is described below. Of course, many economists do not restrict themselves to one technique, but rely on a combination of several, using one to check on another.

Leading Indicators

Perhaps the simplest way to forecast business fluctuations is to use ***leading indicators,*** which are certain economic series that typically go down or up before national output does. The National Bureau of Economic Research, founded by Wesley C. Mitchell (1874–1948), has carried out detailed and painstaking research to examine the behavior of various economic variables over a long period of time, in some cases as long as 100 years. The Bureau has attempted to find out whether each variable goes down before, at, or after the peak of the business cycle, and whether it turns up before, at, or after the trough. Variables that go down before the peak and up before the trough are called ***leading series.*** Variables that go down at the peak and up at the trough are called ***coincident series.*** And those that go down after the peak and up after the trough are called ***lagging series.***

It is worthwhile examining the kinds of variables that fall into each of these three categories, since they give us important facts concerning the anatomy of the cycle. According to the Bureau, some important leading series are business failures, new orders for durable goods, average work week, building contracts, stock prices, certain wholesale prices, and new incorporations. These are the variables that tend to turn down before the peak and turn up before the trough.[9] Coincident series include employment, industrial production, corporate profits, and gross national product, among many others. Some typical lagging series are retail sales, manufacturers' inventories, and personal income.

Economists sometimes use leading series as forecasting devices. There are good economic reasons why these series turn down before a peak or up before a trough. In some cases, they indicate changes in spending in strategic areas of the economy, while in others they indicate changes in businessmen's and investors' expectations. Both to guide the government in determining its economic policies and to guide firms in their planning, it is important to try to spot turning points—peaks and troughs—in advance. This, of course, is the toughest part of economic forecasting. Economists sometimes use these leading indicators as evidence that a turning point is about to occur. If a large number of leading indicators turn down, this is viewed as a sign of a coming peak. If a large number turn up, this is thought to signal an impending trough.

Unfortunately, the leading indicators are not very reliable. It is true that the economy has seldom turned down in recent years without a warning from these indicators. This is fine. But unfortunately these indicators have turned down on several occasions—1952 and 1962, for example—when the economy did not turn down subsequently. Thus they sometimes provide false signals. Also, in periods of expansion, they sometimes turn down too long be-

[8] Paul A. Samuelson, "Economic Forecasting and Science," in his *Readings in Economics,* New York: McGraw-Hill, 1970, pp. 112–13, and reprinted in E. Mansfield, *Economics: Readings, Issues, and Cases,* 2d ed., New York: Norton, 1977.

[9] Of course, business failures turn *up* before the peak and *down* before the trough.

fore the real peak. And in periods of recession, they sometimes turn up only a very short while before the trough, so that we've turned the corner before anything can be done. Nonetheless, these indicators are not worthless. They are watched closely and used to supplement other, more sophisticated forecasting techniques.

Simple Keynesian Models

Leading indicators are used primarily to spot turning points—peaks and troughs. They are of little or no use in predicting GNP (or NNP). To forecast GNP, we need a more sophisticated approach, one more firmly rooted in economic theory. (Leading indicators are largely the product of strictly empirical analysis.) To forecast GNP, it is worthwhile bringing into play the theory we described in Chapters 9 to 11. After all, if the theory is any good, it should help us to forecast GNP. This theory can be used in a variety of ways to help prepare such forecasts, and a first course in economics can provide no more than the most basic introduction to these methods.

One simple way of trying to forecast GNP is to treat certain components of total spending as given and to use these components to forecast the total. This method is sometimes used by the Council of Economic Advisers, among others. For example, suppose that we decide to forecast private investment and government expenditures as a first step, after which we will use these forecasts to predict GNP.[10] Private investment is made up of three parts: expenditures on plant and equipment, residential construction, and changes in inventories. The most important of these parts is expenditure on plant and equipment. To forecast it, the results of surveys of firms' expenditure plans for the next year are helpful. The Department of Commerce and the Securities and Exchange Commission send out questionnaires (at the beginning of each year) to a large number of firms, asking them how much they plan to spend on plant and equipment during the year. The results, which appear in March in the *Survey of Current Business* (a Department of Commerce publication), are pretty accurate. For example, the average error in 1951-63 was only about 3 percent.

These surveys can help us forecast business expenditures on plant and equipment, but what about the other parts of private investment—residential construction and changes in inventories? Lots of techniques are used to forecast them. Some people use construction contracts and similar indicators as the basis for forecasts of residential construction. For inventory changes, some people watch surveys (like those that have been carried out by *Fortune* magazine and the Commerce Department) which ask companies about their inventory plans.

Next, we need a forecast of government expenditures. At the federal level, it is possible to forecast government expenditures on the basis of the president's proposed budget or Congress's appropriations (although these forecasts can sometimes be quite wrong, as in the case of the Vietnam build-up when expenditures were higher than expected). At the state and local level, it is often possible to extrapolate spending levels reasonably well.

Suppose that, having studied as many relevant factors as we can, we finally conclude that in our best estimate private investment plus government expenditure will equal $600 billion next year. How do we go from this estimate to an estimate of GNP? Suppose that consumers in the past have devoted about 90 percent of their disposable income to consumption expenditure, and that disposable income has been about 70 percent of GNP. Assuming that this will also be true again next year, it follows that consumption expenditure will equal 63 percent (90 percent times 70 percent) of GNP. In other words,

[10] We continue to ignore net exports in this part of the book because they are quite small. Chapters 20 and 21 will study them in some detail.

$$C = .63Y, \tag{12.1}$$

where C is consumption expenditure and Y is GNP. Also, by definition,

$$Y = C + I + G,$$

where I is gross private investment and G is government expenditure. Since $I + G = 600$, it follows that

$$Y = C + 600. \tag{12.2}$$

Substituting the righthand side of Equation (12.1) for C,

$$Y = .63Y + 600,$$

or

$$\begin{aligned} Y - .63Y &= 600 \\ .37Y &= 600 \\ Y &= \frac{600}{.37} \\ &= 1{,}622. \end{aligned}$$

Thus our forecast for GNP next year is $1,622 billion.

At this point, our job may seem to be over. But it really isn't; we must check this forecast in various ways. For example, it implies that consumption expenditures next year will be $1,022 billion. (Since $C = .63Y$, according to Equation (12.2), and Y equals 1,622, C must equal 1,022.) Does this seem reasonable? For example, how does it compare with the latest results of the survey of consumer buying plans carried out at the Survey Research Center at the University of Michigan? Also, the forecasted level of GNP must be compared with the productive capacity of the economy. Do we have the physical capacity to produce this much at stable prices? To what extent will the general price level be pushed upward? Moreover, our assumptions concerning investment and government spending must be re-examined in the light of our forecast of GNP. If GNP is $1,622 billion, is it reasonable to assume that I will be the amount we initially forecasted? Or do we want to revise our forecast of investment? A great many steps must be carried out before we finally put forth a GNP forecast, if we are conscientious and professional in our approach. Moreover, even after the forecast is made, it is often updated as new information becomes available, so the process goes on more or less continuously.

Econometric Models

In recent years, more and more emphasis has been placed on econometric models. Twenty years ago, econometric models were in their infancy, but now the Council of Economic Advisers, the Treasury, the Federal Reserve Board, and other parts of the federal government pay attention to the forecasts made by econometric models—and sometimes construct their own econometric models. Business firms too hire economists to construct econometric models for them, to forecast both GNP and their own sales. ***Econometric models*** are systems of equations estimated from past data that are used to forecast economic variables. There are many kinds of econometric models. For example, some are designed to forecast wage rates; others are designed to forecast the sales of a new product; and still others are designed to forecast a particular company's share of the market. We are concerned here only with econometric models designed to forecast GNP.

The essence of any econometric model is that it blends theory and measurement. It is not merely a general, nonquantitative theory. Useful as such a theory may be, it does not in general permit quantitative or numerical forecasts. Nor is an econometric model a purely empirical result based on little or no theoretical underpinning. Although such results may also be useful, they generally are untrustworthy once the basic structure of the economic situation changes. Most econometric models designed to forecast GNP are built, at least in part, on the theoretical foundations described in previous chapters. In other words, they contain a number of equations, one of which is designed to explain consumption expenditures, one to explain investment expenditures, and so forth.

To see what is involved in the construction of an econometric model, let's consider just one of the equations, the consumption equation. The first step in formulating this equation is to ask ourselves what variables influence consumption expenditure. We know from Chapter 9 that one important determinant of consumption expenditure is disposable income. Thus, if the ratio of disposable income to GNP remains constant, consumption expenditure should be closely related to GNP. To keep things simple, let's suppose that this is the only factor that determines consumption expenditure. Needless to say, this is not the case, but it makes it easier to see what is involved in constructing an econometric model.

Economic theory—and hunch and intuition based on experience and insight—suggest the explanatory variables to be used in an equation, but they alone cannot supply the numbers to be used. For example, if the relationship between consumption expenditure and GNP can be represented by a straight line, it follows that

$$C = a + bY, \qquad (12.3)$$

where C is consumption expenditure and Y is gross national product. But what are the numerical values of a and b? At this point, statistical techniques of various sorts come into play. In the simple case considered here, we can plot consumption expenditure (C) against gross national product (Y) in various years in the past, as shown in Figure 12.3. Then we can pick the values of a and b that fit the data best. For example, as shown in Figure 12.3, an equation based on $a = -1{,}400$ and $b = 2$ does not fit the data at all well, while an equation based on $a = 20$ and $b = .6$ does much better. There are standard statistical methods, known as regression techniques, that can be used to determine which values of a and b fit the data best. These values, once determined, can be inserted into Equation (12.3).

A Small Econometric Model[11]

Econometric models, like many of the good things in life, come in various sizes. Some are composed of lots of equations; some contain only a few. Bigger models are not necessarily

[11] This section, and the following one, are optional and can be omitted without loss of continuity.

Figure 12.3
Relationship between Consumption Expenditure and Gross National Product, 1964–74.
The line $C = 20 + .6Y$ fits the data (indicated by the dots) far better than the line $C = -1{,}400 + 2Y$. (C is consumption expenditure and Y is GNP.) No one needs a Ph.D. in mathematical statistics to see this.

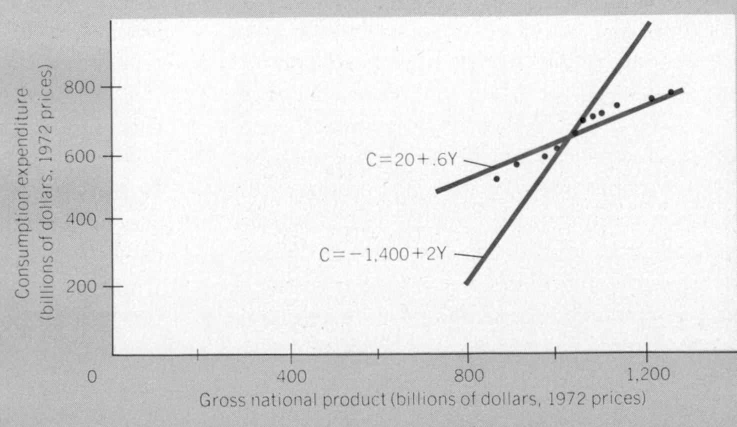

to be preferred to smaller ones, or vice versa. The sort of model that is best for a particular purpose depends on which one predicts best and how costly it is to operate. The best way to get a feel for the nature of an econometric model is to examine one. Let's take a look at a small one designed by Irwin Friend and Paul Taubman of the University of Pennsylvania's Wharton School.[12] Because it contains only five equations, it is an easy one for a student to begin on. More complicated models are discussed in the next section.

Although the discussion in this section and the next one is at an elementary level, the nature of the analysis requires familiarity with the idea of, and notation for, a set of equations. Readers who do not have this familiarity can skip these two sections without losing the thread of the argument.

One of the hardest things to keep track of in econometric models is what each symbol stands for. Let's begin by spelling this out for the Friend-Taubman model. There are nine variables used in the model, and the symbol for each is as follows:

Y = gross national product
C = consumption expenditure
E = plant and equipment expenditures
E^e = expected plant and equipment expenditures, according to surveys
H = residential construction expenditure
L = housing starts (lagged a quarter)
I = inventory investment
S^e = expected business sales, according to surveys
G = government expenditure plus net exports.

Y, C, E, E^e, H, I, G, and S^e are measured in billions of 1954 dollars. L is measured in hundreds of thousands of units. Another symbol that must be explained is Δ, which means the change in a particular variable. For example, ΔY means "the change in Y," or since Y is GNP, it means "the change in GNP." Still another symbol is the subscript $_{-1}$. Any variable with a subscript $_{-1}$ means the value of the variable in the preceding period. Thus a change with a subscript $_{-1}$ means a change occurring between the previous two periods. For example, ΔC_{-1} means the change in consumption expenditure between the last period and the period before. In this model, each period is six months.

Having disposed of the preliminaries, let's look at the model. The first equation explains ΔC, the change in consumption expenditure between this period and last period. According to this equation,

$$\Delta C = 2.18 + .37\Delta Y + .10\Delta C_{-1}. \qquad (12.4)$$

In other words, the change in consumption expenditures equals 2.18 billion (1954) dollars plus .37 times the change in GNP between this period and last period plus .10 times the change in consumption expenditures between last period and the period before. Certainly it is reasonable to expect that the change in consumption will be directly related to the change in GNP. This follows from our discussion of the consumption function in Chapter 9. It is also reasonable to expect that the change in consumption between this period and the last will depend on the change in consumption between the last period and the one before. Basically the reason for this is that there is likely to be a lag in adjustment. The numbers in Equation (12.4), like those in all the equations in the model, were estimated from past data.

The second equation explains ΔE, the change in expenditures on plant and equipment between this period and the last period. According to this equation,

$$\Delta E = -.82 + .63(E^e - E_{-1}) + .08(\Delta Y + \Delta Y_{-1}). \qquad (12.5)$$

[12] Irwin Friend and Paul Taubman, "A Short-Term Forecasting Model," *Review of Economics and Statistics*, August 1964. This model has been revised since publication, and is presented for illustrative purposes only.

In other words, the change in expenditure on plant and equipment equals $-.82$ billion (1954) dollars plus .63 times the difference between expected expenditure on plant and equipment (based on surveys) and actual expenditure on plant and equipment in the previous period, plus .08 times the sum of the change in GNP between this period and the last period and the change in GNP between the last period and the previous period. One would suppose, of course, that the change in actual expenditure on plant and equipment would be directly related to the change indicated by businessmen's expectations concerning their expenditures on plant and equipment. Also, based on the acceleration principle, one would suppose that the amount spent on plant and equipment would be directly related to the rate of change of GNP. Both suppositions are included in Equation (12.5) because neither theory by itself does as well historically as a mixture of both.

The third equation explains ΔH, the change in residential construction between this period and last period. According to this equation,

$$\Delta H = .35 + .58\Delta L + .06(\Delta Y - \Delta Y_{-1}) - .16(E^e - E_{-1}). \qquad (12.6)$$

In other words, the change in expenditure on residential construction equals .35 billion (1954) dollars plus .58 times the change in housing starts (lagged a quarter) plus .06 times the change in the rate of change of GNP minus .16 times the expected change in expenditure on plant and equipment (based on surveys). One would suppose, of course, that the change in expenditure on construction would be directly related to the change in housing starts (lagged a quarter). Also, from the acceleration principle, one would suppose that the amount spent on residential construction would be directly related to the rate of change of GNP. Thus the change in the amount spent on residential construction would be assumed to vary directly with the change in the rate of change of GNP, which of course equals $\Delta Y - \Delta Y_{-1}$. Finally, the change in residential construction is likely to be inversely related to the change in expected expenditures on plant and equipment because if there is a great increase (decrease) in the latter, this will mean higher (lower) interest rates and greater (less) competition for resources which may discourage (encourage) residential construction.

The fourth equation explains ΔI, the change in inventory investment between this period and the last period. According to this equation,

$$\Delta I = 1.51 + .025\Delta S^e + 1.70(E^e - E_{-1}) - 1.15I_{-1}. \qquad (12.7)$$

In other words, the change in inventory investment equals 1.51 billion (1954) dollars plus .025 times the change in total sales expected by businessmen (as given by surveys) plus 1.70 times the difference between expected expenditure on plant and equipment (as given by surveys) and actual expenditure on plant and equipment in the previous period minus 1.15 times the inventory investment in the previous period. The authors of the model argue that the change in inventory investment will be directly related to the change in expected sales, since firms generally want to keep their inventories more or less proportional to their sales. Also, they believe that the change in inventory investment will be directly related to the expected change in expenditure on plant and equipment, since the latter is a good indicator of the general economic outlook. In addition, they state that the change in inventory investment will be inversely related to the level of inventory investment in the previous period. According to their model, if inventory investment was high (low) in the previous period, there will be a smaller (bigger) change in inventory investment than if it was low (high) in the previous period.

Finally, the fifth equation merely states the

obvious fact that the change in GNP must equal the change in consumption expenditures plus the change in each of the parts of gross private investment (expenditures on plant and equipment, residential construction, and inventories) plus the change in government expenditures (plus net exports). In other words,

$$\Delta Y = \Delta C + \Delta E + \Delta H + \Delta I + \Delta G. \quad (12.8)$$

This must be true because Y = consumption + gross private investment + government expenditures (plus net exports). Since gross private investment equals $E + H + I$, it follows that $Y = C + E + H + I + G$. Thus the change in Y must equal the sum of the changes in C, E, H, I, and G.

Econometric models—even small ones like this—are fairly complicated. It is easy to get so engrossed in the details of each equation that we lose sight of the basic purpose of the model—to forecast GNP, in this case. How can we use this model to forecast GNP? As a first step, let's substitute the righthand side of Equation (12.4) for ΔC in Equation (12.8). Also, let's substitute the righthand side of Equation (12.5) for ΔE in Equation (12.8). Let's substitute the righthand side of the Equation (12.6) for ΔH in Equation (12.8), and the righthand side of Equation (12.7) for ΔI in Equation (12.8). All of these substitutions give us an expression for ΔY. In particular,

$$\Delta Y = 3.22 + 2.00\Delta G + 4.34(E_e - E_{-1}) - 2.30I_{-1} + .05\Delta S^e + 1.15\Delta L + .037\,\Delta Y_{-1} + .19\Delta C_{-1}. \quad (12.9)$$

This equation can be used to forecast ΔY—the change in gross national product between the *next* period and the *present* period. To do so, one must insert the appropriate values of ΔC_{-1}, ΔY_{-1}, $(E^e - E_{-1})$, ΔL, ΔS^e, I_{-1}, and ΔG into Equation (12.9). For example, if the change in consumption between this period and the last period was \$1 billion, we would substitute 1 for ΔC_{-1} in Equation (12.9). And if the change in gross national product between this period and the last period was \$2 billion, we would substitute 2 for ΔY_{-1}, and so on for the other variables on the righthand side of Equation (12.9). When the value of each of the variables has been inserted into Equation (12.9), we are the proud possessor of a forecast of ΔY—the change in gross national product between the next period and the present period.

Large Econometric Models

The econometric model just presented is a small one designed to forecast changes in GNP over the next six months. The economists who constructed it did not intend it to be used to estimate the effects of government policy—for example, changes in tax rates or government expenditures—or to forecast prices, income distribution, unemployment, capital utilization, and so forth. In recent years, there has been a remarkable amount of activity in the economics profession here and abroad, aimed at the construction of larger econometric models, which may be able to represent the behavior of the economy in richer and more complete detail. The leading figure in the development of such models has been Lawrence Klein of the University of Pennsylvania. Two of the models that he has constructed—or helped to construct—are known as the Wharton model and the Brookings model.

The original Wharton model, published in 1967, contained about 50 equations: 3 equations that explain various components of consumer spending (consumer nondurable goods, automobiles, and other consumer durable goods), 6 equations to explain various components of private investment (expenditure on plant and equipment, residential housing, and inventory changes), 4 explaining depreciation, 4 explaining tax receipts and transfer payments, 5 explaining the level of output in various sectors of the economy, 7 explaining price level changes in various sectors of the economy, and other equations explaining hours worked, wage rates, unemployment, interest rates, profits, and other variables. This model was used to make quarterly forecasts of GNP, unemployment, changes in the price level, and other variables a year or more ahead. It was also used to forecast the effects on the economy of alternate government policies–for example, to estimate the effects of changes in tax rates on GNP and unemployment. Its forecasts were watched closely and publicized widely in the business commmunity and in government.[13] In recent years, the Wharton model has been extended and refined in numerous ways. It currently contains over 200 equations.

The Brookings model–more formally, the Brookings Quarterly Econometric Model of the United States–was also composed of well over 200 equations. Produced by a team of over 20 well-known economists, headed by Klein and Harvard's James Duesenberry, work on this model went on for over 10 years, and although it was designed largely for experimental purposes, it provided economists with many useful results.[14] Another large model is the Federal Reserve Board-Massachusetts Institute of Technology-Pennsylvania model, which contains over 125 equations. It emphasizes the financial variables that are of importance to the Federal Reserve System.[15] In addition, large econometric models have been built by Data Resources, Inc., Chase Econometrics, the University of Michigan, UCLA, and the Bureau of Economic Analysis of the Department of Commerce, among others.

[13] Michael Evans and Lawrence Klein, *The Wharton Econometric Forecasting Model*, Philadelphia: University of Pennsylvania Press, 1967.

[14] J. Duesenberry, G. Fromm, L. Klein, and E. Kuh, *The Brookings Quarterly Econometric Model of the United States*, Chicago: Rand McNally, 1965.

[15] Some econometric models, such as those developed at the Federal Reserve Bank of St. Louis, have been built largely on monetary factors. In the following three chapters, we shall discuss the effects of monetary factors on national output, employment, and the price level.

Table 12.2
Predictive Record of Some Leading Economic Forecasting Techniques

		Error (in billions of dollars)				
Year	Actual GNP	Average general forecast (Federal Reserve Bank of Philadelphia)	Council of Economic Advisers	Michigan model	Friend-Taubman model	Wharton model
1959	484	−13	—	−19	—	
1960	504	4	—	−10	—	
1961	520	−7	—	2	—	
1962	560	4	14	4	—	1
1963	591	−11	−6	−6	4	1
1964	632	−7	−4	−4	5	1
1965	685	−10	−6	−14	−3	−4
1966	748	−7	−10	−7	—	−4
1967	790	4	6	13	—	3
Average error (1963–67)		7.8	6.4	8.8	4.0	2.8

Source: Michael Evans, *Macroeconomic Activity*, New York: Harper & Row, 1969, p. 516.

Econometric Forecasts: The Track Record

How well can econometric models forecast? Table 12.2 compares the success of the Wharton model, the Friend-Taubman model, and a model constructed at the University of Michigan's Research Seminar in Quantitative Economics in predicting GNP during 1959–67 with the forecasts of the Council of Economic Advisers and a composite forecast of GNP from about 50 economists which is tabulated each year by the Federal Reserve Bank of Philadelphia. With the exception of the Friend-Taubman model, these forecasts were made at the end of the previous year. The Friend-Taubman forecasts were made in mid-March.

In this period, the econometric models seemed to do better than the average forecast of general economists. While the general economists were off, on the average, by about \$8 billion during the period, the econometric models were off by an average of about \$5 billion. The performance of the Wharton model in this period was particularly impressive. Its average error was only about \$3 billion—or less than ½ of 1 percent. In this ball game, that is a very fancy batting average: recall Samuelson's remarks quoted earlier.

However, before you jump to the conclusion that the problem of economic forecasting is now solved, let's turn to the predictive performance of various models in more recent years. Table 12.3 shows how well six well-known models—those of the Bureau of Economic Analysis, Chase Econometrics, Data Resources, Inc., Ray C. Fair, and General Electric, as well as the Wharton model—performed during 1970–74. Also, it shows the performance of the average forecast obtained from the American Statistical Association and National Bureau of Economic Research (ASA-NBER) Survey of a large number of general economists. The figures in Table 12.3 are all average errors. For example, the top line in the table shows that, in forecasting one quarter ahead, the ASA-NBER Survey was in error, on the average, by 1.4 percentage points in forecasting the rate of increase of GNP (in money terms), by 1.8 percentage points in forecasting the rate of increase of GNP (in real terms), by 0.1 percentage points in forecasting the unemployment rate, and by 1.7 percentage points in forecasting the rate of increase of prices.

In this period, there seems to be less difference between the accuracy of the econometric models and that of the average forecast of general economists than in the earlier period. For example, although the Wharton model sometimes has a smaller average error than the ASA-NBER Survey, the reverse is sometimes true. But the date when the various forecasts were made was not the same, and so the results are not entirely comparable. More important is the fact that the GNP forecasts in this later period seem considerably poorer than in the earlier one. Whereas the most accurate models in the earlier period had an average error of only about ½ of 1 percent, the average error in the later period was much higher. In particular, after mid-1973, the forecasting performance of both the econometric models and the general economists declined considerably.

An important reason for this decline in performance was the difficulty in incorporating the effects of the Arab oil embargo, the drastic oil price increase, and the high inflation rate of 1973–74 into such models. The assumption underlying any econometric model is that the basic structure of the economy—the numbers in the equations of the model—will not change much. If this assumption does not hold, the model is in trouble. After all, any econometric model is powered by past data, not magic. Another reason why the models did better during 1959–67 was that this was a period of sustained prosperity. It is easier to forecast GNP during a period when it is steadily rising (or steadily falling) than at a turning point in the business cycle, such as 1970 or 1974. Unfortunately, the turning points are often of major significance to policy makers.

Table 12.3
Average Error (in percentage points) of Forecasts of the Rate of Increase of GNP, the Unemployment Rate, and the Rate of Price Increase, Seven Forecasters, 1970–74.

Forecaster	Rate of increase of GNP (in money terms)	Rate of increase of GNP (in real terms)	Unemployment rate	Rate of price increase
		Forecasts of one quarter ahead		
ASA-NBER Survey	1.4	1.8	0.1	1.7
Bureau of Economic Analysis	1.5	1.6	0.1	1.4
Chase Econometrics	1.3	1.5	0.2	1.4
Data Resources, Inc.	1.7	2.0	0.2	1.8
Ray C. Fair	2.2	2.6	0.2	2.0
General Electric	1.4	1.7	0.1	1.1
Wharton	2.0	1.8	0.2	1.1
		Forecasts of two quarters ahead		
ASA-NBER Survey	1.5	1.4	0.2	1.7
Bureau of Economic Analysis	1.1	1.4	0.2	1.5
Chase Econometrics	1.4	1.5	0.3	1.8
Data Resources, Inc.	1.2	1.6	0.2	1.8
Ray C. Fair	1.9	2.4	0.3	2.1
General Electric	1.3	1.4	0.2	1.4
Wharton	1.3	1.3	0.3	1.6
		Forecasts of three quarters ahead		
ASA-NBER Survey	1.4	1.2	0.3	1.7
Bureau of Economic Analysis	1.3	1.5	0.2	1.7
Chase Econometrics	1.0	1.2	0.3	1.8
Data Resources, Inc.	1.1	1.3	0.2	1.7
Ray C. Fair	1.6	1.9	0.4	2.1
General Electric	1.0	1.3	0.4	1.4
Wharton	1.3	1.2	0.3	1.8
		Forecasts of one year ahead		
ASA-NBER Survey	1.3	1.3	0.3	1.7
Bureau of Economic Analysis	1.2	1.5	0.3	1.7
Chase Econometrics	1.0	1.2	0.3	1.6
Data Resources, Inc.	1.3	1.2	0.3	1.7
Ray C. Fair	1.5	1.9	0.4	2.1
General Electric	1.0	1.2	0.3	1.3
Wharton	1.3	1.0	0.4	1.8

Source: Stephen McNees, "How Accurate Are Economic Forecasts?" *New England Economic Review,* November 1974.

Despite the rather large errors in some recent economic forecasts, neither government nor industry can swear off forecasting. For decades, economic forecasting has played an important role in the decision-making process, both in government and industry. For example, in the recession of 1953-54, President Eisenhower asked Arthur Burns, chairman of the Council of Economic Advisers, to appear at every meeting of the Cabinet until further notice, and summarize developments and prospects. During the 1960s and 1970s, Presidents Kennedy, Johnson, Nixon, Ford, and Carter also paid close attention to economic forecasts. So do most corporation presidents. This isn't because these forecasts are always very good. It's because they are the best available. As Thomas Huxley put it, "If a little knowledge is dangerous, who is the man who has so much as to be out of danger?"

Summary

Changes in sales can result in magnified or accelerated changes in investment; the amount of gross investment depends on the rate of increase of sales. The fact that sales are increasing does not insure that gross investment will increase. On the contrary, if sales are increasing at a decreasing rate, gross investment is likely to fall. This effect of sales on investment is called the acceleration principle. The interaction of the acceleration principle with the multiplier can cause business cycles. Thus turning points can be generated within the economic system. Investment is also determined by many events that occur more or less at random, like innovations, wars, and so on. The effects of these random shocks can also cause business fluctuations. The short cycles are generally inventory cycles. The acceleration principle also applies to inventories.

Although we are not in a position to erase the small dips and pauses in economic activity, it seems extremely unlikely that we will have another depression of the severity of the 1930s. The reason is that policy makers—and the electorate—know that monetary and fiscal policy can be used to push the economy back toward full employment. However, the prospect for price stability is not so bright.

Although economics is by no means an exact science, economic forecasts are useful for many purposes. This does not mean that these forecasts are always very accurate. It means only that they are better than noneconomists' forecasts. Economists have a number of techniques for forecasting. One makes use of leading indicators—variables that historically have turned up or down before GNP. Although of some use, these leading indicators are not very reliable. Another technique is based on the use of simple Keynesian models plus surveys and other data. For example, investment and government expenditures (and net exports) are sometimes estimated as a first step. Then, using the historical relationship between consumption and GNP, it is possible to forecast GNP. A third technique is based on econometric models, which are systems of equations estimated from past data. Econometric models blend theory and measurement.

Econometric models may be big or small. An example of a small model is the Friend-Taubman model; an example of a large model is the Wharton model. During the 1960s, econometric models seemed to do somewhat better than the average forecasts of general economists. However, it is important to recognize that econometric models—like any forecasting device in the social sciences—are quite fallible. During the 1970s, the forecasting performance of both the econometric models and general economists seemed to decline. Nonetheless, economic forecasts continue to receive considerable attention from heads of state and heads of firms. This isn't because these forecasts are always very good: it's because they are the best available.

CONCEPTS FOR REVIEW

Business cycle
Trough
Expansion
Peak
Recession
Depression
Prosperity
Inventory cycle
Net investment
Gross investment
Acceleration principle
Leading indicators
Coincident series
Lagging series
Econometric models
Expectations

QUESTIONS FOR DISCUSSION AND REVIEW

1. "What goes up must come down. There is a cycle in economic activity just as in many other things, and one can use this cycle to forecast quite accurately." Comment and evaluate.

2. Suppose that a firm requires $3 in capital for every $1 of its sales. Suppose that none of its capital ever wears out, and that it had $450,000 in capital at the end of 1970. Its sales in subsequent years were as follows:

Year	Sales (dollars)
1971	150,000
1972	180,000
1973	210,000
1974	220,000
1975	225,000
1976	220,000

How much did the firm invest each year?

3. Describe how the multiplier and acceleration principle can interact to result in business fluctuations. To what extent do you think that this interaction is an adequate explanation of recent fluctuations in the American economy?

4. List the dozen technological innovations that you would regard as being the most important in this century. What effect did each have on the American economy, and to what extent did they contribute to business fluctuations?

5. "The government itself is frequently the cause of business fluctuations." Comment and evaluate.

6. "Many short cycles are basically due to inventory fluctuations." Explain and evaluate. Also, describe how the acceleration principle can be applied to inventories.

7. On p. 261, seven leading series are listed. Explain why each of them would be expected to be a leading series, rather than a coincident or lagging series.

8. Suppose that consumption expenditure was $100 billion in 1970 and $105 billion in 1971, and that GNP increased by $10 billion per year from 1971 to 1976. Based on Equation (12.4), what was the value of consumption expenditure from 1972 to 1976?

PART FOUR

Money, Banking, and Stabilization Policy

13 The Role and Importance of Money

According to the maxim of an ancient Roman, "Money alone sets all the world in motion." Although a statement that leaves so little room for the laws of physics or astronomy may be a mite extravagant, no one would deny the importance of money in economic affairs. The quantity of money is a very significant factor in determining the health and prosperity of any economic system. Inadequate increases in the quantity of money may bring about excessive unemployment, while excessive increases in the quantity of money may result in serious inflation. To some economists, a discussion of business fluctuations and economic stabilization that ignores the money supply is like a performance of *Hamlet* that omits the prince. Most economists would not go quite that far, but almost all would agree that the money supply is very important.

In this chapter, we are concerned with the nature and value of money, as well as with the relationship between a nation's money supply and the extent of unemployment and inflation. In particular, we consider questions like: What is money? What determines its value? What factors influence the demand for money, and what factors influence its quantity? What is the relationship between the quantity of money and the price level? What is the relationship between the quantity of money and the level of net national product? To understand the workings of our economy and the nature of our government's economic policies, you must be able to answer these questions.

What Is Money?

We must begin by defining money. At first blush, it may seem natural to define it by its physical characteristics. You may be inclined to say that money consists of bills of a certain size and color with certain words and symbols printed on them, as well as coins of a certain type. But this definition would be too restrictive, since money in other societies has consisted of whale teeth, wampum, and a variety of other things. Thus it seems better to define money by its functions than by its physical characteristics. Like beauty, money is as money does.

Money's first function is to act as a *medium of exchange*. People exchange their goods and services for something called money, and then use this money to buy the goods and services they want. To see how important money is as a medium of exchange, let's suppose that it did not exist. To exchange the goods and services they produce for the goods and services they want to consume, people would resort to *barter*, or direct exchange. If you were a wheat farmer, you would have to go to the people who produce the meat, clothes, and other goods and services you want, and swap some of your wheat for each of these goods and services. Of course this would be a very cumbersome procedure, since it would take lots of time and effort to locate and make individual bargains with each of these people. To get some idea of the extent to which money greases the process of exchange in any highly developed economy, consider all the purchases your family made last year—cheese from Wisconsin and France, automobiles from Detroit, oil from Texas and the Middle East, books from New York, and thousands of other items from all over the world. Imagine how few of these exchanges would have been feasible without money.

Second, money acts as a *standard of value*. It is the unit in which the prices of goods and services are measured. How do we express the price of coffee or tea or shirts or suits? In dollars and cents, of course. Thus money prices tell us the rates at which goods and services can be exchanged. For example, if the money price of a shirt is $12 and the money price of a tie is $4, a shirt will exchange for 3 ties. Put differently, a shirt will be "worth" 3 times as much as a tie.

Money also acts as a *store of value*. A person can hold on to money and use it to buy things later. You often hear stories about people who hoard a lot of money under their mattresses or bury it in their back yards. These people have an overdeveloped appreciation of the role of money as a store of value. But even those of us who are less miserly often use this function of money by carrying some money with us, and keeping some in the bank to make future purchases.

Finally, it should be recognized that money is a social invention. It is easy to assume that money has always existed, but this is not the case. Someone had to get the idea, and people had to come to accept it. Nor has money always had the characteristics it has today. In ancient Greece and Rome, money consisted of gold and silver coins. By the end of the seventeenth century, paper money was established in England; but this paper currency, unlike today's currency, could be exchanged for gold. Only recently has the transition been made to money that is not convertible into gold or silver. But regardless of its form or characteristics, anything that is a medium of exchange, a standard of value, and a store of value is money.

Three Kinds of Money

Like Caesar's Gaul, all money in modern economies is divided into three parts—coins, currency, and demand deposits. ***Coins*** are not really a very large proportion of the total quantity of money in the United States. In all, they amount to only about $8 billion, or about 2 to 3 percent of the total money supply. This is mainly because coins come in such small denominations. It takes a small mountain of pennies, nickels, dimes, quarters, and half-dollars to make even a billion dollars. Of course, the metal in each of these coins is worth less than the face value of the coin; otherwise people would melt them down and make money by selling the metal. In the 1960s, when silver prices rose, the government stopped using silver in dimes and quarters to prevent coins from meeting this fate.

Currency—paper money like the $5 and $10 bills everyone likes to have on hand—constitutes a second and far larger share of the total money supply than coins. Together, currency and coins outstanding totaled about $74 billion in 1975, as shown in Table 13.1. The Federal Reserve System, described in the next chapter, issues practically all of our currency in the form of Federal Reserve notes. Before 1933, it was possible to exchange currency for gold, but this is no longer the case. All American currency (and coin) is presently "fiat" money. It is money because the government says so and because the people accept it. There is no real metallic backing of the currency anymore. But this does not mean that we should be suspicious of the soundness of our currency, since gold backing is not what gives money its value. (In fact, to some extent, cause and effect work the other way: the use of gold to back currencies has in the past increased the value of gold.) Basically, the value of currency depends on its acceptability by people and on its scarcity.

Table 13.1
Money Supply, December 31, 1975, Seasonally Adjusted

	Amount (billions of dollars)
Demand deposits	222.6
Currency and coins	73.8
Total	296.4

Source: Economic Report of the President.

Third, bank deposits subject to payment on demand—so-called ***demand deposits***—are quantitatively by far the biggest part of our money supply, as shown in Table 13.1. At first you may question whether these demand deposits—or checking accounts, as they are commonly called—are money at all. In everyday speech, they often are not considered money. But economists include demand deposits as part of the money supply, and for good reason. After all, you can pay for goods and services just as easily by check as with cash. Indeed, the public pays for more things by check than with cash. This means that checking accounts are just as much a medium of exchange—and just as much a standard of value and a store of value—as cash. Thus, since they perform all of the functions of money, they should be included as money.

Figure 13.1 shows how the money supply—the sum total of coins, paper currency, and demand deposits—has behaved since World War II. You can see that the quantity of money has generally increased from one year to the next, and that the increase has been at an average rate of about 3 or 4 percent per year. However, the rate of increase of the quantity of money

Figure 13.1
Behavior of Money Supply, United States, 1947–75
The money supply, about $300 billion in 1975, has generally increased from year to year, but the rate of increase has by no means been constant.

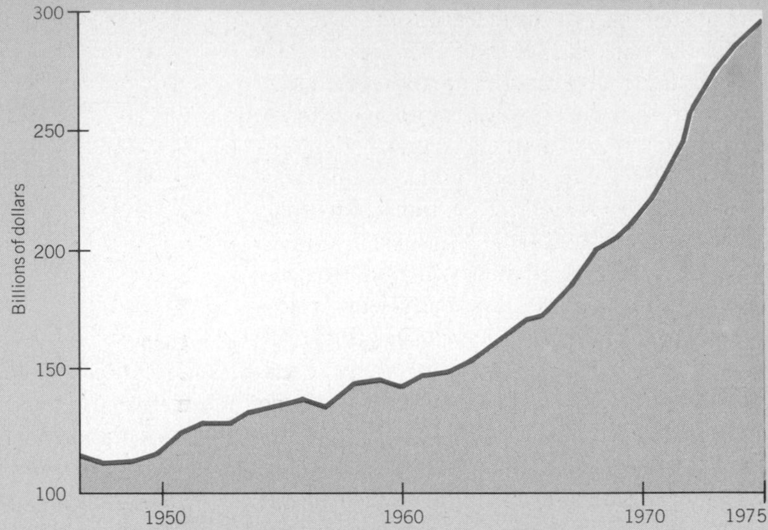

has by no means been constant. In some years, like 1972, the quantity of money increased by about 9 percent; in others, like 1975, it increased by about 4 percent. A great deal will be said later about the importance and determinants of changes in the quantity of money.

Near-Monies

We have just stated that all money is of three kinds—coins, currency, and demand deposits. This is the money supply, narrowly defined. It is not the only definition. There is also the money supply, broadly defined, which includes time or savings deposits as well as coins, currency, and demand deposits. The money supply, narrowly defined, is often called M_1, while the money supply, broadly defined, is often called M_2. Although economists usually use the narrow definition—and when we refer to the money supply in this book, we shall mean this definition—it is sometimes useful to work with the broad definition as well.

Time or savings deposits are excluded from the narrow definition of money because, in most instances, you cannot pay directly for anything with them. For example, suppose that you have a savings account at a commercial bank. You cannot draw a check against it, as you can with a demand deposit. And to withdraw your money from the account, you may have to give the bank a certain amount of notice (although in practice this right may be waived and the bank will ordinarily let you withdraw your money when you want).

On the other hand, economists who use the broad definition feel that time or savings deposits should be included in the money supply because, even if they do not constitute a medium of exchange, they can readily be transformed into cash. You may intend to buy a house sometime in the next year and you may want to keep $5,000 on hand to use as a down payment. You could leave this $5,000 in your checking account, or you could put it in a savings account, where it would earn some interest. Because ordinarily you can withdraw the money from a savings account on short notice, you may decide on this alternative. Since this savings account can so readily be transformed into cash, it is almost like a checking account. Not quite, but almost.

In recent years, the emergence of negotiable order of withdrawal (NOW) accounts has meant that the distinction between checking and savings accounts is even more blurred than in the past. NOW accounts are essentially interest-bearing checking accounts at savings banks and other thrift institutions and banks. First created in 1972 by a Massachusetts savings bank, such accounts are becoming legal in more and more states, particularly in the Northeast. Although they amounted to only about $1.5 billion in 1976, many observers expect them to grow in size. If so, it will no longer be possible to ignore them in the (narrow) definition of the money supply.

Many other assets can also be transformed into cash without much difficulty—though not quite as easily as savings deposits. For example, it is not difficult to convert government bonds into cash. There is no simple way to draw a hard-and-fast dividing line between money and nonmoney, since many assets have some of the characteristics of money. Consequently, there are still other definitions of the money supply that are more inclusive than M_2. But most economists feel that, although assets like government bonds have some of the properties of money, it would be stretching things too far to include them in the money supply. (For one thing, their price varies as interest rates change.)

Economists call such assets ***near-money,*** and recognize that the amount of near-money in the economy has an important effect on spending habits. There is some disagreement among economists as to exactly what is and what isn't near-money, but this needn't concern us here. The major point we want to make is that any dividing line between money and nonmoney must be arbitrary.

The Value of Money

Let's go back to one very important point that was mentioned briefly in a previous section: there is no gold backing for our money. In other words, there is no way that you can exchange a $10 bill for $10 worth of gold. (If you look at a $10 bill, you will see that it says nothing about what the government will give you in exchange for it.) Currency and demand deposits are really just debts, or IOUs. Currency is the debt of the government, while demand deposits are the debts of the commercial banks. Intrinsically, neither currency nor demand deposits have any real value. A $10 bill is merely a small piece of paper, and a demand deposit is merely an entry in a bank's accounts. And, as we have seen, even coins are worth far less as metal than their monetary value.

All this may make you feel a bit uncomfortable. After all, if our coins, currency, and demand deposits have little or no intrinsic value, doesn't this mean that they can easily become worthless? To answer this question, we must realize that basically, *money has value because people will accept it in payment for goods and services.* If your university will accept your check in payment for your tuition, and your grocer will accept a $20 bill in payment for your groceries, your demand deposit and your currency have value. You can exchange them for goods and services you want. And your university or your grocer accepts this money only because they have confidence that they can spend it for goods and services they want.

Thus money is valuable because it will buy things. But how valuable is it? For example, how valuable is $1? Clearly, *the value of a dollar is equivalent to what a dollar will buy. And what a dollar will buy depends on the price level.* If all prices doubled, the value of a dollar would be cut in half, because a dollar would be able to buy only half as many goods and services as it formerly could. On the other hand, if all prices were reduced by 50 percent, the value of a dollar would double, because a dollar would be able to buy twice as many goods and services as it formerly could. You often hear people say that today's dollar is worth only

$.50. What they mean is that it will buy only half what a dollar could buy at some specified date in the past.

It is interesting and important to see how the value of the dollar, as measured by its purchasing power, has varied over time. Figure 13.2 shows how an index of the price level in the United States has changed since 1779. Over time, prices have fluctuated sharply, and the greatest fluctuations have resulted from wars. For example, the price level fell sharply after the Revolutionary War, and our next war—the War of 1812—sent prices skyrocketing, after which there was another postwar drop in prices. The period from about 1820 to about 1860 was marked by relative price stability, but the Civil War resulted in an upward burst followed by a postwar drop in prices. After a period of relative price stability from 1875 to 1915, there was a doubling of prices during World War I and the usual postwar drop. World War II also caused an approximate doubling, but there was no postwar drop in prices.

Clearly, the value of money is inversely related to the price level. In inflationary times, the value of money decreases; the opposite is true when the price level falls (an infrequent phenomenon in the past three decades). Thus the wartime periods when the price level rose greatly were periods when the value of the dollar decreased greatly. The doubling of prices during World War II meant that the value of the dollar was chopped in half. Similarly, the postwar periods when the price level fell greatly were periods when the value of the dollar increased. The 50 percent decline in prices after the Civil War meant a doubling in the value of the dollar. Given the extent of the variation of the price level shown in Figure

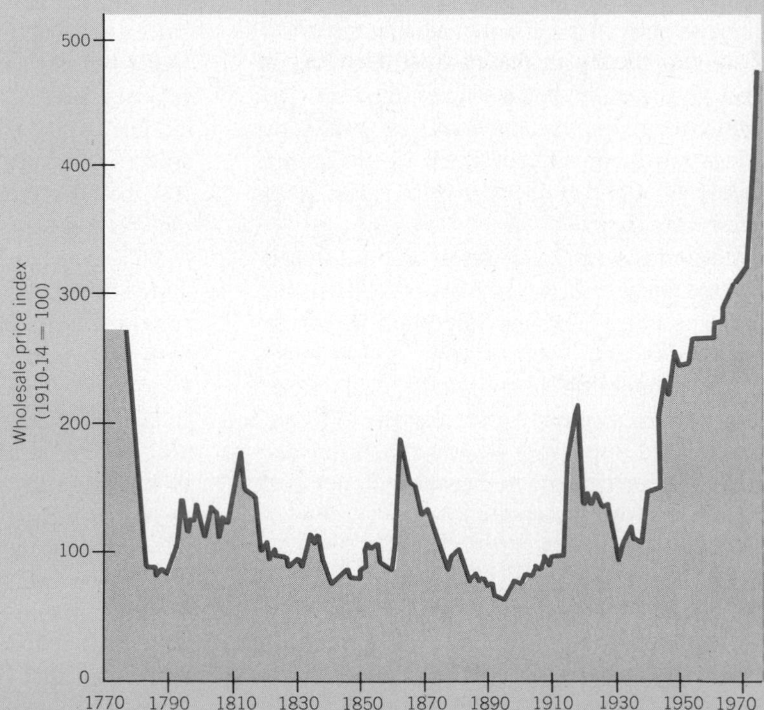

Figure 13.2
Index of Wholesale Prices, United States, 1779–1975 (1910–14 = 100)
The price level has fluctuated considerably, sharp increases generally occurring during wars. Since World War II, the price level has tended to go only one way—up.

13.2, it is clear that the value of the dollar has varied enormously during our history.

Inflation

Runaway Inflation: A Case Study

In periods of inflation, the value of money is reduced. Since inflation means an increase in the price level, and since an increase in the price level means a reduction in the value of money, this proposition seems clear enough. But remember that inflations vary in severity: ***runaway inflations*** wipe out the value of money quickly and thoroughly, while ***creeping inflations*** erode its value gradually and slowly. There is a lot of difference between a runaway inflation and a creeping inflation.

The case of Germany after World War I is a good example of runaway inflation. Germany was required to pay large reparations to the victorious Allies after the war. Rather than attempting to tax its people to pay these amounts, the German government merely printed additional quantities of paper money. This new money increased total spending in Germany, and the increased spending resulted in higher prices because the war-devastated economy could not increase output substantially. As more and more money was printed, prices rose higher and higher, reaching utterly fantastic levels. By 1923, it took a *trillion* marks (the unit of German currency) to buy what one mark would buy before the war. The effect of this runaway inflation was to disrupt the economy. Prices had to be adjusted from day to day. People rushed to the stores to spend the money they received as soon as possible, since very soon it would buy much less. Speculation was rampant. This inflation was a terrible blow to Germany. The middle class was wiped out; its savings became completely worthless. It is no wonder that Germany has in recent years been more sensitive than many other countries to the evils of inflation.

Runaway Inflation and the Quantity of Money

Needless to say, this is not the only case in history of runaway inflation. Our own country suffered from runaway inflations during the Revolutionary War and the Civil War. You may have heard the expression that something is "not worth a continental." It comes from the fact that the inflated dollars in use during the Revolutionary War were called continentals. There have also been runaway inflations in China and Eastern Europe and other parts of the world. Generally, such inflations have occurred because the government increased the money supply at an enormously rapid rate. It is not hard to see why a tremendous increase in the quantity of money will result in a runaway inflation. Other things held constant, increases in the quantity of money will result in increases in total desired spending, and once full employment is achieved, such increases in desired spending will bring about more and more inflation. Eventually, when the inflation is severe enough, households and businesses may refuse to accept money for goods and services because they fear that it will depreciate significantly before they have a chance to spend it. Instead, they may insist on being paid in merchandise or services. Thus the economy will turn to barter, with the accompanying inconveniences and inefficiency.

To prevent such an economic catastrophe, the government must manage the money supply responsibly. As we have stressed in previous sections, the value of money depends basically on the public's willingness to accept it, and the public's willingness to accept it depends on money's being reasonably stable in value. If the government increases the quantity of money at a rapid rate, thus causing a severe inflation and an accompanying precipitous fall in the value of money, public confidence in money will be shaken, and the value of money will be destroyed. The moral is clear: *the gov-*

Is Indexation the Answer to Inflation?

In the mid-1970s, when inflation in the United States was excessive in the eyes of practically all observers, some economists, like Milton Friedman of the University of Chicago, proposed a device called *indexation* to ameliorate the effects of inflation. Indexation is another word for the use of price-escalator clauses in private and public contracts. For example, in many industries, wages now rise automatically in accord with increases in the price level. And many government pensions now have similar provisions. What these economists were proposing was that such provisions be extended throughout the economy, or at least throughout much of it. For example, a person's income tax liability would be geared to the value of his or her income, after correcting for the effects of price-level changes. And interest rates would rise automatically with the rate of inflation.

Without question, indexation would help to reduce some of the harmful effects of inflation. For example, if the U.S. Treasury were to issue bonds where the principal and interest were adjusted to compensate for rises in the price level, it would be possible for small savers to put aside some money for the future, without being victimized by inflation. To see how such bonds might work, suppose that you invested $1,000 in them, and that you cashed them in two years after you bought them. If the price level then was 20 percent higher than when you bought them, you would receive $1,200 in principal plus interest. (Why $1,200? Because, since the price level was 20 percent higher, $1,200 at the time you cashed in the bonds would be the same as $1,000 at the time when you invested in them.)

Indexation really is not a new idea. Such great names of economics as Alfred Marshall of Cambridge and Irving Fisher of Yale were interested in the idea earlier in this century. And it has been tried on a limited scale in Canada and Israel, and to a greater extent in Brazil. But it has not received widespread support in the United States. Undoubtedly, one reason is that many people feel that indexation represents a surrender in the fight against inflation. In their view, it is better to quell inflation than to try to live with it. Also, some people are worried that "indexation will make it easier for the public to recognize changes in the rate of inflation, will thereby reduce the time lag in adapting to such changes, and so will make the . . . price level more sensitive and variable."*

Further, some observers believe that indexation of a comprehensive sort simply is not feasible. For example, as the Council of Economic Advisers has pointed out, "A major obstacle is that many current dollar payment obligations have been incurred in past periods. Furthermore, individuals can hardly be forced to index their future contracts if . . . they wish to make other allowances for the price movements they expect."† As inflation abated somewhat in 1976, talk of indexation died down. But that does not mean that the idea has been abandoned: it might be revived and even applied if the nation suffers more bouts of double-digit inflation.

* Milton Friedman, "Using Escalators to Help Fight Inflation," *Fortune*, July 1974, p. 176.
† Council of Economic Advisers, *Annual Report*, 1975, p. 141.

ernment must restrict the quantity of money, and conduct its economic policies so as to maintain a reasonably stable value of money.

Creeping Inflation and the Value of Money

For the past 40 years, the price level in the United States has tended to go one way only—up. Year after year, prices have risen. Since 1950, there hasn't been a single year when the price level has fallen, and in the 1940s it fell only in 1949. Certainly, this has not been a runaway inflation, but it has resulted in a very substantial erosion in the value of the dollar. Like a beach slowly worn away by the ocean, the dollar has slowly lost a considerable portion of its value. Specifically, prices now tend to be about 4 times what they were 40 years ago. Thus the dollar now is worth about ¼ of what it was worth then. Although a creeping inflation of this sort is much less harmful than a runaway inflation, it has a number of unfortunate social consequences.

For one thing, people with fixed incomes are hit hard by inflation. Although a creeping inflation does not hurt them as much as a runaway inflation, its cumulative effect over a period of years can be substantial. Old people often suffer, since they tend to have fixed incomes derived from public and private pensions, and interest on their savings. In addition, as we pointed out in Chapter 8, inflation hurts lenders and savers. The results can be both devastating and inequitable. The family that works hard and saves for retirement (and a rainy day) finds that its savings are worth far less, when it finally spends them, than the amount it saved. For example, consider the well-meaning souls who invested $1,000 of their savings in United States savings bonds in 1939. By 1949, these bonds were worth only about 800 1939 dollars, including the interest received in the 10-year period. Thus these people had $200 taken away from them, in just as real a sense as if someone picked their pockets.

Although a mild upward creep of prices at the rate of a few percent per year is not likely to result in very disastrous social consequences, any major inflation is a real social problem. (And inflation in the mid-1970s could be more appropriately designated as sprinting, rather than creeping; in 1974, the price level rose by about 12 percent.) Because it has proved difficult to bring inflation under control, some people have argued in recent years that inflation is not as bad as it looks. This, of course, seems quite sensible to those who have gained from inflation. But it does not do justice to the many people, including a disproportionate number of the elderly, who have been "suckered" by inflation. Why should these people have been subjected to such an arbitrary and inequitable tax on their savings and incomes? Moreover, this is not the only consideration. According to some respected economists, inflation tends to feed on itself. That is, a 2 percent rate of inflation tends to grow to a 3 percent rate of inflation, which tends to grow to a 4 percent rate of inflation, and so on. Although the available evidence is too weak to demonstrate this proposition, the possibility should nonetheless be borne in mind.

Inflation has a bad name, both among economists and with the general public. The novelist Ernest Hemingway, overstating his case more than a bit, wrote, "The first panacea for a mismanaged nation is inflation of currency: the second is war. . . . Both are the refuge of political and economic opportunists." [1] Yet we must recognize that under some conditions, full employment can be achieved only if a moderate amount of inflation is tolerated. For example, as we shall see, this seems to have been the case in the 1970s. Under such circumstances, the nation is faced with a painful decision: Should it allow a moderate amount of inflation in order to promote full employment? The im-

[1] Ernest Hemingway, "Notes on the Next War," *Esquire,* September 1935.

portance of maintaining full employment was described in detail in Chapter 8. The answer you give to this question will depend on your own ethical values and political preferences.

Unemployment and the Quantity of Money

In the last two sections, we have been concerned primarily with what happens when the quantity of money grows too rapidly. As we have seen, the result is inflation. But this is only part of the story. The quantity of money can grow too slowly as well as too rapidly; and when this happens the result is increased unemployment. If the money supply grows very slowly, or decreases, there will be a tendency for total desired spending to grow very slowly or decrease. This in turn will cause national output to grow very slowly or decrease, thus causing unemployment to increase. The result will, of course, be the social waste and human misery associated with excessive unemployment.

According to many economists, the recession of 1974-75 was due partly to an inadequate growth of the money supply. The Federal Reserve, trying to stem the inflationary tide in 1974, cut back on the rate of increase of the money supply. Looking back over past business fluctuations, it appears that an inadequate rate of increase in the quantity of money was responsible, at least in part, for many recessions. For example, according to Harvard's James Duesenberry, "Every major depression has been accompanied by a substantial decline in the money supply, and often by a complete collapse of the banking system. Among the many causes responsible for our major depressions, money and banking difficulties have always been prominent."[2] Recall that in our discussion of business fluctuations in the previous chapter, we stressed the importance of monetary factors. In this chapter, as well as Chapters 14 to 16, we will study these factors in detail.

[2] J. S. Duesenberry, *Money and Credit: Impact and Control,* Englewood Cliffs, N.J.: Prentice-Hall, 1972, p. 3.

Determinants of the Quantity of Money

Judging from our discussion thus far, it is clear that to avoid excessive unemployment or excessive inflation, the quantity of money must not grow too slowly or too fast. But what determines the quantity of money? We have already seen that money is of three types: coins, paper currency, and demand deposits. Let's begin by considering the quantity of coins and paper currency in circulation. They make up about ¼ of the total money supply. Practically all the currency is Federal Reserve notes, issued by the Federal Reserve Banks. When the United States was on the gold standard, the amount of money in circulation was determined by the amount of monetary gold in the country. When gold flowed into the country, the money supply increased; when it flowed out, the money supply decreased. This is no longer the case, since we are no longer on the gold standard—and neither is any other major nation.

If gold doesn't determine the amount of coins and currency in circulation, what does? The answer is that this amount responds to the needs of firms and individuals for cash to use or hoard. When people want more coins and currency, they go to their banks and exchange their demand deposits for coins and currency: in other words, they convert part of their checking accounts into cash. When they want less coins and currency, they take their cash to the banks and exchange it for demand deposits, thus converting some of their cash into checking accounts. Although the Federal Reserve System controls the size of the entire money supply, it allows the share of money in coin and currency to be determined by the public's wishes.

Next, consider the quantity of demand deposits, which is of obvious importance, since the bulk of our money supply is composed of demand deposits, not coin and paper currency. Demand deposits are created by commercial banks.[3] The question of how much money banks can create is both fundamental and complicated, and most of the next chapter will be required to present an adequate answer. For the moment, it is sufficient to say that the Federal Reserve System limits the amount of demand deposits the banks can create.

Thus the supply of money is determined to a considerable degree by the Federal Reserve System, which, as we have noted before, is our nation's central bank. Within limits, the Federal Reserve can and does control the quantity of money. But to some extent the private sector of the economy also determines the quantity of money. For example, the nation's commercial banks, through their lending (and other) decisions, can influence the money supply. In the remainder of this chapter, we shall make the simplifying assumption that the money supply is governed solely by the Federal Reserve. In the following chapter, we shall see how the commercial banks also play an important role in this regard.

The Demand for Money

We have discussed in general terms how changes in the quantity of money affect the tempo of economic activity. Now let's look in detail at how changes in the quantity of money affect net national product. The first step in doing this is to discuss the demand for money.

[3] Of course, banks do not create money all by themselves. The public's preferences and actions, as well as bank behavior, influence the amount of demand deposits. Also, commercial banks may not be as unique in this respect as it appears at first sight. See James Tobin, "Commercial Banks as Creators of Money" in D. Carson, ed., *Banking and Monetary Studies*, Homewood, Ill.: Irwin, 1963.

Why does a family or firm want to hold money? Certainly, a family can be wealthy without holding much money. We all know stories about very rich men who hold very little money, since virtually all of their wealth is tied up in factories, farms, and other nonmonetary assets. Unlike assets that yield profits or interest, money produces no direct return; so why do people and firms want to hold money, rather than other kinds of assets? Basically, there are the following three reasons:

Transactions demand for money. To carry out most transactions, money is required. Thus people and firms like to keep some money on their person and in their checking accounts to buy things. Clearly, the higher a person's income—in dollar, not real terms—the more money he or she will want to hold for transactions purposes. For example, in 1976, when a doctor makes about $50,000 a year, the average physician will want to keep more money on hand for transactions purposes than in the days—many, many years ago—when a doctor made perhaps $10,000 a year. Because the quantity of money demanded by a household or firm increases with its income, it follows that the total quantity of money demanded for transactions purposes in the economy as a whole is directly related to net national product. That is, the higher (lower) the level of NNP, the greater (less) the quantity of money demanded for transactions purposes.

Precautionary demand for money. Besides the transactions motive, households and firms like to hold money because they are uncertain concerning the timing and size of future disbursements and receipts. Unpredictable events often require money: for example, people get sick, and houses need repairs. Also, receipts frequently do not come in exactly when expected. To meet such contingencies, people and firms like to put a certain amount of their wealth into money and near-money. In the economy as a whole, the total quantity of money demanded for precautionary purposes (like the quantity demanded for transactions purposes) is likely to vary directly with NNP. For example, if NNP goes up, households and firms will want to hold more money for precautionary purposes, because their incomes and sales will be higher than before the increase in NNP.

Speculative demand for money. Finally, people like to hold some of their assets in a form in which they can be sure of its monetary value and can take advantage of future price reductions. The amount of money individuals and firms will keep on hand for speculative reasons will vary with their expectations concerning future price movements. In particular, if people feel that the prices of bonds and stocks are about to drop soon, they are likely to demand a great deal of money for speculative purposes. By holding money, they can obtain such securities at lower prices than at present. On the other hand, if they believe that the prices of bonds and stocks are about to rise, they are likely to demand much less money for these purposes. Rather than holding money, they will tend to hold these securities, and reap the profit arising from their increase in price.

The Interest Rate and the Demand for Money: The Liquidity Preference Function

Up to this point, we have discussed why individuals and firms want to hold money. But we must recognize that there are disadvantages, as well as advantages, in holding money. One is that the real value of money will fall if inflation occurs. Another is that an important cost of holding money is the interest or profit one loses, since instead of holding money, one might have invested it in assets that would have yielded interest or profit. For example, the annual cost of holding $5,000 in money if one can obtain 6 percent on existing investments, is $300, the amount of interest or profit forgone.

With NNP constant, the amount of money held by individuals and firms is *inversely* related to the interest rate. *The higher the interest rate, the smaller the amount of money demanded. The lower the interest rate, the greater the amount of money demanded.* This is because the cost of holding money increases as the interest rate or yield on existing investments increases. For example, if the interest rate were 7 percent rather than 6 percent, the cost of holding $5,000 in money for one year would be $350 rather than $300. Thus, as the interest rate or profit rate increases, people try harder to minimize the amount of money they hold. So do firms: big corporations like General Motors or U.S. Steel are very conscious of the cost of holding cash balances.

Another reason why the interest rate may be inversely related to the quantity of money demanded is that *bond prices are inversely related to the rate of interest.* If the interest rate goes up, bond prices go down; if the interest rate goes down, bond prices go up. (To see why, suppose that a very long-term bond pays interest of $300 per year. This bond is worth $3,000 if the prevailing interest rate is 10 percent, and $6,000 if it is 5 percent, because with a 10 percent interest rate one can get $300 per year by investing $3,000, whereas with a 5 percent interest rate one must invest $6,000 to get $300 per year.) Thus, if the interest rate is low, bond prices may be so high (relative to speculators' expectations) that speculators may hold money rather than buy bonds. And if the interest rate is high, bond prices may be so low (relative to speculators' expectations) that speculators will want to buy them rather than hold money. Consequently, a high (low) interest rate may result in a lesser (greater) quantity of money demanded.

Figure 13.3 summarizes two important conclusions of our discussion in this and the previous section. Panel A of Figure 13.3 shows that, *holding the interest rate constant, the quantity of money demanded is directly related to NNP.* As

Figure 13.3
The Demand for Money
Holding the interest rate constant, the quantity of money demanded is *directly* related to NNP, as shown in panel A. Holding NNP constant, the quantity of money demanded is *inversely* related to the interest rate, as shown in panel B. The latter relationship is known as the *liquidity preference function.*

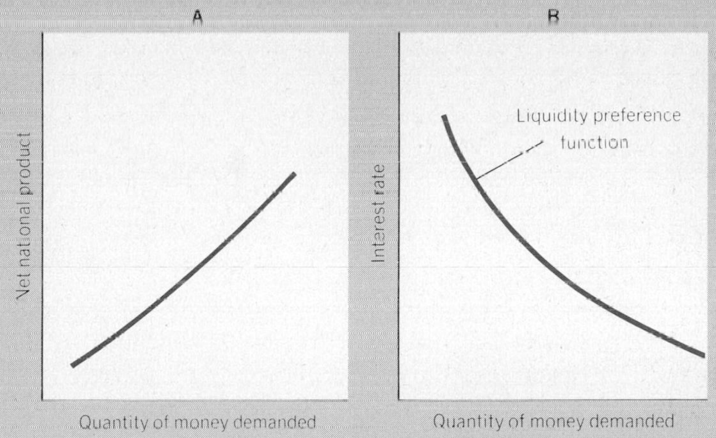

we explained in the previous section, the higher (lower) the level of NNP, the greater (less) the quantity of money demanded. Panel B of Figure 13.3 shows that, *with NNP constant, the quantity of money demanded is inversely related to the interest rate.*[4] This latter relationship, described in this section, is called the ***liquidity preference function.***

Changes in the Money Supply and National Output

Effects of an Increase in the Money Supply: The Keynesian Model

Now that we have investigated the demand for money, we are ready to show how changes in the quantity of money influence the value of NNP. Given the liquidity preference function, it is a simple matter to show how the money supply can be inserted into the Keynesian model (in Chapters 10 and 11) that explains the level of NNP.

To begin with, let's trace the effects of an increase in the money supply from $200 billion to $250 billion. If the liquidity preference function is as shown in panel A of Figure 13.4, the result will be a *decrease in the interest rate* from *d* percent to *c* percent. Why? Because, if the interest rate is *d* percent, people will demand only $200 billion in money, not the $250 billion that is supplied. Having more money on hand than they want, they will invest the excess in bonds, stocks, and other financial assets, with the result that the prices of bonds, stocks, and other financial assets will rise.[5] As pointed out in the previous section, such a price rise is equivalent to a fall in the rate of interest. When the interest rate has fallen to *c* percent, people will be willing to hold the $250 billion in money. At this interest rate, the quantity of money demanded will equal the quantity of money supplied.

The decrease in the interest rate from *d* percent to *c* percent affects the investment func-

[4] However, this relationship between the quantity of money and the interest rate is only short-run. In the long run, increases in the money supply, if they result in increased inflation, may *raise* interest rates, because lenders will require a greater return to offset the greater rate of depreciation of the real value of the dollar. Still, however, the *real* rate of interest—the rate of interest adjusted for inflation—may decline.

[5] For simplicity, we assume that when people have excess money balances, they use the money to buy financial assets. (In the next section, we assume that when people have smaller money balances than they want, they sell financial assets to get more money.) A more complete analysis is provided in Chapter 16. The results are the same as those provided here.

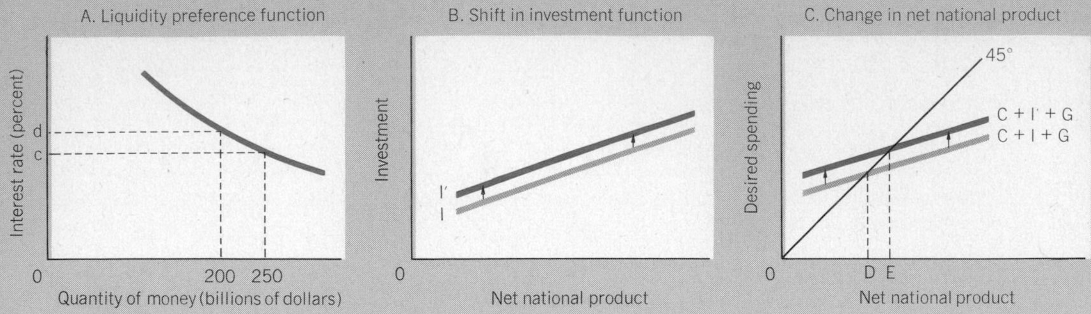

Figure 13.4
Effect of an Increase in the Money Supply.
If the money supply increases from \$200 billion to \$250 billion, the interest rate drops from *d* percent to *c* percent (panel A). Because of the decrease in the interest rate, the investment function shifts upward (panel B), and the equilibrium level of NNP increases from *D* to *E* (panel C).

tion.[6] Recall from Chapter 9 that the level of investment is inversely related to the interest rate. Because it is less costly to invest—and because credit is more readily available[7]—*the investment function will shift upward,* as shown in panel B of Figure 13.4. This occurs because at each level of net national product, firms will want to invest more, since investment is more profitable (because of the cut in the interest rate) and funds are more readily available.[8]

[6] Changes in the money supply, interest rates, and credit availability affect the consumption function and government spending, as well as the investment function. For example, *increases (decreases) in interest rates shift the consumption function and the level of government spending downward (upward).* These factors augment the effect of monetary policy described in the text. We focus attention on the investment function in Figures 13.4 and 13.5 merely because this simplifies the exposition.

[7] Note that it is not just a matter of interest rates: Availability of credit is also important. In times when money is tight, some potential borrowers may find that they cannot get a loan, regardless of what interest rate they are prepared to pay. In times when money is easy, people who otherwise might find it difficult to get a loan may be granted one by the banks. To repeat, both availability and interest rates are important.

[8] Many firms depend to a considerable extent on retained earnings to finance their investment projects. Thus, since they do not borrow externally, the effect on their investment plans of changes in interest rates and credit availability is slight. This factor may reduce the effects of changes in the money supply.

This shift in the investment function then affects the equilibrium level of net national product. As shown in panel C of Figure 13.4, *the equilibrium level of net national product will increase* from *D* to *E,* in accord with the principles discussed in Chapter 10. (Recall that the equilibrium value of NNP is at the point where the $C + I + G$ line intersects the 45-degree line.) Thus *the effect of the increase in the money supply is to increase net national product.*

This, in simplified fashion, is how an increase in the money supply affects NNP, according to the Keynesian model. To summarize, *the increase in the money supply results in a reduction in the interest rate, which results in an increase in investment, which results in an increase in NNP.* Obviously, this theory is of great importance in helping us to understand more completely why our economy behaves the way it does. For example, we can now understand better why vast increases in the quantity of money will result in runaway inflation. Total spending will be pushed upward at a very rapid rate, driving the price level out of sight.

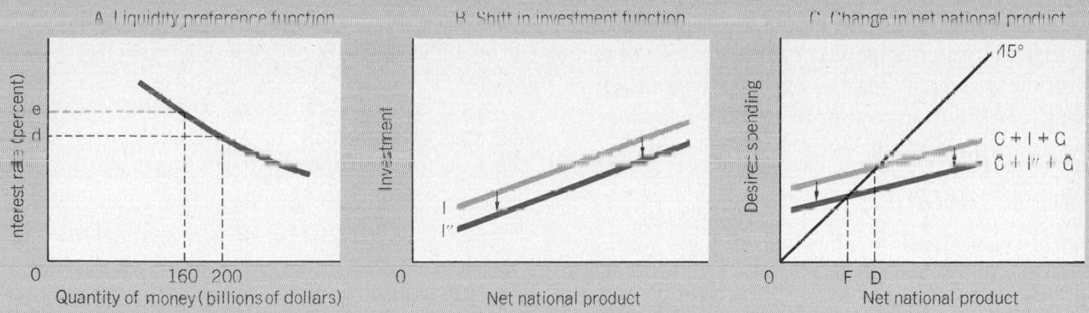

Figure 13.5
Effect of a Decrease in the Money Supply
If the money supply decreases from $200 billion to $160 billion, the interest rate increases from *d* percent to *e* percent (panel A). Because of the increase in the interest rate, the investment function shifts downward (panel B) and the equilibrium level of NNP decreases from *D* to *F* (panel C).

Effects of a Decrease in the Money Supply: The Keynesian Model

Next, let's trace the effects of a decrease in the money supply from $200 billion to $160 billion. If the liquidity preference function is as shown in panel A of Figure 13.5, the result will be an *increase in the interest rate* from *d* percent to *e* percent. Why? Because, if the interest rate is *d* percent, prople will demand $200 billion in money, not the $160 billion that is supplied. Having less money on hand than they want, they will sell some of their bonds, stocks, and other financial assets to build up their money balances, with the result that the prices of bonds, stocks, and other financial assets will fall. As pointed out above, such a fall in price is equivalent to an increase in the interest rate. When the interest rate has increased to *e* percent, people will be willing to hold only the $160 billion in money. At this interest rate, the quantity of money demanded will equal the quantity of money supplied.

The increase in the interest rate from *d* percent to *e* percent affects the investment function. Because it is more costly for firms to invest—and more difficult to obtain credit—*the investment function will shift downward,* as shown in panel B of Figure 13.5. This shift occurs because, at every level of net national product, firms want to invest less. The reasons why an increase in the interest rate reduces investment were given in detail in Chapter 9.

This downward shift in the investment function has an effect in turn on the equilibrium level of net national product. As shown in panel C of Figure 13.5, *the equilibrium level of net national product will decrease from* D *to* F (since the equilibrium level of NNP is at the point where the $C + I + G$ line intersects the 45 degree line). Thus *the effect of the decrease in the money supply is to decrease net national product.*

This, in simplified fashion, is how a decrease in the money supply affects NNP, according to the Keynesian model. To summarize, *the decrease in the money supply results in an increase in the interest rate, which results in a decrease in investment, which results in a decrease in NNP.*

This theory helps to explain, among other things, why an inadequate rate of growth of the money supply can lead to excessive unemployment. If the money supply is too small, NNP will not reach its full employment level.

The Monetarists

Some prominent economists, led by Milton Friedman of the University of Chicago, believe that the quantity of money affects NNP in a different way than was indicated in the previous sections. These economists rely on a theoretical framework generally labeled monetarism; hence they are called monetarists. In their view, monetarism provides more effective tools for forecasting or controlling nominal NNP than the Keynesian model described in Chapters 9 and 10. (***Nominal NNP*** means NNP in money, not real terms. In other words, nominal NNP is NNP measured in current, not constant, dollars.)

Monetarists regard the rate of growth of the money supply as the principal determinant of nominal, or money, net national product. Indeed, they go so far as to say that fiscal policy, although it will alter the composition of net national product, may have little or no long-run effect on the size of nominal NNP unless it influences the money supply. This latter view, explained in more detail in Chapter 16, is not now accepted by most economists.

The monetarists have had a great impact on economic thought in the postwar period, even though theirs remains a minority view. Professor Friedman's most severe critics admit that his research in this area has been pathbreaking and extremely important. According to his findings,

> the rate of change of the money supply shows well-marked cycles that match closely those in economic activity in general and precede the latter by a long interval. On the average, the rate of change of the money supply has reached its peak nearly 16 months before the peak in general business and has reached its trough over 12 months before the trough in general business.[9]

Clearly, findings of this sort must be taken seriously. Moreover, research carried out at the Federal Reserve Bank of St. Louis has shown a close relationship between short-run changes in the quantity of money and short-run changes in NNP. Based on this relationship, the St. Louis Bank has constructed some simple econometric models that have had some success in forecasting NNP. These results have also strengthened the hand of the monetarists. (However, in the 1970s, research suggests that models of this sort have not forecasted as well as the models described in Chapter 12.)

The Velocity of Money and the Equation of Exchange

The monetarists have revived interest in the so-called quantity theory of money, which was developed many years ago by such titans of economics as Alfred Marshall of Cambridge and Irving Fisher at Yale. To understand this theory, it is useful to begin by defining a new term: the velocity of circulation of money. The ***velocity of circulation of money*** is the rate at which the money supply is used to make transactions for final goods and services. That is, it equals the average number of times per year that a dollar is used to buy the final goods and services produced by the economy. In other words,

$$V = \frac{\text{NNP}}{M}, \tag{13.1}$$

where V is velocity, NNP is the nominal net national product, and M is the money supply. For example, if our nominal net national product is $1 trillion and our money supply is $200

[9] Milton Friedman, testimony before the Joint Economic Committee, "The Relationship of Prices to Economic Stability and Growth," 85th Congress, 2d Session, 1958.

billion, the velocity of circulation of money is 5, which means that, on the average, each dollar of our money consummates $5 worth of purchases of net national product.

Nominal net national product can be expressed as the product of real net national product and the price level: In other words,

$$\text{NNP} = P \times Q, \tag{13.2}$$

where P is the price level—the average price at which final goods and services are sold—and Q is net national product in real terms. For example, suppose that national output in real terms consists of 200 tons of steel. If the price of a ton of steel is $100, then nominal NNP equals $P \times Q$, or $100 × 200, or $20,000.[10]

If we substitute $P \times Q$ for NNP in Equation (13.1), we have

$$V = \frac{P \times Q}{M}. \tag{13.3}$$

That is, velocity equals the price level (P) times real NNP (Q) divided by the money supply (M). This is another way to define the velocity of circulation of money—a way that will prove very useful.

Now that we have a definition of the velocity of circulation of money, our next step is to present the so-called equation of exchange. The ***equation of exchange*** is really nothing more than a restatement, in somewhat different form, of our definition of the velocity of circulation of money. To obtain the equation of exchange, all we have to do is multiply both sides of Equation (13.3) by M. The result, of course, is

$$MV = PQ. \tag{13.4}$$

[10] Since real NNP is measured here in physical units (tons), P is the price level. If real NNP had been measured in constant dollars, P would have been a price index. In either event, our conclusions would be basically the same.

To understand exactly what this equation means, let's look more closely at each side. *The righthand side equals the amount received for final goods and services during the period,* because Q is the output of final goods and services during the period and P is their average price. Thus the product of P and Q must equal the total amount received for final goods and services during the period—or nominal NNP. For example, if national output in real terms equals 200 tons of steel, and if the price of a ton of steel is $100, then $100 × 200—that is, $P \times Q$—must equal the total amount received for final goods and services during the period.

The lefthand side of Equation (13.4) equals the total amount spent on final goods and services during the period. Why? Because the lefthand side equals the money supply—M—times the average number of times during the period that a dollar was spent on final goods and services—V. Obviously, $M \times V$ must equal the amount spent on final goods and services during the period. For example, if the money supply equals $10,000 and velocity equals 2, the total amount spent on final goods and services during the period must equal $10,000 × 2, or $20,000.

Thus, since the *amount received for* final goods and services during the period must equal the *amount spent on* final goods and services during the period, the lefthand side must equal the righthand side.

The equation of exchange—Equation (13.4)—is what logicians call a tautology: it holds by definition. Yet it is not useless. On the contrary, economists regard the equation of exchange as very valuable, because it sets forth some of the fundamental factors that influence NNP and the price level. This equation has been used by economists for many years. It is the basis for the crude quantity theory of money used by the classical economists, as well as the recent theories put forth by the monetarists.

The Crude Quantity Theory of Money and Prices

The classical economists discussed in Chapter 9 assumed that both V and Q were constant. They believed that V was constant because it was determined by the population's stable habits of holding money, and they believed that Q would remain constant at its full employment value.[11] On the basis of these assumptions, they propounded the ***crude quantity theory*** of money and prices, a theory that received a great deal of attention and exerted considerable influence in its day.

If these assumptions hold, it follows from the equation of exchange—Equation (13.4)—that the price level (P) must be proportional to the money supply (M), because V and Q have been assumed to be constant. (In the short run, the full-employment level of real net national product will not change much.) Thus we can rewrite Equation (13.4) as

$$P = \left(\frac{V}{Q}\right) M, \qquad (13.5)$$

where (V/Q) is a constant. So P must be proportional to M if these assumptions hold.

The conclusion reached by the crude quantity theorists—namely, *that the price level will be proportional to the money supply*—is very important, if true. To see how they came to this conclusion, one must recognize that they stressed the transaction motive for holding money. Recall from an earlier section that, based on this motive, one would expect the quantity of money demanded to be directly related to the level of nominal NNP. The crude quantity theorists went so far as to assume that it was *proportional* to the level of nominal NNP. This amounted to assuming that velocity was constant.

Suppose that a 10 percent increase occurs in the quantity of money. Why would the crude quantity theorists predict a 10 percent increase in the price level? To begin with, they would assert that, since the quantity of money has increased relative to the value of nominal NNP, households and firms now hold more money than they want to hold. Further, they would argue that households and firms will spend their excess money balances on commodities and services, and that the resulting increase in total desired spending will increase the nominal value, but not the real value of NNP (since full employment is assumed). In other words, the increase in aggregate demand will bid up prices. More specifically, they would argue that prices will continue to be bid up until they have increased by 10 percent, since only then will the nominal value of NNP be big enough so that households and firms will be content to hold the new quantity of money.

Evaluation of the Crude Quantity Theory

The crude quantity theory is true to its name: it is only a crude approximation to reality. One important weakness is its assumption that velocity is constant. Another is its assumption that the economy is always at full employment, which we know from previous chapters to be far from true. But despite its limitations, the crude quantity theory points to a very important truth: if the government finances its expenditures by a drastic increase in the money supply, the result will be drastic inflation. For example, if the money supply is increased tenfold, there will be a marked increase in the price level. If we take the crude quantity theory at face value, we would expect a tenfold increase in the price level; but that is a case of spurious accuracy. Perhaps the price level will

[11] In some cases, they did not really assume continual full employment; instead, they were concerned with the long-run changes in the economy, and compared the peaks of the business cycle, where full employment frequently occurs.

go up only eightfold. Perhaps it will go up twelvefold. The important thing is that it will go up a lot.

There is a great deal of evidence to show that the crude quantity theory is a useful predictor during periods of runaway inflation, such as in Germany after World War I. The German inflation occurred because the German government printed and spent large bundles of additional money. You often hear people warn of the dangers in this country of the government's "resorting to the printing presses" and flooding the country with a vast increase in the money supply. It is a danger in any country. And one great value of the crude quantity theory is that it predicts correctly what will occur as a consequence: rapid inflation.

There is also considerable evidence that the crude quantity theory works reasonably well in predicting long-term trends in the price level. For example, during the sixteenth and seventeenth centuries, gold and silver were imported by the Spanish from the New World, resulting in a great increase in the money supply. The crude quantity theory would predict a great increase in the price level, and this is what occurred. Or consider the late nineteenth century, when the discovery of gold in the United States, South Africa, and Canada brought about a considerable increase in the money supply. As the crude quantity theory would lead us to expect, the price level rose considerably as a consequence.

A More Sophisticated Version of the Quantity Theory

The crude quantity theory was based on two simplifying assumptions, both of which are questionable. One assumption was that real net national product (Q) remains fixed at its full-employment level; the other was that the velocity of circulation of money (V) remains constant. A more sophisticated version of the quantity theory can be derived by relaxing the first assumption. This version of the quantity theory recognizes that the economy is often at less than full employment and consequently that real net national product (Q) may vary a good deal for this reason.

So long as velocity remains constant, the equation of exchange—Equation (13.4)—can be used to determine the relationship between net national product in current dollars and M, even if Q is allowed to vary. On the basis of the equation of exchange, it is obvious that $P \times Q$ should be proportional to M, if the velocity of circulation of money (V) remains constant. Since $P \times Q$ is the nominal net national product, it follows that, if this assumption holds, *the nominal net national product should be proportional to the money supply.* In other words,

$$\text{NNP} = aM, \tag{13.6}$$

where NNP is the nominal net national product and V is assumed to equal a constant—a. Thus, if the money supply increases by 10 percent, the nominal value of NNP should increase by 10 percent. If the money supply increases by 20 percent, the nominal value of NNP should increase by 20 percent. And so forth.

If velocity is constant, this version of the quantity theory should enable us to predict nominal net national product if we know the money supply. Also, if velocity is constant, this version of the quantity theory should enable us to control nominal net national product by controlling the money supply. Clearly, if velocity is constant, Equation (13.6) is an extremely important economic relationship—one that will go a long way toward accomplishing the goals of Chapter 9 to 12, which were to show how net national product could be forecasted and controlled. But is velocity constant? Since Equation (13.6) is based on this assumption, we must find out.

Figure 13.6
Velocity of Circulation of Money, United States, 1920–75
The velocity of circulation of money has generally been between 2.5 and 5.0, except during World War II.

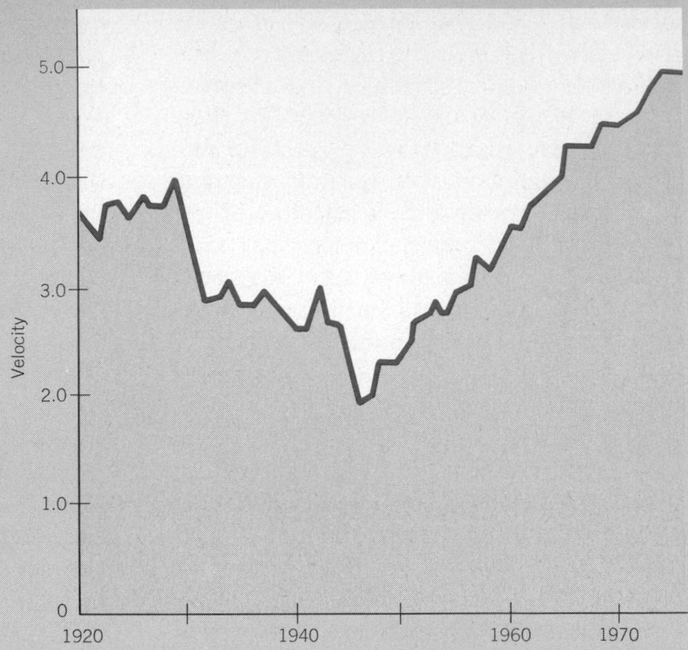

Figure 13.6 shows how the velocity of circulation of money has behaved since 1920.[12] Obviously velocity has not been constant. But on the other hand, it has not varied enormously. Excluding the war years, it has generally been between 2.5 and 5.0 in the United States. Over the long run, it has been reasonably stable, but it has varied a good deal over the business cycle. As shown in Figure 13.6, velocity tends to decrease during depressions and increase during booms. *All in all, one must certainly conclude that, although velocity is fairly stable over the long run, it is not so stable that Equation (13.6) alone can be used in any precise way to forecast or control net national product.*

However, this does not mean that Equation (13.6) is useless, or that the more sophisticated quantity theory is without value. On the contrary, this version of the quantity theory points out a very important truth, which is that *the money supply has an important effect on net national product (in money terms): increases in the quantity of money are likely to increase nominal NNP, while decreases in the quantity of money are likely to decrease nominal NNP.* Because velocity is not constant, the relationship between the money supply and net national product is not as neat and simple as that predicted by Equation (13.6), but there is a relationship—as shown in Figure 13.7[13]

The Importance of Money

Whether one is a Keynesian using the model presented in Figures 13.4 and 13.5 or a monetarist using the more sophisticated form of

[12] The velocity figures in Figure 13.6 are based on gross national product, not net national product. But for present purposes, this makes little real difference.

[13] As we shall see in Chapter 16, sophisticated monetarists often relax the assumption that V is constant, and claim that it is possible to predict V as a function of other variables, like the frequency with which people are paid and the level of business confidence. However, many economists feel that changes in V reflect, rather than cause, changes in NNP.

quantity theory makes a considerable difference, as we shall see in Chapter 16. But it is important to underscore the fact that *the effect of the money supply on nominal NNP is qualitatively the same in both the Keynesian and monetarist models.* Whatever theory you look at, you get the same qualitative result: increases in the money supply would be expected to increase nominal NNP, and decreases in the money supply would be expected to decrease nominal NNP. Thus, whether the Keynesian (majority) view of the world or the monetarist (minority) view of the world is correct, the quantity of money would be expected to influence nominal NNP—and push it in the same direction.

Furthermore, no matter which view is accepted, it would be expected that, as the economy approaches full employment, a bigger and bigger share of the increase in nominal NNP due to increases in the money supply will reflect price increases, not increases in real output. *If the economy is at considerably less than full employment, increases in the money supply would be expected to increase real NNP, while decreases in the money supply would be expected to reduce real NNP.* However, *once full employment is approached, increases in the money supply result more and more in increases in the price level, as distinct from increases in real NNP.*

These expectations are shared both by the monetarists and the Keynesians, which is fortunate since, as we shall see, they are important guides to the formulation of monetary policy, both here and abroad.

Summary

Money performs several basic functions. It serves as a medium of exchange, a standard of value, and a store of value. There are three kinds of money—coins, currency, and demand deposits. Economists include demand deposits as part of the money supply because you can pay for goods and services about as easily by check as with cash. Besides this narrow definition of money, a broader definition includes

Figure 13.7
Relationship between Money Supply and National Product, United States, 1929–75
There is a reasonably close relationship between the money supply and the money value of national product. As one goes up, the other tends to go up too.

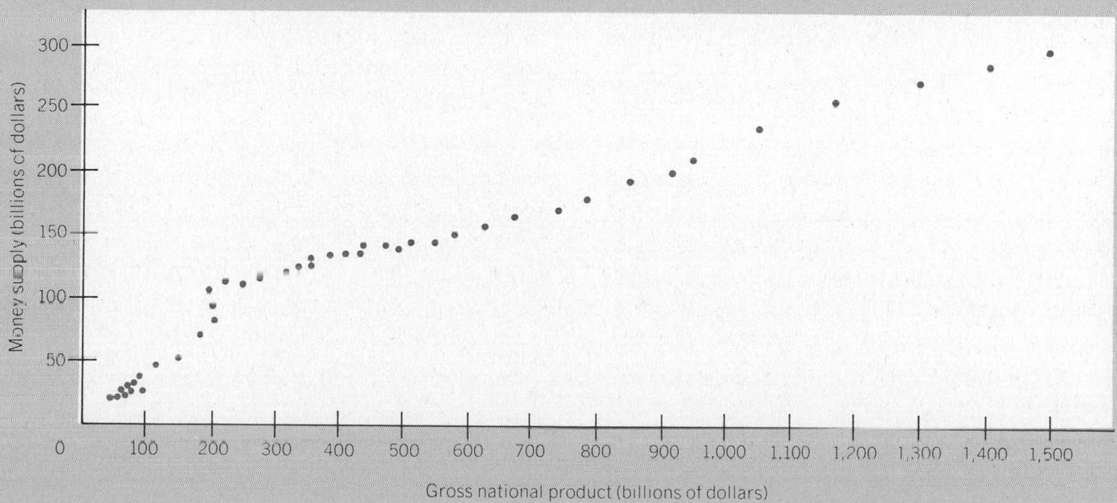

saving and time deposits. Of course, there are lots of other assets—for example, government bonds—that can be transformed without much difficulty into cash. It is not easy to draw a line between money and nonmoney, since many assets have some of the characteristics of money.

America's history has seen many sharp fluctuations in the price level. Wars have generally been periods of substantial inflation, and prices have dropped in the postwar periods. Since World War II, prices have tended to go one way only—up. Although a mild upward creep of prices at the rate of a few percent per year is not likely to result in any disastrous social consequences, runaway inflation is a real social evil that disrupts the economy very seriously. Generally, such inflations have occurred because the government expanded the money supply far too rapidly. However, too small a rate of growth of the money supply can also be a mistake, resulting in excessive unemployment.

Most economists believe that the lower the interest rate, the greater the amount of money demanded. Thus increases in the quantity of money result in lower interest rates, which result in increased investment (and other types of spending), which results in a higher NNP. Conversely, decreases in the quantity of money result in higher interest rates, which result in decreased investment (and other types of spending), which results in a lower NNP. This is the Keynesian approach.

The equation of exchange is $MV = PQ$, where M is the money supply, V is velocity, P is the price level, and Q is net national product in real terms. The velocity of circulation of money is the rate at which the money supply is used to make transactions for final goods and services. Specifically, it equals NNP in money terms divided by the money supply.

If the velocity of circulation of money remains constant and if real net national product is fixed at its full employment level, it follows from the equation of exchange that the price level will be proportional to the money supply. This is the crude quantity theory, which is a reasonably good approximation during periods of runaway inflation, and works reasonably well in predicting long-term trends in the price level.

A more sophisticated version of the quantity theory recognizes that real net national product is often at less than full employment, with the result that Q is not fixed. Thus, if velocity remains constant, net national product in money terms should be proportional to the money supply. In fact, velocity has by no means remained stable over time. However, nominal NNP has been fairly closely related to the money supply.

The monetarists, led by Milton Friedman, prefer the quantity theory over the Keynesian model. There are many important disagreements between the monetarists and the Keynesians, but both approaches agree that increases in the money supply will increase nominal NNP while decreases in the money supply will decrease nominal NNP.

CONCEPTS FOR REVIEW

Demand deposits
Currency
Time deposits
Near-money
Runaway inflation
Transactions demand
Precautionary demand
Speculative demand
Velocity of circulation
Equation of exchange
Crude quantity theory
Liquidity preference function
Federal Reserve notes

QUESTIONS FOR DISCUSSION AND REVIEW

1. "Money, in and of itself, has no value whatsoever. It is valuable only because of what it can buy." Comment and evaluate.

2. Explain in detail why the following items are not money: (a) government bonds, (b) U.S. Steel stock, (c) gold, (d) uranium.

3. Give some reasons why time deposits should be regarded as money. Give some reasons why they should not. Which side of the argument do you find more convincing?

4. Why is the interest rate regarded as the "price" of holding money? What factors will shift the liquidity preference function to the right? To the left?

5. "Creeping inflation inevitably leads to runaway inflation." Comment and evaluate.

6. If the value of NNP (in money terms) increases 10 percent and the money supply remains fixed, does velocity increase? Why or why not? What are some of the factors that might cause an increase in velocity?

7. "The history of the United States is an account of one inflation after another. The currency is being debased further and further. Soon we may experience a runaway inflation." Comment and evaluate.

8. According to Milton Friedman, the monetarists "have always stressed that money matters a great deal for the development of nominal [i.e., money] magnitudes, but not over the long run for real magnitudes." What does he mean? Do you agree or disagree?

9. Describe how the quantity of money influences nominal and real NNP according to (a) the Keynesian model, (b) the crude quantity theory, and (c) the more sophisticated quantity theory. What sorts of tests might be performed to determine which of these models works best?

14 The Banking System and the Quantity of Money

Banking is often viewed as a colorless, dull profession whose practitioners are knee-deep in deposit slips and canceled checks. Also, when the time comes to reject a loan application, the banker is often viewed as a heartless skinflint—even if he advertises that "you have a friend at Chase Manhattan." Yet despite these notions, most people recognize the importance of the banks in our economy, perhaps because the banks deal in such an important and fascinating commodity—money.

In this chapter, we look in detail at how commercial banks operate. We begin by discussing the Federal Reserve System and the functions of commercial banks. Then we describe the nature of commercial banks' loans and investments, as well as the important concept of reserves. After looking into legal reserve requirements we go on to describe how commercial banks create money—a very important and commonly misunderstood process. Finally, we take up the effects of currency

Figure 14.1
Organization of Federal Reserve System
The Federal Reserve System contains about 6,000 commercial banks, the 12 regional Federal Reserve Banks, and the Board of Governors, as well as the Federal Open Market Committee and various advisory councils and committees.

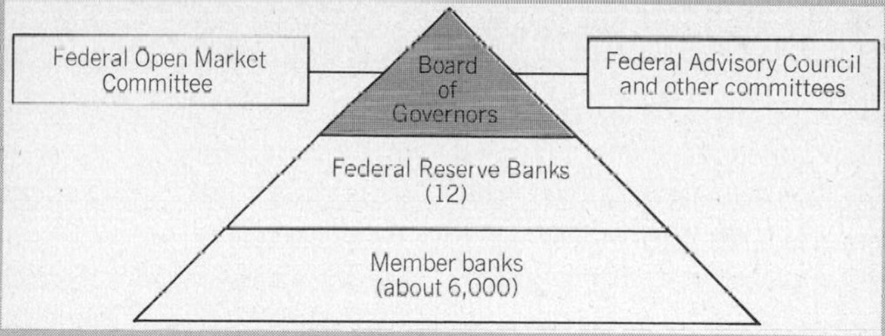

withdrawals and excess reserves on our results. The purpose of this chapter is to introduce you to the operations of the banking system, which is neither as colorless nor as mysterious as is sometimes assumed.

The Federal Reserve System

Any nation must exercise control over the quantity of money. In the United States, the Federal Reserve System is charged with this responsibility. The Federal Reserve System—or "Fed," as it is called by the *cognoscenti*—plays a central role in the American banking system and in the economy as a whole. After a severe financial panic in 1907, when a great many banks failed, there was strong public pressure to do something to strengthen our banking system. At the same time, there was great fear of centralized domination of the nation's banks. The result—after six years of negotiation and discussion—was the establishment by Congress of the ***Federal Reserve System*** in 1913. As shown in Figure 14.1, the organization of this system can be viewed as a triangle. At the base are the commercial banks that belong to the system—the ***member banks.*** All ***national banks*** (so called because they receive their charters from the federal government) have to be members, and many of the larger ***state banks*** (chartered by the states) are members too. Member banks, which number about 6,000 out of the nation's almost 15,000 commercial banks, hold about 80 percent of the nation's demand deposits.

Federal Reserve Banks. In the middle of the triangle in Figure 14.1 are the 12 Federal Reserve Banks, each located in a Federal Reserve district. The entire nation is divided into 12 Federal Reserve districts, with Federal Reserve Banks in New York, Chicago, Philadelphia, San Francisco, Boston, Cleveland, St. Louis, Kansas City, Atlanta, Richmond, Minneapolis, and Dallas. Each of these banks is a corporation owned by the member banks, but, despite this fact, the member banks do not in any sense act as owners of the Federal Reserve Bank in their district. Instead, each Federal Reserve Bank is a public agency. These Federal Reserve Banks act as "bankers' banks," performing much the same sorts of functions for commercial banks that commercial banks perform for the public. That is, they hold the deposits of member banks and make loans to them. In addition, as noted in previous chapters, the Federal Reserve Banks perform a function no commercial bank can perform: they issue Federal Reserve notes, which are the nation's currency.

The Board of Governors. At the top of the triangle in Figure 14.1 is the Board of Governors of the Federal Reserve System. Located in Washington, this board—generally called the Federal Reserve Board—has 7 members appointed by the president for 14-year terms. The board, which coordinates the activities of the Federal Reserve System, is supposed to be independent of partisan politics and to act to promote the nation's general economic welfare. It is responsible for supervising the operation of the money and banking system of the United States. The board is assisted in important ways by the Federal Open Market Committee, which establishes policy concerning the purchase and sale of government securities. The Federal Open Market Committee is composed of the board plus 5 presidents of Federal Reserve Banks. The board is also assisted by the Federal Advisory Council, a group of 12 commercial bankers that advises the board on banking policy.

Functions of the Federal Reserve

The Federal Reserve Board, with the 12 Federal Reserve Banks, constitute the central bank of the United States. Every major country has a central bank: for example, England has the Bank of England, and France has the Bank of France. ***Central banks*** are very important organizations, whose most important function is to help control the quantity of money. One interesting feature of our central bank is that its principal allegiance is to Congress, not to the executive branch of the federal government. This came about because Congress wanted to protect the Fed from pressure by the president and the Treasury Department. Thus the Fed was supposed to be independent of the executive branch. In fact, although the Fed has sometimes locked horns with the president, it has generally cooperated with him and his administration, as we shall see in Chapter 15.

To repeat, any central bank's most important function is to control the money supply. But this is not its only function: a central bank also handles the government's own financial transactions, and coordinates and controls the country's commercial banks. Specifically, the Federal Reserve System is charged with these responsibilities: First, the Federal Reserve Banks hold deposits, or reserves, of the member banks. As we shall see, these reserves play an important role in the process whereby the Fed controls the quantity of money. Second, the Federal Reserve System provides facilities for check collection. In other words, it enables a bank to collect funds for checks drawn on other banks. Third, the Federal Reserve Banks supply the public with currency through the issuance of Federal Reserve notes. Fourth, the Federal Reserve Banks act as fiscal agents for the federal government—they hold some of the checking accounts of the U.S. Treasury, and aid in the purchase and sale of government securities. Finally, the Federal Reserve Banks supervise the operation of the member commercial banks. More will be said about the nature of bank supervision and regulation later in the chapter, and much more will be said about the functions of the Federal Reserve in the next chapter.

Commercial Banks in the United States

In 1975, there were almost 15,000 commercial banks in the United States. This testifies to the fact that, in contrast to countries like England, where a few banks with many branches dominate the banking scene, the United States has promoted the growth of a great many local banks. In part, this has stemmed from a traditional suspicion in this country of "big bankers." ("Eastern bankers" are a particularly suspect breed in some parts of the country.) Most of our banks are state, not national, banks: there are over 9,000 state banks, but only about 5,000 national banks.

Commercial banks have two primary functions. First, *banks hold demand deposits and permit checks to be drawn on these deposits.* This function is familiar to practically everyone. Most people have a checking account in some commercial bank, and draw checks on this account. Second, *banks lend money to industrialists, merchants, homeowners, and other individuals and firms.* At one time or another, you will probably apply for a loan to finance some project for your business or home. Indeed, it is quite possible that some of the costs of your college education are being covered by a loan to you or your parents from a commercial bank.

In addition, commercial banks perform a number of other functions. Often they hold time or savings accounts. You will recall that these accounts bear interest and, although technically one must give a certain amount of notice before withdrawal, in practice they can usually be withdrawn whenever their owner likes. Commercial banks also sell money orders and traveler's checks, and handle estates and trusts. Because of their work with trusts, some banks—for example, the First Pennsylvania Bank and Trust Company, a large Philadelphia bank—include the word *trust* in their title. In addition, commercial banks rent safe-deposit boxes and provide a variety of services for customers.

Needless to say, commercial banks are not the only kind of financial institution. Mutual savings banks and savings and loan associations hold savings and time deposits; "consumer finance" companies lend money to individuals; insurance companies lend money to firms and governments; "factors" provide firms with working capital; and investment bankers help firms sell their securities to the public. All these types of financial institutions play an important role in the American economy. In general, they all act as intermediaries between savers and investors; that is, they all turn over to investors money that they received from savers. As we saw in Chapter 10, this process of converting savings into investment is very important in determining net national product.[1]

The Bank of America: A Case Study

We can learn something about banking in the United States from the history of a particular bank—the Bank of America, the nation's largest commercial bank. In 1904, Amadeo Peter Giannini, a 34-year-old son of an Italian immigrant, founded the Bank of Italy in the Italian district of San Francisco. Giannini was a man of enormous energy and drive. At the age of 12, he had gone to school by day, while working in his stepfather's produce firm for much of each night. At 19, he was a full-fledged member of the produce firm, and at 31 had become rich enough to retire from the produce business—and eventually to turn to banking.

Giannini showed the sort of entrepreneurial zeal in banking that would be expected from his previous track record. As an illustration, consider the following episode:

> In 1906, the city of San Francisco was rocked by earthquake and swept by fire. As the flames approached the little Bank of Italy, the young banker piled his cash and securities into a horse-drawn wagon and with a guard of two soldiers took them to his home at San Mateo, twenty miles from San Francisco, where he buried them in the garden; and then while the ruins of the city were still smoking he set up a desk in the open air down by the waterfront, put up a sign over the desk which read BANK OF ITALY, and began doing business again—the first San Francisco bank to resume.[2]

[1] The relationships among the various types of financial institutions are governed in part by law. In the middle 1970s, legislation has been proposed, and sometimes enacted, that would narrow some of the differences between commercial banks and other financial institutions. For example, in 1976, Congress passed, and President Ford signed, a bill approving NOW accounts for thrift institutions. And the Senate passed a bill in late 1975 to permit commercial banks to pay interest on demand deposits.

[2] Frederick Lewis Allen, *The Lords of Creation,* New York: Harper and Bros., 1935, p. 320. Much of this section is based on Allen's account.

Clearly, Giannini was a banker who did not observe banker's hours.

Giannini's bank prospered and grew. By the time he was 50, it had over 25 branches. During the 1920s, he acquired more and more branches, until old-line California bankers began to realize that the Bank of Italy had become a factor to be reckoned with. They did their best to prevent its further expansion, but to no avail. A man who can turn an earthquake to his advantage is unlikely, after all, to submit to such pressures. Indeed, by 1929, Giannini had 453 banking offices in California alone, as well as a considerable number elsewhere. His was the fourth largest commercial bank in the country.

In 1930, Giannini's bank was renamed the Bank of America. The 1930s were not particularly kind to it, any more than they were to the rest of the economy. But in the past 35 years, the Bank of America has grown and grown. In 1940, its loans (and discounts) totaled $778 million; in 1950, $3.3 billion; in 1960, $6.7 billion; and in 1970, $16 billion. Clearly, the Bank of America was on the move. By 1975, it had deposits of over $50 billion, and was the largest commercial bank in the United States. (The ten largest banks in the United States, in terms of deposits, are listed in Table 14.1.) It had come a long way since the days of the open-air desk on the waterfront.

How Banks Operate

The Bank of America, the biggest in the country, is hardly a typical commercial bank. It has had a remarkable history and a gifted founder. Many commercial banks are very small, as you would guess from the fact that there are almost 15,000 of them in the United States. And there is a great deal of variation among banks in their operating procedures and styles. Some are principally for firms; they do little business with individuals. Others are heavily engaged in lending to consumers. Nonetheless, although it is difficult to generalize about the operations of commercial banks because they vary so much, certain principles and propositions generally hold.

First, *banks generally make loans to both firms and individuals, and invest in securities, particularly the bonds of state and local governments, as well as federal government bonds.* The relationship between a business firm and its bank is often a close and continuing one. The firm keeps a reasonably large deposit with the bank for long periods of time, while the bank provides the firm with needed and prudent loans. The relationship between an individual and his or her bank is much more casual, but banks like consumer loans because they tend to be relatively profitable. In addition, besides lending to firms and individuals, banks buy

Table 14.1
The Ten Largest Commercial Banks in the United States in Terms of Deposits, June 30, 1975

Bank and location	Deposits (billions of dollars)
Bank of America, San Francisco	53.9
First National City Bank, New York	47.1
Chase Manhattan Bank, New York	34.2
Manufacturers Hanover Trust Company, New York	23.2
Chemical Bank, New York	19.2
Morgan Guaranty Trust Company, New York	18.6
Bankers Trust Company, New York	15.1
First National Bank, Chicago	13.8
Continental Illinois National Bank, Chicago	13.7
Security Pacific National Bank, Los Angeles	11.6

Source: American Banker.

large quantities of government bonds. For example, in the early 1970s, commercial banks held about $60 billion of state and local government bonds.

Second, *banks, like other firms, are operated to make a profit.* They don't do it by producing and selling a good, like automobiles or steel. Instead, they perform various services, including lending money, making investments, clearing checks, keeping records, and so on. They manage to make a profit from these activities by lending money and making investments that yield a higher rate of interest than they must pay their depositors. For example, the Bank of America may be able to get 10 percent interest on the loans it makes, while it must pay only 6 percent interest to its depositors. (Commercial banks do not pay interest on demand deposits, but they do pay interest on time deposits.[3] Also, they provide services at less than cost to holders of demand deposits.) If so, it receives the difference of 4 percent, which goes to meet its expenses—and to provide it with some profits.

Third, *banks must constantly balance their desire for high returns from their loans and investments against the requirement that these loans and investments be safe and easily turned into cash.* Since a bank's profits increase if it makes loans or investments that yield a high interest rate, it is clear why a bank favors high returns from its loans and investments. But those that yield a high interest rate often are relatively risky, which means that they may not be repaid in full. Because a bank lends out its depositors' money, it must be careful to limit the riskiness of the loans and investments it makes. Otherwise it may fail.

Until about 40 years ago, banks used to fail in large numbers during recessions, causing depositors to lose their money. Even during the prosperous 1920s, over 500 banks failed per year. It is no wonder that the public viewed the banks with less than complete confidence. Since the mid-1930s, bank failures have been rare, in part because of tighter standards of regulation by federal and state authorities. For example, bank examiners audit the books and practices of the banks. In addition, confidence in the banks was strengthened by the creation in 1934 of the Federal Deposit Insurance Corporation, which insures over 99 percent of all commercial bank deposits. At present, each deposit is insured up to $40,000.

[3] Legislation passed by the Senate in late 1975 would allow banks to pay interest on checking accounts. (See footnote 1.) More will be said on this score in Chapter 15.

The Balance Sheet of an Individual Bank

A good way to understand how a bank operates is to look at its balance sheet. Figure 14.2 shows the Bank of America's balance sheet as

Figure 14.2
Balance Sheet, Bank of America, January 1, 1975

Assets (billions of dollars)		Liabilities and net worth (billions of dollars)	
Cash	15.0	Demand deposits	13.5
Securities	7.6	Savings and time deposits	37.2
Loans	31.3	Other liabilities	7.3
Other assets	6.5	Net worth	2.4
Total	60.4	Total	60.4

Source: Moody's.

of the beginning of 1975. The lefthand side shows that the total assets of the Bank of America were $60.4 billion, and that these assets were made up as follows: $15.0 billion in cash, $7.6 billion in bonds and other securities, $31.3 billion in loans, and $6.5 billion in other assets. In particular, note that the loans included among the assets of the Bank of America are the loans it made to firms and individuals. As we have emphasized repeatedly, lending money is one of the major functions of a commercial bank.

The righthand side of the balance sheet says that the total liabilities—or debts—of the Bank of America were $58.0 billion, and that these liabilities were made up of $50.7 billion in deposits (both demand and time), and $7.3 billion in other liabilities. Note that the deposits at the Bank of America are included among its liabilities, since the Bank of America owes the depositors the amount of money in their deposits. It will be recalled from the previous sections that maintaining these deposits is one of the major functions of a commercial bank. Returning to the balance sheet of the Bank of America, the difference between its total assets and its total liabilities—$2.4 billion—is, of course, its net worth.

One noteworthy characteristic of any bank's balance sheet is the fact that *a very large percentage of its liabilities must be paid on demand.* For example, if all the depositors of the Bank of America tried to withdraw their demand deposits, over ⅕ of its liabilities would be due on demand. Of course, the chance of everyone wanting to draw out his or her money at once is infinitesimally small. Instead, on a given day some depositors withdraw some money, while others make deposits, and most neither withdraw nor deposit money. Consequently, any bank can get along with an amount of cash to cover withdrawals that is much smaller than the total amount of its deposits. For example, the Bank of America's cash equaled about ⅓ of its total deposits. Note that "cash" here includes the bank's deposit with the Federal Reserve System and its deposits with other banks, as well as cash in its vault.

The Bank of America's practice of holding an amount of cash—including its deposits with the Federal Reserve and with other banks—much less than the amount it owes its depositors may strike you as dangerous. Indeed, if you have a deposit at the Bank of America, you may be tempted to go over and withdraw the money in your account and deposit it in some bank that does have cash equal to the amount it owes its depositors. But you won't be able to do this because *all banks hold much less cash than the amount they owe their depositors.* Moreover, this is a perfectly sound banking practice, as we shall see.

Fractional-Reserve Banking

To understand the crucial significance of ***fractional-reserve banking,*** as this practice is called, let's compare two situations—one where a bank must hold as reserves an amount equal to the amount it owes its depositors, another where its reserves do not have to match the amount it owes its depositors. In the first case, the bank's balance sheet might be as shown in Figure 14.3, if demand deposits equal $2 million and net worth equals $500,000. The bank's loans and investments in this case are made entirely with funds put up by the owners of the bank. To see this, note that loans and investments equal $500,000, and that the bank's net worth also equals $500,000. Thus, if some of these loans are not repaid or if some of these investments lose money, the losses are borne entirely by the bank's stockholders. The depositors are protected completely because every cent of their deposits is covered by the bank's reserves.

Now let's turn to the case of fractional-reserve banking. In this case, the bank's balance sheet might be as shown in Figure 14.4, if deposits equal $2 million and net worth equals

Figure 14.3
Bank Balance Sheet: Case Where Reserves Equal Demand Deposits

Assets (millions of dollars)		Liabilities and net worth (millions of dollars)	
Reserves	2.0	Demand deposits	2.0
Loans and investments	0.5	Net worth	0.5
Total	2.5	Total	2.5

$500,000. Some of the loans and investments made by the bank are not made with funds put up by the owners of the bank, but with funds deposited in the bank by depositors. Thus, though depositors deposited $2 million in the bank, the reserves are only $400,000. What happened to the remaining $1.6 million? Since the bank (in this simple case) only has two kinds of assets, loans (and investments) and reserves, the bank must have lent out (or invested) the remaining $1.6 million.

The early history of banking is the story of an evolution from the first to the second situation. The earliest banks held reserves equal to the amounts they owed depositors, and were simply places where people stored their gold. But as time went on, banks began to practice fractional-reserve banking. It is easy to see how this evolution could take place. Suppose that you owned a bank of the first type. You would almost certainly be struck by the fact that most of the gold entrusted to you was not demanded on any given day. Sooner or later, you might be tempted to lend out some of the gold and obtain some interest. Eventually, as experience indicated that this procedure did not inconvenience the depositors, you and other bankers might make this practice common knowledge.

You might use several arguments to defend this practice. First, you would probably point out that none of the depositors had lost any money. (To the depositors, this would be a rather important argument.) Second, you could show that the interest you earned on the loans made it possible for you to charge depositors less for storing their gold. Consequently, you would argue that it was to the depositors' advantage (because of the savings that accrued to them) for you to lend out some of the gold. Third, you would probably argue that putting the money to work benefited the community and the economy. After all, in many cases, firms can make highly productive investments only if they can borrow the money, and by lending out your depositors' gold, you would enable such investments to be made.

Legal Reserve Requirements

Arguments of this sort have led society to permit fractional-reserve banking. In other words,

Figure 14.4
Bank Balance Sheet: Fractional Reserves

Assets (millions of dollars)		Liabilities and net worth (millions of dollars)	
Reserves	0.4	Demand deposits	2.0
Loans and investments	2.1	Net worth	0.5
Total	2.5	Total	2.5

a bank is allowed to hold less in reserves than the amount it owes its depositors. But what determines the amount of reserves banks hold? For example, the Bank of America, according to Figure 14.2, held cash equal to about 30 percent of its total deposits. Probably it could get away with holding much less in reserves, so long as there is no panic among depositors and it makes sound loans and investments. One reason why the Bank of America held this much cash is very simple: *the Federal Reserve System requires every commercial bank that is a member of the system to hold a certain percentage of its deposits as reserves.* This percentage varies with the size of the bank. As of 1976, each member bank had to hold as reserves $7\frac{1}{2}$ percent of its first $2 million of demand deposits, 10 percent of its next $8 million, 12 percent of its next $90 million, 13 percent of its next $300 million, and $16\frac{1}{2}$ percent of its demand deposits in excess of $400 million. These are ***legal reserve requirements;*** they exist for time deposits too, but are lower than for demand deposits.

The Federal Reserve System in recent years has dictated that the average bank should hold about $1 in reserves for every $6 of demand deposits. Most of these reserves are held in the form of deposits by banks at their regional Federal Reserve Bank. Thus, for example, a great deal of the Bank of America's reserves are held in its deposit with the Federal Reserve Bank of San Francisco. In addition, some of any bank's reserves are held in cash on the bank's premises. However, its legal reserves are less than the "cash" entry on its balance sheet since its deposits with other banks do not count as legal reserves. Of course, these legal reserve requirements are binding only on members of the Federal Reserve System, and, as we noted in a previous section, although all national banks are members, not all state banks are. But the banks outside the Federal Reserve System hold only about 20 percent of the nation's deposits, and the Fed seems to believe that it includes a large enough proportion of the banks to accomplish its goals.

The most obvious reason why the Fed imposes these legal reserve requirements would seem to be to keep the banks safe, but in this case the obvious answer isn't the right one. Instead, *the most important reason for legal reserve requirements is to control the money supply.* It will take some more discussion before this becomes clear.

To close with a historical sidelight, until 1972 legal reserve requirements were higher for big-city banks than for small-town banks. Back when the Federal Reserve System was formed, big-city banks often held the reserves of the small-town banks, and thus it seemed reasonable to enforce higher reserve requirements for the big-city banks. But nowadays reserves of all member banks—in big cities or in small towns—are held by the Federal Reserve Banks. Consequently, this difference in legal reserve requirements was like the human appendix and wisdom teeth: a somewhat illogical and useless inheritance from the past. Finally, in 1972, it was jettisoned.

The Safety of the Banks

We have just argued that the reserve requirements imposed by the Federal Reserve System exceed what would be required under normal circumstances to insure the safety of the banks. To support our argument, we might cite some authorities who claim that a bank would be quite safe if it only had reserves equal to about 2 percent of its deposits. Under these circumstances it would be able to meet its depositors' everyday demands for cash. Obviously this level of reserves is much lower than the legally required level.

At the same time, one should recognize that high reserve requirements will not by themselves insure bank safety. For example, suppose that a bank lends money to every budding inventor with a scheme for producing perpetual-motion machines—and that it grants particularly large loans to those who propose to market these machines in the suburbs of Missoula, Montana. This bank is going to fail eventually, even if it holds reserves equal to 20 percent—or 50 percent for that matter—of its demand deposits. It will fail simply because the loans it makes will not be repaid, and eventually these losses will accumulate to more than the bank's net worth. In other words, if the bank is sufficiently inept in making loans and investments it will lose all the owners' money and some of the depositors' money besides.

To promote its safety, a bank must make sensible loans and investments. In addition, it must protect itself against short-term withdrawals of large amounts of money. Although larger-than-usual withdrawals are not very likely to occur, the bank must be prepared to meet a temporary upswing in withdrawals. One way is to invest in securities that can readily be turned into cash. For example, the bank may invest in short-term government securities that can readily be sold at a price that varies only moderately from day to day. Such securities are often referred to as *secondary reserves.*

There can be no doubt that banks are much safer today than they were 50 or 100 years ago. The reason is that the government has put its power squarely behind the banking system. It used to be that "runs" occurred on the banks. Every now and then, depositors, frightened that their banks would fail and that they would lose some of their money, would line up at the tellers' windows and withdraw as much money as they could. Faced with runs of this sort, banks were sometimes forced to close because they could not satisfy all demands for withdrawals. Needless to say, no fractional-reserve banking system can satisfy demands for total withdrawal of funds.

Runs on banks are a thing of the past, for several reasons. One is that the government—including the Federal Deposit Insurance Corporation (FDIC), the Fed, and other public agencies—has made it clear that it will not stand by and tolerate the sorts of panics that used to occur periodically in this country. The FDIC insures the accounts of depositors in practically all banks so that, even if a bank fails, the depositor will get his money back—up to $40,000. Another reason is that the banks themselves are better managed and regulated. For example, bank examiners are sent out to look over the bankers' shoulders and see whether they are solvent. It is a far cry from the situation 60-odd years ago that led to the creation of the Federal Reserve System.

Nonetheless, this does not mean that bank regulation is all that it might be. In the middle 1970s, three big banks—Franklin National, U.S. National, and Security National—failed, and many observers felt that the regulating agencies, such as the FDIC and the Fed, were not doing a proper job. For example, Arthur Burns, chairman of the Fed, cited a "competition in laxity" among the regulators. One criticism was that banks were relying too heavily on debt and too little on equity capital. Some congressional leaders called for the creation of a Federal Bank Commission, which would combine the regulatory functions of the Fed, FDIC, and the Comptroller of the Currency. Despite the advances made in the past 60 years, bank regulation is still an area of some national concern.

The Lending Decision: A Case Study

To get a better feel for the workings of a bank, let's look at an actual decision faced by Robert Swift, the assistant vice-president of the Lone Star National Bank of Houston, Texas. Mr. Swift received a call from Ralph Desmond, president of the Desmond Engineering Corporation. Mr. Desmond wanted to change his bank; he was dissatisfied with the amount he could borrow from his present bank. He wanted to borrow $30,000 from the Lone Star to pay what he owed to his present bank, pay some bills coming up, and buy some material needed to fulfill a contract. Mr. Swift asked Mr. Desmond to come to his office with various financial statements regarding the Desmond Engineering Corporation and its prospects. These included recent profit and loss statements and balance sheets, as well as a variety of other data, including information indicating how rapidly the firm collected its bills and the quality of the debts owed the firm.

Mr. Swift forwarded Mr. Desmond's loan application to the credit department of the bank for further analyses. The credit department added comments on the Desmond Engineering Corporation's solvency and prospects. Besides being secured by a mortgage on some equipment owned by the Desmond Engineering Corporation, this loan was to be personally endorsed by Mr. Desmond and another principal stockholder in the firm. Consequently, Mr. Swift obtained information on the extent and nature of the personal assets of Mr. Desmond and the other stockholder. This information was used, together with all the other data on the firm, to determine whether the bank would make the loan. After a reasonable amount of time, Mr. Swift recommended the acceptance of Mr. Desmond's loan application. In his view, Mr. Desmond had a very good chance of repaying the loan.[4]

[4] This case comes from Leonard Marks and Alan Coleman, *Cases in Commercial Bank Management,* New York: McGraw-Hill, 1962, pp. 168-76. However, the outcome is purely conjectural.

Note two things about this decision. First, if the bank grants Mr. Desmond the loan, it will create a demand deposit for him. In other words, it will create some money. Second, the bank can do this only if it has reserves exceeding the legal reserve requirements. Both of these points are important enough to dwell on for a while.

Two Ways Banks Cannot Create Money

Genesis tells us that God created heaven and earth. Economists tell us that banks create money. To many people, the latter process is at least as mysterious as the former. Even bankers themselves have been known to fall into serious error by claiming that they do not create money. Yet the way banks create money is a relatively simple process, which the next few sections will describe in detail. Suppose that someone receives $10,000 in newly printed currency and deposits it in his local bank. Before we see how the bank can create more than $10,000 from this deposit, we will describe two ways in which banks *cannot* create new money. Since people often jump to the conclusion that one or the other of these two processes is the correct one, it is a good idea to kill off these heresies at the outset.

First, suppose that ours is not a fractional-reserve banking system. In other words, assume that every bank has to maintain reserves equal to its deposits. In this case, the bank receiving the $10,000 deposit cannot create any

Figure 14.5
Changes in Bank Balance Sheet, Where Reserves Equal Demand Deposits

Assets (dollars)		Liabilities and net worth (dollars)	
Reserves	+10,000	Demand deposits	+10,000
Loans and investments	No change	Net worth	No change
Total	+10,000	Total	+10,000

new money. You may be inclined to think that it can be done, but it can't. To see why not, consider the changes in the bank's balance sheet, shown in Figure 14.5. When the $10,000 is deposited in the bank, the bank's deposits go up $10,000. Since the bank must hold $10,000 in reserves to back up the new $10,000 deposit, it must put the $10,000 it receives from the depositor into its reserves. Thus the bank's demand deposits go up by $10,000, and its reserves go up by $10,000. Since demand deposits are on the righthand side of the balance sheet and reserves are on the lefthand side, the balance sheet continues to balance. *No new money is created. All that happens is that the depositor gives up $10,000 in one form of money—currency—and receives $10,000 in another form of money—a demand deposit.*

Next, let's turn to a second way banks cannot create money. Suppose that we have a fractional-reserve banking system and that the legal reserve requirement is 16⅔ percent. In other words, the bank must hold $1 in reserves for every $6 of demand deposits. Suppose that the bank decides to take the crisp, new $10,000 in currency that is deposited and add it to its reserves, thus increasing its reserves by $10,000. Then suppose it reasons (incorrectly) that it can increase its deposits by $50,000, since it has $10,000 in additional reserves. Why $50,000? Because the $10,000 in additional reserves will support $60,000 in demand deposits; and since the person who deposited the $10,000 has a demand deposit of $10,000, this means that it can create additional demand deposits of $60,000 minus $10,000, or $50,000.

The bank will create these additional demand deposits simply by making loans or investments. Thus when a person comes in to the bank for a loan, all the banker has to do is give him a demand deposit—a checking account—that didn't exist before. In other words, the banker can say to his staff, "Establish a checking account of $50,000 for Mr. Smith. We have just lent him this amount to buy a new piece of equipment to be used in his business." At first, this whole process looks a bit like black magic, perhaps even larceny. After all, how can checking accounts be established out of thin air? But they can, and are. In essence, this is how banks create money.

But we prefaced this example by saying that it contains an error: the error is the supposition that the bank can create an additional $50,000 of demand deposits on the basis of the $10,000 deposit. To see why this won't work, consider the changes in the bank's balance sheet, shown in Figure 14.6. After the bank received the $10,000 deposit, its demand deposits and its reserves both increased by $10,000, as shown in the first panel of Figure 14.6. Then, as we noted above, the bank made a $50,000 loan and (in the process of making the loan) created $50,000 in new deposits, as shown in the second panel. So far, so good. The bank's balance sheet continues to balance—in accord with common sense and accounting (in that order). The bank's reserves are ⅙ of its demand deposits; they satisfy the legal reserve requirements established by the Fed.

So what is the problem? None, unless the money lent by the bank is spent. If the man who received the loan—Mr. Smith—never used the money he borrowed, the bank could act this way and get away with it. But people who borrow money are in the habit of spending it; why pay interest on money one doesn't use? Even if Mr. Smith, the recipient of this loan, spent the money, the bank could act in accord with this example and get away with it if the people who received the money from Mr. Smith deposited it in this same bank. But the chances of this occurring are very small. The equipment Mr. Smith plans to buy is likely to be produced by a firm in some other city; and even if it is located in the same city, the firm may well have an account at another bank.

To see the problem that results when the loan is spent, suppose that Mr. Smith spends

Figure 14.6
Changes in Bank Balance Sheet: Fractional Reserves

	Assets (dollars)		Liabilities and net worth (dollars)	
Bank receives deposit	Reserves	+10,000	Demand deposits	+10,000
	Loans and investments	No change	Net worth	No change
	Total	+10,000	Total	+10,000
Bank makes loan	Reserves	No change	Demand deposits	+50,000
	Loans and investments	+50,000	Net worth	No change
	Total	+50,000	Total	+50,000
Mr. Smith spends $50,000	Reserves	−50,000	Demand deposits	−50,000
	Loans and investments	No change	Net worth	No change
	Total	−50,000	Total	−50,000
Total effect	Reserves	−40,000	Demand deposits	+10,000
	Loans and investments	+50,000	Net worth	No change
	Total	+10,000	Total	+10,000

the $50,000 on a machine produced by the Acme Corporation, which has an account at the First National Bank of Boston. He sends the Acme Corporation a check for $50,000 drawn on our bank. When the Acme Corporation receives Mr. Smith's check, it deposits this check to its account at the First National Bank of Boston, which, using the facilities of the Federal Reserve System, presents the check to our bank for payment. Our bank must then fork over $50,000 of its cash—its reserves—to the First National Bank of Boston. Consequently, once the $50,000 check is paid, the effect on our bank's balance sheet is as shown in the third panel of Figure 14.6. Taken as a whole, the bank's demand deposits have increased by $10,000, and its reserves have decreased by $40,000, as shown in the bottom panel of Figure 14.6.

At this point, the error in this example is becoming clear. *If the bank was holding $1 in reserves for every $6 in demand deposits before the $10,000 deposit was made, these transactions must cause the bank to violate the legal reserve requirements.* This is simple to prove. Suppose that, before the $10,000 deposit, our bank had $\$X$ in demand deposits and $\$\frac{X}{6}$ in reserves. Then, after the transactions described above, it must have ($\$X + \$10{,}000$) in demand deposits and $\left(\$\frac{X}{6} - \$40{,}000\right)$ in reserves. Certainly, the reserves $\left(\text{which equal } \$\frac{X}{6} - \$40{,}000\right)$ are now less than $\frac{1}{6}$ of the demand deposits (which equal $\$X + \$10{,}000$). This must be true whatever value X has. (Try it and see.) Thus no bank can create money in this way because, if it did, it would violate the legal reserve requirements after the newly created demand deposits were used. However, as we shall see later, a monopoly bank—that is, the only bank in the country—could create money like this. But monopoly banks do not exist in the United States.

How Banks Can Create Money

Now that you have learned two ways that banks *cannot* create money, let's describe how they *can* create money. Imagine the following scenario. First, suppose once again that someone deposits \$10,000 of newly printed money in our bank, which we'll call Bank *A*. Second, suppose that Bank *A* lends Mr. Smith \$8,333, and that Mr. Smith uses this money to purchase some equipment from Mr. Jones, who deposits Mr. Smith's check in his account at Bank *B*. Third, Bank *B* buys a bond for \$6,944 from Mr. Stone, who deposits the check from Bank *B* to his account at Bank *C*. Fourth, Bank *C* lends \$5,787 to Mr. White, who uses the money to buy a truck from the local General Motors dealer, Mr. Black, who deposits Mr. White's check for \$5,787 to his account at Bank *D*. Fifth, Bank *D* lends Mr. Cohen \$4,823 which Mr. Cohen uses to buy some lumber from Mr. Palucci, who deposits Mr. Cohen's check to his account at Bank *E*. Admittedly, this is a somewhat complicated plot with a substantial cast of characters, but life is like that.

The first step in our drama occurs when someone deposits \$10,000 in newly printed money in Bank *A*. The effect of this deposit is shown in the first panel of Figure 14.7: Bank *A*'s demand deposits and its reserves both go up by \$10,000. Now Bank *A* is far too smart to pull the sort of trick described in the last section. It does not try to make a \$50,000 loan, lest it wind up with less reserves than dictated by the legal reserve requirements. When Mr. Smith asks one of the loan officers of the bank for a loan to purchase equipment, the loan officer approves a loan of \$8,333, not \$50,000. Mr. Smith is given a checking account of \$8,333 at Bank *A*.

How can Bank *A* get away with this loan of \$8,333 without winding up with less than the legally required reserves? The answer is given in the rest of Figure 14.7. The second panel of this figure shows what happens to Bank *A*'s balance sheet when Bank *A* makes the \$8,333 loan and creates a new demand deposit of \$8,333. Obviously, both demand deposits and loans go up by \$8,333. Next, look at the third panel of Figure 14.7, which shows what happens when Mr. Smith spends the \$8,333 on equipment. As pointed out above, he purchases this equipment from Mr. Jones. Mr. Jones deposits Mr. Smith's check to his account in Bank *B* which presents the check to Bank *A* for payment. After Bank *A* pays Bank *B* (through the Federal Reserve System), the result—as shown in the third panel—is that Bank *A*'s deposits go down by \$8,333 since Mr. Smith no longer has the deposit. Bank *A*'s reserves also go down by \$8,333 since Bank *A* has to transfer these reserves to Bank *B* to pay the amount of the check.

As shown in the bottom panel of Figure 14.7, the total effect on Bank *A* is to increase its deposits by the \$10,000 that was deposited originally and to increase its reserves by \$10,000 minus \$8,333, or \$1,667. In other words, reserves have increased by $\frac{1}{6}$ as much as demand deposits. This means that Bank *A* will meet its legal reserve requirements. To see this, suppose that before the deposit of \$10,000, Bank *A* had demand deposits of $\$X$ and reserves of $\$\frac{X}{6}$. Then after the full effect of the transaction occurs on Bank *A*'s balance sheet, Bank *A*'s demand deposits will equal $(\$X + \$10{,}000)$ and its reserves will equal $\left(\$\frac{X}{6} + \$\,\frac{10{,}000}{6}\right)$, since $\$1{,}667 = \frac{\$10{,}000}{6}$. Thus Bank *A* continues to

Figure 14.7
Changes in Bank *A*'s Balance Sheet

	Assets (dollars)		Liabilities and net worth (dollars)	
Bank receives deposit	Reserves	+10,000	Demand deposits	+10,000
	Loans and investments	No change	Net worth	No change
	Total	+10,000	Total	+10,000
Bank makes loan	Reserves	No change	Demand deposits	+ 8,333
	Loans and investments	+ 8,333	Net worth	No change
	Total	+ 8,333	Total	+ 8,333
Mr. Smith spends $8,333	Reserves	− 8,333	Demand deposits	− 8,333
	Loans and investments	No change	Net worth	No change
	Total	− 8,333	Total	− 8,333
Total effect	Reserves	+ 1,667	Demand deposits	+10,000
	Loans and investments	+ 8,333	Net worth	No change
	Total	+10,000	Total	+10,000

hold $1 in reserves for every $6 in demand deposits, as required by the Fed.

Impact on Other Banks

It is important to recognize that *Bank* A *has now created $8,333 in new money.* To see this, note that Mr. Jones winds up with a demand deposit of this amount that he didn't have before; and this is a net addition to the money supply, since the person who originally deposited the $10,000 in currency still has his $10,000, although it is in the form of a demand deposit rather than currency. But this is not the end of the story. The effects of the $10,000 deposit at Bank *A* are not limited to Bank *A*. Instead, as we shall see, other banks can also create new money as a consequence of the original $10,000 deposit at Bank *A*.

Let's begin with Bank *B*. Recall from the previous section that the $8,333 check made out by Mr. Smith to Mr. Jones is deposited by the latter in his account at Bank *B*. This is a new deposit of funds at Bank *B*. As pointed out in the previous section, Bank *B* gets $8,333 in reserves from Bank *A* when Bank *A* pays Bank *B* to get back the check. Thus the effect on Bank *B*'s balance sheet, as shown in the first panel of Figure 14.8, is to increase both demand deposits and reserves by $8,333. Bank *B* is in much the same position as was Bank *A* when the latter received the original deposit of $10,000. Bank *B* can make loans or investments of $6,944. (The way we derive $6,944 is explained in footnote 5 below.)[5] Specifically, it decides to buy a bond for $6,944 from Mr. Stone, who deposits the check from Bank *B* to his account in Bank *C*. Thus, as shown in the

[5] Since Bank *B* has to hold $\frac{\$8,333}{6}$, or $1,389, in legally required reserves, it can lend $8,333 minus $1,389, or $6,944. If it lends more than this amount, it may wind up with less than the legally required reserves.

second panel of Figure 14.8, the effect of this transaction is to increase Bank *B*'s investments by $6,944 and to increase its demand deposits by $6,944 when Bank *B* buys the bond. This transaction increases Bank *B*'s demand deposits by $6,944 because the bank creates a demand deposit of $6,944 to pay for the bond. In other words, the bank in effect creates a deposit for itself and uses it to pay Mr. Stone for the bond. Then Bank *B*'s demand deposits and its reserves are decreased by $6,944 when it transfers this amount of reserves to Bank *C* to pay for the check. When the total effects of the transaction are summed up, Bank *B*, like Bank *A*, continues to meet its legal reserve requirements, since its increased reserves ($1,389) equal $\frac{1}{6}$ of its increased demand deposits ($8,333).

Bank B *has also created some money—$6,944 to be exact.* Mr. Stone has $6,944 in demand deposits that he didn't have before; and this is a net addition to the money supply since the person who originally deposited the currency in Bank *A* still has his $10,000, and Mr. Jones still has the $8,333 he deposited in Bank *B*, and this is still not the end of the story. Bank *C* has experienced an increase of $6,944 in its demand deposits and in its reserves. Thus it—like Banks *A* and *B* before it—can increase its loans and investments. By how much? At this point, the pattern is becoming clear; *it can lend the amount by which its reserves exceed the legally required reserves.* In other words, since Bank *C* must hold $\$\frac{6{,}944}{6}$, or $1,157, in legally required reserves against the new deposit of $6,944, it can lend $6,944 minus $1,157, or $5,787.

According to our plot, Bank *C* lends $5,787 to Mr. White, who buys a truck from the local General Motors dealer, Mr. Black. Mr. Black deposits Mr. White's check for $5,787 to his account at Bank *D*. Figure 14.9 traces out the effects on Bank *C*'s balance sheet. The top panel shows the original increase in its demand deposits and in its reserves of $6,944. The second panel shows the increase of $5,787 in its loans stemming from its loan to Mr. White, as well as the accompanying increase in its demand deposits of $5,787 representing the demand deposit it gave to Mr. White. The third panel shows the $5,787 decrease in demand de-

Figure 14.8
Changes in Bank *B*'s Balance Sheet

	Assets (dollars)		Liabilities and net worth (dollars)	
Bank receives deposit	Reserves	+8,333	Demand deposits	+8,333
	Loans and investments	No change	Net worth	No change
	Total	+8,333	Total	+8,333
Bank buys bond	Reserves	No change	Demand deposits	+6,944
	Loans and investments	+6,944	Net worth	No change
	Total	+6,944	Total	+6,944
Mr. Stone deposits money in Bank *C*	Reserves	−6,944	Demand deposits	−6,944
	Loans and investments	No change	Net worth	No change
	Total	−6,944	Total	−6,944
Total effect	Reserves	+1,389	Demand deposits	+8,333
	Loans and investments	+6,944	Net worth	No change
	Total	+8,333	Total	+8,333

Figure 14.9
Changes in Bank C's Balance Sheet

	Assets (dollars)		Liabilities and net worth (dollars)	
Bank receives deposit	Reserves	+6,944	Demand deposits	+6,944
	Loans and investments	No change	Net worth	No change
	Total	+6,944	Total	+6,944
Bank makes loan	Reserves	No change	Demand deposits	+5,787
	Loans and investments	+5,787	Net worth	No change
	Total	+5,787	Total	+5,787
Mr. White spends $5,787	Reserves	−5,787	Demand deposits	−5,787
	Loans and investments	No change	Net worth	No change
	Total	−5,787	Total	−5,787
Total effect	Reserves	+1,157	Demand deposits	+6,944
	Loans and investments	+5,787	Net worth	No change
	Total	+6,944	Total	+6,944

posits when Mr. White checked out the whole of his account, and the $5,787 decrease in reserves when Bank *C* transferred this amount of reserves to Bank *D* to pay for the check. The bottom panel shows the total effect. As in the case of Banks *A* and *B*, Bank *C* continues to meet the legal reserve requirements when the full effects of the transaction have made themselves felt.

Bank C *also has created some money—$5,787, to be exact.* To see why, note that Mr. Black has $5,787 in demand deposits that he didn't have before; and this is a net addition to the money supply since the original depositor in Bank *A* still has his $10,000, Mr. Jones still has the $8,333 in Bank *B*, and Mr. Stone still has the $6,944 in Bank *C*. But this is still not the end of the story. Bank *D* has experienced an increase of $5,787 in its demand deposits and its reserves. Thus it—like Banks *A*, *B*, and *C* before it—can increase its loans and investments by the amount of its ***excess reserves*** (those in excess of legal requirements). Since it must hold $\frac{\$5{,}787}{6} = \$964$ as legal reserves against its increase in deposits of $5,787, its excess reserves are $5,787 minus $964, or $4,823. Thus Bank *D* can increase its loans and investments by $4,823. As we saw at the beginning of this saga, it decides to lend Mr. Cohen $4,823 to buy some lumber from Mr. Palucci. Mr. Cohen pays Mr. Palucci with a check for $4,823 drawn on Bank *D* and Mr. Palucci deposits the check to his account at Bank *E*. As shown in Figure 14.10, Bank *D* winds up with no excess reserves after it transfers reserves to Bank *E* to pay for the check. (To check your grasp of the material in this section, see if you can fill in the numbers in the top three panels of Figure 14.10; the correct answer is given at the bottom of the facing page.) But Mr. Palucci winds up with a demand deposit of $4,823 that he didn't have before. Thus *Bank* D *also creates some money—$4,823, to be exact.*

The Total Effect of the Original $10,000 Deposit

How big an increase in the money supply can the entire banking system support as a conse-

Figure 14.10
Changes in Bank *D*'s Balance sheet

	Assets (dollars)		Liabilities and net worth (dollars)	
Bank receives deposit	Reserves		Demand deposits	
	Loans and investments		Net worth	
	Total		Total	
Bank makes loan	Reserves		Demand deposits	
	Loan and investments		Net worth	
	Total		Total	
Mr. Cohen spends $4,823	Reserves		Demand deposits	
	Loans and investments		Net worth	
	Total		Total	
Total effect	Reserves	+ 964	Demand deposits	+5,787
	Loans and investments	+4,823	Net worth	No change
	Total	+5,787	Total	+5,787

quence of the original $10,000 deposit in Bank *A*? Clearly, the effects of the original deposit spread from one bank to another, since each bank hands new reserves (and deposits) to another bank, which in turn hands them to another bank. For example, Bank *E* now has $4,823 more in deposits and reserves and so can create $4,019[6] in new money by making a loan or investment of this amount. This process goes on indefinitely, and it would be impossible to describe each of the multitude of steps involved. Fortunately, it isn't necessary to do so. We can figure out the total amount of new money the entire banking system can support as a consequence of the original $10,000 deposit in Bank *A* without going through all these steps.

We do this by computing how much new money each bank creates. Besides the original $10,000, Bank *A* creates $8,333—which is $\frac{5}{6}$ of $10,000. Then Bank *B* creates an additional $6,944—$(\frac{5}{6})^2$ of $10,000. Then Bank *C* creates an additional $5,787—$(\frac{5}{6})^3$ of $10,000. Then Bank *D* creates an additional $4,823—$(\frac{5}{6})^4$ of

[6] Why $4,019? Because it must hold $\frac{\$4,823}{6} = \$804$ as reserves to support the new demand deposit of $4,823. Thus it has excess reserves of $4,019, and it can create another new demand deposit of this amount.

The missing numbers in Figure 14.10 are:

	Assets (dollars)		*Liabilities and net worth (dollars)*	
Bank receives deposit	Reserves	+5,787	Demand deposits	+5,787
	Loans and investments	No change	Net worth	No change
	Total	+5,787	Total	+5,787
Bank makes loan	Reserves	No change	Demand deposits	+4,823
	Loans and investments	+4,823	Net worth	No change
	Total	+4,823	Total	+4,823
Mr. Cohen spends $4,823	Reserves	−4,823	Demand deposits	−4,823
	Loans and investments	No change	Net worth	No change
	Total	−4,823	Total	−4,823

Table 14.2
Increase in Money Supply Resulting from $10,000 Increase in Reserves

Source	Amount (dollars)
Original deposit	10,000
Created by Bank *A*	8,333
Created by Bank *B*	6,944
Created by Bank *C*	5,787
Created by Bank *D*	4,823
Created by Bank *E*	4,019
Created by Bank *F*	3,349
Created by Bank *G*	2,791
Created by Bank *H*	2,326
Created by Bank *I*	1,938
Created by Bank *J*	1,615
Created by other banks	8,075
Total	60,000

$10,000. Then Bank *E* creates an additional $4,019–$(5/6)^5$ of $10,000. The amount of money created by each bank is less than that created by the previous bank, so that the total amount of new money created by the original $10,000 deposit–$10,000 + $8,333 + $6,944 + $5,787 + $4,823 + $4,019 + . . . –tends to a finite limit as the process goes on and on. Elementary algebra tells us what this sum of terms will be. *When the process works itself out, the entire banking system can support $60,000 in money as a consequence of the original $10,000 deposit of new funds.*[7] For a demonstration of this fact, see Table 14.2 and Figure 14.11. Table 14.2 shows the amount of new demand deposits created at each stage of this process, while Figure 14.11 plots the cumulative expansion in demand deposits.

We must note that the banking system as a whole has accomplished what we said in a previous section that an individual bank–Bank *A*–could not do. It has created an additional $50,000 of demand deposits on the basis of the original $10,000 deposit. In other words, given the additional $10,000 in reserves, the banking system can create $60,000 in money. Certainly this seems sensible, since each $1 of reserves can back up $6 in demand deposits. But for the reasons discussed in a previous section, an individual bank cannot do this, unless, of course, it is a monopoly bank. If it is, it need have no fear of losing reserves to other banks, because there are no other banks; so it can behave this way. However, banking in the United States is not monopolized.

In general, *if a certain amount of additional reserves is made available to the banking system, the banking system as a whole can increase the money supply by an amount equal to the amount of additional reserves multiplied by the reciprocal of the required ratio of reserves to deposits.* In other words, to obtain the total increase in the money supply that can be achieved from a certain amount of additional reserves, multiply the amount of additional reserves by the reciprocal of the required ratio of reserves to deposits–or, what amounts to the same thing, *divide the amount of additional reserves by the legally required ratio of reserves to deposits.* Putting it in still another way, the banking system as a whole can increase the money supply by $(1/r)$ dollars–where r is the required ratio of reserves to deposits–for every $1 increase in reserves.[8]

Let's apply this proposition to a couple of specific cases. Suppose that the banking system's reserves increase by $10,000 and that the required ratio of reserves to deposits is $1/6$. To determine how much the banking system can increase the money supply, we must divide the

[7] The proof of this is as follows: the total amount of money supported by the $10,000 in reserves is $10,000 + $8,333 + $6,944 + $5,787 + . . . , which equals $10,000 + 5/6 × $10,000 + $(5/6)^2$ × $10,000 + $(5/6)^3$ × $10,000 + . . . , which equals $10,000 ×

$$(1+5/6+(5/6)^2+(5/6)^3+\ldots)=\$10{,}000\times\frac{1}{1-(5/6)}=\$60{,}000,$$

since $1 + 5/6 + (5/6)^2 + (5/6)^3 + \ldots = \frac{1}{1-(5/6)}$.

[8] The total amount of money supported by $1 of additional reserves is

$$1+(1-r)+(1-r)^2+(1-r)^3+\ldots=\frac{1}{1-(1-r)}=\frac{1}{r}$$

We reach this conclusion by the same method we used in footnote 7.

Figure 14.11
Cumulative Expansion in Demand Deposits on Basis of $10,000 of New Reserves and Legal Reserve Requirement of 16⅔ Percent
The original deposit was $10,000. In the first stage of the expansion process, Bank *A* created an additional $8,333. In the second stage, Bank *B* created an additional $6,944. In the third stage, Bank *C* created an additional $5,787. This process goes on until the final result is $60,000 of demand deposits.

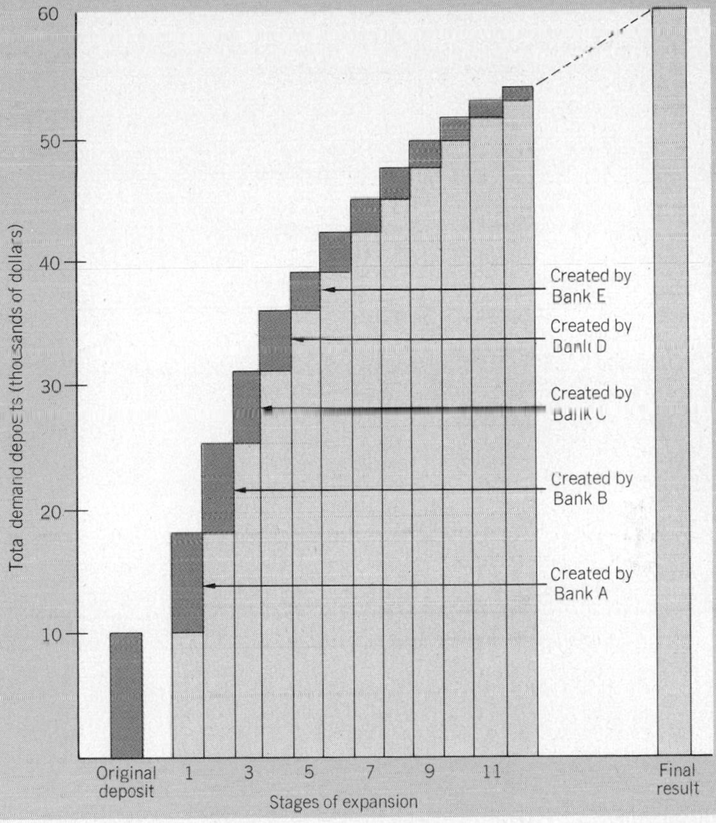

amount of the additional reserves—$10,000—by the required ratio of reserves to deposits—⅙—to get the answer, $60,000. Note, with proper satisfaction, that this answer checks with our earlier results. Now suppose that the required ratio of reserves to deposits is ⅕. By how much can the banking system increase the money supply? Dividing $10,000 by ⅕, we get the answer: $50,000. Note that the higher the required ratio of reserves to deposits, the smaller the amount by which the banking system can increase the money supply on the basis of a given increase in reserves. More will be said about this in the next chapter.

Finally, an increase in reserves generally affects a great many banks at about the same time. For expository purposes, it is useful to trace through the effect of an increase in the reserves of a single bank—Bank *A* in our case. But usually this is not what happens. Instead, lots of banks experience an increase in reserves at about the same time. Thus they all have excess reserves at about the same time, and they all make loans or investments at about the same time. The result is that, when the people who borrow money spend it, each bank tends both to gain and lose reserves. Thus, on balance, each bank need not lose reserves. In real life the amount of bank money often expands simultaneously throughout the banking system until the legally required ratio of deposits to reserves is approached.

The Effect of a Decrease in Reserves

Up to this point, we have been talking only about the effect of an increase in reserves.

Figure 14.12
Change in Your Bank's Balance Sheet

	Assets (dollars)		Liabilities and net worth (dollars)	
You withdraw deposit	Reserves	−10,000	Demand deposits	−10,000
	Loans and investments	No change	Net worth	No change
	Total	−10,000	Total	−10,000
Bank sells bond and gets funds from Bank *Q*	Reserves	+ 8,333	Demand deposits	No change
	Loans and investments	− 8,333	Net worth	No change
	Total	No change	Total	No change
Total effect	Reserves	− 1,667	Demand deposits	−10,000
	Loans and investments	− 8,333	Net worth	No change
	Total	−10,000	Total	−10,000

What happens to the quantity of money if reserves decrease? For example, suppose that you draw $10,000 out of your bank and hold it in the form of currency, perhaps by sewing it in your mattress. You thus reduce the total reserves of the banking system by $10,000. Let us begin with the effect on your bank. Clearly, it will experience a $10,000 decrease in deposits (because of your withdrawal) and, at the same time, a $10,000 decrease in reserves. Thus, if it was holding $1 in reserves for every $6 in deposits before you withdrew the money, it now holds less than the legally required reserves. If its deposits go down by $10,000, its reserves must go down by $1,667, not $10,000, if the 6:1 ratio between deposits and reserves is to be maintained. To observe the legal reserve requirements, your bank must increase its reserves by $10,000 minus $1,667, or $8,333. It has several ways to get this money, one being to sell securities. It may sell a municipal bond to Mrs. Cherrytree for $8,333. To pay for the bond, she writes a check on her bank, Bank *Q*, for the $8,333. Thus, as shown in Figure 14.12, your bank's investments decrease by $8,333, and its reserves increase by $8,333 when Bank *Q* transfers this amount to your bank to pay for the check.

But this is not the end of the story. Because Bank *Q* has lost $8,333 in deposits and $8,333 in reserves, its reserves are now less than the legal minimum. To maintain the legally required reserves, its reserves should have gone down by $\frac{\$8{,}333}{6}$, or $1,389—not by $8,333. Thus Bank *Q* must increase its reserves by $8,333 minus $1,389, or $6,944. To do so, it sells a bond it holds for $6,944. But when the person who buys the bond gives Bank *Q* his check for $6,944 drawn on Bank *R*, Bank *R* loses $6,944 in deposits and $6,944 in reserves. Thus Bank *R*'s reserves are now below the legal requirement. To maintain the legally required reserves, its reserves should have gone down by $\frac{\$6{,}944}{6}$, or $1,157—not by $6,944. So Bank *R* must increase its reserves by \$6,944 minus \$1,157, or \$5,787. And on and on the process goes.

Let us consider the over-all effect on the money supply of the \$10,000 decrease in reserves. Your bank's demand deposits decreased by \$10,000, Bank Q's demand deposits decreased by \$8,333 ($\frac{5}{6}$ of \$10,000), Bank R's demand deposits decreased by \$6,944 ($(\frac{5}{6})^2$ of \$10,000), and so on. The total decrease in the money supply—\$10,000 + \$8,333 + \$6,944 + . . . —tends to a finite limit as the process goes on and on. This limit is \$60,000. Thus, *when the process works itself out, the entire banking system will reduce the money supply by \$60,000 as a consequence of a \$10,000 decrease in reserves.* More generally, *if the banking system's reserves decrease by a certain amount, the banking system as a whole will reduce demand deposits by an amount equal to the reduction in reserves multiplied by the reciprocal of the required ratio of reserves to deposits.*

In other words, to obtain the total decrease in demand deposits resulting from a reduction in reserves, *divide the reduction in reserves by the legally required ratio of reserves to deposits.* Putting it another way, the banking system as a whole will reduce demand deposits by $(1/r)$ dollars—where r is the required ratio of reserves to deposits—for every \$1 decrease in reserves. Of course, there is often a simultaneous contraction of money on the part of many banks, just as there is often a simultaneous expansion. But this doesn't affect the result.

Let's apply this proposition to a particular case. Suppose that the banking system experiences a decrease in reserves of \$10,000 and that the required ratio of reserves to deposits is $\frac{1}{6}$. Applying this rule, we must divide the reduction in reserves—\$10,000—by the required ratio of reserves to deposits—$\frac{1}{6}$—to get the answer, which is a \$60,000 reduction in demand deposits. This answer checks with the result in the next to last paragraph.

Note that the effect of a \$1 decrease in reserves is equal in absolute terms to the effect of a \$1 increase in reserves. Whether the change is an increase or a decrease, a \$1 change in reserves leads to a \$$(1/r)$ change in demand deposits. Or, more precisely, this is the case if certain assumptions, discussed in the next section, are true. To complete our discussion of how banks create money, we turn now to these assumptions.

Currency Withdrawals and Excess Reserves

In discussing the amount of additional demand deposits that can be created by the banking system as a result of injecting \$10,000 of new reserves, we made the important assumption that everyone who received the new demand deposits—from Mr. Palucci back to the person who originally deposited his money in Bank A—wants to keep this money in the form of demand deposits rather than currency. However, this clearly may not be the case. Some people who receive new demand deposits may choose to withdraw some part of this money as currency. For example, Mr. Palucci may decide to withdraw \$1,000 of his new demand deposit in cash.

What effect will this withdrawal of currency have on the amount of demand deposits the banking system can create? To begin with, note that this withdrawal of currency from the entire banking system reduces the reserves of the banking system by \$1,000. Applying the results of the previous section, this means that the banking system can create \$6,000 less in demand deposits (\$1,000 divided by $\frac{1}{6}$) than it could if the currency had not been withdrawn. Consequently, the banking system can create \$60,000 minus \$6,000, or \$54,000, from the combination of the original \$10,000 injection of reserves and the \$1,000 withdrawal of currency. In other words, the banking system can create an amount of demand deposits equal to the amount of additional reserves *left perma-*

nently with the banking system ($10,000 minus $1,000, or $9,000 in this case) divided by the required ratio of reserves to demand deposits.

Similarly, in discussing how much demand deposits will be reduced as a consequence of a $10,000 reduction in reserves, we made the important assumption that everyone who buys a security from a bank pays the bank by check. But some people may pay partly or in full with currency, and this will affect how much the amount of demand deposits must be reduced by the banking system. If somebody pays $1,000 in currency to one of the banks, this restores $1,000 of the $10,000 in reserves that the banking system lost. Thus the banking system really loses $9,000, not $10,000. Then, applying the rule set forth in the previous section, the banking system must reduce its demand deposits by $54,000 ($9,000 divided by 1/6), not $60,000 ($10,000 divided by 1/6). In general, whether the change in reserves is an increase or a decrease, the change in demand deposits equals the change in reserves *left permanently with the banking system* ($9,000 in these cases) divided by the required ratio of reserves to demand deposits. Thus *whether or not a change in reserves has the maximum effect on demand deposits depends on how much of these reserves the public leaves in the banking system.*[9]

Another important assumption lies behind our discussion of the effects of $10,000 of additional reserves—or a $10,000 reduction in reserves—on the amount of demand deposits: *we have assumed that no bank holds excess reserves.* In other words, we have assumed that, whenever a bank has enough reserves to make a loan or investment, it will do so. Recall Bank *A*, which received a new deposit of $10,000. The new deposit enabled Bank *A* to increase its loans and investments by $8,333 without winding up with less than the legally required reserves. Thus we assumed that it would go ahead and make this much in additional loans and investments. In general, this seems to be a reasonable assumption, for the simple reason that loans and investments bring profits (in interest) into the bank while excess reserves bring none. But the matter is not as simple as all that. If a bank cannot find loans and investments it regards as attractive, it may decide to make no such loans. After all, there isn't much profit to be made on a loan that is not repaid. Also, if interest rates are very low, the bank may feel that it isn't losing much by not lending money. During the Great Depression of the 1930s, for example, banks held large excess reserves for this reason. In addition, banks can benefit by maintaining excess reserves, since they constitute insurance against deposit losses.

What difference does it make whether banks hold excess reserves? The answer is plenty. If, for example, Bank *A* decides to lend less than the full $8,333, this will mean that an increase in reserves will have a smaller effect on the amount of demand deposits than we indicated previously. Similarly, if banks hold excess reserves, a decrease in reserves is likely to have a smaller effect on the amount of demand deposits than we indicated above. Thus *whether or not a change in reserves has the maximum effect on demand deposits depends on the lending policies of the bankers. If they do not lend out as much as they can, the effect on demand deposits will be diminished accordingly.*

Summary

The Federal Reserve System is responsible for regulating and controlling the money supply. Established in 1913, the Fed is composed of

[9] Note too that people can convert demand deposits into time deposits, and vice versa. There are legal reserve requirements against time deposits, but they are lower than those against demand deposits. The conversion of demand deposits into time deposits will influence how much money can be supported by a certain amount of reserves. Thus the banking system can support an amount of demand deposits equal to the amount of additional reserves divided by the legally required ratio of reserves to demand deposits (no more, no less) only if there is no conversion of demand deposits into time deposits. In other words, we assume that all the demand deposits created by the banking system are converted into neither cash nor time deposits.

the member banks, 12 regional Federal Reserve Banks, and the Federal Reserve Board, which coordinates the activities of the system. The Federal Reserve System is the central bank of the United States. Commercial banks have two primary functions. First, they hold demand deposits and permit checks to be drawn on them. Second, they lend money to firms and individuals.

Most of our money supply is not coin and paper currency, but bank money—demand deposits. This money is created by banks. Whereas the earliest banks held reserves equal to demand deposits, modern banks practice fractional-reserve banking: that is, their reserves equal only a fraction of their demand deposits. The Federal Reserve System requires every commercial bank that is a member of the system to hold a certain percentage of its demand deposits as reserves; the percentage varies with the size of the bank. Although they increase the safety of the banks, the major purpose of these legal reserve requirements is to control the money supply. Banks have become much safer in recent years, due in part to better management and regulation, as well as to the government's stated willingness to insure and stand behind their deposits. However, bank failures still occur, and bank regulation is not as stringent as it might be.

A bank creates money by lending or investing its excess reserves. If banks had to keep reserves equal to their deposits, they could not create money. A bank cannot lend or invest more than its excess reserves, unless it is a monopoly bank, because it will wind up with less than the legally required reserves. However, the banking system as a whole can support demand deposits equal to its total reserves divided by the legally required ratio of reserves to deposits. Thus, if reserves somewhere in the banking system increase by a certain amount, the banking system as a whole can increase demand deposits by the amount of the increase in reserves divided by the legally required ratio of reserves to deposits.

Similarly, if there is a decrease in reserves somewhere in the banking system, the system as a whole must decrease demand deposits by the amount of the decrease in reserves divided by the legally required ratio of reserves to deposits. Demand deposits are decreased by banks' selling securities or refusing to renew loans, just as demand deposits are increased by banks' making loans and investments.

Our argument so far has assumed that when additional reserves were made available to the banking system, there was no withdrawal of part of them in the form of currency, and that when reserves are decreased, no currency is deposited in banks. If such changes in the amount of currency take place, the change in demand deposits will equal the change in reserves left permanently with the banking system divided by the legally required ratio of reserves to deposits. We have also assumed that the banks hold no excess reserves. Since banks make profits by lending money and making investments, this assumption is generally sensible. But when loans are risky and interest rates are low—for example, in the Great Depression of the 1930s—banks have been known to hold large excess reserves. Clearly, changes in reserves will not have their full, or maximum, effect on demand deposits if the banks do not lend and invest as much as possible.

CONCEPTS FOR REVIEW

Fractional-reserve banking
Legal reserve requirements
Excess reserves
Simultaneous expansion

QUESTIONS FOR DISCUSSION AND REVIEW

1. Suppose that John Smith deposits $50,000 in newly printed currency to his account at Bank *A*. What is the effect on Bank *A*'s balance sheet? Fill in blanks below.

Assets (dollars)		Liabilities and net worth (dollars)	
Reserves	______	Demand deposits	______
Loans and investments	______	Net worth	______
Total	______	Total	______

2. If the legal reserve requirement is that Bank *A* must hold $1 in reserves for every $5 in demand deposits, by how much can Bank *A* increase its loans (after the deposit described in Question 1), if it is not a monopoly bank? By how much can it increase its loans if it is a monopoly bank?

3. Suppose that Bank *A* lends the Bugsbane Music Box Company $30,000. What is the effect on Bank *A*'s balance sheet of both the deposit described in Question 1 and this loan? Fill in the blanks below.

Assets (dollars)		Liabilities and net worth (dollars)	
Reserves	______	Demand deposits	______
Loans and investments	______	Net worth	______
Total	______	Total	______

4. After the Bugsbane Music Box Company receives the $30,000 loan, it uses the money to buy a new piece of equipment from the XYZ Tool Company. The XYZ Tool Company deposits Bugsbane's check on Bank *A* to its account at the Bank of America. What is the total effect on Bank *A*'s balance sheet of the deposit described in Question 1, the loan in Question 3, and the purchase described here? Fill in the blanks below.

Assets (dollars)		Liabilities and net worth (dollars)	
Reserves	______	Demand deposits	______
Loans and investments	______	Net worth	______
Total	______	Total	______

5. If Bank *A* had no excess reserves prior to the transactions described in Questions 1, 3, and 4, and if the legal reserve requirement is as described in Question 2, does Bank *A* have excess reserves after these transactions? If so, how large are these excess reserves?

6. "Banks do not create money. After all, they can only lend out money that they receive from depositors." Comment and evaluate.

7. Suppose that the legally required ratio of reserves to deposits is $\frac{1}{5}$. If the banking system's reserves shrink by $50 million, by how much will the money supply change? What assumptions are you making about excess reserves and currency withdrawals?

8. "Demand deposits are increased by banks when they call in loans and sell investments." Comment and evaluate.

9. Describe the way in which the banking system can create money if there is a single monopoly bank in the nation.

10. Suppose that you were the president of the Bank of America. What rules would you ask your executives to follow in making loans? In other words, what information should they look at, and how should they use this information, to decide whether or not to grant a particular loan?

15

Monetary Policy

Like fiscal policy, monetary policy is no panacea, but it is a very important tool for stabilization of the economy. In recent years, monetary policy has been the subject of considerable controversy. For example, in 1974, when the Federal Reserve held a tight rein on the money supply, many economists claimed that improper monetary policy was pushing the United States into a recession, while others argued that a restrictive monetary policy of this sort was needed to combat the very high rate of inflation. Without doubt, such controversies will continue in the future, since one thing is certain: economists of all persuasions agree that monetary policy has a major impact on the economy.

In this chapter, we are concerned with a variety of basic questions about monetary policy: Who makes monetary policy? What sorts of tools can be employed by monetary policy makers? How does monetary policy affect our national output and the price level? What are some of the problems involved in formulating effective monetary policy? What has been the nature of monetary policy in the United States in recent decades?

The Aims of Monetary Policy

Monetary policy is concerned with the money supply and interest rates. We described in Chapter 13 how the money supply influences net national product and the price level. If the economy is at considerably less than full employment, increases in the money supply tend to increase real NNP, and decreases in the money supply tend to decrease real NNP, with little or no effect on the price level. As full employment is approached, increases in the money supply tend to affect the price level, as well as real output. Finally, once full employment is reached, increases in the money supply result primarily in increases in the price level, since real output cannot increase appreciably.

In formulating monetary policy, the government's objectives are to attain and maintain reasonably full employment without excessive inflation. In other words, when a recession seems imminent and business is soft, the monetary authorities are likely to increase the money supply and push down interest rates. That is, they will "ease credit" or "ease money," as the newspapers put it. This tends to increase net national product. On the other hand, when the economy is in danger of overheating and serious inflation threatens, the monetary authorities will probably rein in the money supply and push up interest rates—in newspaper terms, they will "tighten credit" or "tighten money." This tends to reduce spending, and thus curb the upward pressure on the price level.

At this point, you may be muttering to yourself, "But the aims of monetary policy are essentially the same as those of fiscal policy!" Of course, you are right. Monetary policy and fiscal policy are both aimed at promoting full employment without inflation. But they use different methods to attain this goal. Fiscal policy uses the spending and taxing powers of the government, whereas monetary policy uses the government's power over the money supply.

The Central Role of Bank Reserves

As you will recall from Chapter 13, there is a difference of view concerning the processes by which changes in the money supply affect NNP and the price level. On the one hand, monetarists use the quantity theory of money to link changes in the money supply directly to changes in nominal NNP. On the other hand, Keynesians believe that an increase (decrease) in the money supply decreases (increases) the interest rate, which in turn shifts the investment function upward (downward). This shift in the investment function tends to increase (decrease) national product.[1]

Regardless of which view is closer to the truth, it is essential that we understand how the monetary authorities can promote their aims, since both Keynesians and monetarists acknowledge the importance of monetary policy. Economists of all persuasions would agree that a fundamental and key question is: How can the monetary authorities influence the money supply? And they would agree that the answer is: *by managing the reserves of the banking system.*

To see what this means in practice, suppose that the monetary authorities think that a recession is about to develop, and that, to prevent it, they want to increase the money supply more rapidly than they would otherwise. How can they realize this objective? By increasing the reserves of the banks. As we saw in the previous chapter, an increase in bank reserves enables the banks to increase the money supply.

[1] Keynesians also recognize that spending by consumers and state and local governments, as well as investment, is likely to be affected by changes in the quantity of money. See Chapter 13.

Indeed, we learned that if there were no excess reserves and no currency withdrawals, the banks could increase the money supply by $6 for every $1 of additional reserves.[2] (The ways in which the monetary authorities can increase the reserves of the banking system are discussed at length in subsequent sections.)

On the other hand, suppose that the monetary authorities smell a strong whiff of unacceptable inflation in the economic wind, and so decide to cut back on the rate of increase of the money supply. To do so, they can slow down the rate of increase of bank reserves. As we saw in the previous chapter, this will force the banks to curtail the growth of their demand deposits, by easing off on their loans and investments. Indeed, if the monetary authorities go so far as to reduce the reserves of the banking system, this will tend to reduce the money supply. Under the assumptions made in the previous chapter, the banks must cut back the money supply by $6 for every $1 reduction in reserves.

Makers of Monetary Policy

Who establishes our monetary policy? Who decides that, in view of the current and prospective economic situation, the money supply should be increased (or decreased) at a certain rate? As in the case of fiscal policy, this is not a simple question to answer; many individuals and groups play an important role. Certainly, however, *the leading role is played by the Federal Reserve System—in particular, by the members of the Federal Reserve Board and the Federal Open Market Committee.* The chairman of the Federal Reserve Board is often the chief spokesman for the Federal Reserve System. The recent chairmen—Arthur F. Burns and William McChesney Martin—undoubtedly have had considerable influence over monetary policy.

Although the Federal Reserve is responsible to Congress, Congress has established no clear guidelines for its behavior. Thus the Federal Reserve has had wide discretionary powers over monetary policy. But the Fedeal Reserve System is a huge organization, and it is not easy to figure out exactly who influences whom and who decides what. Formal actions can be taken by a majority of the board and of the Federal Open Market Committee (which is composed of the 7 members of the board plus 5 of the presidents of the 12 regional banks). However, this obviously tells only part of the story.

To get a more complete picture, it is essential to note too that many agencies and groups other than the Fed have an effect on monetary policy, although it is difficult to measure their respective influences. The Treasury frequently has an important voice in the formulation of monetary policy. The Fed must take into account the problems of the Treasury, which is faced with the task of selling huge amounts of government securities each year. Also, congressional committees hold hearings and issue reports on monetary policy and the operations of the Federal Reserve. These hearings and reports cannot fail to have some effect on Fed policy. In addition, beginning in 1975, the Congress has stipulated that the Fed must publish its long-term targets for growth in the money supply, the purpose being to establish somewhat more control over monetary policy. Finally, the president may attempt to influence the Federal Reserve Board. To keep the board as free as possible from political pressure, members are appointed for long terms—14 years—and a term expires every 2 years. But since members frequently do not serve out their full terms, a president may be able to name more than two members during each of his terms in office.

[2] Of course, this assumes that the legal reserve requirement is 16⅔ percent. If the legal reserve requirement were 20 percent, a $5 increase in the money supply could be supported by $1 of additional reserves. Also, as pointed out in the previous chapter, a much smaller increase in the money supply may result from an extra dollar of reserves if banks hold excess reserves and if currency is withdrawn.

Figure 15.1
Consolidated Balance Sheet of the 12 Federal Reserve Banks, March 31, 1976 (billions of dollars).

Assets		Liabilities and net worth	
Gold certificates[a]	12	Reserves of member banks	28
Securities	90	Treasury deposits	7
Loans to commercial banks	1	Outstanding Federal Reserve notes	76
Other assets	18	Other liabilities and net worth	10
Total	121	Total	121

Source: Federal Reserve Bulletin.
[a] Cash is included here too.

The Federal Reserve Banks: Their Consolidated Balance Sheet

We know from a previous section that the Federal Reserve controls the money supply largely by controlling the quantity of member bank reserves. To understand how the Federal Reserve can control the quantity of member bank reserves, one must begin by examining the consolidated balance sheet of the 12 regional Federal Reserve Banks. Such a consolidated balance sheet is shown in Figure 15.1; it pertains to March 31, 1976.

As shown in Figure 15.1, the assets of the Federal Reserve Banks are largely of three kinds: gold certificates, securities, and loans to commercial banks. *Gold certificates* are warehouse receipts issued by the Treasury for gold bullion. Most important for present purposes are *securities* and *loans to commercial banks.* The securities listed on the Federal Reserve Banks' balance sheet are government bonds, notes, and bills. By buying and selling these securities, the Federal Reserve establishes considerable leverage on the quantity of member bank reserves (as we shall see below). The loans to commercial banks listed on the Federal Reserve Banks' balance sheet are loans of reserves that the Fed has made to commercial banks. As pointed out in the previous chapter, the Fed can make such loans if it wants to.

According to the righthand side of the balance sheet in Figure 15.1, the liabilities of the Federal Reserve Banks are largely of three kinds: outstanding Federal Reserve notes, Treasury deposits, and reserves of member banks. The outstanding *Federal Reserve notes* are the paper currency that we use. Since these notes are debts of the Federal Reserve Banks, they are included among the Banks' liabilities. *Treasury deposits* are the deposits which the U.S. Treasury maintains at the Federal Reserve Banks. The Treasury draws checks on these deposits to pay its bills. Finally, the *reserves of member banks* have been discussed in some detail in the previous chapter. Note that, although these reserves are assets from the point of view of the commercial banks, they are liabilities from the point of view of the Federal Reserve Banks.

Tools of Monetary Policy

Open Market Operations

Figure 15.1 shows that government securities constitute about 75 percent of the assets held by the Federal Reserve Banks. As we saw in Chapter 6, the market for government securities is huge and well developed. The Federal Reserve is part of this market: sometimes it buys government securities, sometimes it sells

Figure 15.2
Effect of Fed's Purchasing $1 Million of Government Securities

A. Effect on Fed's balance sheet:

Assets (millions of dollars)		Liabilities and net worth (millions of dollars)	
Government securities	+ 1	Member bank reserves	+ 1

B. Effect on balance sheet of the Chase Manhattan Bank:

Assets (millions of dollars)		Liabilities and net worth (millions of dollars)	
Reserves	+ 1	Demand deposits	+ 1

them. Whether it is buying or selling—and how much—can have a heavy impact on the quantity of bank reserves. Indeed, the most important means the Federal Reserve has to control the quantity of bank reserves are ***open market operations,*** which is the name given to the purchase and sale by the Fed of U.S. government securities in the open market.

Buying securities. Suppose that the Federal Reserve buys $1 million worth of government securities in the open market, and that the seller of these securities is General Motors.[3] To determine the effect of this transaction on the quantity of bank reserves, let's look at the effect on the balance sheet of the Fed and on the balance sheet of the Chase Manhattan Bank, General Motors' bank.[4] In this transaction, the Fed receives $1 million in government securities and gives General Motors a check for $1 million. When General Motors deposits this check to its account at the Chase Manhattan Bank, the bank's demand deposits and reserves increase by $1 million. Thus, as shown in Figure 15.2, the lefthand side of the Fed's balance sheet shows a $1 million increase in government securities, and the righthand side shows a $1 million increase in bank reserves. The lefthand side of the Chase Manhattan Bank's balance sheet shows a $1 million increase in reserves, and the righthand side shows a $1 million increase in demand deposits. Clearly, *the Fed has added $1 million to the banks' reserves.* The situation is entirely analogous to the $10,000 deposit at Bank *A* in the previous chapter.

Selling securities. Suppose that the Federal Reserve sells $1 million worth of government securities in the open market. They are bought by Merrill Lynch, Pierce, Fenner, and Smith, a huge brokerage firm. What effect does this transaction have on the quantity of bank reserves? To find out, let's look at the balance sheet of the Fed and the balance sheet of Merrill Lynch's bank, which we again assume to be the Chase Manhattan. When Merrill Lynch buys the government securities from the Fed, the Fed gives Merrill Lynch the securities in exchange for Merrill Lynch's check for $1 million. When the Fed presents this check to the Chase Manhattan Bank for payment, Chase Manhattan's demand deposits and reserves decrease by $1 million. Thus, as shown in Figure 15.3, the lefthand side of the Fed's balance sheet shows a $1 million decrease in government securities, and the righthand side shows a $1 million decrease in reserves. The lefthand side of the Chase Manhattan Bank's balance sheet shows a $1 million decrease in reserves,

[3] Large corporations often hold quantities of government securities.

[4] For simplicity, we assume that General Motors has only one bank, the Chase Manhattan Bank. Needless to say, this may not be the case, but it makes no difference to the point we are making here. We make a similar assumption regarding the investment firm of Merrill Lynch in the next paragraph.

Figure 15.3
Effect of Fed's Selling $1 Million of Government Securities

A. Effect on Fed's balance sheet:

Assets (millions of dollars)		Liabilities and net worth (millions of dollars)	
Government securities	− 1	Member bank reserves	− 1

B. Effect on balance sheet of the Chase Manhattan Bank:

Assets (millions of dollars)		Liabilities and net worth (millions of dollars)	
Reserves	− 1	Demand deposits	− 1

and the righthand side shows a $1 million decrease in demand deposits. Clearly, *the Fed has reduced the reserves of the banks by $1 million.*

The Federal Open Market Committee

Thus the Federal Reserve adds to bank reserves when it buys government securities and reduces bank reserves when it sells them. Obviously, the extent to which the Federal Reserve increases or reduces bank reserves depends on the amount of government securities purchased or sold. The greater the amount, the greater the increase or decrease in bank reserves. As noted above, open market operations are the Fed's most important technique for controlling the money supply. The power to decide on the amount of government securities the Fed should buy or sell at any given moment rests with the *Federal Open Market Committee.* This group wields an extremely powerful influence over bank reserves and the nation's money supply. Every three or four weeks, the Federal Open Market Committee meets to discuss the current situation and trends, and gives instructions to the manager of the Open Market Account at the Federal Reserve Bank of New York, who actually buys and sells the government securities.

To get some insight into the nature of these discussions, consider the meeting of the Federal Open Market Committee (FOMC) that was held on May 26, 1970. According to Sherman Maisel, a former member of the Federal Reserve Board and one of the participants, much of the meeting was devoted to a discussion of whether the money supply was increasing too rapidly.

> The money supply and bank credit had grown far faster than appeared consistent with the 4 percent growth rate set as policy by prior votes [of the Committee]. The FOMC would now have to make a choice. . . . If the money supply were held to a 4 percent growth rate, interest rates would continue to rise and perhaps at an accelerating rate. . . . Was this what the Committee wanted, or would it prefer to allow reserves and money to grow more rapidly in order to avoid the unsettling effect of a still more rapid run-up in interest rates? . . . As in many similar situations, the Committee was sharply divided in its views. . . . The FOMC finally agreed that it would not change its basic policy stance. Monetary growth above 4 percent was not desirable.[5]

Although no single meeting can be regarded as typical, this brief description gives you some idea of the sort of discussion that takes place every three or four weeks in the meetings of the Federal Open Market Committee.

[5] Sherman Maisel, *Managing the Dollar,* New York: Norton, 1973. A section of this book dealing with Federal Reserve decision making is reprinted in E. Mansfield, *Economics: Readings, Issues, and Cases,* 2d ed., New York: Norton, 1977.

Changes in Legal Reserve Requirements

Open market operations are not the only means the Federal Reserve has to influence the money supply. Another way is *to change the legal reserve requirements.* In other words, *the Federal Reserve Board can change the amount of reserves banks must hold for every dollar of demand deposits.* In 1934, Congress gave the Federal Reserve Board the power to set—within certain broad limits—the legally required ratio of reserves to deposits for both demand and time deposits. From time to time, the Fed uses this power to change legal reserve requirements. For example, in 1958 it cut the legally required ratio of reserves to deposits in big city banks from 17½ percent to 16½ percent, and the ratio remained there until 1968, when it was raised to 17 percent. Table 15.1 shows the change in legal reserve requirements during 1951–73.

Table 15.1
Changes in Legal Reserve Requirements for Demand Deposits in Reserve City Banks, 1951–73.

Year	Reserve requirement (percent of deposits)
1951	20
1953	19
1954	18
1958	16½–17½[a]
1968	17
1969	17½
1973	18

[a] The reserve requirement was reduced from 17½ to 17 to 16½ percent during the year.

The obvious effect of an increase in the legally required ratio of reserves to deposits is that banks must hold larger reserves to support the existing amount of demand deposits. This in turn means that banks with little or no excess reserves will have to sell securities, refuse to renew loans, and reduce their demand deposits to meet the new reserve requirements. For example, suppose that a member bank has \$1 million in reserves and \$6 million in demand deposits. If the legal reserve requirement is 16 percent, it has excess reserves of \$1 million minus \$960,000 (.16 × \$6 million), or \$40,000. It is in good shape. If the legal reserve requirement is increased to 20 percent, this bank now needs \$1.2 million (.20 × \$6 million) in reserves. Since it only has \$1 million in reserves, it must sell securities or refuse to renew loans.

Consider now what happens to the banking system as a whole. Clearly, an increase in the legally required ratio of reserves to deposits means that, with a given amount of reserves, the banking system can maintain less demand deposits than before. For example, if the banking system has \$1 billion in total reserves, it can support $\frac{\$1 \text{ billion}}{.16}$, or \$6.25 billion in demand deposits when the legal reserve requirement is 16 percent. But it can support only $\frac{\$1 \text{ billion}}{.20}$, or \$5 billion in demand deposits when the legal reserve requirement is 20 percent. (See Figure 15.4.)[6] Thus, *increases in the legal reserve requirement tend to reduce the amount of demand deposits—bank money—the banking system can support.*

What is the effect of a decrease in the legally required ratio of reserves to deposits? Obviously, it means that banks must hold less reserves to support the existing amount of demand deposits, which in turn means that banks will suddenly find themselves with excess reserves. For example, if the banking system has \$1 billion in reserves and \$5 billion in demand deposits, there are no excess reserves when the legal reserve requirement is 20 percent. But

[6] We assume arbitrarily in Figure 15.4 that the total net worth of the banks is \$2 billion. Obviously, this assumption concerning the amount of total net worth makes no difference to the point we are making here.

suppose the Federal Reserve lowers the legal reserve requirement to 16 percent. Now the amount of legally required reserves is \$800 million (\$5 billion × .16), so that the banks have \$200 million in excess reserves—which means that they can increase the amount of their demand deposits. Thus *decreases in the legal reserve requirements tend to increase the amount of demand deposits—bank money—the banking system can support.*

Changes in legal reserve requirements are a rather drastic way to influence the money supply—they are to open market operations as a cleaver is to a scalpel, and so are made infrequently. For example, for about ten years—from April 1958 to January 1968—no change at all was made in legal reserve requirements for demand deposits in city banks. Nonetheless, the Fed can change legal reserve requirements if it wants to. And there can be no doubt about the potential impact of such changes. Large changes in reserve requirements can rapidly alter bank reserves and the money supply.

Changes in the Discount Rate

Still another way that the Federal Reserve can influence the money supply is through changes in the discount rate. As shown by the balance sheet of the Federal Reserve Banks (in Figure 15.1), commercial banks that are members of the Federal Reserve System can borrow from the Federal Reserve when their reserves are low (if the Fed is willing). This is one of the functions of the Federal Reserve. The interest rate the Fed charges the banks for loans is called the ***discount rate,*** and the Fed can increase or decrease the discount rate whenever it chooses. Increases in the discount rate discourage borrowing from the Fed, while decreases in the discount rate encourage it.

The discount rate can change substantially and fairly often (Table 15.2). For example, take 1968: the discount rate was changed from $4\frac{1}{2}$ to 5 percent in March, from 5 to $5\frac{1}{2}$ percent in April, and from $5\frac{1}{2}$ to $5\frac{1}{4}$ percent in August. When the Fed increases the discount rate, it obviously makes it more expensive for

Figure 15.4
Consolidated Balance Sheet of All Member Banks, before and after an Increase (from 16 to 20 percent) in the Legal Reserve Requirement

A. Before the increase in the legal reserve requirement:

Assets (billions of dollars)		Liabilities (billions of dollars)	
Reserves	1.00	Demand deposits	6.25
Loans and investments	7.25	Net worth	2.00
Total	8.25		8.25

B. After the increase in the legal reserve requirement:

Assets (billions of dollars)		Liabilities (billions of dollars)	
Reserves	1.00	Demand deposits	5.00
Loans and investments	6.00	Net worth	2.00
Total	7.00		7.00

Table 15.2
Average Annual Value of the Discount Rate, 1960–75

Year	Discount rate (percent)
1960	3.53
1961	3.00
1962	3.00
1963	3.23
1964	3.55
1965	4.04
1966	4.50
1967	4.19
1968	5.17
1969	5.87
1970	5.95
1971	4.88
1972	4.50
1973	6.44
1974	7.83
1975	6.25

Source: Economic Report of the President.

banks to augment their reserves in this way; hence it tightens up a bit on the money supply. On the other hand, when the Fed decreases the discount rate, it is cheaper for banks to augment their reserves in this way, and hence the money supply eases up a bit. However, note that the Fed is largely passive in these relations with the banks. It cannot make the banks borrow. It can only set the discount rate and see how many banks show up at the "discount window" to borrow. Also, it must be recognized that the Fed will not allow banks to borrow on a permanent or long-term basis. They are expected to use this privilege only to tide themselves over for short periods. To discourage banks from excessive use of the borrowing privilege, the discount rate is kept more or less in line with short-term market interest rates.

Most economists agree that changes in the discount rate have relatively little direct impact, and that the Fed's open market operations can and do offset easily the amount the banks borrow. Certainly changes in the discount rate cannot have anything like the direct effect on bank reserves of open market operations or changes in legal reserve requirements. *The principal importance of changes in the discount rate lies in their effects on people's expectations.* When the Fed increases the discount rate, this is generally interpreted as a sign that the Fed will tighten credit and the money supply. A cut in the discount rate is generally interpreted as a sign of easier money and lower interest rates. For example, when in 1969 the Federal Reserve announced an increase in the discount rate, the effect was a sharp drop in the prices of stocks and bonds. People interpreted this increase in the discount rate as a sure sign that the Fed was going to keep the money supply under tight reins to fight inflation.

Other Tools of Monetary Policy

In addition, the Federal Reserve has several other tools it can use, each of which is discussed below. These tools are generally less important than open market operations, changes in legal reserve requirements, and changes in the discount rate.

Moral suasion. This is a fancy term to describe various expressions of pleasure or displeasure by the Fed. In other words, the Fed tells the banks what it would like them to do or not do, and exhorts them to go along with its wishes. It may appeal to the patriotism of the bankers, or it may make some statements that could be regarded as threats. Of course, the Fed does not have the power to force banks to comply with its wishes, but the banks don't want to get into difficulties with the Fed. Thus moral suasion can have a definite impact, particularly for short periods. But banks are profit-oriented enterprises, and when the Fed's wishes conflict strongly with the profit motive, moral suasion may not work very well.

Interest-rate ceilings. The Fed can vary the maximum interest rate commercial banks can pay on time deposits. Since the 1930s, the Fed has had the power, under ***Regulation Q,*** to establish a ceiling on the interest rates commercial banks can pay.[7] And the level at which this ceiling is set can have an important influence on the flow of funds into time deposits, savings and loan associations, and other financial institutions. In particular, by preventing commercial banks from paying more than a certain rate of interest on time deposits, the Fed can protect the savings and loan associations, which are important sources of funds for the construction industry. In other words, the Fed can prevent the commercial banks from drawing too many deposits away from the savings and loan associations. Because it is aimed so directly at the construction industry, Regulation Q is often regarded as a selective credit control, not as a general tool of monetary policy. (A ***selective credit control*** is a control aimed at the use of credit for specific purposes.) Most economists favor the elimination of such interest ceilings on the grounds that they interfere with the functioning of free markets for funds. The Ford administration pressed for passage of legislation, introduced in Congress in 1973, that would phase out these ceilings.

Stock market credit. Another of the Fed's tools is to vary the margin requirements for the purchase of stocks. ***Margin requirements*** set the maximum percentage of the price of stocks that a person can borrow. For example, in the early 1960s, you could borrow 50 percent of the cost of such securities from your broker, but in late 1972, you could borrow only 35 percent from your broker. This is another example of a selective credit control. It may seem odd that margin requirements for the purchase of stocks were singled out for special treatment, but the severity of the stock market crash in 1929 was attributed partly to the fact that people in those days could borrow a large percentage—sometimes even 90 percent—of the value of the stock they purchased. (When stock prices slid, their small equity vanished quickly, and they had to sell out.) Consequently, after the crash, margin requirements were imposed.

Real estate and consumer credit. During and immediately after World War II, the Fed also had two other powers—regulation of mortgage terms and of installment contracts. Until 1953, the Fed could vary the size of down payments for houses and the number of years mortgages could run. This was an effective tool to influence the pace of residential construction. Increases in the size of down payments and decreases in the length of mortgages tended to discourage construction, while decreases in the size of down payments and increases in the length of mortgages tended to encourage construction. Until 1952, the Fed, under Regulation W, could also establish minimum amounts a person had to put up when he bought appliances, automobiles, and other items; and it could impose other restrictions on installment buying. After the Korean War, these restrictions became unpopular, and this power of the Fed was not continued.

When Is Monetary Policy Tight or Easy?

Everyone daydreams about being powerful and important. It is a safe bet, however, that few people under the age of 21 daydream about being members of the Federal Reserve Board or the Federal Open Market Committee. Yet the truth is that the members of the board and

[7] Since the 1930s, no commercial banks have been permitted to pay interest on demand deposits. Some people felt that many of the banks' problems in the 1920s and 1930s were due to too much competition: hence this law. It is easy to see why bankers felt that their earnings would be improved if none of them were allowed to compete for deposits by paying interest, but this is hardly consistent with a competitive philosophy. Legislation passed by the Senate in late 1975 would enable the banks to pay interest on demand deposits.

the committee are among the most powerful people in the nation. Suppose you were appointed to the Federal Reserve Board. As a member, you would have to decide—month by month, year by year—exactly how much government securities the Fed should buy or sell, as well as whether and when changes should be made in the discount rate, legal reserve requirements, and the other instruments of Federal Reserve policy. How would you go about making your choices?

Obviously you would need lots of data. Fortunately, the Fed has a very large and able research staff to provide you with plenty of the latest information about what is going on in the economy. But what sorts of data should you look at? Clearly, one thing you would want is some information on the extent to which monetary policy is inflationary or deflationary—that is, the extent to which it is "tight" or "easy." This is not simple to measure, but there is general agreement that the members of the Federal Reserve Board—and other members of the financial and academic communities—have often used the following four variables as measures.

The level of short-term interest rates. High interest rates are interpreted as meaning that monetary policy is tight; low interest rates are usually thought to mean that monetary policy is easy. The Fed can influence the level of interest rates through its open market operations and other policies. The level of interest rates has been used by the Fed and by the financial and academic communities as a major indicator of the effect of monetary policy on the economy, and the Fed has set as a target increases, decreases, or stability in interest rates. However, to know what the proper interest rate is, you need a forecast of the strength or weakness of investment demand, and an estimate of the extent to which a high interest rate is required to offset inflation. Thus the level of interest rates may be an ambiguous indicator.

The rate of increase of the money supply. When the money supply is growing at a relatively slow rate (much less than 4 or 5 percent per year), this is often interpreted as meaning that monetary policy is tight. A relatively rapid rate of growth in the money supply (much more than 4 or 5 percent per year) is often taken to mean that monetary policy is easy. During the 1960s and 1970s, this has become an increasingly important indicator of the effects of monetary policy on the economy. Its popularity is due to the influence of the monetarists. This indicator has the disadvantage of being influenced by the decisions of the banks and the public about how they want to hold their assets. And it is difficult to know whether the proper definition of the money supply is M_1, M_2, or something else.

The rate of increase of the monetary base. The ***monetary base,*** which by definition equals bank reserves plus currency outstanding, is important because the total money supply is dependent upon—and made from—it. Moreover, as an indicator of the effects of monetary policy, the monetary base has the advantage of being almost completely under the control of the Federal Reserve. A relatively slow growth rate in the monetary base (much less than 4 or 5 percent per year) is often interpreted as a sign of tight monetary policy. A relatively rapid rate of growth (much more than 4 or 5 percent per year) is often taken to mean that monetary policy is easy. This indicator is currently influential, particularly among the monetarists. Before 1960, it was seldom emphasized.

The level of free reserves. ***Free reserves*** are the excess reserves of the banks minus the amounts borrowed by the banks from the Federal Reserve.[8] When free reserves are negative, and the banks owe more to the Fed than they have in excess reserves, this has been used as an indicator that monetary policy is tight. Large and positive free reserves have been used as an

[8] Another measure of money market conditions is the interest rate on federal funds, the interest rate banks receive when they make an overnight loan of reserves to another bank.

indicator that monetary policy is easy. During the 1950s, the Fed used the amount of free reserves as its principal indicator of the effect of monetary policy on the economy, but this method is much less important today. Its shortcomings have been pointed out by many observers. In particular, the banks can influence the amount of free reserves by their lending and borrowing policies.

Decision Making at the Fed: A Case Study

Let's continue to assume that you have been appointed to the Federal Reserve Board, and that the economy suddenly is confronted with what seems to be a dangerously inflationary situation. What sort of action would you recommend? One appropriate action would be to sell a considerable amount of government securities, which would reduce bank reserves. You might also recommend an increase in the discount rate or even an increase in legal reserve requirements. To see how well you were doing, you would watch the variables discussed in the previous section. Specifically, you would look at the rate of increase of the money supply, as well as the rate of increase of the monetary base, and try to reduce both. At the same time you would try to increase interest rates.

Let's compare your recommendations with what the Fed really did in a similar situation. You will recall that the large military build-up associated with the Vietnam War created strong inflationary pressures during the middle and late 1960s. Fiscal policy was not used to curb this inflation, since government spending was highly destablizing and tax changes were painfully slow in coming. Consequently, much of the responsibility for fighting inflation fell to the Federal Reserve. What actions did it take?

In July 1965, when President Johnson announced that 50,000 more men would be sent to Vietnam, it was evident that inflationary pressures would mount unless appropriate fiscal or monetary policies were adopted. William M. Martin, chairman of the Federal Reserve Board, discussed these dangers with administration policy makers during the summer and fall of 1965, and argued publicly for a tax increase. But no such tax increase was in the cards. On December 4, 1965, the Fed decided to fire a highly visible volley against inflation. *The Federal Reserve Board voted to increase the discount rate from 4 to 4½ percent.* President Johnson and many Democrats in Congress were openly critical of this action, but many businessmen and economists agreed with the board's decision to act against inflation.

During 1965, the price level rose by 3 percent. During 1966, inflationary pressures continued unabated, and the government's large expenditures on Vietnam and domestic programs led to a huge budget deficit. As the hopes for a tax increase became dimmer, the Federal Reserve began to resort to sterner and more powerful measures to stem the inflationary tide. During early 1966, the Fed tried to tighten money, but there was a controversy within the board over the proper indicator. Using interest rates as an indicator, money was tight; but the money supply seemed to indicate that money was easy. By the summer of 1966, *the Fed allowed no increase in the monetary base, and the rate of increase in the money supply was cut to zero.* In other words, the Fed did not permit the money supply to increase at all. *Interest rates climbed to very high levels,* in part because of an increase in the demand for credit as people and firms began to fear that soon they would be unable to get credit. Money became extremely tight.

The effects on the financial and housing markets were devastating. Money for mortgages was extremely scarce, and for a time virtually no buyers could be found for municipal bonds. Knowledgeable people began to talk about an impending financial panic. By September 1966, when a crisis seemed imminent, the Fed assured all banks that it would lend them reserves so long as they made only legitimate and socially desirable loans. In addition, the Fed used its open market operations to increase bank reserves, and thus allow some increase in the money supply. By late September, the financial markets were operating reasonably well again.

Clearly, the Fed did pretty much what you would have recommended, and its policies had the intended effect. Indeed, this episode—the so-called credit crunch of 1966—indicates dramatically the potency of monetary policy. For that matter, according to some economists, the Fed may have gone too far. The job of the Fed is often described as "leaning against the wind," and in this case it leaned so heavily that it may almost have caused a panic. However, in its defense it must be pointed out that the Fed was faced with the problem of undoing the mischief caused by inadequate fiscal policies. It was dealt a very bad hand by the fiscal policy makers.

Monetary Policy in the United States

Experience during the 1950s to 1970s

For a more complete—and more balanced—picture of monetary policy in the United States, let's look briefly at the formulation of monetary policy in the past 25 years. When the Eisenhower administration took office in 1952, the economy was prosperous, but the Korean War was ending and the economy would soon have to adapt to peacetime conditions. At first, the Federal Reserve viewed inflation as the big danger, and in January 1953 it raised the discount rate and used open market operations to cut bank reserves. But by the middle of 1953, the Fed changed its course and increased bank reserves by its open market operations and by reducing the legal reserve requirements. This was fortunate because the reduction in government expenditures on the war helped to push the economy into a recession in mid-1953. During this recession, the Fed maintained a stimulative monetary policy.

In 1954, the economy came out of the recession; and by late 1954 and 1955, inflation began to reappear. In late 1955 the Fed moved toward credit restraint. In the middle of 1957, the economy turned down again, partly because of a drop in investment and defense expenditures. Once this became evident, the Fed quickly eased credit; the money supply was permitted to increase more rapidly; and interest rates fell. The recession was short-lived, and by late 1958 the economy was rising once more. But almost as soon as the recovery was under way, both the monetary and fiscal authorities began to put on the brakes. Interest rates rose substantially during much of 1958 and all of 1959. As a consequence of these monetary (and fiscal) policies, the economy began to turn soft once more, and in 1960 another recession began. In early 1960, the Federal Reserve began to ease credit somewhat.

When the Kennedy administration took office in 1961, it inherited a soft economy. To stimulate it, the Federal Reserve added to bank reserves, thus permitting rapid growth in the money supply. However, monetary policy did not play a leading role in economic policy in the Kennedy years. Instead, as described in Chapter 11, the Kennedy administration pushed hard for the tax cut, which was the cornerstone of its economic policy. Monetary policy played a supporting role. Leading administration economists felt that the money supply should grow in such a way as to accommodate the desired growth in national product, but that the growth in national product was to be brought about largely by the tax cut.[9] In fact,

[9] During much of the 1960s, monetary policy was formulated with one eye on the balance of payments, discussed in Chapter 21. If the Fed had attempted to stimulate the economy, interest rates would have fallen, and capital would have gone abroad in response to higher yields there. The result would have been a worsening of our balance of payments problems. In Chapter 21, we discuss the effect of balance of payments problems on domestic economic policy.

the Federal Reserve expanded the money supply during the early 1960s at a substantially higher average annual rate than during the late 1950s. In later years, some monetarists—like Milton Friedman—were to argue that this increase in the money supply, and not the tax cut, was responsible for the growth of national product in the mid-1960s.

When government spending in Vietnam began to skryrocket in 1965, monetary policy began to push itself to the fore. As described in the previous section, the Federal Reserve Board, faced with strong inflationary pressures stemming from a highly destabilizing fiscal policy, committed itself to a strong deflationary stance. The result, as we have seen, was the credit crunch of 1966, after which the Fed eased credit considerably. Indeed, in a rapid about-face, the Fed began to expand credit very rapidly in 1967 and 1968. In the latter part of 1967, the money supply was increasing at 10 percent per year. The tax surcharge was expected (incorrectly) to reduce spending so much that the Fed was encouraged to increase the money supply to offset it partially. Alarmed by this apparent shift to an inflationary posture, critics in Congress and elsewhere belabored the Fed for its "stop-go" policies.

When the Nixon administration came into office in 1969, inflation was unquestionably the nation's principal economic problem. Thus practically everyone, both Republicans and Democrats, agreed that monetary policy should be tight. In accord with this view, the Federal Reserve kept a close rein on the money supply during 1969. The result, however, was to slow the growth of national output and to increase unemployment.

Early in 1970, the Federal Reserve stated that it would adhere to a policy of maintaining steady growth in the money supply. Apparently the target was a 4 percent annual increase in the quantity of money. This decision was in part a reaction to the many criticisms of the Fed's previous "stop-go" policies. During most of 1970, the Fed succeeded in expanding the money supply at this relatively constant rate. During the first half of 1971, the money supply was allowed to expand rapidly: from January to June 1971, the quantity of money increased at a rate of 12 percent. But the second half of 1971 saw little growth in the money supply.

In August 1971, President Nixon announced his New Economic Policy, which, as you will recall from Chapter 11, entailed direct controls of prices, wages, and rents, as well as an expansionary fiscal policy. In line with the more expansionary tone of his economic policies, the president announced in early 1972, that "the Federal Reserve has taken steps to create the monetary conditions necessary for rapid economic expansion." In fact, the money supply grew by about 8 percent in 1972.

After price and wage controls were largely removed in 1973, open inflation occurred with a vengeance. In the *single month* of June 1973, wholesale prices increased by 2.4 percent. President Nixon responded by slapping a 60-day freeze on most prices (but not wages) beginning in mid-June of 1973. And the Federal Reserve tightened money considerably. For example, on June 8, 1973, the Fed raised the discount rate to 6½ percent, its highest level since 1921.

During 1973 and 1974, the Federal Reserve cut back on the rate of increase in the money supply. During 1973, the money supply grew by about 6 percent; during 1974, it grew by about 5 percent. Interest rates reached unprecedented heights in 1974. On the average, the discount rate was almost 8 percent during the year. And the prime bank rate, the interest rate that commercial banks charge their best customers, exceeded 12 percent for a time. Many critics of the Nixon and Ford administrations charged that the Federal Reserve was taking too strong a stance in its fight against inflation.

In the fourth quarter of 1974, there was a sharp, and largely unexpected, drop in real

William McChesney Martin and Arthur F. Burns

According to an old saying, "Where you stand depends on where you sit." This is no less true at 20th and Constitution, the location of the Federal Reserve Board, than elsewhere in Washington. But while internal and external constraints determine the broad outlines of monetary policy, whatever baggage the chairman brings to the job weighs also in setting the Fed's stances vis-á-vis the rest of the government and its stand on specific issues. Consider, for example, former Chairman William McChesney Martin and present Chairman Arthur F. Burns.

Martin associated himself with the New York financial community. Indeed he had served as president of the New York Stock Exchange during the thirties. He believed that good monetary policy required a "feel" for credit markets, an instinct presumably inbred and possibly cultivated, but certainly not acquired by examining thousands of statistics on M_1 and M_2. More importantly, Martin held that the primary responsibility of the Fed was to preserve a sound currency: to stand firm while others were pandering to popular sentiment and calling for cheap money. While elected officials played to the crowd with promises of more employment, the Fed would fight the good fight—against inflation. In order to assure the independence necessary to pursue such a course, Martin virtually removed the Fed from all but the most formal and infrequent contact with the Treasury, the CEA, and Budget Bureau during the Eisenhower administration.

WILLIAM MCCHESNEY MARTIN

ARTHUR F. BURNS

Burns brought a different set of baggage to his new job. Having spent much of his professional life as an economist at Columbia University and with the National Bureau of Economic Research, he was at home, not in a Wall Street club, but with a page of statistics. Thus his chairmanship has meant much more systematic collection and analysis of data on money markets and interest rate movements. (One veteran banker commented, "They may not be making better policy now, but they can certainly tell you better why they're making it.") More significantly, under Burns the Fed became a more active member of the Quadriad and he himself has given informal economic counsel to the president.

In 1974, Burns led the Feb in a very hard fight against the double-digit inflation that occurred then. The rate of growth of the money supply was cut back, and interest rates rose to record levels. Conservatives tended to applaud Burns. (As the president of the Philadelphia National Bank put it, "If the Fed fails again, we will be fighting inflation three years from now at 20 percent.") Liberals criticized him vehemently for helping to bring on the recession that began in the latter part of 1974. Face with this recession, Burns cautioned that the policy goal should be one of "moderation" and "steadiness" in the expansion of money and credit. Before the Senate Banking Committee, he said that the money supply (M_1) would be allowed to grow by between 5 and 7½ percent in the year ending March 1976. Many of his critics felt that this was an inadequate rate of monetary growth. In 1976, there were signs that the Fed was begining to loosen up on monetary policy, as inflation showed at least a temporary drop.

E.A.

NNP. The United States entered the deepest recession in decades. During the first quarter of 1975, there was little or no growth in the money supply, but in subsequent quarters the Fed permitted the money supply to grow more rapidly, with the result that the money supply increased by about 4 percent during the year as a whole. Interest rates declined during the latter part of 1974, and remained relatively stable during 1975. Critics of the Fed maintained that it increased the money supply much too slowly in 1975, thus impeding the recovery. Even in terms of the Fed's own announced targets, the growth in the money supply seemed rather low. In his 1976 campaign, President Carter belabored Arthur F. Burns and the Fed on these grounds, and once Carter became president, there was speculation that he and Burns might clash. Only time will tell how the Fed will behave during the Carter administration.

Problems in Formulating Monetary Policy

Before attempting to evaluate the Fed's record, we must recognize the three major kinds of decisions it must continually make. First, the Fed must maintain a constant watch on the economy, checking for signs that the economy is sliding into a recession, being propelled into an inflationary boom, or growing satisfactorily. As we saw in Chapter 12, there is no foolproof way to forecast the economy's short-term movements. Recognizing the fallibility of existing forecasting techniques all too well, the Fed must nonetheless use these techniques as best it can to guide its actions.

Second, having come to some tentative conclusion about the direction in which the economy is heading, the Fed must decide to what extent it should tighten or ease money. The answer depends on the Fed's estimates of when monetary changes will take effect and the magnitude of their impact, as well as on its forecasts of the economy's future direction. Also, the answer depends on the Fed's evaluation of the relative importance of full employment and price stability as national goals. If it regards full employment as much more important than price stability, it will probably want to err in the direction of easy money. On the other hand, if it thinks price stability is at least as important as full employment, it may want to err in the direction of tight money.

Finally, once the Fed has decided what it wants to do, it must figure out how to do it. Should open market operations do the whole job? If so, how big must be the purchase or sale of government securities? Should a change be made in the discount rate, or in legal reserve requirements? How big a change? Should moral suasion be resorted to? These are the operational questions the Fed continually must answer.

In answering these questions, the Fed must reckon with two very inconvenient facts, both of which make life difficult. First, *there is often a long lag between an action by the Fed and its effect on the economy.* Although the available evidence indicates that monetary policy affects some types of expenditures more rapidly than others, it is not uncommon for the bulk of the total effects to occur a year or more after the change in monetary policy.[10] Thus the Fed may act to head off an imminent recession, but find that some of the consequences of its action are not felt until later, when inflation—not recession—is the problem. Conversely, the Fed may act to curb an imminent inflation, but find that the consequences of its action are not felt until some time later, when recession, not inflation, has become the problem. In either case, the Fed can wind up doing more harm than good.

[10] For example, see Frank de Leeuw and Edward Gramlich, "The Channels of Monetary Policy: A Further Report on the Federal Reserve–MIT Econometric Model," *Federal Reserve Bulletin,* June 1969. However, there is considerable disagreement concerning the length of this lag.

Second, *experts disagree about which of the available measures—such as interest rates, the rate of increase of the money supply, or the rate of increase of the monetary base—is the best measure of how tight or easy monetary policy is.* Fortunately, these measures often point in the same direction; but when they point in different directions, the Fed can be misled. For example, during 1967-68, the Fed wanted to tighten money somewhat. Using free reserves and interest rates as the primary measures of the tightness of monetary policy, it reduced free reserves and increased interest rates. However, at the same time, it permitted a substantial rate of increase in the money supply and the monetary base. By doing so, the Fed—in the eyes of many experts—really eased, not tightened, money.

How Well Has the Fed Performed?

Given the difficult problems the Federal Reserve faces and the fact that its performance cannot be measured by any simple standard, it would be naïve to expect that its achievement could be graded like an arithmetic quiz. Nonetheless, just as war is too important to be left to the generals, so monetary policy is too important to be left unscrutinized to the monetary authorities. According to recent studies of Federal Reserve policy making, what have been the strengths and weaknesses of the Fed's decisions?

Forecasting. If one takes into account the limitations in existing forecasting techniques, the Fed seems to have done a reasonably good job in recent years of recognizing changes in economic conditions. As noted in previous sections, it sometimes was a bit slow to see that the economy was sinking into a recession, or that inflationary pressures were dominant. But hindsight is always much clearer than foresight, which is why Monday morning quarterbacks make so few mistakes—and get paid so little. Because the Fed did a creditable job of recognizing changes in economic conditions, the time interval between changes in economic conditions and changes in policy was rather short, particularly when compared with the corresponding time interval for fiscal policy.

Recognition of lags. The Fed does not seem to have taken much account of the long—and seemingly quite variable—lags between changes in monetary policy and their effects on the economy. Instead, it simply reacted quickly to changes in business conditions. As pointed out in a previous section, such a policy can in reality be quite destabilizing. For example, the Fed may act to suppress inflationary pressures, but find that the consequences of its action are not felt until some time later when recession—not inflation—is the problem. Unfortunately, the truth is that, despite advances in knowledge in the past decade, economists do not have a firm understanding of these lags. Thus the Fed is only partly to blame.

Coordination. With a few notable exceptions, there generally seems to have been reasonably good coordination between the Federal Reserve and the executive branch (the Treasury and the Council of Economic Advisers, in particular). This is important because monetary policy and fiscal policy should work together, not march off in separate directions. Of course, the fact that the Fed and the executive branch have generally been aware of one another's views and probable actions does not mean that there has always been agreement between them. Nor does it mean that, even when they agreed, they could always point monetary and fiscal policy in the same direction. But at least the left hand had a pretty good idea of what the right hand was doing.

Measures. The Fed has been criticized for paying too much attention during the 1950s to free reserves and interest rates as measures of the tightness or looseness of monetary policy, and giving too little attention to the rate of

Is There an Independent Federal Reserve? Should There Be?

A MEETING OF THE FEDERAL OPEN MARKET COMMITTEE.

Some say the Fed is responsible to Congress. Its enabling legislation was passed by Congress in 1913, and it could presumably be reorganized should it sufficiently rouse Congress's wrath. But Congress moves with nothing if not deliberate speed, and not since 1935 has it sought to influence the Federal Reserve through new legislation. The president fills vacancies on the Board of Governors, but since terms on the board run for 14 years, presidents have had to wait until their second terms to appoint a majority of the board.

In fact, as knowledgeable observers often agree, there are two groups that, without appearing prominently on the organization chart, exercise considerable influence over the policies of the Fed. One is the business community—a group with a definite interest in preserving the value of a dollar. The second is the board's professional staff of senior economists. Administrations come and go, but the staff economist remains, and his uniquely detailed knowledge of the workings of the Fed assures him a hearing at 20th and Constitution.

Does it matter that the Fed is a focal point for the forces in the economy who fear inflation and are willing to accept somewhat higher unemployment in the hopes prices will not rise as rapidly? It may matter less than the formal structure suggests. Virtually since its inception, the Federal Reserve has had a crop of antagonistic observers in Congress. Former Secretary of the Treasury John Connally compared one of the Fed's perennial congressional foes to a cross-eyed discus thrower: "He'll never set any records for distance but he certainly keeps the crowd on its toes."

Both William McChesney Martin and the present chairman, Arthur Burns, have been sensitive to the ultimate vulnerability of the Fed's independence, and so have been reluctant to buck administration policy too dramatically. Whether the Federal Reserve's current procedures can survive the general call for more accountability is an open question. In early 1975, Congress passed a resolution that the Federal Reserve must publish its targets for growth in the money supply. But the extent to which this will tie the Fed's hands is by no means clear.

E.A.

growth of the money supply and the monetary base. During the 1960s and 1970s, however, the Fed has paid much more attention to the rate of growth of the money supply and the monetary base. Again, the fault is only partly the Fed's, since the experts cannot agree on the relative importance that should be attached to each measure. But wherever the fault, if any, may lie, the Fed's performance is bound to suffer if it acts on the basis of unreliable measures.

Emphasis. The Fed is often criticized for putting too much emphasis on preventing inflation and too little on preventing unemployment. According to various studies, it probably is true that the Fed has been more sensitive to the dangers of inflation than has the Congress or the administration. Liberals, emphasizing the great social costs of excessive unemployment, tend to denounce the Fed for such behavior. Without question, the costs of unemployment are high, as stressed in Chapter 8. Conservatives, on the other hand, often claim that governments are tempted to resort to inflation in order to produce the short-term appearance of prosperity, even though the long-term effects may be undesirable. They say that, in the short run (when the next election is decided), unemployment is more likely than inflation to result in defeat at the polls. Whether you think that the Fed has put too much emphasis on restraining inflation will depend on the relative importance that you attach to reducing unemployment, on the one hand, and reducing inflation, on the other.[11]

Should the Fed Be Governed by a Rule?

As we have just seen, important criticisms can be made of Federal Reserve policy making. The monetarists, led by Milton Friedman, go so far as to say that the Fed's attempts to "lean against the wind"—by easing money when the economy begins to dip and tightening money when the economy begins to get overheated—really do more harm than good. In their view, the Fed actually intensifies business fluctuations by changing the rate of growth of the money supply. Why? Partly because the Fed sometimes pays too much attention to measures other than the money supply. But more fundamentally, it is because the Fed tends to overreact to ephemeral changes, and because the effects of changes in the money supply on the economy occur with a long and highly variable lag. In their view, this lag is so unpredictable that the Fed—no matter how laudatory its intent—tends to intensify business fluctuations.

According to Professor Friedman and his followers, the Fed should abandon its attempts to "lean against the wind." *They propose that the Fed conform to a rule that the money supply should increase at some fixed, agreed-upon rate, such as 4 or 5 percent per year. The Fed's job would be simply to see that the money supply grows at approximately this rate.* The monetarists do not claim that a rule of this sort would prevent all business fluctuations, but they do claim that it would work better than the existing system. In particular, they feel that it would prevent the sorts of major depressions and inflations we have experienced in the past. Without major decreases in the money supply (such as occurred during the crash of 1929-33), major depressions could not occur. Without major increases in the money supply (such as occurred during World War II), major inflations could not occur. Of course, it would be nice if monetary policy could iron out minor business fluctuations as well, but in their view this simply cannot be done at present.

This proposal has received considerable attention from both economists and politicians. A number of studies have been carried out to try to estimate what would have happened if Friedman's rule had been used in the past. The

[11] For a good discussion of recent monetary and fiscal policy, see G. L. Bach, *Making Monetary and Fiscal Policy,* Washington, D.C.: Brookings Institution, 1971. Also, see the papers by Milton Friedman and Walter W. Heller in E. Mansfield, *Economics: Readings, Issues and Cases,* 2d ed., New York: Norton, 1977.

results, although by no means free of criticism, seem to indicate that such a rule might have done better than discretionary action did in preventing the Great Depression of the 1930s and the inflation during World War II. But in the period since World War II, the evidence in favor of such a rule is less persuasive. Most economists seem to believe that it would be a mistake to handcuff the Fed to a simple rule of this sort. They think that a discretionary monetary policy can outperform Friedman's rule.

Nonetheless, the debate over rules versus discretionary action goes on, and the issues are still very much alive. Professor Friedman has been able to gain important converts, including the Federal Reserve Bank of St. Louis and members of the Joint Economic Committee of Congress. Indeed, after the Fed's "stop-go" policies of 1966–68 (when the Fed tightened money sharply in 1966 and loosened it rapidly in 1967–68), the Joint Economic Committee urged the Fed to adopt a rule of the sort advocated by Friedman. In 1968, the committee complained that its advice was not being followed, and special hearings were held. The Council of Economic Advisers and the secretary of the Treasury sided with the Fed against adopting such a rule. Some academic economists favor such a rule, others oppose it, and considerable economic research is being carried out to try to clarify and resolve the questions involved.

Monetary Policy: Advantages and Disadvantages

Just as sensible wine drinkers value both Bordeaux and Burgundy (and both France and California), so most economists believe that both monetary and fiscal policy can and should play an important role in our nation's economic stabilization policies. However, this does not mean, of course, that monetary policy does not have certain advantages over fiscal policy, and vice versa. One disadvantage of monetary policy, according to many economists, is that it may be less dependable than fiscal policy when the government wants to stimulate the economy. All that monetary policy can do is to increase bank reserves. The monetary authorities cannot make the banks lend out the excess reserves—as illustrated by the situation during the 1930s when banks held huge excess reserves. And if the banks don't lend them out or invest them, there is little or no stimulation to the economy. Thus monetary policy may be less effective as a stimulant than as a rein on the economy. However, the 1970s are not the 1930s, and this assymetry may be less pronounced than has sometimes been assumed.

On the other hand, one of the most important advantages of monetary policy is that the monetary authorities can react much more quickly to changed economic conditions than can the fiscal authorities. Changes in monetary policy can be put into effect relatively quickly if the Fed wants to do so, but no matter what the Treasury, the Council of Economic Advisers, and other administration officials want to do, changes in tax and expenditure policy must be approved by the Congress. Proposed fiscal policies can be delayed and even made into a political football, as happened to the tax surcharge of 1968, which had been kicked around for a couple of years before it finally was enacted.

According to some observers, another advantage of monetary policy is that it is nondiscriminatory. In other words, the Fed does not favor particular classes of borrowers or activities; it just tightens or eases money and credit, and lets the market determine which people and industries will be benefited or hurt. But other observers retort that monetary policy is highly discriminatory, since it can hit a particular group or industry or type of borrower harder than anyone would intend. For example, the home construction industry has sometimes been clobbered by tight monetary policy.

Because of the importance of mortgage funds to the construction industry, tight money can have a big impact on its output and profits.

Summary

Monetary policy is concerned with the money supply and interest rates. Its purpose is to attain and maintain full employment without inflation. When a recession seems imminent and business is soft, the monetary authorities are likely to increase the money supply and reduce interest rates. On the other hand, when the economy is in danger of overheating and inflation threatens, the monetary authorities are likely to rein in the money supply and push up interest rates. Monetary policy and fiscal policy are aimed at much the same goals, but they use different methods to promote them. One advantage of monetary policy is that the lag between decision and action is relatively short. In view of the time involved in getting tax (and spending) changes enacted, this is an important point.

Although monetary policy is influenced by Congress, the Treasury, and other parts of the government and the public at large, the chief responsibility for the formulation of monetary policy lies with the Federal Reserve Board and the Federal Open Market Committee. To a very large extent, monetary policy operates by changing the quantity of bank reserves. The most important tool of monetary policy is open market operations, which involve the buying and selling of government securities in the open market by the Federal Reserve. When the Fed buys government securities, this increases bank reserves. When the Fed sells government securities, this reduces bank reserves. The Fed can also tighten or ease money by increasing or decreasing the discount rate or by increasing or decreasing legal reserve requirements. In addition, the Fed can use moral suasion, and it has power over maximum interest rates on time deposits and margin requirements for the purchase of stock.

As indicators of how tight or easy monetary policy is, the Fed has looked at the level of short-term interest rates, the quantity of free reserves, the rate of growth of the money supply, and the rate of growth of the monetary base. During the 1950s, the Fed paid most attention to the first two indicators; in the 1960s and 1970s, the Fed increased the amount of attention paid to the last two. To provide some idea of how monetary policy has been used, we presented a brief description of the nature and course of monetary policy during the past two decades. Also, to provide a richer picture of the use of monetary policy to stem inflation, we described in some detail the credit crunch of 1966. This episode (like the developments in 1974) is a dramatic example of the potency of monetary policy.

The Federal Reserve is faced with many difficult problems in formulating and carrying out monetary policy. It must try to see where the economy is heading, and whether–and to what extent–it should tighten or ease money to stabilize the economy. This task is made very difficult by the fact that there is often a long–and highly variable–lag between an action by the Fed and its effect on the economy. There is also considerable disagreement over the best way to measure how tight or easy monetary policy is.

There has been criticism of various kinds regarding the performance of the Federal Reserve. Often, the Fed is criticized for paying too little attention to the long lags between its actions and their effects on the economy. Also, some critics claim that the Fed puts too much emphasis on fighting inflation and too little on preventing unemployment. Some monetarists, led by Milton Friedman, believe that monetary policy would be improved if discretionary policy were replaced by a rule that the Fed should increase the money supply at some fixed, agreed-on rate, such as 4 or 5 percent per year.

The Fed, the Council of Economic Advisers, the Treasury, and many academic economists have argued against the adoption of such a rule, but Friedman's proposal has won some support in the Joint Economic Committee and elsewhere. The debate over rules versus discretionary policy goes on, and is one of the liveliest in present-day economics.

CONCEPTS FOR REVIEW

Monetary policy
Federal Reserve Board
Federal Open Market Committee
Discount rate
Changes in legal reserve requirements
Easy money
Moral suasion
Selective credit control
Free reserves
Monetary base
Margin requirements
Credit crunch
Tightening money

QUESTIONS FOR DISCUSSION AND REVIEW

1. Suppose that the Federal Reserve buys $5 million worth of government securities from U.S. Steel. Insert the effects in the blanks below.

Effects on Fed's balance sheet:

Assets	Liabilities and Net Worth
Securities ______	Member bank reserves ______

Effects on balance sheet of U.S. Steel's bank:

Assets	Liabilities and net worth
Reserves ______	Demand deposits ______

2. Suppose that the Federal Reserve sells $5 million worth of government securities to U.S. Steel. What is the effect on the quantity of bank reserves?

3. "When the Fed increases legal reserve requirements, it loosens credit, because the banks have more reserves." Comment and evaluate.

4. "Regulation Q interferes with the functioning of free markets, and should be abandoned. By establishing a floor under interest rates, it promotes inflation." Comment and evaluate.

5. Suppose that you have $5,000 to invest. At a restaurant you overhear someone saying that the Fed is almost certain to increase the discount rate dramatically. If this rumor is correct, do you think that you should invest now, or wait until after the increase in the discount rate? Or doesn't it matter? Be sure to explain the reasons for your preference (or lack of it) in this regard.

6. "The Fed should keep interest rates low to promote prosperity. Unfortunately, however, it is dominated by bankers who like high interest rates because they increase bank profits." Comment and evaluate.

7. "The Fed is like a driver whose steering wheel takes about a minute to influence the car's wheels." Comment and evaluate.

8. According to Walter W. Heller, "In the imperfect world in which we actually operate, beset by all sorts of rigidities, . . . [Friedman's] money supply rule might, in fact, be destabilizing."[12] Comment and evaluate.

9. According to Henry Wallich, a member of the Fed's Board of Governors, although "monetary policy has so often been wrong that it [may seem] preferable to deprive it of discretion and subject it to a fixed rule, . . . this reasoning is fallacious." Do you agree? Why or why not? How would you go about testing this proposition?

10. According to Sherman Maisel, William McChesney Martin, former chairman of the Federal Reserve Board, felt "that the primary function of the Federal Reserve Board was to determine what was necessary to maintain a sound currency. . . . [To Martin] it is as immoral for a country today to allow the value of its currency to fall as it was for kings of old to clip coinage." Do you agree with Martin's views? Why or why not?

[12] Milton Friedman and Walter W. Heller, *Monetary vs. Fiscal Policy,* New York: Norton, 1969.

16 Problems of Economic Stabilization Policy

Despite the advances in economic knowledge during the past 30 years, the United States, like other countries, finds it very difficult to achieve full employment with stable prices. Monetary policy is an important means toward that end. And in the eyes of most economists, so is fiscal policy. Yet, despite the power of monetary and fiscal policies, we are still a long way from the desired degree of economic stability. Judging from the experience of the past 30 years, we have learned how to avoid very serious depressions, but we have not yet learned how to attain full employment with stable prices. Excessive unemployment and excessive inflation persist.

Two important reasons why our performance has been less than satisfactory are evident. First, economists are still uncertain about many effects of monetary and fiscal policies. For one thing, as pointed out in previous chapters, the views of the monetarists differ from those of the Keynesians. Second, if some of the inflationary pressures in our society stem from an upward push of costs (or profits), some form of incomes policy may be needed to quell undesirable inflation. In this chapter, we discuss both of these problems at length.

The General Problem of Achieving Economic Stability

As a first step, let's review how fiscal and monetary policies can be used to promote full employment without inflation. We begin with fiscal policy. With a given level of potential output or capacity, actual net national product is determined by desired spending. Fiscal policy uses the government's expenditures and taxes to influence desired spending. Specifically, when NNP is at less than its full-employment level, increases in government expenditures or reductions in taxes can be used to push it up to this level, and thus reduce excessive unemployment. Or when there is excessive inflation, decreases in government expenditures or increases in taxes can reduce total spending, and thus curb inflation.

Monetary policy uses the government's power over the quantity of money to influence NNP. Increases in the money supply tend to increase the money value of NNP, whereas reductions in the money supply tend to reduce the money value of NNP. The route by which the quantity of money has this effect on NNP is a subject of controversy. The majority, or Keynesian, view is that increases in the money supply reduce interest rates, which stimulates investment, which increases NNP. Conversely, decreases in the money supply increase interest rates, which cuts investment, which reduces NNP. (Many Keynesians, at least in more recent years, also recognize that changes in the money supply influence the net worth of consumers, and thus have an impact on consumption expenditures.) Monetarists, relying heavily on the quantity theory of money, relate changes in the money supply more directly to changes in nominal, or money, NNP.

The controversy between the monetarists and the Keynesians has received so much attention in recent years that one might think that, if it were resolved, the problem of formulating monetary and fiscal policies to achieve full employment with stable prices would be licked. This is by no means true. However the controversy is resolved, no existing economic model can give policy makers reliable quantitative estimates of how much the money supply should be altered, or government expenditures should be changed, or tax rates should be modified, to achieve full employment with stable prices. To a considerable extent, the knowledge we have is qualitative, not quantitative. Until we can better estimate the quantitative effects of policy changes of various magnitudes, it will be unreasonable to expect that monetary and fiscal policies can be used with precision to achieve our national goals.

In addition, it must be emphasized that both the Keynesian and the monetarist models are just that—models. In other words, they are convenient and useful simplifications; and, as such, they abstract from many important aspects of reality. In particular, they take little or no notice of the possibility that inflation may arise because of an upward push of costs, and they tell us very little about what to do when there is both excessive unemployment and excessive inflation. Nor do they say much about the extent of the lags between the time when policy makers want to act and the time when such action is approved and taken, or the lags between the time when action is taken and the time when its economic effects are felt.

Further, it must be recognized that government decisions are not dictated by considerations of economic stabilization alone. Thus, even if economic models were completely accurate and the government knew how to achieve full employment at stable prices, it would not always choose to do so. For example, the political party in power may be committed to a particular policy designed to alleviate a certain social ill, like poverty or discrimination. To carry out this objective, it may increase government expenditures at a time when, from the point of view of economic stabilization, it would be better to reduce them. Or in wartime, modern military needs require enormous outlays, but the political party in power may not be willing to take the unpopular step of raising taxes, even though this would be desirable for economic stabilization. Or consider an upcoming presidential election. The incumbent president may initiate or expand programs to make people feel prosperous in the short run, even though this may be destabilizing in the longer run. After all, the important thing is to win the election and prevent that other fellow, whoever he may be, from ruining the country!

Monetarists versus Keynesians

The debate between the monetarists and the Keynesians has not been limited to the classroom and scholarly gatherings. It has spilled over onto the pages of the daily newspapers and aroused considerable interest in Congress and other parts of the government. At heart, the argument is over what determines the level of output, employment, and prices. The Keynesians put more emphasis on the federal budget than do the monetarists, who put more emphasis on the money supply than do the Keynesians. To understand this debate fully, we need to know something about the recent development of economic thought. Up until the Great Depression of the 1930s, the prevailing theory was that NNP, expressed in real terms, would tend automatically to its full-employment value. (Recall from Chapter 9 the classical economists' reasons for clinging to this belief.) Moreover, the prevailing theory was that the price level could be explained by the crude quantity theory of money. In other words, the price level, P, was assumed to be proportional to the quantity of money, M, because $MV = PQ$, and real NNP, Q, and the velocity of money, V, were thought to be essentially constant.

During the Great Depression of the 1930s, this body of theory was largely discredited and abandoned. Clearly, NNP was not tending automatically toward its full-employment level. And the crude quantity theory seemed to have little value. In contrast, Keynes's ideas, which stressed the importance of fiscal policy, seemed to offer the sort of theoretical guidance and policy prescriptions that were needed. Keynesians did not neglect the use of monetary policy entirely, but they felt that it played a subsidiary role. Particularly in depressions, monetary policy seemed to be of relatively little value, since "you can't push on a string." In other words, monetary policy can make money available, but it cannot insure that it will be spent.

During the 1940s, 1950s, and early 1960s, the Keynesian view was definitely predominant, here and abroad. But by the mid-1960s, it was being challenged seriously by the monetarists, led by Professor Milton Friedman and his supporters. The monetarist view harked back to the pre-Keynesian doctrine in many respects. In particular, it emphasized the importance of the equation of exchange as an analytical device and the importance of the quantity of money as a tool of economic policy. The monetarist view gained adherents in the late 1960s. Partly responsible was the long delay in passing the surtax of 1968, for the reluctance of the administration to propose and of Congress to enact the new levy vividly illustrated some of the difficulties in using fiscal policy for stabilization. In contrast, monetary policy seemed to assure only a short lag between policy decisions and their implementation. Another factor favoring the monetarists was that the economy was plagued by inflation, not unemployment. Monetary policy, by controlling the quantity of money, can quite effectively restrain inflation, even if, under certain circumstances, it may not be so effective in reducing unemployment. "You may be able to pull on a string," even if "you can't push on a string."

Causes of Business Fluctuations: The Opposing Views

Monetarists and Keynesians tend to disagree over the basic causes of business fluctuations. As seen by monetarists, major depressions, such as the Great Depression of the 1930s, are due to decreases in the money supply. In the Great Depression, for example, the money supply contracted by over ¼. Similarly, major inflations, in their view, are due to increases in the money supply. Looking at recent developments, they assert that the inflation of the late 1960s and early 1970s was due to the increases that occurred in the money supply.

Keynesians, on the other hand, reject the monetarist view that money is the predominant factor accounting for business fluctuations. To the Keynesians, this view is simplistic and inadequate. The Keynesian view is that both monetary and nonmonetary factors cause business fluctuations. Among the important nonmonetary factors are changes in desired investment or shifts in the consumption function. (We have discussed many of these nonmonetary factors in Chapter 12.) The Keynesians do not deny that there is a correlation between changes in the money supply and changes in NNP, but they believe that the monetarists tend to mix up cause and effect. The Keynesians argue that increases in desired spending may bring about a greater demand for money, which in turn causes the money supply to increase. Under these circumstances, the line of causation may be the opposite of that posited by the monetarists.

Monetarists and Keynesians also tend to differ over the extent to which our economy is stable. The monetarists are generally more inclined to believe that, if the money supply is managed properly by the government, the free-market economy will tend automatically toward full employment with reasonably stable prices. Although the monetarists are by no means unanimous in this respect, they tend to emphasize the self-regulating characteristics of a free-enterprise economy. In their view, business fluctuations must often be laid at the door of the monetary authorities, whose well-meaning attempts to stabilize the economy frequently do more harm than good.

In contrast, the Keynesians are convinced that a free-enterprise economy has relatively weak self-regulating mechanisms. Like Keynes himself, they argue that the equilibrium level of national output may remain for a long time below the level required for full employment. (See Chapter 9 for Keynes's views.) Also, they argue that there is nothing in the modern economy to prevent considerable inflation, even if the money supply does not increase greatly. Thus, in their view, the government has a much more positive discretionary role to play in stabilizing the economy than visualized by the monetarists.

Effects of the Interest Rate: The Opposing Views

Many of the basic disagreements between the Keynesians and monetarists center about the quantitative effects of the interest rate.[1] These disagreements are of three kinds:

Demand for money. The first disagreement is over the demand for money. Recall from Chapter 13 that, because the cost of holding money is the interest forgone, the quantity of money demanded goes down as the interest

[1] Both the Keynesian and monetarist groups contain a variety of opinions; thus it is somewhat misleading to refer to *the* Keynesian view or *the* monetarist view. All that we can do here is summarize and contrast one major version of each of these theories, leaving a more detailed treatment to more advanced texts.

Figure 16.1
Keynesian and Monetarist Assumptions Concerning the Demand for Money
Keynesians tend to believe that the quantity of money demanded is more sensitive to the interest rate than do monetarists. Thus, if the interest rate falls from r to r', the quantity of money demanded increases from D_0 to D_3 under Keynesian assumptions, but only from D_1 to D_2 under monetarist assumptions.

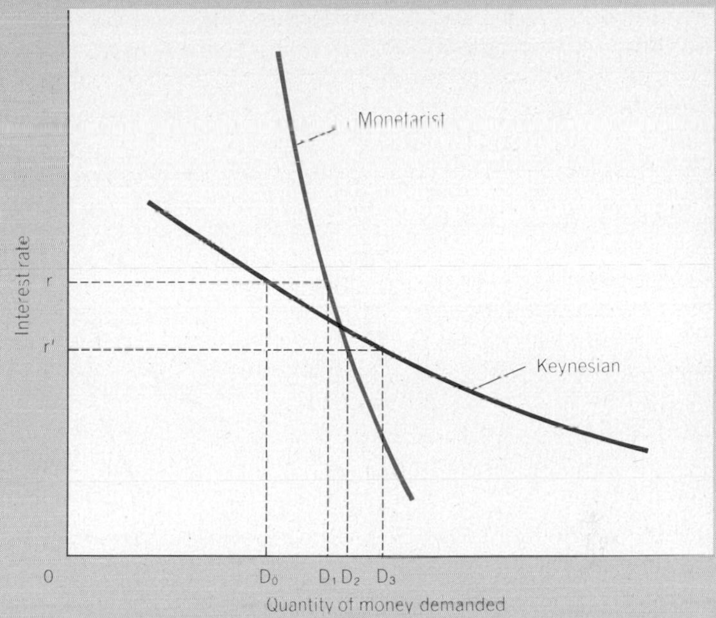

rate goes up—as shown in Figure 13.3. *According to the monetarists, the quantity of money demanded is relatively insensitive to changes in the interest rate; whereas to Keynesians, it is very sensitive to such changes.* Thus, as shown in Figure 16.1, monetarists believe that the relationship between the quantity of money demanded and the interest rate is more nearly vertical than do Keynesians. The reason is that the monetarists believe that the transactions motive for holding money is particularly important, and the interest rate is less important than people's incomes in determining the transactions demand for money. Keynesians, on the other hand, put more emphasis on the speculative motive for holding money, where the interest rate plays a major role.

Supply of money. The second disagreement is over the extent to which the supply of money is influenced by the interest rate. *According to the monetarists, the supply of money is relatively insensitive to changes in the interest rate; whereas to Keynesians, it is quite sensitive to such changes.* In other words, the monetarists believe that the relationship between the money supply and the interest rate shown in Figure 16.2 is nearly vertical, whereas the Keynesians do not. The reason is the monetarists believe that banks will generally keep few excess reserves, with the result that they will be unable to vary the money supply in response to changes in loan demand and in interest rates. Keynesians, on the other hand, believe that banks generally hold considerable excess reserves during depressions, and that they can and do increase the money supply when loan demand and interest rates are high.

Total desired spending. The third disagreement is over the extent to which total desired spending is sensitive to changes in the interest rate. *According to the monetarists, total expenditure is very sensitive to changes in the interest rate; whereas to some Keynesians, it is not so sensitive to such changes.* Thus the monetarists believe that the relationship between total desired spending and the interest rate shown in Figure 16.3 is close to horizontal, whereas the Keynesians believe that it is closer to vertical. The

Figure 16.2
Keynesian and Monetarist Assumptions Concerning the Supply of Money
Keynesians tend to believe that the supply of money is more sensitive to the interest rate than do monetarists. Thus, if the interest rate falls from r to r', the supply of money drops from S_3 to S_0 under Keynesian assumptions, but only from S_2 to S_1 under monetarist assumptions.

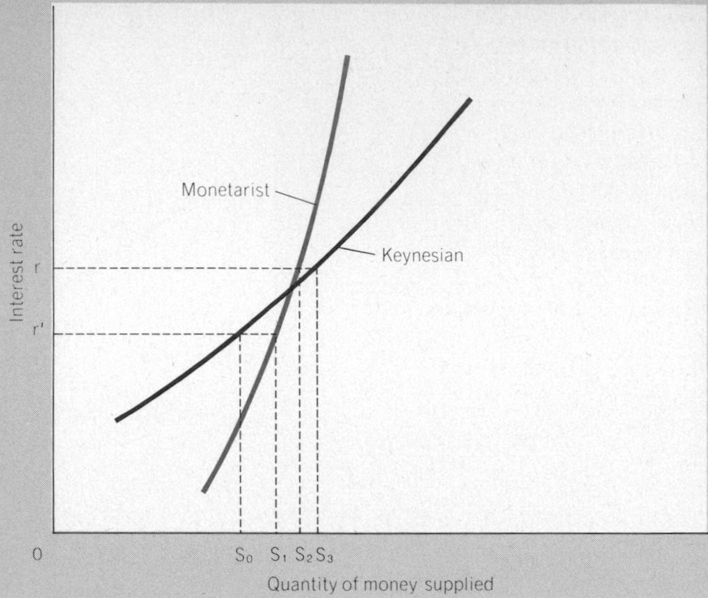

reason is that the monetarists are convinced that firms' investment decisions, as well as investment in residential housing and expenditure on consumer durable goods, depend considerably on the interest rate, whereas the Keynesians feel that, although the interest rate has an effect, it is smaller than the monetarists assume. According to the Keynesians, other factors, such as existing business conditions and businessmen's expectations, are far more important than the interest rate in determining total expenditure.

The Effect of Monetary Policy: The Opposing Views

Given the three disagreements described in the preceding section, it is easy to see why monetarists believe that monetary policy is of preeminent importance, whereas Keynesians tend to believe that it is of lesser importance. As a first step toward understanding why this is so, one must recognize that *the equilibrium interest rate must be at the level where the quantity of money demanded equals the quantity of money supplied.* If the public wants to hold less money than is supplied, the interest rate will tend to decline in order to encourage people to demand more money. If the public wants to hold more money than is supplied, the interest rate will tend to increase in order to make people cut back on their demand for money. Only if the quantity of money demanded equals the quantity of money supplied is the interest rate at its equilibrium level.

Suppose that the monetary authorities increase the money supply, with the result that the *money supply curve* (that is, the relationship between the money supply and the interest rate in Figure 16.2) shifts to the right. Under both the Keynesian and monetarist assumptions, there will be a fall in the equilibrium interest rate, since the quantity of money supplied will exceed the quantity of money demanded at the existing interest rate. But, as shown in Figure 16.4, there will be a greater fall in the interest rate under the monetarist assumptions (shown in panel B of Figure 16.4) than under the Keynesian assumptions (shown in panel A). Under the monetarist assumptions, the interest

Figure 16.3
Keynesian and Monetarist Assumptions Concerning the Effect of the Interest Rate on Total Desired Spending
Keynesians tend to believe that total desired spending is less sensitive to the interest rate than do monetarists. Thus, if the interest rate falls from r to r', total desired spending increases from T_0 to T_3 under monetarist assumptions, but only from T_1 to T_2 under Keynesian assumptions.

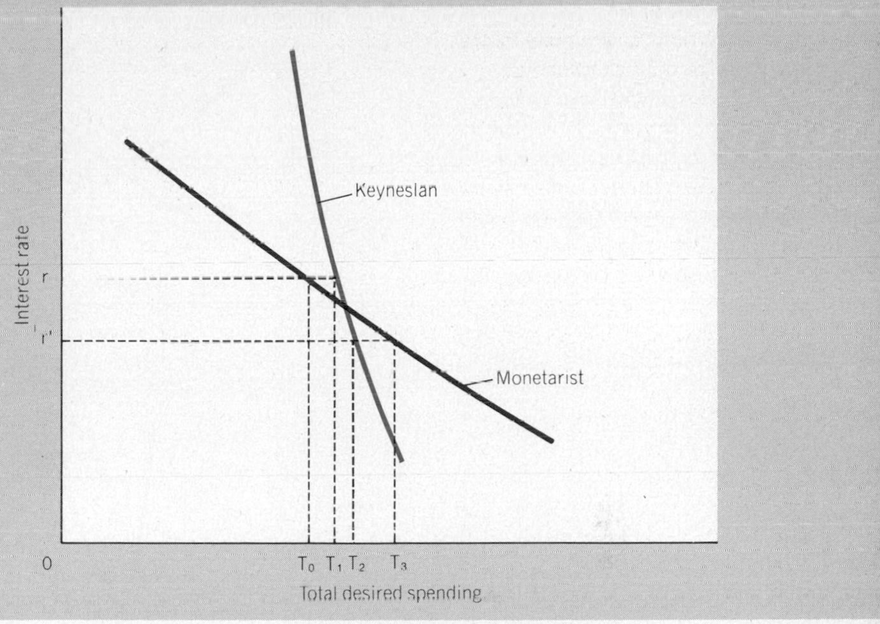

rate will fall to r_1, whereas under the Keynesian assumptions, it will fall to r_2.

Further, the resulting fall in the interest rate will have a greater effect on total expenditure under the monetarist assumptions than under the Keynesian assumptions. Under the monetarist assumptions, the fall in the interest rate to r_1 results in total expenditure increasing to X_1. Under the Keynesian assumptions, the fall in the interest rate to r_2 results in total expenditure increasing to X_2. Clearly, *the effect of the increase in the money supply on total expenditure is greater under the monetarist assumptions than under the Keynesian assumptions*—and it is not hard to see why monetarists tend to be more enthusiastic about the effects of monetary policy than are the Keynesians.[2]

The Effect of Fiscal Policy: The Opposing Views

The monetarists attack the Keynesian view that fiscal policy works in the way we described in Chapter 11. According to the monetarists, whether the government runs a surplus or deficit has little or no long-run effect on NNP, except insofar as the government finances the surplus or deficit in a way that affects the stock of money. For example, if the government runs a deficit and finances it by borrowing from the public, the money supply will be unchanged. Thus the monetarists would argue that such a deficit has little or no long-run expansionary effect on NNP. On the other hand, if the government finances its deficit by increasing the money supply, the monetarists would expect NNP to increase, but as a result of the expansion of the money supply, not of the deficit. Thus the monetarists claim that the expansion of NNP after the tax cut of 1964 was due to considerable increases in the money supply, not to the tax cut.

Given the assumptions that they make, it is not difficult to see why the monetarists come to this conclusion. Suppose, for example, that an increase occurs in government expenditure. The result, of course, will be a shift to the right of the expenditure function in the righthand

[2] In Figure 16.4, the analysis is simplified in a number of respects. For a more complete analysis of the topics discussed in this and the following sections, see the Appendix to this chapter.

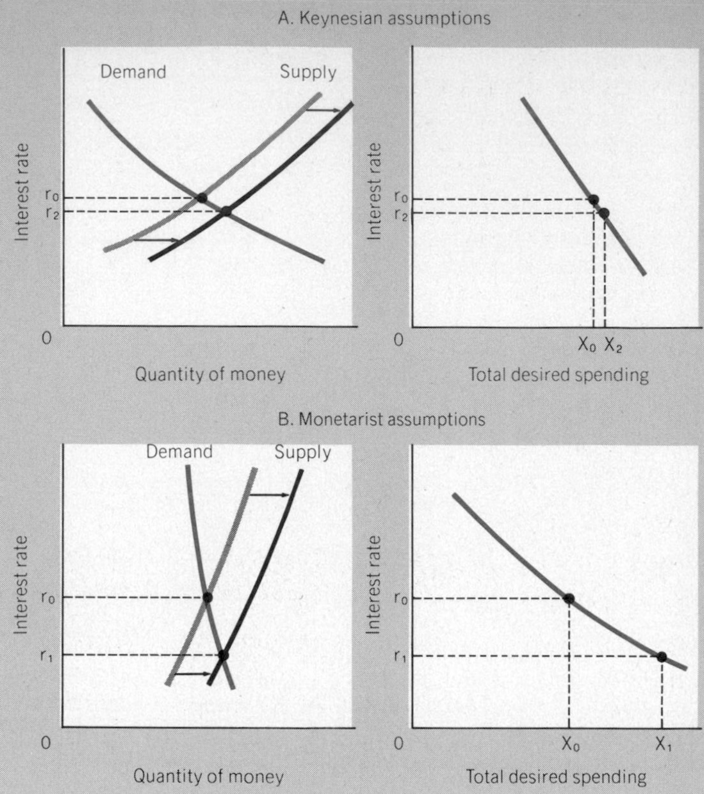

Figure 16.4
Effects of Monetary Policy under Keynesian and Monetarist Assumptions
An increase in the money supply results in a bigger drop in the interest rate, and a bigger increase in spending, under monetarist assumptions than under Keynesian assumptions.

panel of Figure 16.5B. (Note that the B panels in Figure 16.5 are the relevant ones here, since we are concerned with the monetarist assumptions.) If this function shifts from E_1 to E_2, the public will demand more money for transaction purposes, and the *demand curve for money*—that is the relationship between the quantity of money demanded and the interest rate (which we called the liquidity preference function in Chapter 13)—will shift to the right, as shown in the lefthand panel of Figure 16.5B. Thus the interest rate will increase to r_3. This relatively great increase in the interest rate will cut private expenditure on consumption goods and investment, and total expenditure will be X_3. (If the interest rate had not risen, total expenditure would have been X_5.) Since X_3 is not appreciably greater than X_0, the increase in government expenditure has little effect on total expenditure: its principal effect is to substitute public for private expenditure.

Based on their own quite different assumptions, the Keynesians conclude, of course, that fiscal policy is very effective. To see why, assume once again that an increase occurs in government expenditure, the result being a shift from E_1 to E_2 of the expenditure function in the righthand panel of Figure 16.5A. (This time, the A panels are the relevant ones, since they contain the Keynesian assumptions.) Once again, as total expenditure rises, the public will demand more money for transactions purposes, thus increasing the interest rate. But according to the Keynesians the increase in the interest rate will be relatively small, since there will be an expansion in the money supply and the quantity of money demanded is relatively sensitive to the interest rate. Thus the interest

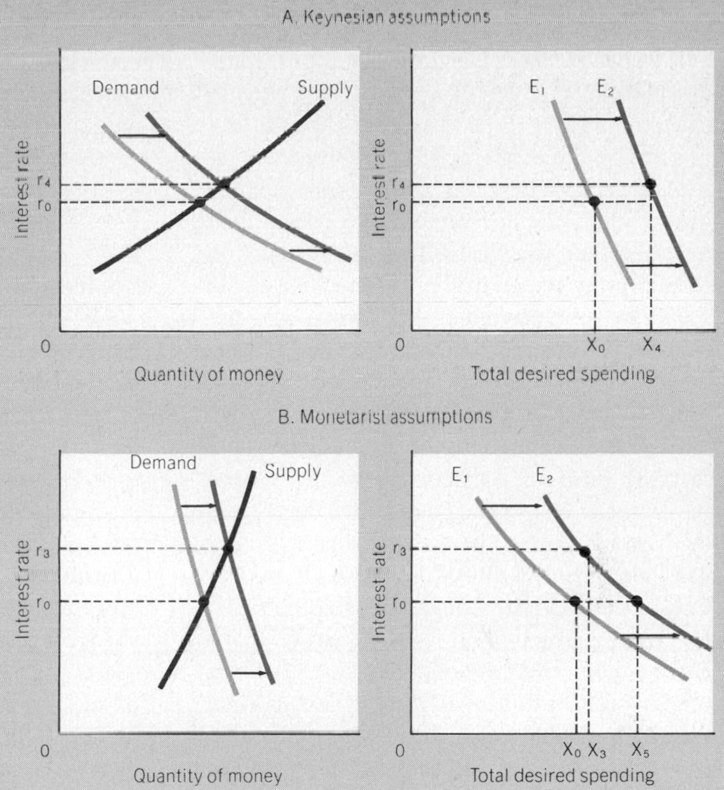

Figure 16.5
Effects of Fiscal Policy under Keynesian and Monetarist Assumptions.
An increase in government expenditure results in a bigger rise in the interest rate, and a smaller increase in spending, under monetarist assumptions than under Keynesian assumptions.

rate rises only to r_4, and total expenditure will be X_4. Since X_4 is much greater than X_0, the increase in government expenditure has a great effect on total expenditure, based on the Keynesian assumptions.

Policy Recommendations: Keynesians and Monetarists

Many, but not all, leading monetarists advocate the establishment of a rule to govern monetary policy. In the previous chapter, we discussed the arguments of Milton Friedman and his supporters for such a rule. You will recall their charge that the Federal Reserve's monetary policies have often caused economic instability. Because of the difficulties in forecasting the future state of the economy and the fairly long and variable time lag in the effect of changes in the money supply, the Fed, in the eyes of many leading monetarists, frequently has caused excessive inflation or unemployment by its discretionary policies. According to the monetarists, we would be better off with a rule stipulating that the money supply should grow steadily at a constant rate, say 4 or 5 percent per year.

The Keynesians retort that such a rule would handcuff the monetary authorities and contribute to economic instability, since discretionary monetary policies are required to keep the economy on a reasonably even keel. The Keynesians grant that the Fed sometimes makes mistakes, but they assert that things would be worse if the Fed could not pursue the policies that a given set of circumstances seems to call for.

The monetarists and Keynesians also differ

over many aspects of fiscal policy. The monetarists claim that the Congress is very slow to change tax rates and government expenditures to stabilize the economy, and that for this reason monetary policy is much more flexible than fiscal policy. Further, they argue that temporary tax changes will have little effect on consumption expenditures because household spending is determined by permanent, not transitory, income. Recall the permanent-income hypothesis regarding the consumption function, discussed in Chapter 9.

To these arguments, the Keynesians reply that the budgetary machinery in the federal government has been altered considerably in the past few years. The new budgetary apparatus, built around the Congressional Budget Committees and the Congressional Budget Office, has the potential at least to sharpen legislative action on fiscal policy. As for the effects of temporary tax changes, the Keynesians deny that such changes have little or no effect on consumer spending. In particular, they tend to feel that expenditures on consumer durable goods are affected considerably by such tax changes.

An Overview of the Debate

The debate between the monetarists and the Keynesians is important and illuminating. It has forced the entire economics profession to review its thinking about the effects of monetary and fiscal policies. This is the sort of ferment that keeps a discipline healthy and vital. Chances are that it will be many years before the issues are completely resolved, but in the past decade, considerable strides have been taken toward understanding the real differences between these two schools of thought.

The Keynesian theory, in its simplest form, emphasizes that the economy will be in equilibrium only when consumers are spending at the rate they desire, given their income, and when firms are investing at the rate they desire. The monetarist theory, in its simplest form, emphasizes that the economy will be in equilibrium only when consumers and firms are willing to hold the existing quantity of money, given their income and the quantity of other assets that they hold. In truth, of course, both these conditions for equilibrium must be fulfilled: neither alone is sufficient to guarantee equilibrium.

For example, what happens when the government increases the quantity of money by handing out some newly printed money to the public? Let's begin with the public's asset holdings. Since the public has more money than before, it will rearrange its portfolio of assets, assuming that it had the portfolio it desired prior to the increase in the money supply. Consumers and firms, finding themselves with more money than they want to hold, will exchange money for other types of assets. In other words, they will spend some of their money holdings—and will continue to spend money until, once again, their portfolio of assets is balanced so as to maximize their satisfaction.

Second, consider how the increase in the public's income due to the increase in the money supply will affect spending. The people who receive the newly printed money, finding that their disposable incomes have risen, want to spend more on consumption goods. Firms that receive the new money are also likely to want to increase their investment expenditures. Both consumers and firms will continue to spend more until, once again, their expenditures are in the desired relationship to their incomes. Note that this adjustment process, stressed by Keynesian theory, goes on simultaneously with the adjustment process described in the previous paragraph, which is related to the monetarist theory.

Once one recognizes that both processes go on simultaneously, it is easy to see that much of the debate between the Keynesians and monetarists is really over which of two simplifications is more fruitful—or does less violence

Milton Friedman versus Walter W. Heller

Seldom do the *New York Times,* the *Wall Street Journal,* and *Vogue* cover a debate between two economists. That they covered the seventh annual Arthur K. Salomon Lecture at New York University in November 1968 is a tribute to the impact each of the protagonists—Milton Friedman and Walter W. Heller—has had on presidents, potential presidents, and public opinion in the monetary versus fiscal debate.

Friedman, a professor at the University of Chicago, has written on as wide a range of subjects as any living economist. A staunch conservative, he nevertheless originated such "liberal" proposals as the educational voucher (used experimentally in Vermont and North Dakota districts) and the negative income tax. In keeping with his conservative philosophy, he has attacked the evils of Social Security and the minimum wage, praised the virtues of abolishing licensing of professions, and argued the intimate connection between capitalism and freedom. Although never a full-time government employee since his World War II stint with the Treasury Department, he has served in his spare time as economic adviser to presidential candidate Barry Goldwater and to President Nixon (before Nixon left the faith and imposed price and wage controls).

FRIEDMAN-HELLER DEBATE, NOVEMBER 1968.

But Friedman is most prominently identified, at least within the economics profession, as the defender (and in large part the creator) of monetarism. While Keynesianism triumphant swept the economics profession in the postwar years, Friedman and a few University of Chicago colleagues were investigating the historical connection between money and U.S. economic history, eventually persuading the Federal Reserve Bank of St. Louis to gather and publish statistics using their concepts and fortifying the monetarist arguments until the inflation of the late sixties made monetarism fashionable again. In 1976, Friedman won the Nobel Prize for his work.

By contrast, Walter W. Heller, a professor at the University of Minnesota, has been a liberal and a political activist (at least by economists' standards). As chairman of the Council of Economic Advisers under both Presidents Kennedy and Johnson, he was a principal architect of the 1962 investment tax credit and the 1964 tax cut. He enjoyed a close and sympathetic relationship with the New Frontiersmen, and as a consequence, the council assumed a broader, more activist role than it has enjoyed before or since. He was a leading spokesman for the use of fiscal and monetary policies, not merely to avoid major depressions and inflations, but to smooth out the smaller fluctuations in the economy.

In their debate, Heller posed many basic questions concerning monetarism: "Which money-supply indicator do you believe? Can one read enough from money supply without weighing also shifts in demand and interest rates? Don't observed variations in monetary time lags and velocity cast serious doubt on any simple relation between money supply and GNP? Can a rigid monetary rule find happiness in a world beset with rigidities and rather limited adjustment capabilities? That is, is the rigid Friedman rule perhaps a formula made in heaven, that will work only in heaven?" These questions remain at the heart of the continuing debate between Keynesians and monetarists. E.A.

to reality. According to the Keynesians, the multiplier is more stable than the velocity of money, so that changes in taxes or government spending have a more predictable effect on total spending than changes in the quantity of money.[3] According to the monetarists, the velocity of money is more predictable than the multiplier, which means that the effects of changes in the quantity of money on total spending are more predictable than changes in taxes or government spending. Much econometric work is being done at present to try to resolve this issue. Although the evidence as yet is inconclusive, it is reasonable to expect that in the foreseeable future we will be much better able to answer this question.

Cost-Push Inflation and the Phillips Curve

Whether they lean toward the monetarist or the Keynesian route to economic stability, policy makers have found inflation to be a stubborn foe. In previous chapters, we described ***demand-pull inflation,*** a situation in which there is too much aggregate spending. The $C + I + G$ line is too high, resulting in inflationary pressure. Or, put in terms of the equation of exchange, $M \times V$ is too high, so that P is pushed up: too much money is chasing too few goods. This kind of inflation stems from the demand or spending behavior of the nation's consumers, firms, and government. We have had many inflations of this kind. The major inflations during the Revolutionary and Civil Wars were basically caused by demand-pull factors; and so, much more recently, was the inflation arising from the Vietnam War. In these extreme cases, the rise in the price level can be treated as a matter of arithmetic: with all resources fully utilized, national output is fixed, and prices rise in proportion to the increase in total spending.

However, in the view of many economists, demand-pull inflation is not the only kind of inflation. There is also a different kind—***cost-push inflation.*** The process underlying cost-push inflation is not as well understood as it should be, but, according to many economists, it works something like this: costs are increased, perhaps because unions push up wages, and in an attempt to protect their profit margins, firms push up prices. These price increases affect the costs of other firms and the consumer's cost of living. As the cost of living goes up, labor feels entitled to, and obtains, higher wages to offset the higher living costs. Firms again pass on the cost increase to the consumer in the form of a price increase. This so-called ***wage-price spiral*** is at the heart of cost-push inflation.

Basically, in cost-push inflation, *the culprits are unions and firms with considerable market power.* In a world of perfect competition, both in product and input markets, cost-push inflation could not occur. In such a world, labor could not increase wages in the face of appreciable unemployment. If it tried, competition would bring wages back down. Nor could firms increase prices to protect their profits. Competition would put a tight ceiling on their pricing policy. Under perfect competition, inflation could occur (make no mistake about that), but it would have to be of the demand-pull type. Whether big labor or big business initiates the wage-price spiral is very difficult to determine in practice, and may well vary from case to case. But whoever makes the first move, the result is inflation.

In some cases, increases in materials prices may play a major role in cost-push inflation. When the oil-producing countries increased the price of crude oil in early 1974, this resulted in price increases in a wide variety of

[3] Data we have seen (recall Figure 13.6) confirm that velocity is far from constant. For one thing, it varies with interest rates and with people's expectations. However, sophisticated monetarists would say that the velocity function—a functional relationship derived from the demand for money—is stable. This is different from saying that velocity as a calculated number is stable.

products that are made (directly or indirectly) from petroleum. Because these price increases were not offset by price reductions elsewhere in the economy, the over-all price level increased (and at a very rapid rate) in 1974. Of course, the price hike for crude oil (and other materials) was by no means the sole reason for this inflation. But unquestionably it did play a noteworthy role in exacerbating it. More will be said on this score in subsequent sections.

Generally it is difficult, if not impossible, to sort out cost-push inflation from demand-pull inflation. However, one case of fairly pure cost-push inflation occurred in the late 1950s. This was a period of considerable slack in the economy. You will recall from Chapter 12 that a recession occurred in 1957-58. By 1958 6.8 percent of the labor force was unemployed. Nonetheless, wage increases took place during the late 1950s—and at a rate in excess of the rate of increase of labor productivity (output per man-hour).[4] For example, average earnings (outside agriculture) went up by 4 percent between 1957 and 1961, while labor productivity went up by 2½ percent. Moreover, prices increased each year—by 3 percent from 1956 to 1957, and by 2 percent from 1957 to 1958.

Certainly this seemed to be a different phenomenon than the demand-pull inflation described in previous chapters. There was no evidence that too much money was chasing too few goods. Instead, this was apparently a case of cost-push inflation. Commenting on the situation in the middle and late 1950s, the Council of Economic Advisers concluded, "The movement of wages during this period reflected in part the power exercised in labor markets by strong unions and the power possessed by large companies to pass on higher wage costs in higher prices."[5]

[4] In the next section, we shall discuss the importance of the rate of increase of output per man-hour. For present purposes, it is sufficient to note that the greater the rate of increase of output per man-hour, the larger the rate of increase of cost per man-hour that can be absorbed without an increase in unit cost.

[5] *1962 Annual Report of the Council of Economic Advisers,* Washington, D.C.: Government Printing Office, p. 175.

The Phillips Curve

What determines the rate at which labor can push up wages? If you think about it for a while, you will probably agree that *labor's ability to increase wages depends on the level of unemployment. The more unemployment, the more difficult it is for labor to increase wages.* Although perfect competition by no means prevails in the labor market, there is enough competition so that the presence of a pool of unemployed workers puts some damper on wage increases. In nonunion industries and occupations, workers are much less inclined to push for wage increases—and employers are much less inclined to accept them—when lots of people are looking for work. In unionized industries and occupations, unions are less likely to put their members through the hardship of a strike—and firms have less to lose from a strike—when business is bad and unemployment is high.

Because wages tend to be increased at a greater rate when unemployment is low, one would expect the rate of increase of wages in any year to be inversely related to the level of unemployment. This expectation is borne out by the available evidence. In a particular period of time in the United States, suppose that the rate of increase in wages tends to be related to the level of unemployment in the way shown in Figure 16.6. According to this figure, which is based on hypothetical, but reasonable, numbers, wages tend to rise by about 7 percent per year when 9 percent of the labor force is unemployed, by about 8½ percent per year when 7 percent of the labor force is unemployed, and by about 10 percent per year when 6 percent of the labor force is unemployed. *The relationship between the rate of increase of wages and the level of unemployment is the* ***Phillips curve.*** It was named after A. W. Phillips, the British economist who first called attention to it.

Given the Phillips curve in Figure 16.6 it is

Figure 16.6
The Phillips Curve
The Phillips curve shows the relationship between the rate of increase of wages and the level of unemployment. This curve is drawn on the assumption that little or no inflation is expected.

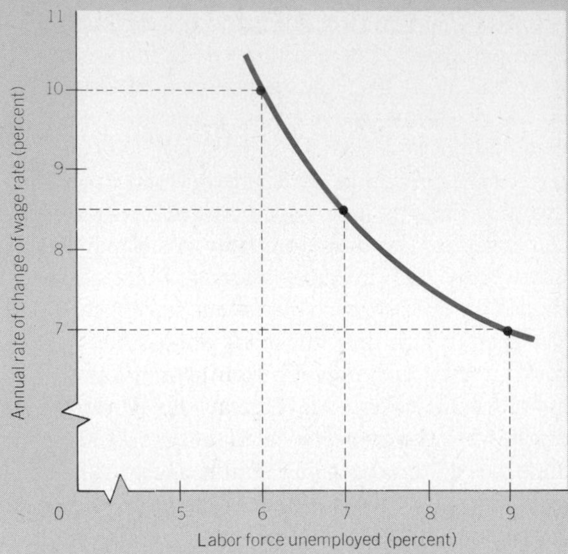

a simple matter to determine the relationship between the rate of inflation and the level of unemployment. If C is the total cost—wage and nonwage—per man-hour, the total cost per unit of output equals $C \times M \div O$, where M is the total number of man-hours worked and O is total output. This says no more than that total cost per unit of output equals total cost per man-hour times the number of man-hours divided by the number of units of output. Thus total cost per unit of output equals total cost per man-hour divided by output per man-hour. (Output per man-hour is often called ***labor productivity.***) Since the rate of increase of a ratio is the rate of increase of the numerator minus the rate of increase of the denominator, it follows that the *rate of increase of total cost per unit of output equals the rate of increase of total cost per man-hour minus the rate of increase of output per man-hour.*

Suppose that the rate of increase of prices equals the rate of increase of total cost per unit of output, and that the rate of increase of total cost per man-hour equals the rate of increase of wages. Then *the rate of increase of prices equals the rate of increase of wages minus the rate of increase of output per man-hour.* Suppose too that the rate of increase of output per man-hour (that is, labor productivity) is 3 percent per year. Then the rate of increase of prices equals the rate of increase of wages minus 3 percent. Consequently, the relationship between the rate of increase in prices and the level of unemployment is as shown in Figure 16.7.

There is, of course, a simple relationship between the curve in Figure 16.6 and the curve in Figure 16.7. The curve in Figure 16.7 (which shows the relationship between *price* increases and unemployment) is always 3 percentage points below the curve in Figure 16.6 (which shows the relationship between *wage* increases and unemployment). Why? Because the rate of increase of prices—under the assumptions set forth above—always equals the rate of increase of wages minus 3 percent.

At this point it should be clear that the curve in Figure 16.7 is none other than the curve encountered before, in Figure 8.3. Our present discussion has added an account of how this relationship is related to, and based on, the Phillips curve.

Shifts in the Phillips Curve

Before we get too impressed by the apparent accuracy of the Phillips curve, we must remind ourselves that the world is more complicated than Figure 16.7 indicates. In fact, predictions based on this curve may be quite wrong. Why? *Because the Phillips curve tends to be unstable.* For example, it may shift from position 1 to position 2 in Figure 16.8, thus causing the relationship between the rate of price increase and unemployment to shift from position 1 to position 2 in Figure 16.9. If you make a prediction based on the curve's being in position 1 in Figure 16.9, when in fact it is in position 2, you can make a substantial mistake. For example, suppose that you want to predict the rate of price increase if unemployment is 7 percent. Assuming that the curve is in position 1, you will predict a 6 percent increase in prices, but in fact there will be an 8 percent increase. The moral is clear enough: we need to look at the factors that can cause the Phillips curve to move.

Education. An important factor that can shift the Phillips curve is education or training. As more and more of the labor force is trained and equipped with relevant and basic skills, there is less upward pressure on wages at any level of unemployment. An important reason why wages are pushed upward as unemployment falls is that the economy tends to run out of skilled workers, so that poorly educated and untrained workers constitute a large percentage of the unemployed. When aggregate demand gets strong enough to absorb these workers, other workers experience so strong a demand that their wages are pushed up. Thus it follows that programs to train the labor force, particularly the unemployed, will shift the Phillips curve downward. That is, the rate of increase of wages associated with a given level of unemployment will fall.

Mobility. Increased mobility of workers will also shift the Phillips curve. As the labor force becomes able and willing to move from place to place, there is less pressure on wages at any level of unemployment. Thus it follows that measures designed to increase the mobility of workers—such as employment services and preferential tax treatment of moving expenses—tend to shift the Phillips curve downward.

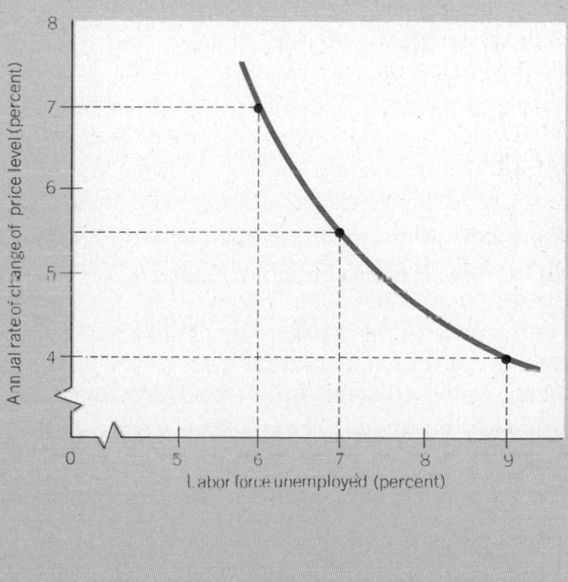

Figure 16.7
Relationship between Unemployment Rate and Rate of Inflation
This relationship can, under the conditions specified in the text, be deduced from the Phillips curve.

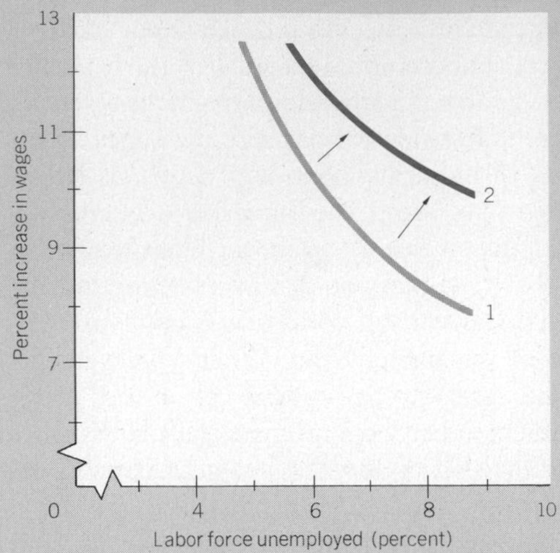

Figure 16.8
Shift in Phillips Curve
The Phillips curve can shift over time, as from position 1 to position 2.

Figure 16.9
Shift in Relationship between Price Increase and Unemployment Rate
If the Phillips curve shifts, as in Figure 16.8, the relationship between the unemployment rate and the rate of inflation will shift from position 1 to position 2.

Discrimination. Still another factor that will shift the Phillips curve is reduced discrimination against blacks, women, and others who historically have fared poorly in the labor force. With intense discrimination, labor markets must be very tight (and wages must be under considerable upward pressure) to make employers willing to hire women, blacks, and other minorities. With less discrimination, there is less upward pressure on wages at any level of unemployment, because the minorities are now in a position to compete on a more equal basis with other workers. Thus reductions in discrimination tend to shift the Phillips curve downward.

Demography and unions. The Phillips curve can also be shifted by changes over time in the demographic composition of the labor force (such as the proportion of women, teenagers, or blacks), as well as by changes in the bargaining power of unions.

Expectations. Finally, shifts occur in the Phillips curve because of changes in people's expectations. If people expect a great deal of inflation, this will be reflected in the wage demands of labor (and the pricing policies of management). Thus wages will rise more rapidly at a given unemployment level than if people expect less inflation. In other words, the more inflation people expect, the further upward and out from the origin the Phillips curve is likely to be. And the less inflation people expect, the further downward and close to the origin the Phillips curve will be. If we experience a great deal of inflation—as we have in the 1970s—the Phillips curve is likely to be pushed upward because it is likely that people will come to expect inflation to continue. This phenomenon undoubtedly was important in explaining our experience with high unemployment and high rates of inflation in the 1970s.

The Phillips Curve: Short versus Long Run

According to some economists, among them Milton Friedman of the University of Chicago and Edmund Phelps of Columbia, the Phillips curve in Figure 16.6 is only a short-run relationship. In the long run, the Phillips curve is vertical, as shown in panel A of Figure 16.10. Thus expansionary monetary and fiscal policies that result in inflation will only reduce unemployment temporarily. The only permanent way to reduce it is through manpower and training policies that will make the unemployed better suited to the available jobs. This is because labor comes to recognize that its wage gains are being eroded by inflation, so that it builds its expectations of inflation into its wage demands, thus pushing the Phillips curve upward and outward from the origin. Eventually, labor bargains with reference to the real, not the money wage.

This challenge to the conventional Phillips curve has itself been challenged by many economists. (This entire area is one of continuing controversy.) As indicated by panel B of Figure 16.10, there may be a range of unemployment, perhaps above 5 percent, where an inverse relationship exists in the long run between unemployment and inflation; but below this range, the Phillips curve may be essentially vertical. This view has been put forth by Yale's James Tobin and Northwestern University's Robert Gordon, among others. If this is the case, monetary and fiscal policies may not be the right tools to reduce unemployment in the range where the curve is essentially vertical. Manpower and retraining programs might be emphasized instead.

"Stagflation"

In recent years, and particularly during the mid-1970s, the American economy has been characterized by "stagflation"—a combination of high unemployment and high inflation. (The term *stagflation* was coined by putting together *stag*nation and in*flation*.) Apparently, the Phillips curve shifted upward; that is, at a given unemployment rate, the inflation rate has been higher than it formerly was. Why did this shift occur? Economists are by no means in agreement on this score. Indeed, the combination of excessive unemployment and excessive inflation in the mid-1970s has been an embarrass-

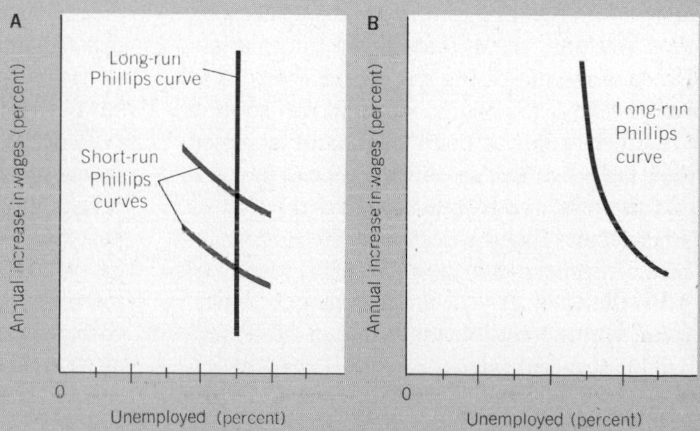

Figure 16.10
The Phillips Curve, Short and Long Run
Some economists argue that the long-run Phillips curve is vertical, as in panel A; others argue that it is shaped like that in panel B.

ment to economists, since they have neither a universally accepted explanation for it nor a well-developed cure for it. Nonetheless, the following account seems to be a reasonably accurate sketch of what occurred during the mid-1970s.

Let's begin in the summer of 1972. Although the economy was not in rosy shape then, it was far healthier than in the next few years. The unemployment rate then was about 5 percent, and the inflation rate in 1972 was about 3 percent. What occurred to propel the economy into the subsequent stagflation? Basically, several factors were at work. First, food prices shot up, beginning in late 1972, because of bad crops around the world (and the disappearance of Peruvian anchovies, which caused a drop in the fish catch off the South American coast). Second, many other raw material prices increased rapidly, due to a world-wide expansion of economic activity and the devaluation of the dollar. Third, the price of crude oil increased greatly in 1974, as pointed out in a previous section. These three factors together with a relatively great increase in the money supply in late 1972, were responsible for pushing the inflation rate up to 9 percent in 1973 and 12 percent in 1974.

At the same time, these three factors set in motion serious recessionary forces. The oil price hike acted like an excise tax levied on the consumer; it reduced the amount that consumers could spend on other things. The general inflation raised people's money incomes, thus pushing them into higher income tax brackets and increasing the amount they had to pay in taxes. (Similarly, the inflation swelled the paper profits of many firms, and increased their tax bills.) Because of the oil price increase and the effective increase in taxes, as well as other factors like the decline in the stock market, consumers cut back on their spending. Thus the $C + I + G$ line was pushed downward, and the equilibrium value of NNP fell.

This scenario can explain our being afflicted simultaneously with both the highest inflation rate (12 percent in 1974) and the highest unemployment rate ($8\frac{1}{2}$ percent in 1975) in postwar history. And many economists believe this to be the explanation. But other economists emphasize additional factors as well, such as changes in the structure of the American economy. To explain the evident upward shift in the Phillips curve, it is frequently claimed that our economy does not work the way it used to. According to this view, there is less competition than formerly, and a more pervasive public expectation that inflation may accelerate. As pointed out above, such factors could push the Phillips curve upward. The extent to which they in fact have done so is largely unknown.

Attacks on Market Power and Controls on Prices: Two Suggested Remedies

The government would, of course, like to shift the Phillips curve downward, for example from position C to position D in Figure 16.11. Programs to train manpower, increase labor mobility, reduce discrimination, and change expectations can have this effect. Unfortunately, however, programs of this sort take a considerable amount of time to make an impact, and, as we have seen in the previous section, the evidence of recent years seems to indicate that the Phillips curve has shifted upward, not downward. In this section, we take up two other remedies—the reduction of market power, and price and wage controls.

Reduction of market power. Since the market power of unions and firms is the basic cause of cost-push inflation, it would seem logical to attack cost-push inflation in this way. To some extent, the government is, of course, committed to a policy of this sort. Antitrust policy is a basic part of our nation's economic policy. But as we shall see in Chapter 26, antitrust policy is

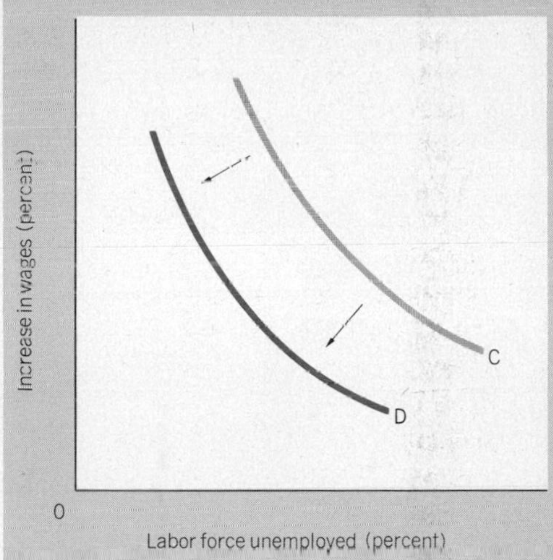

Figure 16.11
Shift in Phillips Curve
The government would like to shift the Phillips curve downward, as from position *C* to position *D*.

not designed to root out market power in all forms and degrees. This would be foolish in any case, because economies of scale and other considerations require that firms in many industries—to be efficient and innovative—must have a certain amount of market power. Moreover, even when the existing size of firms or concentration of industries cannot be defended on these grounds, the government is not seriously attempting to break up existing firms. Some economists would favor such a policy, both to quell cost-push inflation and to obtain the other advantages (discussed in Chapters 26 and 30) of a competitive economy. But it does not seem at all likely that such a radical—and politically difficult—policy will be adopted.

Price and wage controls. During World War II—and other wartime emergencies—the government has imposed controls on wages and prices. In other words, the government intervened directly in the market place to see that wages and prices did not increase by more than a certain amount. Some distinguished economists argue that price and wage controls should also be used to control cost-push inflation in peacetime. According to a former president of the American Economic Association,

> A complete attack on inflation requires that both causes of inflation—both the excess of demand or spending, and the wage-price spiral—be brought under control. . . . The defense against the wage-price spiral (i.e., cost-push inflation) . . . is the direct control over prices and wages. These direct controls are not a substitute for a strong fiscal policy; they perform a different task. . . . To tie down the wage-price spiral, with reasonable justice and equity, we need to do three things. They are (1) Effectively stabilize basic living costs. This is necessary if wages are to be stabilized. (2) Maintain a general ceiling on wages and prices in that part of the economy where wages are determined by collective-bargaining contracts and where prices normally move in response to wage movements. I have reference here to what may properly be called the great industrial core of the American economy—the steel, automobile, electrical goods, construction, transport, and like industries. (3) As a contribution to over-all stability, place firm ceiling prices on basic raw materials.[6]

But most economists do not share this view. The economics profession has little enthusiasm for direct controls of wages and prices, for several reasons. First, such controls are likely to result in a distortion of the allocation of resources. Recall from Chapter 4 our discussion of the functions of the price system in allocating resources. Price and wage controls do not permit prices to perform these functions, and the result is inefficiency and waste. Second, such controls are likely to be expensive to administer. For example, during the Korean War, the Economic Stabilization Agency had 16,000 employees; and even so, it was difficult to prevent violation or evasion of the controls.

[6] John Kenneth Galbraith, testimony before the Joint Committee on the Economic Report, 82d Congress, 1st Session.

Are Price and Wage Controls Desirable? Inevitable?

According to some respected economists, such as Robert Lekachman of the City University of New York, price and wage controls are desirable. In his view, there is a need for a permanent federal agency to establish and apply criteria concerning wages and prices. As he puts it, "The continuing concentration of economic power and the proliferation of conglomerates and multinational corporations as recent embodiments of that power dictate the creation of a countervailing source of power operating in the public interest. Hence, the sooner economists and politicians shed the delusion that controls are required only in exceptional circumstances, the better."*

Most economists, however, are skeptical of the desirability of such controls. As C. Jackson Grayson, Jr., of Southern Methodist University (and former chairman of President Nixon's Price Commission) has said, "The lessons of history seem pretty clear. . . . In A.D. 301, the emperor Diocletian imposed the first extensive price-wage program. His edict (referred to as 'commanded cheapness') set schedules for 76 different wage categories and for 890 different price categories (222 of which were for food!). The penalty for an offense was death. Thirteen years later, the program, in shambles, was abandoned."† Turning from ancient Rome to modern times, the recent experience with incomes policies has not been very encouraging either. As Lloyd Ulman and Robert Flanagan of the University of California concluded from their study of Western European experiences after World War II, "Incomes policy, to generalize from the experience of the countries in this account, has not been very successful. . . . Experience . . . suggests that in none of the variations so far turned up has incomes policy succeeded in . . . making full employment consistent with a reasonable degree of price stability."‡

Perhaps the most frequent criticism of controls is that they interfere with the price system's ability to allocate resources, the result being bottlenecks, shortages, and waste. Other points emphasized by critics of controls are that a wage-price controls program will not work unless both labor and business cooperate, and that incomes policies will not work for long, since they erode with time. According to Grayson, voluntary programs have limited success, with the result that they tend to become mandatory, and getting into controls is easier than getting out. Both critics and defenders of controls accept that, unless monetary and fiscal policies are formulated responsibly, controls can have little durable effect. As Lekachman says, "Controls will fail except in the context of appropriate fiscal, monetary, and employment programs."[§]

Although they differ in their evaluation of the desirability of controls, both defenders of them, like Lekachman, and critics, like Grayson, feel that, for better or worse, controls will eventually be tried again in this country. Thus Grayson predicts that "We will turn again in the United States, in desperation, to some form of controls over wages and prices—just as people have done over the centuries. And the answer will still be the same—they make some short-term gains, but at the expense of the long-run welfare."[‖] It is also a safe bet that the controversy over the desirability of controls will continue for a long time to come, since inflationary pressures are unlikely to disappear.

[*] R. Lekachman, "The Inevitability of Controls," *Challenge*, November–December 1974.
[†] C. J. Grayson, "Controls Are Not the Answer," *Challenge*, November–December 1974.
[‡] L. Ulman and R. Flanagan, *Wage Restraint: A Study of Incomes Policies in Western Europe*, Berkeley: University of California Press, 1971.
[§] Lekachman.
[‖] Grayson.

Third, there is widespread opposition to detailed government regulation and control of this sort, on the grounds that it impairs our economic freedom. The Council of Economic Advisers undoubtedly spoke for most of the economics profession when it said in 1968,

> The most obvious—and least desirable—way of attempting to stabilize prices is to impose mandatory controls on prices and wages. While such controls may be necessary under conditions of an all-out war, it would be folly to consider them as a solution to the inflationary pressures that accompany high employment under any other circumstance. . . . Although such controls may be unfortunately popular when they are not in effect, the appeal quickly disappears once people live under them.[7]

Wage and Price Controls under the Nixon Administration: A Case Study

Despite the disadvantages of price controls, the Nixon administration adopted them in the summer of 1971. Wholesale prices were rising then at about 5 percent per year. The wage-price spiral was very much in evidence. Collective bargaining agreements were reached calling for wage increases far in excess of productivity increases, and there was no question but that firms would boost prices in an attempt to cover the resulting increase in costs. Since it took office in 1969, the Nixon administration had been opposed to wage and price guidelines, or wage and price controls, although a number of congressmen and others had suggested the adoption of controls or some form of incomes policy. However, in August 1971, President Nixon reversed his previous stand. He froze wages and prices for a three-month period. Then he appointed a 15-member Pay Board and a 7-member Price Commission, both of which were supervised by the government's Cost of Living Council.

The Pay Board was given the responsibility of administering wage controls, and the Price Commission was to administer price controls. In November 1971, these two bodies announced their initial policies. The Pay Board stated that pay increases had to be kept under 5.5 percent per year. A company could increase some employees' pay by more than this amount, but other employees would have to get less since total increases could not exceed this figure. The Price Commission ruled that

[7] *1968 Annual Report of the Council of Economic Advisers*, Washington, D.C.: Government Printing Office, p. 119.

price increases had to be kept under 2.5 percent. Both for prices and wages, exceptions could be made in some areas. Large firms were required to notify the Pay Board and Price Commission of intended wage or price increases.

From November 1971 to January 1973, this program of price and wage controls continued. Although it did not eliminate inflation, prices seemed to go up more slowly than before the freeze. (The consumer price index went up by about 3 percent during 1972.) By early 1973, it appeared that controls might safely be relaxed. In January 1973, the Pay Board and the Price Commission became part of the Cost of Living Council, headed by Harvard's labor economist, John Dunlop. And controls were eliminated or relaxed for most prices and wages, with the major exceptions of the health, food, and construction industries. To a considerable extent, the Nixon administration phased out the first peacetime wage and price controls in our history.

Unfortunately, inflation occurred subsequently at a bewildering pace. During the first half of 1973, wholesale prices of farm products and processed foods and feeds rose at the unbelievable rate of 48 percent per year. At the same time, the prices of lumber, fuel, and other industrial goods rose at alarming rates. President Nixon responded by imposing a 60-day freeze on prices (but not wages), beginning in mid-June of 1973. This was only a breather, an interim measure designed to give the administration some time to deal with the serious inflationary pressures that were evident through the economy.

In August 1973, the administration announced that price increases could not exceed cost increases. This was the core of the new postfreeze program. But it soon became obvious that this new program was not proving effective, and that there was growing criticism and skepticism concerning price controls. In April 1974, Congress allowed the control authority to expire. This phase of the program was widely acknowledged to be a failure.

It is difficult to evaluate the effects of the price and wage controls established between 1971 and 1974. According to many observers, the price level rose, once controls were relaxed, to the level that it would have attained in any event, if there had been no controls. Thus, to these observers, the effects of the controls were short-term and largely cosmetic. To other observers, the controls had a significant longer-term effect. According to the Council of Economic Advisers, "regardless of the overall effect of the program, whatever contribution it may have made was probably concentrated in its first 16 months, when the economy was operating well below its potential. As various industrial sectors reached capacity operations in 1973 under the stimulus of a booming domestic and world economy, the controls system began to obstruct normal supplier-purchaser relationships, and in some cases the controls became quite unworkable."[8] Still others maintained that the administration, by frequently voicing its distaste for controls, had a hand in undermining its own program.

Incomes Policies

Most economists regard neither direct controls not the reduction of market power as effective, practical devices to fight cost-push inflation. Faced with this fact, there has been considerable interest, both here and abroad, in using incomes policies to stem cost-push inflation. According to one common definition, an ***incomes policy*** contains three elements. *First, it has some targets for wages (and other forms of income) and prices for the economy as a whole.* For example, the target may be to stabilize the price level, or to permit the consumer price

[8] *1975 Annual Report of the Council of Ecomonic Advisers,* Washington, D.C.: Government Printing Office, pp. 228–29.

index to increase by less than 2 percent per year, or to allow wage increases not exceeding a certain percentage.

Second, an incomes policy gives particular firms and industries some more detailed guides for decision making on wages (and other forms of income) and prices. These guides are set in such a way that the over-all targets for the entire economy will be fulfilled. For example, if the aim is price stability, these guides tell firms and unions what kinds of decisions are compatible with this target. To be useful, the guides must be specific and understandable enough to be applied in particular cases. There obviously is little point in telling firms and unions to avoid "inflationary" wage and price decisions if they don't know whether a particular decision is "inflationary" or not.

Third, an incomes policy contains some mechanisms to get firms and unions to follow the guides. An incomes policy differs from price and wage controls in that it seeks to induce firms and unions to follow these guides voluntarily. But if it is to have any effect, clearly the government must be prepared to use certain forms of "persuasion" beyond moral suasion. In fact, governments sometimes have publicly condemned decisions by firms and unions that were regarded as violating the guides. Government stockpiles of materials and government purchasing policies have also been used to penalize or reward particular firms and industries. Other pressures too have been brought to bear in an attempt to induce firms to follow the established guides. Thus the difference between an incomes policy and price and wage controls is one of degree and emphasis, not a clear-cut difference in kind.

An example of an incomes policy in the United States was the so-called Kennedy-Johnson guidelines. Although earlier administrations (for example, the Eisenhower and Truman Administrations) had often appealed to business and labor to limit wage and price increases, the first systematic attempt at a fairly specific incomes policy in the United States occurred during the Kennedy administration. In 1961, President Kennedy's Council of Economic Advisers issued the following wage-price guidelines:

> The general guide for noninflationary wage behavior is that the rate of increase in wage rates (including fringe benefits) in each industry be equal to the trend rate of *over-all productivity advance.* General acceptance of this guide would maintain stability of labor cost per unit of output for the economy as a whole—though not of course for individual industries. The general guide for noninflationary price behavior calls for price reduction if the industry's rate of productivity increase exceeds the over-all rate—for this would mean declining unit labor costs; it calls for an appropriate increase in price if the opposite relationship prevails; and it calls for stable prices if the two rates of productivity increase are equal. [Note once again that productivity equals output per man-hour.][9]

To see just what this meant, let's consider prices and wages in the auto industry. Suppose that labor productivity in the economy as a whole was increasing at 3.2 percent per year. Then according to the guidelines, *wages in the automobile industry should increase by 3.2 percent per year.* If labor productivity in the auto industry increased by 4.2 percent per year, then, if the auto makers applied this guideline, the labor cost of producing a unit of output would decrease by 1 percent per year in the auto industry (since the 3.2 percent rate of increase of wages minus the 4.2 percent rate of increase of labor productivity equals −1 percent). Thus the guidelines specified that *prices in the auto industry should decrease,* perhaps by about 1 percent per year.

The Council of Economic Advisers specified several situations where these general guidelines would have to be modified. In particular, if there was a shortage of labor in a particular industry or if an industry's wages were

[9] *1962 Annual Report of the Council of Economic Advisers,* Washington, D.C.: Government Printing Office, p. 189.

lower than those earned elsewhere by similar labor, higher wage increases (than specified in general) would be warranted. Or if an industry's profits were insufficient to attract needed infusions of capital, or if an industry's nonwage costs rose greatly, higher price increases than specified in general would be justified. However, the Council did not attempt to set forth detailed, quantitative provisions about the extent to which higher wages or prices would be warranted under these circumstances.

The Steel Price Increase of 1962: A Case Study

To conform to our definition of an incomes policy, the Kennedy-Johnson wage-price policy had to have an over-all target, more detailed guides for wage and price decisions, and a mechanism to get firms and unions to observe these guides. The over-all target was the stabilization of prices, and the more detailed guides for price and wage decisions were described in the previous section. But what about the mechanisms to induce acceptance of these guides? How did the government get industry and labor to go along?

The famous confrontation in 1962 between President Kennedy and the steel industry is an interesting case study of how pressure was brought to bear. Before the wage-price guidelines were issued, President Kennedy asked the major steel companies to avoid raising prices, and no price increases occurred. Then, after the issuance of the guidelines, he asked the steel union for restraint in the wage negotiations coming up in March 1962. Arthur Goldberg, Kennedy's secretary of labor, played an important role in persuading the union to accept a 2.5 percent increase in compensation, which was clearly noninflationary. At this point, government and the press felt quite optimistic about the apparent success of the president's program.

In the week following the wage agreement, however, the United States Steel Corporation increased all its prices by $3\frac{1}{2}$ percent, and most of the major steel companies followed suit. The price increase was clearly a violation of the president's guidelines. It almost seemed as if the steel companies were trying to demonstrate once and for all that pricing was up to them, and them alone. Their action elicited a wrathful speech by the president publicly denouncing them. Roger M. Blough, chairman of the United States Steel Corporation, tried to rebut the president's arguments by claiming that U.S. Steel's profits were too low to attract new capital.

Three of the major steel producers—Armco, Inland, and Kaiser—did not follow U.S. Steel's lead in the day or so after its price increase. Government officials, noting this fact as well as prior public arguments against price increases by Inland officials, quickly began to apply pressure on these three producers to hold their prices constant. Government officials who knew executives of these firms called them and tried to persuade them to do so. The firms were also informed that government contracts would be directed to firms that held their prices constant. Apparently, the government's campaign succeeded. Inland and Kaiser made public statements that they would not raise prices. Faced with this fact, the other steel companies had no choice but to rescind the price increase.

This is an example of how presidential pressure can induce firms to go along with the guidelines. Often the Council of Economic Advisers tried to head off price increases before they were announced. In one way or another, sometimes from the companies themselves, the Council often learned of an impending price increase. The Council then asked the firms to meet to discuss the situation. In these meetings, the Council explained the importance of price stability and both parties discussed the proposed increase. It is difficult, of course, to measure the impact of such discussions, but, according to the Council, they sometimes resulted in the postponement or reduction of the planned price increases.

The Kennedy-Johnson Guidelines: Criticism and Experience

Soon after the announcement of the guidelines, critics began to point out problems in them. The criticism was of several types:

Inefficiency. Some observers feared that the guidelines would result in inefficiency and waste. In a free-enterprise economy, we rely on price changes to direct resources into the most productive uses and to signal shortages or surpluses in various markets. If the guidelines were accepted by industry and labor, prices would not be free to perform this function. Of course, the guidelines specified that modifications of the general rules could be made in case of shortages, but critics of the guidelines felt that this escape hatch was too vague to be very useful.

Freedom. Many observers were concerned about the reduction in economic freedom. Of course, the guidelines were presented in the hope that they would be observed voluntarily. But a time was sure to come when they would be in serious contradiction with the interests of firms and unions. In such a situation, what would happen if the firms or unions decided not to follow them? To the extent that the government applied pressure on the firms or unions, there would certainly be a reduction in economic freedom; and to some observers, it seemed likely that the next step might well be direct government controls. Moreover, the nonlegislated character of the guidelines and the arbitrary choice of whom to pursue by the government raised important questions of a political nature.

Feasibility. Many people felt that the guidelines really were not workable. In other words, even if the public would go along with them, in many cases they would be impossible to use, because accurate and relevant data on changes in labor productivity in particular industries were often unobtainable, and the situations where exceptions were allowed were so vaguely specified.

Symptoms. Some economists felt that reliance on the guidelines was dangerous because it focused attention on symptoms rather than causes of inflation. In their view, inflation was largely the result of improper monetary and fiscal policies. In other words, the basic causes had to be laid at the government's own door. But by setting up guidelines, the government seemed to be saying that the fault lay with industry and labor. Thus some critics felt that the guidelines tended to cloud the real issues and so let the government escape responsibility for its actions.

After the government's bout with the steel industry in 1962, there was no major public fight over wages and prices for a couple of years; and the government claimed that the guideposts were working well. To a considerable extent, this may have been because the economy still had considerable slack, as well as because of the noninflationary expectations of firms and individuals engendered by several years of relative price stability. By 1965, as labor markets tightened and prices rose in response to the Vietnam build-up (see Chapter 11), it became much more difficult to use the guidelines. Union leaders fought the guidelines tooth and nail, mainly because consumer prices were rising. In various important labor negotiations, unions demanded and got higher wage increases than the guidelines called for. For example, the airline machinists got a 4.9 percent increase in 1966. By 1968, the guidelines were dead: no one was paying any attention to them.

What effect did the guidelines have? Some people claim that they had no real effect at all, while others claim that they reduced cost-push inflation in the early 1960s by a considerable amount. Since it is difficult to separate the effects of the guidelines from the effects of other factors, there is considerable dispute over the question. Considering the level of unemployment in the early 1960s, wages increased less rapidly then than in earlier or later periods. Prices too increased less rapidly during that period—holding unemployment constant—than earlier or later. But whether these developments were due to the guidelines, or to noninflationary expectations or some other factor, is very hard to say.

Perhaps the most important reason why the guidelines broke down was that they could not deal with the strong demand-pull inflation of the late 1960s. Even the strongest defenders of the guidelines are quick to point out that they are no substitute for proper monetary and fiscal policy. *If fiscal or monetary policy is generating strong inflationary pressures, such as existed in the late 1960s, it is foolish to think that guidelines can save the situation.* Perhaps they can cut down on the rate of inflation for a while; but in the long run, the dike is sure to burst. If the guidelines are voluntary, as in this case, firms and unions will ignore them, and the government will find it difficult, if not impossible, to do anything about it. *Even price and wage controls are no adequate antidote to strong inflationary pressures by an overly expansive fiscal or monetary policy. Such controls may deal temporarily with the symptoms of inflation, but over the long haul these inflationary pressures will have an effect.*

Economic Stabilization: Where We Stand

Where do we stand in the struggle to achieve full employment without inflation? Clearly, we know much more than we did 30 years ago about how to use monetary and fiscal policies to attain this objective. Given the more advanced state of economics, it is very, very unlikely that a catastrophe like the Great Depression of the 1930s will occur again. But on the other hand, economists were overly optimistic in the mid-1960s when they talked about "fine-tuning" the economy. Our experience since then makes it clear that we have a long way to go before we understand the workings of the economy well enough to achieve continuous full employment without inflation. Equally important, we have seen that, even if the advice of its economists were always correct, the government might still pursue destabilizing policies, as it did in the late 1960s.

The mid-1970s have been characterized by both excessive inflation and excessive unemployment. Throughout the Western industrialized world, governments have been perplexed by this phenomenon of "stagflation." The standard economic remedies—monetary and fiscal policy—are not very effective in dealing with this combination of ailments. Although they can deal with either excessive unemployment or excessive inflation, they are not well designed to deal simultaneously with both of them.

To some economists, the answer (or at least a partial answer) is to rely more heavily on some form of incomes policy to fight inflation. But the evidence, here and abroad, seems to emphasize the problems in formulating an effective incomes policy. The unfortunate truth is that we do not have an adequate understanding of the factors causing "stagflation." Until we obtain a better basic understanding of this phenomenon, the chances are that policy makers, both here and abroad, will continue to have problems with regard to economic stabilization—and that there will be a good deal of floundering. If we experience severe inflation (á la 1974) once again, it is likely that some form of incomes policy will be applied in the United States. But it must be recognized that such policies have had limited success in restraining inflation in the past, in the United States as in other countries.

Summary

An important debate has been going on between the monetarists and Keynesians. The monetarists believe that changes in the money supply are the basic reason for business fluctuations. Keynesians believe that both monetary and nonmonetary factors cause business fluctuations. Many of the basic disagreements between the Keynesians and monetarists center about the quantitative effects of the interest rate. (1) According to the monetarists, the quantity of money demanded is relatively insensitive to changes in the interest rate; whereas to Keynesians, it is very sensitive to such changes. (2) According to the monetarists, the supply of money is relatively insensitive to changes in the interest rate; whereas to Keynesians, it is quite sensitive to such changes. (3) According to the monetarists, total expenditure is very sensitive to changes in the interest rate; whereas to some Keynesians, it is not so sensitive to such changes.

Because of these differing points of view, monetarists believe that monetary policy is of pre-eminent importance, whereas Keynesians tend to believe that it is of lesser importance. There also are differences of view concerning the effects of fiscal policy. The monetarists attack the Keynesian view that fiscal policy works as described in Chapter 11. According to the monetarists, whether the government runs a surplus or a deficit does not have much long-run effect on NNP, except insofar as the government finances the deficit or surplus in a way that alters the quantity of money. Monetarists and Keynesians come to quite different policy conclusions. In particular, many leading monetarists favor the establishment of a rule to govern monetary policy, an idea most Keynesians oppose.

An important barrier to achieving economic stability through monetary and fiscal policy is cost-push inflation. The Phillips curve shows the relationship between the rate of increase of wages and the level of unemployment. Given the Phillips curve, it is a simple matter to determine the relationship between the rate of inflation and the level of unemployment. If the Phillips curve remains fixed, it poses an awkward dilemma for policy makers. To the extent that they use fiscal and monetary policy to fight unemployment, they fuel the fires of inflation; to the extent that they use monetary and fiscal policy to fight inflation, they contribute to greater unemployment.

The available evidence indicates that the Phillips curve is unstable. The Phillips curve shifts in response to increased education or training of the work force, increased mobility of workers, reduced discrimination, demographic changes, changes in union bargaining power, and changes in people's expectations. Also, it can shift, at least temporarily, in response to various government policies, such as wartime controls on wages and prices. Although a few economists favor such controls during peacetime, most do not agree. Such controls are likely to distort the allocation of resources, to be difficult to administer, and to run counter to our desire for economic freedom. Another way to shift the Phillips curve is to attack market power, but although many economists favor some such action, it does not seem practically or politically feasible.

Many countries have experimented with various kinds of incomes policies. An incomes policy contains targets for wages and prices for the economy as a whole, more detailed guides for wage and price decisions in particular industries, and some mechanisms to get firms and unions to follow these guides. The Kennedy-Johnson guidelines were one form of incomes policy. Further, wage and price controls have been instituted in some countries. For the first time, the United States resorted to such controls in peacetime in 1971–74. Although controls of this sort have a short-term effect on the price level, how much effect they have in the long run is hard to say.

In recent years, and particularly during the mid-1970s, the American economy has been characterized by "stagflation," a combination of high unemployment and high inflation. Apparently, the Phillips curve shifted upward; that is, at a given unemployment rate, the inflation rate has been higher than it formerly was. Among the most important factors responsible for this shift were bad crops, the devaluation of the dollar, and the marked increase in the price of crude oil in the early and mid-1970s. These factors combined both to cause serious inflation and severe recession. In addition, according to some economists, there is less competition than formerly, and a more pervasive public expectation that inflation will go on. These factors, too, could have pushed the Phillips curve upward.

CONCEPTS FOR REVIEW

Monetarists	Cost-push inflation	Incomes policy
Keynesians	Wage-price spiral	Price freeze
Demand-pull inflation	Phillips curve	

QUESTIONS FOR DISCUSSION AND REVIEW

1. According to Juanita Kreps, "It is the function of manpower programs to improve the terms of the tradeoff—that is, to shift the Phillips curve to the left." Suggest as many kinds of manpower programs as you can that might help in this regard. What sorts of manpower programs have been launched in this country?

2. According to Milton Friedman, "It is far better that inflation be open than that it be suppressed [by price guidelines]." Do you agree? Why or why not?

3. "The Kennedy-Johnson guidelines for noninflationary price behavior called for price reduction if an industry's rate of productivity increase exceeded the over-all rate. It is unrealistic to expect price cuts of this sort." Do you agree? Why or why not?

4. "The inflations arising from the Revolutionary, Civil, and Vietnam Wars were largely cost-push." Comment and evaluate.

5. "Keynesians believe that the demand curve for money is close to vertical; consequently, they feel that monetary policy has less effect on NNP than monetarists." Comment and evaluate.

6. Suppose that the relationship between the annual rate of change of the wage rate and the percent of the labor force unemployed is as shown below:

Rate of change of wage rate (percent per year)	Unemployment rate (percent)
5	8
6	7
7	6
8	5

Plot the Phillips curve on a graph. Would Milton Friedman accept this curve as a long-run Phillips curve? Why or why not?

7. Suppose that output per man-hour is growing at 2 percent per year. Based on the data in Question 6, plot the relationship between the annual rate of change of the price level and the unemployment rate. State the assumptions you are making.

8. "The Phillips curve shifts position so much that it is an unreliable tool for the determination of public policy." Comment and evaluate.

9. "Reliance on incomes policies is dangerous because it looks at symptoms, not the basic causes of our problems." Comment and evaluate.

10. John Kenneth Galbraith has written that "the defense against the wage-price spiral . . . is the direct control over prices and wages." Using the experience of the United States with such controls during the early 1970s as a guide, evaluate Galbraith's position. Would Galbraith accept such evidence as conclusive? Why or why not?

APPENDIX: *IS* and *LM* Curves—A More Complete Model

To understand more completely the argument between the Keynesians and the monetarists, it is worthwhile to enlarge the model of national output determination in Chapters 10 and 11 to include monetary factors. The simplest extension of this sort involves the use of *IS* and *LM* curves, both of which will be discussed in detail below. These curves, originated by Oxford's Nobel laureate, Sir John Hicks, help to put the debate between the monetarists and the Keynesians into somewhat deeper perspective.

Before describing how *IS* and *LM* curves are constructed, it is important to be clear concerning the basic assumptions that are being made. First, it is assumed that the price level is fixed, and that the public has a fixed demand curve for real money balances, a fixed consumption function, and a fixed investment function. Second, foreign trade is ignored. Third, the money supply is fixed by the monetary authorities, and does not vary with NNP or the interest rate. Fourth, tax rates are fixed, and fiscal policy takes the form of varying government expenditure.

The IS *Curve: Definition and Derivation*

The IS *curve shows, for each possible level of the interest rate, the level of NNP that will satisfy the equilibrium condition that desired spending on output must equal NNP.* (If this equilibrium condition is a bit hazy, review Chapter 10.) This equilibrium condition is equivalent to saying that the public must be spending the desired amount relative to its income. (We put a great deal of stress on this equilibrium condition in Chapter 10.) To construct the *IS* curve,

Figure 16.12
Derivation of the *IS* Curve
If the interest rate is i_1, desired investment is I_1. If the interest rate is i_2, desired investment is I_2.

If desired investment is I_1, equilibrium NNP is Y_1. If desired investment is I_2, equilibrium NNP is Y_2.

The *IS* curve shows, for each level of the interest rate, the level of NNP that will satisfy the equilibrium condition that desired spending on output must equal NNP. Points *A* and *B* are derived in the panels above, which show that equilibrium NNP equals Y_1 if the interest rate is i_1 and Y_2 if the interest rate is i_2.

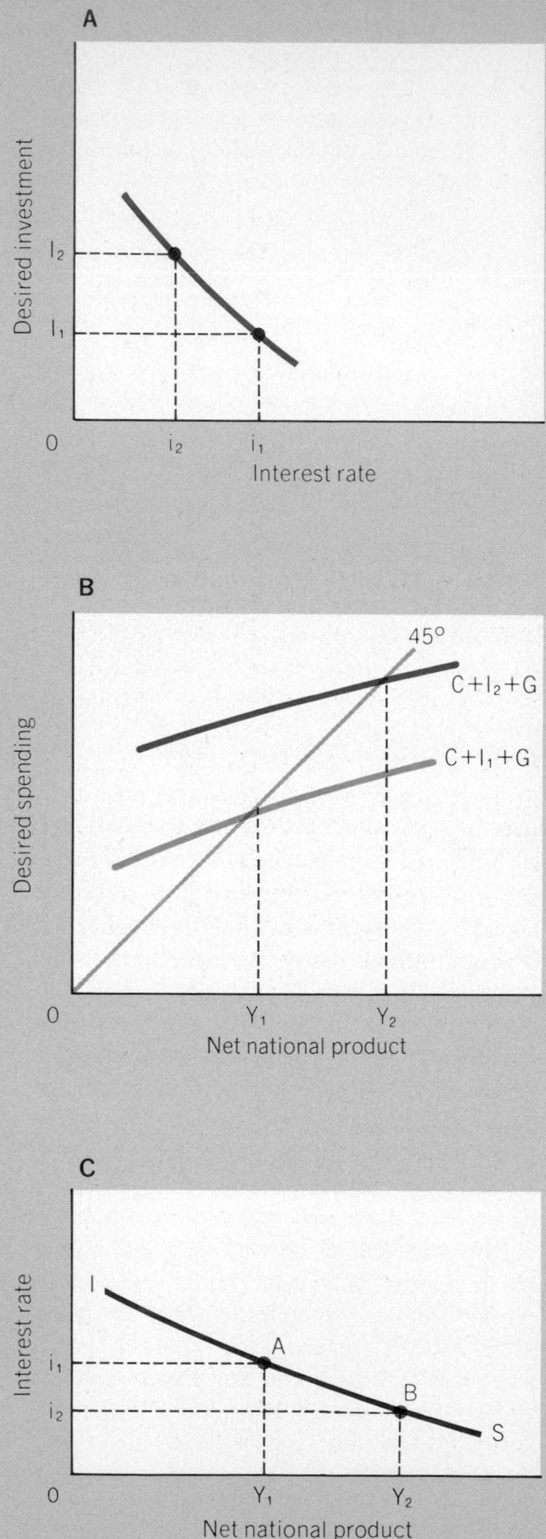

it is essential to recognize two things. First, the level of desired investment is inversely related to the interest rate. (In other words, for reasons described in Chapter 9, the higher the rate of interest, the lower the amount of desired investment, as shown in panel A of Figure 16.12.) Second, the level of desired investment (as well as consumption and government expenditure) will determine the equilibrium level of NNP. (See panel B of Figure 16.12.) Thus, since the interest rate determines the level of desired investment, and the level of desired investment determines the equilibrium level of NNP, there will be a relationship between the level of the interest rate and the equilibrium level of NNP; this relationship is the *IS* curve, shown in panel C of Figure 16.12.

To see more precisely what the *IS* curve is, it is useful to derive some points on such a curve. Let's derive two points—*A* and *B*—on the *IS* curve in panel C of Figure 16.12. To derive point *A*, note that, if the interest rate is i_1, desired investment will be I_1, according to panel A of Figure 16.12. And if desired investment is I_1, total desired spending at each level of NNP will be as shown by the $C + I_1 + G$ line in panel B of Figure 16.12, with the result that the equilibrium level of NNP will be Y_1. Thus, if the interest rate is i_1, the equilibrium level of NNP is Y_1—which explains the coordinates of point *A*.

To explain point *B*, note that if the interest rate is i_2, desired investment will be I_2, according to panel A of Figure 16.12. And if desired investment is I_2, total desired spending at each level of NNP will be as shown by the $C + I_2 + G$ line in panel B of Figure 16.12, with the result that the equilibrium level of NNP will be Y_2. Thus, if the interest rate is i_2, the equilibrium level of NNP is Y_2—which explains the coordinates of point *B*.

Note that *the* IS *curve slopes downward to the right.* That is, the lower the interest rate, the higher the level of NNP on the *IS* curve. For example, when the interest rate fell from i_1 to i_2 in Figure 16.12, panel A, desired investment increased from I_1 to I_2. And when desired investment rose from I_1 to I_2, the equilibrium level of NNP increased from Y_1 to Y_2, as shown in panel B of Figure 16.12. More generally, since the level of desired investment is inversely related to the interest rate, but directly related to the equilibrium level of NNP, it follows that the interest rate must be inversely related to the level of NNP on the *IS* curve.

The LM Curve: Definition and Derivation

The LM *curve shows, for each possible level of the interest rate, the level of NNP that will satisfy the equilibrium condition that the public be satisfied to hold the existing quantity of money.* We have stressed the importance of this equilibrium condition, and have pointed out that two of the principal reasons why the public wants to hold cash is the transaction motive and the speculative motive. Clearly, the quantity of money demanded for transactions purposes is dependent upon the value of NNP. Further, the quantity of money demanded for speculative (and other) purposes is dependent on the rate of interest. Thus, as stressed in Chapter 13, the total quantity of money demanded by the public is dependent both on the value of NNP and on the interest rate.

More specifically, the total quantity of money demanded by the public is *directly* related to the value of NNP and *inversely* related to the interest rate. (Recall the discussion in Chapter 13.) As NNP increases (and incomes rise), people want to keep more money on hand to buy things. Thus the quantity of money demanded by the public is directly related to the value of NNP (as shown in panel A of Figure 16.13). On the other hand, the higher the inter-

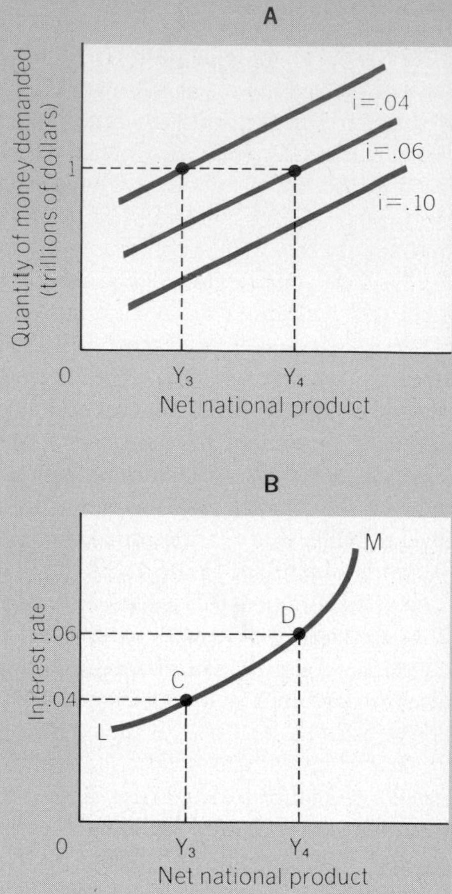

Figure 16.13
Derivation of the *LM* Curve
Holding constant the interest rate, *i*, the quantity of money demanded increases as NNP increases. Holding constant NNP, the quantity of money demanded increases as the interest rate decreases. If $i = .04$ and NNP $= Y_3$, the quantity of money demanded equals \$1 trillion. If $i = .06$ and NNP $= Y_4$, the quantity of money demanded equals \$1 trillion. These correspond to points *C* and *D* in panel B.

The *LM* curve shows, for each possible level of the interest rate, the level of NNP that will satisfy the equilibrium condition that the quantity of money demanded equal the supply of money. Points *C* and *D* are derived in panel A.

est rate, the more costly it is to hold money (because the more interest is forgone by holding money rather than investing it). Thus the higher the interest rate the smaller the amount of money that is demanded. In other words, the quantity of money demanded by the public is inversely related to the interest rate. (This is shown in panel A of Figure 16.13 by the fact that, if NNP is held constant, the quantity of money demanded increases as *i* decreases.)

Let's derive two points, *C* and *D*, on the *LM* curve, shown in panel B of Figure 16.13. Recall that any *LM* curve is based on the supposition that the money supply is *fixed*, and that the money supply must be just equal to the quantity of money demanded (for an equilibrium to occur). The *LM* curve in panel B of Figure 16.13 shows, for each interest rate, the value of NNP that will result in the public demanding this fixed amount of money, say \$1 trillion. If the relationships in panel A of Figure 16.13 hold, the quantity of money demanded will equal \$1 trillion if the interest rate is 4 percent and NNP is Y_3. Thus, if the interest rate is 4 percent, NNP (on this *LM* curve) must be Y_3—which explains the coordinates of point *C*. Panel A of Figure 16.13 shows that the quantity of money demanded will also equal \$1 trillion if the interest rate is 6 percent and the NNP is Y_4. Thus, if the interest rate is 6 percent, NNP (on this *LM* curve) must be Y_4—which explains the coordinates of point *D*.

Note that to maintain the quantity of money demanded equal to the fixed money supply ($1 trillion in this case), an increase in the interest rate must be accompanied by an increase in NNP. Why? Because, holding NNP constant, an increase in the interest rate will reduce the quantity of money demanded, as shown in panel A of Figure 16.13. Thus, unless NNP is increased, the quantity of money demanded will be less than the fixed money supply. To bring it back into equality with the fixed money supply, and thus to maintain the equilibrium on which the *LM* curve is based, NNP must be increased. Similarly, a decrease in the interest rate must be accompanied by a decrease in NNP, if the quantity of money demanded is to equal the fixed money supply. For these reasons, *the* LM *curve slopes upward to the right.* That is, the higher the interest rate, the higher the level of NNP that satisfies the equilibrium condition underlying the *LM* curve.

The Equilibrium Level of NNP

As pointed out in an earlier section of this chapter, a full-scale equilibrium requires *both* that households and firms be spending the desired amounts relative to their incomes *and* that they be satisfied to hold the existing amount of money. In other words, both the equilibrium condition underlying the *IS* curve and the equilibrium condition underlying the *LM* curve must be satisfied. For this to be so, the equilibrium combination of NNP and interest rate must be at a point lying both on the *IS* curve (which means that it satisfies the equilibrium condition underlying this curve) and on the *LM* curve (which means that it satisfies the equilibrium condition underlying this curve).

If we plot the IS *and* LM *curves on the same diagram, as in Figure 16.14, the equilibrium combination of NNP and interest rate must therefore be the one that is given by the intersection of the two curves.* Only this combination

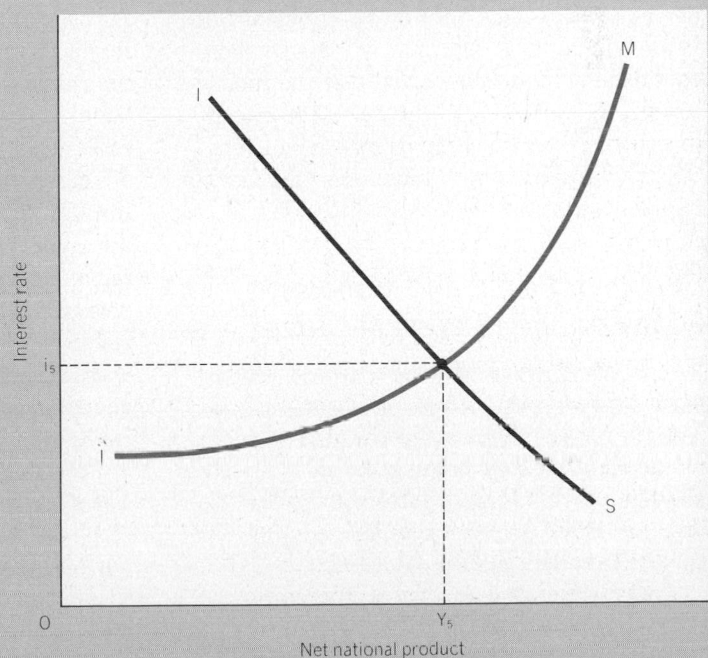

Figure 16.14
Determination of Equilibrium NNP and Interest Rate
The equilibrium level of NNP (and of the interest rate) must be at the intersection of the *IS* and *LM* curves. The equilibrium NNP equals Y_5, and the equilibrium interest rate equals i_5.

Figure 16.15
Effect of a \$10 Billion Increase in Government Expenditures on *IS* Curve
If government expenditures are increased by \$10 billion, and the interest rate is i_1, equilibrium NNP increases from Y_1 to Y_1'. If the interest rate is i_2, it increases from Y_2 to Y_2'. Since the level of NNP on the *IS* curve corresponding to any level of the interest rate is increased, the effect of the increase in government expenditures must be to shift the *IS* curve to the right.

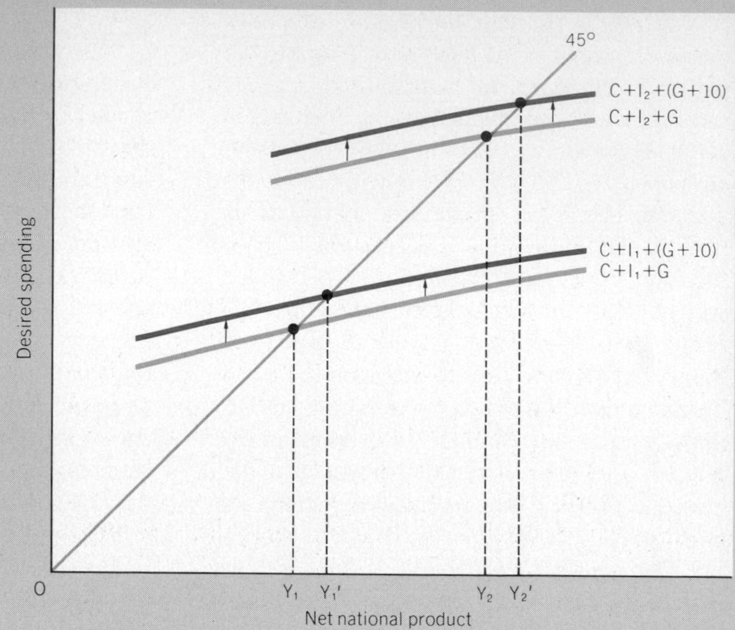

lies on both curves, and thus satisfies both equilibrium conditions. For example, in Figure 16.14, the equilibrium level of NNP must be Y_5, and the equilibrium level of the interest rate must be i_5. This is the only combination of NNP and interest rate that will satisfy both equilibrium conditions, given that the money supply, the public's demand curve for money, its consumption function, its investment function, and government expenditures (and taxes) remain fixed.

Effects of Fiscal and Monetary Policy on the IS and LM Curves

The IS *curve will shift to the right if government expenditures increase or taxes decrease.* The reason why these factors shift the *IS* curve to the right is that, holding the interest rate constant, each of these factors increases the level of NNP that satisfies the equilibrium condition underlying the *IS* curve.

To see why this is so, take as an example the effect of a \$10 billion increase in government expenditures in Figure 16.12. Before the increase occurs, what is the equilibrium level of NNP corresponding to an interest rate of i_1? As we saw in Figure 16.12, it is Y_1. But after the increase occurs, it is no longer Y_1. Due to the increased government expenditure, the $C + I + G$ line in panel B of Figure 16.12 is raised from $C + I_1 + G$ to $C + I_1 + (G + 10)$, as shown in Figure 16.15. Thus the equilibrium level of NNP is increased to Y_1', as shown in Figure 16.15. Similarly, if the interest rate is i_2, the equilibrium level of NNP is increased to Y_2'. Since the level of NNP on the *IS* curve corresponding to each level of the interest rate is increased, the effect of the increase in government expenditure is to shift the *IS* curve to the right.

The LM *curve will shift to the right if the monetary authorities increase the money supply, and it will shift to the left if they decrease the money supply.* To see why, consider first an increase in the money supply. Under such circumstances, if the interest rate stays the same, NNP must increase in order to bring the quantity of money demanded into equality with the new money supply. Why? Because the quantity of money demanded, if it is to equal the new money supply, must increase, and an increase in NNP will result in such an increase in the quantity of money demanded. Thus, since the level of NNP where this equality holds (the interest rate being unchanged) is greater than before, the effect of the increase in the money supply must be to shift the *LM* curve to the right.

Next, consider a decrease in the money supply. If the interest rate stays the same, NNP must decrease in order to bring the quantity of money demanded into equality with the new money supply. Why? Because decreases in NNP will decrease the quantity of money demanded, which is required if the quantity of money demanded is to equal the diminished money supply. Thus, since the level of NNP where this equality holds (the interest rate being unchanged) is smaller than before, the effect of the decrease in the money supply must be to shift the *LM* curve to the left.

Effects of Fiscal Policy on NNP

To understand the difference between Keynesian and monetarist views concerning the effects of fiscal policy on NNP, it is useful to consider three alternative assumptions. First, let's assume that the economy is operating at a point where *the* LM *curve has a positive slope and is neither close to being vertical nor close to being horizontal.* Since an increase in government expenditures shifts the *IS* curve to the right, an expansionary fiscal policy will increase both NNP and the interest rate, if the *LM* curve has such a shape. Panel A of Figure 16.16 shows that this is the case. A shift to the right of the *IS* curve (such as from I_1S_1 to $I_1'S_1'$) increases both NNP (from Y_6 to Y_7) and the interest rate (from i_6 to i_7).

Second, let's assume that the economy is operating at a point where *the* LM *curve is close to being vertical.* Indeed, to make things simple, let's assume that it is vertical. If so, an expansionary fiscal policy results in an increase in the interest rate, but no increase in NNP. For example, in panel B of Figure 16.16, a shift to the right of the *IS* curve (such as from I_2S_2 to $I_2'S_2'$) increases the interest rate (from i_8 to i_9), but not NNP. This is the so-called *classical range* of the *LM* curve, where fiscal policy cannot increase NNP.

Third, let's assume that the economy is operating at a point where *the* LM *curve is horizontal (or nearly so).* If so, an expansionary fiscal policy results in an increase in NNP, but no increase in the interest rate. For example, in panel C of Figure 16.16, a shift to the right of the *IS* curve (such as from I_3S_3 to $I_3'S_3'$) increases NNP (from Y_8 to Y_9), but not the interest rate. This is sometimes called the *liquidity-trap range.*

Although both a perfectly vertical and a perfectly horizontal *LM* curve are polar extremes, they are useful in indicating the differences between the monetarists and the Keynesians. *The monetarists believe that the* LM *curve is close to vertical, whereas the Keynesians believe that it is much closer to horizontal.* (Why? Because of the differences in their assumptions, indicated in Figures 16.1 to 16.3.) Given their different views concerning the shape of the *LM* curve, it is easy to see why they come to quite different conclusions concerning the effects of fiscal policy on NNP. Clearly, the monetarists, based on their assumptions, will conclude that fiscal policy has less impact on NNP than will the Keynesians.

Effects of Monetary Policy on NNP

To understand the difference between Keynesian and monetarist views concerning the effects of monetary policy on NNP, it is useful to consider three alternative assumptions.

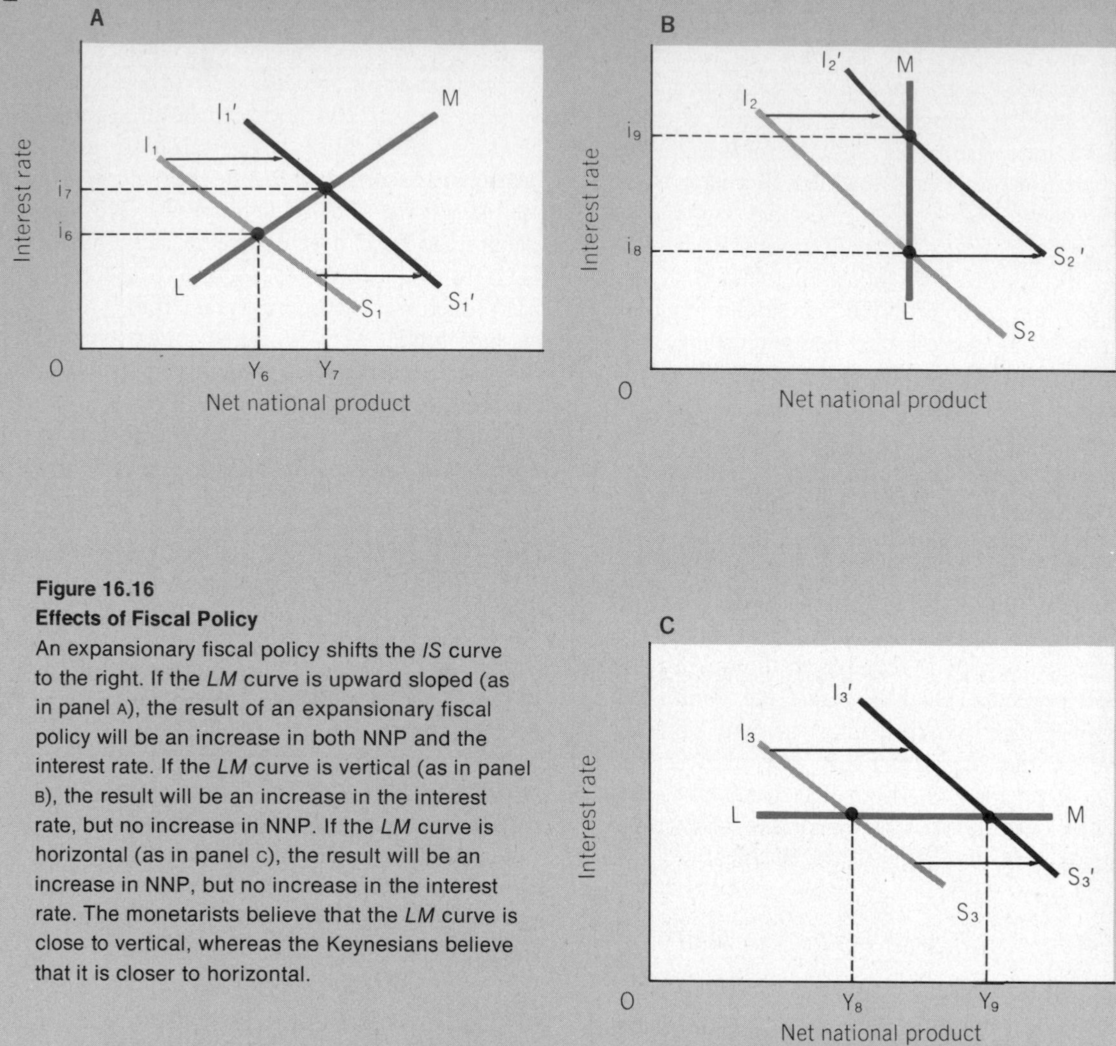

Figure 16.16
Effects of Fiscal Policy
An expansionary fiscal policy shifts the *IS* curve to the right. If the *LM* curve is upward sloped (as in panel A), the result of an expansionary fiscal policy will be an increase in both NNP and the interest rate. If the *LM* curve is vertical (as in panel B), the result will be an increase in the interest rate, but no increase in NNP. If the *LM* curve is horizontal (as in panel C), the result will be an increase in NNP, but no increase in the interest rate. The monetarists believe that the *LM* curve is close to vertical, whereas the Keynesians believe that it is closer to horizontal.

First, let's assume that the economy is operating at a point where the IS *curve has a negative slope and is neither close to being horizontal nor close to being vertical.* Since an increase in the money supply shifts the *LM* curve to the right, an expansionary monetary policy will increase NNP and reduce the interest rate, if the *IS* curve has this shape. Panel A of Figure 16.17 shows that this is the case. A shift to the right of the *LM* curve (from L_1M_1 to $L_1'M_1'$) increases NNP (from Y_{10} to Y_{11}) and reduces the interest rate (from i_{10} to i_{11}).

Second, let's assume that the economy is operating at a point where *the* IS *curve is horizontal (or very nearly so).* If so, expansionary monetary policy results in an increase in NNP, but little or no decrease in the interest rate. For example, in panel B of Figure 16.17, a shift to the right of the *LM* curve (from L_2M_2 to $L_2'M_2'$) increases NNP (from Y_{12} to Y_{13}) but does not reduce the interest rate.

Third, let's assume that the economy is operating at a point where *the* IS *curve is close to being vertical.* If so, an expansionary mone-

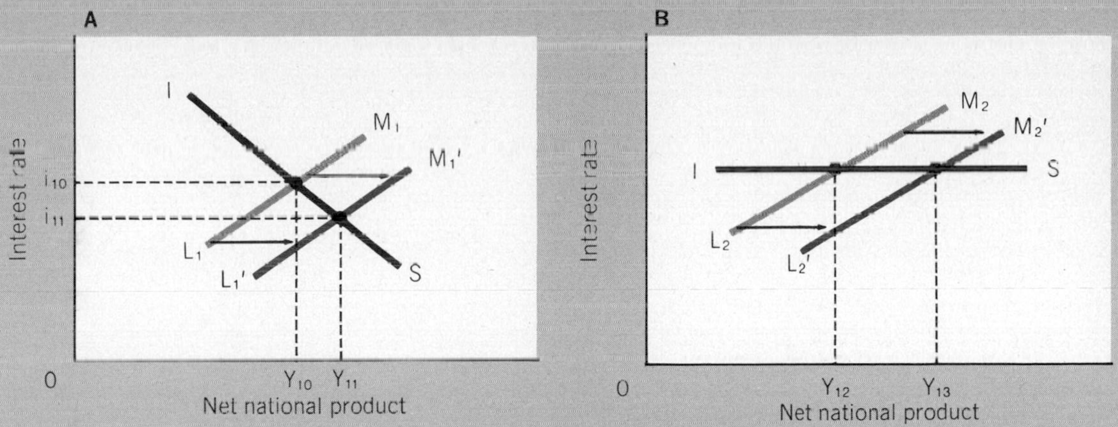

Figure 16.17
Effects of Monetary Policy
An increase in the money supply shifts the *LM* curve to the right. If the *IS* curve is downward sloped (as in panel A), an increase in the money supply will increase NNP and reduce the interest rate. If the *IS* curve is horizontal (as in panel B), it will increase NNP, but have no effect on the interest rate. If the *IS* curve is vertical (as in panel C), it will reduce the interest rate, but have no effect on NNP. The monetarists believe that the *IS* curve is close to horizontal, whereas some Keynesians believe that it is closer to vertical.

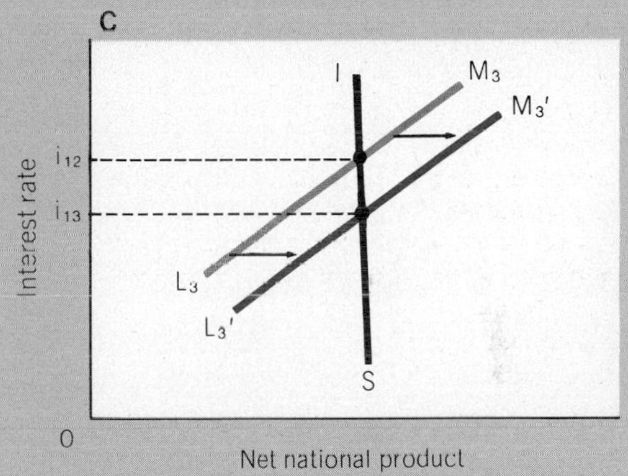

tary policy results in a decrease in the interest rate, but little or no increase in NNP. For example, in panel C of Figure 16.17, a shift to the right of the *LM* curve (from L_3M_3 to $L_3'M_3'$) decreases the interest rate (from i_{12} to i_{13}), but does not affect NNP.

Although both a perfectly horizontal and a perfectly vertical *IS* curve are polar extremes, they are useful in indicating the differences between the monetarists and the Keynesians. *Some Keynesians believe that the* IS *curve is close to vertical, whereas the monetarists believe that it is closer to horizontal.* (Why? Because of the differences in their assumptions, indicated in Figures 16.1 to 16.3.) Given their different views concerning the shape of the *IS* curve, it is easy to see why they come to different conclusions concerning the effects of monetary policy on NNP. Clearly, the monetarists, based on their assumptions, will conclude that monetary policy has a greater impact on NNP than will the Keynesians.

PART FIVE

Economic Growth, Energy, and the Environment

17

Economic Growth

Until fairly recently in human history, poverty was the rule, not the exception. As Sir Kenneth Clark puts it in his famous lectures on *Civilisation*,

> Poverty, hunger, plagues, disease: they were the background of history right up to the end of the nineteenth century, and most people regarded them as inevitable—like bad weather. Nobody thought they could be cured: St. Francis wanted to sanctify poverty, not abolish it. The old Poor Laws were not designed to abolish poverty but to prevent the poor from becoming a nuisance. All that was required was an occasional act of charity.[1]

Clearly, the human condition has changed considerably during the past century, at least in the industrialized nations of the world. Rising living standards have brought a decline in poverty, though by no means its disappearance. How has this increase in per capita output been achieved? This question has fascinated econo-

[1] K. Clark, *Civilisation*, New York: Harper & Row, 1970.

mists for a long time. Although we still are far from completely understanding the process of economic growth, our knowledge has increased considerably through the efforts of economic researchers, here and abroad. In this chapter, we discuss the process of economic growth in industrialized countries. A discussion of economic growth in less developed countries will be presented in Chapter 22.

Economic Growth: Definition and Evaluation

What Is Economic Growth?

There are two common measures of the rate of economic growth. The first is the rate of growth of a nation's real gross national product (or net national product),[2] which tells us how rapidly the economy's total real output of goods and services is increasing. The second is the rate of growth of *per capita* real gross national product (or net national product), which is a better measure of the rate of increase of a nation's standard of living. We shall use the second measure unless we state otherwise.

Two aspects of the rate of growth of per capita real gross national product should be noted from the start. First, *this measure is only a very crude approximation to the rate of increase of economic welfare.* For one thing, gross national product does not include one good that people prize most highly—leisure. For another, gross national product does not value at all accurately new products and improvements in the quality of goods and services, and does not allow properly either for noneconomic changes in the quality of life or for the costs of environmental pollution. Nor does gross national product take account of how the available output is distributed. Clearly, it makes a difference whether the bulk of the population gets a reasonable share of the output, or whether it goes largely to a favored few.

Second, *small differences in the annual rate of economic growth can make very substantial differences in living standards a few decades hence.* For example, per capita GNP in the United States was about $7,000 in 1975. If it grows at 3 percent per year, it will be about $14,600 (1975 dollars) in the year 2000, whereas if it grows at 4 percent per year, it will be about $18,700 (1975 dollars) in the year 2000. Thus an increase of 1 percentage point in growth rate means a $4,100—or 30 percent—increase in per capita GNP in the year 2000. Even an increase of ¼ of 1 percentage point can make a considerable difference. If the growth rate increases from 1¾ percent to 2 percent per year, per capita GNP in the year 2000 will increase from $10,800 to $11,500. Of course, this is no more than simple arithmetic, but that doesn't make it any less important.

Economic Growth as a Policy Objective

Following World War II, governments throughout the world became much more involved in trying to stimulate economic growth. In the United States, the government was not much inclined to influence the growth rate before the war. Of course, the government did many things that had some effect on the rate of economic growth, and in a general sort of way was interested in promoting economic growth. But it was normally taken for granted that, left to its own devices, our economy would manage to grow at more or less the proper rate. In the late 1950s and early 1960s, the climate of opinion began to change. To a considerable extent, this was because the U.S. rate of economic growth during the 1950s was rather low compared to that of other industrialized nations. From 1950 to 1959, per capita GNP grew by

[2] Either net national product or gross national product will do. As pointed out in Chapter 8, NNP has certain conceptual advantages, but GNP is more frequently used. It makes little difference since they do not differ by much. We use gross national product in this chapter, because data on GNP are more easily available.

about 2 percent per year in the United States, whereas it grew by about 6 percent in Japan, 5 percent in Italy and Germany, 4 percent in France, and 3 percent in the Netherlands, Norway, and Sweden. Moreover, our growth rate seemed to be less than that of the Soviet Union, the leading economic power in the Communist world.

The Call for Faster Economic Growth

During the late 1950s and early 1960s, many American economists and politicians drew attention to these facts, and called for an explicit public policy designed to increase our growth rate. In response, President Kennedy set as a target the attainment of a $4\frac{1}{2}$ percent annual increase in total output during the 1960s. Three principal arguments were given at that time for government stimulation of the rate of economic growth. First, it was argued that we had to increase our rate of economic growth to stay ahead of the Communist countries, the Soviet Union in particular. Economic growth was regarded as important for national defense and national prestige. In 1958, a report by the Rockefeller Brothers Fund concluded that growth was the most feasible way to provide for the defense outlays it envisioned as necessary in the future.

Second, it was argued that we should increase our rate of economic growth in order to increase public expenditures for schools, urban renewal, transportation, hospitals, and other such services. As we saw in Chapter 6, some observers, led by John Kenneth Galbraith, believed that there was a serious underinvestment in the public sector. Since it is very difficult politically to increase the percentage of GNP devoted to such services, it was felt that the only realistic way to remedy the situation was to increase the GNP. Then the absolute amount spent on the public sector could increase even if its percentage of GNP remained much the same.

Third, it was argued that we should increase our rate of economic growth in order to impress the neutral nations, many of which are relatively poor, with the benefits of our type of society. The emphasis here, as in the first argument, was on economic competition with the Communist world. According to many observers, the neutral countries were watching the growth rates of the Communist and capitalist countries, and the results would help decide which way these countries jumped. As the Council of Economic Advisers put it in 1962, "The less developed nations . . . need a further demonstration of the ability of a free economy to grow."[3]

During the 1970s, the enthusiasm for growth abated somewhat, for reasons discussed in the next section. But growth was by no means abandoned as a policy objective, in the United States or elsewhere. One important reason was that growth was viewed as a means by which poverty, here and abroad, might be reduced. If output per capita is rising, it is more likely that the electorate will vote to redistribute some of its income to the poor than if output per capita is constant. With growth, such a redistribution means that the poor can be made better off without cutting into the living standards of the more affluent. Without growth, this is impossible.

Skepticism toward Growth

Not all economists and policy makers agree that the government should alter the growth rate. Particularly in the past few years, there has been increasingly a feeling among economists (as well as the public at large) that economic growth should not be force-fed. Those who feel this way fall into two broad groups. One school of economists—including people like the University of Rochester's W. Allen Wallis, a prominent adviser to Presidents

[3] *1962 Annual Report of the Council of Economic Advisers,* Washington, D.C.: Government Printing Office, p. 110.

Nixon and Eisenhower—believes that the proper rate of economic growth is that which would emerge from private decisions. In their view, there is no reason to "force" growth on the economy, since there is no real possibility that the USSR will catch up with us soon, and the "unmet social needs" argument is little more than a slogan.

Another group of economists—led by E. J. Mishan of the London School of Economics—feels that economic growth, as usually measured, is a mirage. In their view, it has resulted in the degradation of the environment, the congestion and noise of our cities, the ugliness of some of the countryside, and the dullness of much of our work. They argue that the added production is not really of much value to society, and that people must be convinced by producers (through advertising and other sales techniques) that they want it. This viewpoint has appealed to many young people in recent years. However, it should be noted that if we are to reduce poverty, clean up the environment, and improve the quality of life, we shall need productive capacity, and economic growth is an important way to get it.

Whether or not the government should increase the rate of economic growth is, of course, a political decision; and your opinion of such a government policy will depend on many things, including your attitude toward present sacrifice for future material gain. As we shall see in subsequent sections, *a more rapid rate of growth can often be achieved only if consumers are willing to give up some consumption now so that they and their children can have more goods and services in the future.* To the extent that you believe that private decisions place too little weight on the future and too much weight on the present, you may be inclined to support a government policy designed to increase the growth rate. Otherwise you may not favor such a policy. In the next chapter, we shall discuss the pros and cons of economic growth in much more detail. Here we are concerned with its determinants.

The Aggregate Production Function

Economic Growth and the Product Transformation Curve

To represent the process of economic growth, it is convenient to use the product transformation curve which, as you will recall from Chapter 3, shows all efficient combinations of output an economy can produce. For example, suppose that a society produces only two goods, food and tractors. Then if this society has at its disposal a fixed amount of resources and if technology is fixed, the product tranformation curve (like the one in Figure 17.1) shows the maximum quantity of food that can be produced, given each amount of tractors produced.

Clearly, *a nation's potential output increases when its product transformation curve shifts outward,* for example, from position *A* to position *B* in Figure 17.2. This happens because the society can produce (and consume) more of one good without having to produce (and consume) less of the other good. Thus its productive capacity must be greater. If the product transformation curve shifts outward, if the economy is efficient, and if population remains constant, per capita GNP increases and economic growth occurs. Moreover, the faster the product transformation curve shifts outward, the greater the rate of economic growth.

Even if a nation's product transformation curve does not shift outward, economic growth can occur if unemployment or inefficiency is reduced. If a nation allows some of its resources to be unemployed or underutilized because of an insufficiency of desired spending, this will cause the economy to operate at a point *inside* the product transformation curve rather than *on* the curve. The same thing will happen if a nation allocates its resources inefficiently. Clearly, a nation can achieve some economic growth by getting closer to the product transformation curve through a reduction in unemployment or inefficiency.

A nation's potential output is directly related to the amount of resources it possesses and the extent to which they are used. These resources, or inputs, are of various kinds, including labor, capital, and land. The relationship between the amount used of each of these inputs and the resulting amount of potential output is often called the ***aggregate production function.*** It is analogous to the production function discussed in Chapter 7, which is the relationship between a firm's inputs and its output. However, the aggregate production function pertains to the entire economy, not a single firm.

Given that a nation's potential output depends on the amount of labor, capital, and land it uses, then the rate of growth of a nation's potential output must depend, in part at least, on the changes that occur in the amount of each of these inputs that is used. For example, if a nation invests heavily in additional capital, we would expect this to result in a substantial increase in potential output. Thus *a nation's rate of economic growth depends on the extent of the changes in the amounts of the various inputs used.* In addition, *a nation's rate of economic growth depends on the rate of technological change.* The aggregate production function is constructed on the assumption that technology is fixed. Changes in technology result in shifts in the production function, since more output is obtained from a given amount of resources.

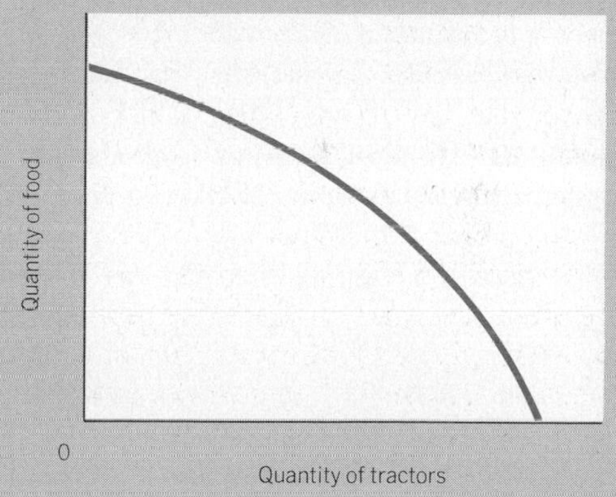

Figure 17.1
Product Transformation Curve
The product transformation curve shows all efficient combinations of output an economy can produce.

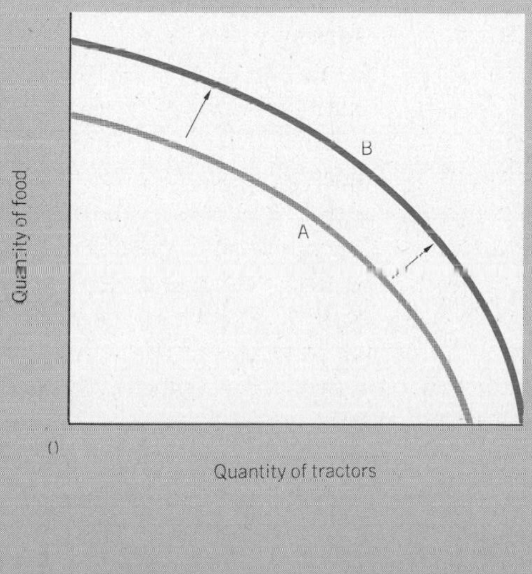

Figure 17.2
Outward Shift of Product Transformation Curve
A nation's potential output increases when its product transformation curve shifts outward, for example, from position *A* to positon *B*.

The Law of Diminishing Marginal Returns

If a nation's land, labor, and capital increase, one would certainly expect its output to increase as well. But suppose the nation cannot increase the amount used of all of its resources at the same rate. Instead, suppose it can increase the quantity of one resource, say labor, while the amount of other resources, like land, is held constant. In this situation, what will be the effect on output if the nation uses more and more of the resource that can be augmented? This is an important question, which occurs both in the present context and in the study of the production processes of the business firm.

To help answer it, economists have formulated the famous ***law of diminishing marginal returns,*** which states that, *if more and more of a resource is used, the quantities of other resources being held constant, the resulting increments of output will decrease after some point has been reached.* To see what this means, suppose that we obtain data concerning the amounts of output resulting from the utilization of various amounts of one resource, holding constant the amounts of other resources. For example, suppose that data are obtained concerning the amounts of output resulting from various amounts of labor, holding constant the amounts of capital and land. Then suppose that we determine the *extra* amount of output resulting from the addition of each *extra* unit of labor. According to the law of diminishing marginal returns, this extra amount of output will eventually *decrease,* as more and more labor is utilized with the fixed amounts of capital and land. In other words, beyond some point, *an additional unit of labor will add less and less to total output.*

To illustrate the workings of this law, consider Table 17.1, which shows the total output—or GNP—of a simple agricultural society under a set of alternative assumptions concerning the number of man-hours of labor used. For simplicity, we assume that this society produces only one product, corn, so that total output can be measured in bushels of corn. Also, we assume that the amount of land and capital that can be used is fixed in quantity. Column 1 in the table shows various alternative numbers of man-hours of labor that can be used with this fixed amount of land and capital. Column 2 shows the total output in each case.

Column 3 shows the additional output resulting from the addition of an extra man-hour of labor; this is called the ***marginal product***

Table 17.1
The Law of Diminishing Marginal Returns

(1) Man-hours of labor (millions)	(2) Bushels of corn (millions)	(3) Marginal product of labor (bushels per man-hour)	(4) Average product of labor (bushels per man-hour)
1	1.5		1.50
2	3.5	2.0	1.75
3	6.0	2.5	2.00
4	9.0	3.0	2.25
5	11.0	2.0	2.20
6	13.0	2.0	2.17
7	14.0	1.0	2.00
8	14.0	0.0	1.75

of labor. For example, if the quantity of labor is between 2 million man-hours and 3 million man-hours, the marginal product of labor is 2.5 bushels per man-hour of labor, because each extra man-hour of labor results in an extra 2.5 bushels of output.

In Table 17.1, the marginal product of labor increases as more and more labor is used, but only up to a point: beyond 4 million man-hours of labor, the marginal product of labor goes down as more and more labor is used. Specifically, the marginal product of labor reaches a maximum of 3.0 bushels per man-hour when between 3 and 4 million man-hours of labor are used. Then it falls to 2.0 bushels per man-hour when between 4 and 5 million man-hours of labor are used, remains at 2.0 bushels per man-hour when between 5 and 6 million man-hours of labor are used, and falls once again to 1.0 bushel per man-hour when between 6 and 7 million man-hours of labor are used.

Thus, as predicted by the law of diminishing marginal returns, *the marginal product of labor eventually declines.* Moreover, as shown in column 4 of Table 17.1, the ***average product*** of labor, which is defined as total output per man-hour, also falls beyond some point as more and more labor is used with a fixed amount of other resources. This too stems from the law of diminishing marginal returns.

It is easy to see why the law of diminishing marginal returns must be true. For example, imagine what would happen in the simple economy of Table 17.1 if more and more labor were applied to a fixed amount of land. Beyond a point, as more and more labor is used, the extra labor has to be devoted to less and less important tasks. If enough labor is used, it even becomes increasingly difficult to prevent the workers from getting in one another's way! For such reasons, one certainly would expect that, beyond some point, extra amounts of labor would result in smaller and smaller increments of output.

Finally, note several important things about this law. First, at least one resource must be fixed in quantity. The law of diminishing marginal returns does not apply to cases where there is a proportional increase in all resources. Second, technology is assumed to be fixed. Third, the law of diminishing marginal returns is an empirical generalization, not a deduction from physical or biological laws.

Thomas Malthus and Population Growth

A nation's rate of economic growth depends on, among other things, how much the quantities of inputs of various kinds increase. To illuminate the nature of the growth process, we discuss the effect on the rate of economic growth of increasing each kind of input, holding the others constant. We begin by looking at the effects of changes in the quantity of labor. Economists have devoted a great deal of attention to the effects of population growth on the rate of economic growth. The classic work was done by Thomas Malthus (1776–1834), a British parson who devoted his life to academic research. The first professional economist, he taught at a college established by the East India Company to train its administrators—and was called "Pop" by his students behind his back. Whether "Pop" stood for population or not, Malthus's fame is based on his theories of population growth.

Malthus believed that the population tends to grow at a geometric rate. In his *Essay on the Principle of Population,* published in 1798, he pointed out the implications of such a constant rate of growth:

> If any person will take the trouble to make the calculation, he will see that if the necessities of life could be obtained without limit, and the number of people could be doubled every twenty-five years, the population which might have been produced from a single pair since the

THOMAS MALTHUS

on Population

Throughout the animal and vegetable kingdoms Nature has scattered the seeds of life abroad with the most profuse and liberal hand; but has been comparatively sparing in the room and the nourishment necessary to rear them. . . . Necessity, that imperious, all-pervading law of nature, restrains them within the prescribed bounds. The race of plants and the race of animals shrink under this great restrictive law; and man cannot by any efforts of reason escape from it.

In plants and irrational animals, the view of the subject is simple. . . . The effects of this check on man are more complicated.

It may safely be pronounced that population, when unchecked, goes on doubling itself every twenty-five years, or increases in a geometrical ratio. The rate according to which the productions of the earth may be supposed to increase, will not be so easy to determine. Of this, however, we may be perfectly certain, that the ratio of their increase in a limited territory must be of a totally different nature from the ratio of the increase of population. A thousand millions are just as easily doubled every twenty-five years by the power of population as a thousand. But the food to support the increase from the greater number will by no means be obtained with the same facility. Man is necessarily confined in room. When acre has been added to acre til all the fertile land is occupied, the yearly increase of food must depend upon the melioration of the land already on possession. This is a fund, which, from the nature of all soils, instead of increasing, must be gradually diminishing. But population, could it be supplied with food, would go on with unexhausted vigor; and the increase of one period would furnish the power of a greater increase the next, and this without any limit. . . .

It may be fairly pronounced, therefore, that considering the present average state of the earth, the means of subsistence, under circumstances the most favorable to human industry, could not possibly be made to increase faster than in an arithmetical ratio. . . . The ultimate check to population appears then to be a want of food, arising necessarily from the different ratios according to which population and food increase.

Thomas Malthus, *An Essay on the Principle of Population,* London: Reeves and Turner, 1888, pp. 4–6. Originally published in 1798.

> Christian era, would have been sufficient, not only to fill the earth quite full of people, so that four should stand in every square yard, but to fill all the planets of our solar system in the same way, and not only them but all the planets revolving around the stars which are visible to the naked eye, supposing each of them . . . to have as many planets belong to it as our sun has.[4]

In contrast to the human population, which tends to increase at a geometric rate,[5] the supply of land can increase slowly if at all. And land, particularly in Malthus's time, was the source of food. Consequently, it seemed to Malthus that the human population was in danger of outrunning its food supply: "Taking the whole earth," he wrote, ". . . and supposing the present population to be equal to a thousand millions, the human species would increase as the numbers 1, 2, 4, 8, 16, 32, 64, 128, 256, and subsistence as 1, 2, 3, 4, 5, 6, 7, 8, 9. In two centuries, the population would be to the means of subsistence as 256 to 9; in three centuries as 4096 to 13, and in two thousand years the difference would be incalculable."[6]

Certainly, Malthus's view of humanity's prospects was bleak, as he himself acknowledged (in a masterpiece of British understatement) when he wrote that "the view has a melancholy hue." Gone is the optimism of Adam Smith: according to Malthus, the prospects for economic progress are very limited. Given the inexorable increase in human numbers, the standard of living will be kept at a minimum level required to keep body and soul together. If it exceeds this level, the population will increase, driving the standard of living back down. On the other hand, if the standard of living is less than this level, the population will decline because of starvation. Certainly, the long-term prospects were anything but bright. Thomas Carlyle, the famous historian and essayist, called economics "the dismal science." To a considerable extent, economics acquired this bad name through the efforts of Parson Malthus.

Malthus's theory can be interpreted in terms of the law of diminishing marginal returns. Living in what was still largely an agricultural society, he emphasized the role of land and labor as resources, and assumed a relatively fixed level of technology. Since land is fixed, increases in labor—due to population growth—will eventually cause the marginal product of

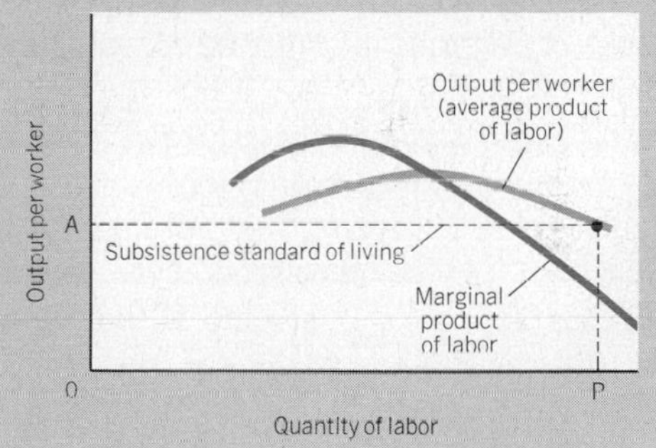

Figure 17.3
Diminishing Marginal Returns and the Effect of Population Growth
According to Malthus, the labor force will tend to *OP* because, if output per worker exceeds *OA*, population will increase, and if output per worker is less than *OA*, starvation will reduce the population.

[4] T. Malthus, *Essay on the Principle of Population,* as quoted by R. Heilbroner, *The Worldly Philosophers,* New York: Simon and Schuster, 1961, p. 71. For those who would like to read more concerning the history of economic thought, Heilbroner's book is highly recommended.
[5] Of course, it does not matter to Malthus's argument whether the population doubles every 25 years or every 40 years: the important thing is that it increases at a geometric rate.
[6] T. Malthus, "The Principle of Population Growth," reprinted in E. Mansfield, *Economics: Reading, Issues, and Cases,* 2d ed., New York: Norton, 1977. See also the full *Essay on the Principle of Population,* Philip Appleman, ed. New York: Norton, 1976, which contains critical commentary from Malthus's own time to the present.

labor to get smaller and smaller because of the law of diminishing marginal returns. In other words, because of this law, the marginal product of labor will behave as shown in Figure 17.3, with the result that continued growth of the labor force will ultimately bring economic decline—that is, a reduction in output per worker. This happens because as the marginal product of labor falls with increases in the labor force, the average product of labor will eventually fall as well—and the average product of labor is another name for output per worker.

Of course, Malthus recognized that various devices could keep the population down—war, famine, birth-control measures, among others. In fact, he tried to describe and evaluate the importance of various checks on population growth. For example, suppose that population tends to grow to the point where output per worker is at a subsistence level—just sufficient to keep body and soul together. If this is the case, and if the subsistence level of output per worker is *OA,* then the labor force will tend to equal *OP* in Figure 17.3. Why? Because, as noted above, Malthus believed that if the standard of living rises appreciably above *OA,* population will increase, thus forcing it back toward *OA.* On the other hand, if the standard of living falls below *OA,* some of the population will starve, thus pushing it back toward *OA.*

Effects of Population Growth

Was Malthus right? Among the less developed nations of the world, his analysis seems very relevant today. During the past 30 years, the population of the less developed nations has grown very rapidly, in part because of the decrease in death rates attributable to the transfer of medical advances from the industrialized countries to the less developed countries. Between 1940 and 1970, the total population of Asia, Africa, and Oceania almost doubled. There has been a tendency for growing populations to push hard against food supplies in some of the countries of Africa, Latin America, and Asia; and the Malthusian model can explain important elements of the situation.

However, Malthus's theory seems far less relevant or correct for the industrialized countries. In contrast to his model, population has not increased to the point where the standard of living has been pushed down to the subsistence level. On the contrary, the standard of living has increased dramatically in all of the industrialized nations. The most important mistake Malthus made was to underestimate the extent and importance of technological change. Instead of remaining fixed, the marginal-product-of-labor curve in Figure 17.3 moved gradually to the right, as new methods and new products increased the efficiency of agriculture. In other words, the situation was as shown in Figure 17.4. Thus, as population

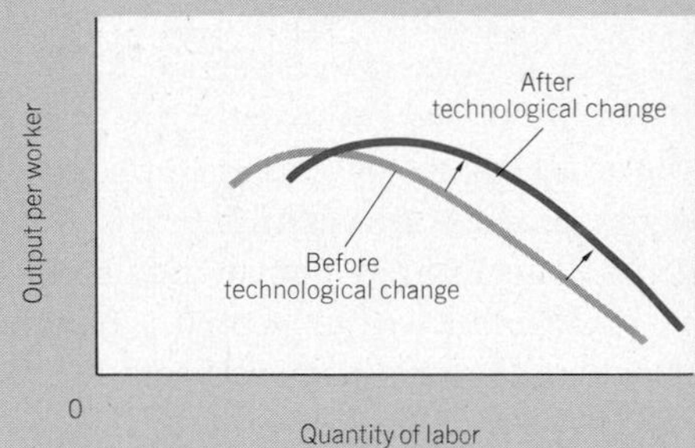

Figure 17.4
Shift over Time in the Marginal Product of Labor
Technological change has shifted the marginal-product-of-labor curve to the right.

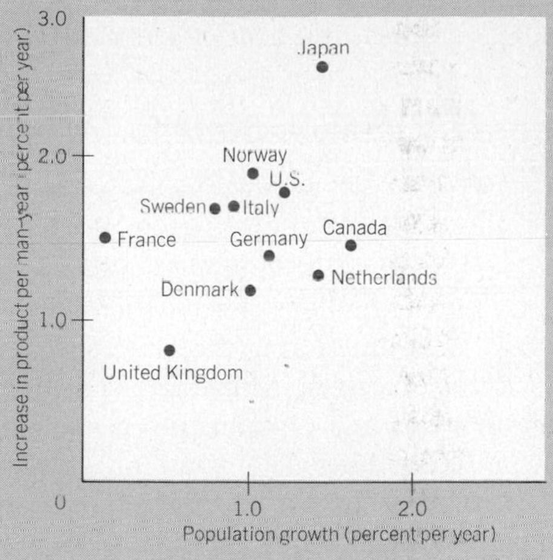

Figure 17.5
Relationship between Population Growth and Increases in National Product per Man-year, 11 Industrialized Nations, 1913–59
In industrialized nations, there is little or no relationship between a nation's rate of population growth and its rate of economic growth.

increased, the marginal product of labor did not go down. Instead, technological change prevented the productivity of extra agricultural workers from falling.

Among the industrialized nations, have countries with relatively high rates of growth of population had relatively low—or relatively high—rates of economic growth? In general, there seems to be little or no relationship between a nation's rate of population increase and its rate of economic growth. For example, Figure 17.5 plots the rate of population increase against the rate of growth of output per man-year in 11 industrialized nations between 1913 and 1959. The results suggest that there is little or no relation between them; and the relationship that exists appears to be direct rather than inverse.

David Ricardo and Capital Formation

Ricardo on Trade and Economic Growth

A contemporary and good friend of Malthus's who also contributed to the theory of economic growth was David Ricardo (1772–1823). Of all the titans of economics, he is probably least known to the general public. Smith, Malthus, Marx, and Keynes are frequently encountered names. Ricardo is not, although he made many brilliant contributions to economic thought. An extremely successful stockbroker who retired at the age of 42 with a very large fortune, he devoted much of his time to highly theoretical analyses of the economic system and its workings. In contrast to Malthus, who was reviled for his pessimistic doctrines. Ricardo and his writings were widely admired in his own time. He was elected to the House of Commons and was highly respected there.

Ricardo was concerned in much of his work with the distribution of income. Unlike Adam Smith, who paid much less attention to the conflict among classes, Ricardo emphasized the struggle between the industrialists—a relatively new and rising class in his time—and the landowners—the old aristocracy that resisted the rise of the industrial class. This clash was reflected in the struggle in Britain around 1800 over the so-called Corn Laws (*corn* being a general term covering all types of grain). Because of the increase in population, the demand for grain increased in Britain, causing the price of grain to rise greatly. This meant higher profits for the landowners. But the industrialists complained bitterly about the increase in the price of food, because higher food prices meant that they had to pay higher wages. As the price of grain increased, merchants began to import cheap grain from abroad. But the landowners, who dominated Parliament, passed legislation—the Corn Laws—to keep cheap grain out of Britain. In effect, the Corn Laws imposed a high tariff or duty on grain.

According to Ricardo's analysis, the landlords were bound to capture most of the benefits of economic progress, unless their control of the price of grain could be weakened. As national output increased and population expanded, poorer and poorer land had to be brought under cultivation to produce the extra food. As the cost of producing grain increased, its price would increase too—and so would the rents of the landlords. The workers and the industrialists, on the other hand, would benefit little, if at all. As the price of grain increased, the workers would have to get higher wages—but only high enough to keep them at a subsistence level (since Ricardo agreed entirely with his friend Malthus on the population issue). Thus the workers would be no better off; and neither would the industrialists, who would wind up with lower profits because of the increase in wage rates.

Ricardo felt that the Corn Laws should be repealed and that free trade in grain should be permitted. In a beautiful piece of theoretical analysis that is still reasonably fresh and convincing 150 years after its publication, he laid out the basic principles of international trade and pointed out the benefits to all countries that can be derived by specialization and free trade. For example, suppose that England is relatively more efficient at producing textiles, and France is relatively more efficient at producing wine. Then, on the basis of Ricardo's analysis, it can be shown that each country is likely to be better off by specializing in the product it is more efficient at producing—textiles in England, wine in France—and trading this product for the one the other country specializes in producing. In Chapter 20, we shall discuss this argument in considerable detail; it is a very important part of economics.

Ricardo's View of Capital Formation

Let's turn to the effect on economic growth of increases in physical capital, holding other inputs and technology fixed. Ricardo constructed some interesting theories concerning the effects of capital formation—i.e., investment in plant and equipment—on economic growth. Other things held constant, a nation's output depends on the amount of plant and equipment that it has and operates. Moreover, one can draw a curve showing the marginal product of capital—the extra output that would result from an extra dollar's worth of capital—under various assumptions about the total amount of capital in existence. This curve will slope downward to the right, as shown in Figure 17.6, because of the law of diminishing marginal returns. As more and more capital is accumulated, its marginal product eventually must decrease. For example, if $100 billion is the total investment in plant and equipment (or total capital), the extra output to be derived from an extra dollar of investment is worth $*A*; whereas if the total investment is increased to $150 billion, the economy must resort to less productive investments, and the extra output to be derived from an extra dollar of investment is only worth $*B*.

The curve in Figure 17.6 leads to the conclusion that investment in plant and equipment, although it will increase the growth rate up to some point, will eventually be unable to increase it further. As more and more is invested in new plant and equipment, less and less productive projects must be undertaken. Finally, when all the productive projects have been carried out, further investment in plant and equipment will be useless. At this point—

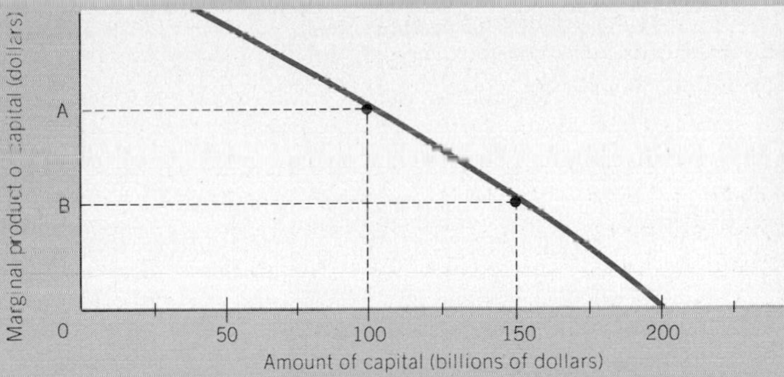

Figure 17.6
Marginal Product of Capital
This curve shows the marginal product of capital, under various assumptions concerning the total amount of capital. For example, if there is $100 billion of capital, the marginal product of capital is $*A*, whereas if there is $150 billion of capital, the marginal product of capital is $*B*.

$200 billion of total capital in Figure 17.6—further investment in plant and equipment will not increase output at all.

This kind of analysis led Ricardo to the pessimistic conclusion that the economy would experience decreases in the profitability of investment in plant and equipment, and eventual termination of economic growth. Also, he expected increases in the ratio of capital to output, because he expected increases in the total amount of capital to be accompanied by decreases in the marginal product of capital. To illustrate this, suppose that an economy's output equals $1 trillion and its total capital is $3 trillion. Suppose too that $100 billion of extra capital will result in $30 billion in extra output, another $100 billion of extra capital will result in $20 billion in extra output, and still another $100 billion in extra capital will result in $10 billion in extra output. Then the amount of capital per dollar of output will be (3,000 + 100)/(1,000 + 30) if $100 billion is invested, (3,000 + 200)/(1,000 + 50) if $200 billion is invested, and (3,000 + 300)/(1,000 + 60) if $300 billion is invested. Since the marginal product of capital is decreasing, the amount of capital per dollar of output is increasing—from 3 to 3.01 to 3.05 to 3.11.

Was Ricardo right? Have we seen increases in the amount of capital per dollar of output, decreases in the profitability of investment in plant and equipment, and eventual termination of economic growth? Clearly, no. Ricardo, like Malthus, was led astray by underestimating the extent and impact of future changes in technology. Suppose that, because of the development of major new products and processes, lots of new opportunities for profitable investment arise. Obviously, the effect on the curve in Figure 17.6 is to shift it to the right, because there are more investment opportunities than before above a certain level of productivity. But if this curve shifts to the right, as shown in Figure 17.7, we may be able to avoid Ricardo's pessimistic conclusions.

To see how this can occur, note that, if *XX′* in Figure 17.7 is the relevant curve in a particular year and if $100 billion is the total amount of capital, an extra dollar of investment in plant and equipment would have a marginal product of $*C*. A decade later, if *YY′* is the relevant curve and if the total amount of capital has grown to $150 billion, the marginal product of an extra dollar of investment in plant and equipment is still $*C*. Thus there is no reduction in the productivity of investment opportunities despite the 50 percent increase in the total amount of capital. Because of technological change and other factors, productive and profitable new investment opportunities are opened up as fast as old ones are invested in.

Figure 17.7
Effects of Technological Change on the Marginal Product of Capital
Technological change has shifted the marginal-product-of-capital curve to the right. (Actually, Ricardo's variable input was a combined dose of capital and labor.)

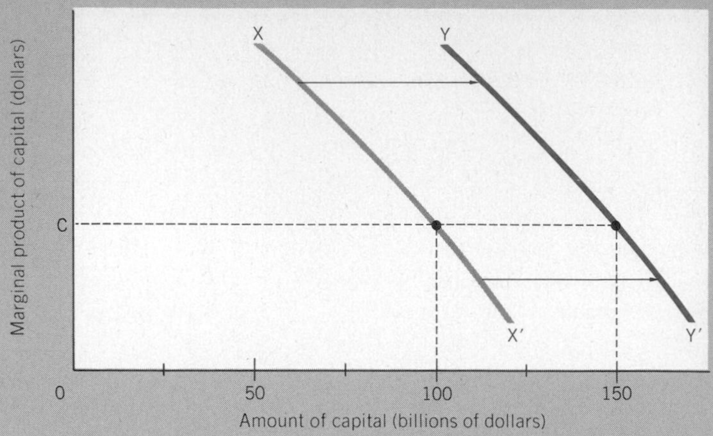

The history of the United States is quite consistent with this sort of shift in investment opportunities over time. Even though we have poured an enormous amount of money into new plant and equipment, we have not exhausted or reduced the productivity or profitability of investment opportunities. The rate of return on investment in new plant and equipment has not fallen. Instead, it has fluctuated around a fairly constant level during the past 70 years. Moreover, the amount of capital per dollar of output has remained surprisingly constant. It has not increased.

Effects of Capital Formation

To see more clearly the role of investment in the process of economic growth, let's extend the Keynesian model we discussed in Chapter 10. Suppose we ignore the government and consider only the private sector of the economy. Suppose that the full-employment, noninflationary NNP this year is $1,000 billion, and that the consumption function is such that consumption expenditure is $900 billion if NNP is $1,000 billion. If desired investment this year is $100 billion, with the result that NNP is in fact $1,000 billion, *next year's full-employment NNP will increase because this year's investment will increase the nation's productive capacity.* In other words, this year's investment increases next year's full-employment NNP. The amount of the increase in full-employment NNP depends on the ***capital-output ratio,*** which is the number of dollars of extra investment required to produce an extra dollar of output. For example, if the capital-output ratio is 2, $2 of investment is required to increase full-employment NNP by $1.

Let's look more closely at the effect of investment on full-employment NNP. If the capital-output ratio is 2, full-employment NNP will increase by $50 billion as a consequence of the $100 billion of investment: thus full-employment NNP next year is $1,050 billion. On the other hand, suppose that this year's investment is $200 billion rather than $100 billion, and that the consumption function is such that consumption expenditure is $800 billion rather than $900 billion if NNP is $1,000 billion. What will full-employment NNP be next year? If the capital-output ratio is 2, it will be $1,100 billion. Why? Because the $200 billion in investment will increase full-employment NNP by $100 billion—from $1,000 billion to $1,100 billion.

Thus the full-employment NNP will be

larger if investment is $200 billion than if it is $100 billion. Similarly, the full-employment NNP will be larger if investment is $300 billion than if it is $200 billion. If the capital-output ratio is 2, the full-employment NNP will be $1,150 billion next year, if investment is $300 billion. Why? Because the $300 billion in investment will increase full-employment NNP by $150 billion—from $1,000 billion to $1,150 billion.

In general, the greater the percent of NNP that the society devotes to investment this year, the greater will be the increase in its full-employment NNP. Thus, *so long as the economy sustains noninflationary full employment and the capital-output ratio remains constant, the rate of growth of national output will be directly related to the percent of NNP devoted to investment.*[7]

Certainly, this result seems sensible enough. If a country wants to increase its growth rate, it should produce more blast furnaces, machine tools, and plows, and less cosmetics, household furniture, and sports cars. But all this is theory. What do the facts suggest? Table 17.2 shows the rate of investment and the growth rate in the six major industrialized nations of the non-Communist world in 1955-64. The growth rate was highest in Japan, so was the investment rate. The growth rates were lowest in the United States and the United Kingdom, and so were the investment rates. Of course, this does not prove that there is any simple cause-and-effect relationship between the investment rate and the growth rate, but it certainly is compatible with the view that investment influences growth.

Table 17.2
Rate of Growth of Output per Man and Percent of GNP Invested in Physical Capital, 1955–64

Nation	Rate of growth of output per man (percent)	Percent of GNP invested
	Annual Average	
France	4.7	15.7
Germany	4.4	20.1
Italy	5.7	16.9
Japan	8.8	30.2
United Kingdom	2.6	13.7
United States	1.9	13.9

Source: Angus Maddison, *Lloyds Bank Review*, January 1966, and E. Phelps, *The Goal of Economic Growth*, rev. ed., New York: Norton, 1969.

As revealed in the historical record of the United States, between 1929 and 1947 the amount of U.S. plant and equipment increased at about the same rate as the labor force. On the other hand, between 1947 and 1965, the amount of U.S. plant and equipment increased much more rapidly than the labor force. These facts would lead one to expect that the rate of economic growth would be more rapid in the latter period; and, in keeping with the theory, this turns out to be true. Again, one must be cautious about interpreting such comparisons. Lots of other things besides the investment rate were different in 1947-65 than in 1929-47, and these other things, not the investment rate, may have been responsible for the difference in growth rates. However, it seems likely that the difference in investment rates was at least partially responsible.

The Role of Human Capital

A nation's rate of economic growth is influenced by the rate at which it invests in

[7] It can be shown that the rate of growth of NNP equals s/b, where s is the proportion of NNP that is saved (and invested), and b is the capital-output ratio, assuming that both s and b are constant and that full employment is maintained. For example, if b is 2 and $s = .10$, NNP will grow at 5 percent per year, since $.10/2 = .05$. This result is part of the so-called Harrod-Domar growth model developed by Sir Roy Harrod of Oxford and Evsey Domar of M.I.T. Although useful, this result must be used with caution since it is based on highly simplified assumptions.

human capital as well as physical capital. It may seem odd to speak of *human* capital, but every society builds up a certain amount of human capital through investments in formal education, on-the-job training, and health programs. You often hear people talk about investing in their children's future by putting them through college. For the economy as a whole, the expenditure on education and public health can also be viewed—at least partly—as an investment, because consumption is sacrificed in the present in order to make possible a higher level of per capita output in the future.

The United States invests in human capital on a massive scale. For example, in 1960 expenditures for schools at all levels of education were about $25 billion, or about 5 percent of our gross national product. Moreover, our total investment in the education of the population—the "stock" of educational capital—has grown much more rapidly than has the stock of plant and equipment. For example, whereas the stock of physical capital was about 4 times as big in 1956 as in 1900, the stock of educational capital was about 8 times as big. These enormous and rapidly growing investments in human capital have unquestionably increased the productivity, versatility, and adaptability of our labor force. They have certainly made a major contribution to economic growth.

Income tends to rise with a person's education. Using this relationship to measure the influence of education on a person's productivity, some economists, notably the University of Chicago's Theodore Schultz and Gary Becker, have tried to estimate the profitability, both to society and to the person, of an investment in various levels of education. For example, Becker has tried to estimate the rate of return from a person's investment in a college education. According to his estimates, the typical urban white male in 1950 received about a 10 percent return (after taxes) on his investment in tuition, room, books, and other college expenses (including the earnings he gave up by being in college rather than at work). This was a relatively high return—much higher, for example, than if the student (or his family) simply put the equivalent amount of money in a savings bank or in government bonds.

By the mid-1970s, however, the return from the investment in a college education seemed to have fallen considerably. According to Richard Freeman of Harvard University and Herbert Hollomon of M.I.T., it declined from about 11 or 12 percent in 1969 to about 7 or 8 percent in 1974. In part, this was due to the increase in college tuition, as well as the recession experienced by the economy that year. Also, the income differential between college-educated and other workers seems to have narrowed. For example, in 1969, full-time, male workers with four years of college earned 53 percent more than male workers with only four years of high school, but in 1974, the differential was only about 40 percent. Whether this decrease in the return from a college education is temporary is hard to say.

The Role of Technological Change

A nation's rate of economic growth depends on the rate of technological change, as well as on the extent to which quantities of inputs of various kinds increase. Indeed, the rate of technological change is perhaps the most important single determinant of a nation's rate of economic growth. Recall from Chapter 1 that technology is knowledge concerning the industrial and agricultural arts. Thus technological change often takes the form of new methods of producing existing products; new designs that make it possible to produce goods with important new characteristics; and new techniques of organization, marketing, and management. Two examples of technological change are new ways of producing power (for example, atomic energy) and new fibers (for example, nylon or dacron).

We have already seen that technological change can shift the curves in both Figure 17.4 and 17.7, thus warding off the law of diminishing marginal returns. But note that new knowledge by itself has little impact. *Unless knowledge is applied, it has little effect on the rate of economic growth.* A change in technology, when applied for the first time, is called an ***innovation,*** and the firm that first applies it is called an ***innovator.*** Innovation is a key stage in the process leading to the full evaluation and utilization of a new process or product. The innovator must be willing to take the risks involved in introducing a new and untried process, good, or service; and in many cases, these risks are high. Once a change in technology has been applied for the first time, the ***diffusion process***—the process by which the use of the innovation spreads from firm to firm and from use to use—begins. How rapidly an innovation spreads depends heavily on its economic advantages over older methods or products. The more profitable the use of the innovation is, the more rapidly it will spread.

Joseph Schumpeter, Harvard's distinguished economist and social theorist, stressed the important role played by the innovator in the process of economic growth. In Schumpeter's view, the innovator is the mainspring of economic progress, the man with the foresight to see how new things can be brought into being and the courage and resourcefulness to surmount the obstacles to change. For his trouble, the innovator receives profit; but this profit eventually is whittled down by competitors who imitate the innovator. The innovator pushes the curves in Figure 17.4 and 17.7 to the right, and once his innovation is assimilated by the economy, another innovator may shove these curves somewhat further to the right. For example, one innovator introduces vacuum tubes, a later innovator introduces semiconductors; one innovator introduces the steam locomotive, a later innovator introduces the diesel locomotive. This process goes on and on—and is a main source of economic growth.

The Electronic Computer: A Case Study[8]

To get a better feel for the nature of technological change and the process of innovation, let's consider one of the most important technological advances of the twentieth century—the electronic computer. Many of the basic ideas underlying the computer go back to Charles Babbage, a brilliant nineteenth-century British inventor; but not until 1946 was the first electronic computer, the ENIAC, designed and constructed. John Mauchly and J. Presper Eckert, both professors at the Moore School of Electrical Engineering at the University of Pennsylvania, were responsible for the ENIAC's design and construction. The work was supported by the U.S. Army. John von Neumann, a famous mathematician at the Institute for Advanced Study at Princeton, added the important concepts of stored programming and conditional transfer.

After the war, Mauchly and Eckert established a small firm to produce electronic computers. Their firm was acquired by Remington Rand, which in 1951 marketed the Univac I, a machine used by the Census Bureau. The International Business Machines Corporation (IBM), the leading company in office machinery and data processing, which before this had been cautious about the potential market for computers, was spurred into action by Remington Rand's success. Once it entered the field, IBM's financial resources, strong marketing organization, and engineering strength enabled it to capture a very large share of the

[8] This and the following section are based to a considerable extent on E. Mansfield, *The Economics of Technological Change,* New York: Norton, 1968; and my paper in the International Economic Association's *Science and Technology in Economic Growth,* London: Macmillan, 1973.

computer market, here and abroad. In the United States, IBM's share of the market grew to about 90 percent during the 1960s.

The electronic computer has been an extremely important stimulus to economic growth. By 1966, the total number of computers installed in the Western world exceeded 50,000 at a total value of about $20 billion. These computers have had important effects on production techniques in many industries. For example, in the chemical, petroleum, and steel industries, digital computers were an important step in the evolution of control techniques. Computers helped to determine and enforce the best conditions for process operation, as well as acting as data loggers. They could also be programmed to help carry out the complex sequence of operations required to start up or shut down a plant. They have increased production, decreased waste, improved quality control, and reduced the chance of damage to equipment. In another quite different industry, banking, computers have had an important effect too. They have made it possible to eliminate conventional machines and processes for sorting checks, balancing accounts, and computing service charges. With high-speed sorters, it is possible now to process more than 1,500 checks per minute.

Obviously, the electronic computer has enabled us to produce more output from a given amount of resources. In other words, it has enabled us to push the product transformation curve outward, thus increasing our rate of economic growth. But it must be recognized that the process by which the computer has had this effect has by no means been simple or straightforward. Many people in many countries were involved in the development of the basic ideas. Many organizations, public and private, funded the experimental work. Firms of various types were the innovators with respect to particular aspects of the modern computer. And countless individuals and organizations had to be willing to accept, work with, and invest in computers.

Technological Change: Determinants and Measurement

What determines the rate of technological change and the rate at which changes in technology are applied and spread? Clearly, the nature and extent of a nation's scientific capability, and the size and quality of its educational system are of fundamental importance. The first thing that must be said about the influence of a nation's scientific capability on its rate of technological change is that science and technology are two quite different things that have drawn together only recently. Until the twentieth century, it simply was not true that technology was built on science. Even today, many technological advances rely on little in the way of science. However, in more and more areas of the economy (such as aircraft, electronics, and chemicals), the rapid application of new technology has come to depend on a strong scientific base. Merely to imitate or adapt what others have developed, a firm in these areas needs access to high-caliber scientists.

A nation's educational system also has a fundamental influence on the rate of technological change. First, and perhaps most obviously, it determines how many scientists and engineers are graduated, and how competent they are. Clearly, the rate of technological change depends on the quantity and quality of scientific and engineering talent available in the society. Second, the educational system influences the inventiveness and adaptability of the nation's work force. Despite the closer links between technology and science, workers and independent inventors remain important sources of inventions in many areas. Third, the educational system also influences the rate of technological change and innovation via the training of managers.

Industrial managers are a key agent in the innovative process. We must emphasize that the proper management of innovation is much more than establishing and maintaining a research and development laboratory that produces a great deal of good technical output. In many industries, most important innovations are not based in any significant degree on the firms' research and development. And even when the basic idea does come from a firm's own R and D, the coupling of R and D with marketing and production is crucial. Many good ideas are not applied properly because the potential users do not really understand them, and many R and D projects are technically successful but commercially irrelevant because they were not designed with sufficient comprehension of market realities. Typically, successful technological innovations seem to be stimulated by perceived production and marketing needs, not by technological opportunities. In other words, most of the time it takes a market-related impetus to prompt work on a successful innovation.

In addition, the rate of technological change depends on the organization of industry and the nature of markets. Although a certain amount of industrial concentration may promote more rapid technological change, increases in concentration beyond a moderate level probably reduce rather than increase the rate of technological change. The rate of technological change also depends on the scale and sophistication of available markets. The scale of the market influences the extent to which a firm can spread the fixed costs of developing and introducing an innovation. This factor has often been cited as a reason for America's technological lead over many other countries. Finally, it is extremely important to note that a country that is not a technological leader can still achieve considerable technological change by borrowing and transferring technology from the leaders.

It is difficult to measure the rate of technological change. Perhaps the most frequently used measure is the rate of growth of labor productivity—that is, the rate of growth of output per man-hour. Unfortunately, this measure is influenced by lots of other factors besides the rate of technological change. Nonetheless, despite its inadequacies, it is worthwhile to look briefly at how rapidly productivity has increased in the United States over the long run. Since about 1890, the nation's real output per man-hour increased by about 2 percent per year—and these productivity gains were widely diffused, real hourly earnings growing about as rapidly, on the average, as output per man-hour.

In part because of differing rates of technological change, there have been considerable

Table 17.3
Average Annual Rates of Increase of Labor Productivity, Selected Manufacturing Industries, 1947–73.

Industry	Productivity increase (percent per year)
Canning and preserving	3.2
Flour	4.1
Bakery products	2.4
Sugar	4.2
Candy	3.2
Malt liquors	5.1
Soft drinks	3.5
Tobacco products	3.1
Hosiery	5.4
Paper	4.0
Boxes	3.4
Man-made fibers	5.7
Drugs[a]	4.9
Paints	2.5
Petroleum refining	5.8
Tires	3.9
Footwear	1.3
Glass containers	1.7
Cement	4.5
Steel	1.8
Copper, lead, and zinc	2.3
Aluminum	4.5
Household appliances	5.3
Motor vehicles	3.9

Source: National Commission on Productivity and Work Quality, *Fourth Annual Report*, March 1975.
[a]1960–73.

differences among industries in the rate of growth of output per man-hour. As shown in Table 17.3, labor productivity increased after World War II in some industries—like man-made fibers—by more than 5 percent per year, and in other industries—like footwear—by only about 1 percent per year. To some extent, these differences can be explained by interindustry differences in the amount spent on *research and development.* In addition, a number of other factors—like the amount spent by *other industries* to improve the capital goods and other inputs the industry uses, the extent of *competition* in the industry, the attitudes of *unions* toward change, and the quality of *management*—undoubtedly played important roles too in explaining these interindustry differences in productivity increase.

Entrepreneurship and the Social Environment

Still another set of basic factors influencing a nation's level of potential output and its rate of economic growth is the economic, social, political, and religious climate of the nation. It is difficult, if not impossible, to measure the effect of these factors, but there can be no doubt of their importance. Some societies despise material welfare and emphasize the glories of the next world. Some societies are subject to such violent political upheavals that it is risky, if not foolish, to invest in the future. Some societies are governed so corruptly that economic growth is frustrated. And some societies look down on people engaged in industry, trade, or commerce. Obviously, such societies are less likely to experience rapid economic growth than others with a more favorable climate and conditions.

The relatively rapid economic growth of the United States was undoubtedly stimulated in part by the attitude of its people toward material gain. It is commonplace to note that the United States is a materialistic society, a society that esteems business success, that bestows prestige on the rich, that accepts the Protestant ethic (which, crudely stated, is that work is good), and that encourages individual initiative. The United States has been criticized over and over again for some of these traits—often by nations frantically trying to imitate its economic success. Somewhat less obvious is the fact that, because the United States is a young country whose people came from a variety of origins, it did not inherit many feudal components in the structure of society. This too was important.

The United States has also been characterized by great economic and political freedom, by institutions that have been flexible enough to adjust to change, and by a government that has encouraged competition in the market place. This has meant fewer barriers to new ideas. Also, the United States has for a long time enjoyed internal peace, order, and general respect for property rights. There have been no violent revolutions since the Civil War, and for many years we were protected from strife in other lands by two oceans—which then seemed much broader than they do now. All these factors undoubtedly contributed to rapid economic growth.

The American economy also seems to have been able to nurture a great many entrepreneurs and a vast horde of competent businessmen. During the nineteenth century, American entrepreneurs were responsible for such basic innovations as the system of interchangeable parts, pioneered by Eli Whitney and others. In many areas, the United States gained a technological lead over other nations, and the available evidence seems to indicate that, to a significant extent, this lead has been maintained. It must be recognized that much of this lead has come from superior management as well as superior technological resources. For example, the Organization for Economic Cooperation and Development recently concluded, "In the techniques of *management,* including the management of research, and of combined technological and market forecasting, the United States appears to have a significant lead."[9]

The Gap between Actual and Potential Output

Up to this point, our discussion of economic growth has centered on the factors that determine how rapidly a nation's potential output grows—factors like technological change, increased education, investment in plant and equipment, and increases in the labor force. Now we must examine the factors that determine how close a nation's actual output comes to its potential output. As we already know, a nation's potential output is its output under full employment. Thus, as we also know, whether or not the economy operates close to full employment is determined by the level of the $C + I + G$ line. If the $C + I + G$ line is too low, the economy will operate with considerable unemployment, and actual output will be substantially below potential output. Or, in terms of the equation of exchange, if $M \times V$ is too small, the economy will operate with considerable unemployment, and actual output will be substantially below potential output.

From previous chapters, we also know how the government can use fiscal and monetary policies to push actual output close to potential output. Cuts in tax rates, increases in government spending, incentives for private investment in plant and equipment, increases in the money supply, reductions in interest rates; all these devices can be used to push actual output closer to potential output. Such devices promote economic growth, in the sense that actual per capita output is increased. However, only so much growth can be achieved by squeezing the slack out of the economy. For example, if there is a 7 percent unemployment rate, output per capita can be increased by perhaps 9 percent simply by reducing the unemployment rate to 4 percent, as we saw in Chapter 8. *But this is a one-shot improvement.* To get any further growth, the nation must increase its potential output.

Of course this doesn't mean that it isn't important to maintain the economy at close to full employment. On the contrary, as we stressed in Chapter 8, one of the major objectives of public policy must be full employment, and a reduction of unemployment will have a significant effect on the rate of economic growth in the short run. (Much of the economic growth in the United States in the early 1960s was caused by the transition to full employment.) But the point we are making is that, once the economy gets to full employment, no further growth can occur by this route. If a nation wants further growth, it must influence the factors responsible for the rate of growth of potential output.

Japan: A Case Study of Rapid Economic Growth

Japan has experienced a very high rate of economic growth for a long time. Especially after World War II, the Japanese economy increased per capita GNP very rapidly. For example, between 1955 and 1964 gross national product per man increased at an average rate of 8.8 percent per year. Some of the most important reasons for this rapid growth are as follows:[10]

High investment. After World War II, the

[9] Organization for Economic Cooperation and Development, *Technology Gap: General Report,* Paris, 1968, p. 25. However, according to many observers, our lead in this respect is being reduced.

[10] For further discussion, see K. Ohkawa and H. Rosovsky, "Recent Japanese Growth in Historical Perspective," *American Economic Review,* May 1963, pp. 578–88; and M. Peck (with the collaboration of S. Tamura), "Infusion of Technology and the Mysteries of the Catch-Up," unpublished, 1974.

rate of investment in plant and equipment was extremely high. For example, in 1954 the Japanese devoted over 20 percent of their GNP to the formation of physical capital; and in 1961 and 1964, they devoted 35 and 33 percent, respectively. While this high rate of capital formation was due, particularly in the early postwar years, to the dislocations caused by the war, this was not the only reason. To a considerable extent, the rate was high because Japan was catching up with technological developments elsewhere in the world. Japan invested heavily in newer industries based on innovations in other countries—television, electronic devices, synthetics, and others—as well as in older industries like steel, machinery, and chemicals.

Technological transfer. A second very important contributor to Japan's economic growth was the borrowing and application of technology developed in other countries. The Japanese were skilled borrowers of Western technology. Their success illustrates a very important point often overlooked by nations interested in increasing their growth rates. To benefit from technology, a nation does not have to develop or invent it. Conversely, because a country develops or invents a new product or process, it does not follow that the product or process will do much for its rate of economic growth. If another country is quicker to apply and exploit the innovation, it may get more of the economic benefits. The Japanese concentrated their energies and resources on transferring Western technology rather than developing or inventing their own. This strategy paid off well.

Education and other factors. Japan has also had an abundant supply of educated labor, which has made it much easier to assimilate new technology. The importance of such an investment in human capital has been emphasized in previous sections. And Japan undoubtedly benefited from the fact that its burden of national defense was largely assumed by the United States, so that Japanese resources could be devoted to economic development rather than to defense. Last, Japan's level of per capita GNP was lower than that of most of the nations with which it is generally compared. It is often argued that countries at a relatively low level of economic development find it easier to achieve a high growth rate than do more affluent societies. In other words, a high rate of growth may be easier to achieve from a low economic base.

In conclusion, it is worth noting that the recession of the mid-1970s hit Japan, as it did other major industrialized countries. Despite the emphasis in Japan upon lifetime employment, firms had to lay off many workers; indeed, the unemployed swelled to 1.2 million in January 1976, a postwar high. Some Japanese seemed to believe that the days of rapid growth were over. But as is clear from the previous section, whether or not this is true depends to a considerable extent on how fast Japan can get back to full employment. If the Japanese can squeeze the slack out of their economy relatively quickly, their growth rate may not suffer greatly over the long run.

Summary

Economic growth is measured by the increase of per capita real gross national product, an index that does not measure accurately the growth of economic welfare, but is often used as a first approximation. In the recent past, many economists and politicians called for an explicit public policy designed to increase our growth rate. A nation's rate of economic growth depends on the increase in the quantity and quality of its resources (including physical and human capital) and the rate of technological change. In addition, the rate of economic growth depends on the extent to which a society maintains full employment and on the efficiency with which its resources are allocated and managed.

One factor that may influence a nation's rate of economic growth is the rate at which its population grows. In Malthus's view, population growth, unless checked in some way, ultimately meant economic decline, since output could not grow in proportion to the growth in population. The law of diminishing marginal returns insured that beyond some point, increases in labor, holding the quantity of land constant, would result in smaller and smaller increments of output. However, Malthus underestimated the extent and importance of technological change, which offset the law of diminishing marginal returns.

Another factor that determines whether per capita output grows rapidly or slowly is the rate of expenditure on new plant and equipment. Without technological change, more and more of this sort of investment would result in increases in the amount of capital per dollar of output and decreases in the profitability of investment in plant and equipment, as Ricardo pointed out. But because of technological change, none of these things has occurred. According to the available evidence, a nation's rate of economic growth seems directly related to its rate of investment in plant and equipment.

To a considerable extent, economic growth here and abroad has resulted from technological change. A change in technology, when applied for the first time, is called an innovation, and the firm that first applies it is called an innovator. Innovation is a key stage in the process leading to the full evaluation and utilization of a new process or product. Unless knowledge is used, it has little effect on the rate of economic growth. The rate of technological change and the rate at which new technology is applied depend on a number of factors, including the nature and extent of a nation's scientific capability, the size and quality of its educational system, the quality of its managers, the attitude and structure of its firms, the organization of its industries, and the nature of its markets.

Another factor with an important effect on a nation's rate of economic growth is the rate at which it invests in human capital. The United States invests in human capital on a massive scale, and these enormous and rapidly growing investments have unquestionably increased the productivity, versatility, and adaptability of our labor force. Still another set of basic factors influencing the rate of economic growth is the economic, social, and political climate of the nation. Some societies despise material welfare, are subject to violent political upheavals, and are governed by corrupt groups. Such societies are unlikely to have a high rate of economic growth. Finally, the rate of economic growth is also affected by the extent and behavior of the gap between actual and potential GNP. However, once a nation gets to full employment, it cannot grow further by reducing this gap.

CONCEPTS FOR REVIEW

Economic growth
Capital formation
Population increase
Marginal product of labor
Average product of labor
Law of diminishing marginal returns
Technological change
Innovation
Innovator
Diffusion process
Aggregate production function

QUESTIONS FOR DISCUSSION AND REVIEW

1. Suppose that a society produces only two goods, food and tractors, and that its product transformation curve in 1976 and 1977 is given below:

Quantity of food (millions of tons)	Quantity of tractors (thousands of tractors)
0	9
1	8
2	7
3	5
4	3
5	0

If this society produces 4,000 tractors and 3 million tons of food in 1976 and 5,000 tractors and 3 million tons of food in 1977 (its population remaining constant), has any economic growth occurred between 1976 and 1977? If so, to what is it due?

2. Suppose that the society in Question 1 produces 6,000 tractors and 3 million tons of food in 1978 (its population remaining the same as in 1977), has any economic growth occurred between 1977 and 1978? If so, is it due entirely to a shift in the product transformation curve? How can you tell?

3. Suppose that a society produces only one commodity, wheat, and that it has the following aggregate production function:

Man-hours of labor (millions)	Bushels of wheat (millions)
0	0
1	2
2	4
3	6
4	7
5	7

What is the marginal product of labor when between 1 and 2 million man-hours of labor are used? When between 2 and 3 million man-hours of labor are used? When between 4 and 5 million man-hours of labor are used? Do the results conform to the law of diminishing marginal returns? Why or why not?

4. Suppose that an advance in technology doubles the output that can be obtained from each amount of labor in Question 3. Under these new conditions, what is the marginal product of labor when between 1 and 2 million man-hours of labor are used? When between 4 and 5 million man-hours of labor are used? Do the results conform to the law of diminishing marginal returns? Why or why not?

5. In Question 3, suppose that the subsistance wage was 1,400 bushels of wheat. According to Malthus, what would have been the equilibrium labor force? What factors would push the labor force toward this level? What would be the effect of the technological advance in Question 4 on the equilibrium labor force?

6. Suppose that a society's full-employment NNP increases between 1975 and 1976 by $100 billion. During the same period, its corporations floated $20 billion in stocks and bonds, and it invested $200 billion. What is the capital-output ratio in this society? Will the capital-output ratio in this society always be the same? Why or why not?

7. Suppose that a society's capital-output ratio is 3 and that it invests 10 percent of its NNP. If full employment is maintained, by what percentage will its NNP grow?

8. "Ricardo's pessimistic view of the prospects for economic growth stemmed from his assumptions concerning the capital-output ratio. If he had recognized that it was not fixed, he would have been closer to correct." Comment and evaluate.

9. In 1971, Herbert Stein wrote, "During the past 4 years the rates of growth in productivity . . . slowed down." What are some possible reasons why this occurred? What is the significance of this slowdown?

10. Describe in as much detail as you can the ways in which capital formation, population growth, technological change, and education are interrelated. Show how these interrelationships make it difficult to sort out the effect of each of these factors on the rate of economic growth.

18 American Economic Growth: History, Policies, Problems, and Prospects

About a century ago, Benjamin Disraeli, the famous British prime minister, said that "increased means and increased leisure are the two civilizers of man." Although one might add to Disraeli's list of "civilizers," there can be little doubt that economic growth has helped to improve man's lot. Since World War II, the rate of economic growth has become a major index, both here and abroad, of how well an economy is performing; and many governments have tried to increase their rate of economic growth. In 1960 John F. Kennedy ran for president on a platform emphasizing the need for faster economic growth in the United States; and in subsequent elections—here and abroad—economic growth frequently has been a campaign issue.

However, bigger may not always be better. More and more often, observers in recent years have stressed that economic growth may not be an unalloyed blessing. It too has its costs. Indeed, the pros and cons of more rapid economic growth have been the subject of much debate. In this chapter, we are concerned with four basic questions about economic growth in the United States. What has been our rate of economic growth in the past? What are the advantages and disadvantages of a faster rate of economic growth? If faster growth is desired, what measures can the government take to promote it? And, assuming that present trends continue, what rate of economic growth can we expect in the future?

Economic Growth in the United States

Let's begin by looking at the salient facts about the rate at which the American economy has grown in the past. Soon after its emergence as an independent nation, the United States reached a relatively high level of economic development. By 1840, it ranked fourth in per capita income, behind England, France, and Germany. During the next 30 years, the United States experienced relatively rapid economic growth. By 1870, it ranked second only to England in per capita income. In the next 40 years, the American economy continued to grow rapidly. National product per person employed grew by about 2.2 percent per year between 1871 and 1913. This growth rate was higher than for practically any other major industrialized nation; and well before the turn of the century, income per capita was greater in the United States than in any other nation in the world.

Between 1913 and 1959, the American growth rate was somewhat lower than in previous years. National product per person employed grew by about 1.8 percent per year. Nonetheless, although we grew less rapidly than in earlier years, we pulled further ahead of most other industrialized countries, because we continued to grow faster than they did. Of course, our rate of economic growth varied from decade to decade: economic growth does not proceed at a steady rate. In some decades (like the 1920s), our economy grew rapidly, while in others (like the 1930s), it grew little, if at all. During periods of recovery and prosperity, the growth rate was high; during depressions, it was low. In the 1950s, the growth rate in the United States was lower than in many other countries. As pointed out in the previous chapter, this caused considerable controversy and some alarm.

During the 1960s, our growth rate increased perceptibly. But our present growth rate is by no means the highest among the major industrialized nations. That honor belongs to Japan, which, as we saw in the previous chapter, has long experienced rapid economic growth. Table 18.1 shows the annual rates of growth of per capita real GNP in the United States and other major Western industrialized countries during the last century. You can see that, for the period as a whole, per capita real GNP in the United States grew at an average rate of about 2 percent per year. Compared with Germany, France, Italy, Canada, and the United Kingdom, our growth rate was quite impressive. In recent years, however, many industrialized countries have shown growth rates larger than or equal to ours.

Table 18.1
Average Annual Growth Rates of Per Capita Real GNP, Selected Western Industrialized Countries (percent)

Country	1870–1964	1929–70
United States	1.9	1.9
Canada	1.7	2.1
France	1.5	2.0
Germany	1.7	3.0
Italy	1.4	2.5
United Kingdom	1.3	1.7

Source: U.S. Department of Commerce, *Long-Term Economic Growth*, 1966, and *Statistical Abstract of the United States.*

Figure 18.1
Population and Labor Force, United States, 1900–75.
The American population in 1975 was over double what it was in 1920, and about triple what it was in 1900.

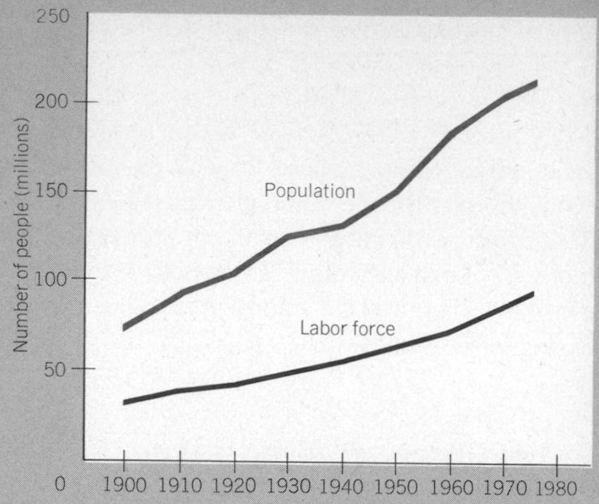

Population and Human Resources

As we have seen, a nation's rate of economic growth is influenced, among other things, by its rate of population growth and the extent of its investment in human capital. As shown in Figure 18.1, the population of the United States has grown substantially during our history, because of a fairly high birth rate as well as considerable immigration from other parts of the world.[1] Indeed, our population in 1975 was over double what it was in 1920, and about triple what it was in 1900.

In the past 15 or 20 years, the birth rate has fallen considerably, due partly to changes in attitudes toward women's role in society. However, according to official forecasts, the American population will continue to grow for at least the next 10 or 20 years, and perhaps for much longer. Of course, increases in population do not necessarily bring about economic growth. As we saw in the previous chapter, population increases, carried beyond a certain point, can lower per capita GNP, unless they are offset by other factors, such as advances in technology.

Equally important, it is not sheer numbers alone that count. The quality as well as the quantity of the population determines how much is produced. Measured by its education and skill, the quality of the American population is among the highest in the world. Moreover, as indicated by Table 18.2, the educational level of the population has increased dramatically during the past 70 years. To a considerable extent, our economic growth seems to have been due to this large investment in human capital.

Is it possible to make any quantitative estimate of the contribution of increased education to economic growth in the United States? Because the effects of education, technological change, and investment in plant and equipment intertwine in various ways, it is very difficult to sort out any one of them. Yet it is worthwhile to give the best estimates currently available. According to Edward Denison of the Brookings Institution, increased education seemed to account for about $\frac{1}{8}$ of the growth in real output in the United States during 1909–29, and for about $\frac{1}{4}$ of this growth during 1929–57.

[1] As shown in Figure 18.1, the percent of the population in the labor force does not remain constant over time, and changes in this percentage can, of course, influence a country's rate of economic growth. Increases in the number of years of schooling and more liberal attitudes toward working wives, as well as changes in the age distribution of the population and in income levels, will influence this percentage.

Table 18.2
Percent of 17-Year-Olds That Graduated from High School, United States, 1900–80

Year	Percent graduated from high school
1900	6.4
1920	16.8
1940	50.8
1950	59.0
1960	65.1
1970	78.0
1980 (projected)	82.5

Source: Statistical Abstract of the United States, 1972.

Moreover, he forecasts that increased education will account for about $\frac{1}{10}$ of this growth during 1969–80. Thus, if these estimates, shown in Table 18.3, can be trusted, increased education has been a major contributor to economic growth in the United States.

Technological Change

America's economic growth has also been due in very considerable part to technological change. For example, as shown in Table 18.3, Denison concludes that the "advance of knowledge" contributed about $\frac{1}{8}$ of the growth in real output during 1909–29, and about $\frac{1}{5}$ of this growth during 1929–57. Also, he forecasts that it will contribute about $\frac{1}{4}$ of this growth during 1969–80. Such estimates are rough, but useful. It is very difficult to separate the effects on economic growth of technological change from those of investment in physical capital, since to a considerable extent new technology must be embodied in physical capital—new machines and equipment—to be used. For example, a nuclear power plant must obviously be built to take advantage of nuclear power plant technology. Nor can the effects of technological change easily be separated from those of education. After all, the returns from increased education are enhanced by technological change, and, as we saw in the previous chapter, the rate of technological change is influenced by the extent and nature of a society's investment in education.

In interpreting America's economic growth, we must recognize that the United States has long been a technological leader. Even before 1850, scattered evidence gives the impression that the United States was ahead of other countries in many technological areas. And after 1850, the available evidence indicates that productivity was higher in the United States than in Europe, that the United States had a strong export position in technically progressive industries, and that Europeans tended to

Table 18.3
Estimated Sources of Growth in Real National Income in the United States, 1909–80

Source	Period 1909–29	1929–57	1969–80
	[Percent of total growth]		
Increase in quantity of labor	39	27	26
Increase in quantity of capital	26	15	25
Improved education and training	13	27	7
Technological change	12	20	28
Other factors	10	11	14
Total	100	100	100

Source: E. Denison, *The Sources of Economic Growth in the United States*, New York: Committee for Economic Development, 1962, and his paper in T. Khachaturov, ed., *Methods of Long-Term Planning and Forecasting*, London, Macmillan, 1976.

Table 18.4
Expenditures on Research and Development, United States, 1945–74 (millions of dollars)

Year	Total R and D expenditure	Sources of funds: Government	Industry	Universities and nonprofit institutions
1945	1,520	1,070	430	20
1950	2,870	1,610	1,180	80
1955	6,270	3,490	2,510	270
1960	13,551	8,752	4,508	291
1965	20,439	13,033	6,539	519
1974[a]	32,045	16,955	13,916	1,174

Source: Statistical Abstract of the United States, 1970, and National Science Foundation, *Science Indicators,* 1974. The data for the earlier years may not be entirely comparable with those for the later years.
[a]Estimated by National Science Foundation.

imitate American techniques. Needless to say, the United States did not lead in all fields, but it appears to have held a technological lead in many important aspects of manufacturing. This was in contrast to pure science where, until World War II, the United States was not a leader.

Toward the end of the nineteenth century, as the connection between science and technology gradually became closer, commercial research laboratories began to appear. The first organized research laboratory in the United States was established by Thomas Edison in 1876. Eastman Kodak (1893), B. F. Goodrich (1895), General Electric (1900), DuPont (1902), and the Bell Telephone System (1907) were some of the earliest firms to establish laboratories. The industrial R and D laboratory constituted a significant departure from the past, when invention was mainly the work of independent inventors like Eli Whitney (interchangeable parts and cotton gin), Robert Fulton (steamboat), Samuel Morse (telegraph), Charles Goodyear (vulcanization of rubber), and Cyrus McCormick (reaper). These men were responsible for a very rich crop of inventions, some of which established whole new industries. Since the advent of the industrial laboratory, the relative importance of independent inventors seems to have declined, but they continue to produce a significant share of the important inventions in many areas. For example, xerography was invented by an independent inventor, Chester Carlson.

Recent decades have witnessed a tremendous growth in the amount spent on research and development. Table 18.4 shows that R and D expenditures in the United States in 1974 were over 20 times what they were in 1945. Although the bulk of these expenditures go for rather minor improvements rather than major advances, this vast increase in research and development has generated much economic growth. But, as the table shows, the federal government is the source of most R and D funds, which are heavily concentrated on defense and space technology. In the eyes of many economists, this vast investment in R and D would probably have had a bigger impact on the rate of economic growth if more of it had been directed at civilian rather than military and political objectives.

Capital Formation and Natural Resources

As pointed out in the previous chapter, a nation's rate of economic growth depends partially on how much of its GNP is invested in new plant and equipment. In recent years, we have devoted over 10 percent of our GNP to this purpose. In the United States, the average worker has more equipment to work with than his counterpart in any other country of the world. In manufacturing, for example, the average American worker has at his disposal about $30,000 worth of plant and equipment. Moreover, the government has invested huge amounts in highways, harbors, dams, and other forms of social capital; and the public has invested heavily in residential construction.

America's great natural resources have also been an important factor underlying our economic growth. We have an abundance of fertile soil and of various kinds of ores and minerals; a reasonably good climate; and coal, oil, and other sources of power. Few nations have as plentiful a supply of natural resources, and obviously they have been a great boon to our economic development. Although countries with limited natural resources can offset this limitation by importing raw materials, by irrigation and drainage projects, and by the use of modern technology, a good supply of natural resources is a valuable asset in achieving rapid economic growth.

In recent years, some fear has been expressed that if the world economy continues to grow at current rates, we shall begin to run out of basic raw materials. For example, in 1972, Dennis and Donella Meadows and their colleagues at M.I.T. conducted a study sponsored by the Club of Rome on *The Limits to Growth*,[2] in which they concluded that unless we curb our growth rate the world will run out of raw materials in the foreseeable future. However, this ignores the fact that the price system encourages producers to conserve raw materials as they become increasingly scarce, and that it provides a strong incentive for producers to invent and adopt new techniques that use less of these resources. The price system accomplishes these things simply by seeing to it that the price of a raw material increases as it becomes scarcer. More will be said about these "doomsday models" in a subsequent section of this chapter.

The Social and Entrepreneurial Environment, the GNP Gap, and Allocative Efficiency

As we stressed in the previous chapter, America's relatively rapid long-term economic growth has also been a result of its social and entrepreneurial environment. In general, American society places considerable emphasis on materialistic considerations, values hard work, allows a great deal of economic and political freedom, and is flexible enough to adjust to change. Also, the United States has not been wracked (in the past century) by internal armed conflict or widespread confiscation of private property. These factors have been important in promoting economic growth. In addition, the price system, which has been relied on to channel resources into the proper uses, seems to have worked quite well. It has provided the incentives required to get labor, land, and capital to move from less productive to more productive uses.

However, not all aspects of the American economy have been conducive to rapid economic growth. For one thing, as we saw in Chapter 8, in many periods actual GNP fell short of potential GNP because desired spending was too low. For example, in the Great Depression of the 1930s, actual GNP was far below our potential GNP. When a large gap develops between actual and potential GNP, this reduces the growth rate, as we saw in the previous chapter. Moreover, it has indirect as well as direct effects. As this gap grows, and there is substantial unemployment, firms are

[2] For example, see Donella Meadows, Dennis Meadows, J. Randers, and William Behrens, "The Limits to Growth," reprinted in E. Mansfield, *Economics: Readings, Issues, and Cases*, 2d ed., New York: Norton, 1977.

discouraged from investing in new technology or capital formation, and unions are more inclined to resist adopting new techniques that might replace men with machines, so that the growth rate in subsequent years may be reduced as well.

Another factor that can reduce our economic growth rate is the increased strength of monopolistic forces that prevent resources from being allocated efficiently. For example, some labor unions resist the adoption of new techniques that would increase productivity and growth. Thus the compositors' union has restricted the use of the teletypesetter by requiring that the machine be operated by a journeyman printer or apprentice. Also, groups that are adversely affected by changes that would promote economic growth often try to convince the government to stop or offset them. For example, the farm programs discussed in Chapter 5 impeded past economic growth by making it more difficult to transfer resources out of agriculture and into more productive uses. Also, many industries that cannot compete with foreign producers lobby for and obtain tariffs, with the result that resources are misallocated.

Finally, if resources tend to be more immobile, this too will hamper economic growth. As tastes, technology, and population change, resources often should move from one use or location to another, if society's output is to be maximized. But there are many barriers to the mobility of resources. In the case of labor, people often are reluctant to pick up stakes; sever their ties to friends, family, and neighbors; and move to another location. Similarly, they often are unwilling or unable to learn a new occupation or trade, even though it might increase their income. The immobility of capital is even more obvious. A particular piece of capital is built for specific purposes—for example, to cut metal or to refine oil—and cannot be used for other purposes. However, when this piece of capital wears out, it can be replaced with capital of another type.

The Pros and Cons of Economic Growth

Past and Present Views of Economic Growth

Despite an imperfect record, the American economy has strongly adhered to a pattern of growth. Should we try to increase our rate of economic growth? Some economists answer yes, some answer no. Before presenting the issues, several points should be noted about the attitudes of economists, past and present, toward economic growth. First, the great economists of the past were deeply concerned with the poverty and economic misery of their times; and they tried in various ways to help set humanity on a course whereby output per capita might rise. Smith, Malthus, and Ricardo all wanted to ameliorate the meager lot of the average Englishman of their day; Marx was distressed and angered by the misery of the working classes; and Keynes spent much of his time and energy trying to find a way out of the poverty and misery arising from the Great Depression.

Second, except for Smith and Keynes, these great economists of the past were not very optimistic about how much output per capita could be increased. Malthus and Ricardo were about as pessimistic as one reasonably could get. In their view, population would expand whenever the standard of living poked its head above the subsistence level, with the result that more and more people would be working a relatively fixed amount of land. Given the law of diminishing marginal returns, it appeared certain to them that output per capita would eventually fall. As for Marx, we have seen that he believed the capitalistic system was headed for collapse, and that the bulk of the population was doomed to increased misery so long as capitalism survived.

With all the advantages of hindsight, it is relatively easy to see where the pessimists went wrong, at least for the industrialized nations. As pointed out in the previous chapter, Malthus and Ricardo vastly underestimated the power of technological change. They could not visualize the sorts of innovations that were to occur. New techniques and new products were destined to offset the dreaded law of diminishing marginal returns and to allow food supplies to more than keep pace with increases in population. Moreover, because of innovations in birth control and changes in attitudes, population has not grown as rapidly as many people forecasted. Marx could not visualize the sorts of changes that were to occur in capitalism. Nor could he avoid the consequences of the basic flaws in his economic theories.

It is important to recognize that, for a variety of reasons, the attitudes of most economists today are quite different from the attitudes of their great predecessors. The difference does not lie in a lack of concern for the underprivileged. Most economists today are just as interested in eradicating poverty as were Smith or Marx. *The big difference is that today's economists are reasonably confident that we can increase output per capita. Indeed, they expect, almost as a matter of course, that output per capita will increase in the industrialized nations of the world.* Of course, some wish that it could be made to increase a little faster (and some would like to slow it down) but, in general, the present view is decidedly optimistic.

The Case for Economic Growth

Having reached a level of affluence that would have astonished Smith, Ricardo, Malthus, or Marx (but not Keynes), the industrialized nations are now at a point where some observers question the wisdom of further economic growth. For example, in the United States, the attitude toward economic growth has changed perceptibly in the decade or so since President Kennedy made it a target of public policy. More emphasis is placed today on the "costs" of economic growth. There are more statements to the effect that we really are rich enough, and more questions about the desirability of technological change, which is one of the principal mainsprings of economic growth. But many people continue to favor rapid economic growth. What arguments do they use?

Higher living standards. It is often argued that economic growth means a higher standard of living, which is important in and of itself. But before accepting this uncritically, one should stress the limitations of the customary growth measures. A decade or so ago, people tended uncritically to accept increases in per capita GNP as a measure of increases in economic welfare, despite the many warnings of economists. People now are more conscious of the frailties of the GNP—the fact that it does not count as "product" many benefits that are a part of the productive process (such as increased leisure) and that it does not count as "costs" many problems (such as the human and environmental costs) that arise as a consequence of the productive process. Some economists are currently trying to improve the statistics to take better account of some of these factors, such as environmental pollution (see Chapter 8). But since it is unlikely that we will ever have very precise measures of economic welfare, the available figures need to be treated with caution.

Reduction of poverty. It is argued that economic growth provides the means to reduce poverty and attain other national objectives. In the words of Peter Passell and Leonard Ross,

> "Growth is the only way that America will ever reduce poverty. . . . While the relative share of income that poor people get seems to be frozen, their incomes do keep pace with the economy. . . . Even allowing for inflation, the average income of the bottom 10th of the population has increased about 55 percent since 1950. Twenty more years of growth could do for the poor what the Congress won't do."[3]

[3] P. Passell and L. Ross, "Don't Knock the $2-Trillion Economy," *New York Times,* March 5, 1972.

Also, it is argued that economic growth makes it easier to achieve other national goals, because they can be achieved without reducing the production and consumption of other goods and services. For example, as mentioned in the previous chapter, it has been maintained that economic growth makes it easier to expand needed government and social services, since such an expansion can be achieved without cutting private consumption.

Defense and prestige. Many maintain that economic growth contributes to national prestige and national defense. As pointed out in the previous chapter, this was one of the most important reasons for the emphasis on economic growth in the early 1960s. People were worried that we were losing the "growth race" to the Soviet Union, and that Premier Nikita Khrushchev's claim that the Russians would "bury" us economically might be more than an idle boast. In recent years, as our relations with the Communist countries have improved, these reasons for economic growth have been given less importance, but they still are cited by some proponents of economic growth.

The Case against Economic Growth

Basically, there are four arguments made by those who question the wisdom of further economic growth in our society:

Quality of life. It is argued that increases in per capita GNP really will not make us any happier: on the contrary, they will only be achieved by reducing the quality of our lives. For example, according to E. J. Mishan of the London School of Economics, economic growth results in "the appalling traffic congestion in our towns, cities, and suburbs, . . . the erosion of the countryside, the 'uglification' of coastal towns, . . . and a wide heritage of natural beauty being wantonly destroyed."[4] In his view, to strain for further economic growth is simply to put ourselves on a meaningless treadmill, since it prevents us from enjoying what we have. Relatively few economists share this rather extreme view.

Pollution. It is argued that economic growth is likely to result in additional environmental pollution. Of course, increases in per capita GNP do not necessarily have to entail increases in pollution. On the contrary, as we shall see in the next chapter, it is possible to increase output without increasing pollution. Nonetheless, the fact seems to be that economic growth in the past has been associated with increases in pollution, and some observers feel that this association is likely to persist in the future. Thus they regard increases in environmental pollution as a likely "cost" of economic growth. Among those who argue against further economic growth on environmental grounds is biologist Barry Commoner of Washington University, who concludes that

> in most of the technological displacements which have accompanied the growth of the economy since 1946, the new technology has an appreciably greater environmental impact than the technology which it has displaced, and the postwar technological transformation of productive activities is the chief reason for the present environmental crisis. . . . If we are to survive economically as well as biologically, much of the technological transformation of the United States economy since 1946 will need to be, so to speak, redone in order to bring the nation's productive technology much more closely into harmony with the inescapable demands of the ecosystem.[5]

Solving social and political problems. It is argued that economic growth is not the solver of social problems that its proponents claim. For example, critics point out that we are rich enough now to solve the problem of poverty in the United States. In their view, what we need is the will and courage to eliminate poverty,

[4] E. Mishan, *Technology and Growth,* New York: Praeger, 1969.

[5] B. Commoner, "The Environmental Costs of Economic Growth," in R. and N. Dorfman, *Economics of the Environment,* 2d ed., New York: Norton, 1977.

not extra output. In reply to the argument that economic growth is needed for reasons of national prestige and defense, the critics retort that it is not the size of a country's GNP, but its composition, that counts in determining military strength. For example, the Soviet Union's military strength is roughly equal to ours, although its GNP is about 50 percent smaller. Moreover, the critics question whether the less developed countries are much impressed by a simple comparison of our growth rate with that of the Soviet Union.

Current sacrifices. It is pointed out that, to increase our growth rate, it may be necessary for us to make sacrifices now. For example, we may have to sacrifice leisure or postpone the consumption of goods and services in order to invest in capital goods. Many economists have stressed that one cannot make the naive assumption that more growth is costless, or that it will always be worth the sacrifices involved. Thus some economists argue that there is no reason to "force" growth on the economy. To them, the proper rate of economic growth is that which would emerge from private decisions. Whether the increase in the growth rate is worth the sacrifices depends upon the tastes and preferences of the people: it is a political issue.

Is Doomsday at Hand?

Most critics of economic growth believe that it is not worth its costs, for the sorts of reasons discussed above. But some go further and argue that *sustained economic growth for an additional century will not be possible.* This arresting conclusion has been put forth by Dennis and Donella Meadows and their colleagues in the book, *The Limits to Growth.* Specifically, they say that

> if the present growth trends in world population, industrialization, pollution, food production, and resource depletion continue unchanged, the limits to growth on this planet will be reached sometime within the next one hundred years. The most probable result will be a rather sudden and uncontrollable decline in both population and industrial capacity.[6]

In view of the world-wide interest in their study, it is worth looking in some detail at the model they use. (This model is related closely to the work of Jay Forrester at M.I.T.) According to this model, per capita output is determined by the supply of natural resources and the amount of capital per worker. Technological change doesn't enter into the model, and the supply of resources is seen as largely fixed. There is no allowance for the fact that new resources may be discovered, that resources may be made more useful by new technologies, or that plentiful resources may be substituted for scarce ones. Given these assumptions, it is easy to see why they came to their very pessimistic conclusions.

Critics have directed a great many salvoes at these so-called doomsday models. For one thing, they point out that the assumption of no technological change is at odds with reality, and that it tends to insure that economic growth will slow down. As we saw in the last chapter, increases in capital will eventually result in diminishing marginal returns. Unless technological change occurs, less and less productive projects must be undertaken as more and more is invested in capital. The eventual result is a cessation of economic growth. But this result is due to the assumption of no technological change–a strange assumption for M.I.T. faculty members to make.

Another disturbing assumption is that there is a relatively small and readily exhaustible amount of resources. This assumption seems to ignore the fact that, as particular resources become increasingly scarce, their prices go up, and there is an incentive to find more of them, to find substitutes for them, and to economize on their use. Given this assumption, it is not hard to see why economic growth eventually

[6] D. Meadows et al, "The Limits to Growth."

will be impossible, according to the model. After all, if there is only a finite amount of resources, and if economic growth means using them at current rates, we eventually will run out of them. No question about it.

But this assumption seems oversimplified and overly pessimistic. As Peter Passell and Leonard Ross point out,

> before we run out of Arabian oil, we will begin extracting petroleum from the vast reserves of oil-shale rocks and tar sands. And long before we run out of those reserves, cars will be powered with other sources of energy. Appeals to faith in technical change are more than a cheap debating trick to counter the Forrester school. The technology of substituting plentiful materials for scarce ones grows every day. Silicates made from sand replace copper and silver radio circuitry; European cattle feeds are enriched with nutrients made of natural gas converted by bacteria; mattresses are filled with polyurethane which never was closer to a Liberian rubber tree than Bayonne, N.J.[7]

Perhaps the most fundamental criticism of their model is that it fails to recognize the workings of the price system. As Robert Solow has pointed out, the price system leads us to economize on various raw materials as they become scarce.

> Higher and rising prices of exhaustible resources lead competing producers to substitute other materials that are more plentiful and therefore cheaper. To the extent that it is impossible to design around or find substitutes for expensive natural resources, the prices of commodities will rise relative to the prices of other goods and services that don't use up a lot of resources. Consumers will be driven to buy fewer resource-intensive goods and more of other things. All of these effects work automatically . . . to reduce resource requirements per unit of GNP.[8]

Because of these criticisms, most economists do not accept the conclusions of the doomsday models. However, Dennis and Donella Meadows and their colleagues unquestionably have focused attention on some very important issues, and for this we must be grateful. But until their models are free of the objections noted above, they will have difficulty in convincing economists of the wisdom of their policy recommendations—which are to curb economic growth and population growth drastically.

Public Policies to Stimulate Economic Growth

Although the critics of growth have made some headway, there has been no renunciation of economic growth as a goal of public policy. On the contrary, most government officials, in the United States and elsewhere, continue to press for further economic growth. All nations have important social objectives that seem more likely to be attained if they can increase per capita output. Thus most would like to effect such an increase, notwithstanding Mishan's views concerning the hollowness of it all. But the more sophisticated question of how far the government should go in promoting or forcing growth is not easy to answer. And as you would expect, there are very substantial differences of opinion on this score among politicians in this country (and other countries as well). Whether or not we should stimulate growth is essentially a political question, and your own view will depend on your political preferences.

But whether you are for or against the stimulation of growth, you should know how the government's policies can influence the growth rate. Suppose that the American people, registering their opinions through the proper democratic process, indicate that they want to increase the nation's rate of economic growth. What sorts of programs would lead to that goal?

First, the nation might *increase expenditures on research and development* (R and D), since

[7] P. Passell and L. Ross, "Don't Knock the $2-Trillion Economy."
[8] R. Solow, "Is the End of the World At Hand?" in E. Mansfield, *Economics: Readings, Issues, and Cases*, 2d ed., New York: Norton, 1977.

increases in such expenditures are likely to increase the rate of technological change, which in turn will increase the growth rate.[9] The government can either increase R and D expenditures by directly financing more R and D, or it can provide tax credits or other inducements to get private firms to increase their R and D expenditures. It is important to recognize, however, that the added R and D must be carried out in areas where the social payoffs are high: otherwise there will be little impact on the growth rate. Moreover, we must also note that the government can stimulate the growth rate by encouraging the application and diffusion of existing technology, as well as by encouraging the development of new technology.

Second, measures might be taken to *increase investment in education and training.* If there is a high rate of return from such an investment, increased education and training would increase the nation's potential output considerably. To foster such increases, the federal government could spend larger amounts on scholarships and provide more loans for potential students. (Since 1965, the Department of Health, Education, and Welfare has helped students with grants, loans, and loan guarantees.) Also, the government could provide more financial support to the nation's colleges and universities. But a major question is how high the rate of return from increased education really is. Until the early 1970s, the evidence indicated that it was relatively high, but, as we saw in the previous chapter, recent studies suggest that it now may be lower than it used to be.

Third, steps might be taken to *increase investment in plant and equipment.* Increases in aggregate investment will increase the growth rate, assuming, of course, that the extra investment is in areas of high productivity. Again, we must recognize that this policy, like the others described above, imposes costs. Increases in investment can occur—under full employment—only at the expense of current consumption. Assuming that the people understand these costs and are willing to pay them, the government can increase investment in plant and equipment by keeping interest rates low (to encourage investment) and personal tax rates high (to choke off consumption). Also, the government can give tax credits for investment in plant and equipment and allow firms to depreciate their plant and equipment more rapidly.[10]

Fourth, if the economy is operating at considerably less than full employment, the government might step in *to narrow the gap between actual and potential output.* As we saw in the previous chapter, this can be a very effective way to grow, at least in the short run. To do it, the government must use its fiscal and monetary policies to reduce unemployment. The goal of full employment is widely accepted—more widely, for that matter, than the goal of increasing the rate of economic growth. Unfortunately, however, when the economy approaches full employment, there may be a tendency for the goal of full employment to conflict with the goal of price stability, as we saw in Chapter 8. Thus an attempt to close completely the gap between actual and potential output may lead to undesirable inflationary pressures.

Policies for Economic Growth in the Early 1960s: A Case Study

As we have noted, in the early 1960s, the Kennedy administration set out to spur the rate of economic growth in the United States. We

[9] It is interesting to contrast this attitude toward R and D with the view of the French revolutionaries, who said, as they led the famous scientist, Lavoisier, to the guillotine, "The Republic has no need of scientists." Clearly, scientists are viewed differently—and treated more gently—today.

[10] A tax credit is a device whereby a firm's income tax liability is smaller if it invests a great deal in plant and equipment than if it invests little. Obviously, such a tax credit increases the profitability of investing in plant and equipment. More rapid depreciation of plant and equipment also encourages investment because, if a firm can write off a new piece of equipment more rapidly for tax purposes, the new piece of equipment is more profitable to the firm than it otherwise would be.

now can take a closer look at the set of economic policies designed to accomplish this goal. These policies were formulated by members of the Council of Economic Advisers, and others, inside and outside the government. To be put into effect, some of these policies and programs had to be approved by the Congress.

For research and development, the Kennedy administration proposed a Civilian Industrial Technology program to encourage and support additional R and D in industries that it regarded as lagging technologically. It also proposed an industrial extension service—analogous to the agricultural extension service that distributes technological information and advice—to increase the rate of diffusion of innovations. Congress eventually approved the industrial extension service,[11] but not the Civilian Industrial Technology program. An important reason for its defeat was that some industrial groups feared that government sponsorship of industrial R and D could upset existing competitive relationships.

In the field of education too, the administration proposed new measures. For example, in his 1962 *Economic Report,* President Kennedy stated,

> Public education has been the great bulwark of equality of opportunity in our democracy for more than a century. . . . There can be no better investment in equity and democracy—and no better instrument for economic growth. For this reason, I urge action by the Congress to provide Federal aid for more adequate public school facilities, higher teachers' salaries, and better quality in education. I urge early completion of congressional action on the bill to authorize loans for construction of college academic facilities and to provide scholarships for able students who need help. The talent of our youth is a resource which must not be wasted.[12]

To encourage investment in plant and equipment, the administration pushed through an "investment tax credit" that permitted firms to deduct from their income tax statements 7 percent of the amount they invested in new plant and equipment. Obviously, this made such investment more profitable. Also, the administration revised the depreciation schedules so that firms could write off such investments more quickly for tax purposes, thus increasing their profitability still more. But it did not lower interest rates or increase taxes to choke off consumption. In its *1962 Annual Report,* the Council of Economic Advisers recognized that such actions might promote growth, but felt that other considerations, such as our balance of payments (discussed in Chapter 21), ruled them out.

Finally, turning to the reduction of the gap between actual and potential output, the administration used fiscal and monetary policies to push the economy toward full employment. An important part of this policy in the eyes of most economists was the tax cut of 1964, described in Chapter 11. Between 1962 and 1966, the United States achieved a high rate of growth, in considerable part because of the reduction of the gap between actual and potential output.

Thus, taken as a whole, the Kennedy administration's policies to stimulate economic growth conformed to the elementary principles discussed in this and the previous chapter. In the area of growth policy—just as in fiscal, monetary, and incomes policy—the basic principles of economics take you a long way toward understanding the policies of government, whether Democratic or Republican.

Adjustment to Technological Change

Technological Unemployment

Up to now, we have stressed that rapid technological change is an important stimulus to economic growth. But this stimulus to growth can

[11] The industrial extension service, embodied in the State Technical Services Act, was passed in 1965, but was later killed.
[12] *Economic Report of the President,* Washington, D.C.: Government Printing Office, 1962, p. 10.

Is There a Capital Crisis?

Assuming that the American people desire continued economic growth, American firms must invest an enormous amount in plant, equipment, and other forms of capital in the next decade. For example, according to Roger Brinner and Allen Sinai of Data Resources, Inc., about $1.9 trillion will have to be invested in machinery between 1975 and 1985, compared with about $670 billion invested in this way between 1965 and 1975. This accelerated rate of investment is due partly to the fact that our investment rate was not very high during the past decade, partly to the increased capital requirements to satisfy the antipollution and safety regulations that recently have been enacted, and partly to a variety of other factors.

If these estimates are at all reliable, the required investment is enormous by any standards. And many people, particularly in industry and on Wall Street, are worried that we won't be able to augment our capital stock at the required rate. One reason for this concern is inflation. According to some economists, many companies will have trouble increasing their capital stock at the desired rate because their allowances for depreciation will be too small to permit them to replace worn-out equipment. (Why? Because, as we saw in Chapter 7, depreciation allowances are based on historical cost—and in times of rapid inflation, historical cost is much less than the cost of replacing equipment.) Moreover, they will have a difficult time borrowing money for this purpose, because they already have amassed a very large amount of debt. According to some estimates, American firms in 1975 had about $2 of owner-provided capital per $1 of debt, whereas in 1965 they had about $4 of owner-provided capital per $1 of debt.

Some economists believe that these apparent problems can be avoided if the federal government runs a surplus in the late 1970s. Among the leading supporters of this view are James Duesenberry of Harvard University and Barry Bosworth and Andrew Carron of the Brookings Institution.* The reason why a surplus tends to ease the situation is that the government, if it runs a surplus, is spending less than it takes in. Thus a surplus, like individual or corporate saving, results in resources being available for investment. However, critics of this view point out that the federal budget has generally been biased toward deficits, not surpluses.

Other economists, like Robert Eisner of Northwestern University, are inclined to minimize the seriousness of this whole matter. In their view, no capital crisis exists. They point out that, if the quantity of capital supplied is less than the quantity demanded, then interest rates should rise to induce more saving. And if markets are working properly, there is no reason, they say, why the quantity demanded should be less than the amount that is socially optimal. As evidence that there is no capital shortage, some people cite the fact that the rate of return on invested capital has been falling during the late 1960s and early 1970s. They say that, if there were a shortage of capital, it should be rising. But other economists, such as Federal Reserve Board member Henry Wallich, point out that the rate of return from newly invested capital may be higher than that from old capital.

Thus far there is no indication that the Congress will reduce taxes on business to encourage firms to invest more, even though some of the Ford administration's highest officials, notably Secretary of the Treasury William Simon, have clamored for greater incentives for capital formation.

* B. Bosworth, J. Duesenberry, and A. Carron, *Capital Needs in the Seventies*, Washington, D.C.: Brookings Institution, 1975.

be offset, at least partially, if rapid technological change results in technological unemployment. Economists have long recognized that new technology can throw people out of work. Karl Marx, in particular, gave technological change—and technological unemployment—a significant role in his theoretical system. (As we saw in Chapter 9, he believed that capitalists would adopt new technologies that would result in more and more technological unemployment.) Workers too have long recognized and feared technological unemployment. As long ago as the mid-1700s, a mob of worried English spinners entered James Hargreaves's mill and smashed the first workable multispindle frames.

Although the dread of technology-induced mass unemployment is not new, it was revived with great effect in the late 1950s and early 1960s. The new scare word was *automation.* For example, Professor Crossman of Oxford University, addressing an international conference in 1964, said that "unemployment due to automation will grow steadily over the next four decades, perhaps centuries, and in the end it is likely to reach a very high figure, say 90 percent of the labor force, unless radical changes are made in the present pattern of working."[13] Although ***automation*** means different things to different people, it generally refers to processes designed to mechanize the the human cognitive, conceptual, and informational processes.

Do increases in the rate of technological change necessarily result in increases in aggregate unemployment? To make a long story short, the answer is *no.* Rapid technological change need not have this effect if the government increases total spending at the proper rate. When total spending rises too slowly, increased aggregate unemployment takes place. If it rises too rapidly and resources are already fully employed, inflation will result. As we know, the job of choosing and carrying out appropriate fiscal and monetary policies is not easy; but used with reasonable finesse, such policies should prevent any large increase in aggregate unemployment from technological change.

To see how large-scale technological unemployment can occur—and how it can be avoided—consider Figure 18.2, which shows the $C + I + G$ line at a particular point in time. (If you are a bit hazy about the meaning and significance of this line, review Chapter 11.) Since this line intersects the 45-degree line at point A, the equilibrium level of net national product is \$400 billion. If the high-employment level of net national product is also \$400 billion, the economy enjoys a high level of employment. Now suppose that there is a significant amount of technological change. What will be the result? To begin with, the advance in technology will almost certainly result in an increase in productivity. In other words, it will enable the labor force to produce more than it formerly could. Thus the high-employment level of net national product will increase—say to \$450 billion. Given this increase, it is obvious that there will be substantial unemployment if the $C + I + G$ line stays put. This is obvious enough. After all, if output remains the same and output per man-hour increases, fewer workers will be needed and there will be unemployment.

But there is no reason why the $C + I + G$ *line should remain constant.* The advance in technology itself may increase the profitability of investment, thus raising I. Moreover, the advance in technology may result in new consumer products, which prompt consumers to spend more of a given level of income, thus raising C. Suppose that, by virtue of these changes in C and I, the $C + I + G$ line shifts to $C' + I' + G'$ (shown in panel B of Figure 18.2). The new equilibrium level of net national product is \$425 billion, as shown in

[13] Organization for Economic Cooperation and Development, *The Requirements of Automated Jobs,* Paris, 1965, p. 21.

Figure 18.2
Possible Effects of Technological Change on Equilibrium Level of Net National Product.

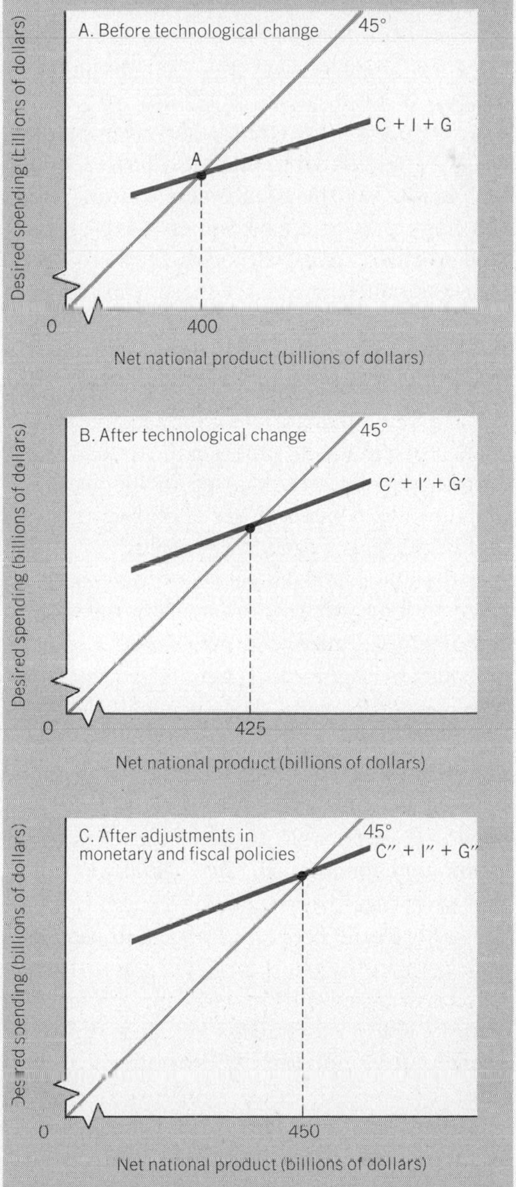

panel B. Unfortunately, in this particular case (but not necessarily in other cases), the new equilibrium level of NNP is less than the new high-employment level of NNP. Thus, without some change in public policy, there would be some technological unemployment. But as we know, the Federal Reserve can increase I by increasing the money supply and reducing interest rates, and the government can push C upward by reducing tax rates and increase G by increasing its own expenditures. Thus there is no reason why the government cannot raise the $C + I + G$ line to the point where it intersects the 45-degree line at $450 billion. For example, the government might nudge the $C + I + G$ line up to $C'' + I'' + G''$ in panel C of Figure 18.2. And if it does this, the equilibrium level of net national product equals the high-employment level of net national product. Thus it should be possible to avoid large amounts of technological unemployment, although transitional problems, discussed in a subsequent section, will remain.

Structural Unemployment

The considerable concern during the 1950s and early 1960s that technological change would result in massive technological unemployment was heightened by fears that workers and jobs were becoming more and more mismatched. According to one group of economists, technological change and other factors were increasing the skill and educational requirements of available jobs, and making it more likely that shortages of highly educated workers would coexist with unemployed pools of unskilled workers. Unemployment of this sort—unemployment that occurs because the workers available for employment do not possess the qualities that employers require—is called ***structural unemployment.*** The economists who asserted that structural unemployment was growing in the late 1950s and early 1960s were often called the structuralists.

In opposition to the structuralists, another

large group of economists denied that structural unemployment was increasing. An important and lively debate took place, both inside and outside the government, over the important question of how unemployment would respond to an increase in total spending. If an increase in total spending would reduce unemployment, then evidently at least that much unemployment was not structural. If it would fail to reduce unemployment, then the unemployment that remained could be called structural. To put the issue to a test, attempts were made to compare various periods when the general pressure of total spending was about the same, to see whether the level of unemployment was higher or more strongly concentrated in certain skill categories, industries, or regions in more recent periods than in the past.

Although neither side had a monopoly on the truth, the results of these tests, as well as the course of events after the 1964 tax cut, provided little support for the structuralist view. There was no evidence that unemployment was becoming more concentrated in particular geographic regions. Moreover, after adjusting for the effect of the over-all unemployment rate on the unemployment rate in particular occupations and industries, very few occupations or industries showed an unambiguous tendency for unemployment to increase with time. Also, after adjusting for the effects of the over-all unemployment rate, there was no significant tendency for unemployment rates among blacks to rise during the late 1950s and early 1960s. Thus, although a substantial portion of all unemployment may have been structural, there was no evidence that unemployment of this type increased greatly during that period.

Labor Displacement

Economic growth often occurs as a consequence of innovation and the redeployment of resources, which in turn means that *people*—workers, managers, owners of capital—*must adapt to these innovations and redeployments of resources.* Some people lose their jobs, some must move to other places, and some must enter new occupations. For example, consider the movement of people from agricultural to urban areas in the United States—a movement that has been part of the process of economic growth. During the postwar period, the number of farm owners and farm workers declined by over 40 percent. Innovations in agriculture—ranging from chemical fertilizers and insecticides to the mechanical cotton picker and huge harvesting combines—have contributed to this exodus, although they are by no means the only reason. Of those who left agriculture, many wound up in urban ghettos, many lacked the skills and education needed to fill urban jobs, and many who adapted to their new surroundings did so at considerable cost in psychological and emotional terms. Such human costs do not show up in the gross national product. Yet they are important costs, or disadvantages, of economic growth.

Although an adequate level of total spending can go a long way toward assuring that aggregate unemployment will not exceed a socially acceptable minimum, it cannot prevent labor from being displaced from particular occupations, industries, and regions, and being drawn to others. Nor would we want to eliminate all such movements of labor, without which it would be impossible to adjust to changes in technology, population, and consumer tastes. However, regardless of the long-run benefits of this adjustment process, important problems may arise in the short run, and great distress may be imposed on the workers who are displaced. These movements of labor must be carried out as efficiently and painlessly as possible.

The most serious adjustment problems have occurred when massive displacement has occurred in isolated areas among workers with specialized skills and without alternative sources of employment. Coal miners are a good example. About ⅔ of the nation's bituminous coal miners in 1960 were located in West Virginia, Pennsylvania, and Kentucky, and most of the coal mining was concentrated in isolated towns. Employment in bituminous coal started to decline after World War II, partly because of shifting demand and the adoption of new techniques. Between 1947 and 1959, total employment in the industry declined by more than 60 percent, leading to an unemployment rate of roughly 10 percent of the labor force in 5 major bituminous coal areas during most of the 1950s. In 25 smaller areas where there were few job opportunities outside coal mining, the unemployment rate was even higher.

Displaced older workers have encountered particularly serious problems. Seniority rights have helped hold down the displacement of older workers; but once unemployed, they are less likely than younger workers to be reemployed. For example, one year after the shutdown of the Packard automobile plant in Detroit, 77 percent of the workers under 45 were working at another job, whereas the percentages were 67 for the 45-to-54 age group and 62 for the 55-to-64 age group. Even if skill is held constant, the older workers had more serious unemployment problems than the younger workers, at least as measured by length of unemployment. Another study obtained similar results for a period when the general level of employment was higher than in the Packard case. It is easy to understand why older workers have more trouble finding another job. Many of their skills are specific to a particular job, and much of their income and status may be due to seniority, so that they cannot command as high a wage on the open market as they previously earned. Moreover, employers naturally are reluctant to invest in hiring and training a worker who will only be available for a relatively few years and who often has relatively limited education. Finally, because of their roots in the community, older workers are less likely to move to other areas where jobs are more plentiful.

Displaced black workers seem to find it even more difficult than older workers to obtain suitable re-employment at their previous status and earnings. For example, among workers who had been earning the same wage at Packard, blacks experienced a higher average length of unemployment than whites. Moreover, the prestige and economic level of the new job were more likely to be lower for blacks than whites. Needless to say, prejudice often plays an important role in preventing displaced blacks from obtaining new jobs.

Manpower and Training Policies

Beyond insuring an adequate level of total spending, perhaps the most important way that the government can facilitate adjustment to the adoption of new techniques is by promoting the necessary adaptability of the labor force through education and training. Education can increase the versatility and flexibility of the work force and increase its ability to adjust to change. It can open up greater opportunities and improve the productivity of workers at any level of skill or ability. The available evidence indicates the importance of a broad-based, secondary education rather than a narrow vocational education. The training for many—perhaps most—specific jobs can and should be done on the job.

Turning from the education of tomorrow's work force to the retraining of today's, it is generally agreed that the government should help workers who are casualties of technological (and other) change to obtain the skills required to return to productive employment. A coordinated, integrated system of adult retraining, which takes proper account of nationwide needs and supplies and reaches the underprivileged and hard-core unemployed, is useful and important. However, it should be recognized that industry quite properly plays the predominant role in the vocational training and retraining of the work force, and that the government plays only a residual role. The dif-

JOHN MAYNARD KEYNES

on "Economic Possibilities for Our Grandchildren"

Let us, for the sake of argument, suppose that a hundred years hence we are all of us, on the average, eight times better off in the economic sense than we are today. Assuredly there need be nothing here to surprise us.

Now it is true that the needs of human beings may seem to be insatiable. But they fall into two classes—those needs which are absolute in the sense that we feel them whatever the situation of our fellow human beings may be, and those which are relative in the sense that we feel them only if their satisfaction lifts us above, makes us feel superior to, our fellows. Needs of the second class, those which satisfy the desire for superiority, may indeed be insatiable; for the higher the general level, the higher still are they. But this is not so true of the absolute needs—a point may soon be reached, much sooner perhaps than we are all of us aware of, when these needs are satisfied in the sense that we prefer to devote our further energies to non-economic purposes.

Now, for my conclusion, which you will find, I think, to become more and more startling to the imagination the longer you think about it.

I draw the conclusion that, assuming no important wars and no important increase in population, the *economic problem* may be solved, or be at least within sight of solution, within a hundred years. This means that the economic problem is not—if we look into the future—*the permanent problem of the human race.*

Why, you may ask, is this so startling? It is startling because—if, instead of looking into the future we look into the past—we find that the economic problem, the struggle for subsistence, always has been hitherto the primary, most pressing problem of the human race—not only of the human race, but of the whole of the biological kingdom from the beginnings of life in its most primitive forms.

Thus we have been expressly evolved by nature—with all our impulses and deepest instincts—for the purpose of solving the economic problem. If the economic problem is solved, mankind will be deprived of its traditional purpose.

Will this be a benefit? If one believes at all in the real values of life, the prospect at least opens up the possibility of benefit. Yet I think with dread of the readjustment of the habits and instincts of the ordinary man, bred into him for countless generations, which he may be asked to discard within a few decades.

John Maynard Keynes, *Essays in Persuasion*, London: Macmillan, 1933. Originally published in 1930.

ficulties faced by government-sponsored training programs are considerable, given the limitations of capacity of the vocational education system and the lack of basic education among the trainees.

The government can also promote greater efficiency of labor markets and better adjustment to change by providing better labor market information and by experimenting, in its role as employer, with new adjustment techniques. Job seekers typically have relatively little information about alternative job openings. The federal government should do what it can to expand the amount and quality of available information—keeping in mind that the costs incurred must bear a reasonable relationship to the benefits attained. As well as exploring new ways of disseminating information to those who need and want work, the government might also investigate new education technologies to recognize individual potential and to promote faster and better learning.

Visions of the Economic Future

Finally, let's turn to the rate of economic growth in the future. What sort of economic growth rate is the United States likely to experience between now and the year 2000? Long-range economic forecasting is a hazardous business—unless, of course, the forecaster is so old and the forecast so far in the future that he can be sure of being dead before anyone can tell whether the forecast was right or wrong. As we saw in Chapter 12, it is difficult enough to forecast what will happen next year, let alone 20 years from now. Nonetheless, for some purposes, long-range economic forecasts are useful and need to be made. What do they indicate about the future rate of economic growth in the United States?

In 1967, Herman Kahn, the well-known physicist and strategic theorist, collaborated with sociologist Anthony Wiener to produce some forecasts of what the world will be like by the year 2000. In their view, economic growth will probably have resulted in a per capita gross national product of at least $17,000 (in terms of 1975 prices) in the United States. This is a very, very high standard of living. For comparison, recall that per capita GNP in 1975 was about $7,000. Thus Kahn and Weiner believe that per capita GNP will be more than twice as high in 2000 as in 1975. In their view the United States will have become a "postindustrial society." There will be a reduction in society's emphasis on efficiency and production, less attention paid to traditional work-oriented values, much more leisure, and a much looser relationship between work and income.[14]

Certainly, if these are truly the characteristics of the future, it is not at all what was anticipated by many of the great economists of the past. Malthus and Ricardo never dreamed of such affluence, and Marx never dreamed it could happen under capitalism. Only Keynes, who lived much later than the others, could see the handwriting on the wall. In a famous article written in 1930, he concluded that "assuming no important wars and no important increase in population, the *economic problem* may be solved, or be at least within sight of solution, within a hundred years."[15] Specifically, he hazarded the guess that we might then be eight times better off economically than at the time he was writing.

At first glance, it may seem that if Keynes and Kahn and Wiener are right, we are on the threshold of solving practically all our problems. But upon closer examination, one cannot escape the feeling that there are likely to be important problems in adjusting to such a level of affluence. As Keynes put it so well,

> I think with dread of the readjustment of the habits and instincts of the ordinary man, bred into him for countless generations, which he may be asked to discard within a few decades. . . .

[14] Herman Kahn and Anthony J. Weiner, *The Year 2000*, New York: Macmillan, 1967.

[15] John Maynard Keynes, "Economic Possibilities for our Grandchildren," reprinted in *Essays in Persuasion*.

> [For] the first time since his creation man will be faced with his real, his permanent problem—how to use his freedom from pressing economic cares, how to occupy his leisure, which science and compound interest will have won for him, to live wisely and agreeably and well.

Nonetheless, one must be very pessimistic about the intelligence and imagination of our people if he regards such problems as outweighing the benefits of this economic freedom. Admittedly, the rich have their problems, but there are few poor people who wouldn't trade places with them. In time, is it too much to expect that we will learn how to use these riches to build a better life than we, or others, have known before? I think not. In time, is it too much to expect that we will become more willing and able to share these riches with the poorer nations of the world? I hope not. On this latter point, it is important to understand that the forecasts of milk and honey by the year 2000 are for the industrialized countries, not the less developed countries. The prospects for the latter are less cheerful, as we shall see in Chapter 22.

Summary

Compared with that of other major industrial countries, America's rate of economic growth has been quite impressive over the past century, although in recent years many industrialized countries have experienced higher growth rates than we have. Our relatively rapid economic growth has been due to a variety of important factors, such as rapid technological change, increases in education and training, investment in plant and equipment, plentiful natural resources, and our social and entrepreneurial climate. However, not all aspects of the American economy have been conducive to rapid economic growth. Actual GNP has fallen short of potential GNP, and monopolies and immobilities have prevented efficient resource allocation.

Having reached a level of affluence that would have astonished Smith, Ricardo, Malthus, or Marx (but not Keynes), the industrialized nations are now at a point where some observers question the wisdom of further economic growth. The critics of growth assert that more output does not bring more happiness, that economic growth is likely to result in additional environmental pollution, that we are rich enough now to solve our major social problems, and that extra growth is not worth the sacrifices it requires. On the other hand, the proponents of growth argue that it will bring higher living standards, that it will enable us to solve such national problems as poverty, and that it is important for reasons of national defense and national prestige. Although the critics of growth have made some headway, there has been no renunciation of economic growth as a goal of public policy. To stimulate the rate of economic growth, governments encourage investment in technology, education, and plant and equipment, as well as reduce the gap between actual and potential GNP.

Although rapid technological change is an important stimulus to economic growth, it can also result in technological unemployment. If the government increases total spending at the proper rate, there is no reason why technological unemployment should be large. But an adequate level of total spending cannot prevent labor from being displaced from particular occupations, industries, and regions, and being drawn to others. This adjustment process, which results in long-run benefits, may impose great distress on the workers who are involved. It is important that these movements of labor be carried out as efficiently and painlessly as possible. Through its manpower and training policies, the government can help to distribute the "costs of change" more equitably. Finally, according to various long-term forecasts, per capita real GNP in the United States is likely to be more than twice as high in 2000 as in 1975. If this turns out to be true, many economic problems will be solved, but many will still remain.

CONCEPTS FOR REVIEW

Benefits from economic growth
Costs of economic growth
Limits to economic growth
Automation
Structural unemployment
Technological unemployment
Investment tax credit

QUESTIONS FOR DISCUSSION AND REVIEW

1. "Increases in population mean increases in output, because more people can produce more. Further, they mean economic growth because, with more people, there can be greater specialization of labor." Comment and evaluate.

2. During the middle-1970s, there was much public concern that the United States might experience a "capital shortage." According to *Business Week,* "the capital shortage problem . . . [is] part of the whole question of economic growth, and once the capital shortage is looked at in this way, it begins to take on some real meaning." Explain. Do you agree? Why or why not?

3. According to some scientists and engineers, the United States is losing its technological lead over other countries in many areas of industrial technology. If this is true, what, if anything, does it portend for our rate of economic growth?

4. "The world has only a fixed amount of copper, manganese, tin, iron, and other resources. If we continue using them at current rates, we're bound to run out of them. Thus it is inevitable that economic growth can only be sustained for a limited amount of time." Comment and evaluate.

5. "The arguments against economic growth are foolish. Who can be against higher living standards?" Comment and evaluate.

6. Discuss the effects on the U.S. economic growth rate of each of the following: (a) the investment tax credit, (b) government support of higher education, (c) the development of birth-control pills, (d) government support of basic research, (d) increases in featherbedding.

7. "Technological change almost always results in a loss of jobs. No wonder organized labor opposes it." Comment and evaluate.

8. Contrast the views of Karl Marx and John Maynard Keynes concerning economic growth in the non-Communist world. Whose views have been closer to correct?

9. According to E. J. Mishan, "If the moving spirit behind economic growth were to speak, its motto would be 'Enough does not suffice.' " Comment and evaluate.

10. According to Robert Solow, "The Doomsday Models [by Forrester et al.] . . . say that continued economic growth is impossible . . . because (a) the earth's natural resources will soon be used up; (b) increased industrial production will soon strangle us in pollution; and (c) increased population will eventually outrun the world's capacity to grow food." Do you agree with these models? Why or why not?

19 Environmental and Energy Problems

Environmental pollution and energy are two important problems in the United States—and both are related to economic growth. According to many scientists and social observers, one of the costs of economic growth is environmental pollution. For many years, people in the United States paid relatively little attention to the environment and what they were doing to it, but this attitude has changed markedly in the last decade. Now the public seems genuinely concerned about environmental problems. However, in the effort to clean up the environment, choices are not always clear, nor solutions easy. In particular, the energy crisis that surfaced in the fall of 1973 has brought home the fact that a cleaner environment is not costless. Many measures that would reduce pollution would increase the demand for energy.

America's energy problems are related only partly to environmental matters. To a considerable extent, they stem from the fact that oil reserves in this country are being depleted, and that we face increasing dependence on foreign sources of oil—a rather worrisome prospect, since these foreign sources have banded together in an international cartel which raised the price of crude oil enormously in 1974. Also, there is the related question of developing safe and reliable alternatives to fossil fuels. In this chapter, we consider the economic aspects of both environmental decay and the nation's energy needs. Our purpose is to indicate the extent and seriousness of these problems, the factors that are responsible for them, and the sorts of public policies that might be adopted to help deal with them.

Our Environmental Problems

The Nature and Extent of Environmental Pollution

To see what we mean by environmental pollution, let's begin with one of the most important parts of man's environment, our water supplies. As a result of human activities, large amounts of pollutants are discharged into streams, lakes, and the sea. Chemical wastes are released by industrial plants and mines, as well as by farms and homes when fertilizers, pesticides, and detergents run off into waterways. Oil is discharged into the waters by tankers, sewage systems, oil wells, and other sources. Organic compounds enter waterways from industrial plants and farms, as well as from municipal sewage plants; and animal wastes, as well as human wastes, contribute substantially to pollution.

To reduce the ill effects of water pollution, waste water is sometimes subjected to a treatment process, in which the water is separated from the solid waste, and both are treated so as to protect public health and in-stream life. Generally, the treatment occurs in one or two phases. Primary treatment takes large particles out of the water and lets some of the smaller particles settle out as sludge before releasing the water to a nearby stream or river. Secondary treatment employs a controlled sequence of aeration and settling processes. According to the Environmental Protection Agency, the wastes of about 30 percent of the population served by sewerage facilities received only primary treatment (or no treatment at all) in 1973.

Obviously, we cannot continue to increase the rate at which we dump wastes into our streams, rivers, and oceans. A river, like everything else, can bear only so much. The people of Cleveland know this well: in 1969, the Cuyahoga River, which flows through Cleveland, literally caught fire, so great was its concentration of industrial and other wastes. Of course, the Cuyahoga is an extreme case, but many of our rivers, including the Hudson and the Ohio, are badly polluted, as Table 19.1 shows. Water pollution is a nuisance and perhaps a threat: for example, according to the Public Health Service, we may be approaching a crisis with respect to drinking water.[1]

If clean water is vital to man's survival, so too is clean air. Yet the battle being waged against air pollution in most of our major cities has not been won. Particles of various kinds are spewed into the air by factories that utilize combustion processes, grind materials, or produce dust. Motor vehicles release lead compounds from gasoline and rubber particles worn from tires, helping to create that unheavenly condition known as smog. Citizens of Los Angeles are particularly familiar with smog, but few major cities have escaped at least periodic air pollution. No precise measures have been developed to gauge the effects of air pollution on public health and enjoyment, but some rough estimates suggest that perhaps 25 percent of all deaths from respiratory disease

[1] See *Fortune*, February 1970; D. Rohrer, D. Montgomery, M. Montgomery, D. Eaton, and M. Arnold, *The Environment Crisis*, Skokie, Ill.: National Textbook, 1970; and Enviromental Protection Agency, *The Economics of Clean Water, 1973*, Washington, D.C.: Government Printing Office, 1973.

Table 19.1
Water Pollution for Major Drainage Areas, United States, 1970 and 1971

Major watershed	Stream miles	Polluted miles 1970	Polluted miles 1971	Polluted miles Change
Ohio	28,992	9,869	24,031	+14,162
Southeast	11,726	3,109	4,490	+ 1,381
Great Lakes	21,374	6,580	8,771	+ 2,191
Northeast	32,431	11,895	5,823	− 6,072
Middle Atlantic	31,914	4,620	5,627	+ 1,007
California	28,277	5,359	8,429	+ 3,070
Gulf	64,719	16,605	11,604	− 5,001
Missouri	10,448	4,259	1,839	− 2,420
Columbia	30,443	7,443	5,685	− 1,758
United States	260,324	69,739	76,299	+ 6,560

Source: Council on Environmental Quality, *Third Annual Report,* August 1972.

could be avoided by a 50 percent reduction in air pollution.

One of the most important contributors to air pollution is the combustion of fossil fuels, particularly coal and oil products: by-products of combustion comprise about 85 percent of the total amount of air pollutants in the United States. Most of these pollutants result from impure fuels or inefficient burning. Among the more serious pollutants are sulphur dioxide, carbon monoxide, and various oxides of nitrogen. Table 19.2 shows the total amount of major air pollutants emitted by various sources, and Figure 19.1 shows the upward trend in the amount of these emissions. According to some observers, the worst air pollution threat for the future lies in the tremendous growth of the electric power industry. Of course, nuclear energy, which may provide more of our future energy needs, does not pollute the air. However, the rate of growth of nuclear power is hard to forecast (for reasons

Table 19.2
Estimated Emissions of Air Pollutants by Weight, Nationwide, 1971

Source	Carbon monoxide	Particulates	Sulphur oxides	Hydrocarbons	Nitrogen oxides
	(millions of tons per year)				
Transportation	77.5	1.0	1.0	14.7	11.2
Fuel combustion in stationary sources	1.0	6.5	26.3	0.3	10.2
Industrial processes	11.4	13.6	5.1	5.6	0.2
Solid waste disposal	3.8	0.7	0.1	1.0	0.2
Miscellaneous	6.5	5.2	0.1	5.0	0.2
Total	100.2	27.0	32.6	26.6	22.0

Source: Council on Environmental Quality, *Fourth Annual Report,* August 1973.

Figure 19.1
Weight of Emission of Air Pollutants, United States, 1940–70
Among the most serious air pollutants are carbon monoxide, sulphur oxides, nitrogen oxides, particulates, and hydrocarbons. In the past 30 years, the amount of these pollutants emitted in the United States has increased.

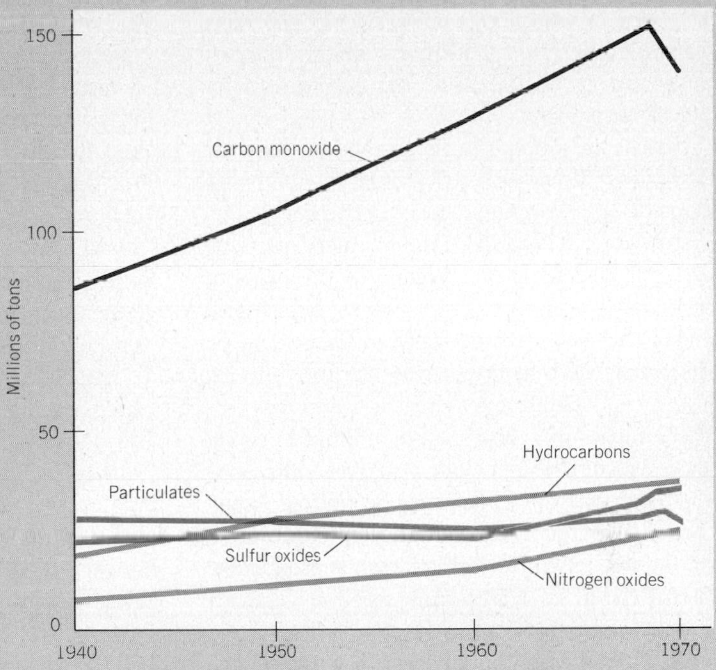

discussed below), and in any event nuclear energy is not free of environmental difficulties. Nuclear reactors can cause thermal pollution of rivers and streams, and radiation may be a threat despite various preventive measures.

At present, the automobile is the principal source of air pollution in the United States. According to some estimates, human activities pump into the air over 200 million tons of waste each year, and automobiles can be credited with the dubious honor of contributing about 40 percent of this figure. Spurred on by the public interest in pollution control, some technologists have been hard at work on substitutes for the internal combustion engine. Attempts have been—and are being—made to devise economical and convenient electric and steam-driven automobiles. To date, however, these efforts have not succeeded. Thus it seems likely that in the near future at least, we shall have to rely heavily on modifications of the internal combustion engine and its fuel to reduce air pollution.[2] (More use of nonpolluting transport like bicycles and feet would help too.)

Unfortunately, the air and water are not the only parts of man's environment that are being polluted. Each year, we produce an enormous amount of solid waste. Junk heaps testify to the quantity of superannuated cars left, like mechanical corpses, to mar the scenery. Each year industry produces literally mountains of waste and refuse. And picnic lovers and beer drinkers the world over are engaged in what sometimes seems a conspiracy to distribute cans, bottles, and other trash in every conceivable quarter. (Indeed, they sometimes even deposit some in a trash basket!) And it must be noted that the

[2] Ibid. Also, see L. Lave and E. Seskin, "Air Pollution and Human Health," *Science*, August 21, 1970.

problem is not merely an aesthetic one. Our nation's cities are buckling under the strain of disposing of all the solid waste generated by the affluent society.

There are other problems too. In many of our cities, the noise level is annoying and perhaps dangerous. Then there is thermal pollution. Water is used to cool machinery, particularly in electric power plants; in the process, the water is heated and, when discharged, raises the water temperature in the stream or lake into which it flows. Thus the solubility of certain substances may rise, the water may become more toxic and unable to hold as much oxygen, and the behavior patterns and reproductive capacities of fish may be altered. As for fish, so perhaps for man. There are questions about the extent to which man's production and disposal of wastes may render the earth uninhabitable for various kinds of life. To be sure, many of the most pessimistic and shocking predictions are probably little more than science fiction, but the questions are too important to be dismissed without careful consideration.

The Important Role of External Diseconomies

The reason why our economic system has tolerated pollution of the environment lies largely in the concept of external diseconomies, which we mentioned in Chapter 5. An ***external diseconomy*** occurs when one person's (or firm's) use of a resource damages other people who cannot obtain proper compensation. When this occurs, a market economy is unlikely to function properly. The price system is based on the supposition that the full cost of using each resource is borne by the person or firm that uses it. If this is not the case and if the user bears only part of the full costs, then the resource is not likely to be directed by the price system into the socially optimal use.

To understand why, we might begin by reviewing briefly how resources are allocated in a market economy. As we saw in Chapter 4, resources are used in their socially most valuable way because they are allocated to the people and firms who find it worthwhile to bid most for them, assuming that prices reflect true social costs. For example, under these circumstances, a paper mill that maximizes its profits will produce the socially desirable output of paper and use the socially desirable amounts of timber, labor, capital, and other resources.

Suppose, however, that because of the presence of external diseconomies people and firms do not pay the true social costs for resources. For example, suppose that some firms or people can use water and air for nothing, but that other firms or people incur costs as a consequence of this prior use. In this case, the ***private costs*** of using air and water differ from the ***social costs:*** *the price paid by the user of water and air is less than the true cost to society.* In a case like this, users of water and air are guided in their decisions by the private cost of water and air—by the prices they pay. Since they pay less than the true social costs, water and air are artificially cheap to them, so that they will use too much of these resources, from society's point of view.

Note that the divergence between private and social cost occurs if and only if the use of water or air by one firm or person imposes costs on other firms or persons. Thus, if a paper mill uses water and then treats it to restore its quality, there is no divergence between private and social cost. But when the same mill dumps wastes into streams and rivers (the cheap way to get rid of its by-products), the towns downstream that use the water must incur costs to restore its quality. The same is true of air pollution. An electric power plant uses the atmosphere as a cheap and convenient place to dispose of wastes, but people living and working nearby may incur costs as a result, since the incidence of respiratory and other diseases may increase.

We said above that pollution-causing activities that result in external diseconomics represent a malfunctioning of the market system. At this point, the nature of this malfunctioning should be clear. *Firms and people dump too much waste material into the water and the atmosphere. The price system does not provide the proper signals because the polluters are induced to use our streams and atmosphere in this socially undesirable way by the artificially low price of disposing of wastes in this manner. Moreover, because the polluters do not pay the true cost of waste disposal, their products are artificially cheap, so that too much is produced of them.*

Consider two examples. Electric power companies do not pay the full cost of disposing of wastes in the atmosphere. They charge an artificially low price, and the public is induced to use more electric power than is socially desirable. Similarly, since the owners of automobiles do not pay the full cost of disposing of exhaust and other wastes in the atmosphere, they pay an artificially low price for operating an automobile, and the public is induced to own and use more automobiles than is socially desirable.[3]

The Polluted Hudson and the Tin Can: Two Case Studies[4]

Richmond is a village of about 2,000 people about 10 miles south of Albany. It is situated at a very badly polluted place on the Hudson River. The water is brown with the human and industrial wastes of Albany, Troy, and other cities upstream, as well as with the wastes dumped into the river locally. In the area immediately around Richmond, two of the principal polluters are the village of Richmond itself and the Smith Paper Company. The village's sewer mains dump their contents into the river, and the Smith Paper Company discharges its untreated wastes into a creek that flows into the river.

The people of Richmond have dragged their heels about building a sewage treatment system because they have felt that unless towns upstream took action, their own efforts would be fruitless. After some prodding by New York State, a referendum was held in 1968 to vote on a sewer district, but it was turned down by the voters. Needless to say, part of the reason was that the people of the village would have to pay about $85 per family per year for the water treatment system. Despite the state's nudging, the officials of Richmond admit that it will be a long time before the problem is taken care of.

The Smith Paper Company has also been slow to do anything about water pollution. State health officials ordered it to clean up its effluent by July 1970, but the company did not formulate a preliminary plan for a treatment system until April 1970. According to many reports, the Company was not in healthy financial condition, and Smith's treatment costs, according to some of its engineers, could run as high as $300,000–or about 10 percent of the value of its plant. Obviously, one reason why this plant remains in business is that it does not pay the full social costs of waste disposal. Obviously, too, the price of its paper is artificially low for this reason. This is no criticism of the company. In a free enterprise economy, firms are expected to be motivated by profit. The problem is that, because of external diseconomies, the market system does not insure that the private costs of waste disposal equal the social costs. The result is a polluted river.

Richmond is an example of one type of pollution. To understand how external diseconomies can result in another type of pollution, consider the cans and bottles that are so conspicuous a part of our nation's litter problem.

[3] L. Ruff, "The Economic Common Sense of Pollution," *The Public Interest*, Spring 1970; R. Solow, "The Economist's Approach to Pollution and Its Control," *Science*, August 6, 1971; and M. Goldman, *Controlling Pollution*, Englewood Cliffs, N.J.: Prentice-Hall, 1967.

[4] The names Richmond and Smith are fictitious, but otherwise the case study given in the first part of this section, taken from an article in the *New York Times*, is factual.

Years ago, beer, soft drinks, and other such liquids came in relatively expensive bottles on which there was a deposit. Typically, when you purchased a bottle of beverage, you had to deposit $.05 for the bottle. If you didn't bring back the bottle, you didn't get the $.05 back. If someone else found—or stole—your bottle, he could take it back and get the money. Since $.05 was a significant amount in those days, there were few bottles lying around as unsightly litter. Kids—and more than a few adults—were only too glad to pick them up and take them back to the store to get the deposit. Thus, in those days, the system worked in such a way that the purchaser of the beverage paid for the cost of bringing the bottle back to the store. Either he took it back himself (and got his deposit back), or in effect he paid someone else $.05 to do it for him.

But this situation changed abruptly about 40 years ago, when producers of beer and soft drinks introduced a packaging innovation: the can. Unlike the old-fashioned bottle, there was no deposit on the can. Indeed, one of the advantages to consumers was that they didn't have to bother to take the cans back; they could simply throw them away. Consumers preferred the can for its convenience, and bottle manufacturers were forced to develop a cheaper no-deposit bottle to compete with cans. The result has been trash and litter, because there is no longer the same incentive to pick up cans and bottles or to return them to stores or manufacturers. Moreover, since bottles are no longer used over and over, there are more bottles and cans to dispose of.

It is important to note that, once the cans and no-deposit bottles were introduced, the consumer of beverages no longer had to pay for the cost of disposing of the cans or bottles. Basically, this was the reason for the litter problem. In other words, there was now an external diseconomy, since purchasers and consumers of beverages imposed costs on other people, who had to bear the expense of disposing of the litter. Of course, this was not always the case, since many people were public-spirited enough to dispose of their own cans and bottles, even without financial incentive. But our highways and parks testify to the fact that many people are not so public-spirited; as a result, certain states (like Oregon and Vermont) have passed laws requiring the sale of deposit bottles.

Economic Growth and Environmental Pollution

According to many authorities, economic growth—defined as increases in total economic output per capita—has been associated with increases in the level of environmental pollution. This is not very surprising, since practically all the things that are produced must eventually be thrown away in one form or another. Thus, as output per capita goes up, the level of pollution is likely to go up as well. For example, as we grow more affluent and increase the number of automobiles per capita, we also increase the amount of such air pollutants as nitrogen oxide and tetraethyl lead, both of which are emitted by automobiles. We also increase the number of automobiles that eventually must be scrapped.

But it is important to recognize that pollution is not tied inextricably to national output. Although increases in national output in the past have been associated with increases in pollution, there is no reason why this correlation must continue unchanged in the future. Clearly, we can produce things that are heavy polluters of the environment—like electric power and automobiles—or we can produce things that do not pollute the environment nearly so much—like pianos and bicycles.

In recent years, some people have suggested that we curtail our economic growth in order to reduce pollution: ***Zero Economic Growth*** is their goal. Very few economists seem to favor such a policy. Opponents of Zero Economic Growth point out that more productive capacity would help produce the equipment required to reduce pollution. As we shall see, this equipment will not be cheap. Moreover, with proper public policies, we should be able to increase output without increasing pollution, if this is what our people want. In addition, as pointed out by Walter Heller of the University of Minnesota,

> Short of a believable threat of extinction, it is hard to believe that the public would accept the tight controls, lowered material living standards, and large income transfers required to create and manage a [no-growth] state. Whether the necessary shifts could be accomplished without vast unemployment and economic dislocation is another question. It may be that the shift to a no-growth state would throw the fragile ecology of our economic system so out of kilter as to threaten its breakdown. Like it or not, economic growth seems destined to continue.[5]

Some people have also argued that technological change is the real villain responsible for pollution, and that the rate of technological change should be slowed. Certainly, technological change has made people more interdependent, and brought about more and stronger external diseconomies. Technological change also results in ecological changes, some of which are harmful. For example, detergents have contained phosphate, which induced water pollution by causing heavy overgrowths of algae.

But technological change is also a potential hero in the fight against pollution, because the creation of new technology is an important way to reduce the harmful side effects of existing techniques—assuming, of course, that we decide to use our scientists and engineers to this end. Contrary to some people's views, pollution is not the product of some mindless march of technology, but of human action and inaction. There is no sense in blaming technology, when pollution is due basically to economic, social, and political choices and institutions.

Finally, it is frequently suggested that, as our population increases, we must expect more pollution. Many who advocate a policy of ***Zero Population Growth*** advance the argument that it would help reduce the level of pollution. The available evidence indicates some relationship between a nation's population and its pollution levels. But there are important differences in the amount of pollution generated by people in various countries. The average American is responsible for much more pollution than the average citizen of most other countries, because the average American is a much bigger user of electric power, detergents, pesticides, and other such products. It has been estimated that the United States, with less than $\frac{1}{10}$ of the world's population, produces about $\frac{1}{3}$ of the wastes discharged into the air and water. Clearly, much more than economics is involved in the discussion of the optimal level of poulation. Although it is only one of a number of important factors, a nation's population does affect the level of pollution; but as we shall see in subsequent sections, pollution can be reduced considerably even if our population continues to grow.[6]

Public Policy toward Pollution

Pollution is caused by defects in our institutions, not by malicious intent, greed, or corruption. In cases where waste disposal causes significant external diseconomies, economists generally agree that government intervention may be justifiable. But how can the govern

[5] W. Heller, "Economic Growth and Ecology—An Economist's View," *Monthly Labor Review,* November 1971.

[6] It must also be noted that pollution is not confined to capitalist countries; the Soviet Union and other Communist countries are afflicted by serious pollution problems. Nor is pollution anything new: for example, the ancient Romans complained of water pollution.

ment intervene? Perhaps the simplest way is ***direct regulation,*** through the issuance of certain enforceable rules for waste disposal. For example, the government can prohibit the burning of trash in furnaces or incinerators, or the dumping of certain materials in the ocean; and make any person or firm that violates these restrictions subject to a fine, or perhaps even imprisonment. Also, the government can ban the use of chemicals like DDT, or require that all automobiles meet certain regulations for the emission of air pollutants. Further, the government can establish quality standards for air and water.

The government can also intervene by establishing effluent fees. An ***effluent fee*** is a fee a polluter must pay to the government for discharging waste. In other words, a price is imposed on the disposal of wastes into the environment; and the more a firm or individual pollutes, the more he must pay. The idea behind the imposition of effluent fees is that they can bring the private cost of waste disposal closer to the true social costs. Faced with a closer approximation to the true social costs of his activities, the polluter will reduce the extent to which he pollutes the environment. Needless to say, many practical difficulties are involved in carrying out this seemingly simple scheme, but many economists believe that this is the best way to deal with the pollution problem.[7]

Still another way for the government to intervene is to establish ***tax credits*** for firms that introduce pollution-control equipment. There are, of course, many types of equipment that a plant can introduce to cut down on pollution—for example, "scrubbers" for catching poisonous gases, and electrostatic precipitators for decreasing dust and smoke. But such pollution-control equipment costs money, and firms are naturally reluctant to spend money on purposes where the private rate of return is so low. To reduce the burden, the government can allow firms to reduce their tax bill by a certain percentage of the amount they spend on pollution-control equipment. Tax incentives of this sort have been discussed widely in recent years, and some have been adopted.

Direct Regulation

Let's look more closely at the advantages and disadvantages of each of these major means by which the government can intervene to remedy the nation's pollution problems. At present we rely mostly on direct regulation of waste disposal (and the quality of the environment); and despite the many problems involved, it has undoubtedly done much good. As Allen Kneese, one of the country's top experts in this area, says about water pollution, "The control of water discharges through administrative orders regulating individual waste disposers has been a useful device and cannot be abandoned until we have a better substitute."[8]

However, economists agree that direct regulation suffers from some serious disadvantages. First, such regulations have generally taken the form of general, across-the-board rules. For example, if two factories located on the same river dump the same amount of waste material into the river, such regulations would probably call for each factory to reduce its waste disposal by the same amount. Unfortunately, although this may appear quite sensible, it may in fact be very inefficient. Suppose, for example, that it is much less costly for one factory to reduce its waste disposal than for the other. Clearly, in such a case, it would be more efficient to ask the factory that could reduce its wastes more cheaply to cut down more on its waste disposal than the other factory. For reasons of this sort, reductions in pollution are

[7] Another possibility is for the government to issue a certificate or license to pollute. The government might issue a limited number of certificates, to be auctioned off to the highest bidders. Although it has theoretical possibilities, this technique is not being used to any appreciable extent at present.

[8] A. Kneese, "Public Policy toward Water Pollution," in E. Mansfield, *Microeconomics: Selected Readings,* 2d ed., New York: Norton, 1975, p. 467.

likely to be accomplished at more than minimum cost, if they are accomplished by direct regulation.

Second, to formulate such regulations in a reasonably sensible way, the responsible government agencies must have access to much more information than they are likely to obtain or assimilate. Unless the government agencies have a detailed and up-to-date familiarity with the technology of hundreds of industries, they are unlikely to make sound rules. Moreover, unless the regulatory agencies have a very wide jurisdiction, their regulations will be evaded by the movement of plants and individuals from localities where regulations are stiff to localities where they are loose. In addition, the regulatory agencies must view the pollution problem as a whole, since piecemeal regulation may simply lead polluters to substitute one form of pollution for another. For example, New York and Philadelphia have attempted to reduce water pollution by more intensive sewage treatment. However, one result has been the production of a lot of biologically active sludge that is being dumped into the ocean—and perhaps causing problems there.[9]

Effluent Fees

The use of effluent fees is the approach most economists seem to prefer, for the following reasons: First, it obviously is socially desirable to use the cheapest way to achieve any given reduction in pollution. A system of effluent fees is more likely to accomplish this objective than direct regulation, because the regulatory agency cannot have all the relevant information (as we noted above), whereas polluters, reacting in their own interest to effluent fees, will tend to use the cheapest means to achieve a given reduction in pollution.

To see why this is the case, consider a particular polluter. Faced with an effluent fee—that is, a price it must pay for each unit of waste it discharges—the polluter will find it profitable to reduce its discharge of waste so long as the cost of doing so is less than the effluent fees it saves. Thus, if this firm can reduce its discharge of wastes relatively cheaply, it will be induced to make such a reduction by the prospect of increased profits. On the other hand, if it cannot reduce its discharge of wastes at all cheaply, it will not make such a reduction, since the costs will exceed the saving in effluent fees. Thus a system of effluent fees induces firms that can reduce waste disposal more cheaply to cut down more on their waste disposal than firms where such a reduction is more expensive. This means that a given reduction of pollution will occur at a relatively low cost.

Economists also favor effluent fees because this approach requires far less information in the hands of the relevant government agencies than does direct regulation. After all, when effluent fees are used, all the government has to do is meter the amount of pollution a firm or household produces (which admittedly is sometimes not easy) and charge accordingly. It is left to the firms and households to figure out the most ingenious and effective ways to cut down on their pollution and save on effluent fees. This too is a spur to inventive activities aimed at developing more effective ways to reduce pollution. Also, economists favor the use of effluent fees because financial incentives are likely to be easier to administer than direct regulation. Witness the case of Richmond, which illustrates the gap between regulation and enforceable performance.

To illustrate how effluent fees can produce more efficient ways to reduce pollution, consider a recent proposal by the state of Washington for reducing emission of sulphur oxides. The proposed regulation would oblige copper smelters to control 90 percent of the sulphur content of ore entering smelters. There is considerable disagreement over the cost of the regulation. The state says it would

[9] Solow, "The Economist's Approach."

cost the smelters about $.02 per pound of copper to comply, whereas the smelters say it is technologically impossible to comply. Some people have suggested that one way to resolve this controversy might be to impose a fee equivalent to $.03 per pound of copper if the emission of sulphur oxide were not controlled. Then if the smelters could achieve 90 percent control for $.02 per pound, they would have every incentive to do so, thus increasing their profits. If they could not reach the goal, they would have an incentive to adopt other control measures or to develop new and less costly control devices.

While economists tend to favor the use of effluent fees, they are not always against direct regulation. Some ways of disposing of certain types of waste are so dangerous that the only sensible thing to do is to ban them. For example, a ban on the disposal of mercury or arsenic in places where human beings are likely to consume them—and die—seems reasonable enough. In effect, the social cost of such pollution is so high that a very high penalty—imprisonment—is put on it. In addition, of course, economists favor direct regulation when it simply is not feasible to impose effluent fees—for example, in cases where it would be prohibitively expensive to meter the amount of pollutants emitted by various firms or households.

The Ruhr: A Case Study[10]

Let's consider a well-known case of effluent fees in use—the Ruhr valley in West Germany. The Ruhr is one of the world's most industrialized areas. It includes about ⅓ of West Germany's industrialized capacity, and about 70 to 90 percent of West Germany's coal, coke, and iron and steel outputs. It contains about 10 million people and about 4,300 square miles. Water supplies in the Ruhr are quite limited: 5 small rivers supply the area. The amazing amount of waste materials these rivers carry is indicated by the fact that the average annual natural low flow is less than the volume of effluent discharged into the rivers. Yet the local water authorities have succeeded in making this small amount of water serve the needs of the firms and households of this tremendous industrial area, and at the same time the streams have been used for recreation. Moreover, all this has been achieved at a remarkably low cost. The success of water management in the Ruhr seems to be due in considerable part to institutional arrangements that allowed the German water managers to plan and operate a relatively efficient regional system. Collective water quality improvement measures are used. Water quality is controlled by waste treatment in over 100 plants, regulation of river flow by reservoir, and a number of oxidation lakes in the Ruhr itself.

Effluent fees are an integral part of the institutional arrangements governing water quality. The amount a firm has to pay depends upon how much waste—and what kind—it pumps into the rivers. A formula has been devised to indicate how much a polluter must pay to dispose of a particular type of waste. In simple terms, the formula bases the charge on the amount of clean water needed to dilute the effluent in order to avoid harm to fish. Using this formula, the local authorities can determine, after testing the effluent of any firm, the amount the firm should pay. Specifically, the amount depends on the amount of suspended materials that will settle out of the effluent, the amount of oxygen consumed by bacteria in a sample of effluent, the results of a potassium permanganate test, and the results of a fish toxicity test. You need not understand the nature or specific purposes of these measurements and tests. The important thing is that you understand their general aim—which is to measure roughly the amount of pollution caused by various kinds of wastes. Having made these

[10] This section is based on A. Kneese and B. Bower, *Managing Water Quality: Economics, Technology, Institutions,* Washington, D.C.: Resources for the Future, 1968, Chapter 12.

measurements and tests, the local authorities use their formula to determine how much a firm must pay in effluent fees.

Tax Credits for Pollution-Control Equipment

Many tax inducements to encourage firms and individuals to install pollution-control equipment have been proposed. A typical suggestion is that the government offer a tax credit equal to 20 percent of the cost of pollution-control equipment, and allow a firm to depreciate such equipment in only one to five years. In this way, the government would help defray some of the costs of the pollution-control equipment by allowing a firm that installed such equipment to pay less taxes than if no such tax inducements existed.

However, such schemes have a number of disadvantages. For one, subsidies to promote the purchase of particular types of pollution-control equipment may result in relatively inefficient and costly reductions in pollution. After all, other methods that don't involve special pollution-control equipment—such as substituting one type of fuel for another—may sometimes be a more efficient way to reduce pollution. Also, subsidies of this sort may not be very effective. Even if the subsidy reduces the cost to the firm of reducing pollution, it may still be cheaper for the firm to continue to pollute. In other words, subsidies of this sort make it a little less painful for polluters to reduce pollution; but unlike effluent fees, they offer no positive incentive.

Furthermore, it seems preferable on grounds of equity for the firms and individuals that do the polluting—or their customers—to pay to clean up the mess that results. Effluent fees work this way, but with tax credits for pollution-control equipment, the government picks up part of the tab by allowing the polluter to pay lower taxes. In other words, the general public, which is asked to shoulder the additional tax burden to make up for the polluters' lower taxes, pays part of the cost. But is this a fair allocation of the costs? Why should the general public be saddled with much of the bill?

Pollution-Control Programs in the United States

In recent years, there has been considerable growth in government programs designed to control pollution. To take but one example, federal expenditures to reduce water pollution increased in the period from the mid-1950s to 1970 from about $1 million to $300 million annually. To curb water pollution, the federal government has for years operated a system of grants-in-aid to state, municipal, or regional agencies to help construct treatment plants; and grants are made for research on new treatment methods. In addition, the 1970 Water Quality Improvement Act authorizes grants to demonstrate new methods and techniques and to establish programs to train people in water control management. (The federal government has also regulated the production and use of pesticides.) The states, as well as the federal government, have played an important role in water pollution control. They have set standards for allowable pollution levels, and many state governments have provided matching grants to help municipalities construct treatment plants.

In 1969, the Congress established a new agency—the Council on Environmental Quality—to oversee and plan the nation's pollution control programs. Modeled to some extent on the Council of Economic Advisers, the Council on Environmental Quality, which has three members, is supposed to gather information on considerations and trends in the quality of the environment, review and evaluate the federal government's programs in this area, develop appropriate national policies, and conduct needed surveys and research on environmental quality. The tasks assigned to the council are obviously important ones. The extent to which this relatively new agency can carry out these tasks is difficult to say. It will be some time before the council's effectiveness can be appraised at all fully.

In 1970, the federal government established another new agency, the Environmental Protection Agency (EPA). Working with state and local officials, this agency establishes standards for desirable air and water quality, and devises rules for attaining these goals. The 1970 Clean Air Amendments directed EPA to establish minimum ambient standards for air quality, and it set limits on the emission of carbon monoxide, hydrocarbons, and nitrous oxides from automobiles. But after a number of clashes between EPA and the auto makers, the EPA relaxed the deadlines when these limits were supposed to be met. The 1972 amendments to the Water Pollution Act authorized EPA to set effluent standards for both privately and publicly owned plants. A stated goal of the amendments was to eliminate the discharge of pollutants into water by 1985, but, for reasons discussed in the next section, this goal seems unrealistically stringent. In general, recent legislation has emphasized direct regulation, although there has been some study of the use of effluent fees. For example, the government has considered imposing a fee on the emission of sulphur oxide into the air.

Some people believe that public policy is moving too rapidly in this area; others believe that it is moving too slowly. It is not easy to determine how fast or how far we should go in attempting to reduce pollution. Those who will bear the costs of pollution-control projects—towns like Richmond, firms like the Smith Paper Company—have an understandable tendency to emphasize (and perhaps inflate) the costs and discount the benefits of such projects. Those who are particularly interested in enjoying nature and outdoor recreation—like the Sierra Club—are understandably inclined to emphasize (and perhaps inflate) the benefits and discount the costs of such projects. Politics inevitably plays a major role in the outcome of such cases. The citizens of the United States must indicate, through the ballot box as well as the market place, how much they are willing to pay to reduce pollution. We must also decide at what level of government the relevant rules are to be made. Since many pollution problems are local, it often seems sensible to determine the appropriate level of environmental quality locally. (However, there are obvious dangers in piecemeal regulation, as pointed out above.)

How Clean Should the Environment Be?

One of the most fundamental questions about pollution control is: How clean do we want the air, water, and other parts of our environment to be? At first glance, it may seem that we should restore and maintain a pristine pure environment, but this is not a very sensible goal, since the costs of achieving it would be enormous. The Environmental Protection Agency has estimated that it would cost about $60 billion to remove 85 to 90 percent of water pollutants from industrial and municipal sources by the mid-1980s. This is hardly a trivial amount, but it is far less than the cost of achieving zero discharge of pollutants, which would be about $320 billion—a truly staggering sum.

Fortunately, however, there is no reason to aim at so stringent a goal. It seems obvious that, as pollution increases, various costs to society increase as well. Some of these costs were described at the beginning of this chapter. For example, we pointed out that increases in air pollution result in increased deaths, and that increases in water pollution reduce the recreational value of rivers and streams. Suppose that we could get accurate data on the cost to society of various levels of pollution. Of course, it is extremely difficult to get such data, but if we

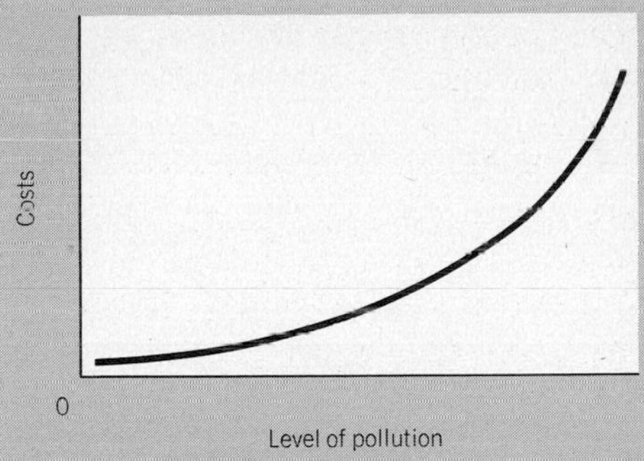

Figure 19.2
Costs to Society of Pollution
The costs to society of pollution increase with the level of pollution.

could, we could determine the relationship between the amount of these costs and the level of pollution. Clearly, it would look like the hypothetical curve in Figure 19.2: the greater the level of pollution, the higher these costs will be.

But these costs are not the only ones that must be considered. We must also take into account the costs of controlling pollution. In other words, we must look at the costs to society of maintaining a certain level of environmental quality. These costs are not trivial, as we saw at the beginning of this section. To maintain a very low level of pollution, it is necessary to invest heavily in pollution-control equipment and to make other economic sacrifices.[11] If we could get accurate data on the cost to society of controlling pollution, we could find the relationship between the amount of these costs and the level of pollution. Clearly, it would look like the hypothetical curve in Figure 19.3; the lower the level of pollution, the higher these costs will be.

At this point, it should be obvious why we should not try to achieve a zero level of pollution. *The sensible goal for our society is to minimize the sum of the costs of pollution and the costs of controlling pollution.* In other words, we should construct a graph, as shown in Figure 19.4, to indicate the relationship between the sum of these two types of costs and the level of pollution. Then we should choose the level of pollution at which the sum of these two types of costs is a minimum. Thus, in Figure 19.4, we should aim for a pollution level of A. There is no point in trying for a lower level; such a reduction would cost more than it would be worth. For example, the cost of achieving a zero pollution level would be much more than it would be worth. Only when the pollution level exceeds A is the extra cost to society of the additional pollution greater than the cost of

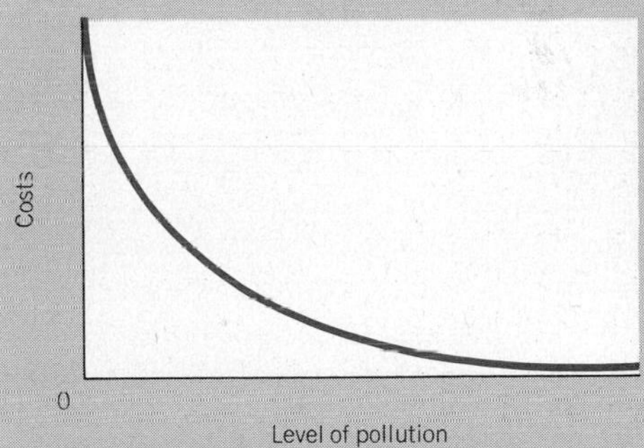

Figure 19.3
Costs to Society of Pollution Control
The more pollution is reduced, the higher are the costs to society of pollution control.

[11] It is important to recognize that the costs of pollution control extend far beyond the construction of more and better water treatment plants, or the more extensive control of gas emission, or other such steps. A serious pollution-control program can put firms out of business, put people out of work, and bring economic trouble to entire communities. Further, a pollution control system can result in a redistribution of income. For example, automobiles, electric power, and other goods and services involving considerable pollution are likely to increase in price relative to other goods and services involving little pollution. To the extent that polluting goods and services play a bigger role in the budgets of the poor than of the rich, pollution controls hurt the poor and help the rich.

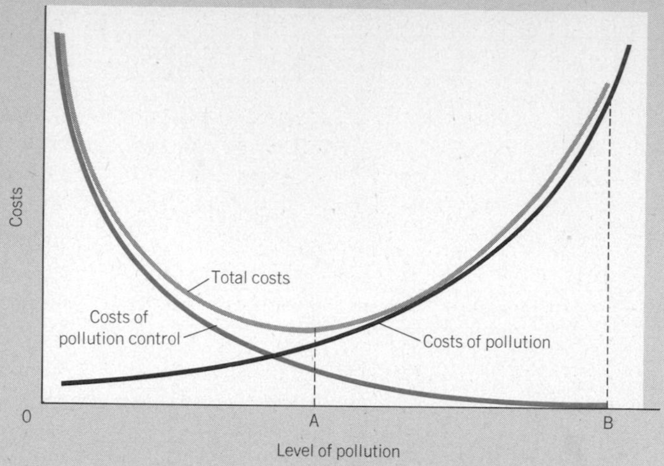

Figure 19.4
Determining Optimal Level of Pollution
The optimal level of pollution is at point *A*, since this is where the total costs are a minimum. Below point *A*, the cost to society of more pollution is less than the cost of preventing it. Above point *A*, the cost to society of more pollution is greater than the cost of preventing it.

preventing it. For example, the cost of allowing pollution to increase from *A* to *B* is much greater than the cost of prevention.

It is easy to draw hypothetical curves, but not so easy actually to measure these curves. Unfortunately, no one has a very clear idea of what the curves in Figure 19.4 really look like—although we can be sure that their general shapes are like those shown there. Thus no one really knows just how clean we should try to make the environment. Under these circumstances, expert opinion differs on the nature and extent of the programs that should be carried out. Moreover, as pointed out in the previous section, political considerations and pressures enter in. But one thing is for sure: we will continue to live with some pollution—and that, for the reason just given, will be the rational thing to do.

Our Energy Problems

OPEC and the Energy Crisis

During the early 1970s, even as it began to dawn on Americans that our environment was not indestructible, other urgent concerns arose about our natural resources. A nation that had taken its abundant energy supplies for granted suddenly was confronted by the prospect of shortages. In late 1973, there was the Arab oil embargo; then in 1974, there was a tremendous increase in the price of imported crude oil. In September 1973, imported crude oil cost American petroleum refiners about $4.50 per barrel; a year later, it cost them about $12.50 per barrel. This great and sudden increase in the price of imported crude oil had a very substantial effect on both the national and international economy. It helped to create inflation at home, and transferred tens of billions of dollars from the oil-consuming nations to the oil-producing nations.

Why did the price of imported crude oil increase so spectacularly? Because the Organization of Petroleum Exporting Countries (OPEC) upped the price of crude oil. OPEC is an international cartel—that is, an association of national petroleum producers that gets together and sets prices for oil.[12] In other words, OPEC operates like a monopoly, or close to it. Formed in the early 1960s, OPEC's charter says that "members shall study and formulate a

[12] Although many of the oil-exporting countries are in the Middle East, OPEC also includes countries in Africa, Latin America, and other continents.

system to ensure the stabilization of prices by, among other means, the regulation of production, with due regard to the interests of the producing and the consuming nations, and to the necessity of securing a steady income to the producing countries." In the 1960s, OPEC gained strength; in the 1970s, it lowered the boom on the oil-consuming nations.

The Arab oil embargo in late 1973 called attention to another aspect of our energy problems—the fact that the United States is coming to depend to an increasing extent on foreign sources of supply of crude oil. Gross imports of petroleum and petroleum products were about 36 percent of U.S. consumption in 1974, as compared to about 21 percent in 1965. Some people are disturbed that we may be approaching the point where our national security might be imperiled by a cutoff of foreign oil. They assert that a sudden interruption of oil imports would disrupt our economy and perhaps have military consequences as well. They are particularly fearful on this score, since many of the oil producers are Arab nations, hostile to Israel, a country we have supported.

The argument that we should try to avoid being dependent on foreign sources of oil is by no means new. Until 1973, this argument was used to justify the adoption of oil import quotas in the United States. These import quotas set a limit on the amount of foreign oil that could be imported. Many economists were opposed to these quotas because they increased the price of petroleum and petroleum products to consumers. (See Chapter 20.) Whether self-sufficiency with regard to energy is as important a goal as some policy makers seem to believe is hard to say. But recent events—the Arab oil embargo in particular—have made the potential threat more credible.

Energy and Economic Growth

U.S. policy makers have proclaimed the importance of guaranteeing energy supplies that will meet the nation's growing energy demands. According to some observers, such as the authors of the *Limits to Growth*[13] (discussed in the previous chapter), this will not be possible. Why? Because there is only a finite supply of energy resources like oil and coal. If economic growth continues, the demand for these resources will increase exponentially. Eventually, according to these observers, we shall run out of such resources, with the result that both output and production will decline. Moreover, although this outcome is not around the corner, it is not so far off either: in their view, it will occur in the next 100 years.

Many people regard this as one of the most serious and fundamental of our energy problems. However, few economists accept the assumptions underlying these arguments. In the first place, economists charge that the authors of *Limits to Growth* underestimate very substantially the amount of the world's energy resources. Between 1944 and 1969, total world economic reserves of crude oil increased by about 12 times, due to producers' efforts to find and develop new sources of supply. Since annual world consumption rose about 6 times, this meant that reserves more than kept pace with oil consumption. Yet the authors of *Limits to Growth* assumed that known economic reserves of energy resources would increase only 5 times between now and the year 2100.

More fundamentally, economists charge that the authors of *Limits to Growth* do not take proper account of the workings of the price system. When the supply of a resource becomes tight, its price rises, with the result that firms have a greater financial incentive to find more of it. Also, as the price of this resource rises, firms have an incentive to develop new technology that permits less of this resource to be used. These mechanisms have resulted in the elimination of many apparent

[13] Dennis and Donella Meadows et al, *The Limits to Growth,* New York: New American Library, 1972.

shortages in the past, and most economists tend to believe that they will play a major role in attacking our energy problems as well.[14]

Energy and the Environment

Still another aspect of our current energy problem is related to the environment. As stressed in earlier sections of this chapter, energy production is responsible for a considerable amount of environmental pollution. One senator has put it this way: "Airborne pollutants, concentration of nuclear wastes, oil spills, thermal pollution from power plants, extensive modification of the landscape by the increased construction of transmission lines, refineries, pumped storage facilities, and marine transmission facilities are illustrative causes of environmental problems related to energy production and use."[15] In recent years, it has become increasingly obvious that our environmental and energy problems are intertwined.

To illustrate, consider the case of the trans-Alaskan pipeline. Atlantic-Richfield and Exxon discovered the Prudhoe Bay oil field, the largest known field in North America, in 1967. The cheapest way to deliver this oil seemed to be to build a 900-mile pipeline from the North Slope to Valdez. However, there were objections from environmentalists, who argued that a trans-Canadian pipeline would result in less ecological damage. The Interior Department, after issuing the required environmental impact statement in March 1972, recommended that the trans-Alaskan pipeline be built. This ruling was appealed to the courts. Finally, in late 1973, Congress passed legislation to end the legal battle and to go ahead with the trans-Alaskan pipeline, which was supposed to get oil flowing from Alaska by 1978.

The choice here was between building the trans-Alaskan pipeline or a 2,500-mile pipeline across Canada into the Midwest (assuming Canada approved). What were the arguments for the trans-Alaskan pipeline? The most important seemed to be that construction costs would be about $3 billion less than for the trans-Canadian pipeline, and that the trans-Canadian pipeline would take one to three years longer to complete. Unquestionably, these were important arguments. However, as some environmentalists pointed out, oil prices tend to be much higher in the Midwest (where the trans-Canadian pipeline would deliver oil) than on the West Coast (where the trans-Alaskan pipeline would deliver oil). This fact might have helped to offset the higher delivery costs associated with the trans-Canadian route.

The arguments against the trans-Alaskan pipeline were environmental in considerable part. The trans-Alaskan pipeline will go through earthquake-prone regions, and the oil will have to be carried by tanker from Valdez to the West Coast. Thus the danger of an oil spill is much larger than if the trans-Canadian pipeline were built. Supporters of the trans-Alaskan pipeline argued that mandatory safety measures would reduce this danger to a very low level, whereas its critics challenged this claim. When the final decision had to be made, it was to build the trans-Alaskan pipeline. Only time will tell what the environmental consequences will be.

The Shortage of Natural Gas

Still another facet of our recent energy problems has been a reported shortage of one of our most important fuels, natural gas. As shown in Table 19.3, natural gas accounts for about 30 percent of total energy consumption in the United States. It is a very desirable fuel because it is relatively nonpolluting. According to many economists, this shortage is due to the regulatory policies of the Federal Power Commission. Only recently has the Federal Power Commission been required to set prices of gas

[14] This section, as well as others in this chapter, are based in part on R. Mancke, *The Failure of U.S. Energy Policy,* New York: Columbia University Press, 1974.
[15] Ibid., p. 43.

Table 19.3
Total Gross Consumption of Energy, and Percent from Each Major Source, United States, 1966–74

Year	Total energy consumption (quadrillion Btus)	Oil	Natural gas	Coal	Hydropower	Nuclear
				(percent of total)		
1966	56.4	43.2	30.9	22.1	3.7	0.1
1968	61.8	43.8	31.7	20.5	3.8	0.2
1970	67.1	44.0	32.8	18.9	4.0	0.3
1972	71.9	45.8	32.0	17.3	4.1	0.8
1973	74.7	46.4	30.6	17.9	3.9	1.2
1974	72.7	46.0	30.1	18.3	4.2	1.4

Source: Economic Report of the President, 1975.

producers in sales to pipelines. Before 1954, there was no such regulation. But in that year, the Supreme Court found that the Federal Power Commission should determine whether prices of gas sold in interstate commerce were "reasonable." Since then, there has been continual controversy over whether such regulation is really necessary or desirable, and if so, over what form it should take.

The Supreme Court ruled that the price of natural gas should be regulated because it felt that the price was not determined under competitive conditions. It believed that the producers of natural gas had appreciable monopoly power. However, this belief was not shared by many observers, including a number of distinguished academic economists. For example, Morris Adelman of M.I.T. testified that "it is my conclusion that the production of natural gas is a competitive industry." Adelman's view was based in part on the fact that the industry contains thousands of producers and that there is relatively little concentration of employment or sales. Nonetheless, other eminent economists argued that the industry did contain serious monopolistic elements, and the court seemed to agree.

In response to its new responsibility, the Federal Power Commission established "area prices" for each of 23 natural-gas-producing regions of the United States. Any producer of gas was allowed to agree to a contract for a price less than or equal to the "area price" for his region. If he wanted a higher price, he had to prove its "necessity and convenience" to the commission. According to many observers, the commission set these "area prices" in such a way as to keep the price of natural gas artificially low. In other words, the commission has been accused of "freezing" the price at less than its equilibrium level. At first glance, this may seem to be a boon to the nation and the consumer. After all, who can be against low prices? But the truth is that a price that is too low can be just as bad for society as one that is too high.

To see what is wrong with a price that is too low, we must hark back to our discussion of how the price system works. Recall that a product's price influences how much of it firms will supply. Clearly, if the price set by the commission is lower than would be the case in a competitive market, firms will supply less natural gas in the long run than they would under competition. That is, they will invest fewer resources in exploring for natural gas, with the result that there may be a "shortage" of natural gas, in the sense that the quantity supplied may be less than the quantity demanded. In other words, the situation would be like that in Figure 19.5, where OP_r is the price set by the commission. At this price, the quantity supplied is less than the quantity demanded. According to some observers, the remedy is to end the regulation of natural gas prices. More will be said on this score below.[16]

Public Policy toward Energy

Reduction of Energy Demand

What can we do to help solve our energy problems? One suggestion made by some economists is that we should reduce our demand for energy. Without question, there are many areas where energy could be saved with little inconvenience. One way that a reduction in energy demand could be accomplished is through the imposition of a tax on fuel. A number of economists have suggested such a measure. To see how it might work, consider Figure 19.6, which shows the demand and supply curves for fuel. Without the tax, the price of fuel would be OP_0, and the quantity consumed would be OQ_0.

Suppose that a tax of $.20 per gallon[17] of fuel were imposed. If so, the supply curve would shift upward by the amount of the tax. To see why, note that, if the pretax price had to be OP_0 per gallon to induce sellers to supply OQ_0 gallons of fuel, the posttax price would have to be $.20 higher to induce the same supply. Similarly, if the pretax price had to be OP_1 per gallon to induce sellers to supply OQ_1 gallons of fuel, the posttax price would have to be $.20 higher to induce the same supply. The reason why the sellers require $.20 more per gallon to supply the pretax amount is that they must pay the tax of $.20 per gallon to the gov-

[16] Note that in 1975 the Federal Power Commission abandoned the establishment of area rates, and that in the summer of 1976 it raised the nation-wide price of gas to $1.42 per 1,000 cubic feet, pending court review. Nonetheless, there is continuing pressure for deregulation. For a more complete discussion, see P. MacAvoy, *Crisis of the Regulatory Commission*, New York: Norton, 1970.

[17] We assume here that fuel is measured in gallons. For some fuels (like coal), this is not the case; but this simplification can easily be removed. It is used here only for convenience.

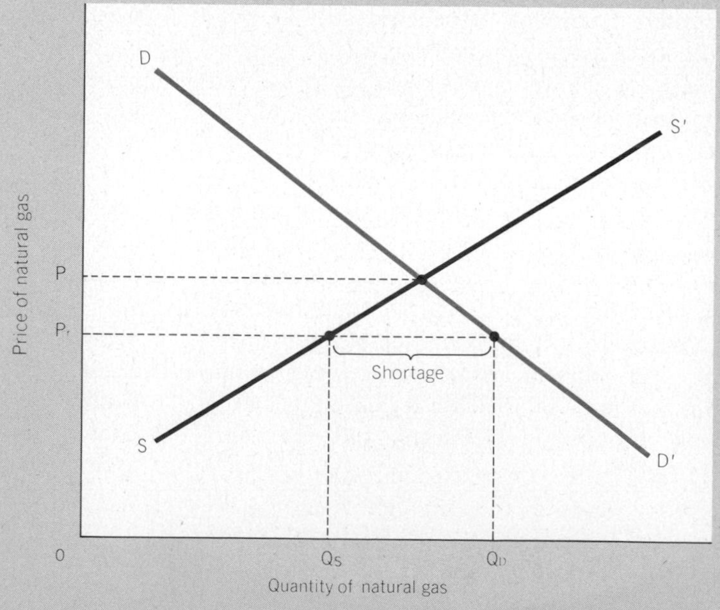

Figure 19.5
Shortage of Natural Gas
If the regulated price of natural gas is OP_r, the quantity supplied will be OQ_S and the quantity demanded will be OQ_D. Since the quantity demanded exceeds the quantity supplied, there is a shortage. This is because OP_r is below the equilibrium price, OP.

Figure 19.6
Effect of a Tax on Fuel
If a tax of $.20 per gallon is imposed on fuel, the supply curve for fuel shifts from SS' to S_1S_1'. Since the demand curve for fuel is DD', the quantity of fuel consumed is cut from OQ_0 to OQ_2.

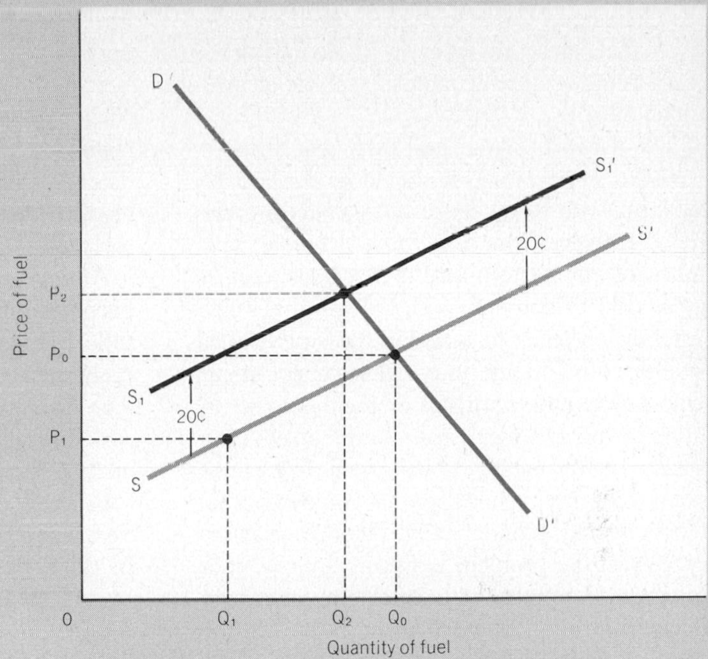

ernment. Thus they need the extra $.20 to wind up with the same amount as before.

Since the tax shifts the supply curve upward by $.20, the posttax supply curve is S_1S_1'—and the posttax equilibrium price and quantity are OP_2 and OQ_2, respectively. The effect of the tax on the quantity of fuel consumed is just what one would expect: it reduces fuel consumption. In Figure 19.6, the reduction is from OQ_0 to OQ_2. According to calculations by Dale Jorgensen of Harvard University and Edward Hudson of Data Resources, Inc., a tax equal to 3 percent of sales in 1985 and increasing gradually to about 15 percent in the year 2000 would result in no growth whatsoever in the quantity of energy consumed between 1985 and 2000. However, it is by no means clear that the United States should seek to maintain energy consumption at a constant level. For one thing, such a policy would reduce our rate of economic growth, although considerable growth would still occur.

Development of New Energy Technologies

Another way that we can avoid increased dependence on foreign oil is to develop new technologies that can produce energy economically from our domestic resources. One important resource of this kind is shale, which is found in Colorado, Wyoming, and Utah. For many years, shale has been regarded as a promising source of synthetic oil, but so far the costs of producing oil by this route have been too high to make it economical. Also, there are many unresolved environmental problems, since it is difficult to dispose of the spent shale. In Canada, a potentially important source of synthetic oil is the tar sands located in Alberta. Here too, the costs of producing oil in this way are relatively high—about $9 per barrel in 1975, according to some estimates. But some production is occurring. In both the cases of shale and tar sands, perhaps additional investments in research and development can solve the problems that presently prevent these resources from being a more economical source of synthetic oil.

The United States has vast quantities of coal. To some extent, it should be possible to substitute our relatively plentiful coal for other fuels. However, one important problem with much of our Eastern coal is that it contains a great deal of sulphur, with the result that its combustion leads to a rise in the emission of sulphur dioxide, an important air pollutant. One way to cope with this problem is to scrub most of this chemical from power plants' flue stacks. Unfortunately, however, there does not seem to be any technology that can do this effectively and economically. Another way to cope with the problem is to convert coal to a clean gas. A number of technologies have been developed to do this, but many are still in the pilot-plant stage. Here is another area where research and development have a promising role to play.

Still another promising source of energy is the sun. Techniques for harnessing solar energy have been known for a long time. For example, flat plate collectors can be used to heat water or air, which can then be used to heat buildings. But solar energy is still very costly, and there are problems in storing it for use on cloudy days and at night. According to some experts, solar energy is potentially of great economic significance, and too little has been invested to try to develop it and reduce its cost. This is an obvious area for further research and development.

Is Nuclear Power the Answer?

In 1938, Otto Hahn and Fritz Strassmann "discovered" nuclear fission in their studies of the substances obtained when neutrons impinge on the uranium nucleus. Their work, as well as that of Fermi, Bohr, Wheeler, and others, formed the basis for nuclear reactors. A nuclear reactor produces electricity by producing heat. Generally, a reactor will contain fissionable material, control rods, a moderator, shielding, and structural materials and mechanisms for removing the heat that is generated. The capital cost of a nuclear power reactor tends to be high because of the complexity of the plant.

Atomic energy came into being for military purposes during World War II, and for some time, private industry in the United States was prohibited from developing nuclear power. The Atomic Energy Commission Act of 1954 permitted private industry to own and operate nuclear reactors, but the ownership of nuclear fuels (and certain important elements of nuclear technology) resided with the government. In 1964, the AEC Act was amended to allow private ownership of nuclear fuels. The first commercial nuclear power plant in the United States was Duquesne Light Company's Shippingport plant in Pennsylvania, which began operations in 1957.

The federal government and private industry have invested billions of dollars in nuclear power, and by 1974, it accounted for almost 7 percent of the nation's electrical generating capacity. (See Figure 19.7.) Yet nuclear power remains controversial. For one thing, there has been considerable discussion of possible dangers to the environment and to public safety. As critics of nuclear power point out, reactors release some amount of irradiated wastes, the disposal of nuclear wastes can cause problems, and thermal pollution can pose an environmental threat. Further, there are possible dangers associated with the use of fissionable materials to make bombs, and with the sabotage of nuclear power plants by terrorists. Although the probability of these disastrous events unquestionably is low, some citizens regard it as too high to be acceptable. Others, however, feel that the risks have been greatly exaggerated.

In addition, there has been considerable con-

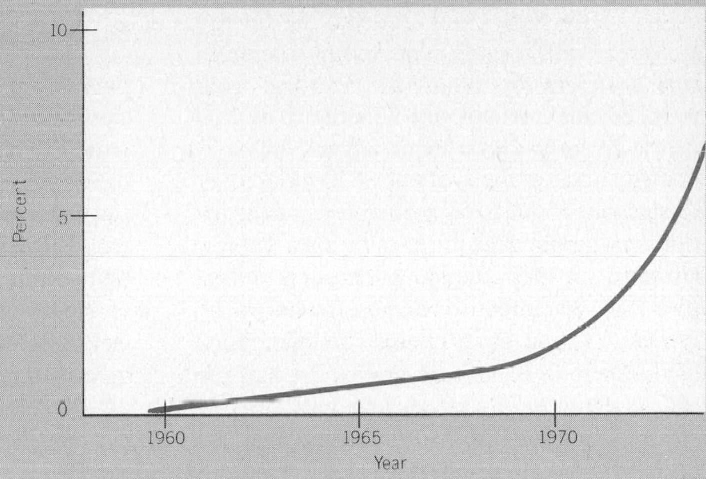

Figure 19.7
Nuclear Capacity as a Percent of All Installed Electrical Generating Capacity, United States, 1959–74
Government and private investment since 1959 in nuclear power has resulted in its increase to almost 7 percent of U.S. electrical generating capacity. *Source: Statistical Abstract of the United States and Federal Power Commission.*

troversy over how the production costs of nuclear power compare with those of conventional power. Many advocates of nuclear power have insisted that it is competitive with conventional power—or that it soon would be. Critics, on the other hand, have claimed that this is not true. For example, Philip Sporn estimated in 1970 that the cost of switchboard delivered nuclear power was 7.06 mills per kilowatt-hour as against 6.65 mills for coal-fired energy, with coal at $.25 per Btu. And in the mid-1970s, many electric utilities began canceling or postponing orders for nuclear plants, as they re-examined the economics of nuclear power.

Due both to the environmental and economic uncertainties surrounding nuclear power, it appears that it is a very incomplete answer to our energy problems. However, here too advances in technology may alter the picture considerably. The federal government has invested huge sums in the development of a Liquid Metal Fast Breeder Reactor, which, if successful, could produce more plutonium than it consumes. Also, the government has invested considerable sums in research concerning fusion. However, according to expert opinion, neither the breeder reactor nor the fusion reactor could affect the energy picture in an important way before the end of this century.[18]

Government Policies and Proposals

Faced with the energy problems described above, the government has taken or proposed a number of actions. First, it has tried in a variety of ways to encourage the conservation of fuel. For example, President Ford recommended in 1975 that the price of oil, some of which was under federal controls, be allowed to increase, thus reducing oil consumption and stimulating oil output. But this suggestion was viewed with considerable skepticism in Congress, since it would aggravate existing inflationary pressures. Faced with congressional opposition, the Ford administration did not push hard for removing federal controls in 1975, although action along this line may occur in the future.

Second, the government has increased its expenditures on energy research and development. In President Ford's revised request to

[18] Parts of this section are taken from my "The Diffusion of Eight Major Industrial Innovations in the United States," in *The State of Science and Research: Some New Indicators*, Washington, D.C., National Planning Association, 1975.

Congress, he asked authority for the Energy Research and Development Administration to sign contracts for almost $2 billion in fiscal 1976. Of this total amount, about $620 million would go for nuclear fission, about $140 million for nuclear fuels, about $620 million for fossil fuels, about $260 million for nuclear fusion, and about $80 million for solar energy. However, in 1976, the House defeated a bill to give loan guarantees for demonstration plants. President Carter has proposed a reorganization of the nation's energy programs, but it is too early to say what its effects may be.

Third, there have been proposals that the price of natural gas should be decontrolled. President Ford, the Federal Energy Administration, and the Federal Power Commission have favored such a step on the grounds that it would end the natural gas shortage and result in a less wasteful use of gas. On the other hand, congressional liberals and consumers groups have resisted, arguing that the market for natural gas is not competitive. As Michigan's Senator Philip Hart put it, "I can't agree that we can lift price regulation in the natural gas industry until we take steps to make this a competitive market."

Finally, some observers have proposed a variety of measures to weaken the power of the OPEC oil cartel. One proposal is that the major oil-consuming nations should get together and bargain collectively with OPEC in an effort to reduce oil prices. However, the prevailing view seems to be that this is not feasible (even if it would work, which is by no means clear) since several major oil-consuming nations do not want to join such a group. Another proposal is that the United States should try to drive a wedge among the various members of OPEC and get them to compete with one another. Although some ingenious schemes have been put forth to help accomplish this, there was little evidence (up to 1976, at least) that OPEC was so disunited that the price of oil was about to crumble.

Summary

One of the major social issues of the 1970s is environmental pollution. To a considerable extent, environmental pollution is an economic problem. Waste disposal and other pollution-causing activities result in external diseconomies. Specifically, the firms and individuals that pollute the water and air (and other facets of the environment) pay less than the true social costs of disposing of their wastes in this way. Part of the true social cost is borne by other firms and individuals who must pay to clean up the water or air, or who must live with the consequences. Because of the divergence of private from social costs, the market system does not result in an optimal allocation of resources. Firms and individuals create too much waste and dispose of it in excessively harmful ways. Because the polluters do not pay the full cost of waste disposal, their products are artificially cheap, with the result that too much is produced of them.

The government can intervene in several ways to help remedy the breakdown of the market system in this area. One way is to issue regulations for waste disposal and other activities influencing the environment. Another is to establish effluent fees, charges a polluter must pay to the government for discharging wastes. In recent years, there has been considerable growth in government programs designed to control pollution. It is extremely difficult to determine how clean the environment should be. Of course, the sensible goal for society is to permit the level of pollution that minimizes the sum of the costs of pollution and the costs of controlling pollution; but no one has a very clear idea of what these costs are, and to a large extent the choices must be made through the political process.

Another major issue of the 1970s has been energy. There are several aspects of this issue. First, the Arab oil embargo in late 1973 and OPEC's huge price increase in early 1974 called attention to the growing dependence of the United States on foreign sources of crude oil. Second, according to some observers (but few economists), we will "run out" of energy resources unless we cut back on energy consumption. Third, energy production is responsible for a considerable amount of environmental pollution. Fourth, according to some economists and public officials, the regulatory policies of the Federal Power Commission have resulted in a shortage of natural gas.

A variety of policy measures have been carried out or proposed to help deal with our energy problems. One proposal is that we enact a tax on fuel to reduce energy demand. Another approach is to develop new energy technologies that can produce energy economically from our domestic energy resources. The Energy Research and Development Administration has begun work along this line. Still another proposal is that the price of natural gas be decontrolled. Finally, a variety of measures has been proposed to try to weaken the power of the OPEC oil cartel.

CONCEPTS FOR REVIEW

External diseconomies
Private costs
Social costs
Water pollution
Primary treatment
Secondary treament
Air pollution
Thermal pollution
Noise pollution
Effluent fees

QUESTIONS FOR DISCUSSION AND REVIEW

1. Suppose that the paper industry emits wastes into rivers and streams, and that municipalities or firms downstream must treat the water to make it usable. Do the paper industry's private costs equal the social costs of producing paper? Why or why not?

2. Suppose that each ton of paper produced results in pollution that costs municipalities and firms downstream $1.00, and that a law is passed that requires the paper industry to reimburse the municipalities and firms downstream for these costs. Prior to this law, the supply curve for paper was:

Price of paper (dollars per ton)	Quantity supplied (million tons)
1.00	10.0
2.00	15.0
2.50	17.5
3.00	20.0
4.00	25.0

After the law takes effect, what will be the quantity supplied at each price?

3. If the demand curve for paper is as shown below, what will be the equilibrium output of paper before and after the paper industry has to reimburse the municipalities and firms downstream (as indicated in Question 2)?

Price of paper (dollars per ton)	Quantity demanded (million tons)
1.00	30.0
2.00	25.0
3.00	20.0
3.50	17.5
4.00	15.0

4. In Question 3, which output—the one prevailing before the industry has to reimburse others, or the one prevailing afterward—is socially more desirable? Why?

5. Suppose that the social cost (in billions of dollars) due to pollution equals $5P$, where P is the level of pollution, and that the cost (in billions of dollars) of pollution control equals $10 - 2P$. What is the optimal level of pollution?

6. "A tax on fuel will reduce the quantity consumed by a greater amount if the quantity of fuel demanded is relatively insensitive to its price than if it is relatively sensitive to it." Comment and evaluate.

7. "The apparent shortage of natural gas really has been due to the fact that natural gas producers, expecting higher prices in the future, have been holding supplies off the market." Comment and evaluate.

8. "The only dependable way to cut down on pollution is to ban certain kinds of polluting activities." Do you agree? Why or why not?

9. The *1971 Annual Report of the Council of Economic Advisers* states that "new rules for use of the environment are bound to affect competitive relationships within and among industries, localities, and nations." Give examples of these effects, and ways that society can make the transition easier.

10. Smoke is a classic case of an external diseconomy. (It was cited by Alfred Marshall and others.) Describe what actions can and should be taken to eliminate socially undesirable effects of smoke.

PART SIX

International Economics

20 International Trade

It takes the average human being little time to realize that he is not an island unto himself and that he benefits from living with, working with, and trading with other people. Exactly the same is true of nations. They too must interact with one another, and they too benefit from trade with one another. No nation can be an island unto itself—not even the United States. To understand how the world economy functions, you must grasp the basic economic principles of international trade.

This chapter discusses many of the fundamental questions about international trade. What is the nature of American foreign trade? What are the effects of international trade? What determines the sorts of goods a nation will import or export? What are the advantages of free trade and the arguments against it? What are the social costs of tariffs and quotas, and what has been their history in the United States? What are some of the major issues regarding protectionism in the United States today? Some of these questions have occupied the attention of economists for hundreds of years; some are as current as today's newspaper.

America's Foreign Trade

America's foreign trade, although small relative to our national product, plays a very important role in our economic life. Many of our industries depend on other countries for markets or for raw materials (like coffee, tea, or tin). Our ***exports***—the things we sell to other countries—amount to about 5 to 10 percent of our gross national product, which seems small relative to other countries like Germany, France, Italy, and the United Kingdom, where exports are about 15 to 20 percent of gross national product. But this is because our domestic market is so large. In absolute terms, and relative to those of other countries, our exports seem very large indeed. In recent years, they have represented about 15 percent of total world trade. Without question, our way of life would have to change considerably if we could not trade with other countries.

When we were a young country, we exported raw materials primarily. For example, during the 1850s about 70 percent of our exports were raw materials and foodstuffs. But the composition of our exports has changed with time. More are now finished manufactured goods and less are raw materials. In the 1960s, about 60 percent of our exports were finished manufactured goods, and only about 20 percent were raw materials and foodstuffs. Table 20.1 shows the importance of machinery and industrial supplies in our merchandise exports. Table 20.2 indicates to whom we sell: Western Europe and Canada take almost ½ of our exports, and Latin America takes about 15 percent.

What sorts of goods do we buy from abroad? About 10 percent of our ***imports*** are agricultural commodities like coffee, sugar, bananas, and cocoa. Almost 30 percent are petroleum and its products. But a considerable proportion is neither raw materials nor foodstuffs. Over ⅓ of our imports, as shown in Table 20.3, are manufactured goods like bicycles from England or color TVs from Japan. Just as we sell more to Canada and Western Europe than any other area, so we buy more from these countries too (see Table 20.4). But the pattern varies, of course, from product to product. For example, Canada is our leading foreign source for wood pulp and nonferrous metals, while Latin America is our leading source of imported coffee and sugar.

Finally, several general observations on the pattern of world trade are worth making. First, *much of world trade involves the industrialized richer countries.* This is no surprise, since these countries account for so large a share of the world's productivity and purchasing power. Second, *the industrialized, richer countries of the world tend to trade with one another, while the nonindustrialized, poorer countries tend to trade with the industrialized countries, not with one another.* The reasons for this are clear enough. The nonindustrialized countries supply the industrialized countries with raw materials and foodstuffs, and receive manufactures in return. The nonindustrialized countries have little reason to trade with one another since they cannot get from one another the manufactures they need. Third, *neighboring nations tend to trade with one another.* This too is predictable: lower transportation costs and greater familiarity tend to promote trade between neighbors.

Specialization and Trade

We have discussed the extent and nature of our trade with other countries, but not *why* we trade with other countries. Do we—and our trading partners—benefit from this trade? And if so, what determines the sorts of goods we

Table 20.1
U.S. Merchandise Exports, 1975

Product	Amount (millions of dollars)
Food, feed, and beverages	19,239
Industrial supplies and materials	30,776
Machinery	29,193
Automotive vehicles and parts	10,599
Consumer goods (excluding autos)	6,563
Aircraft	3,225
Other	7,589
Total	107,184

Source: Survey of Current Business, March 1976. These figures exclude military items.

Table 20.2
U.S. Exports, by Area, 1975

Country	Amount (millions of dollars)
Japan	9,570
Australia, New Zealand, and South Africa	3,509
Latin America	17,096
Canada	23,635
Eastern Europe	2,859
United Kingdom	4,807
European Economic Community	17,862
Other Western Europe	7,595
Other	20,251
Total	107,184

Source: See Table 20.1.

Table 20.3
U.S. Merchandise Imports, 1975

Product	Amount (millions of dollars)
Food, feed, and beverages	9,683
Petroleum and oil products	26,522
Other industrial supplies and materials	24,694
Capital goods	9,693
Automotive vehicles and parts	11,871
Consumer goods (excluding autos)	13,739
Other	1,937
Total	98,139

Source: See Table 20.1.

Table 20.4
U.S. Imports, by Area, 1975

Country	Amount (millions of dollars)
Japan	11,257
Australia, New Zealand, and South Africa	2,243
Latin America	16,177
Canada	21,877
Eastern Europe	737
United Kingdom	3,737
European Economic Community	12,151
Other Western Europe	4,883
Other	25,077
Total	98,139

Source: See Table 20.1.

should export and import? These are very important questions, among the most fundamental in economics. The answers are by no means new. They have been well understood for considerably more than a century, due to the work of such great economists as David Hume, David Ricardo, Adam Smith, and John Stuart Mill.

As a first step, it is useful to recognize that the benefits *nations* receive through trade are essentially the same as those *individuals* receive through trade. Consider the hypothetical case of John Barrister, a lawyer, with a wife and two children. The Barrister family, like practically all families, trades continually with other families and with business firms. Since Mr. Barrister is a lawyer, he trades his legal services for money which he and his wife use to buy the food, clothing, housing, and other goods and services his family wants. Why does the Barrister family do this? What advantages does it receive through trade? Why doesn't it attempt to be self-sufficient?

To see why the Barrister family is sensible indeed to opt for trade rather than self-sufficiency, let's compare the current situation—where Mr. Barrister specializes in the production of legal services and trades the money he receives for other goods and services—with the situation if the Barrister family attempted to be self-sufficient. In the latter case, the Barristers would have to provide their own transportation, telephone service, foodstuffs, clothing, and a host of other things. Mr. Barrister is a lawyer—a well-trained, valuable, productive member of the community. But if he were to try his hand at making automobiles—or even bicycles—he might be a total loss. Thus, if the Barrister family attempted to be self-sufficient, it might be unable to provide many of the goods it now enjoys.

Clearly, *trade permits specialization, and specialization increases output:* this is the advantage of trade, both for individuals and for nations. In our hypothetical case, it is obvious that, because he can trade with other families and with firms, Mr. Barrister can specialize in doing what he is good at—law. Consequently, he can be more productive than if he were forced to be a Jack-of-all-trades, as he would have to be if he could not trade with others. The same principle holds for nations. For example, because the United States can trade with other nations, it can specialize in the goods and services it produces particularly well. Then it can trade them for goods that other countries are especially good at producing. Thus both we and our trading partners benefit.

Some countries have more and better resources of certain types than others. Saudi Arabia has oil, Canada has timber, Japan has a skilled labor force, and so on. *International differences in resource endowments, and in the relative quantity of various types of human and nonhuman resources, are important bases for specialization.* For example, countries with lots of fertile soil, little capital, and much unskilled labor are likely to find it advantageous to produce agricultural goods, while countries with poor soil, much capital, and highly skilled labor will probably do better to produce capital-intensive, high-technology goods. We must recognize, however, that the bases for specialization do not remain fixed over time. Instead, as technology and the resource endowments of various countries change, the pattern of international specialization changes as well. For example, as we saw in the previous section, the United States specialized more in raw materials and foodstuffs about a century ago than it does now.

Absolute Advantage

To clarify the benefits of trade, consider the following example. Suppose that the United States can produce 2 electronic computers or 5,000 cases of wine with 1 unit of resources.

Suppose that France can produce 1 electronic computer or 10,000 cases of wine with 1 unit of resources. Given the production possibilities in each country, are there any advantages in trade between the countries? And if so, what commodity should each country export, and what commodity should each country import? Should France export wine and import computers, or should it import wine and export computers?

To answer these questions, assume that the United States is producing a certain amount of computers and a certain amount of wine—and that France is producing a certain amount of computers and a certain amount of wine. If the United States shifts 1 unit of its resources from producing wine to producing computers, it will increase its production of computers by 2 computers and reduce its production of wine by 5,000 cases of wine. If France shifts 1 unit of resources from the production of computers to the production of wine, it will increase its production of wine by 10,000 cases and reduce its production of computers by 1 computer.

Table 20.5 shows the *net* effect of this shift in the utilization of resources on *world* output of computers and of wine. World output of computers increases (by 1 computer) and world output of wine increases (by 5,000 cases) as a result of the redeployment of resources in each country. Thus *specialization increases world output.*

Table 20.5
Case of Absolute Advantage

	Increase or decrease in output of: Computers	Wine (thousands of cases)
Effect of U.S.'s shifting 1 unit of resources from wine to computers	+2	− 5
Effect of France's shifting 1 unit of resources from computers to wine	−1	+10
Net effect	+1	+ 5

Moreover, if world output of each commodity is increased by shifting 1 unit of American resources from wine to computers and shifting 1 unit of French resources from computers to wine, it follows that world output of each commodity will be increased further if each country shifts *more* of its resources in the same direction. This is because the amount of resources required to produce each good is assumed to be constant, regardless of how much is produced.

Thus, in this situation, one country—the United States—should specialize in producing computers, and the other country—France—should specialize in producing wine. This will maximize world output of both wine and computers, permitting a rise in both countries' standards of living. Of course, complete specialization of this sort is somewhat unrealistic, since countries often produce some of both commodities, but this simple example illustrates the basic principles involved.

Comparative Advantage

The case just described is a very special one, since one country (France) has an absolute advantage over another (the United States) in the production of one good (wine), whereas the second country (the United States) has an absolute advantage over the first (France) in the production of another good (computers). What do we mean by the term *absolute advantage?* Country *A* has an ***absolute advantage*** over Country *B* in the production of a good when Country *A* can produce a unit of the good with less resources than can Country *B*. Since the

United States can produce a computer with fewer units of resources than France, it has an absolute advantage over France in the production of computers. Since France requires fewer resources than the United States to produce a given amount of wine, France has an absolute advantage over the United States in the production of wine.

But what if one country is more efficient in producing both goods? If the United States is more efficient in producing both computers and wine, is there still any benefit to be derived from specialization and trade? At first glance, you are probably inclined to answer no. But if this is your inclination, you should reconsider—because you are wrong.

To see why specialization and trade have advantages even when one country is more efficient than another at producing both goods, consider the following example. Suppose the United States can produce 2 electronic computers or 5,000 cases of wine with 1 unit of resources, and France can produce 1 electronic computer or 4,000 cases of wine with 1 unit of resources. In this case, the United States is a more efficient producer of both computers and wine. Nonetheless, as we shall see, world output of both goods will increase if the United States specializes in the production of computers and France specializes in the production of wine.

Table 20.6 demonstrates this conclusion. If 2 units of American resources are shifted from wine to computer production, 4 additional computers and 10,000 fewer cases of wine are produced. If 3 units of French resources are shifted from computer to wine production, 3 fewer computers and 12,000 additional cases of wine are produced. Thus the combined effect of this redeployment of resources in both countries is to increase world output of computers by 1 computer and to increase world output of wine by 2,000 cases. Even though the United States is more efficient than France in the production of both computers and wine, world output of both goods will be maximized if the United States specializes in computers and France specializes in wine.

Table 20.6
Case of Comparative Advantage

	Increase or decrease in output of: Computers	Wine (thousands of cases)
Effect of U.S.'s shifting 2 units of resources from wine to computers	+4	−10
Effect of France's shifting 3 units of resources from computers to wine	−3	+12
Net effect	+1	+ 2

Basically, this is so because, although the United States is more efficient than France in the production of both goods, it has a greater advantage in computers than in wine. It is twice as efficient as France in producing computers, but only 25 percent more efficient than France in producing wine. To derive these numbers, recall that 1 unit of resources will produce 2 computers in the United States, but only 1 computer in France. Thus the United States is twice as efficient in computers. On the other hand, 1 unit of resources will produce 5,000 cases of wine in the United States, but only 4,000 cases in France. Thus the United States is 25 percent more efficient in wine.

A nation has a ***comparative advantage*** in those products where its efficiency relative to other nations is highest. Thus, in this case, the United States has a comparative advantage in the production of computers and a comparative disadvantage in the production of wine. So long as a country has a comparative advantage in the production of some commodities and a comparative disadvantage in the production of others, it can benefit from specialization and trade. A country will specialize, of course, in products where it has a comparative advantage, and import those where it has a comparative disadvantage. The point is that *specialization and trade depend on comparative, not absolute advantage.* One of the first economists to understand the full significance of this fact was David Ricardo, the famous English economist of the early nineteenth century.

A Geometric Representation of Comparative Advantage

The principle of comparative advantage, like so many important economic concepts, can be displayed diagrammatically. Again, we suppose that in the United States 1 unit of resources will produce 2 electronic computers or 5,000 cases of wine. Consequently, the ***product transformation curve*** in the United States—the curve that shows the maximum number of computers that can be produced, given various outputs of wine—is the one in panel A of Figure 20.1. The United States must give up 1 computer for every additional 2,500 cases of wine that it produces; thus the slope of the American product transformation curve is $-\frac{1}{2,500}$.[1] Also, as in the previous section, we suppose that in France 1 unit of resources will produce 1 electronic computer

[1] As we know from Chapter 3, the product transformation curve shows the maximum amount of one commodity that can be produced, given various outputs of the other commodity. Since the United States must give up 1/2,500 computer for each additional case of wine that it produces, the slope must be −1/2,500.

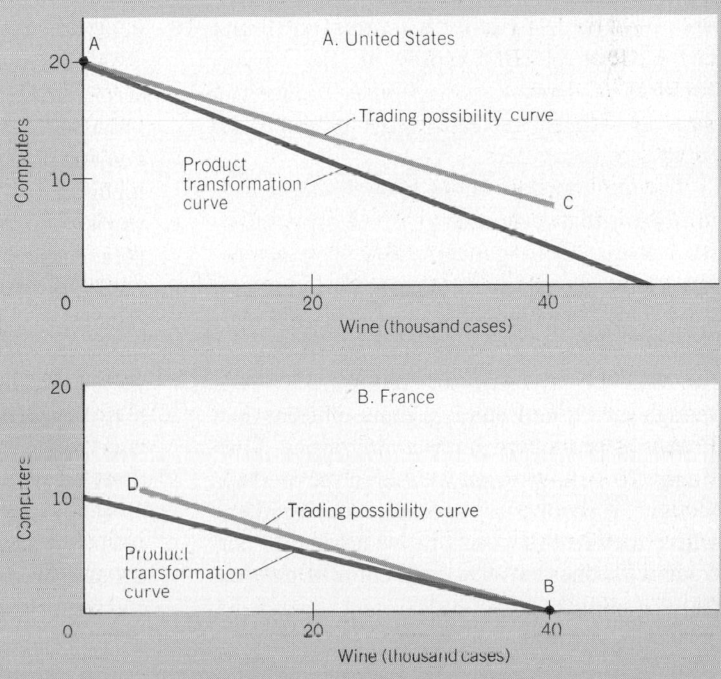

Figure 20.1
Benefits of Specialization and Trade
AC represents the various amounts of computers and wine that the United States can end up with, if it specializes in computers and trades them for French wine. The slope of *AC* equals −1 times the ratio of the price of a case of wine to the price of a computer, assumed to be $\frac{1}{3,333}$. *BD* represents the various amounts of computers and wine that France can wind up with, if it specializes in wine and trades for U.S. computers. *AC* lies above America's product transformation curve and *BD* lies above France's product transformation curve. Thus both countries can have more of both commodities by specializing and trading than by attempting to be self-sufficient.

or 4,000 cases of wine. Thus the product transformation curve in France is as shown in panel B of Figure 20.1. France must give up 1 computer for every additional 4,000 cases of wine it produces; thus the slope of France's product transformation curve is $-\frac{1}{4{,}000}$.

Now suppose that the United States uses all its resources to produce computers and that France uses all its resources to produce wine. In other words, the United States operates at point A on its product transformation curve and France operates at point B on its product transformation curve. Then suppose that the United States trades its computers for France's wine. AC in panel A of Figure 20.1 shows the various amounts of computers and wine the United States can end up with if it specializes in computers and trades them for French wine. AC is called the ***trading-possibility curve*** of the United States. The slope of AC is minus 1 times the ratio of the price of a case of wine to the price of a computer, since this ratio equals the number of computers the United States must give up to get a case of French wine. Similarly, the line BD in panel B of Figure 20.1 shows France's trading-possibility curve. That is, BD represents the various amounts of computers and wine France can wind up with if it specializes in wine and trades it for U.S. computers.

The thing to note about both panels of Figure 20.1 is that each country's trading-possibility curve—AC in panel A, BD in panel B—lies above its product transformation curve. This means that *both countries can have more of both commodities by specializing and trading than by trying to be self-sufficient*—even though the United States is more efficient than France at producing both commodities. Thus Figure 20.1 shows what we said in the previous section: if countries specialize in products where they have a comparative advantage and trade with one another, each country can improve its standard of living.

The Terms of Trade and Incomplete Specialization

The ***terms of trade*** are defined as the quantity of domestic goods that a country must give up in order to get a unit of imported goods. Thus, in Figure 20.1, the terms of trade are measured by the ratio of the price of a computer to the price of a case of wine—since this ratio shows how many cases of its wine France must give up to get an American computer. In Figure 20.1, we assume that this ratio equals 3,333:1. It is important to note that this ratio must be somewhere between 2,500:1 and 4,000:1. By diverting its own resources from computer production to wine production, the United States can exchange a computer for 2,500 cases of wine. Since this is possible, it will not pay the United States to trade a computer for less than 2,500 cases of wine. Similarly, since France can exchange a case of wine for 1/4,000 of a computer by diverting its own resources from wine to computers, it clearly will not be willing to trade a case of wine for less than 1/4,000 of a computer.

But where will the price ratio lie between 2,500:1 and 4,000:1? The answer depends on *world supply and demand for the two products.* The stronger the demand for computers (relative to their supply) and the weaker the demand for wine (relative to its supply), the higher the price ratio. On the other hand, the weaker the demand for computers (relative to their supply) and the stronger the demand for wine (relative to its supply), the lower the price ratio.

Figure 20.1 shows that the United States should specialize completely in computers, and that France should specialize completely in wine. This result stems from the assumption that the cost of producing a computer or a case of wine is constant. If, on the other hand, the cost of producing each good increases with the amount produced, the result is likely to be incomplete specialization. In other words, although the United States will continue to specialize in computers and France will continue to specialize in wine, each country will also produce some of the other good as well. This is a more likely outcome, since specialization generally tends to be less than complete.

Comparative Advantage and Actual Trade Patterns: A Case Study

The principle of comparative advantage is useful in explaining and predicting the pattern of world trade, as well as in showing the benefits of trade. For example, consider the exports of Great Britain and the United States. Robert Stern of the University of Michigan compared British and American exports of 39 industries in 1950.[2] In some of these industries, Britain exported much more than we did, while in others we exported more than the British. In all these industries, labor productivity—output per man-hour—was higher in the United States than in Great Britain. But in some industries labor productivity in the United States was over three times as great as in Britain, whereas in other industries labor productivity was less than three times as great as in Britain. According to the principle of comparative advantage, the industries where the United States is most efficient relative to the British should be the ones where the United States exports more than the British.

To what extent is this hypothesis borne out by the facts? In 21 of the 24 industries where our labor productivity was more than three times that of the British, our exports exceeded British exports. In 11 of the 15 industries where our labor productivity was less than three times that of the British, our exports were less than British exports. Thus, in 32 out of 39 industries, the principle of comparative advantage, as interpreted by Stern, predicted correctly which country would export more. This is a high batting average, since labor is not the only input and labor productivity is an imperfect measure of true efficiency. Moreover, as we shall see in subsequent sections, countries raise barriers to foreign trade, preventing trade from taking place in accord with the principle of comparative advantage.

[2] Robert M. Stern, "British and American Productivity and Comparative Costs in International Trade," *Oxford Economic Papers,* October 1962.

International Trade and Individual Markets

We have emphasized that nations can benefit by specializing in the production of goods for which they have a comparative advantage and trading these goods for others where they have a comparative disadvantage. But how do a nation's producers know whether they have a comparative advantage or disadvantage in the production of a given commodity? Clearly, they do not call up the local university and ask the leading professor of economics (although that might not always be such a bad idea). Instead, as we shall see in this section, the market for the good provides the required signals.

To see how this works, let's consider a new (and rather whimsical) product—bulletproof suspenders. Suppose that the Mob, having run a scientific survey of gunmen and policemen, finds that most of them wear their suspenders over their bulletproof vests. As a consequence, the Mob's gunmen are instructed to render a victim immobile by shooting holes in his suspenders (thus making his trousers fall down and trip him). Naturally, the producers of suspenders will soon find it profitable to produce a new bulletproof variety, an innovation which, it is hoped, will make a solid contribution to law and order. The new suspenders are demanded only in the United States and England, since the rest of the world wears belts. The demand curve in the United States is *DD,* as shown in panel A of Figure 20.2, and the de-

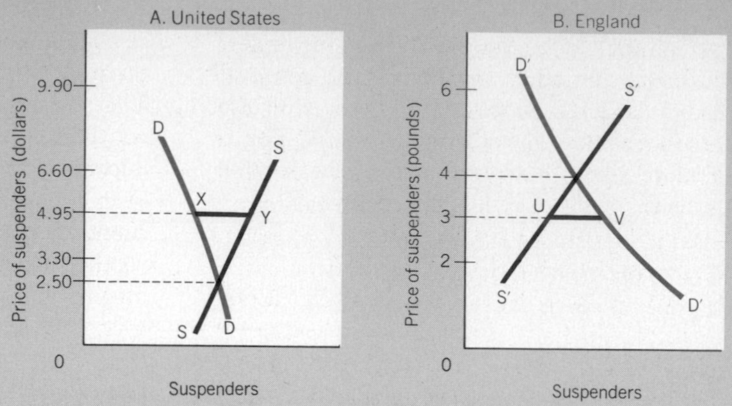

Figure 20.2
Determination of Quantity Imported and Exported under Free Trade
Under free trade, price will equal \$4.95, or £3. The United States will export *XY* units, the English will import *UV* units, and $XY = UV$.

mand curve in England is *D′D′*, as shown in panel B. Suppose further that this product can be manufactured in both the United States and England. The supply curve in the United States is *SS*, as shown in panel A, and the supply curve in England is *S′S′*, as shown in panel B.

Take a closer look at Figure 20.2. Note that prices in England are expressed in pounds (£) and prices in the United States are expressed in dollars (\$). This, of course, is quite realistic. Each country has its own currency, in which prices in that country are expressed. As of early 1977, £1 was equal to \$1.65. In other words, you could exchange a pound note for \$1.65—or \$1.65 for a £1 note. For this reason, the two panels of Figure 20.2 are lined up so that a price of \$1.65 is at the same level as a price of £1, \$3.30 is at the same level as £2, and so on.

To begin with, suppose that bulletproof suspenders can not be exported or imported, perhaps because of a very high tariff (tax on imports) imposed on them in both the United States and England. (One can readily imagine members of both Congress and Parliament defending such a tariff on the grounds that a capacity to produce plenty of bulletproof suspenders is important for national defense.) If this happens, the price of bulletproof suspenders will, of course, be \$2.50 in the United States and £4 in England. Why? Because, as shown in Figure 20.2, these are the prices at which each country's demand curve intersects its supply curve.

Next, suppose that international trade in this product is permitted, perhaps because both countries eliminate the tariff. Now what will happen? Since the price is lower in the United States than in England, people can make money by sending this product from the United States to England. After all, they can buy it for \$2.50 in this country and sell it for £4 (= \$6.60) in England. But they will not be able to do so indefinitely. As more and more suspenders are supplied by the United States for the English market, the price in the United States must go up (to induce producers to produce the additional output) and the price in England must go down (to induce consumers to buy the additional quantity).

When an equilibrium is reached, *the price in the United States must equal the price in England.* If this did not happen, there would be an advantage in increasing American exports (if the price in England were higher) or in decreasing American exports (if the price in the United States were higher). Thus only if the prices are equal can an equilibrium exist.

At what level will this price—which is common to both countries—tend to settle? Obviously, *the price must end up at the level where the amount of the good one country wants to ex-*

port equals the amount the other country wants to import. In other words, it must settle at \$4.95 or £3. Otherwise, the total amount demanded in both countries would not equal the total amount supplied in both countries. And any reader who has mastered the material in Chapter 4 knows that such a situation cannot be an equilibrium.

At this point, we can see how market forces indicate whether a country has a comparative advantage or a comparative disadvantage in the production of a certain commodity. *If a country has a comparative advantage, it turns out—after the price of the good in various countries is equalized and total world output of the good equals total world demand for it—that the country exports the good under free trade and competition.* For example, in Figure 20.2, it turns out—as we've just seen—that the United States is an exporter of bulletproof suspenders under free trade, because the demand and supply curves in the United States and England take the positions they do. The basic reason why the curves take these positions is that the United States has a comparative advantage in the production of this good. Thus, to put things in a nutshell, a nation's producers can tell (under free trade) whether they have a comparative advantage in the production of a certain commodity by seeing whether it is profitable for them to export it. If they can make a profit, they have a comparative advantage.[3]

Economies of Scale, Learning, and Technological Change

Specialization and trade may be advantageous even if there is no difference among countries in the efficiency with which they can produce goods and services. In a case like this, although no nation has a technological advantage over any other, specialization and trade may still be of benefit, because there may be economies of scale in producing some commodities. Thus, if one country specializes in one good and another country specializes in another good, firms can serve the *combined* markets of both countries, which will make their costs *lower* than if they could only reach their domestic markets. This is a major argument for forming an international economic association like the European Common Market, discussed below.

Another reason for specialization is that it may result in learning. It is well known that the cost of producing many articles goes down as more and more of the articles are produced. For example, in the aircraft and machine tool industries, producers are well aware of the reduction in costs from learning. The unit costs of a new machine tool tend to be reduced by 20 percent for each doubling of cumulated output, due to improved efficiency through individual and organizational learning. Clearly, if such learning is an important factor in an industry, there are advantages in having one nation's producers specialize in a certain good. Specialization can reduce costs to a lower level than if each nation tries to be self-sufficient. Longer production runs cut costs since *the more a producer makes, the lower the unit costs.*

International trade also arises because of technological change. Suppose, for example, that a new product is invented in the United States and an American firm begins producing and selling it in the American market. It catches on, and the American innovator decides to export the new product to Europe and other foreign markets. If the new product meets European needs and tastes, the Europeans will import it from the United States; and later, when the market in Europe gets big enough, the American firm may establish a branch plant in Europe. For a time at least, Eu-

[3] In reality, of course, things are not quite so simple. For one thing, high transport costs are often involved in moving goods from one country to another. These costs can impede trade in certain commodities. Also, tariffs or quotas can be enacted by governments to interfere with free trade.

ropean firms do not have the technological know-how to produce the new product, which is often protected to some extent by patents.

Trade of this sort is based on a *technology gap* between countries. Consider the plastics industry. After the development of a new plastic, there is a period of 15 to 25 years when the innovating country has a decisive advantage and is likely to lead in per capita production and exports. It has a head start, as well as the benefits of patents and commercial secrecy. Production may be licensed to other countries, but usually on a limited scale and only after a number of years. Soon after the patents expire, a different phase begins. Imitation is easier, technical know-how spreads more readily, direct technical factors lose importance, and such other factors as materials costs become much more important. Industry from other countries may challenge the innovator in export markets, and sometimes in the innovator's home market as well, although the innovator still benefits to some extent from his accumulated knowledge and experience and his ongoing research and development.

The United States tends to export products with a high technological component—relatively new products based on considerable research and development. For example, if the 5 U.S. industries with the largest research programs are compared with the 14 other major industries, we see that the high-research industries export 4 times as much per dollar of sales as the others.[4] During the 1960s, Europeans expressed considerable concern over the technological gap between the United States and Europe. They asserted that superior know-how stemming from scientific and technical development in the United States had allowed American companies to obtain large shares of European markets in areas like aircraft, space equipment, computers, and other electronic products.

It is difficult to separate technical advantages from other competitive factors in explaining why American firms left their European rivals far behind in some fields. Differences in educational levels and managerial skills, economies of scale, and other such factors may have been very important. As we shall see in the following chapter, our technological lead seems to have narrowed in recent years, as the Japanese, Germans, and others have upgraded their technology. According to many observers, some American exports will be, and are being, hurt as a consequence.[5]

Multinational Firms

One of the most remarkable economic phenomena of the last 20 years has been the growth of multinational firms—firms that make direct investments in other countries and produce and market their products abroad. For example, Coca-Cola is produced and bottled all over the world. Most multinational firms are American, but companies like Shell in petroleum and Hoffman-LaRoche in drugs are examples of foreign-based multinational firms. The available data indicate that the multinational firms have grown by leaps and bounds, and that their shipments have become a bigger and bigger proportion of international trade. Indeed, according to economists like Lawrence Krause of the Brookings Institution, they are "now having a revolutionary effect upon the international economic system."[6]

[4] Charles Kindleberger, *International Economics,* Homewood, Ill.: Irwin, 1968, p. 67. Also, see R. Vernon, "International Investment and International Trade in the Product Cycle," *Quarterly Journal of Economics,* May 1966.

[5] Besides differences in technology, another reason for trade is a difference in national tastes. If Country *A* likes beef and Country *B* likes pork, it may pay both countries to produce beef and pork, and Country *A* may find it advantageous to import beef from Country *B* and Country *B* may find it advantageous to import pork from Country *A*.

[6] Lawrence Krause, "The International Economic System and the Multinational Corporation," *The Annals,* 1972. Some of this and the previous section is based on my "Technology and Technological Change" in J. Dunning, ed., *Economic Analysis and the Multinational Enterprise,* London: Allen and Unwin, 1974.

The reasons why firms have become multinational are varied. In some cases, firms have established overseas branches to control foreign sources of raw materials. In other cases, they have invested overseas in an effort to defend their competitive position. Very frequently, firms have established foreign branches to exploit a technological lead. After exporting a new product (or a cheaper version of an existing product) to foreign markets, firms have decided to establish plants overseas to supply these markets. Once a foreign market is big enough to accommodate a plant of minimum efficient size, this decision does not conflict with economies of scale. Moreover, transport costs often hasten such a decision. Also, in some cases, the only way a firm can introduce its innovation into a foreign market is through the establishment of overseas production facilities.

By carrying its technology overseas, the multinational firm plays a very important role in the international diffusion of innovations. A firm with a technological edge over its competitors often prefers to exploit its technology in foreign markets through wholly owned subsidiaries rather than through licensing or other means. To some extent, this is because of difficulties in using ordinary market mechanisms to buy and sell information. The difficulties of transferring technology across organizational, as well as national, boundaries also contribute to the decision. For these and other reasons, the innovating firm may find it advantageous to transfer its technology to other countries by establishing subsidiaries abroad.

One of the most important effects of the multinational firm has been to integrate the economies of the world more closely into a world-wide system. In other words, multinational firms have tended to break down some of the barriers between nations. Besides speeding the diffusion of new technology, they have linked the capital markets of many countries and promoted the international transfer of important managerial labor. However, a number of problems are also associated with multinational firms. One is the possibility that they will attain undesirable monopoly power in some industries. In addition, as we shall see in the following chapter, they may put undesirable stress on the international financial system and threaten the sovereignty of some nation-states. In the latter connection, recent evidence of their bribing foreign officials has not contributed to their popularity, here or abroad.

Arguments Against Tariffs and Quotas

The Social Costs of Tariffs

Despite its advantages, not everyone benefits from free trade. On the contrary, some firms and workers may feel that their well-being is threatened by foreign competition; and they may press for a ***tariff,*** a tax the government imposes on imports. The purpose of a tariff is to cut down on imports in order to protect domestic industry and workers from foreign competition. A secondary reason for tariffs is to produce revenue for the government.

To see how a tariff works, consider the market for wristwatches. Suppose that the demand and supply curve for wristwatches in the United States are *DD* and *SS,* as shown in panel A of Figure 20.3, and that the demand and supply curves for wristwatches in Switzerland are *D′D′* and *S′S′*, as shown in panel B. Clearly, Switzerland has a comparative advantage in the production of wristwatches, and under free trade the price of a wristwatch would tend toward $10 in the United States and toward 30 Swiss francs in Switzerland. (Note that 3 Swiss francs are assumed to equal $1.) Under free trade, the United States would import 10 million wristwatches from Switzerland.

Now if the United States imposes a tariff of

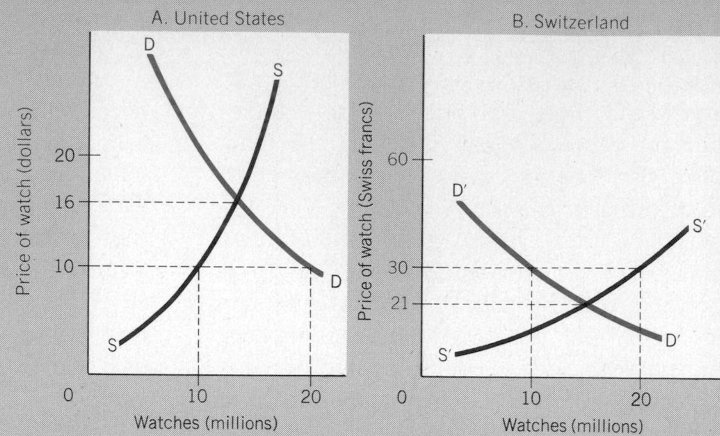

Figure 20.3
Effect of a Tariff on Swiss Watches
Under free trade, price would equal $10, or 30 Swiss francs. If a tariff of $10 is imposed on each watch imported from Switzerland, there will be a complete cessation of imports. Price in the U.S. will increase to $16, and price in Switzerland will fall to 21 Swiss francs.

$10 on each wristwatch imported from Switzerland, the imports will completely cease. Any importer who buys watches in Switzerland at the price (when there is no foreign trade) of 21 Swiss francs—which equals $7—must pay a tariff of $10; this makes his total costs $17 per watch. But this is more than the price of a watch in the United States when there is no foreign trade (which is $16). Consequently, there is no money to be made by importing watches—unless Americans can be persuaded to pay more for a Swiss watch than for an identical American watch.

What is the effect of the tariff? Clearly, the domestic watch industry receives a higher price—$16 rather than $10—than it would without a tariff. And the workers in the domestic watch industry may have more jobs and higher wages than without the tariff. The victim of the tariff is the American consumer, who pays a higher price for wristwatches.

Thus the domestic watch industry benefits at the expense of the rest of the nation. But does the general public lose more than the watch industry gains? In general, the answer is yes. The tariff reduces the consumption possibilities open to the nation. For example, suppose that wristwatches and bread were the only two commodities. A nation's ***consumption-possibility curve*** shows the various combinations of goods that can be consumed. Under free trade, the consumption-possibility curve is higher, as shown in Figure 20.4, than it is with the tariff. Clearly, the tariff reduces the consumption possibilities open to the nation.

The tariff in Figure 20.3 is a ***prohibitive tariff***—a tariff so high that it stops all imports of the good in question. Not all tariffs are pro-

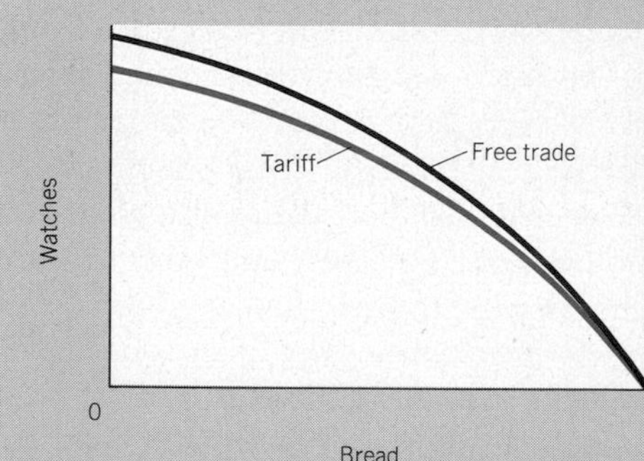

Figure 20.4
Consumption-Possibility Curves, Given Tariff and Free Trade
Under free trade, the consumption-possibility curve is farther from the origin than with the tariff. Consequently, society as a whole is better off under free trade.

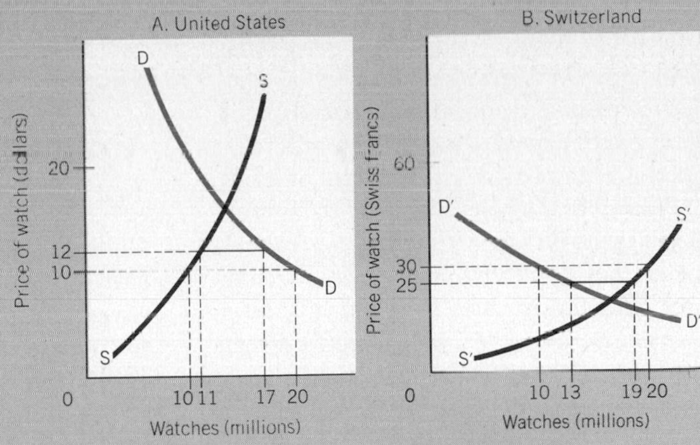

Figure 20.5
Effect of a Quota on Swiss Watches
Before the quota is imposed, the price is $10, or 30 Swiss francs. After a quota of 6 million watches is imposed, the price in the United States rises to $12, and the price in Switzerland falls to 25 Swiss francs.

hibitive. (If they were, the government would receive no revenue at all from tariffs.) In many cases, the tariff is high enough to stop some, but not all, imports; and, as you would expect, the detrimental effect of a nonprohibitive tariff on consumption possibilities and living standards is less than that of a prohibitive tariff. But this does not mean that nonprohibitive tariffs are harmless. On the contrary, they can do lots of harm to domestic consumption and living standards.

The detrimental effects of tariffs have long been recognized, even in detective stories. For example, in the course of solving the mystery concerning the Hound of the Baskervilles, Sherlock Holmes expressed his enthusiastic approval of a newspaper editorial that read as follows:

> You may be cajoled into imagining that your own special trade or your own industry will be encouraged by a protective tariff, but it stands to reason that such legislation must in the long run . . . lower the general conditions of life on this island.[7]

Of course, Holmes considered this point elementary (my dear Watson) but worth hammering home.

[7] Arthur Conan Doyle, *The Hound of the Baskervilles*, in *The Complete Sherlock Holmes*, Garden City, N.Y.: Garden City Publishing Co., 1938, p. 802.

The Social Costs of Quotas

Besides tariffs, other barriers to free trade are ***quotas,*** which many countries impose on the amount of certain commodities that can be imported annually. For example, the United States sets import quotas on sugar and exerts pressure on foreigners to get them to limit the quantity of steel and textiles that they will export to us. To see how a quota affects trade, production, and prices, let's return to the market for wristwatches. Suppose the United States places a quota on the import of wristwatches: no more than 6 million wristwatches can be imported per year. Figure 20.5 shows the effect of the quota. Before it was imposed, the price of wristwatches was $10 (or 30 Swiss francs), and the United States imported 10 million wristwatches from Switzerland. The quota forces the United States to reduce its imports to 6 million.

What will be the effect on the U.S. price? The demand curve shows that, if the price is $12, American demand will exceed American supply by 6 million watches; in other words, we will import 6 million watches. Thus, once the quota is imposed, the price will rise to $12, since *this is the price that will reduce our imports to the amount of the quota.* Clearly, a quota—like a tariff—increases the price of the good. (Note too that the price in Switzerland will fall to 25 francs. Thus the quota will reduce the price in Switzerland.)

Both a quota and a tariff reduce trade, raise prices, protect domestic industry from foreign competition, and reduce the standard of living of the nation as a whole. But most economists tend to regard quotas with even less enthusiasm than they do tariffs. Under many circumstances, a quota insulates local industry from foreign competition even more effectively than a tariff does. Foreigners, if their costs are low enough, can surmount a tariff barrier; but if a quota exists, there is no way they can exceed the quota. Moreover, a (nonprohibitive) tariff provides the government with some revenue, while quotas do not even do that. The windfall price increase from a quota accrues to the importer who is lucky enough or influential enough—or sufficiently generous with favors and bribes—to get an import license. (However, if the government auctions off the import licenses, it can obtain revenue from a quota.)

Export Subsidies and Other Barriers to Free Trade

Finally, ***export subsidies,*** another means by which governments try to give their domestic industry an advantage in international competition, are also a major impediment to free trade. Such subsidies may take the form of outright cash disbursements, tax exemptions, preferential financing or insurance arrangements, or other preferential treatment for exports. Export subsidies, and other such measures, frequently lead to countermeasures. For example, to counter foreign export subsidies, the U.S. government has imposed duties against such subsidies on goods sold here.

Other barriers to free trade include licensing requirements and unreasonable product quality standards. By granting few licenses (which are required in some countries to import goods) and by imposing unrealistically stringent product quality standards, governments discourage imports.

Arguments for Tariffs and Quotas

Given the disadvantages to society at large of tariffs and other barriers to free trade, why do governments continue to impose them? There are many reasons, some sensible, some irrational. One of the most convincing is the desirability of maintaining a domestic industry for purposes of *national defense.* For example, even if the Swedes had a comparative advantage in producing airplanes, we would not allow free trade to put our domestic producers of aircraft out of business if we felt that a domestic aircraft industry was necessary for national defense. Although the Swedes are by no means unfriendly, we would not want to import our entire supply of such a critical commodity from a foreign country, where the supply might be shut off for reasons of international politics. (Recall the Arab oil embargo of 1973.)

This is a perfectly valid reason for protecting certain domestic industries, and many protective measures are defended on these grounds. To the extent that protective measures are in fact required for national defense, economists go along with them. Of course the restrictions entail social costs (some of which were described in previous sections), but these costs may well be worth paying for enhanced national security. The trouble is that many barriers to free trade are justified on these grounds when in fact they protect domestic industries only tenuously connected with national defense. Moreover, even if there is a legitimate case on defense grounds for protecting a domestic industry, subsidies are likely to be a more straightforward and efficient way to do so than tariffs or quotas.

Besides national defense, there are other noneconomic reasons for protecting particular domestic industries. Some countries—Canada, for one—use a tariff to protect certain industries that they feel help them to be more independent of foreign domination and influence. Many Canadians, for understandable reasons, are intent on maintaining their traditions and values, and on resisting the penetration of American ways. Such noneconomic reasons for protection are perfectly reasonable if the nation as a whole understands the economic cost and agrees that the game is worth the candle (and if the reasons are sufficiently understood by foreigners that the measures do not provoke retaliation).

The Pre-1973 Oil Import Quotas: A Case Study

As we pointed out in Chapter 19, the United States has been concerned about its energy supplies. To illustrate the nature and effect of barriers to free trade, as well as to shed light on this problem, let's consider the oil import quotas that existed until 1973 in the United States. These quotas were the subject of great controversy. First established by President Eisenhower in 1959, the Mandatory Oil Import Quota allowed firms to import only a certain amount of oil. Supporters of the quota argued that we could not afford to depend on foreigners for our oil because foreign sources might be cut off in war or other emergencies. Opponents argued that the costs to the consumer of these quotas were very high and that the oil requirements for national security were overstated.

Economists at Charles River Associates estimated the costs to the consumer in a study prepared for President Nixon's Office of Science and Technology.[8] Figure 20.6 shows the demand curve for petroleum in the United States, labeled *DD′*. The supply curve for domestically produced petroleum was *SS′*. The supply curve for foreign-produced petroleum

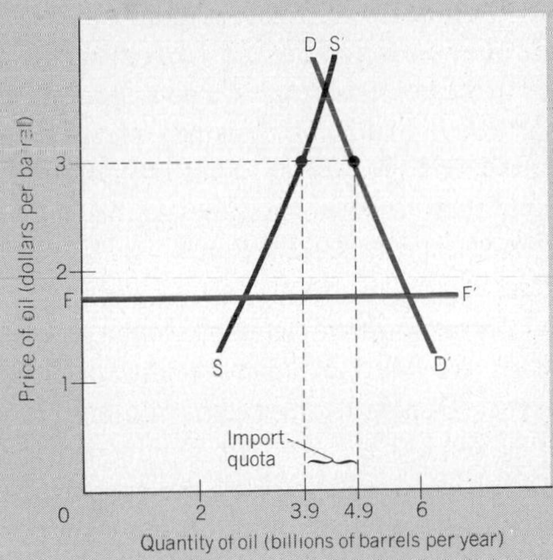

Figure 20.6
Effect of the pre-1973 Import Quota
SS′ is the supply curve for domestically produced petroleum, *FF′* is the supply curve for foreign produced petroleum, and *DD′* is the demand curve for petroleum in the United States. With an import quota of 1 billion barrels, the price will be $3; the price would be $1.75 if the import quota were removed.

at that time was *FF′*, a horizontal line at $1.75. Clearly, the price of petroleum under the import quota was set at the level—$3.00 per barrel—where the horizontal distance between the quantity demanded and the quantity supplied was equal to the import quota. If there were free trade, the price of petroleum would have been at the intersection of the *FF′* and *DD′* curves—or $1.75 per barrel.

Thus, in 1968, for example, consumers paid about $5.6 billion more for petroleum than they would have under free trade. We arrive at this figure by noting that consumers bought about 4.9 billion barrels of oil in 1968. If they paid $1.25 extra for each barrel, they paid 4.9

[8] James Burrows and Thomas Domencich, *An Analysis of the United States Oil Import Quota*, Lexington, Mass.: Heath, 1970.

billion times $1.25—or $5.6 billion—more than under free trade. Moreover, this does not include all the costs to the consumers. Additional costs arise because some consumers used less oil at the price of $3.00 than they would have if the price had been $1.75. They would have increased their satisfaction if they could have expanded their oil consumption.[9]

This was an enormous cost. Could it be justified on grounds of national security? It was difficult to tell, but many economists were doubtful. During his first term in office, President Nixon asked for a "full review of the nation's oil-import policies by the executive offices of the president." A task force—composed of the secretaries of labor, defense, state, interior, and commerce, as well as the director of the Office of Emergency Preparedness—was appointed to study the issue. Though many questions were raised concerning the merits of the oil import quota, it was continued nonetheless.

In 1973, when government officials became increasingly concerned about impending fuel shortages, opposition to the oil import quota mounted. Finally, in April 1973, President Nixon announced he was suspending direct control over the quantity of crude oil and refined products that could be imported. The oil import quota was dead. But in late 1973 and early 1974, the situation changed drastically, as the Arabs first cut back oil exports to us and then increased the price of oil by an enormous amount. No longer was *FF′* the supply curve for foreign oil; instead, the supply curve jumped off the graph. The days of relatively cheap foreign oil were over, at least for the foreseeable future.

Other Arguments for Tariffs

Besides national defense, several other arguments for tariffs or quotas can make sense. First, *tariffs or other forms of protection can be justified to foster the growth and development of young industries.* For example, suppose that Japan has a comparative advantage in the production of a certain semiconductor, but Japan does not presently produce this item. It may take Japanese firms several years to become proficient in the relevant technology, to engage in the learning described in a previous section and to take advantage of the relevant economies of scale. While this industry is "growing up," Japan may impose a tariff on such semiconductors, thus shielding its young industry from competition it can not yet handle. This "infant industry" argument for tariffs has a long history; Alexander Hamilton was one of its early exponents. Needless to say, it is *not* an argument for *permanent* tariffs, since infant industries are supposed to grow up—and the sooner the better. (Moreover, a subsidy for the industry would probably be better and easier to remove than a temporary tariff, according to many economists.)

Second, *tariffs sometimes may be imposed to protect domestic jobs and to reduce unemployment at home.* In the short run the policy may succeed, but we must recognize that other nations are likely to retaliate by enacting or increasing their own tariffs, so that such a policy may not work very well in the long run. A more sensible way to reduce domestic unemployment is to use the tools of fiscal and monetary policy described in Chapters 11 and 15 rather than tariffs. If workers are laid off by industries that cannot compete with foreign producers, proper monetary and fiscal policy, together with retraining programs, should enable these workers to switch to other industries that can compete.

Third, *tariffs sometimes may be imposed to prevent a country from being too dependent on only a few industries.* For example, consider a Latin American country that is a major producer of bananas. Under free trade, this

[9] Of course, one must distinguish between the costs to the consumer and the costs to the nation as a whole. For example, some of the costs to the consumer represented the transfer of money to the oil producers. See ibid.

country might produce bananas and little else, putting its entire economy at the mercy of the banana market. If, for instance, the price of bananas fell, the country's national income would decrease drastically. To promote industrial diversification, this country may establish tariffs to protect other industries, for example, certain types of light manufacturing. In a case like this, the tariff protects the country from having too many eggs—or bananas (if you want to avoid mixing a metaphor)—in a single basket.

Fourth, *tariffs may sometimes improve a country's terms of trade—that is, the ratio of its import prices to its export prices.* For example, the United States is a major importer of bananas. If we impose a tariff on bananas, thus cutting down on the domestic demand for them (because the tariff will increase their price), the reduction in our demand is likely to reduce the price of bananas abroad. Consequently, foreign producers of bananas will really pay part of the tariff. However, other countries may retaliate; and if all countries pursue such policies, few, if any, are likely to find themselves better off.

Frequently Encountered Fallacies

Although, as we have just seen, tariffs can be defended under certain circumstances, many of the arguments for them frequently encountered in political oratory and popular discussions are misleading. Although no field of economics is free of popular misconceptions and fallacies, this one is particularly rich in pious inanities and thunderous *non sequiturs.* For example, one frequently encountered fallacy is that, if foreigners want to trade with us, they must be benefiting from the trade. Consequently, according to this argument, we must be giving them more than we get—and it must be in our interest to reduce trade. This argument is, of course, entirely erroneous in its assumption that trade cannot be beneficial to *both* trading partners. On the contrary, as we have seen, the heart of the argument for trade is that it can be mutually beneficial.

Another fallacy one often encounters in polite conversation—and not-so-polite political debate—is that a tariff is required to protect our workers from low-wage labor in other countries. According to this argument, since American labor (at $5 an hour) clearly cannot compete with foreign labor (which works at "coolie" wage levels), we have no choice but to impose tariffs. If we do not, cheap foreign goods will throw our high-priced laborers out of work. This argument is wrong on two counts. First, *high wages do not necessarily mean high unit costs of production.* Because the productivity of American workers is high, unit labor costs in the United States are roughly in line with those in other countries. (Recall from Chapter 16 that unit labor cost equals the wage rate divided by labor productivity. Obviously, unit labor cost may be no higher here than abroad, even though the wage rate here is much higher, if labor productivity here is also much higher than abroad.) Second, *if our costs were out of line with those of other countries, there should be a change in exchange rates, which would tend to bring them back into line.* As we shall see in Chapter 21, exchange rates should move to bring our exports and imports into balance.

Still another fallacy that makes the rounds is that it is better to "buy American" because then we have both the goods that are bought and the money, whereas if we buy from foreigners we have the goods but they have the money. Like some jokes, this fallacy has an ancient lineage—and one that borders on respectability, since Abraham Lincoln is supposed to have subscribed to it. Basically, the flaw is the implicit assumption that money is somehow valued for its own sake. In reality, all the foreigners can do with the money is buy some of our goods, so that really we are just swapping some of our goods for some of theirs. If such a trade is mutually advantageous, fine.

Why do politicians (both Democrats and Republicans) sometimes utter these fallacies? No doubt an important reason is simply ignorance. There is no law that prevents people with little understanding of economics from holding public office. But this may not be the only reason. Special-interest groups—particular industries, unions, and regions—have a lot to gain by getting the government to enact protective tariffs and quotas. And Congress and the executive branch of the government are often sensitive to the pressures of these groups, which wield considerable political power.

Faced with a choice between helping a few powerful, well-organized groups and helping the general public—which is poorly organized and often ignorant of its own interests—politicians frequently tend to favor the special-interest groups. After all, these groups have a lot to gain and will remember their friends, while the general public—each member of which loses only a relatively small amount—will be largely unaware of its losses anyhow. Having decided to help these groups, a congressman or senator may not exert himself unduly to search out or expose the weakness in some of the arguments used to bolster their position. For example, there is the story of a well-known senator who, about to deliver a certain oration, wrote in the margin of one section of his speech: "Weak point here. Holler like hell."

Tariffs in the United States

How high are American tariffs, now and in the past? In our early years, we were a very protectionist nation. The argument for protecting our young industry from the competition of European manufacturers was, of course, the "infant industry" argument, which, as we saw above, can be perfectly sensible. However, our own industries understandably found it advantageous to prolong their childhood for as long as possible—and to press for continuation of high tariffs. During the nineteenth century and well into the twentieth, the industrial Northeast was particularly strong in its support of tariffs. Furthermore, the Republican party, which generally held sway in American politics between the Civil War and the New Deal, favored a high tariff. Thus, as shown in Figure 20.7, the tariff remained relatively high from about 1870 until the early 1930s. With the exception of the period around World War I, average tariff rates were about 40 to 50 percent. With the enactment of the Smoot-Hawley Tariff of 1930, the tariff reached its peak—about 60 percent. Moreover, these tariff rates understate the extent to which the tariff restricted trade: some goods were completely shut out of the country by the tariff, and do not

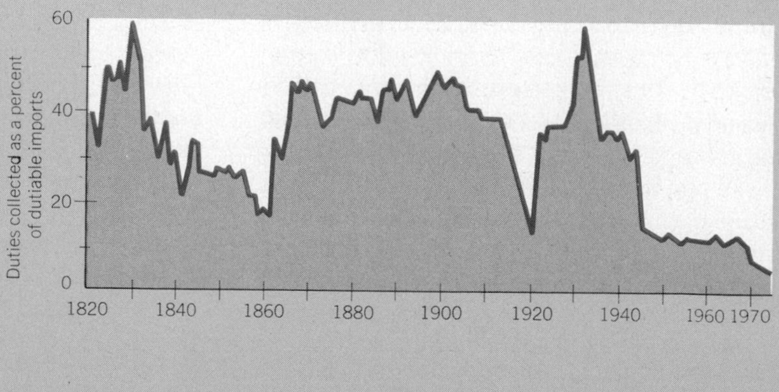

Figure 20.7
Average American Tariff Rates
The tariff generally remained high from about 1870 to the early 1930s; in recent years it has decreased substantially.

show up in the figures.

With the Democratic victory in 1932, a movement began toward freer trade. The Trade Agreements Act of 1934 allowed the president to bargain with other countries to reduce barriers to trade. He was given the power to lower U.S. tariffs by as much as 50 percent. In 1945, he was given the power to make further tariff reductions. Between 1934 and 1948, tariff rates fell substantially, as shown in Figure 20.7. By 1948, the United States was no longer a high-tariff country; the average tariff rate was only about 10 percent.

During the 1950s, there were no further decreases in the tariff—but there were no substantial increases either. The movement toward freer trade was continued by President Kennedy in 1962, and during the 1960s, the "Kennedy Round" negotiations took place among about 40 nations in an attempt to reduce tariffs. In 1967, the United States agreed to cut tariffs by about ⅓ on a great many items.

The negotiations during the 1960s were prompted by the establishment of the European Economic Community—or "Common Market." The EEC was composed originally of Belgium, France, West Germany, Holland, Italy, and Luxembourg; and in the 1970s, Britain, Denmark, and Ireland joined. When the EEC was formed, the member countries agreed to reduce the tariff barriers against one another's goods—but not against the goods of other nations, including the United States.

The formation and success of the Common Market—and the likelihood that other European countries would join—posed a problem for the United States. The Common Market is a large and rich market, with over 200 million people and a combined gross national product exceeding $800 billion. With the reduction of tariff barriers *within* the Common Market, trade *among* the members of the Common Market increased rapidly, and prices of many items were cut. But American exporters were less than ecstatic about all of this, because the members of the Common Market still maintained their tariff barriers against American goods. While the "Kennedy Round" negotiations succeeded in reducing some of the tariff barriers between the United States and the Common Market, important tariff barriers remain, particularly for agricultural products.

In 1973, over 100 nations met in Tokyo to plan a new round of trade negotiations. The aim was to make further progress toward the reduction of tariffs and nontariff barriers to trade. In 1974, the Congress passed the Trade Reform Act of 1974, which enabled the president, after international negotiations, to reduce any tariff presently above 5 percent by ⅗ and to abolish any tariff presently equal to 5 percent or less. Also, the act allowed workers, firms, and communities that are hurt by import competition to obtain payments and other forms of assistance. In 1975, a new round of negotiations was begun in Geneva. As in previous years, one of the important problem areas was agriculture, where the European Economic Community is reluctant to reduce tariffs.

Recent years have seen some increase in protectionist feelings in the United States. As Western Europe and Japan have become more formidable competitors abroad and at home, many industries have begun to press for quotas and higher tariffs. The textile and steel industries have been particularly vocal and have managed to increase trade barriers. Some unions have joined the protectionist forces in an effort to hold on to jobs. The Hartke-Burke bill, which attempted to increase trade barriers and to impede the international diffusion of technology, received considerable attention in Congress in the early 1970s. And the Trade Reform Act of 1974 was not free of protectionist features. It is to be hoped that this upsurge of protectionist spirit will be short-lived, and developments here and abroad will enable us and our trading partners to move closer to the realization of the benefits of free trade.

The European Economic Community

The EEC, born in the embers of World War II, was fathered by a desire to bind Germany to the rest of Europe. The success of the European Steel and Coal Community and the Benelux union encouraged the "Europeanists," and in 1957 the Treaty of Rome formally proclaimed the birth of a six-country free-trade area in which labor, capital, and goods were to move freely. None of this was to happen instantaneously, but the six countries—France, Germany, Italy, Belgium, the Netherlands, and Luxemborg—did agree on a timetable for the removal of centuries-old barriers and on a commission and council to manage the details of the process.

There are ample statistics to tell the story since 1958—growth rates of above 4 percent, increased competitiveness by European firms, increases in per capita incomes, and increased membership (including Great Britain). But the flavor of this customs union comes through best by seeing what it has meant to three prototype economic men.

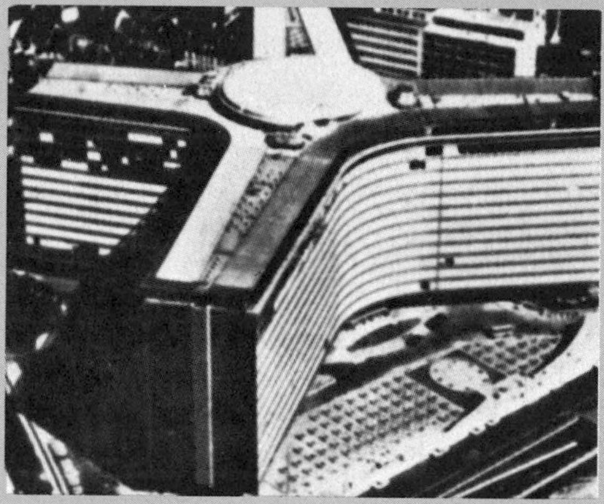

HEADQUARTERS OF THE EUROPEAN ECONOMIC COMMUNITY, BRUSSELS

Nino T. was born in southern Italy, where reported unemployment is 14 percent.* If disguised unemployment were included, the rate might run as high as double that. Wages, for those with jobs, averaged about $20 per week. In 1965, he migrated to Germany to work in an automobile plant in Frankfort, where he could make $75 a week, and send back $40 to his family. He planned to stay for another two years—perhaps until he had saved enough to buy a small business.

John C. works for a leather-goods firm in London. As a new member of the Common Market, he was able to migrate to the Continent and find a job, at considerably higher wages. He has no plans to do so, however, and when Britain joined the Common Market, his chief worry was that it would mean higher food prices. Why? Because the technologically inefficient but politically powerful French farmer was able to demand protection from cheap American and Canadian food. Thus, while French wheat would flow freely into Great Britain, the high external tariff would now keep out North American wheat.

Richard B., an American businessman, now lives in Paris, managing the French subsidiary of a large New-York-based corporation. He was moved to Paris about ten years ago, when company officials decided that the removal of internal barriers by the EEC would allow U.S. companies to operate on the scale to which they were accustomed. To stay compet itive in the European market, they decided to build production facilities inside the EEC, rather than producing in the U.S. and shipping abroad. Richard now finds himself very much at home in France, and seriously considers living out his days in Paris. E.A.

* George Hildebrand, *The Italian Economy*, New York: Harper and Row, 1967, p. 337.

Summary

International trade permits specialization, and specialization increases output. This is the advantage of trade, both for individuals and for nations. Country *A* has an absolute advantage over Country *B* in the production of a good when Country *A* can produce a unit of the good with less resources than can Country *B*. Trade can be mutually beneficial even if one country has an absolute advantage in the production of all goods.

Specialization and trade depend on comparative, not absolute advantage. A nation is said to have a comparative advantage in those products where its efficiency relative to other nations is highest. Trade can be mutually beneficial if a country specializes in the products where it has a comparative advantage and imports the products where it has a comparative disadvantage.

The principle of comparative advantage is of use in predicting the pattern of world trade, as well as in showing its benefits. If markets are relatively free and competitive, producers will automatically be led to produce in accord with comparative advantage. If a country has a comparative advantage in the production of a certain good, it will turn out—after the price of the good in various countries is equalized and total world output of the good equals total world demand—that this country is an exporter of the good under free trade.

Specialization may occur because of economies of scale and learning. Also, some countries develop new products and processes, which they export to other countries until the technology becomes widely available.

A tariff is a tax imposed by the government on imports, the purpose being to cut down on imports in order to protect domestic industry and workers from foreign competition. Tariffs benefit the protected industry at the expense of the general public, and, in general, a tariff costs the general public more than the protected industry (and its workers and suppliers) gains. Quotas are another barrier to free trade. They too reduce trade, raise prices, protect domestic industry from foreign competition, and reduce the standard of living of the nation as a whole.

Tariffs, quotas, and other barriers to free trade can sometimes be justified on the basis of national security and other noneconomic considerations. Moreover, tariffs and other forms of protection can sometimes be justified to protect infant industries, to prevent a country from being too dependent on only a few industries, and to carry out other national objectives. But many arguments for tariffs are fallacious.

In our early years, we were a very protectionist country. Our tariff remained relatively high until the 1930s, when a movement began toward freer trade. Between 1934 and 1948, our tariff rates dropped substantially. Again during the 1960s, there was a significant reduction in our tariffs. But more recently, as some of our industries (like steel) have been hit hard by imports, there has been some tendency to push for more protectionist measures.

Although it has equaled only about 5 to 10 percent of our gross national product, foreign trade is of very considerable importance to the American economy. Many of our industries rely on foreign countries for raw materials or for markets, and our consumers buy many kinds of imported goods. In absolute terms, our exports are large and have represented about 15 percent of total world trade. Both our exports and imports are mostly finished manufactured goods.

CONCEPTS FOR REVIEW

Comparative advantage
Absolute advantage
Product transformation curve
Trading-possibility curve
Tariff
Quota
Prohibitive tariff
Export subsidy
Technology gap
Multinational firm
European Economic Community

QUESTIONS FOR DISCUSSION AND REVIEW

1. According to Hendrik Houthakker, "Our workers get high real income not because they are protected from foreign competition, but because they are highly productive, at least in certain industries." Do you agree? Why or why not?

2. According to Richard Cooper, "Technological innovation can undoubtedly strengthen the competitive position of a country in which the innovation takes place, whether it be one which enlarges exports or displaces imports." Give examples of this phenomenon, and discuss various ways that one might measure the effects of technological innovation on a country's competitive position.

3. Discuss the effects of the multinational firm on the world economy. Do you think that the activities of multinational firms should be regulated in new ways? If so, why?

4. Suppose that the United States can produce 3 electronic computers or 3,000 cases of wine with 1 unit of resources, while France can produce 1 electronic computer or 2,000 cases of wine with 1 unit of resources. Will specialization increase world output?

5. Suppose that the United States has 100 units of resources while France has 50 units. Based on the data in Question 4, draw the product transformation curve in each country. Without international trade, what will be the ratio of the price of an electronic computer to the price of a case of wine in each country?

6. Given the information in Questions 4 and 5, how will firms in France and the United States know whether they should produce wine or electronic computers? Must the government instruct them on this score? Why or why not?

7. Under the circumstances described in Questions 4 and 5, will each country specialize completely in the production of one or the other good? Why or why not? What factors result in incomplete specialization in the real world?

8. "The United States doesn't export electronic computers because we have a comparative advantage in producing them. It's because we're better at producing them than any other country." Comment and evaluate.

9. "The principle of comparative advantage doesn't work. The U.S. exports electronic computers to Japan and imports electronic consumer goods like TV sets from Japan." Comment and evaluate.

10. Would you favor a high tariff on imported steel if you were: (a) an automobile worker, (b) a steel worker, (c) an automobile buyer, (d) a plastics worker? Explain your reasoning in each case.

21 Exchange Rates and the Balance of Payments

During the early 1970s, any American at all acquainted with the financial or international news became aware that the United States was having "balance of payments difficulties"—or, a bit more specifically, we were experiencing deficits in our balance of payments. In response to these deficits, President Nixon devalued the dollar twice between 1971 and 1973, and then, together with the other major trading nations of the world, agreed in 1973 to allow exchange rates to "float." These were important developments by any standard. Even in the nation's less prestigious and more sensational newspapers, they managed to crowd the juiciest sports and criminal news off the front pages.

To understand these developments, we must consider several questions. What are exchange rates, and how are they determined? How are international business transactions carried out? Should there be fixed or flexible exchange rates? What is the balance of payments, and what is its significance? What problems has the United States had with its balance of payments in recent years? These questions, which are both fundamental and timely, are taken up in this chapter.

International Transactions and Exchange Rates

Suppose you want to buy a book from a German publisher, and that book costs 20 marks. (The German currency consists of marks, not dollars.) To buy the book, you must somehow get marks to pay the publisher, since this is the currency in which he deals. Or, if he agrees, you might pay him in dollars; but he would then have to exchange the dollars you give him for marks, since he must pay his bills in marks. Whatever happens, either you or he must somehow exchange dollars for marks, since international business transactions, unlike transactions within a country, involve two different currencies.

If you decide to exchange dollars for marks to pay the German publisher, how can you make the exchange? The answer is simple. You can buy German marks at a bank, just as you might buy lamb chops at a butcher shop. Just as the lamb chops have a price (expressed in dollars), so the German marks have a price (expressed in dollars). The bank may tell you that each mark you buy will cost you $.40. This makes the ***exchange rate*** between dollars and marks .4 to 1, since it takes .4 dollars to purchase 1 mark (or 2½ marks to purchase 1 dollar).

In general, *the exchange rate is simply the number of units of one currency that exchanges for a unit of another currency.* The obvious question is what determines the exchange rate. Why is the exchange rate between German marks and American dollars what it is? Why doesn't a dollar exchange for 10 marks, rather than 2½ marks? This basic question will occupy us in the next three sections.

Exchange Rates under the Gold Standard

As a starter, let's see how exchange rates were determined under the ***gold standard,*** which prevailed before the 1930s. *If a country was on the gold standard, a unit of its currency was convertible into a certain amount of gold.* For example, before World War I the dollar was convertible into $\frac{1}{20}$ ounce of gold, and the British pound was convertible into ¼ ounce of gold. Thus, since the pound exchanged for 5 times as much gold as the dollar, the pound exchanged for $5. The currency of any other country on the gold standard was convertible into a certain amount of gold in the same way; and *to see how much its currency was worth in dollars, you divided the amount of gold a unit of its currency was worth by the amount of gold ($\frac{1}{20}$ ounce) a dollar was worth.*

Why did the exchange rate always equal the ratio between the amount of gold a foreign currency was worth and the amount of gold a dollar was worth? For example, why did the price of a British pound stay at $5 before World War I? To see why, suppose that the price (in dollars) of a pound rose above this ratio—above $5. Instead of exchanging their dollars directly for pounds, Americans would have done better to exchange them for gold and then exchange the gold for pounds. By this indirect process, Americans could have exchanged $5 for a pound, so they would have refused to buy pounds at a price above $5 per pound.

Similarly, if the price of a pound fell below $5, the British would have refused to sell pounds, since they could have obtained $5 by converting the pound into gold and the gold into dollars. Thus, *because Americans would refuse to pay more than $5, and the British would refuse to accept less, for a pound, the price of a pound had to remain at about $5.* (In practice, the pound could be a few cents above or below $5, because it costs money to transport gold in order to carry out the conversion.)

But what insured that this exchange rate, dictated by the gold content of currencies, would result in a rough equality of trade between countries? For example, if one pound exchanged for $5, perhaps the British might find our goods so cheap that they would import a great deal from us, while we might find their goods so expensive that we would import little from them. Under these circumstances, the British would have to ship gold to us to pay for the excess of their imports from us over their exports to us, and eventually they would run out of gold. Could this happen? If not, why not? These questions occupied the attention of many early economists. The classic answers were given by David Hume, the famous Scottish philosopher, in the eighteenth century.

Hume pointed out that under the gold standard a mechanism insured that trade would be brought into balance and that neither country would run out of gold. This mechanism was as follows: If, as we assumed, the British bought more from us than we bought from them, they would have to send us gold to pay for the excess of their imports over their exports. As their gold stock declined, their price level would fall. (Recall the quantity theory of money.) As our gold stock increased, our price level would rise. Thus, because of our rising prices, the British would tend to import less from us; and because of their falling prices, we would tend to import more from them. Consequently, the trade between the two countries would tend toward a better balance. Eventually, when enough gold had left Britain and entered the United States, prices here would have increased enough, and prices in Britain would have fallen enough, to put imports and exports in balance.

Flexible Exchange Rates

The gold standard is long gone; and after many decades of fixed exchange rates (discussed in the next section), the major trading nations of the world began to experiment with flexible exchange rates in early 1973. Let's consider a situation where exchange rates are allowed to fluctuate freely, like the price of any commodity in a competitive market. In a case of this sort, exchange rates—like any price—are determined by supply and demand. There is a market for various types of foreign currency—German marks, British pounds, French francs, and so on—just as there are markets for various types of meat.

In the case of the German mark, the demand and supply curves may look like those shown in Figure 21.1. The demand curve shows the amount of German marks that people with dollars will demand at various prices of a mark. The supply curve shows the amount of German marks that people with marks will supply at various prices of a mark. Since the amount of German currency supplied must equal the

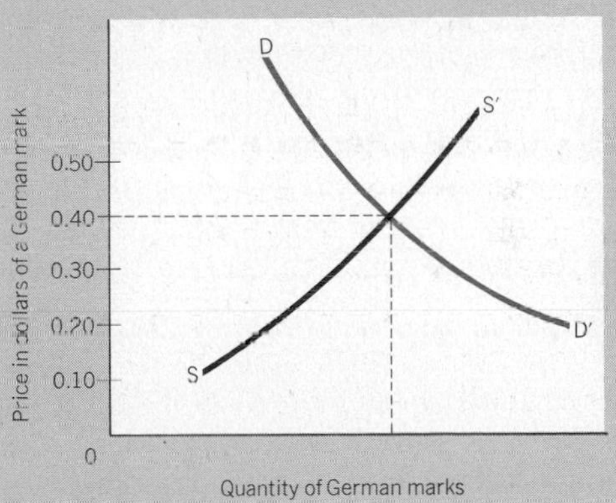

Figure 21.1
Determination of the Exchange Rate between Dollars and German Marks under Freely Fluctuating Exchange Rates
Under freely fluctuating exchange rates, the equilibrium price of a German mark would be $.40 if *DD′* is the demand curve for marks and *SS′* is the supply curve.

amount demanded in equilibrium, *the equilibrium price (in dollars) of a German mark is given by the intersection of the demand and supply curves.* In Figure 21.1, this intersection is at $.40.

Let's look in more detail at the demand and supply sides of this market. On the *demand* side are people who want to import German goods (like the book you want to buy) into the United States, people who want to travel in Germany (where they'll need German money), people who want to build factories in Germany, and others with dollars who want German currency. The people on the *supply* side are those who want to import American goods into Germany, Germans who want to travel in the United States (where they'll need American money), people with marks who want to build factories in the United States, and others with marks who want American currency.

Thus it is obvious that *when Americans demand more German cameras or Rhine wine (causing the demand curve to shift upward and to the right), the price (in dollars) of the German mark will tend to increase.* Conversely, *when the Germans demand more American cars or computers (resulting in a shift of the supply curve downward and to the right), the price (in dollars) of the German mark will tend to decrease.*

To see why an increase in German demand for American cars or computers shifts the supply curve downward and to the right, recall that the supply curve shows the amount of marks that will be supplied at each price of a mark. Thus a shift downward and to the right in the supply curve means that more marks will be supplied at a given price (in dollars) of the mark. Given the posited increase in German demand for American goods, such a shift in the supply curve would be expected.

Changes in Exchange Rates: Determinants and Effects

Under a system of flexible exchange rates, changes in tastes, among other things, affect the equilibrium level of the exchange rate, as shown by the usual sorts of supply-and-demand diagrams that we introduced in Chapter 4. For example, as we have just seen, if Americans become fonder and fonder of German goods and less fond of their domestic goods, there will be an increase in the demand for goods imported from Germany, and an attendant increase in the demand for German marks. As shown in Figure 21.2, the demand curve for marks shifts from *DD′* to *EE′*, causing a rise in the price (in dollars) of a German mark from $.40 to $.44.

Also, differences between the two countries in many other factors, including the rate of inflation and the rate of economic growth, will affect the exchange rate. *If the rate of inflation in the United States is relatively high, this is likely to result in an increase in the price (in dollars) of a German mark, because of its effect on these supply and demand curves.* On the other

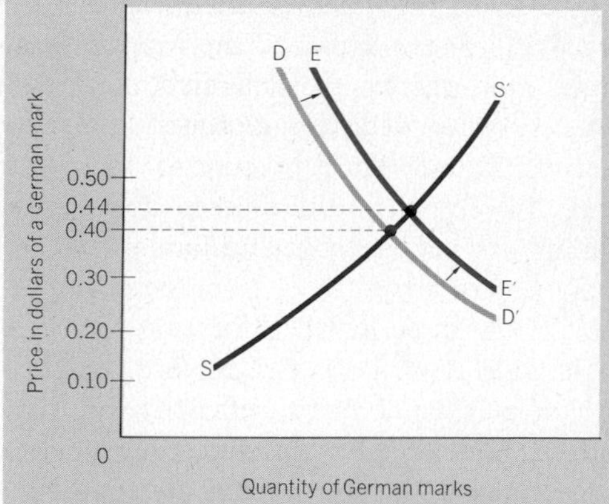

Figure 21.2
Effect of Shift in Demand Curve for German Marks
If the demand curve shifts from *DD′* to *EE′*, the equilibrium price of a German mark increases from $.40 to $.44.

hand, *a relatively low rate of inflation in the United States, and a high rate of inflation in Germany, is likely to cause a decrease in the price (in dollars) of a German mark.*

Two terms frequently encountered in discussions of exchange rates are ***appreciation*** and ***depreciation.*** When Country *A*'s currency becomes more valuable relative to Country *B*'s currency, Country *A*'s currency is said to appreciate relative to that of Country *B*, and Country *B*'s currency is said to depreciate relative to that of Country *A*. In Figure 21.2, the mark appreciated relative to the dollar and the dollar depreciated relative to the mark. This use of terms makes sense. Since the number of dollars commanded by a mark increased, the mark clearly became more valuable relative to the dollar and the dollar became less valuable relative to the mark.

Note that such a change in exchange rates would not have been possible under the gold standard. Unless a country changed the amount of gold that could be exchanged for a unit of its currency, exchange rates were fixed under the gold standard. Sometimes governments did change the amount of gold that could be exchanged for their currencies. For example, in 1933 the United States increased the price of gold from $21 an ounce to $35 an ounce. When a country increases the price of gold, this is called a ***devaluation*** of its currency.

Under flexible exchange rates, what insures a balance in the exports and imports between countries? The situation differs, of course, from that described by David Hume, since Hume assumed the existence of the gold standard. Under flexible exchange rates, the balance is achieved through changes in exchange rates. For example, suppose once again that for some reason Britain is importing far more from us than we are from Britain. This will mean that the British, needing dollars to buy our goods, will be willing to supply pounds more cheaply. In other words, the supply curve for British pounds will shift downward and to the right from S_1S_1' to S_2S_2', as shown in Figure 21.3. This will cause the price of a pound to decline from P_1 dollars to P_2 dollars. Or, from Britain's point of view, the price (in pounds) of a dollar will have been bid up by the swollen demand for imports from America.

Because of the increase in the price (in pounds) of a dollar, our goods will become more expensive in Britain. Thus the British will tend to reduce their imports of our goods. At the same time, since the price (in dollars) of a pound has decreased, British goods will become cheaper in the United States, and this, of course, will stimulate us to import more from Britain. Consequently, as our currency appreciates in terms of theirs—or, to put it another way, as theirs depreciates in terms of ours—the British are induced to import less and export

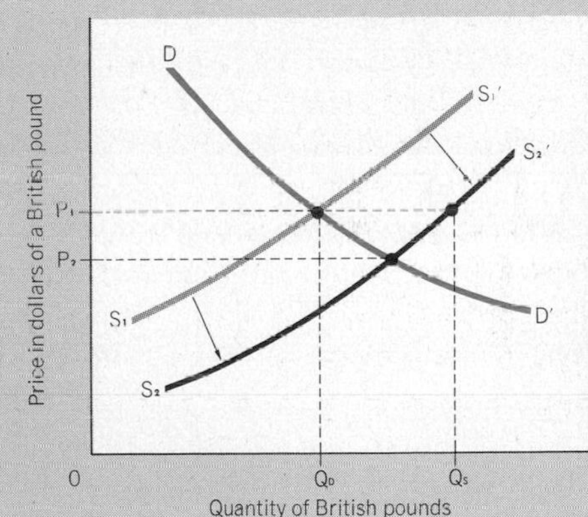

Figure 21.3
Adjustment Mechanism
If Britain imports more from us than we do from Britain, the supply curve will shift from S_1S_1' to S_2S_2', resulting in a decline of the price of the pound from P_1 to P_2 dollars. If Britain tries to maintain the price at $\$P_1$, the British government will have to exchange dollars for $(Q_S - Q_D)$ pounds.

more. Thus there is an automatic mechanism (just as there was under the gold standard) to bring trade between countries into balance.

Fixed Exchange Rates

Although many economists believed that exchange rates should be allowed to fluctuate, very few exchange rates really did so in the period from the end of World War II up to 1973. Instead, *most exchange rates were fixed by government action and international agreement.* Although they may have varied slightly about the fixed level, the extent to which they were allowed to vary was small. Every now and then, governments changed the exchange rates, for reasons discussed below; but for long periods of time, they remained fixed.

If exchange rates remain fixed, the amount demanded of a foreign currency may not equal the amount supplied. For example, consider the situation in Figure 21.4. If *DD′* and *SS′* are the demand and supply curves for German marks, the equilibrium price of a mark is $.40. But suppose the fixed exchange rate between dollars and marks is .35 to 1: that is, each mark exchanges for $.35. Unless the government intervenes, more German marks will be demanded at a price of $.35 per mark than will be offered. Specifically, the difference between the quantity demanded and the quantity supplied will be $Q_D - Q_S$. Unless the government steps in, a black market for German marks may develop, and the real price may increase toward $.40 per mark.

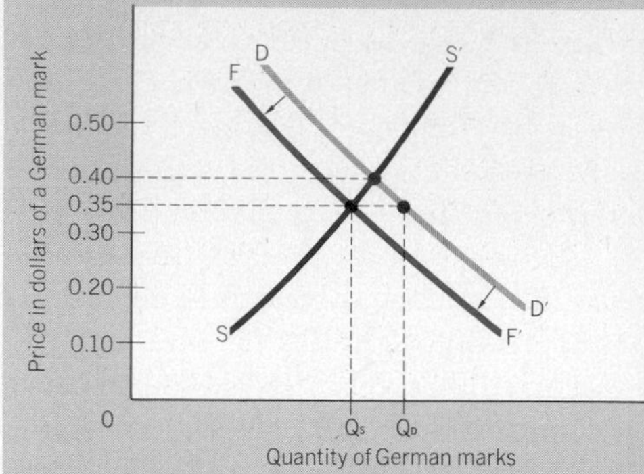

Figure 21.4
Fixed Exchange Rate
The equilibrium price of a German mark is $.40, if *DD′* is the demand curve. If $.35 is the fixed exchange rate, the U.S. government may try to shift the demand curve for marks from *DD′* to *FF′*, thus bringing the equilibrium exchange rate into equality with the fixed exchange rate.

To maintain exchange rates at their fixed levels, governments can intervene in a variety of ways. For example, they may reduce the demand for foreign currencies by reducing defense expenditures abroad, by limiting the amount that their citizens can travel abroad, and by curbing imports from other countries. Thus, in the case depicted in Figure 21.4, the American government might adopt some or all of these measures to shift the demand curve for German marks downward and to the left. If the demand curve can be pushed from *DD′* to *FF′*, the equilibrium price of a German mark can be reduced to $.35, the fixed exchange rate. For the time being, there will no longer be any mismatch between the quantity of marks demanded and the quantity supplied.

However, when exchange rates are fixed, such mismatches cannot be eliminated entirely and permanently. To deal with temporary mismatches of this sort, governments enter the market and buy and sell their currencies in order to maintain fixed exchange rates. This happened in post-World-War-II Britain. At times the amount of British pounds supplied exceeded the amount demanded. Then the British government bought up the excess at the fixed exchange rate. At other times, when the quantity demanded exceeded the amount supplied, the British government supplied the pounds desired at the fixed exchange rate. As long as the equilibrium exchange rate was close to (sometimes above and sometimes below) the fixed exchange rate, the amount of its currency the government sold at one time equaled, more or less, the amount it bought at another time.

But in some cases governments tried to maintain a fixed exchange rate far from the equilibrium exchange rate. For example, the British government might have tried to maintain the price (in dollars) of the pound at P_1 in the situation in Figure 21.3, when the supply curve for British pounds was S_2S_2'. Since the quantity of British pounds supplied exceeded the quantity demanded at that exchange rate, the British government would have to buy the difference. That is, it would have to buy ($Q_S - Q_D$) pounds with dollars. Moreover, it would have to keep on exchanging dollars for pounds in these quantities for as long as the demand and supply curves remained in these positions. Eventually, the government would run out of dollars and would have to impose restrictions to shift the supply or demand curves (as described above) or change the exchange rate. How long it could maintain the price of the pound at P_1 would depend on how big its reserves of foreign currency were.

Fixed versus Flexible Exchange Rates

Why, until 1973, did most countries fix their exchange rates, rather than allow them to fluctuate? One important reason was the feeling that flexible exchange rates might vary so erratically that it might be difficult to carry out normal trade. For example, an American exporter of machine tools to Britain might not know what British pounds would be worth six months from now, when he would collect a debt in pounds. According to the proponents of fixed exchange rates, fluctuating rates would increase uncertainties for people and firms engaged in international trade and thus reduce the volume of such trade. Moreover, they argued that the harmful effects of speculation over exchange rates would increase if exchange rates were flexible, because speculators could push a currency's exchange rate up or down, and destabilize the exchange market. Further, they argued that flexible exchange rates might promote more rapid inflation.

Many economists disagreed, feeling that flexible exchange rates would work better. They asked why flexible prices are used and trusted in other areas of the economy, but not in connection with foreign exchange. They pointed out that a country would have more autonomy in formulating its fiscal and monetary policy if exchange rates were flexible, and they claimed that speculation regarding exchange rates would not be destabilizing. But until 1973, the advocates of flexible exchange rates persuaded few of the world's central bankers and policy makers.

However, considerable attention was devoted to a compromise between fixed and completely flexible exchange rates the so-called *crawling peg.* According to the crawling peg (which admittedly sounds more like an insect than a system of exchange rates), the exchange rate between currencies would be allowed to change, but only up to a certain amount—perhaps 1 or 2 percent per year. Thus, if supply and demand dictated that the dollar should depreciate relative to the German mark, the price (in dollars) of the mark could increase 10 or 20 percent over a decade.

The advantage of the crawling peg is, of course, that it allows exchange rates to move in a way that eventually results in international equilibrium. However, in contrast to flexible exchange rates, the crawling peg insures that changes in exchange rates will be gradual enough to preserve many of the benefits of fixed exchange rates. In particular, the risks and uncertainties involved in international

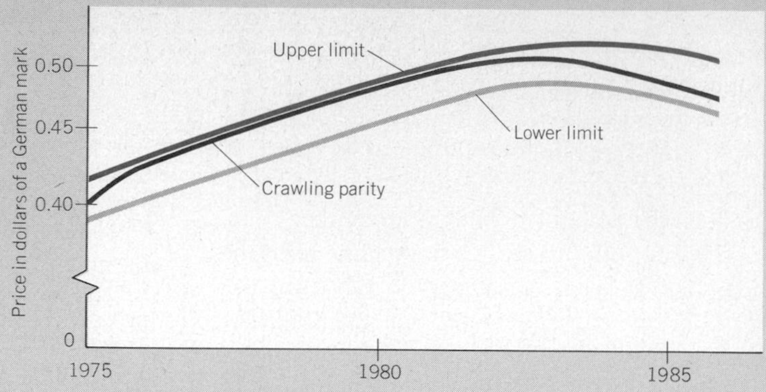

Figure 21.5
The Crawling Peg
According to the crawling peg, the exchange rate can vary by a certain amount each year. The upper and lower limits and crawling parity are shown here for a hypothetical case. Supply and demand can push the exchange rate between the upper limit and lower limit.

trade might be less than under flexible rates (see Figure 21.5).

In early 1973, after a series of attempts to alter the system of fixed exchange rates to maintain its viability, the major trading nations of the world agreed to allow exchange rates to fluctuate–in other words, to float. However, they did not go so far as to establish completely flexible exchange rates. Instead, the float was to be managed. Central banks would step in to buy and sell their currency. For example, the United States agreed that "when necessary and desirable" it would support the value of the dollar. Also, some European countries decided to maintain fixed exchange rates among their own currencies, but to float jointly against other currencies. This new system of fluctuating exchange rates seems to have worked reasonably well, despite the fact that the international monetary system received some major jolts, such as the oil crisis (described below) in the mid-1970s.

Experience with the Gold Standard and Gold Exchange Standard

What has been our experience with various types of exchange rates? During the latter part of the nineteenth century, the gold standard seemed to work very well, but serious trouble developed after World War I. After going off the gold standard during World War I, for reasons we will discuss in the next chapter, some countries tried to re-establish the old rates of exchange in the postwar period. Because the wartime and postwar rates of inflation were greater in some countries than in others, under the old exchange rates the goods of some countries were underpriced and those of other countries were overpriced. According to the doctrines of David Hume, this imbalance should have been remedied by increases in the general price level in countries where goods were underpriced and by reductions in the general price level in countries where goods were overpriced. But wages and prices proved to be inflexible, and, as one would expect, it proved especially difficult to adjust them downward. When the adjustment mechanism failed to work quickly enough, the gold standard was abandoned.

During the 1930s, governments tried various schemes. This was, of course, the time of the Great Depression, and governments were trying frantically to reduce unemployment. Sometimes a government allowed the exchange rate to be flexible for a while, and when it found what seemed to be an equilibrium level, fixed the exchange rate there. Sometimes a government depreciated the value of its own currency relative to those of other countries in an attempt to increase employment by making its goods cheap to other countries. Of course, when one country adopted such policies, others retaliated, causing a reduction in international trade and lending, but little or no benefit for the country that started the fracas.

In 1944, the Allied governments sent representatives to Bretton Woods, New Hampshire, to work out a more effective system for the postwar era. It was generally agreed that competitive devaluations, such as occurred in the 1930s, should be avoided. Out of the Bretton Woods conference came the ***International Monetary Fund*** (IMF), which was set up to maintain a stable system of fixed exchange rates and to insure that when exchange rates had to be changed because of significant trade imbalances, disruption was minimized.

The system developed during the postwar period is generally labeled the *gold-exchange standard,* as opposed to the gold standard. Under this system, the dollar—which had by this time taken the place of the British pound as the world's key currency—was convertible into gold at a fixed price (not, however, for monetary purposes by private American citizens, as we saw in Chapter 13). And since other currencies could be converted into dollars at fixed exchange rates, other currencies were convertible indirectly into gold at a fixed price.

During the early postwar period, this system worked reasonably well. However, throughout the 1960s our gold stock decreased substantially, as year in, year out, we had a deficit in our balance of payments, described below. To prevent speculators and others from depleting our gold stock, the major central banks agreed in 1968 to establish a ***"two-tier" gold system***—an ***official tier*** in which gold, used solely for monetary purposes, was traded back and forth between central banks at the official exchange rates, and a ***private tier*** in which the rest of the world's gold supply was traded on a free market. The central banks agreed not to sell gold to the private tier.

But this remedy could only postpone the breakdown of the gold-exchange standard. In August 1971, President Nixon announced that the United States would no longer convert dollars into gold for foreign central banks. Thus the link between gold and exchange rates was shattered. Also, pressure was exerted on other countries, particularly Japan and Germany, to allow their currencies to appreciate in terms of our own. Since this would make their goods more expensive to us and cut down on their exports, they resisted such changes. But eventually they allowed their currencies to become more expensive in terms of ours, and (what amounts to the same thing) we allowed our currency to become cheaper in terms of theirs. A new system of fixed exchange rates was approved in 1971, when representatives of the major trading nations met at the Smithsonian Institution.

Although President Nixon hailed the Smithsonian agreement as "the greatest international monetary agreement in the history of the world," events were to prove it unequal to the tasks it faced. In February 1973, scarcely more than a year after the agreement, the United States felt obliged to devalue the dollar again, as the outflow of dollars to other countries continued. Then, in March 1973, representatives of the major trading nations met in Paris to establish a system of fluctuating exchange rates, thus abandoning the Bretton Woods system of fixed exchange rates. This was a major break with the past, and one that was greeted with considerable apprehension as well as hope.

The Fight to Save the Pound: A Case Study

From this discussion it is clear that although exchange rates were generally fixed until 1973, from time to time they were altered to respond to changes in basic economic conditions. To illustrate how these alterations occurred, consider the case of Great Britain in the mid-1960s. Since 1949, the exchange rate between dollars and pounds had been 2.8 to 1, which meant that a British pound was worth $2.80. But at this exchange rate, Britain found it very difficult to export as much as she bought from foreigners. In other words, at this exchange rate the quantity of pounds supplied exceeded the quantity demanded. If the market for pounds had been free, the price of the pound would have dropped. That is, the pound would have depreciated relative to the dollar.

Britain's Labor government, elected in 1964, declared that it would not depreciate the pound. Prime Minister Harold Wilson claimed that maintaining the exchange rate at $2.80 was of primary importance and called the fight to maintain the exchange rate a "second battle of Britain." (The original battle of Britain occurred early in World War II, when Britain fought off air attacks by Nazi Germany.) In 1964, the government slapped a 15 percent tax on imports to shift the supply curve for pounds to the left. In 1965, the government restricted foreign travel and exports of capital. Finally, in 1966, the government froze wages, increased taxes, and cut government expenditures to curb inflation in an attempt to promote exports. All these measures were designed to push the equilibrium exchange rate—the rate at which the demand and supply curves for pounds intersect—up toward $2.80.

But it was to no avail. In 1967, the British were forced to devalue the pound. The exchange rate was reduced from $2.80 to $2.40, a depreciation of about 14 percent. It was hoped that this change would expand British exports, now cheaper to non-Britons, and discourage foreign imports, now more expensive to Britons. In other words, it was hoped that $2.40 was close to the equilibrium exchange rate. From 1967 to 1971, when the Smithsonian agreement took place, the exchange rate remained at this level. During 1975 and 1976, the pound fell once again, to below $1.65 in October 1976. But this decline occurred under a regime of floating, not fixed, exchange rates. In considerable degree, it reflected Britain's very high rate of inflation. (In early 1975, prices were rising at more than 30 percent per year.) As we noted above, a relatively high rate of inflation pushes down the value of a nation's currency when exchange rates are flexible.[1]

Experience with Floating Exchange Rates

From 1973 to date, exchange rates have been flexible, not fixed. As noted above, there has been some intervention by central banks to keep the movement of exchange rates between broad bounds, but this intervention generally has not been very great. The result has been considerable volatility in exchange rates. For example, the exchange rate between the dollar and the German mark has sometimes varied by 2 percent or more from one day to the next, and by 15 percent or more over a period of several months. Figure 21.6 shows the changes in the value of the dollar relative to selected foreign currencies during 1973–75. Clearly, the dollar depreciated considerably relative to the French franc, the German mark, the British pound, and the Italian lira in late 1974 and early 1975. But in late 1975, the dollar appreciated considerably relative to all of them, particularly the pound and the lira.

Unquestionably, the variations in exchange rates, some of which are erratic and without fundamental economic significance, have made international transactions more difficult. For example, Renault, the French auto manufacturer, is reported to have hesitated to launch an export drive into the U.S. market because of the erratic behavior of the dollar-franc ex-

[1] For further discussion, see Richard Cooper's contribution to R. Caves, *Britain's Economic Prospects,* Washington, D.C.: Brookings Institution, 1968, and J. B. Cohen, *Balance-of-Payments Policy,* Baltimore: Penguin, 1969.

Figure 21.6
Changes over Time in Foreign Exchange Rates, 1973–75
Since 1973, exchange rates have been floating. The dollar depreciated relative to the French franc, the German mark, the British pound, and the Italian lira in late 1974 and early 1975, but appreciated relative to them in late 1975.
Source: Board of Governors of the Federal Reserve System.

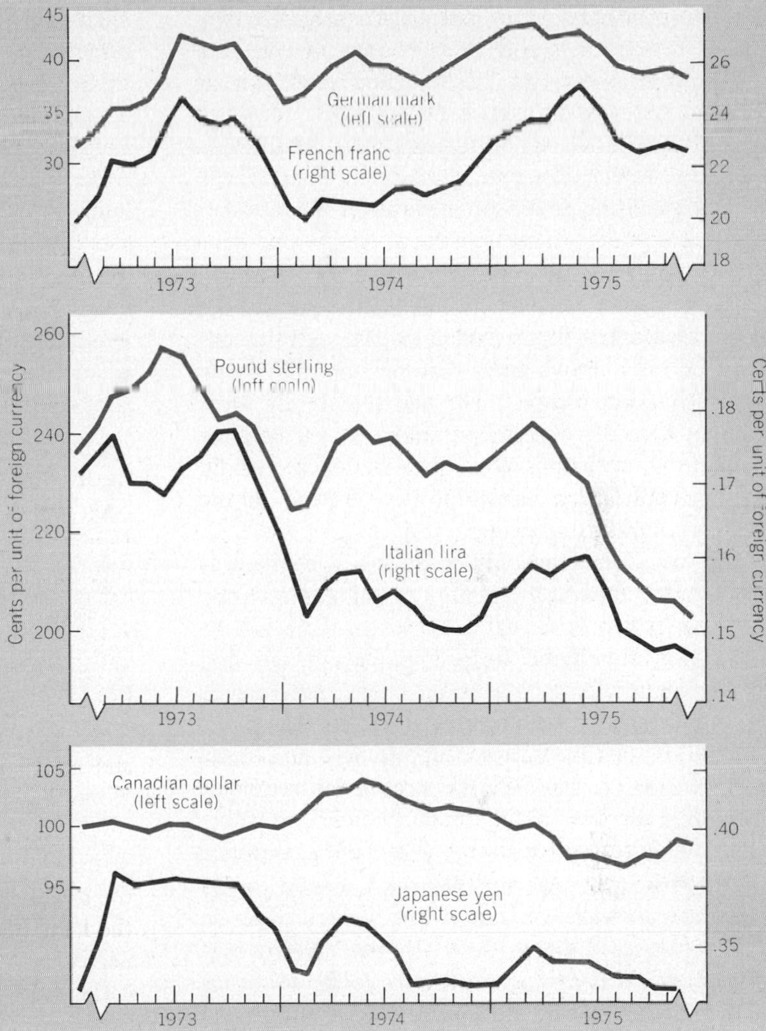

change rate. However, businessmen seem to have coped rather successfully with such exchange rate variation, as reflected in the following statement in late 1975 by the National Foreign Trade Council: "[Floating exchange rates have] . . . responded well to the shocks of the fast-moving developments of recent years, . . . [although] at times business has been unfavorably affected by sharp fluctuations of key currencies."

One of the greatest "shocks" of recent years was the increase in oil prices at the beginning of 1974. This sharp price increase meant that oil-importing countries suddenly had to pay unprecedented bills to the oil-producing countries, with the result that massive strain was put on the international financial system. Although the difficulties were not surmounted easily, the new system of floating exchange rates seems to have shown the required resilience to overcome this crisis.

During 1973 and 1974, there was considerable disagreement, particularly between the United States and France, over how flexible exchange rates should be. The French wanted to go back to fixed exchange rates; the U.S. wanted little or no impediment to the flexibility of exchange rates. In November 1975, the French and American governments agreed to a compromise whereby central banks would intervene to prevent "disorderly," or "erratic," fluctuations in exchange rates. Secretary of the Treasury William Simon defined such fluctuations as "movements that have no underlying economic reason." He said that in the year prior to this agreement, there were perhaps one or two occasions when the Federal Reserve did not intervene, but would have done so on the basis of this agreement.

An important aspect of this agreement is that it foreshadows more consultation among nations in this area. Every week, there will be contact between high Treasury officials and their counterparts in about a dozen other major countries to determine whether "disorderly" or "erratic" fluctuations are in evidence. This should allow decisions concerning government intervention in the exchange markets to be made on the basis of better and more complete information. Of course, it is too soon to tell how these new arrangements will turn out in practice. How frequently the relevant governments will agree to intervene is by no means obvious. But on the surface at least, this agreement seems to indicate somewhat more stability for exchange rates.

The Balance of Payments

We have referred repeatedly in this chapter to the balance of payments. Now we will discuss it in some detail. *Any country's* ***balance of payments*** *measures the flow of payments between it and other countries.* Consider the U.S. balance of payments in 1975, reproduced in Table 21.1. There are two types of items in the balance of payments: debit items and credit items. ***Debit items*** are items for which we must pay foreigners—items that use up the foreign currency we have. ***Credit items*** are items for which foreigners pay us—items that provide us with a stock of foreign currency. For example, if a French importer buys an American car to sell in France, this is a credit item in the U.S. balance of payments because a foreigner—the French importer—must pay us for the car. On the other hand, if an American importer buys some French wine to sell in the United States, this is a debit item in the U.S. balance of payments. We must pay the foreigner—the French winemaker—for the wine.

It is essential to understand at the outset that *the balance of payments always balances.* The total of credit items must always equal the total of debit items, because the sum of the debit items is the total value of goods, services, and assets we received from foreigners. These goods, services, and assets must be paid for with credit items, since credit items provide the foreign currency required by foreigners. Since the debit items must be paid for by the credit items, *the sum of the credit items must equal the sum of the debit items.*

To see exactly what the balance of payments tells us, let's look at each of the entries in Table 21.1, starting with the debits column. During 1975, we imported about $98 billion worth of merchandise. This, of course, is a debit item, since it requires payments to manufacturers abroad. Also, we spent about $1 billion for net military transactions, about $2 billion for remittances abroad (such as Social Security payments to Americans now living abroad), about $2 billion for net government grants and long-term capital outflows (such as our foreign aid programs and government finance for exports), about $9 billion for net private long-term capital outflows, about $3 billion for net nonliquid short-term private capital outflows, and about $6 billion for net liquid private capital outflows. These items (each of which will be described in some detail below) are all debit items, since they entail payments by us to foreigners.

Table 21.1
United States Balance of Payments, 1975

	Credit (billions of dollars)	Debit
Goods and services		
Merchandise exports	107	
Merchandise imports		98
Net services (including travel and transportation)	2	
Net military transactions		1
Net investment income	6	
Transfers, capital movements, and movements of reserve assets		
Remittances		2
Net U.S. government grants and capital outflows		2
Net U.S. private long-term capital outflows		9
Net nonliquid short-term private capital outflows		3
Errors and omissions	4	
Net liquid private capital outflows		6
Net change in liabilities to foreign official agencies	3	
Net change in U.S. reserves		1
Total	122	122

Source: Survey of Current Business, March 1976.

To see how we paid for these debit items, we must look at the credits column. We exported about $107 billion worth of merchandise. This, of course, is a credit item, since it represents payments to us by foreign purchasers of American goods. Also, we received $2 billion (net) for services abroad, and about $6 billion in net income from foreign investments; both of these are credit items. Thus, adding up these credit items and these debit items (and noting that we must add $4 billion to the credit items to offset errors and omissions), our payments abroad totaled about $121 billion and payments to us equaled about $119 billion. The remaining items in the balance of payments show how we paid for the difference of $2 billion. As shown by the last two items in Table 21.1, foreigners accepted $3 billion in additional IOUs from us, and our reserves increased by $1 billion. This covered the $2 billion difference.

Goods and Services

Having looked briefly at the entire balance of payments, let's break the table into two parts: (1) goods and services; and (2) transfers, capital movements, and movements of reserve assets. First, consider goods and services. As you can see from Table 21.1, this part of the balance of payments shows the amount of goods and services we exported and imported. Note that exports and imports include *invisible* items, as well as *visible* items (that is, merchandise). Among the invisible items are transportation services, tourist expenditures, military sales and expenditures, and earnings on investments in other countries. They must be accounted for in the balance of payments, since they entail payments by one country to another. For example, when a British vessel carries our merchandise, we must pay for this service. Or when an American tourist stays at the George

V Hotel in Paris, we must pay for this service—and judging from the George V's rates, pay dearly at that. Or when foreigners lend us capital, we must pay them interest.

You will recall from the previous section that credit items supply us with foreign currency while debit items use up our foreign currency. Thus it is clear that when foreign carriers transport our goods or people, this is a debit item, but when we carry other countries' goods or people, this is a credit item in our balance of payments. Similarly, expenditures by American tourists traveling abroad are debit items, but money spent here by foreign tourists is a credit item. Further, interest we pay to foreigners on money they lent us is a debit item, but interest foreigners pay us on money we lent them is a credit item.

Besides the transactions made by private citizens, the government's transactions must be included too in our balance of payments. The United States government supports a vast network of military bases around the world. Every now and then, we become involved in "police actions" and other euphemisms and circumlocutions which, to the naked eye, look very much like wars. We also engage in a host of other government activities abroad (like the work of the United States Information Service, the Peace Corps, and so on), and all these programs affect our balance of payments. In the main, they result in debit items since they involve payments abroad. For example, money spent by U.S. military authorities stationed in Wiesbaden, Germany, to buy supplies from local German companies is a debit item.

We can tell a great deal about America's transactions with other countries by looking at the individual figures for goods and services in Table 21.1. First, it is clear that in 1975 we exported about $9 billion more merchandise than we imported. Second, we spent about $2 billion less on foreign transportation and other services and on tourism abroad than foreigners spent on our transportation and other services and on tourism here. Third, foreigners paid us far more—about $6 billion more—in interest and dividends on money we invested abroad than we paid foreigners for similar investments here. Fourth, the U.S. government spent (net) about $1 billion abroad for military transactions.

The Balance of Trade

The newspapers often mention the balance of trade. The ***balance of merchandise trade*** refers only to a part of the balance of payments. A nation is said to have a *favorable* balance of merchandise trade if its exports of merchandise are more than its imports of merchandise, and an *unfavorable* balance of merchandise trade if its exports of merchandise are less than its imports of merchandise. As Table 21.1 shows, the United States had a favorable balance of merchandise trade of about $9 billion in 1975. But obviously the balance of merchandise trade tells only part of what we want to know about a country's transactions with other countries. As shown in Table 21.1, there is much more to the balance of payments than a comparison of merchandise exports with merchandise imports. Moreover, a "favorable" balance of trade is not necessarily a good thing, since imports, not exports, contribute to a country's standard of living.

Also, note that the United States had a *net surplus with respect to goods and services* of about $16 billion in 1975. In other words, the credit items for goods and services added up to $115 billion, while the debit items added up to $99 billion. This means that we spent about $16 billion less on foreign goods and services than foreigners spent on our goods and services. Any surplus with respect to goods and services must be offset by a deficit in the rest of the balance of payments. This is because, as stressed in the previous section, the total of the debit items must equal the total of the credit items. Similarly, any deficit with respect to goods and services must be offset by a surplus in the rest of the balance of payments. In the following sections, we shall see exactly how the deficit with respect to goods and services was offset in 1975.

Transfers, Capital Movements, and Reserve Assets

Let's turn now to the rest of the balance of payments, which shows transfers (gifts, pensions, etc.), capital movements, and movements of reserve assets from one country to another. Take a close look at the second part of our 1975 balance of payments, reproduced in Table 21.2. You will see that the entries regarding capital movements are classified as transactions by the government or by private parties. This classification seems self-explanatory; for example, when an American lends money to a German firm by buying its long-term bonds, this is clearly a *private* capital outflow. In Table 21.2, the term, *capital outflow,* is used repeatedly. A capital outflow is a loan or investment abroad. For example, Americans may buy plants in foreign countries, or purchase the securities of foreign firms, or make deposits in foreign banks.

Recall from previous sections that a credit item supplies us with foreign currency and a debit item uses up our foreign currency. Let's apply this rule to a case where we lend money abroad. Clearly, such a transaction requires that we use foreign currency, since we will be buying foreign bonds or other securities. Thus lending abroad results in a debit item. On the other hand, borrowing from abroad supplies us with foreign currency, since foreigners pay us with their currency when they buy our bonds or other securities. Thus borrowing abroad results in a credit item.

Table 21.2 shows that in 1975 the United States government granted or lent (long-term) about $2 billion abroad (net of repayments), and private citizens and firms made long-term capital outflows of about $9 billion, net nonliquid short-term capital outflows of about $3 billion, and net liquid capital outflows of about $6 billion. Also, we sent $2 billion abroad in remittances—for example, gifts and pensions. As we just pointed out, these are all debit items. Combined with the $16 billion net surplus for goods and services (and the credit item of $4 billion to offset errors and omissions), this meant a total of about $2 billion of debits to be financed, one way or another, by the United States. This is frequently referred to as the "deficit on an official-settlements basis" in our balance of payments. The use of the term

Table 21.2
Transfers, Capital Movements, and Movements of Reserve Assets, 1975

	Credit (billions of dollars)	Debit
Remittances		2
Net U.S. government grants and long-term capital outflows		2
Net U.S. private long-term capital outflows		9
Net nonliquid short-term private capital outflows		3
Errors and omissions	4	
Net liquid private capital outflows		6
Net change in liabilities to foreign official agencies	3	
Net change in U.S. reserves		1

Source: Table 21.1.

Table 21.3
Deficit in U.S. Balance of Payments, 1975

	Credit	Debit
	(billions of dollars)	
Merchandise exports	107	
Merchandise imports		98
Net services	2	
Net military transactions		1
Net investment income	6	
Remittances		2
Net U.S. government grants and capital outflows		2
Net U.S. private long-term capital outflows		9
Net nonliquid short-term private capital outflows		3
Errors and omissions	4	
Net liquid private capital outflows		6
Total	119	121

Deficit on official-settlements basis = \$121 billion − \$119 billion = \$2 billion

Source: Survey of Current Business, March 1976.

deficit does not mean that our entire balance of payments is in deficit. That could never be the case, since by definition the total of the debits must always equal the total of the credits. What this deficit really means is that we spent about \$2 billion more on foreign goods, services, and investments than foreigners spent on our goods, services, and investments. This is shown in Table 21.3.

Financing the Deficit

Next we must consider how this deficit (on an official-settlements basis) of about \$2 billion was financed. What credit items in other parts of the balance of payments offset this debit balance? To answer this question, we must look at the last two items in the balance of payments—net change in U.S. liabilities to foreign official agencies, and net change in U.S. reserves. First, consider the net change in U.S. liabilities to foreign central banks. As you can see from Tables 21.1 and 21.2, our debt to foreign central banks increased by about \$3 billion during 1975. In other words, foreign central banks built up their short-term investments here. They invested about \$3 billion in our short-term debt, which is how we financed the deficit.

Next, let's look at the change in the level of U.S. monetary reserves, including gold. Such changes are another way the deficit could have been financed. For example, in 1970, foreign central banks asked us for about \$3 billion in reserves. Thus the 1970 deficit was financed partly by transferring our reserves to other countries and partly by our increased liabilities. Of course, as noted above, the situation now is different than it was in 1970. The U.S. government will no longer exchange gold for dollars held by foreign central banks. But other reserve assets, including foreign exchange, can be used to make settlements. In 1975, however, there was no reduction in U.S. reserves; instead, our reserves increased by \$1 billion.

Finally, when we get down to the bottom of the balance of payments, we achieve the balance between debit items and credit items that logic—and arithmetic—assures us will prevail, since we must pay in cash or IOUs for what we get from other nations.[2]

Interpretation of a Deficit or Surplus: Fixed versus Floating Exchange Rates

To prevent confusion, it is important to point out that the interpretation of a deficit or surplus in our balance of payments is different under floating exchange rates than under fixed exchange rates. Under fixed exchange rates, a deficit (on an official-settlements basis) meant that foreign central banks had bought dollars because at the fixed exchange rates the private demand for dollars by foreigners was less than the available supply. This was viewed as a measure of pressure on the dollar in foreign exchange markets. Under floating exchange rates, on the other hand, exchange rates are allowed to change in response to such pressure. Thus a deficit of this sort can not be interpreted as evidence of such pressure. The size of the deficit is determined now by factors such as the preference of the oil-exporting countries (which garnered a huge amount of investable funds in the mid-1970s) for putting their funds in the United States. In May 1976, *the federal government stopped publishing figures on the deficit or surplus in our balance of payments because such figures no longer mean what they used to.*

U.S. Balance of Payments Deficits, 1950–72

As noted in the previous section, when exchange rates were fixed, a balance of payments deficit was evidence of pressure on the dollar in foreign exchange markets. Figure 21.7 shows that, *during the period from 1950 to 1972 (the last full year when exchange rates were fixed), the United States showed a chronic deficit in its balance of payments.* This chronic deficit caused considerable uneasiness and concern, both here and abroad. Several factors were responsible for it.

Postwar recovery of Western Europe and Japan. As the Western European and Japanese economies recovered from the devastation of World War II, they adopted new technology, and became tough competitors. To cite but one example, the Japanese were particularly adept at absorbing modern electronic technology and

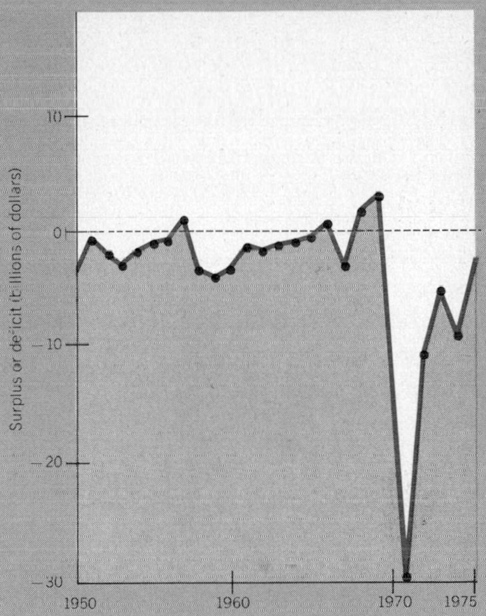

Figure 21.7
Deficit or Surplus in U.S. Balance of Payments, 1950–75

[2] However, even this certainty is clouded a bit by the fact that there are errors and omissions in the statistics that mean that a perfect balance is never achieved. But this only reflects the limitations of the data: logic dictates that if complete data could be obtained, a perfect balance would always be achieved.

at producing electronic goods for civilian markets. In many areas of technology, the United States continued to enjoy a lead, but the gap seemed to be narrowing. As productivity in Western Europe and Japan rose more rapidly than ours, their costs fell relative to ours, and they were able to undersell us much more in their own markets, third markets, and sometimes even our own market.

Military and foreign aid. We spent enormous amounts abroad for military purposes and for foreign aid. Our military expenditures abroad were particularly high during the Vietnam War. For example, they were about $4.5 billion in 1968. Not only did this war take a heavy toll in lives and in social disruption; it also helped keep our balance of payments in deficit. Note, however, that some of our government spending abroad has involved the use of "tied" funds, which can be used only to buy American goods. Since these programs result in exports that would not otherwise be made, the elimination of some of these programs would not reduce the deficit. If the government spending were cut, the exports it financed would be cut as well.

Private investment abroad. American firms invested enormous amounts of money abroad. U.S. investors acquired oil refineries, assembly lines, and hundreds of other types of plants. The rate of private investment abroad increased spectacularly during the 1950s and 1960s. In the early 1950s, new American private investment abroad was about $2 billion per year; in the late 1950s, over $3 billion per year; in the early 1960s, over $4 billion per year; and in the late 1960s, over $8 billion per year. The reason for this growth is fairly obvious. The markets of Western Europe (and other parts of the world) were growing rapidly and the construction of plants abroad was a profitable move. To help reduce our balance of payments deficit, the government introduced a voluntary program to limit such investment abroad in 1965, and made the program compulsory in 1968. (It lapsed in the 1970s.)

Inflation and discrimination. A number of other factors, including inflation in the United States and discrimination abroad against U.S. products, also contributed to our balance of payments deficits. Clearly, inflation in the United States—such as occurred in the late 1960s and early 1970s in particular—makes our exports more expensive abroad. It is true, of course, that inflation in the United States was not as great as in many other countries, but in many industries, like steel, our prices rose relative to those abroad. Also, foreigners maintained various quotas, tariffs, and other devices to keep out American exports. Many of these discriminatory regulations were enacted during earlier days when such policies were more understandable than during the period under consideration.

Autonomous and Accommodating Transactions

One of life's certainties is that the balance of payments of any nation will balance, but this, like many of the certainties of life, is merely a tautology. The important point is not that a balance is achieved, but *how it is achieved.* Sometimes a balance is achieved in a way that results in a stable equilibrium. In other cases, a balance is achieved in a way that results in disequilibrium, which, as we know, is a situation that cannot be maintained indefinitely. In the latter cases, something has to change; things cannot go on as they are. In the late 1960s and early 1970s, economists and bankers generally agreed that the U.S. balance of payments was in disequilibrium.

To see more clearly what disequilibrium means, it is convenient to distinguish between autonomous transactions and accommodating transactions. *Autonomous transactions* occur for reasons quite independent of the balance of payments. Exports, imports, and net capital movements occur because of people's tastes, comparative costs, and relative rates of return in various countries. Government expenditures abroad are made for military, political, and other reasons. Thus it is customary to treat these transactions as autonomous. On the other hand, *accommodating transactions* are made to bring about the necessary balance that must occur in the balance of payments. They compensate for differences between the total credits and total debits resulting from the autonomous transactions. For example, changes in a country's gold stock and other reserve assets, as well as short-term investments in the country's currency and other assets by foreigners, may be accommodating transactions.

Accommodating transactions are evidence of disequilibrium in a country's balance of payments. The United States's autonomous transactions—exports, imports, government expenditures abroad, long-term capital movements—resulted in a debit balance during the 1960s and early 1970s. This meant that certain accommodating transactions (reductions in our gold stock and other reserve assets, and increases in foreign investments in our currency and short-term investments) had to occur. These accommodating transactions were evidence of disequilibrium. They could not go on forever.

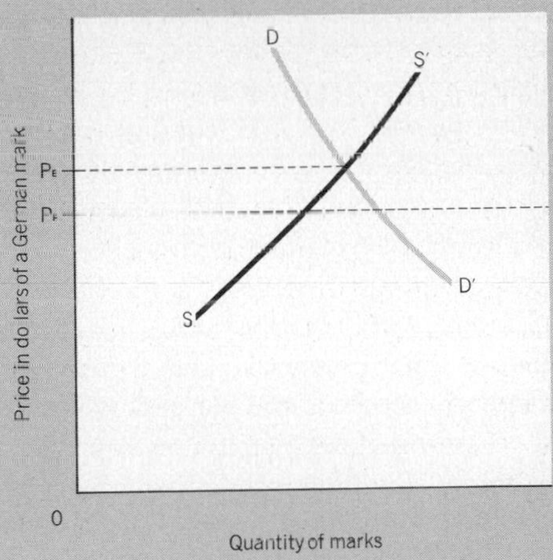

Figure 21.8
"Overvaluation" of the Dollar
Whereas the fixed exchange rate was only $\$P_F$ for a German mark, the equilibrium price was $\$P_E$.

Restoring Equilibrium in the Early 1970s

Under a regime of fixed exchange rates, what can a country do to restore equilibrium in its balance of payments? In general there are three routes it can take. (1) It can adjust its exchange rate. (2) It can change its price level. (3) It can adopt various kinds of controls to interfere with market forces. To illustrate each of these ways to restore equilibrium, consider the situation facing the United States in 1970. The dollar at that time was overvalued relative to other currencies, like the German mark. The situation was as shown in Figure 21.8, where *DD'* and *SS'* are the demand and supply curves for marks. In a free market for foreign exchange, the price (in dollars) of a German mark would have risen from the fixed exchange rate, P_F, to P_E. This would have discouraged American imports, encouraged American exports, and brought the U.S. balance of payments into equilibrium. In other words, it would have increased the autonomous transactions resulting in credits and decreased the autonomous transactions resulting in debits.

Thus one step the United States might have taken in 1970 to restore equilibrium was to *depreciate the dollar.* But the United States was reluctant to depreciate its currency relative to others. Depreciation of our currency would hurt friendly nations who had been willing to hold large dollar balances. The United States wanted to discourage speculation against the dollar. And there was a chance that depreciation of the world's leading currency would seriously disrupt the entire world monetary system. Also, it must be noted that depreciation would have required the cooperation of other countries. For example, unless the Germans were prepared to let the mark rise in value relative to the dollar, they could stop it by also depreciating the mark.

A second way to restore equilibrium was to *change the price level.* This was the sort of mechanism the gold standard used to restore equilibrium. In a country with a chronic deficit, like the United States, the remedy would be a lowering of its general price level relative to that of other countries. This would reduce our imports and promote our exports. In contrast to the previous alternative, it would not have meant any alteration in exchange rates. However, it might well have led to a depression in the United States. Because wages and prices are very difficult to push downward, any serious attempt to reduce aggregate spending in an effort to reduce the price level would probably cut output and increase unemployment. For this reason, economists were not enthusiastic about this route to equilibrium. However, they may well have counseled the president to keep inflation to a minimum—for balance of payments reasons as well as others discussed in previous chapters. In an inflationary world, all that the United States really had to do was have a lower inflation rate than other countries, not reduce its price level.

A third way to restore equilibrium was to *adopt various types of controls.* For example, a country might impose controls over the exchange market. Thus the United States government might have required all foreign exchange received by exporters (or others) to be sold to the government, and the government might have rationed this foreign exchange among importers and others who wanted it. By so doing, the government would see that equilibrium in the balance of payments was restored. However, this kind of scheme has many disadvantages. For example, it obviously limits freedom of choice and is difficult for the government to enforce.

Another type of government control is aimed at trade rather than the exchange markets. In this case, the government tries to influence imports and exports through quotas, tariffs, subsidies, and other such controls. For example, the United States might have raised tariffs and imposed quotas to cut its imports, and subsidized some of its exports to increase their volume. It might also have imposed limits on the amount American tourists could spend abroad. Of course, an important difficulty with such interference with free trade is that it reduces world efficiency, as we saw in Chapter 20.

In addition, the government might have discouraged American investment abroad—and in fact it did so in various ways, including the imposition in 1963 of an "interest equalization tax" of 15 percent (later reduced to $11\frac{1}{2}$ percent) on any purchase of a foreign stock or bond by an American from a foreigner. Also, in the special circumstances facing the United States, one way to restore equilibrium to our balance of payments might have been to convince other countries to increase their share of the responsibilities for defense and foreign aid. For example, Western Europe might pay a larger share of the costs of maintaining a defensive shield that protects us all. The United States has been pressing for this for many years, with some success. Also, the United States might have tried to persuade other countries to remove discriminatory barriers to our goods. And finally, the United States might have tried to step up its rate of productivity increase and product innovation. This would have made our exports more competitive.

In fact, what did the United States do in the early 1970s to restore equilibrium in its balance of payments? As you might expect, we adopted many of the measures described above. In December 1971, we depreciated the dollar relative to all major foreign currencies. On the average, the dollar was depreciated by about 10 to 15 percent. Moreover, throughout

The International Money Game

Q: During the early 1970s, what contributed to, or aggravated, an international monetary crisis?

A: It's not a what, but a who. In periods of international financial stress, speculators moved vast sums of money out of weak currencies into strong currencies, and forced the central banks to intervene in order to maintain orderly foreign exchange markets.

Q: Why did speculators do a thing like that?

A: Because it was very profitable.

Q: Who were the speculators?

A: Right after the war (World War II, that is), the "in" speculator was a small Swiss banker (sometimes referred to as a Gnome of Zurich). More recently, much of the speculation business was rumored to be centered in OPEC (Organization of Petroleum Exporting Countries). As long as the U.S. kept exchanging billions of U.S. dollars for oil, the sheiks had plenty to speculate with.

Q: Were there other speculators?

A: Sure. Multinational corporations.

Q: I thought companies dealt in foreign exchange only to cover costs of their imports. Aren't they the honest merchants?

INTERNATIONAL MONEY DESK AT A SWISS BANK, ZURICH.

A: Some do. Most small companies deal in foreign exchange only when converting receipts from an overseas customer into dollars. But a select group of multinationals have come to be major powers in foreign exchange markets. The biggest 200 American-based MNFs (multinational firms) own about $25 billion in cash, and have another $100 billion or so in inventories and receivables. In comparison, West Germany's reserves—the largest of any Western nation—amount to about $31 billion. During the currency crises of the sixties, these MNFs learned that it was not wise to be caught in pounds sterling or dollars, and so began to move money on a large scale.

Q: By ship?

A: No, by prepayment and borrowings. For example, branches of a multinational continuously buy and sell from each other. If a treasurer saw an appreciation of the mark coming on, he urged the German subsidiaries to pay its sister subsidiaries as slowly as possible.

Q: It sounds unpatriotic.

A: Depends on whom you ask. The treasurer would claim enlightened profit-maximizing. Isn't that what you want a firm to do?

E.A.

the early 1970s a serious effort was made to contain inflation at home, and, for better or worse, some protectionist controls were established or continued. Also, the president's special assistant on international economic policy, Peter Peterson (later secretary of commerce), beat the drum for subsidies or encouragement for added research and development by American industry. In February 1973, the dollar was depreciated again, this time by about 10 percent. And when renewed speculation against the dollar caused a further crisis in March 1973, other countries decided to allow the dollar to float, and an international agreement was reached to this effect in Paris. Thus far, the new system of floating exchange rates seems to be working reasonably well, as we have seen in previous sections.

International Lending

Before concluding this chapter, we must discuss international capital movements in somewhat more detail. The factors underlying international transactions with regard to goods and services are clear enough. For example, we saw in the previous chapter why countries find it profitable to import and export goods and services. But we need to know more about the reasons why nations lend to one another. What factors are responsible for the capital movements shown in the balance of payments?

If the world were free of political problems and nationalist fervor, the answer would be easy. Because different parts of the world are endowed with different amounts and qualities of land and other resources, and have different population densities and amounts of capital, the rate of return to be derived from investments will vary from place to place. Consequently, nations where savings rates are high and investment opportunities are relatively poor will invest their capital in nations where the investment opportunities are better.

Such international lending helps both the lender and the borrower. The lender receives a higher rate of return than it would otherwise, and the borrower gains by having more capital to work with, so that the borrower's output and wages are higher than they would be otherwise. So long as the lender receives a relatively high return from the borrowing country, there is no reason why it should ask for repayment. It may continue to lend money to the borrowing country for years and years. For example, England was a net lender to the United States for about a century. To pay interest to the lender, the borrowing country must sell the lender more goods than it buys, thus building up a credit in its balance of payments that it can use to finance the interest, which is, of course, a debit item.

But the world is not free of political problems and nationalist fervor. Wars occur, governments topple, devastating inflations take place, property is confiscated. Only a fool contemplates investment in another country without taking some account of these and other risks; and because these risks are present, international lending that would otherwise be profitable and beneficial—and would take place if only economic considerations were involved—is sometimes stymied. Suppose that you had $1 million to invest, and that you could invest it at 15 percent interest in a country with an unstable government, where the chances were substantial that your investment would be confiscated and that you would get back only a fraction of the $1 million. Would you make the loan? Maybe; maybe not. Unfortunately, such risks discourage many international loans that would otherwise be advantageous to both lender and borrower.

America's Role as International Lender

As a country grows and develops, its balance of

payments tends to go through four stages. First, *a country, when it is relatively undeveloped, is often a net borrower with an "unfavorable" balance of trade.* Its imports exceed its exports, and it borrows from other countries to finance the difference between its imports and exports. It needs the goods, supplies, and equipment it imports to put it on the road to economic development. For example, during the first century of American history we were a substantial net borrower of capital from Europe. This capital helped fuel the early economic growth of the United States, described in Chapter 18.

Second, *as the country pays back more and more of its debts, it gets to the stage where debt repayment exceeds new borrowing, and its balance of trade becomes "favorable."* In other words, its exports exceed its imports, with the difference being used to reduce the country's outstanding debts and to pay interest on them. The United States entered this stage in the 1870s and remained in it for about half a century.

Third, *as the country becomes richer and more advanced, it becomes a net lender to other countries, and its balance of trade continues to be "favorable."* This excess of exports over imports is to be expected, since other countries borrow to finance such a net flow to them of goods and services. The United States entered this stage during and after World War I, when it lent huge amounts to its wartime allies for equipment and relief. Although the 1920s were a period when the United States erected high tariffs and barriers to imports, so long as we continued to lend abroad, foreigners could get the dollars to buy our exports. (However, when we cut back our foreign lending in the 1930s, serious trouble developed.)

Fourth, *the country becomes a mature creditor.* At this point, the interest it receives from its foreign investments is so great that it exceeds the new loans made to foreigners. Thus its balance of trade must become "unfavorable." Its imports will exceed its exports. In real terms, this difference represents payment of goods and services by foreigners for the use of capital. This "unfavorable" balance of trade is not unfavorable at all, since a country consumes imports, not exports. England reached this stage years ago; the United States is currently heading in this direction.

The United States is now the world's great creditor country—the great international lender. We continue to invest vast amounts abroad, both as private firms and individuals take advantage of profitable opportunities and as our government engages in large foreign aid and military programs. The United States is now entering the fourth stage; it is becoming a mature creditor. Our interest from foreign investments made in previous years helps to finance our net imports and our military and aid programs.

Summary

An important difference between international business transactions and business transactions within a country is that international business transactions involve more than one currency. The exchange rate is simply the number of units of one currency that exchanges for a unit of another currency. Before the 1930s, many major countries were on the gold standard, which meant that their currency was convertible into a certain amount of gold, and that the relative gold content of currencies determined exchange rates.

The gold standard is long gone. Another way to determine exchange rates is to allow the market for foreign exchange to function like any other free market, the exchange rate being determined by supply and demand. Under such a system, exchange rates, which are flexible, tend to move in a way that removes imbalances among countries in exports and imports. In 1973, many major countries, including the United States, allowed their currencies to float, resulting in much more flexibility of exchange rates.

Until 1973, when exchange rates became more flexible, most exchange rates were fixed by government action and international agreement. They were allowed to vary slightly, but only slightly, about the official rate. If exchange rates are fixed, the amount of a foreign currency demanded may not equal the amount supplied. To maintain exchange rates at the official levels, governments enter the market and buy and sell their currencies as needed. They also intervene by curbing imports, limiting foreign travel, and other measures. There has been considerable discussion over the relative advantages of fixed and flexible exchange rates.

A country's balance of payments measures the flow of payments between it and other countries. Debit items result in a demand for foreign currency, whereas credit items supply foreign currency. The total of the debit items must equal the total of the credit items because the total of the debit items is the total amount of goods, services, and assets we received from foreigners, and these goods, services, and assets must be paid for with credit items. The balance of merchandise trade refers only to part of the balance of payments. A nation is said to have a favorable (unfavorable) balance of merchandise trade if its exports of merchandise exceed (are less than) its imports of merchandise.

If a country's balance with regard to goods and services, transfers, and capital movements is negative, it is said to have a deficit in its balance of payments. The United States experienced a chronic deficit during the 1950s, 1960s, and early 1970s. This deficit—the result of the growing productivity of other economies, our large investments abroad, and our military and foreign aid expenditures abroad—was financed by reductions in our gold stock and by foreigners' acceptance of our short-term debt. Our balance of payments was in disequilibrium. To bring it into equilibrium, we could depreciate the dollar, curb inflation at home, impose controls of various kinds, or try to step up domestic productivity and innovation. Several steps along this line were attempted, including devaluations of the dollar in 1971 and 1973 and allowing the dollar to float in 1973. Under floating exchange rates, a deficit in our balance of payments is not an indication of pressure on the dollar in foreign exchange markets, because exchange rates are allowed to change in response to such pressure.

The United States is now the world's great creditor country. As a country develops, its balance of payments tends to go through four stages. The United States seems to be entering the fourth stage, where the balance of trade becomes "unfavorable."

CONCEPTS FOR REVIEW

Exchange rate
Devaluation of currency
Appreciation
Depreciation
Crawling peg
International Monetary Fund
Gold exchange standard
Official tier
Private tier
Balance of merchandise trade
Balance of payments
Gold standard
Deficit on an official-settlements basis
Autonomous transactions
Accommodating transactions
Debit items
Credit items

QUESTIONS FOR DISCUSSION AND REVIEW

1. Do you think that we should return to the gold standard? Why or why not? Do you think that this is a live possibility?

2. "Exports finance imports. Unless we export to other countries, we cannot get the imports we need." Comment and evaluate.

3. Suppose that the demand curve for German marks is as follows:

Quantity demanded (billions of marks)	Price (in dollars) of a mark
20	0.20
15	.30
10	.40
5	.50

Plot this demand curve on a graph. What sorts of groups, organizations, and individuals are part of the demand side of this market?

4. Suppose that the supply curve for German marks is as follows:

Quantity supplied (billions of marks)	Price (in dollars) of a mark
8	0.20
9	.30
10	.40
11	.50

Plot this supply curve on the same graph as the demand curve in Question 3. What sorts of groups, organizations, and individuals are part of the supply side of this market?

5. Based on the information in Questions 3 and 4, what is the equilibrium value of the exchange rate, if it is completely flexible? Why? Is the exchange rate between the U.S. dollar and the German mark completely flexible at present?

6. Suppose that the exchange rate is fixed, and that the price (in dollars) of a mark is set at $0.30. Based on the data in Questions 3 and 4, will the quantity of marks demanded equal the quantity supplied? What sorts of government actions will have to be taken?

7. The United States had an unfavorable balance of merchandise trade of about $7 billion in 1972. What does this mean? Of what importance is this fact?

8. Explain in detail why the balance of payments must balance. Indicate the significance of a payments deficit under a regime of fixed exchange rates.

9. During the 1950s and 1960s, the British government reacted to deficits in its balance of payments by adopting deflationary monetary and fiscal policies (temporarily at least). Was this sensible? Why or why not?

10. Under what circumstances would you be willing to invest $10,000 (if you had $10,000) in (a) Chile, (b) Angola, (c) Japan, (d) India? What interest rate would you expect? What guarantees would you expect? Why?

22 The Less Developed Countries

Fresh from a raid on the well-stocked family refrigerator or comfortably placed in front of a television set, the average American finds it difficult to believe that hunger is a problem in the world. Yet it is. The industrialized countries—like the United States, Western Europe, Japan, and the USSR—are really just rich little islands surrounded by seas of poverty in Asia, Africa, and much of Latin America. This chapter deals with the problems of these so-called "less developed countries" (LDCs)—the poor countries of the world. We take up several questions. Which countries are poor and why? How badly do they need additional capital? How great is the danger of overpopulation? To what extent do they lack modern technology? How can they stimulate their rate of economic growth? What can the United States do to help them? These questions are crucial, both to the people in the less developed countries and to us.

Less Developed Countries: Definition and Characteristics

What Is a Less Developed Country?

Economics abounds with clumsy terms. A profession responsible for cross elasticity of demand and average propensity to consume cannot claim a prize for elegant language. The term *less developed country* is not a model of clarity. For a country to be less developed it must be poor, but *how* poor? Any answer has to be arbitrary. We shall define any country with a per capita income of $750 or less as less developed. Although the $750 cut-off point is arbitrary, it certainly is low enough so that any country unfortunate enough to qualify is most certainly poor. Recall that per capita income in the United States is about $7,000.

Table 22.1 shows that many countries have a per capita income of $750 or less. Thus much of the world is, by this definition, less developed. Indeed, *the staggering fact is that more people live in the less developed countries than in the developed countries (with per capita incomes of over $3,000) or the intermediate countries (with per capita incomes of $751 to $3,000).* Specifically, about 1/5 of the world's people live in the developed countries, about 1/8 live in the intermediate countries, and 2/3 live in the less developed countries.

Imagine what life might be like if you grew up in a country with per capita income of $750 or less per year.[1] Chances are that you would be illiterate. You would probably work on a farm with meager tools and little technology. You would have few possessions (and sometimes only enough food to keep body and soul

[1] It must be noted that these income figures *overestimate* the gap between the rich and poor nations, since the procedure used to translate local currencies into dollars is to look at prices of internationally traded goods, which are generally more expensive than goods and services consumed locally. Thus a per capita income of $750 or less isn't as low as it seems, but is still very low.

Table 22.1
Countries Classified by Level of Per Capita Income, 1974

A. Countries with per capita income exceeding $3,000			
Australia	Finland	Luxembourg	Sweden
Austria	France	Netherlands	Switzerland
Belgium	Germany	New Zealand	United Kingdom
Canada	Iceland	Norway	United States
Denmark	Japan	Soviet Union	
B. Countries with per capita income of $751 to $3,000			
Argentina	Hong Kong	Panama	Spain
Chile	Jamaica	Portugal	Uruguay
Costa Rica	Lebanon	Saudi Arabia	Venezuela
Greece	Malta	South Africa	
C. Countries with per capita income of $750 or less			
Afghanistan	China	Iraq	Peru
Algeria	Congo	Kenya	Philippines
Angola	Egypt	Laos	Sri Lanka
Bangladesh	Ethiopia	Malaysia	Thailand
Brazil	Ghana	Morocco	Turkey
Burma	India	Nigeria	Uganda
Cambodia	Indonesia	Pakistan	Zaire

Source: Agency for International Development

together) and be likely to die young. This is the life in most of Asia, Africa, and Latin America.

The unpleasant fact is that this harsh existence—not the affluent way of life portrayed in *Better Homes and Gardens* or even the *Jersey City Journal*—is the lot of most earth dwellers. Of course this does not mean that the less developed countries do not have rich citizens: indeed they do. But the rich are a tiny minority surrounded by masses of poor people. Nor does it mean that many of these people do not live in cities. Bombay, for example, is the home of over 4 million, most of them poor.

It must also be recognized that many of the less developed countries have gained their political independence in recent years. Before World War II, the major European powers had substantial empires. For example, the British had colonies all over the globe. In the postwar period, many colonies have achieved independence. These new countries are often fiercely nationalistic. They resent what they regard as exploitation at the hands of the former European colonists and demand power and status. Although weak individually, together they represent a force that must be reckoned with.

Moreover, because of better communications and altered religious and cultural beliefs, the expectations and demands of people in less developed countries have changed enormously. Years ago, they were more likely to accept a life of privation and want, since their eye was on the next world. Now the emphasis has shifted to this world, and to material comforts—and getting them quickly. People in less developed countries have become aware of the high standards of living in the industrialized societies, and they want to catch up as fast as they can.

Although the available data on the less developed countries are not as accurate as one would like, these countries seem to have increased their per capita output in recent years. As Table 22.2 shows, the average rate of growth of per capita output in 15 major less developed countries was about 2½ percent per year during 1950-73. But since the average growth rate in the major developed countries was somewhat higher, *the gap between income per capita in the less developed countries and in the developed countries has been increasing.* This is a disturbing fact. Apparently, the gap between rich and poor will not decrease, unless recent trends are altered.

Table 22.2
Annual Rate of Growth of Per Capita National Product, 1950–67 and 1970–73

Less developed country	Average annual growth rate 1950–67	1970–73[a]
Brazil	2.1	3.9
Sri Lanka	0.8	-0.6
Colombia	1.3	2.8
Egypt	2.7	1.6
Ghana	1.3	5.1
India	1.6	-0.9
Malaya	0.8	n.a.
Mexico	2.8	3.5
Pakistan	1.5	-2.4
Peru	2.9	2.6
Philippines	1.8	3.1
South Korea	3.8	8.7
Taiwan	5.3	n.a.
Thailand	3.2	2.3
Turkey	2.8	5.9
Average	2.3	2.7

Source: A. Maddison, *Economic Progress and Policy in Developing Countries,* New York: Norton, 1970; and United Nations.
[a] Where figures for 1970–73 were unavailable, 1970–72 (or the most recent period for which data were available) was used.

A Closer Look at the LDCs

Needless to say, the less developed countries vary enormously. Some, like China, are huge; others, like Paraguay, are small. Some, like Taiwan, have lots of people jammed into every square mile of land; others, like Brazil, have relatively few people spread over lots of land. Some, like Iraq, have important natural resources (notably oil); others have few resources. Some, like India, have had great civilizations many, many centuries old; others have had ruder histories. Nonetheless, although it is not easy to generalize about the less developed countries, many of them, besides suffering from relatively low productivity, have the following characteristics:

Stress on agriculture. The less developed countries generally devote most of their resources to food production. Agriculture is by far their largest industry. This contrasts markedly with industrialized countries like the United States, where only a small percentage of output is food. Moreover, food makes up most of the goods consumed in less developed countries. They are so poor that the typical family has very little besides food, a crude dwelling, some simple clothing, and other such necessities.

Dual economy. Many less developed countries have two economies, existing side by side. One of these is a *market-oriented* economy much like that in developed countries. This economy is generally found in the big cities, where there may be some modern manufacturing plants, as well as government agencies, wholesale and retail outlets, and services for the small number of rich people in the country. Coexisting with this relatively modern economy is a *subsistence* economy based largely on barter, innocent of all but the crudest technology and capable of producing little more—and sometimes less—than a subsistence wage for the inhabitants. This subsistence economy often includes most of the rural areas. It has little or no capital, few decent roads, only the most rudimentary communications. Unfortunately, this is the economy in which the bulk of the population exists.

Political problems. Some of the less developed countries have relatively weak, unstable governments. Thus the climate for long-term investment and planning is relatively poor in such countries. Moreover, some governments are controlled by a small group of wealthy citizens or by other groups with a vested interest in resisting social change. Corruption among government officials is encountered too often, and honest officials are sometimes not very well trained or experienced in their duties. To some extent these problems stem from the relative youth of many of these countries. But whatever the reasons, they hamper the effect of government on economic development.

Income inequality. Most of the less developed countries have a relatively high degree of income inequality. Indeed, there is much more income inequality than in the industrialized countries. Typically, a few landowners or industrialists in a less developed country are rich, sometimes enormously rich. But all outside this tiny group are likely to be very poor. The middle class, so important in the industrialized countries, is very small in most less developed countries.

Barriers to Development and the Need for Capital Formation

Why are the less developed economies so poor, and what can they do to raise their income levels? These are very difficult questions, both because the answers vary from country to country and because the answers for any single country are hard to determine. A variety of factors generally is responsible for a country's poverty, and these factors are so intermeshed that it is difficult to tell which are most important. Nonetheless, certain factors stand out; among these is the lack of capital in less developed countries.

Without exception, the people in the less developed countries have relatively little capital to work with. There are few factories, machine tools, roads, tractors, power plants, miles of railroad, and so on. If you visited one of these countries, you would be struck by the absence of mechanical aids to production. Workers use their hands, legs, and simple tools, often as their ancestors did long ago.

There are several reasons why the less developed countries have not accumulated much capital. First, a country must usually reduce consumption to accumulate capital, but for the less developed countries, with their very low income levels, a reduction in consumption can be painful. Equally important, much of the saving that does go on in less developed countries is not utilized very effectively. Second, there are important barriers to domestic investment, such as the smallness of local markets, the lack of skilled labor, and the lack of qualified entrepreneurs (faced with the right incentives) who are willing and able to take the risks involved in carrying out investment projects. Third, fear that property will be confiscated deters industrialized countries from investing in the less developed countries. As we pointed out above, many of the less developed countries are relatively young nations, filled with nationalistic fervor and fearful of becoming economically dependent. They are suspicious of foreign investment in their countries—and in some cases are quite capable of confiscating foreign-owned property. Needless to say, this does not make foreigners particularly anxious to invest in some of them.

Recognizing their need for additional capital, the less developed countries have used three principal methods to increase investment. First, they have *taxed away part of the nation's resources and used them for investment purposes or made them available to private investors.* Second, they have tried to *mobilize "surplus labor" from agriculture to carry out investment projects.* Third, they have *increased government spending on investment projects without increasing taxes, thus producing inflation.* Although effective within limits, each of these methods has important limitations. Taxes may dull incentives and in any event are often evaded; "surplus labor" is difficult to transfer and utilize; and a little inflation may soon develop into a big inflation. (As shown in Table 22.3, the rate of inflation in some less developed countries has been impressive indeed.) Besides these three methods, a country can *use foreign aid to increase investment.* It too has its problems and limitations, but it is hard to see how many less developed countries can scrape up the capital they need without it.

Methods of this sort have enabled many less developed countries to increase the proportion of their national output devoted to capital formation. For example, Table 22.4 shows that in major LDCs the average proportion of national output devoted to capital formation was about 16 percent in 1973 (whereas it was less

Table 22.3
Annual Rate of Increase of the Domestic Price Level, 1950–65 and 1971–73

	Average annual rate of increase (percent)	
Country	1950–65	1971–73[a]
Brazil	30.1	21
Sri Lanka	−0.1	7
Colombia	9.3	18
Egypt	1.6	3
Ghana	5.7	9
India	2.3	9
Malaya	1.4	5
Mexico	6.2	9
Pakistan	2.3	5
Peru	8.2	8
Philippines	1.8	18
South Korea	19.8	10
Taiwan	6.6	n.a.
Thailand	1.6	6
Turkey	8.2	18
Average	7.1	10

Source: See Table 22.2.
[a] 1970–71 for Brazil and Pakistan.

Table 22.4
Gross Fixed Capital Formation as a Percentage of National Product, 1973[a]

Less developed countries: Country	Percentage	Developed countries: Country	Percentage
Brazil	16	France	26
Sri Lanka	17	Germany	25
Colombia	19	Italy	19
Egypt	11	Japan	37
Ghana	9	United Kingdom	18
India	15		
Malaya	16	Average	24
Mexico	19		
Pakistan	13		
Peru	13		
Phillipines	18		
South Korea	24		
Thailand	20		
Turkey	18		
Average	16		

Source: United Nations.
[a] Where 1973 figures are unavailable, these data pertain to 1972, 1971, or whatever is the latest year for which data are given.

than 10 percent in 1950). This proportion is still significantly less than in the developed countries, where it averaged about 24 percent in 1973, but it is increasing. Needless to say, these figures are very rough, and not too much reliance should be placed on them. But they do indicate that the less developed countries are progressing in their attempts to increase their rate of capital formation.

The Population Explosion

Another very important reason why per capita income is so low in some (but by no means all) less developed countries is that they suffer from overpopulation. Many less developed countries have sizably increased their total output. In Latin America, Africa, and Southeast Asia, it may have grown at about 5 percent per year in recent years. If population in these areas had remained approximately constant, output per capita would also have increased at about 5 percent per year. But population has not remained constant. It has grown at almost 3 percent per year, so that output per capita has increased at only about 2 percent per year.

Table 22.5 shows the rate of population growth in a variety of less developed countries, as well as some major developed countries. Clearly the rate has been higher, without exception, in the less developed countries than in the developed ones. The most important reason is that modern methods of preventing and curing diseases have been introduced into the LDCs, thus reducing the death rate, particularly among children. It used to be that although the birth rate in the less developed countries was higher than in the developed countries, the death rate was also higher, so that the rate of population growth was about

Table 22.5
Annual Rates of Growth of Population, Less Developed and Developed Countries, 1950–67 and 1970–73 (percentages)

Less developed		
Country	1950–67	1970–73
Brazil	3.1	2.8
Sri Lanka	2.5	1.9
Colombia	3.2	3.2
Egypt	2.5	2.2
Ghana	2.7	2.7
India	2.2	2.1
Malaya	3.0	3.7
Mexico	3.3	3.5
Pakistan	2.4	3.6
Peru	2.6	3.2
Philippines	3.2	3.0
South Korea	2.8	2.0
Taiwan	3.1	n.a.
Thailand	3.0	3.2
Turkey	2.7	2.5
Average	2.8	2.8

Developed		
Country	1950–67	1970–73
France	1.1	0.9
Germany	1.2	0.7
Italy	0.7	0.8
Japan	1.1	1.3
United Kingdom	0.5	0.3
United States	1.6	0.9
Average	1.0	0.8

Source: See Table 22.2.

the same in the less developed countries as in the developed ones. But in recent years, the death rate in the LDCs has been reduced by better control of malaria and other diseases, whereas the birth rate has remained high. The result has been a population explosion. For example, in parts of Latin America the population is doubling every 20 years.

This growth of sheer numbers, which recalls the work of Thomas Malthus (Chapter 17), is only part of the problem. The populations of the less developed countries also tend to be illiterate and ill-nourished. Thus they do not have the skills required to absorb much modern technology. In addition, many workers have little or nothing to do. They live with their relatives and occasionally hold a job. Although they may not be included in the official unemployment figures, they represent a case of *disguised unemployment.* In sum, the population of many less developed countries is large (relative to the available capital and natural resources), fast-growing, of relatively poor economic quality, and poorly utilized.

The less developed countries have responded to the population explosion in at least two ways. Where birth control is opposed on religious or cultural grounds, the LDCs often concentrate on the widespread unemployment that results from population increase. The rapidly expanding labor force cannot be employed productively in agriculture, since there is already a surplus of farm labor in many LDCs, and the capital stock is not increasing rapidly enough to employ the growing numbers in industry. Governments faced with serious unemployment of this sort often are induced to *create public works programs and other projects to make jobs, even if these projects do not really promote economic growth.*

The LDCs have also responded to the population explosion by *attempting to lower the birth rate through the diffusion of contraceptive devices and other birth control techniques.* In many of the less developed countries, there is no religious barrier to the adoption of such techniques. For example, Hinduism does not frown on birth control. However, their adoption has been slow. One reason is the medical drawbacks of existing contraceptive devices. Also, there are obvious problems in communicating the necessary information to huge numbers of illiterate and often superstitious people. India has made considerable efforts to disseminate birth control information, but the problems are enormous. In some of the smaller LDC's, such as Singapore, South Korea, and Taiwan, birth control programs seem to have had a more definite effect on the rate of population increase.

Besides trying to cope with or influence the growth rate of their populations, the LDCs have also tried to increase the economic quality of their human resources. In other words, *they have been investing in human capital.* Such an investment seems warranted; educational and skill levels in many less developed countries have been quite low. Table 22.6 shows that in 15 major less developed countries, the proportion of the population aged 5 to 19 in primary or secondary school increased, on the average, from about 30 percent in 1950 to about 50 percent in 1964. This was certainly a step in the right direction, although enrollment in school is obviously only a crude measure of the quality of the labor force. In order to absorb and utilize, and eventually develop, modern technology, the LDCs must continue to invest in a more productive labor force.

Table 22.6
Percentage of Population Aged 5 to 19 Enrolled in Primary and Secondary Education, 1950 and 1964

Country	1950	1964
	(percentage)	
Brazil	22	46
Sri Lanka	54	65
Colombia	22	45
Egypt	20	41
Ghana	14	57
India	19	38
Malaya	35	50
Mexico	30	52
Pakistan	16	25
Peru	34	50
Philippines	59	57
South Korea	43	53
Taiwan	38	64
Thailand	38	48
Turkey	24	40
Average	31	52
United States	80	84

Source: Statistical Yearbook, UNESCO.

Technology: A Crucial Factor

Still another very important reason why per capita income is so low in the less developed countries is that these countries use rudimentary and often backward technology. In previous chapters, we have seen that to a considerable extent the increase in per capita income in the developed countries has resulted from the development and application of new technology. Too often, the less developed countries still use the technology of their forefathers—the agricultural and manufacturing methods of long, long ago. Why is this the case? Why don't the less developed countries copy the advanced technology of the industrialized countries, following the examples of the Japanese and Russians, among others, who promoted their economic development during the twentieth century by copying Western technology?

There are several reasons. One is that some types of modern technology require considerable capital. Modern petroleum refining technology, to choose one, cannot be used without lots of capital, which the less developed countries, with their low rates of investment, find difficult to scrape up. But many technological improvements do not require substantial capital. Indeed, some technological improvements are capital-saving. That is, they reduce the amount of capital needed to produce a given amount of output.

A second reason why the less developed countries find it difficult to copy and use modern technology is that they lack both a skilled labor force and entrepreneurs. Imagine the difficulties in transplanting a complicated technology—for example, that involved in steel production—from the United States to a less developed country where there are few competent engineers, fewer experienced and resourceful managers, and practically no laborers with experience in the demanding work required to operate a modern steel plant.

Even more fundamental is the fact that much of our advanced Western technology is really not very well suited to circumstances in the less developed countries. Because the industrialized countries have relatively great amounts of capital and relatively little labor, they tend to develop and adopt technology that substitutes capital for labor. But this technology may not be appropriate for less developed countries where there is little capital and lots of labor. Thus *it is very important that the less developed countries pick and choose among the technologies available in the industrialized countries, and that they adapt these technologies to their own conditions.* Mindless attempts to ape the technologies used in the industrialized countries can result in waste and failure.

In agriculture, important technological advances have taken place in the less developed countries in recent years. In particular, new types of seeds have been developed, increasing the yields of wheat, rice, and other crops. Some of this research was supported by the Rockefeller and Ford Foundations. The resulting increase in agricultural productivity has been so impressive that many observers call it a "green revolution." There is no question that wheat and rice production has increased greatly in countries like Mexico, the Philippines, Iran, Sri Lanka, India, and Pakistan. Plenty of opportunity remains for improvements in livestock yields as well, but religious beliefs and traditional prejudices are sometimes an important barrier to change.

In industry, most of the new technology adopted by the less developed countries is taken from the developed countries. Very little attempt is being made to devise new technologies more appropriate to conditions in the less developed countries, both because the less developed countries do not have the engineering and scientific resources to develop them, and because such attempts have not been very successful in the past. In countries where the private sector finds it unprofitable to carry out research and development, government research institutes sometimes try to fill the void, but these institutes frequently devote too much of their limited resources to projects not closely related to economic development. In addition, productivity centers have been created in some countries to teach managers and supervisory personnel how to make better use of new technology. Such centers have helped promote the diffusion of new technology in Mexico and Taiwan, among other countries.

Entrepreneurship, Social Institutions, and Natural Resources

Yet another important reason why per capita income is so low in the less developed countries is that they lack entrepreneurs and favorable social institutions. This point was noted in the previous section but needs more discussion. In some LDCs there is a rigid social structure. One "knows one's place" and stays in it, people distrust and resist change, and things are done in the time-honored way they have always been done (as far as anyone can remember). No wonder these countries lack entrepreneurs! The basic social and political institutions discourage entrepreneurship. Moreover, these institutions also are at least partially responsible for the ineffective utilizations of savings, relatively high birth rates, and difficulties in transferring technology noted above. As Richard Gill of Harvard University has put it, "In many underdeveloped countries, a complete social and political revolution is required while the industrial revolution is getting underway."

The governments of many less developed countries are relatively weak and unstable. It is difficult enough for any government to give these countries an effective tax system and a rational program of public expenditures, including proper provision for the highways, public utilities, communications, and other "social overhead capital" they need. But the problems are made even more difficult when the government is weak, unstable, and perhaps somewhat corrupt. Further, the population's value systems and attitudes sometimes do little to promote economic development. Again quoting Gill, "A sharp desire for material betterment, a willingness to work hard and in a regular, punctual manner, an awareness of the future benefits of present sacrifices—these attitudes may be the prerequisites of economic growth; yet they may be largely absent in many underdeveloped countries."[2]

Finally, it should also be pointed out that some of the LDCs have little in the way of natural resources. Moreover, technological change has made some of their resources less valuable, as in the case of synthetic rubber, which affected the market for natural rubber, an important natural resource of Malaya. But this is not true of all the less developed countries: Iraq and Indonesia, among others, are endowed with oil, which (as members of the OPEC cartel) they are using to propel themselves into affluence. In any event, the skimpiness of natural resources in some less developed countries does not mean that they are condemned to poverty. Neither Denmark nor Switzerland is endowed with great natural resources, but both are prosperous.

The important thing is how a country uses what it has. International trade allows a country to compensate, at least in part, for its deficiencies in natural resources. Thus, although some of the less developed countries have been dealt a poor hand by Mother Nature, this lack alone does not explain their poverty. Of course, they might have been more prosperous with more natural resources; but even with what they have, they might have done much better.

There are several ways for them to use their resources more effectively. In many of the less developed countries, a peasant may farm several strips of land that are very small and distant from one another, working a small patch here and a small patch there. Obviously, this procedure is very inefficient. If these small plots could be put together into larger farms, output and productivity could be increased. In other LDCs, huge farms are owned by landlords and worked by tenant farmers. This system too tends to be inefficient, because the tenant farmers have little incentive to increase productivity (since the extra output will accrue to the landlord) and the landlords have little incentive to invest in new technology (since they often fear that the tenant farmers will not know how to use the new equipment).

Land reform is a very lively—indeed an explosive—issue in many less developed countries, and one of the issues the Communists try to exploit. Recall that agriculture is a very important part of the economy of most of the less developed countries. Thus the land is the major form of productive wealth. No wonder

[2] Richard Gill, *Economic Development: Past and Present,* Englewood Cliffs, N.J.: Prentice-Hall, 1967, p. 87.

there is a bitter struggle in some countries over who is to own and work it.

The Role of Government

There are several opinions on the role the governments of the less developed countries should play in promoting economic growth. Some people go so far as to say that these countries would fare best if they allowed market forces to work with a minimum of government interference. But the less developed countries themselves believe a free enterprise system would produce results too slowly, if at all. Thus the prevailing view in the less developed countries is that the government must intervene—and on a large scale.

In some less developed countries—China, for example—the government exercises almost complete control over the ecomony. The government makes the basic decisions on what is produced, how it is produced, and who gets it. But even in the non-Communist LDCs, such as India, the government makes many decisions on what sorts of investment projects will be undertaken, and it controls foreign exchange. And, needless to say, the government has the responsibility for providing the important social overhead capital—roads, public utilities, schools, and so on—that is so badly needed.

Further, the government may also foster social and political change. As Nobel laureate Simon Kuznets has put it, "The problem of strategy is essentially the problem of how fast you can change an inadequate set of social and political institutions, without provoking a revolution internally, or losing allies and partners externally. The question is to know what institutions you want to change, and how."

Most economists would agree that the government has a very important role to play in promoting economic development. But there is a tendency to put less weight on the government's role than in the past. Experience has made it clear that some of the less developed countries are plagued by incompetent and corrupt government officials and by a plethora of bureaucratic red tape. Moreover, many governments have gone on spending sprees that have resulted in serious inflation. Even those who are very mistrustful of free markets find it difficult to put their complete faith in such governments, well-intentioned though they may be. Recent years have seen more and more emphasis on self-interest and individual action as contributors to growth. (If Adam Smith is peering down from the Great Beyond, he probably is smiling in agreement.) But this in no way denies the fact that governments have a key role to play.

Balanced Growth

An important issue facing the governments of most less developed countries is the extent to which they want to maintain a balance between the agricultural and industrial sectors of the economy. That is, how much more rapidly should they expand industry than agriculture? According to some economists, less developed countries should invest heavily in industry, since the long-term trend of industrial prices is upward, relative to agricultural prices. In addition, advocates of unbalanced growth argue that the development of certain sectors of the economy will result in pressures for development elsewhere in the economy. Advocates of this approach point to the Soviet Union, which stressed industrialization in its growth strategy.

Other economists argue that industry and agriculture should be expanded at a more nearly equal rate. Successful industrial expansion requires agricultural expansion as well, because industry uses raw materials as inputs and because, as economic growth takes place, the people will demand more food. Balanced growth has other advantages. Various sectors of the economy are closely linked and an attempt to expand one sector in isolation is unlikely to succeed. Proponents of balanced growth deny that the long-term trend of industrial prices is upward, relative to agricultural prices. And to illustrate the wisdom of their approach, they cite as examples the United States and Britain, where industry and agriculture both expanded in the course of the development process.

In practically all of the 13 LDCs included in Table 22.7, industrial employment has increased more rapidly than agricultural employment in recent years. Without question, the less developed countries are expanding industry relative to agriculture. In some cases, such as India and Pakistan, it is generally agreed that more balance—more emphasis on agriculture—would have been preferable. Moreover, in many cases, the allocation of resources within industry could certainly have been improved. Countries have sometimes put too much emphasis on substituting their own production—even when it is not efficient—for imports. For example, Chile has prohibited the import of fully assembled cars to promote domestic production, but Chile's automobile plants have been uneconomic.

One reason why the less developed countries tend to push industrialization is that they see heavy industrialization in the wealthier countries. The United States, Western Europe, Japan, the USSR, all have lots of steel plants, oil refineries, chemical plants, and other kinds of heavy industry. It is easy for the less developed countries to jump to the conclusion that, if they want to become richer, they must become heavily industrialized too. It certainly

Table 22.7
Average Annual Rate of Growth of Product, by Sector, 1960–70

Country	Industry	Agriculture	Wholesale and retail trade
		(percentage)	
Brazil	6.4	3.9	5.3
Sri Lanka[a]	7.2	2.7	6.8
Colombia	5.5	3.6	5.4
Egypt	6.0	4.7	4.0
Ghana[b]	8.4	5.2	6.1
India	5.2	2.0	4.2
Mexico	9.3	3.9	8.2
Pakistan[c]	8.7	3.7	6.1
Peru[b]	4.6	6.1	n.a.
Phillipines	5.8	4.0	4.3
South Korea	16.6	4.5	10.2
Thailand	11.9	5.5	9.4
Turkey	10.3	2.5	8.7
Average	8.1	4.0	6.6

Source: United Nations.
[a]1963–70.
[b]1968–70.
[c]1960–69.

seems sensible enough—until you think about the theory of comparative advantage. After all, if the less developed countries have a comparative advantage in areas other than heavy industry, they may do better to put more of their resources where their comparative advantage lies.

Another reason why the leaders of some less developed countries are fascinated by steel plants, airlines, and other modern industries, is that they think such industries confer prestige on their countries and themselves. Such prestige may be costly. Given their current situation, many of these countries might be well advised to invest much of their scarce resources in promoting higher productivity in agriculture, where they have a comparative advantage. Of course, we are not saying that many of these countries should not attempt to industrialize. We *are* saying that some of them have pushed industrialization too far—and that many have pushed it in uneconomic directions.

Development Planning in Less Developed Countries

The governments of many LDCs have established development plans to specify targets or goals for the economy. In some countries, these goals are set forth in very specific, detailed form; in others, they are more generally formulated. An important purpose of these plans is to allocate scarce resources, such as capital, in order to achieve rapid economic growth (or whatever the country's social objectives may be). For example, in India, estimates have been made of the amount of capital that would be generated internally, as well as the capital that could be imported from abroad. Then the plan attempted to set a system of priorities for the use of this capital.

Some plans are merely window dressing, full of bold words and little else. But others are the result of careful investigation and hard work. Clearly, to be useful, a plan must set realistic goals, which take proper account of the country's resources, available capital, and institutions. An unrealistically ambitious plan, if actually put in effect, is likely to lead to inflation, while a plan that is too easily satisfied is likely to mean a less than optimal rate of economic growth.

A useful plan should specify the policies to be used to reach the plan's goals, as well as the goals themselves. It should also forecast carefully how the various components of gross national product will change over time, the extent to which inflationary pressures will develop, the adequacy of the supply of foreign exchange, and the effects of the development program on various regions and parts of the population.

Planning techniques have benefited from the application of many tools of modern economic analysis, among them linear programming and input-output analysis. Linear programming can be used to determine how resources should be allocated to maximize output, and input-output analysis can determine how much capacity there must be in various industries to satisfy certain consumption targets. These modern tools have undoubtedly helped in formulating development plans, but their importance should not be exaggerated. It would be a great mistake to think that making a good plan is merely a job for an electronic computer.

If the plan is realistic, it can be a useful tool, but unless it is implemented properly, it will achieve very little for the economy. How well it is implemented will depend on the government's ability to marshal resources through taxation and foreign aid, to work effectively with the private sector, and to pick productive public investment projects. In some countries, like India, "the plan" has sometimes become a political symbol, but in many others, like Mexico, planning has been politically less visible. Countries where economic growth has been most rapid seem to have viewed "the plan" less as holy writ, and planning has tended to be more modest and low-key.

Planning in Action: The Case of India

Perhaps the best way to understand the operation of development plans is to look at the nature of a particular country's plans and how they have been fulfilled. For example, consider the interesting case of India, which has had a series of five-year plans.[3] The First Five-Year Plan was for 1951–56. Its targets were to increase net investment in India from 5 to 6.75 percent of national income, to reduce income inequality, to cut the rate of population increase to 1 percent per year, and to lay the groundwork for a doubling of per capita output in a generation. To achieve these targets, the government relied heavily on capital formation. In particular, it sought to carry out many of the investment projects that had been discussed and planned under the British for 50 years or more. The First Five-Year Plan was accompanied by moderate growth. Per capita output grew by about 1.7 percent per year, and net investment rose from 5 to 8 percent of national income.

At the beginning of 1956, the Indian Planning Commission published its Second Five-Year Plan, which called for much heavier investments—and more emphasis on investment in industry and mining, rather than agriculture and power—than the First Plan. Moreover, the Second Plan relied more heavily on deficit financing than did the First Plan, and devoted much more attention to the expansion of employment opportunities, since unemployment was a considerable problem. Unfortunately, the Second Plan ran into severe difficulties. One big problem was the loss of foreign exchange, as imports grew much more rapidly—and exports less rapidly—than expected. But perhaps more important was the fact that output did not grow as rapidly as the plan called for. By the end of the Second Five-Year Plan, all sectors of the economy, other than the service sector, were producing less than the planned targets. Nonetheless, per capita output grew by about 1.8 percent per year.

India's Third Five-Year Plan—for 1961–66—involved bigger investments and somewhat more emphasis on agriculture than the Second Plan. Responding to the fact that agricultural imports had been much higher than expected under the Second Plan, the Third Plan called for more investment in agriculture. Unfortunately, however, agricultural production during the Third Plan did not come up to expectations. Indeed, India might have experienced a serious famine in 1966 if it had not received substantial food imports from the United States. During the course of the Third Plan, India did increase the percentage of national income devoted to investment from 11 to 14 percent, but a substantial proportion of her investment was financed by foreign aid. Unfortunately, India's output grew by 1/6, instead of the planned 1/3, during the Third Plan, and there was little or no increase in per capita output.

Although the failure of the Third Plan was due in considerable measure to India's involvement in two wars and to two bad harvests, it nonetheless shook many Indians' confidence in the planning process. There was a three-year delay before the Fourth Five-Year Plan was unveiled, and its political significance was played down. The Fourth Plan shifted the emphasis to agricultural development, including irrigation and fertilizers; it stressed a large birth control program; and it called for a 5½ percent increase per year in national output, as

[3] It is worthwhile emphasizing that the development strategies of *small* LDCs, because of their necessarily greater reliance on foreign trade, must be quite different from that of *large* LDCs, like India.

well as further increases in investment. The Fourth Plan put somewhat more emphasis on the price system and somewhat less on detailed planning. In practice, however, the latter changes seemed to have been slow to occur.

In 1975, when Prime Minister Indira Gandhi declared a national emergency, she claimed that many of the stern measures taken at that time were designed to help improve India's economic condition. She put forth a 20-Point Economic Program which emphasized the reduction of inflation, the encouragement of agriculture, and the reduction of the birth rate. How much impact this program will have on India's serious economic problems is hard to say.[4]

Choosing Investment Projects in Less Developed Countries

Clearly, one of the crucial problems any less developed country must face is how the available capital should be invested. Countless investment projects could be undertaken—roads, irrigation projects, power plants, improvements in agricultural equipment, and so on. Faced with this menu of alternatives, how should a country choose?

One procedure often used is to accept projects resulting in high output per unit of capital invested. That is, projects are ranked by the ratio of the value of the output they produce to the capital they require. For example, if a project yields \$2 million worth of output per year and requires \$1 million of capital, its ratio would be 2. Projects with high values of this ratio are accepted. This procedure, which is crude but sensible, is based on the correct idea that capital is the really scarce resource in many of the less developed countries. It is aimed at maximizing the output to be derived from a certain amount of capital.

However, a better technique for choosing projects is the concept of rate of return, which is used by profit-maximizing firms to choose among alternative investment opportunities. A less developed country, like a firm, can compute the rate of return from each investment opportunity. That is, it can estimate the rate of interest that will be obtained from each investment. Then it, like a firm, should choose the *projects with the highest rates of return.*

In computing the rate of return from each investment project, it is necessary to attach values to the resources it uses and to the returns it produces. At first glance, it may seem adequate to use market prices of inputs and outputs as these values. For example, if unskilled labor's market price is \$.10 an hour, this would be the value attached to unskilled labor. Unfortunately, there are some important pitfalls in using market prices in this way. In particular, *market prices of inputs in the less developed countries often do not indicate social costs properly.* For example, although the market price of unskilled labor may be \$.10 an hour, there may be lots of unskilled labor doing essentially nothing in the countryside, with the result that the social cost—the true alternative cost—of using such labor is zero, not \$.10 an hour. Moreover, *the market prices of some outputs may not indicate their social worth.* Because of tariffs and quotas, domestic prices may differ significantly from world prices, which may be closer to the appropriate price for some analyses of this sort.

Thus, when computing each project's rate of return, it is important to make proper adjustments so that inputs are valued at their social cost and outputs are valued at their social worth. This is easier said than done, but even crude adjustments in the right direction can be worthwhile.

[4] Much of the material in the section comes from Benjamin Higgins, *Economic Development,* New York: Norton, 1968; J. Bhagwati and P. Desai, *India: Planning for Industrialization,* Oxford: Oxford University Press, 1970; R. Gill, *Economic Development,* A. Maddison, *Economic Progress and Policy,* and W. Malenbaum, *Modern India's Economy,* Columbus, Ohio: Charles Merrill, 1971.

OPEC: A Model for Other Less Developed Countries?

The OPEC oil cartel, when it precipitously raised the price of crude oil, transformed a group of less developed countries, like Saudi Arabia, Iran, and Libya, from relative poverty to relative affluence. Some economists believe that other less developed countries will attempt to form cartels to raise the price of raw materials over which they have significant control. Indeed, there has already been some activity in this direction. For example, the seven leading bauxite exporters have formed the International Bauxite Association, and have pushed for significant increases in the price of this major raw material (used to make aluminum). And the leading tin producers have asked for substantial price increases.

The circumstances under which such cartels are likely to be successful are relatively easy to enumerate. First, the cartel must be able to control the supply of the commodity, or at least a very substantial portion of it. Unless the cartel can reduce the amount supplied, it cannot increase the price. Second, the members of the cartel must be able to agree on policy and coordinate their actions.

If some countries cheat on the cartel agreements and secretly cut prices, the cartel may fall apart. Third, the demand for the product must be relatively insensitive to price changes. If, for example, close substitutes exist for the product, the cartel may not find it worthwhile to raise prices very far.

The accompanying table lists the raw materials where the chances seem highest that a cartel of this sort might be successful. Let's look more closely at a few of the most likely cases—bauxite, copper, and tin. In the case of bauxite (and alumina), about 75 percent of the world's exports come from the seven members of the International Bauxite Association—Australia, Guinea, Guyana, Jamaica, Sierra Leone, Surinam, and Yugoslavia. Like OPEC, the members of this group have pressed for higher taxes on the multinational firms that process the raw material. In the view of many knowledgeable economists, this is the case where the probability of OPEC-type action is greatest.

With regard to copper, four leading producing countries have formed CIPEC (a French acronym for the copper council). They accounted for about $\frac{1}{2}$ of the world's exports of copper in 1971, and if other less developed countries, like Papua, New Guinea, and the Philippines, joined CIPEC, its share would increase to about $\frac{2}{3}$. Until 1975 at least, there was considerable disagreement among CIPEC members concerning the desirability of raising copper prices. Some economists think it unlikely that they will be able to achieve sufficient agreement to engage in OPEC-like action.

As for tin, only four countries—Bolivia, Indonesia, Malaysia, and Thailand—account for $\frac{4}{5}$ of the non-Communist world's production of this metal. This, of course, makes collusion relatively easy. But there are many substitutes for tin, and the United States has a stockpile of it, both of which should discourage considerable price increases.

Faced with these prospects, what can the United States do? According to many economists, an important measure that we might take is to form a stockpile of each of these commodities equal to our total imports over one or two years. In this way, we could be sure that our economy would not be disrupted for a year or two, and by then the cartel (weakened by the reduced American market for its product) might no longer be effective. Other economists are not so optimistic. In their view, we are likely to be confronted with higher raw materials prices and possible interruptions of supply, due to OPEC-like action in some of these areas, the result being further inflationary pressures and discord in our relations with other countries.

Some Major Commodities with over $\frac{1}{3}$ of U.S. Imports from Less Developed Countries.

Commodity	Major sources of U.S. imports	Projected annual rate of growth of U.S. demand	Net imports as percent of U.S. domestic use (1970)
			(percent)
Bauxite	Jamaica, Surinam, Canada, Australia	7	86
Chromium	South Africa, USSR, Turkey	5	100
Cobalt	Zaire, Zambia, Norway, Finland	2	96
Copper	Canada, Peru, Chile	4–5	30
Iron ore	Canada, Venezuela	2	30
Lead	Canada, Australia, Peru, Mexico	1.6	40
Manganese	Brazil, Gabon, South Africa, Zaire	3	94
Tin	Malaysia, Thailand, Bolivia	4	71
Tungsten	Canada, Bolivia, Peru, Australia, Thailand	8	50

Source: R. Mikesell, "More Third World Cartels Ahead?" *Challenge*, November 1974, p. 28.

Foreign Aid

American Programs

The plight of the less developed countries is of concern to Americans, both because it is good morality and good policy to help them. From the point of view of humanitarianism, the United States and the other rich nations have a moral responsibility to help the poor nations. From the point of view of our self-interest, the promotion of growth in the less developed countries should help to preserve and encourage political and international stability and to make them more effective trading partners.

How can the United States be of help? With regard to many of their problems, we can do relatively little. But one thing that we can do is to provide badly needed capital. Responding to that need, we have given and lent a substantial amount of capital to the less developed countries in the past 20 years.

One important type of foreign aid consists of loans and gifts made by the United States government. It has amounted to almost $200 billion since World War II. At first, the emphasis was on aid to Europe, but since the late 1950s, the emphasis has been on the less developed countries. About ⅓ has been for military aid; about ⅔ for nonmilitary aid. As noted in Chapter 21, much of this aid has been in the form of loans or grants that must be spent on American goods and services. Also, much of this consisted of our giving away part of what were then surplus stocks of food. (Recall the agricultural programs discussed in Chapter 5.) India has been a leading recipient of U.S. agricultural surpluses. Table 22.8 shows the flow of resources from the United States (and other developed non-Communist nations) to the LDCs in 1973. As you can see, American official development assistance amounted to about $3 billion in that year.

In addition, the United States has established various kinds of technical assistance programs designed to help the less developed countries borrow some of our technology, administrative techniques, medical knowledge, educational methods, and so on. The emphasis frequently is on training people from the less developed countries to the point where they can teach their fellow countrymen. Often the costs of these programs are shared by the United States and by the recipient of the aid. Most observers seem to believe that these technical assistance programs have been worthwhile and successful.

Some other aspects of American policy are also important, although they are not aid programs. For one thing, the United States and other developed countries can help the LDCs by reducing trade barriers, thus allowing them to increase their national incomes through trade. However, it seems unlikely that trade alone can substitute for aid, and the situation is clouded by the trade barriers the LDCs themselves have been erecting to protect their own industry. Another way that the United States can help is through private investment. American corporations have invested an enormous amount in the less developed countries—over $3 billion in 1973 alone, according to Table 22.8. To the less developed countries, this is a significant source of capital.

Besides providing capital, the multinational corporations have also been a source of needed technology. However, these firms have faced much more difficult problems in transmitting technology to less developed countries than to industrialized countries. Many of the techniques of the multinational firms are not very well suited to the less developed countries, with their plentiful unskilled labor, few skills, and little capital. Moreover, there is sometimes little incentive for multinational firms to adapt their products, production techniques, and marketing methods to the conditions present in developing countries. And when they do manage to make a technological transplant, its effects are often restricted to narrow segments of the economy. Still further, it should be noted that the multinational firms are often viewed with some suspicion and fear by the host governments.

In recent years, American foreign aid has been reduced because of considerable feeling in Congress and elsewhere that our aid programs were not working very well. During the early 1960s an average of about $4 billion per year was spent on such aid programs, but by the early 1970s this figure had been cut to about $3 billion. Foreign aid has been a controversial subject in the United States for some time. Many critics argue that the money could better be spent at home to alleviate domestic poverty. They claim that other industrialized countries–like Germany and Japan–should contribute a bigger share of the aid to the less developed countries. And they assert that our aid programs have not had much impact on the less developed countries so far.

Many suggestions have been made for ways to improve the effectiveness of our foreign aid. One prominent suggestion is that we go further in concentrating the bulk of our aid on a relatively few countries–those that really want to do what is necessary to develop, that can use the money well, and that are important from the point of view of size and international politics. Obviously adopting this suggestion means reducing aid to some other countries. Another suggestion is that, rather than impose political conditions on aid, we should give money with no strings attached. This suggestion entails a great deal more than economics. To evaluate it, one must decide what the goals of foreign aid should be. To what extent should it be aimed at raising the standard of living of the world's population, whatever the effect on the United States? To what extent should it be aimed at furthering American goals and American foreign policies? In practice, foreign aid has been bound up closely with our foreign policy. Given the political facts of life, it is difficult to see how it could be otherwise.

The World Bank and Other Aid Programs

The United States has provided a large percentage of the aid that has flowed from the industrialized countries to the less developed countries, but, as shown in Table 22.8, it has

Table 22.8
Flow of Resources from Individual Developed Market Economies to Less Developed Countries, 1973[a]

Country	Official development assistance	Other official flows of funds	Private capital	Total
		(millions of dollars)		
United States	2,993	318	3,733	7,044
Japan	988	1,216	3,522	5,726
France	1,487	93	1,186	2,766
Germany	965	150	251	1,366
United Kingdom	588	41	354	983
Canada	510	34	434	978

Source: United Nations.
[a] Note that private capital flows are included here. Also, this table and Table 22.9 are based on the United Nations' definition of a less developed country.

by no means been the sole contributor. Other industrialized nations also have aid programs. For example, France contributed about $1.5 billion in official development assistance in 1973, and Japan and Germany contributed about $1 billion. Moreover, the Soviet Union has formulated a significant aid program. Table 22.9 shows that the Soviet Union committed over $1 billion in capital to the LDCs in 1973. Indeed, it is often claimed that the Russian programs have had more political effect than our own because they allow the recipient countries more freedom to build "prestige" projects like steel mills and because they make their aid look somewhat less like charity.[5]

In addition, the International Bank for Reconstruction and Development (more frequently referred to as the World Bank) has channeled large amounts of capital into the less developed countries. The World Bank is set up to lend money to finance development projects and to insure private loans made for this purpose. In the late 1950s and early 1960s, the World Bank set up the International Finance Corporation and the International Development Association, affiliated agencies that have become increasingly important as sources of funds for the poor nations. The bank's activities have grown substantially: in 1965, its loan authorizations were about $1 billion; in 1974, they were about $4 billion. Nonetheless, despite its achievements, many economists believe that in the past the World Bank has sometimes been too conservative and that it should have been willing to take bigger risks. Since the late 1960s, when Robert McNamara became its head, the bank has become less conservative in this respect.

Table 22.10 shows the amount of aid received per capita by various countries in the early 1970s. The largest amounts were received by Israel and Vietnam, both political allies of the United States. Excluding these two countries, the amount of annual aid received per capita ranged from less than $1 in Brazil and Mexico to about $10 in South Korea.

To illustrate the size and nature of foreign aid, consider the case of India. In 1951, foreign aid equaled about 1 percent of India's national product; by 1958, it had risen to about 2.7 per-

[5] Since the mid-1970s, the oil-exporting countries have established aid programs too. As a percent of GNP, their programs are bigger than those of the industrialized countries.

Table 22.9
Bilateral Commitments of Capital by Centrally Planned Economies to Less Developed Countries

Source	1954–69	1970	1971	1972	1973
			(millions of dollars)		
Bulgaria	157	82	55	40	43
China	883	685	492	498	351
Czechoslovakia	1,166	55	14	100	303
East Germany	684	125	25	23	—
Hungary	375	79	42	45	148
Poland	529	25	65	100	243
Romania	373	10	141	385	36
Soviet Union	5,977	197	677	921	1,236
Total	10,144	1,258	1,511	2,112	2,360

Source: United Nations.

Table 22.10
Per Capita Disbursements to Individual Countries of Official Assistance from Developed Market Economies and Multilateral Institutions, 1971–73 Annual Average

Country	Amount of aid per person (dollars per year)	Country	Amount of aid per person (dollars per year)
Congo	8.80	Israel	37.07
Egypt	1.40	South Korea	9.98
Ethiopia	2.06	India	1.41
Ghana	5.70	Sri Lanka	4.18
Zaire	5.37	Peru	3.41
Brazil	0.93	Philippines	3.87
Chile	3.48	Thailand	1.52
Colombia	5.04	Pakistan	5.11
Mexico	0.31	Vietnam	25.80

Source: United Nations.

cent; and by 1965, it had increased to about 3.8 percent. Clearly, India has received vast amounts of foreign aid, most of it as loans, but some as grants and assistance under Public Law 480, which involved the transfer of commodities like wheat and was close to being a grant. An interesting feature of the foreign aid India has received is that it has come from so many sources. Non-Communist aid to India has been channeled in through the Aid-India Consortium, composed of Canada, Japan, the United Kingdom, the United States, West Germany, Belgium, France, Italy, Holland, the World Bank, and others. (In 1976, the consortium pledged $1.8 billion in aid.) Until 1971, the United States put up the bulk of the consortium's aid funds—over 70 percent in the First Plan, over 55 percent in the Second Plan, and over 58 percent in the Third Plan. India has also received some aid from the Soviet Bloc countries. During the Second Plan, about 6 percent of India's aid came from the Soviet Bloc, and during the Third Plan, about 12 percent came from this source. Soviet Bloc aid generally has been used for heavy industrial projects.

What are the maturity of the loans and the interest rate for the loan segment of India's aid? The average maturity for loans authorized during the Third Five-Year Plan was 36 years for American loans, 25 years for British loans, 17 years for German loans, 15 years for Japanese loans, and 12 years for Russian loans. The average interest rate was 1.9 percent for American loans, 4.4 percent for British loans, 4.8 percent for German loans, 5.8 percent for Japanese loans, and 2.5 percent for Russian loans. Thus American lenders set the easiest terms. Aside from commodity assistance, the bulk of the aid received by India has been used for power projects, harbor development, railroads, and industrial projects such as iron and steel plants. This reflects India's emphasis on industrialization. This emphasis also has meant that India has had to rely on substantial technical assistance programs to provide the necessary skills and training. The United States has provided much of this assistance, and the United Nations has sponsored trips to India by foreign experts, as well as fellowships enabling Indians to study and gain experience abroad.[6]

[6] For further discussion, see Bhagwati and Desai, *India*.

Summary

A country is defined here as a less developed country if its per capita income is $750 or less. Over 2 billion people live in the less developed countries, which include most of the countries in Asia, Africa, and Latin America. In recent years, there has been a great increase in the expectations and material demands of the people in these countries. The less developed countries vary greatly, but they generally devote most of their resources to the production of food, are composed of two economies (one market-oriented, the other subsistence), and often have relatively weak, unstable governments and a relatively high degree of income inequality.

One obvious reason why income per capita is so low is that the people in the less developed countries have so little capital to work with. The less developed countries, with their low incomes, do not save much, they lack entrepreneurs, and the climate for investment (domestic or foreign) often is not good. Also, some less developed countries suffer from overpopulation; and as total output has increased, these gains have been offset by population increases. Modern medical techniques have reduced the death rate, while the birth rate has remained high. The result is a population explosion.

Another very important reason why per capita income is so low in these countries is that they often use backward technology. The transfer of technology from one country to another is not as easy as it sounds, particularly when the recipient country has an uneducated population and little capital. Also, these countries lack favorable social institutions and sometimes have few natural resources.

To promote development, most of the less developed countries seem to believe that the government must intervene on a large scale. An important issue facing the governments of most less developed countries is the extent to which they want to maintain a balance between the agricultural and industrial sectors of the economy. Without question, the LDCs are expanding industry relative to agriculture. In some cases, such as India and Pakistan, more balance—less emphasis on industry, more on agriculture—would have been preferable. Moreover, some countries have put too much emphasis on substituting their own production for imports, even when their own production is uneconomic.

Many of the less developed countries have established development plans that specify targets or goals for the economy and policies designed to attain them. One criterion often used to determine whether a given investment project should be accepted or rejected is the ratio of the value of the output produced to the capital used. Only projects with high values of this ratio are accepted. A more sophisticated criterion is the rate of return from the project, the method used by firms in capital budgeting. However, when computing each project's rate of return, it is important that inputs be valued at their social cost and that outputs be valued at their social worth. Modern tools of economic analysis—like linear programming and input-output analysis—are used in formulating some plans.

The United States has been involved in a number of major aid programs to help the less developed countries. During the early 1960s, our government gave or lent about $4 billion per year to the LDCs and carried out a variety of technical assistance programs. In recent years, these aid programs have come under increasing attack, and expenditures have been reduced. One suggestion frequently made is that we go further in concentrating our aid on a relatively few countries that really want to do what is necessary to develop, can use the money well, and are important in terms of size and politics. Besides the United States, other countries—including the Soviet Union—have carried out significant aid programs. And the World Bank has channeled major amounts of capital into the less developed countries.

CONCEPTS FOR REVIEW

Less developed country	Birth control	Population explosion
Balanced growth	Development plan	International Finance Corporation
Green revolution	Foreign aid	International Development Association
Comparative advantage	World Bank	Multinational corporation

QUESTIONS FOR DISCUSSION AND REVIEW

1. Between 1950 and 1967, the annual rate of growth of per capita national product was 5.3 percent in Taiwan, and 1.6 percent in India. Suggest as many hypotheses as you can to explain this difference.

2. In 1950, gross nonresidential investment was 9.8 percent of national product in Taiwan, and 7.4 percent of national product in India. In 1966, it was 16.7 percent of national product in Taiwan, and 13.8 percent of national product in India. Does this help to explain the difference in Question 1? Why or why not?

3. Between 1950 and 1967, the annual rate of growth of population was 3.1 percent in Taiwan and 2.2 percent in India. Does this help to explain the difference in Question 1? Why or why not?

4. "It is always a good idea for less developed countries to substitute their own production for imports. This is the only way they can become economically independent." Comment and evaluate.

5. Why don't some market prices of inputs correspond closely to social costs in less developed countries? Give examples. What implications does this have for the economic analysis of investment projects in LDCs?

6. Angus Maddison has written that "the so-called crisis in planning which has caused so much heart-searching amongst Indian economists, is in reality a move towards a more sophisticated policy mix in which the price mechanism is being restored to a more realistic role." Explain and evaluate.

7. When the United States was a young country, was there disagreement among the founding fathers concerning the strategy we should adopt to promote economic development? If so, describe some of the positions taken by our leaders at that time.

8. "Foreign aid is of limited use; it goes into the pockets of the rich and powerful, not the poor." Comment and evaluate.

9. According to Simon Kuznets, "A substantial economic advance in the less developed countries may require modification in the available stock of material technology, and probably even greater innovations in political and social structure." What does he mean? If he is correct, what are the implications for the less developed countries? For the developed countries?

10. According to Hans Morgenthau, "Foreign aid for economic development has a chance to be successful only within relatively narrow limits which are raised by cultural and political conditions impervious to direct outside influence." Do you agree? If he is correct, what are the implications for the less developed countries? For the developed countries?

INDEX

Definitions of terms appear on pages set in **boldface** type.